A PEOPLE AND A NATION

Brief Seventh Edition

A **P**EOPLE AND A **N**ATION

A History of the United States

Volume 1   To 1877

Brief Seventh Edition

Mary Beth Norton
Cornell University

David M. Katzman
University of Kansas

David W. Blight
Yale University

Howard P. Chudacoff
Brown University

Fredrik Logevall
Cornell University

Beth Bailey
Temple University

Thomas G. Paterson
University of Connecticut

William M. Tuttle, Jr.
University of Kansas

Houghton Mifflin Company   Boston New York

Publisher: Charles Hartford
Sponsoring Editor: Sally Constable
Senior Development Editor: Jeffrey Greene
Editorial Assistant: Arianne Vanni
Senior Project Editor: Bob Greiner
Editorial Assistant: Katherine Leahey
Senior Art and Design Coordinator: Jill Haber Atkins
Senior Photo Editor: Jennifer Meyer Dare
Composition Buyer: Chuck Dutton
Manufacturing Buyer: Florence Cadran
Senior Marketing Manager: Sandra McGuire

Cover Image: Arthur Miller, Frontiersman and Child, ca. 1840. Courtesy Michael Altman Fine Art, New York.

Printed in the U.S.A.

Library of Congress Catalog Number: 2005926283

Instructor's exam copy:
ISBN 13: 978-0-618-73026-1
ISBN 10: 0-618-73026-5

For orders, use student text ISBNs:
ISBN 13: 978-0-618-61151-5
ISBN 10: 0-618-61151-7

2 3 4 5 6 7 8 9-VH-09 08 07 06

Brief Contents

CONTENTS

SPECIAL FEATURES

PREFACE TO THE BRIEF SEVENTH EDITION

Creation of the Brief Edition

More than two decades have passed since the publication of the first brief edition of *A People and a Nation*. In that initial brief edition, as well as each subsequent one, the intent was to preserve the uniqueness and integrity of the complete work while condensing it. This Brief Seventh Edition once again reflects the scholarship, readability, and comprehensiveness of the full-length version. It also maintains the integration of social, cultural, political, economic, and foreign relations history that has been a hallmark of *A People and a Nation*.

The authors collectively mourn the death of William J. Brophy, who prepared the brief text for the previous six editions. His successors, though, have worked closely with us, ensuring that the changes in content and organization incorporated in the full-length Seventh Edition were retained in the condensation. The authors attained reductions by paring down details rather than deleting entire sections. The Brief Seventh Edition thus contains fewer statistics, fewer quotations, and fewer examples than the unabridged version. A sufficient number of quotations and examples were retained, however, to maintain the richness in style created by the authors.

The Brief Seventh Edition is available in both one- and two-volume formats. The two-volume format is divided as follows: Volume 1 contains Chapters 1 through 16, beginning with a discussion of three cultures—American, African, and European—that intersected during the exploration and colonization of the New World, and ending with a discussion of the Reconstruction era. Volume 2 contains Chapters 16 through 33, beginning its coverage at Reconstruction and extending the history of the American people to the present. The chapter on Reconstruction appears in both volumes to provide greater flexibility in matching a volume to the historical span covered by a specific course.

Changes in This Edition

While the preface to the full-length Seventh Edition elaborates on specific content changes, we note here that the authors paid increased attention to the following: ethnic and religious diversity in the United States; the environment and technology; the domestic, political, economic, and social impact of the nation's wars; and popular culture. The discussion of the relationship between America and the rest of the world from the colonial period to the present has been expanded throughout the book, as is exemplified in a feature now appearing in each chapter, "Links to the World." These emphases and the complete reorganization of the post-1960 chapters, as well as the updated scholarship on which they are based, are retained in the Brief Seventh Edition.

Although each author feels answerable for the whole of *A People and a Nation*, we take primary responsibility for particular chapters: Mary Beth Norton, Chapters 1–8; David M. Katzman, Chapters 9–12; David Blight, Chapters 13–16; Howard P. Chudacoff, Chapters 17–21 and 24; Fredrik Logevall, Chapters 22, 23, 26, 28, and shared responsibility for 30–33; Beth Bailey, Chapters 25, 27, 29, and shared responsibility for 30–33.

Teaching and Learning Aids

These supplements have been created with the diverse needs of today's students and instructors in mind.

For the Instructor

■ The **Online Teaching Center** (http://college.hmco.com/pic/nortonbrief7e) includes PowerPoint slides of hundreds of maps, images, and other media related to each chapter in the book as well as web links and questions for use with Personal Response Systems. Instructors have access to 100 interactive maps and over 500 primary sources to use for assignments. In addition, there is an Instructor's Resource Manual that can aid in encouraging classroom discussions or constructively enhance a class presentation.

■ A **Class Prep CD-ROM** contains a computerized test bank prepared by George Warren of Central Piedmont Community College that includes search functions that allow instructors to design tests thematically by entering keywords. This CD contains the maps and images that are on the Online Teaching Center web site.

■ The **Blackboard/WebCT CD** provides instructors who want to offer all or part of their entire course online with much of the fundamental material for their course, including graded homework questions organized by topic. From this base, instructors can customize the course to meet their needs.

■ **Eduspace** provides the ability for instructors to create part or all of their courses online, using the widely recognized tools of Blackboard Learning System and content from Houghton Mifflin. Instructors can quickly and easily assign homework exercises, quizzes and tests, tutorials, and supplementary study materials and can modify or add content of their own. A powerful grade book in Eduspace allows instructors to monitor student progress and easily tabulate grades.

■ The **Houghton Mifflin U.S. History Transparency Set, Volumes I and II**, is a set of standard U.S. history transparencies, taken from illustrations and maps in the Houghton Mifflin survey texts. It includes 150 full-color maps.

■ **BiblioBase for U.S. History** is a database of hundreds of primary source documents—including speeches, essays, travel accounts, government documents, and memoirs—covering U.S. history from the fifteenth century to the present. This comprehensive database enables you to create a customized course pack of primary sources to complement any U.S. history text. You can search for documents by period, region, approach, theme, and type and then view the documents in their entirety before choosing your course pack selections.

■ The **Rand McNally Atlas of American History** is offered for packaging with the textbook. Please contact your sales representative for additional information.

For the Student

■ The **Online Study Center** (http://college.hmco.com/pic/nortonbrief7e) is a student web site that includes a wide array of interactive study content such as pre-class quizzes, ACE Practice Tests, vocabulary-building exercises, identification exercises, and interactive map activities, among other resources. This web site also contains the same primary sources and interactive maps that are on the Online Teaching Center.

■ **Icons** in the text direct students to interactive maps, primary sources, and ACE Practice Test questions.

Acknowledgments

For essential assistance in the preparation of this abridged edition, we are grateful to Jan Fitter and Debra Michals.

Author teams rely on review panels to help create and execute successful revision plans. For the revision of this Brief Seventh Edition, we were guided by the many historians whose thoughtful insights and recommendations helped us with the preparation of the full-length Seventh Edition. Their names appear in the preface to that edition that follows.

Finally, we want to thank the many people who have contributed their thoughts and labors to this work, especially the talented staff at Houghton Mifflin.

For the authors,
Mary Beth Norton,
Coordinating Author

PREFACE TO THE FULL-LENGTH SEVENTH EDITION

Some readers might think that a book entering its seventh edition would be little changed from the previous version. Nothing could be further from the truth. In this seventh edition, *A People and a Nation* has undergone major revisions, while still retaining the narrative strength and focus that characterized its earlier editions and made it so popular with students and teachers alike. In the years since the publication of the sixth edition, new documents have been uncovered, new interpretations advanced, and new themes (especially globalization) have come to the forefront of American historical scholarship. The authors—including two new members of our team—have worked diligently to incorporate those findings into this text.

Like other teachers and students, we are always re-creating our past, restructuring our memory, rediscovering the personalities and events that have influenced us, injured us, and bedeviled us. This book represents our continuing rediscovery of America's history—its diverse people and the nation they created and have nurtured. As this book demonstrates, there are many different Americans and many different memories. We have sought to present all of them, in both triumph and tragedy, in both division and unity.

About *A People and a Nation*

A People and a Nation, first published in 1982, was the first major textbook in the United States to fully integrate social and political history. Since the outset, the authors have been determined to tell the story of *all* the people of the United States. This book's hallmark has been its melding of social and political history, its movement beyond history's common focus on public figures and events to examine the daily life of America's people. All editions of the book have stressed the interaction of public policy and personal experience, the relationship between domestic concerns and foreign affairs, the various manifestations of popular culture, and the multiple origins of America and Americans. We have consistently built our narrative on a firm foundation in primary sources—on both well-known and obscure letters, diaries, public documents, oral histories, and artifacts of material culture. We have long challenged readers to think about the meaning of American history, not just to memorize facts. Both students and instructors have repeatedly told us how much they appreciate and enjoy our approach to the past.

As has been true since the first edition, each chapter opens with a dramatic vignette focusing on an individual or a group of people. These vignettes develop key questions, which then frame the chapters in succinct introductions and summaries. Numerous maps, tables, graphs, and charts provide readers with the necessary geographical and statistical context for observations in the text. Carefully selected illustrations—many of them unique to this book—offer readers visual insight into the topics under discussion, especially because the authors have written the captions. In this edition, as in all previous ones, we have sought to incorporate up-to-date scholarship, readability, a clear structure, critical thinking, and instructive illustrative material on every page.

What's New in This Edition

Planning for the seventh edition began at a two-day authors' meeting at the Houghton Mifflin headquarters in Boston. There we discussed the most recent scholarship in the field, the reviews of the sixth edition solicited from instructors, and the findings of our own continuing research. For this edition, we added two new colleagues, who experienced the intellectual exhilaration and rigor of such an authors' meeting for the first time. Beth Bailey, who has written acclaimed works on sexuality and popular culture in modern America, now writes the chapters and sections dealing with domestic matters after the 1920s. Fredrik Logevall, whose scholarship on the Vietnam War has won international recognition, now writes all the chapters and sections on foreign policy since the Civil War. These new authors have substantially reworked and reorganized the post-1945 chapters, in ways outlined below.

This seventh edition enhances the global perspective on American history that has characterized the book since its first edition. From the "Atlantic world" context of European colonies in North and South America to the discussion of international terrorism, the authors have incorporated the most recent globally oriented scholarship throughout the volume. We have worked to strengthen our treatment of the diversity of America's people by examining differences within the broad ethnic categories commonly employed and by paying greater attention to immigration, cultural and intellectual infusions from around the world, and America's growing religious diversity. At the same time, we have more fully integrated the discussion of such diversity into our narrative, so as not to artificially isolate any group from the mainstream. Treatments of environmental history and the history of technology have both been expanded. Finally, we have streamlined the useful chronologies that appear near the beginning of each chapter.

As always, the authors reexamined every sentence, interpretation, map, chart, illustration, and caption, refining the narrative, presenting new examples, and bringing to the text the latest findings of scholars in many areas of history, anthropology, sociology, and political science. More than a quarter of the chapter-opening vignettes are new, as is also true of the popular "Legacy" features introduced in the sixth edition.

To students who question the relevance of historical study, the legacies offer compelling and timely answers. Those brief essays, which follow the chapter summaries, explore the historical roots of contemporary topics. New subjects of legacies include the "self-made man" ideal, states' rights, reparations for slavery, Planned Parenthood, the Social Security system, the concern for human rights, and the Americans with Disabilities Act.

New "Links to the World"

In keeping with the emphasis on globalization in this edition, and building on the long-standing strength of this text in the history of American foreign relations, we have introduced a new feature in each chapter: "Links to the World." Examining both inward and outward ties between America (and Americans) and the rest of the world, the "Links" appear at appropriate places in each chapter to explore specific topics at considerable length. Tightly constructed essays detail the often little-known connections between developments here and abroad. The topics range broadly over economic, political, social, technological, medical, and cultural history, vividly demonstrating that the geographical region that is now the United States has never lived in isolation from other peoples and countries. Examples include the impact of American maize (corn) on the rest of the world, the introduction of coffee and tea into the American colonies, the discovery of gold in California, proposals to annex Cuba, baseball in Japan, Pan American Airways, the influenza pandemic of 1918, the 1936 Olympics, Barbie dolls, CNN, and the AIDS epidemic. Each "Link" highlights global interconnections with unusual and lively examples that will both intrigue and inform students.

Themes in This Book

Several themes and questions stand out in our continuing effort to integrate political, social, and cultural history. We study the many ways Americans have defined themselves—gender, race, class, region, ethnicity, religion, sexual orientation—and the many subjects that have reflected their multidimensional experiences. We highlight the remarkably diverse everyday lives of the American people—in cities and on farms and ranches, in factories and in corporate headquarters, in neighborhoods and in legislatures, in love relationships and in hate groups, in recreation and in work, in the classroom and in military uniform, in secret national security conferences and in public foreign relations debates, in church and in voluntary associations, in polluted environments and in conservation areas. We pay particular attention to lifestyles, diet and dress, family life and structure, labor conditions, gender roles, migration and mobility, childbearing, and child rearing. We explore how Americans have entertained and informed themselves by discussing their music, sports, theater, print media, film, radio, television, graphic arts, and literature, in both "high" culture and popular culture. We study how technology has influenced Americans' lives, such as through the internal combustion engine and the computer.

Americans' personal lives have always interacted with the public realm of politics and government. To understand how Americans have sought to protect their different ways of life and to work out solutions to thorny problems, we emphasize their expectations of governments at the local, state, and federal levels; governments' role in providing answers; the lobbying of interest groups; the campaigns and outcomes of elections; and the hierarchy of power in any period. Because the United States has long been a major participant in world affairs, we explore America's participation in wars, interventions in other nations, empire-building, immigration patterns, images of foreign peoples, cross-national cultural ties, and international economic trends.

Section-by-Section Changes in This Edition

Mary Beth Norton, who had primary responsibility for Chapters 1 through 8 and served as coordinating author, expanded coverage of ancient North America (the Anasazi and Mississippians); Brazil, the Caribbean islands, and Nova Scotia; witchcraft, especially the 1692 Salem crisis; migration to the colonies from England, Ireland, and Germany; the trade in African and Indian slaves and the impact of that trade on African and Native American societies; the trans-Appalachian west in peace and war; and slavery and gradual emancipation after the Revolution. She also reorganized Chapter 3 to consolidate related materials on politics and the imperial context, and extensively revised and expanded Chapter 6 to reflect recent scholarship. There are new sections on the West during the revolutionary era and on the experiences of ordinary Americans in wartime, both in and out of the military.

David M. Katzman, with responsibility for Chapters 9 through 12, has continued (as in the sixth edition) to sharpen the chronological flow in these chapters. He has broadened the discussion of political culture and emerging partisanship in the young republic, reflecting the current rethinking of politics at that time. He has expanded coverage of religious life and the links between religion and social and political reform. The discussions of families, immigrant lives (especially the Irish), and African American identity, culture, and communities have all been completely revised. Throughout, there is greater attention paid to technology, global ties, and popular culture.

David W. Blight, who had primary responsibility for Chapters 13 through 16, enhanced the discussion of women and gender throughout these chapters. He also added material on the lives of freed people, before, during, and after the Civil War; the impact of the Fugitive Slave Law; the West in the Civil War and Reconstruction eras; and the home front during wartime. He revised the interpretation of the Denmark Vesey slave rebellion and increased coverage of the Underground Railroad, and of the role of the Mormons and westward expansion in the slavery crisis. In Chapter 15, he developed new sections on how the Civil War shaped the future of Indians in the far West, as well as the conflict's significance abroad, especially in England.

Howard P. Chudacoff, responsible for Chapters 17 through 21 and 24, has increased the coverage of technology throughout his chapters, adding discussions of farming technology, the machine tool industry, technological education in universities, birth-control devices, and the automobile. He has included new material on the environment as well, expanding his discussion of such topics as water supply and sewage disposal, the unanticipated effects of national parks, and the conservation movement. Topics related to ethnicity—including anti-Chinese violence and exclusion laws, Mexican immigration, and holiday celebrations by ethnic groups—also receive increased attention. He has reconfigured portions of Chapters 18, 19, and 21 to clarify the narrative.

Fredrik Logevall, with primary responsibility for Chapters 22, 23, 26, and 28, worked to internationalize the treatment of America's foreign relations by giving greater attention to the perspectives of nations with which we interacted, and by examining the foreign policy aims of such leaders as Joseph Stalin, especially in Chapters 23 and 26. He significantly expanded the coverage of U.S. relations with the Middle East, showing the increasing importance of America's dealings with that region during the past four decades. He has also brought a sense of contingency to the narrative of American foreign relations, suggesting that matters might have turned out quite differently at various key junctures had policymakers reached different decisions. He made major changes in Chapter 28 (formerly Chapter 29), creating greater thematic unity and incorporating much new scholarship on the Cold War and relations with China and the Soviet Union. Throughout, Logevall builds on the excellent foundation laid by Thomas G. Paterson, who wrote these and the post-1960 foreign policy chapters in the previous six editions of this textbook, and who also served as the coordinating author for all six of those editions.

Beth Bailey, primarily responsible for Chapters 25, 27, and 29, integrated the experiences and actions of various groups into the main narrative while still focusing on the diversity of the American people in the modern era. In general, she enhanced coverage of the South and West (especially Latinos and Mexican immigrants in the Southwest) and added material on gender, sexuality, and popular culture. Throughout these chapters she placed Americans' fears about their nation's future in an international context. In Chapter 25, she strengthened the discussion of New Deal policies, showing how assumptions about race and gender structured these important social programs. Chapter 27 has a stronger chronological framework, as well as new treatments of culture and daily life during WWII, in combat and on the home front. Chapter 29 (formerly Chapter 28) has been extensively revised, assessing the myriad transformations of American society and culture in the 1950s, with particular attention to race, labor, masculinity, McCarthyism, and the impact of new federal policies. Bailey's work updates the domestic policy chapters written superbly in the previous six editions by William M. Tuttle, Jr.

Post-1960 Chapters

Bailey and Logevall shared responsibility for the new Chapters 30 through 33. In these completely revamped chapters, domestic and foreign topics are discussed in tandem rather than separately, demonstrating the extensive linkages between them. The two authors collaborated closely to create a fresh and lively, comprehensive, chronologically based narrative that places events in the United States in their appropriate international setting. The coverage of foreign relations includes increased attention to the Middle East and to the motivations of America's allies and opponents alike. The treatment of the Vietnam War now draws on Logevall's own scholarship, just as the discussion of recent popular culture and sexuality is based on Bailey's original research. Increased attention is given to the civil rights movement, the rise of second- and third-wave feminism, new patterns of immigration, and the growth of grassroots conservatism.

Teaching and Learning Aids

The supplements listed here accompany this Seventh Edition of *A People and a Nation*. They have been created with the diverse needs of today's students and instructors in mind, with extensive print and non-print resources available.

We are proud to announce the **History Companion**, your new primary source for history technology solutions. The *History Companion* has three components: the **Instructor Companion**, the **Student Study Companion**, and the **Student Research Companion**. Each of these components is described below: the *Instructor Companion* under instructor resources, and the *Student Research Companion* and *Student Study Companion* under student resources.

For the Instructor:

■ The *Instructor Companion* is an easily searchable CD-ROM that makes hundreds of historical images and maps instantly accessible in PowerPoint format. Each image is accompanied by notes that place it in its proper historical context and tips for ways it can be presented in the classroom. With this edition of *A People and a Nation*, this CD also includes a wealth of additional resources, including testing, lecture, and course planning tools. A computerized test bank is included complete with search functions, which allows instructors to design tests thematically by entering keywords to bring up particular questions. An Instructor's Resource Guide is also included that can aid in encouraging classroom discussions or constructively enhance a class presentation. This CD is free to instructors with the adoption of this Houghton Mifflin textbook.

■ A print **Test Bank,** prepared by George Warren of Central Piedmont Community College, also accompanies the text and contains many multiple choice, identification, geography, and essay questions for use in creating exams.

■ In addition, a series of **PowerPoint** slides, created by Barney Rickman of Valdosta State University, is included to assist in instruction and discussion of key topics and material.

■ The **Blackboard/WebCT Basic CD** provides instructors who want to offer all or part of their entire course online with much of the fundamental material for their course. From this base, instructors can customize the course to meet their needs.

■ The **Houghton Mifflin U.S. History Transparency Set, Volumes I and II,** is a set of standard U.S. history transparencies, taken from illustrations and maps in the Houghton Mifflin survey texts. It includes 150 full-color maps.

■ **BiblioBase for U.S. History** is a database of hundreds of primary source documents—including speeches, essays, travel accounts, government documents, and memoirs—covering U.S. history from the fifteenth century to the present. This comprehensive database enables you to create a customized course pack of primary sources to complement any U.S. history text. You can search for documents by period, region, approach, theme, and type and then view the documents in their entirety before choosing your course pack selections.

■ The **Rand McNally Atlas of American History** is offered for packaging with the textbook. Please contact your sales representative for additional information.

For the Student:

The **Houghton Mifflin History Companion** for *A People and a Nation,* Seventh Edition, has two student components.

■ The *Student Study Companion* is a free online study guide that contains ACE self-tests, flashcards, timelines, chronology exercises, graphic organizer exercises, map exercises, text feature exercises, web links, and Internet exercises. These study tools will help your students to be more successful.

- The *Student Research Companion* is a free Internet-based tool with 100 interactive maps and 500 primary sources. The primary sources include headnotes that provide pertinent background information, and both the maps and the primary sources include questions that students can answer and e-mail to their instructors.

- **Study Guide Volumes I and II**, by George Warren, offers students learning objectives, vocabulary exercises, identification suggestions, skill-building activities, multiple choice questions, essay questions, and map exercises in two volumes.

- **American Ethnic Identities: Online Activities**
  By using examples throughout American history, these informative and lively activities will broaden your understanding of the different ethnic groups that make up the United States.

Acknowledgments

The authors would like to thank the following persons for their assistance with the preparation of this edition: Shawn Alexander, David Anthony Tyeeme Clark, Mike Ezra, David Farber, Max Bailey/Farber, Steve Jacobson, Andrea Katzman, Eric Katzman, Julee Katzman, Theo Katzman, Ariela Katzman-Jacobson, Elieza Katzman-Jacobson, Iris Jane Katzman, Sharyn Brooks Katzman, Danyel Logevall, Chester Pach, Cheryl Ragar, Ann Schofield, Daniel Williams, and Norman Yetman.

At each stage of this revision, a sizable panel of historian reviewers read drafts of our chapters. Their suggestions, corrections, and pleas helped guide us through this momentous revision. We could not include all of their recommendations, but the book is better for our having heeded most of their advice. We heartily thank:

Marynita Anderson, *Nassau Community College*
Erica R. Armstrong, *University of Delaware*
Jim Barrett, *University of Illinois at Urbana-Champaign*
Virginia R. Boynton, *Western Illinois University*
Robert Cottrell, *California State University, Chico*
Bruce Dierenfield, *Canisius College*
Lisa Lindquist Dorr, *University of Alabama*
Latricia E. Gill-Brown, *Pensacola Junior College*
Melanie Gustafson, *University of Vermont*
Jorge Iber, *Texas Tech University*
Anthony E. Kaye, *Pennsylvania State University, University Park*
Carol A. Keller, *San Antonio College*
Kathleen Kennedy, *Western Washington University*
Anne Klejment, *University of St. Thomas*
Carolyn J. Lawes, *Old Dominion University*
Patrick K. Moore, *University of West Florida*
Jared Orsi, *Colorado State University*

Chester Pach, *Ohio University*
Marie Jenkins Schwartz, *University of Rhode Island*
Erik R. Seeman, *SUNY-Buffalo*
Sayuri G. Shimizu, *Michigan State University*
Manisha Sinha, *University of Massachusetts,
     Amherst*
Evelyn Sterne, *University of Rhode Island*
Benson Tong, *Wichita State University*
Michael M. Topp, *University of Texas, El Paso*

The authors once again thank the extraordinary Houghton Mifflin people who designed, edited, produced, and nourished this book. Their high standards and acute attention to both general structure and fine detail are cherished in the publishing industry. Many thanks, then, to Jean Woy, editor-in-chief; Sally Constable, sponsoring editor; Ann Hofstra Grogg, freelance development editor; Bob Greiner, senior project editor; Sandra McGuire, senior marketing manager; Henry Rachlin, senior designer; Carol Merrigan, senior production/design coordinator; Marie Barnes, senior manufacturing coordinator; Pembroke Herbert, photo researcher; Charlotte Miller, art editor; and Kisha Mitchell and Trinity Peacock-Broyles, editorial assistants.

THREE OLD WORLDS CREATE A NEW 1492–1600

*a*s they neared the village called Cofitachequi on May 1, 1540, the band of Spanish explorers led by Hernán de Soto beheld a surprising scene. Villagers came to meet the Europeans, carrying their female chief, or *cacica*. The Lady of Cofitachequi, a Spanish chronicler recorded, welcomed the weary Spaniards to her domain in today's western South Carolina, giving Soto a string of pearls from her neck. Later, she gave the hungry men huge quantities of corn and, seeing that they especially valued pearls, suggested they take the ones they would find in nearby burial chambers.

The Spanish explorers had landed at Tampa Bay, Florida, about a year earlier. They would wander through what is now the southeastern United States for three more years, encountering many different peoples, whom they often treated with great cruelty. Always they sought gold and silver. The people of Cofitachequi told the Spaniards they might find these treasures in another ruler's domain, about twelve days' travel away. When Soto left, he took the Lady with him as a captive, but she escaped and presumably returned home.

Why had the Lady greeted Soto's band so kindly? Perhaps she did not have enough men to resist the Europeans; her people had been devastated by an unknown "pestilence" two years earlier. Or possibly messengers had informed the Lady about Soto's vicious treatment of villages he had previously encountered. Whatever her reasoning, the strategy worked: Soto and his men moved on, and Cofitachequi survived to be recorded by Spanish, French, and finally English visitors over the next 130 years.

For thousands of years before 1492, human societies in the Americas had developed in isolation from the rest of the world. The era that began in the Christian fifteenth century brought that long-standing isolation to an end. As Europeans sought treasure and trade, peoples from different cultures came into regular contact for the first time. All were profoundly changed. The brief encounter between Soto and the Lady of Cofitachequi illustrates many of the

Online Study Center
This icon will direct you to interactive map and primary source activities on the website http://college.hmco.com/pic/nortonbrief7e

CHRONOLOGY

12,000–10,000 B.C.E. • Paleo-Indians begin migrating from Asia to North America across the Beringia land bridge

7000 B.C.E. • Cultivation of food crops begins in America

c. 1000 B.C.E. • Olmec civilization appears

c. 300–600 C.E. • Height of influence of Teotihuacán

c. 600–900 C.E. • Classic Mayan civilization

1000 C.E. • Anasazi build settlements in modern states of Arizona and New Mexico

1001 • Norse establish settlement in "Vinland"

1050–1250 • Height of influence of Cahokia; prevalence of Mississippian culture in midwestern and southeastern United States

14th century • Aztec rise to power

1450s–80s • Portuguese explore and colonize islands in the Mediterranean Atlantic and São Tomé in Gulf of Guinea

1477 • Publication of Marco Polo's *Travels,* describing China

1492 • Columbus reaches Bahamas

1494 • Treaty of Tordesillas divides land claims between Spain and Portugal in Africa, India, and South America

1496 • Last Canary Island falls to Spain

1497 • Cabot reaches North America

1513 • León explores Florida

1518–30 • Smallpox epidemic devastates Indian population of West Indies and Central and South America

1519 • Cortés invades Mexico

1521 • Tenochtitlán surrenders to Cortés; Aztec Empire falls to Spaniards

1524 • Verrazzano sails along Atlantic coast of United States

1534–35 • Cartier explores St. Lawrence River

1539–42 • Soto explores southeastern United States

1540–42 • Coronado explores southwestern United States

1587–90 • Raleigh's Roanoke colony vanishes

1588 • Harriot publishes *A Briefe and True Report of the New Found Land of Virginia*

elements of contact: cruelty and kindness, greed and deception, trade and theft, surprise and sickness, captivity and enslavement. By the time Soto and his men landed in Florida in 1539, the age of European expansion and colonization was already well under way. The history of the tiny colonies that would become the United States must be seen in this broad context of European exploration and exploitation.

The continents that European sailors reached in the late fifteenth century had their own history. The residents of the Americas were the world's most skillful plant breeders; they had developed vegetable crops more nutritious and productive than those grown in Europe, Asia, or Africa. They had invented systems of writing and mathematics and had created calendars as accurate as those used on the other side of the Atlantic. In the Americas, as in Europe, states rose and fell as leaders succeeded or failed in expanding their political and economic power. But the arrival of Europeans immeasurably altered the Americans' struggles with one another.

After 1400, European nations tried to acquire valuable colonies and trading posts elsewhere in the world. Initially they were interested primarily in Asia and Africa, but many Europeans eventually focused their attention on the Americas. Their contests for trade and conquest changed the course of history on four continents. Even as Europeans slowly achieved dominance, their fates were shaped by the strategies of Americans and Africans. In the Americas of the fifteenth and sixteenth centuries, three old worlds came together to produce a new. ■

American Societies

*H*uman beings originated on the continent of Africa, where humanlike remains about 3 million years old have been found in what is now Ethiopia. Over many millennia, the growing population slowly dispersed to the other continents. Scholars have long believed that all the earliest inhabitants of the Americas crossed a land bridge known as Beringia (at the site of the Bering Strait) approximately 12,000 to 14,000 years ago. Yet striking new archaeological discoveries in both North and South America suggest that some parts of the Americas may have been settled much earlier, perhaps by seafarers crossing from northern Europe by island hopping from Iceland to Greenland to Baffin Island, much as the Vikings did many millennia later (see Map 1.1).

The first Americans are called Paleo-Indians. Nomadic hunters of game and gatherers of wild plants,

ANCIENT AMERICA they spread throughout North and South America, probably moving as bands composed of extended families. By about 11,500 years ago the Paleo-Indians were making fine stone projectile points, which they attached to wooden spears and used to kill the large mammals then living in the Americas. But as the Ice Age ended and the human population increased, all the large American mammals except the bison (buffalo) disappeared. As their meat supply decreased, the Paleo-Indians found new ways to survive.

By approximately 9,000 years ago, the residents of what is now central Mexico began to cultivate food crops, especially maize (corn), squash, beans, and peppers. In the Andes Mountains of South America, people started to grow potatoes. As knowledge of agricultural techniques improved and spread throughout the Americas, vegetables and maize proved a more reliable source of food than hunting and gathering. Thus, most Americans started to adopt a more sedentary style of life so that they could tend fields regularly. Some established permanent settlements; others moved several times a year among fixed sites. All the American cultures emphasized producing sufficient food to support themselves. Trade existed, but no society ever became dependent on another group for items vital to its survival.

Wherever agriculture dominated the economy, complex civilizations flourished. Such societies, assured of steady supplies, were able to accumulate wealth, produce ornamental objects, trade with other groups, and create elaborate rituals and ceremonies. In North America, the successful cultivation of nutritious crops seems to have led to the growth and development of all the major civilizations: first the large city-states of Mesoamerica (modern Mexico and Guatemala), and then the urban clusters known collectively as the Mississippian culture and located in the present-day United States. Each of these societies reached its height of population and influence only after achieving success in agriculture. Each later collapsed after reaching the limits of its food supply.

Little is known about the first major Mesoamerican civilization, that of the Olmecs, who about 3,000

MESOAMERICAN CIVILIZATIONS years ago lived near the Gulf of Mexico in cities dominated by temple pyramids. Two societies that developed approximately 1,000 years later, those of the Mayas and of Teotihuacán, are better recorded. Teotihuacán, founded in the Valley of Mexico about 300 B.C.E. (Before the Common Era), eventually became one of the largest urban areas in the world, housing perhaps 100,000 people in the fifth century C.E. (Common Era). Teotihuacán's commercial network extended hundreds of miles; many peoples prized its obsidian (a green glass), used to make fine knives and mirrors. Pilgrims must also have traveled long distances to visit Teotihuacán's impressive pyramids and the great temple of Quetzalcoatl—the feathered serpent, primary god of central Mexico.

On the Yucatán Peninsula, in today's eastern Mexico, the Mayas built urban centers containing tall pyramids and temples. They studied astronomy and created the first writing system in the Americas.

Their city-states, though, engaged in near-constant warfare with one another. Warfare and an inadequate food supply caused the collapse of the most powerful cities by 900 C.E., thus ending the classic era of Mayan civilization. By the time Spaniards arrived five hundred years later, only a few remnants of the once-mighty society remained.

Ancient native societies in what is now the United States learned to grow maize, squash, and beans from Mesoamericans, but the

ANASAZI AND MISSISSIPPIANS

exact relationship of the various cultures is unknown. (No Meso-american artifacts have been found north of the Rio Grande, but some items resembling Mississippian objects have been excavated in northern Mexico.) The Hohokam, Mogollon, and Anasazi peoples of the modern states of Arizona and New Mexico subsisted by combining hunting and gathering with agriculture in an arid region. Hohokam villagers constructed extensive irrigation systems, but even so, they occasionally had to relocate when water supplies failed. Between 900 and 1150 C.E., the Anasazi built fourteen "Great Houses" in Chaco Canyon, each a massive multistoried stone structure averaging two hundred rooms. The canyon served as a major regional trading and processing center for turquoise, used then as now to create beautiful ornamental objects. Scholars have not determined why the Anasazi disappeared or where they went, but a major drought could well have been responsible.

At almost the same time, the unrelated Mississippian culture flourished in what is now the midwestern and southeastern United States. Relying largely on maize, squash, nuts, pumpkins, and venison for food, the Mississippians lived in substantial settlements. The largest of their urban centers was the City of the Sun (now called Cahokia), near modern St. Louis. Located near the confluence of the Illinois, Missouri, and Mississippi Rivers, Cahokia, like Teotihuacán and Chaco Canyon, served as a focal point for both religion and trade. At its peak (in the eleventh and twelfth centuries C.E.), the City of the Sun covered more than 5 square miles and had a population of about twenty thousand—small by Mesoamerican standards but larger than London in the same era.

Although the Cahokians never seem to have invented a writing system, these sun worshippers developed an accurate calendar, evidenced by a woodhenge—a large circle of timber posts aligned with the solstices and the equinox. The city's main pyramid (one of 120 of varying sizes), today called Monks Mound, was at the time of its construction the third largest structure in the Western Hemisphere; it remains the largest earthwork ever built in the Americas. It sat at the northern end of the Grand Plaza, surrounded by seventeen other mounds, some used for burials. Yet after 1250 C.E., the city was abandoned. Archaeologists believe that climate change and degradation of the environment, caused by overpopulation and the destruction of nearby forests, brought about the city's collapse.

The Aztecs' histories tell of the long migration of their people (who called themselves Mexica) into the

AZTECS

Valley of Mexico during the twelfth century. The uninhabited ruins of Teotihuacán, which by then had been deserted for at least two hundred years, awed and mystified the migrants. Their chronicles record that their primary deity, Huitzilopochtli—a war god represented by an eagle—directed them to establish their capital on an island where they saw an eagle eating a serpent, the symbol of Quetzalcoatl. That island city became Tenochtitlán, the center of a rigidly stratified society composed of hereditary classes of warriors, merchants, priests, common folk, and slaves.

The Aztecs conquered their neighbors, forcing them to pay tribute, including human beings who could be sacrificed to Huitzilopochtli. The war god's taste for blood was not easily quenched. At the 1502 coronation of Motecuhzoma II (Montezuma to the Spaniards), five thousand people are thought to have been sacrificed by having their still-beating hearts torn from their bodies.

The Aztecs believed that they lived in the age of the Fifth Sun. Four times previously, they wrote, the earth and all the people who lived on it had been destroyed. They predicted that their own world would end in earthquakes and hunger. In the Aztec year Thirteen Flint, volcanoes erupted, sickness and hunger spread, and an eclipse of the sun darkened the sky. Did some priest wonder whether the Fifth Sun was approaching its end? In time, the Aztecs learned that Thirteen Flint was called 1492 by the Europeans.

North America in 1492

*O*ver the centuries, the Americans who lived north of Mexico adapted their once-similar ways of life to very different climates and terrains, thus creating the diverse cultures that the Europeans encountered when they first arrived (see Map 1.1). Scholars often refer to such cultures by language group (such as Algonquian or Iroquoian), since neighboring Indian nations commonly spoke related languages. Bands that lived in environments not well suited to agriculture followed a nomadic lifestyle. Within the area of the present-day United States, these groups included the Paiutes and Shoshones, who inhabited the Great Basin (now Nevada and Utah). Because of the difficulty of finding sufficient food for more than a few people, such hunter-gatherer bands were small. The men hunted small animals, and the women gathered seeds and berries. Where large game was more plentiful and food supplies therefore more certain, as in present-day central and western Canada and the Great Plains, bands of hunters were somewhat larger.

In more favorable environments, larger groups combined agriculture with gathering, hunting, and fishing. Those who lived near the seacoasts, like the Chinooks of present-day Washington State and Oregon, consumed fish and shellfish in addition to growing crops and gathering seeds and berries. Residents of the interior (for example, the Arikaras of the Missouri River valley) hunted large animals while also cultivating maize, squash, and beans. The peoples of what is now eastern Canada and the northeastern United States also combined hunting and agriculture.

Societies that relied primarily on hunting large animals assigned that task to men and allotted food preparation and clothing production to women. Agricultural societies, by contrast, differed in their assignments of work to the sexes. The Pueblo peoples (descendants of the Anasazi) defined agricultural labor as men's work. In the east, large clusters of peoples speaking Algonquian, Iroquoian, and Muskogean languages allocated most agricultural chores to women. In all the farming societies, women gathered wild foods and prepared food for consumption or storage, while men were responsible for hunting.

SEXUAL DIVISION OF LABOR IN NORTH AMERICA

Everywhere in North America, women cared for young children, while older youths learned adult skills from the parent of the same sex. Young people usually chose their own marital partners, and in most societies couples could easily divorce. Populations in these societies remained at a level sustainable by existing food supplies, largely because of low birth rates. Mothers nursed infants and toddlers until the age of two or even longer, and taboos prevented couples from having sexual intercourse during that period.

The southwestern and eastern agricultural peoples had similar social organizations. The Pueblos lived in multistory buildings constructed on terraces along the sides of cliffs or other easily defended sites. Northern Iroquois villages (in modern New York State) were composed of large, rectangular, bark-covered structures, or longhouses. In the present-day southeastern United States, Muskogeans and southern Algonquians lived in large houses made of thatch. Defensive wood palisades and ditches surrounded most of the eastern villages.

SOCIAL ORGANIZATION

In all the agricultural societies, each dwelling housed an extended family defined matrilineally (through a female line of descent). Mothers, their married daughters, and their daughters' husbands and children all lived together. Matrilineal descent did not imply matriarchy, or the wielding of power by women, but rather served as a way to reckon kinship. Extended families were linked into clans defined by matrilineal ties. The nomadic bands of the Great Plains, by contrast, were most often related patrilineally (through the male line).

Long before Europeans arrived, residents of the continent fought one another for control of the best hunting and fishing territories, the most fertile agricultural lands, or the sources of essential items like salt (for preserving meat) and flint (for making knives and arrowheads). People captured in such wars were sometimes enslaved, but slavery was never an important source of labor in pre-Columbian America.

WAR AND POLITICS

American political structures varied considerably. Among Pueblo and Muskogean peoples, the village council was the highest political authority; no

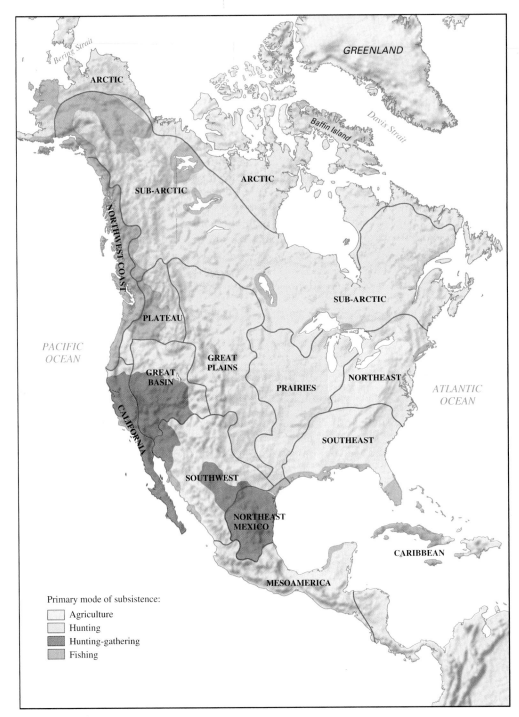

Map 1.1 Native Cultures of North America

The natives of the North American continent effectively used the resources of the regions in which they lived. As this map shows, coastal groups relied on fishing, residents of fertile areas engaged in agriculture, and other peoples employed hunting (often combined with gathering) as a primary mode of subsistence.

government structure connected the villages. Nomadic hunters also lacked formal links among separate bands. The Iroquois, by contrast, had an elaborate political hierarchy incorporating villages into nations and nations into a confederation; a council comprising representatives from each nation made crucial decisions concerning war and peace for the entire confederacy. In all the North American cultures, political power was divided between civil and war leaders, who wielded authority only so long as they retained the confidence of the people. Women assumed leadership roles more often among agricultural peoples than among nomadic hunters. Female sachems (rulers) led Algonquian villages in what is now Massachusetts, but women never became heads of Great Plains hunting bands. Iroquois women did not become chiefs, yet the clan matrons of each village chose its chief and could both start wars (by calling for the capture of prisoners to replace dead relatives) and stop them (by refusing to supply warriors with necessary foodstuffs).

Online Study Center
Improve Your Grade
   Primary Source: Dekanawida Myth & the
   Achievement of Iroquois Unity

Americans' religious beliefs varied even more than did their political systems, but all the peoples were

RELIGION

polytheistic, worshiping a multitude of gods. Each group's most important beliefs and rituals were closely tied to its means of subsistence. The major deities of agricultural peoples like the Pueblos and Muskogeans were associated with cultivation. The most important gods of hunters (such as those living on the Great Plains) were associated with animals. A band's economy and women's role in it helped to determine women's potential as religious leaders. Women held the most prominent positions in agricultural societies in which they were also the chief food producers, whereas in hunting societies, men took the lead in religious as well as political affairs.

A wide variety of cultures, comprising more than 5 million people, thus inhabited mainland North America when Europeans arrived. The diverse inhabitants of North America spoke well over one thousand different languages. For obvious reasons, they did not consider themselves one people, nor did they—for the most part—think of uniting to repel the European invaders.

African Societies

Fifteenth-century Africa also housed a variety of cultures adapted to different terrains and climates. In the north, along the Mediterranean Sea, lived the Berbers, who were Muslims, followers of the Islamic religion founded by the prophet Mohammed in the seventh century C.E.

On the east coast of Africa, Muslim city-states traded extensively with India, the Moluccas (part of modern Indonesia), and China. Waterborne commerce between the eastern Mediterranean and East Asia passed through the East African city-states; the rest followed the long land route across Central Asia known as the Silk Road.

South of the Mediterranean coast in the African interior lie the great Saharan and Libyan deserts. Below the deserts, much of the continent is divided between tropical rain forests (along the coasts) and grassy plains (in the interior). People speaking a variety of languages and pursuing different subsistence strategies lived in a wide belt south of the deserts. South of the Gulf of Guinea, the grassy landscape came to be dominated by Bantu-speaking peoples, who left their homeland in modern Nigeria about 2,000 years ago and slowly migrated south and east across the continent.

Online Study Center   **Improve Your Grade**
   Interactive Map: Africa and Its Peoples, c. 1400

West Africa was a land of tropical forests and savanna grasslands where fishing, cattle herding, and

WEST AFRICA (GUINEA)

agriculture supported the inhabitants. The northern region of West Africa, or Upper Guinea, was heavily influenced by the Islamic culture of the Mediterranean. Trade via camel caravans between Upper Guinea and the Muslim Mediterranean was sub-Saharan Africa's major connection to Europe and West Asia. In return for salt, dates, silk, and cotton cloth, Africans exchanged ivory, gold, and slaves with northern merchants.

The people of Upper Guinea's northernmost region, the so-called Rice Coast (present-day Gambia, Senegal, and Guinea), fished and cultivated rice. The Grain Coast, the next region to the south, was thinly populated and not readily accessible from the sea because it had only one good harbor (modern Freetown,

Sierra Leone). Its people concentrated on farming and raising livestock.

In the fifteenth century, most Africans in Lower Guinea were farmers who practiced traditional religions, not the precepts of Islam. As did the agricultural peoples of the Americas, they developed rituals intended to ensure good harvests. Throughout the region, individual villages composed of kin groups were linked into hierarchical kingdoms characterized by decentralized political and social authority.

The societies of West Africa, like those of the Americas, assigned different tasks to men and women.

COMPLEMENTARY GENDER ROLES

In general, the sexes shared agricultural duties. Men also hunted, managed livestock, and did most of the fishing. Women were responsible for child care, food preparation, and cloth manufacture. Everywhere in West Africa, women were the primary local traders.

Despite their different economies and the rivalries among states, the peoples of Lower Guinea had similar social systems organized on the basis of what anthropologists have called the dual-sex principle. In Lower Guinea, each sex handled its own affairs: just as male political and religious leaders governed men, so females ruled women. In the Dahomean kingdom, for example, every male official had his female counterpart; in the thirty little Akan States on the Gold Coast, chiefs inherited their status through the female line, and each male chief had a female assistant who supervised other women.

Throughout Upper Guinea, religious beliefs stressed complementary male and female roles. Both women and men served as heads of the cults and secret societies that directed the spiritual life of the villages. Young women were initiated into the Sandé cult, young men into Poro. Although West African women rarely held formal power over men, female religious leaders did govern other members of their sex within the Sandé cult.

West African law recognized both individual and communal landownership, but men seeking to

SLAVERY IN GUINEA

accumulate wealth needed access to labor, including slaves. West Africans held in slavery on their own continent therefore made up essential elements of the economy. Africans could be enslaved for life as punishment for crimes, but more often slaves were enemy captives or people who voluntarily enslaved themselves or their children to pay debts. An African who possessed bondspeople had a right to the products of their labor, although the degree to which slaves were exploited varied greatly. Some slaves were held as chattel; others could engage in trade, retaining a portion of their profits; and still others achieved prominent political or military positions. All, however, found it difficult to overcome the social stigma of enslavement, and they could be traded or sold at the will of their owners.

■ This decorative brass weight, created by the Asante peoples of Lower Guinea, was used for measuring gold dust. It depicts a family pounding fu-fu, a food made by mashing together plantains (a kind of banana), yams, and cassava. The paste was then shaped into balls to be eaten with soup. This weight, probably used in trading with Europeans, shows a scene combining foods of African origin (plantains and yams) with an import from the Americas (cassava), thus bringing the three continents together in ways both symbolic and real.   (© Trustees of the British Museum. Photo by Michael Holford)

European Societies

ﬁn the fifteenth century, Europeans too were agricultural peoples. Split into numerous small, warring countries, Europe was divided linguistically, politically, and economically, yet in social terms Europeans' lives were more similar than different. European societies were hierarchical: a few families wielded autocratic power over the majority of the people. At the base of such hierarchies were people held in various forms of bondage. Although Europeans were not subjected to perpetual slavery, Christian doctrine permitted the enslavement of "heathens" (non-Christians), and serfdom restricted some Europeans' freedom, tying them to the land, if not to specific owners. In short, Europe's kingdoms resembled those of Africa and Mesoamerica but differed greatly from the more egalitarian societies found in America north of Mexico (see Map 1.2).

Most Europeans, like most Africans and Americans, lived in small villages. European farmers, who

Map 1.2   Europe in 1490

The Europeans who ventured out into the Atlantic came from countries on the northwestern edge of the continent, which was divided into numerous competing nations.

SEXUAL DIVISION OF LABOR IN EUROPE

were called peasants, owned or leased separate landholdings, but they worked the fields communally. Because fields had to lie fallow (unplanted) every second or third year to regain fertility, a family could not ensure itself a regular food supply unless all villagers shared each year's work and crops. Men did most of the fieldwork; women helped out chiefly at planting and harvest. In some areas, men concentrated on herding livestock. Women's duties consisted primarily of child care and household tasks, including preserving food, milking cows, and caring for poultry. Since Europeans kept domesticated pigs, goats, sheep, and cattle for meat, hunting had little economic importance in their cultures.

In contrast to African and American societies, in which women often played prominent roles in politics and religion, men dominated all areas of life in Europe. A few women—notably Queen Elizabeth I of England—achieved status or power by right of birth, but the vast majority were excluded from positions of political authority. Husbands and fathers expected to control their families. European women generally held inferior social, economic, and political positions, yet within their own families they wielded power over children and servants.

Christianity was the dominant religion in Europe. In the West, authority rested in the Catholic

CHRISTIANITY

Church, based in Rome and led by the pope. The Catholic Church had an uneasy relationship with both secular rulers and the populace at large. Although European peoples were nominally Catholic, many adhered to local belief systems that the church deemed heretical and could not extinguish. Kings would ally themselves with the church when it suited their needs but often acted independently. Even so, the Christian nations of Europe from the twelfth century on publicly united in a goal of driving nonbelievers (especially Muslims) not only from European domains but also from the holy city of Jerusalem, which caused the series of wars known as the Crusades.

When the fifteenth century began, European nations were slowly recovering from the devastating

EFFECTS OF PLAGUE AND WARFARE

epidemic of plague known as the Black Death, which seems to have arrived in Europe from China, traveling with long-distance traders along the Silk Road to the eastern Mediterranean. From 1346 through the 1360s and 1370s, the plague killed an estimated one-third of Europe's people. A precipitous economic decline followed, as did severe social, political, and religious disruption because of the deaths of clergymen and other leading figures.

As plague ravaged the population, England and France waged the Hundred Years' War (1337–1453) over the English monarchy's claim to the French throne. The war interrupted overland trade routes through France that connected England and the Netherlands to the Italian city-states and thence to Central Asia. Merchants in the eastern Mediterranean found a new way to reach their northern markets by forging a regular maritime link with the Netherlands to replace the overland route. The use of a triangular, or lateen, sail (rather than the then-standard square rigging) improved the maneuverability of ships. Also of key importance was the perfection of navigational instruments like the astrolabe and the quadrant, which allowed oceangoing sailors to estimate their position (latitude) by measuring the relationship of the sun, moon, or certain stars to the horizon.

In the aftermath of the Hundred Years' War, European monarchs forcefully consolidated their previously diffuse political power

POLITICAL AND TECHNOLOGICAL CHANGE

and raised new revenues through increased taxation of an already hard-pressed peasantry. In England, Henry VII in 1485 founded the Tudor dynasty and began uniting a previously divided land. In France, the successors of Charles VII unified the kingdom. Most successful of all were Ferdinand of Aragón and Isabella of Castile, who married in 1469, founding a strongly Catholic Spain. In 1492 they defeated the Muslims, who had lived in Spain and Portugal for centuries, and thereafter expelled all Jews and Muslims from their domain.

The fifteenth century also brought technological change to Europe. Movable type and the printing press, invented in Germany in the 1450s, made information more accessible than ever before. Printing stimulated the Europeans' curiosity about fabled lands across the seas—lands they could now read about in books. The most important such work was Marco Polo's *Travels,* first published in 1477, which recounted a Venetian merchant's adventures in thirteenth-century China and, most intriguing, described that nation as bordered on the east by an ocean. Polo's account led

Nova zemla

Strate de Naſſauwe

Matflo Delgo

SAMVE TEN LANT

■ In the fifteenth and sixteenth centuries, caravels ventured into the open oceans, thereby changing the contours of the known world. This illustration from a manuscript account of William Barents's 1594 expedition into the Arctic Ocean shows the combination of square rigging and lateen sails that gave ships greater maneuverability and allowed them to navigate along unfamiliar coastlines far from their home ports.   (Bridgeman Art Library)

many Europeans to believe that they could trade directly with China in oceangoing vessels instead of relying on the Silk Road or the route through East Africa.

Technological advances and the growing strength of newly powerful national rulers made possible

MOTIVES FOR EXPLORATION

the European explorations of the fifteenth and sixteenth centuries. Each country craved easy access to African and Asian goods—spices like pepper, cloves, cinnamon, and nutmeg (to season the bland European diet), silk, dyes, perfumes, jewels, sugar, and gold. A desire to spread Christianity around the world supplemented the economic motive. This linking of materialist and spiritual goals might seem contradictory today, but fifteenth-century Europeans saw no necessary conflict between the two. Explorers and colonizers—especially Roman Catholics—honestly sought to convert "heathen" peoples, while at the same time hoping to increase their nation's wealth and standing among other countries.

Early European Explorations

Before European mariners could discover new lands, they had to explore the oceans. To reach Asia, seafarers needed not just maneuverable vessels and navigational aids, but also knowledge of the sea, its currents, and especially its winds. How did the winds run? Where would Atlantic breezes take their ships?

Europeans answered these questions in the "Mediterranean Atlantic": the expanse of the Atlantic Ocean that is south and west of Iberia, the peninsula that includes Spain and Portugal, and bounded by the island groups of the Azores (on the west) and the Canaries (on the south), with the Madeiras in their midst. Europeans reached all three sets of islands during the fourteenth century. From their experience sailing in the Mediterranean Atlantic, mariners learned to exploit the prevailing winds—the Northeast Trades that would push them south along the coast of Africa and eventually toward the Caribbean; and the Westerlies, farther north, that returned them to Europe.

SAILING IN THE MEDITERRANEAN ATLANTIC

During the fifteenth century, armed with knowledge of the winds and currents of the Mediterranean Atlantic, Iberian seamen regularly visited the three island groups, all of which they could reach in two weeks or less. By the 1450s Portuguese colonists in the Madeiras were employing slaves (probably Jews and Muslims brought from Iberia) to grow large quantities of sugar for export to the mainland. By the 1470s Madeira had developed into a colonial plantation economy. For the first time in world history, a region had been settled explicitly to cultivate a valuable crop—sugar—to be sold elsewhere, and only a supply of enslaved laborers to do the backbreaking plantation work could ensure the system's continued success.

ISLANDS OF THE MEDITERRANEAN ATLANTIC

Meanwhile, the Guanche people of the Canary Islands fought the assaults of the French, Portuguese, and Spanish. However, the Guanches were weakened by European diseases, and one by one the islands fell to Europeans, who carried off the Guanches as slaves to the Madeiras or the Iberian Peninsula. Spain conquered the last island in 1496 and subsequently devoted the land to sugar cultivation. Collectively, the Canaries and Madeira became known as the Wine Islands because much of their sugar production was directed to making sweet wines.

For Portugal's Prince Henry the Navigator, the islands were steppingstones to Africa. He knew that vast wealth awaited the first European nation to tap the riches of Africa and Asia directly. Each year he dispatched ships southward along the African coast, attempting to discover an oceanic route to Asia. But not until after Prince Henry's death did Bartholomew Dias round the southern tip of Africa (1488) and Vasco da Gama finally reach India (1498).

PORTUGUESE TRADING POSTS IN AFRICA

Long before that, West African states had allowed the Portuguese to establish trading posts along their coasts. Charging the traders rent and levying duties on goods they imported, the African kingdoms set the terms of exchange and benefited considerably from their new, easier access to European manufactures. The Portuguese gained too, for they no longer had to rely on trans-Saharan camel caravans. Their vessels earned immense profits by swiftly transporting African gold, ivory, and slaves to Europe. By bargaining with African masters to purchase their slaves and then carrying those bondspeople to Iberia, the Portuguese introduced black slavery into Europe.

In the 1480s the Portuguese colonized an island off the African coast, previously uninhabited: São Tomé, located in the Gulf of Guinea. The soil of São Tomé proved ideal for raising sugar, and plantation agriculture there expanded rapidly. Planters imported large numbers of slaves from the mainland to work in the cane fields, thus creating the first economy based primarily on the bondage of black Africans.

By the 1490s, Europeans had learned three key lessons of colonization in the Mediterranean Atlantic. First, they had learned how to transplant their crops and livestock successfully to exotic locations. Second, they had discovered that the native peoples of those lands could be either conquered (the Guanches) or exploited (the Africans). Third, they had developed a viable model of plantation slavery and a system for supplying nearly unlimited quantities of such workers. The stage was set for a pivotal moment in world history.

LESSONS OF EARLY COLONIZATION

The Voyages of Columbus, Cabot, and Their Successors

Christopher Columbus was well schooled in the lessons of the Mediterranean Atlantic. Born in 1451 in the Italian city-state of Genoa, Columbus was by the 1490s an experienced sailor and mapmaker. Like many mariners of the day, he was drawn to Portugal and its islands, especially Madeira, where he commanded a merchant vessel. At least once he voyaged to the Portuguese outpost on the Gold Coast. There he acquired an obsession with gold and came to understand the economic potential of the slave trade.

Like all accomplished seafarers and most educated people, Columbus knew the world was round. However, he differed from other cartographers in his estimate of the earth's size: he thought that China lay only 3,000 miles from the southern European coast. Thus, he argued, it would be easier to reach Asia by sailing west than by making the difficult voyage around the southern tip of Africa. Experts scoffed at this crackpot notion, accurately predicting that the two continents lay 12,000 miles apart. When Columbus in 1484 asked the Portuguese authorities to back his plan to sail west to Asia, they rejected the proposal.

Ferdinand and Isabella of Spain, jealous of Portugal's successes in Africa, were more receptive to Columbus's ideas. Urged on by some Spanish noblemen and a group of Italian merchants residing in Castile, the monarchs agreed to finance the risky voyage. And so, on August 3, 1492, in command of the *Pinta*, the *Niña*, and the *Santa Maria*, Columbus set sail from the Spanish port of Palos.

COLUMBUS'S VOYAGE

On October 12, he and his men landed on an island in the Bahamas, which he renamed San Salvador. Later he went on to explore the islands now known as Cuba and Hispaniola. Because he thought he had reached the Indies, Columbus referred to the inhabitants of the region as Indians.

Three themes predominate in Columbus's log. First, he insistently asked the Taínos, the islands' residents, where he could find gold, pearls, and valuable spices. Each time, his informants replied (largely via signs) that such products could be

COLUMBUS'S OBSERVATIONS

obtained on other islands, on the mainland, or in cities in the interior. Second, he wrote repeatedly of the strange and beautiful plants and animals. Columbus's interest was more than aesthetic. "I believe that there are many plants and trees here that could be worth a lot in Spain for use as dyes, spices, and medicines," he observed, adding that he was carrying home to Europe "a sample of everything I can," so that experts could examine them.

Third, Columbus described the Taíno people, and he seized some to take back to Spain. The Taínos were, he said, very handsome, gentle, and friendly. He believed they would be likely converts to Catholicism. He also thought the islanders "ought to make good and skilled servants."

These records of the first encounter between Europeans and America and its residents revealed the themes that would be of enormous significance for centuries to come. Above all, Europeans wanted to extract profits from North and South America by exploiting their natural resources: plants, animals, and peoples alike. Christopher Columbus made three more voyages, exploring most of the major Caribbean islands and sailing along the coasts of Central and South America. Until the day he died in 1506 at the age of fifty-five, Columbus believed that he had reached Asia. Even before his death, others knew better. Because the Florentine Amerigo Vespucci, who explored the South American coast in 1499, was the first to publish the idea that a new continent had been discovered, Martin Waldseemüller in 1507 labeled the land "America." By then, Spain, Portugal, and Pope Alexander VI had signed the Treaty of Tordesillas (1494), confirming Portugal's dominance in Africa—and later Brazil—in exchange for Spanish preeminence in the rest of the Americas.

EUROPEANS AND "AMERICA"

Five hundred years before Columbus, about the year 1001, the Norseman Leif Ericsson and other Norse explorers sailed to North America across the Davis Strait, which separated their villages in Greenland from Baffin Island (see Map 1.1), settling at a site they named Vinland. Attacks by local residents forced them to depart after just a few years. In the 1960s, archaeologists determined that the Norse had established an outpost at

NORSE AND OTHER NORTHERN VOYAGERS

what is now L'Anse aux Meadows, Newfoundland, but Vinland itself was probably located farther south.

Later Europeans did not know of the Norse explorers, but some historians argue that European sailors may have found the rich Newfoundland fishing grounds in the 1480s but kept their discoveries a secret so that they alone could fish there. Whether or not fishermen crossed the entire width of the Atlantic, they thoroughly explored its northern reaches, voyaging among the European continent, England, Ireland, and Iceland. Those who explored what would become the United States and Canada built on their knowledge. They learned that in the spring at the northernmost reaches of the Westerlies, sporadic shifts to easterly winds would push them west. Thus, those taking the northern route usually reached America along the coast of what is now Maine or the Canadian maritime provinces.

The European generally credited with "discovering" North America is John Cabot. More precisely,

JOHN CABOT'S EXPLORATIONS

Cabot brought to Europe the first formal knowledge of the northern coastline of the continent and claimed the land for England. Like Columbus, Cabot was a master mariner from the Italian city-state of Genoa, and he was in Spain when Columbus returned from his first trip to America. Calculating that England—which traded with Asia only through a long series of middlemen stretching from Belgium to Venice to the Muslim world—would be eager to sponsor exploratory voyages, Cabot sought and won the support of King Henry VII. He set sail from Bristol in late May 1497, reaching his destination on June 24. Scholars disagree about the location of his landfall (some say it was Cape Breton Island, others Newfoundland), but all recognize the importance of his month-long exploration of the coast.

The voyages of Columbus, Cabot, and their successors finally brought the Eastern and Western Hemispheres together. The Portuguese explorer Pedro Álvares Cabral reached Brazil in 1500; John Cabot's son Sebastian followed his father to North America in 1507; France financed Giovanni da Verrazzano in 1524 and Jacques Cartier in 1534; and in 1609 and 1610 Henry Hudson explored the North American coast for the Dutch West India Company. These men were primarily searching for the legendary, nonexistent "Northwest Passage" through

the Americas, but their discoveries interested European nations in exploring North and South America.

Spanish Exploration and Conquest

*O*nly in the areas that Spain explored and claimed did colonization begin immediately. On his second voyage in 1493, Columbus brought to Hispaniola seventeen ships loaded with twelve hundred men, seeds, plants, livestock, chickens, and dogs—along with microbes, rats, and weeds. The settlement named Isabela (in the modern Dominican Republic) and its successors became the staging area for the Spanish invasion of America.

At first, Spanish explorers fanned out around the Caribbean basin. In 1513 Juan Ponce de León reached Florida, and Vasco Núñez de Balboa crossed the Isthmus of Panama to the Pacific Ocean. In the 1530s and 1540s, conquistadors traveled farther, exploring many regions claimed by the Spanish monarchs: Francisco Vásquez de Coronado journeyed through the southwestern portion of what is now the United States at approximately the same time as Hernán de Soto explored the southeast and encountered the Lady of Cofitachequi. Juan Rodriguez Cabrillo sailed along the California coast, and Francisco Pizarro acquired the richest silver mines in the world by conquering and enslaving the Incas in western South America. But the most important conquistador was Hernán Cortés.

Cortés, an adventurer who first arrived in the West Indies in 1504, embarked for the mainland in

CORTÉS AND MALINCHE

1519 in search of the wealthy cities rumored to exist there. As he moved his force inland from the Gulf of Mexico, local Mayas presented him with a gift of twenty young female slaves. One of them, Malinche, who had been sold into slavery by the Aztecs and raised by the Mayas, became Cortés's translator. Malinche bore Cortés a son, Martín—one of the first *mestizos*, or mixed-blood children—and eventually married one of his officers. When the Aztec capital Tenochtitlán fell to the Spaniards in 1521, Cortés and his men seized a fabulous treasure of gold and silver. Thus, not long after Columbus's first voyage, the Spanish monarchs controlled the richest, most extensive empire Europe had known since ancient Rome.

Spain established the model of colonization that other countries later attempted to imitate, a model with three major elements. First, the Crown maintained tight control over the colonies, imposing a hierarchical government that allowed little autonomy to New World jurisdictions. Second, most of the colonists sent from Spain were male. They took Indian—and later African—women as their sexual partners, thereby creating the racially mixed population that characterizes much of Latin America to the present day.

SPANISH COLONIZATION

Third, the colonies' wealth was based on the exploitation of both the native population and slaves imported from Africa. The *encomienda* system, which granted tribute from Indian villages to individual conquistadors as a reward for their services to the Crown, in effect legalized Indian slavery. Yet in 1542 a new code of laws reformed the system, forbidding Spaniards from enslaving Indians. In response, the conquerors, familiar with slavery in Spain, began to import Africans to increase the labor force under their direct control.

Spanish wealth derived from American suffering. The Spaniards deliberately leveled American cities, building cathedrals and monasteries on sites once occupied by Aztec, Incan, and Mayan temples. Some conquistadors sought to erase all vestiges of the great Indian cultures by burning the written records they found. With their traditional ways of life in disarray, devastated by disease, and compelled to labor for their conquerors, many demoralized residents of Mesoamerica accepted the Christian religion brought to New Spain by friars of the Franciscan and Dominican orders.

The friars devoted their energies to persuading Mesoamerican people to move into new towns and build Roman Catholic churches. In such towns, Indians were exposed to European customs and religious rituals designed to assimilate Catholic and pagan beliefs. Friars deliberately juxtaposed the cult of the Virgin Mary with that of the corn goddess, and the Indians adeptly melded aspects of their traditional worldview with Christianity, in a process called syncretism. Thousands of Indians residing in Spanish territory embraced Catholicism,

CHRISTIANITY IN NEW SPAIN

at least partly because it was the religion of their new rulers.

The Columbian Exchange

 broad mutual transfer of diseases, plants, and animals (called the Columbian Exchange by the historian Alfred Crosby) resulted directly from the European voyages of the fifteenth and sixteenth centuries and from Spanish colonization. The Eastern and Western Hemispheres had evolved separately for thousands of years, developing widely different forms of life. Many large mammals like cattle and horses were native to the connected continents of Europe, Asia, and Africa, but the Americas had no domesticated beasts larger than dogs and llamas. The vegetable crops of the Americas—particularly corn, beans, squash, cassava, and potatoes—were more nutritious and produced higher yields than those of Europe and Africa, such as wheat, millet, and rye. In time, native peoples learned to raise and consume European livestock, and Europeans and Africans became accustomed to planting and eating American crops. The diets of all three peoples were consequently vastly enriched.

Diseases carried from Europe and Africa, though, had a devastating impact on the Americas. Indians fell victim to microbes that had long infested the other continents and had repeatedly killed hundreds of thousands but had also left survivors with some measure of immunity. The statistics are staggering. When Columbus landed on Hispaniola in 1492, approximately half a million people resided there. Fifty years later, fewer than two thousand native inhabitants were still alive. Overall, historians estimate that the alien microorganisms could have reduced the American population by as much as 90 percent.

SMALLPOX AND OTHER DISEASES

The greatest killer was smallpox, spread primarily by direct human contact. One epidemic began on Hispaniola in December 1518 and was carried to the mainland by Spaniards in 1520. There it fatally weakened the defenders of Tenochtitlán. As an old Aztec man recalled, "It spread over the people as great destruction." Largely as a consequence, Tenochtitlán surrendered, and the Spaniards built Mexico City on its site.

Maize, to Mesoamericans, was a gift from Quetzalcoatl, the plumed serpent god. Cherokees told of an old woman whose blood produced the prized stalks after her grandson buried her body in a cleared, sunny field. For the Abenakis, the crop began when a beautiful maiden ordered a youth to drag her by the hair through a burned-over field. The long hair of the Cherokee grandmother and the Abenaki maiden turned into silk, the flower on the stalks that Europeans called Indian corn.

Sacred to all the Indian peoples who grew it, maize was a cereal crop, a main part of their diet. They dried the kernels; ground into meal, maize was cooked as a mush or shaped into flat cakes and baked, the forerunners of modern tortillas. Indians also heated the dried kernels until they popped open, just as is done today. Although the European invaders of North and South America initially disdained maize, they soon learned that it could be cultivated in a wide variety of conditions— from sea level to twelve thousand feet, from regions with abundant rainfall to dry lands with as little as twelve inches of rain a year. Corn was also highly productive, yielding almost twice as many calories per acre as wheat. So Europeans too came to rely on corn, growing it not only in their American settlements but also in their homelands.

Maize cultivation spread to Asia and Africa. Today, China is second only to the United States in total corn production, and corn is more widely grown in Africa than any other crop. Still, the United States produces 45 percent of the world's corn—almost half of it in the three states of Illinois, Iowa, and Nebraska—and corn is the nation's single largest crop. More than half of American corn is consumed by livestock. Much of the rest is processed into syrup, which sweetens carbonated beverages and candies, or into ethanol, a gasoline additive that reduces both pollution and dependence on fossil fuels. Corn is an ingredient in light beer and toothpaste. It is used in the manufacture of tires, wallpaper, cat litter, and aspirin. Remarkably, of the ten thousand products in a modern American grocery store, about one-fourth rely to some extent on corn.

Today this crop bequeathed to the world by ancient American plant breeders provides one-fifth of all the calories consumed by the earth's peoples. The gift of Quetzalcoatl has linked the globe.

The earliest known European drawing of maize, the American plant that was to have such an extraordinary impact on the entire world. (Typ 565.42. 409 F[B], Department of Printing and Graphic Arts, Houghton Library, Harvard College Library)

Far to the north, where smaller American populations encountered only a few Europeans, disease also ravaged the countryside. A great epidemic, probably smallpox coupled with measles, swept through the villages along the coast north of Cape Cod from 1616 to 1618. Again the mortality rate may have been as high as 90 percent. Because of this dramatic depopulation of the area, English colonists were able to establish settlements virtually unopposed just a few years later.

The Americans, though, took a revenge of sorts. They gave the Europeans syphilis, a virulent venereal disease. The first recorded European case of the new ailment occurred in Barcelona, Spain, in 1493, shortly after Columbus's return from the Caribbean. Carried by soldiers, sailors, and prostitutes, it spread quickly through Europe and Asia, reaching as far as China by 1505.

The exchange of three commodities had significant impacts on Europe and the Americas. Sugar,

SUGAR, HORSES, AND TOBACCO which was first domesticated in the East Indies, was being grown on the islands of the Mediterranean Atlantic by 1450. The insatiable European demand for sugar led Columbus to take Canary Island sugar canes to Hispaniola on his 1493 voyage. By the 1520s, plantations worked by African slaves in the Greater Antilles (the major Caribbean islands) regularly shipped cargoes of sugar to Spain. Half a century later, the Portuguese colony in Brazil (founded in 1532) was producing sugar on an even larger scale for the European market, and after 1640, sugar cultivation became the crucial component of English and French colonization in the Caribbean.

Horses, which like sugar were brought to America by Columbus in 1493, fell into the hands of North American Indians during the seventeenth century. Through trade and theft, horses spread among the peoples of the Great Plains, reaching most areas by 1750. Lakota, Comanches, and Crows, among others, came to use horses for transportation and hunting, calculated their wealth in the number of horses owned, and waged wars primarily from horseback. Women no longer had to carry the bands' belongings on their backs. And a mode of subsistence that had been based on hunting several different animals, in combination with gathering and agriculture, became one focused almost wholly on hunting buffalo.

In America, Europeans encountered tobacco, which at first they believed had beneficial medicinal effects. Smoking and chewing the "Indian weed" became a fad in Europe. Despite the efforts of such skeptics as King James I of England, who in 1604 pronounced smoking "harmfull to the brain, [and] dangerous to the Lungs," tobacco's popularity climbed.

The European and African invasion of the Americas therefore had a significant biological component, for the invaders carried plants and animals with them. Some creatures, such as livestock, they brought deliberately. Others, including rats, weeds, and diseases, arrived unexpectedly. And upon their return home, the Europeans deliberately took back such crops as corn, potatoes, and tobacco, along with that unanticipated stowaway, syphilis.

Europeans in North America

*N*orthern Europeans, denied access to the wealth of Mesoamerica by the Spanish and beaten to South America by the Portuguese, were initially more interested in exploiting North America's abundant natural resources than in the difficult task of establishing colonies on the mainland. Following John Cabot's report of a plentiful supply of fish along the North American coast, Europeans rushed to reap the sea's bounty. By the 1570s, more than 350 ships, primarily from France and England, were capitalizing on the fisheries of the Newfoundland Banks each year.

European fishermen soon learned that they could augment their profits by exchanging cloth and metal

TRADE AMONG INDIANS AND EUROPEANS goods like pots and knives for the native trappers' beaver pelts, which Europeans used to make fashionable hats. At first the Europeans conducted their trading from ships sailing along the coast, but later they established permanent outposts on the mainland to centralize and control the traffic in furs.

The Europeans' demand for furs, especially beaver, was matched by the Indians' desire for European goods that could make their lives easier and establish their superiority over their neighbors. Some bands began to concentrate so completely on trapping for the European market that they abandoned their traditional economies. The intensive trade in pelts also had serious ecological consequences. In some regions, beavers were completely wiped out. The disappearance of their dams led to soil erosion, especially when combined with the extensive clearing of forests by later European settlers.

Although their nation reaped handsome profits from fishing, English merchants and political leaders

CONTEST BETWEEN SPAIN AND ENGLAND

watched enviously as Spain's American possessions enriched that country immeasurably. In the mid-sixteenth century, English "sea dogs" like John Hawkins and Sir Francis Drake began to raid Spanish treasure fleets sailing home from the West Indies. Their actions helped to foment a war that in 1588 culminated in the defeat of a huge invasion force—the Spanish Armada—off the English coast. As part of the contest with Spain, English leaders started to think about planting colonies in the Western Hemisphere, thereby gaining better access to valuable trade goods and simultaneously preventing their enemy from dominating the Americas.

The first English colonial planners hoped to reproduce Spanish successes by dispatching to America men who would similarly exploit the native peoples for their own and their nation's benefit. In the mid-1570s, a group that included Sir Humphrey Gilbert and his younger half-brother, Sir Walter Raleigh, began to promote a scheme to establish outposts that could trade with the Indians and provide bases for attacks on New Spain. Approving the idea, Queen Elizabeth I authorized first Gilbert, and then Raleigh, to colonize North America.

Gilbert died trying, unsuccessfully, to plant a colony in Newfoundland, and Raleigh was only briefly

ROANOKE

more successful. After two preliminary expeditions, in 1587 he sent 117 colonists to the territory he named Virginia, after Elizabeth, the "Virgin Queen." They established a settlement on Roanoke Island, in what is now North Carolina, but in 1590 a resupply ship—delayed in leaving England because of the Spanish Armada—could not find them. The colonists had vanished, leaving only the name of a nearby island carved on a tree.

Thus, England's first attempt to plant a permanent settlement on the North American coast failed, as had similar efforts by Portugal on Cape Breton Island (in the early 1520s) and France in northern Florida (in the mid-1560s). All three enterprises collapsed because of the hostility of their neighbors and their inability to be self-sustaining in food.

The explanation for such failures becomes clear in Thomas Harriot's *A Briefe and True Report of the New Found Land of Virginia*, pub-

HARRIOT'S BRIEFE AND TRUE REPORT

lished in 1588 to publicize Raleigh's colony. Harriot, a noted scientist who sailed with the second of the preliminary voyages to Roanoke, described the animals, plants, and people of the region for an English readership. His account revealed that although the explorers depended on nearby villagers for most of their food, they needlessly antagonized their neighbors by killing some of them for what Harriot himself admitted were unjustifiable reasons. The scientist advised later colonizers to deal with the native peoples of America more humanely than his comrades had.

Harriot's *Briefe and True Report* depicted for his English readers a bountiful land full of opportunities for quick profit. The people already residing there would, he thought, "in a short time be brought to civilitie" through conversion to Christianity, admiration for European superiority, or conquest—if they did not die from disease, the ravages of which he witnessed. Thomas Harriot's prediction was far off the mark: European dominance of North America would be difficult to achieve.

Summary   Online Study Center   ACE the Test

*T*he process of initial contact between Europeans and Americans that ended near the close of the sixteenth century began approximately 250 years earlier when Portuguese sailors first set out to explore the Mediterranean Atlantic and settle its islands. That region of the Atlantic so close to European and African shores nurtured mariners who, like Christopher Columbus, ventured into previously unknown waters. When Columbus first reached the Americas, he thought he had found Asia, his intended destination. Later explorers knew better but, except for the Spanish, regarded the Americas primarily as a barrier to their long-sought goal of an oceanic route to the riches of China and the Moluccas. Ordinary European fishermen were the first to realize that the northern coasts had valuable products to offer: fish and furs, both much in demand in their homelands.

The wealth of the north could not compare to that of Mesoamerica. The Aztec Empire, heir to the trading networks of Teotihuacán as well as to the intellectual sophistication of the Mayas, dazzled the conquistadors with the magnificence of its buildings and its seemingly unlimited wealth. The Aztecs believed that their Fifth Sun would end in earthquakes and hunger. Hunger they surely experienced after Cortés's invasion; and if there were no earthquakes, the great temples tumbled to the ground nevertheless, as the Spaniards used their stones (and Indian laborers) to construct cathedrals honoring their God and his son, Jesus, rather than Huitzilopochtli. The conquerors employed first American and later enslaved African workers to till the fields, mine the precious metals, and herd the livestock that earned immense profits for themselves and their mother country.

The initial impact of Europeans on the Americas proved devastating. Flourishing civilizations were, if not entirely destroyed, markedly altered in just a few decades. By the end of the sixteenth century, fewer people resided in North America than had lived there before Columbus's arrival, even taking into account the arrival of many Europeans and Africans. And the people who did live there—Indian, African, and European—resided in a world that was indeed new—a world engaged in the unprecedented process of combining foods, religions, economies, styles of life, and political systems that had developed separately for millennia. Understandably, conflict and dissension permeated that process.

LEGACY FOR A PEOPLE AND A NATION
Columbus Day

Each year, the United States celebrates the second Monday in October as a tribute to Christopher Columbus's landing in the Bahamas in 1492. The first known U.S. celebration of Columbus's voyage occurred in New York City on October 12, 1792, when a men's social club gave a dinner to mark its three hundredth anniversary. In the late 1860s, Italian American communities in New York City and San Francisco began to celebrate October 12, but not until 1892 did a congressional resolution order a one-time national commemoration. Columbus Day was first observed as a national holiday in 1971.

Today, the annual observances can arouse strong emotions. The American Indian Movement, founded in 1968, has declared that "from an indigenous vantage point, Columbus' arrival was a disaster" and that he "deserves no recognition or accolades." At the same time, people of Hispanic descent have claimed Columbus as their own, insisting that his voyage was "a thoroughly Spanish event." In some cities, most notably New York, their celebrations rival those long organized by Italian Americans; in others, such as Miami, Hispanics control the official commemorations. Still other Latinos, especially those of Mexican descent living in Los Angeles, call October 12 Día de la Raza and use it as an occasion to protest current U.S. immigration policy.

As ethnic diversity has increased in the nation and as peoples of different origins have sought to claim a share of the American heritage, holidays have unsurprisingly become the occasion for heated contests. Each fall, the American people and nation continue to confront the controversial legacy of Columbus's 1492 voyage.

EUROPEANS COLONIZE NORTH AMERICA 1600–1640

Captain William Rudyerd seemed like a man any Puritan colony in the Americas would prize, so when his older brother urged the planners of the new settlement to appoint him muster master general, they readily agreed. Rudyerd, a veteran of European wars, followed the new dissenting English faith, as did the planners and many of the settlers. In the colony's first years, Rudyerd proved to be a vigorous soldier who worked hard to train the settlers to defend themselves. But he also proved to be a vigorous defender of his own status, and his actions wreaked havoc in the fragile community. The captain beat to death a servant suffering from scurvy (thinking the servant merely lazy), and he also quarreled continually with other settlers, believing they failed to show the proper respect to a gentleman of noble birth.

Similar conflicts occurred in all the Anglo-American settlements, as gentlemen accustomed to unquestioning deference from their inferiors learned that in a colonial setting, their inherited social standing could be challenged. But in Rudyerd's colony, the disputes were especially dangerous, because the settlers lived on Providence Island, an isolated Puritan outpost off the coast of modern Nicaragua.

Providence Island, founded by a company of Puritan adventurers in 1630, sought to establish an English beachhead that could lead to successful colonization of the Central American mainland. Yet the outpost's failure to establish a viable economy and, ultimately, its desperate attempts to stay afloat financially by serving as a base for English privateers caused its downfall. That decision led the Spaniards to conclude that the Puritans must be removed. In May 1641, a large Spanish fleet captured the island, and the English survivors scattered to other Caribbean settlements or returned to England.

By this time, though, Spain no longer predominated in the Americas. France, the Netherlands, and England all had permanent colonies in North America by the 1640s. The French and Dutch colonies, like the Spanish out-

Online Study Center
This icon will direct you to interactive map and primary source activities on the website
http://college.hmco.com/pic/nortonbrief7e

C H R O N O L O G Y

1533 • Henry VIII divorces Catherine of Aragon; English Reformation begins

1558 • Elizabeth I becomes queen

1565 • Founding of St. Augustine (Florida), oldest permanent European settlement in present-day United States

1598 • Oñate conquers Pueblos in New Mexico for Spain

1603 • James I becomes king

1607 • Jamestown founded, first permanent English settlement in North America

1608 • Quebec founded by the French

1610 • Founding of Santa Fe, New Mexico

1611 • First Virginia tobacco crop

1614 • Fort Orange (Albany) founded by the Dutch

1619 • Virginia House of Burgesses established, first representative assembly in the English colonies

1620 • Plymouth colony founded, first permanent English settlement in New England

1622 • Powhatan Confederacy attacks Virginia

1624 • Dutch settle on Manhattan Island (New Amsterdam)
 • English colonize St. Kitts, first island in Lesser Antilles to be settled by Europeans
 • James I revokes Virginia Company's charter

1625 • Charles I becomes king

1630 • Massachusetts Bay colony founded

1634 • Maryland founded

1636 • Williams expelled from Massachusetts Bay, founds Providence, Rhode Island
 • Connecticut founded

1637 • Pequot War in New England

1638 • Hutchinson expelled from Massachusetts Bay colony, goes to Rhode Island

c. 1640 • Sugar cultivation begins on Barbados

1642 • Montreal founded by the French

1646 • Treaty ends hostilities between Virginia and Powhatan Confederacy

posts, were settled largely by European men who interacted regularly with indigenous peoples, using their labor or seeking to convert them to Christianity. Like the conquistadors, French and Dutch merchants and planters hoped to make a quick profit and then perhaps return to their homelands. The English, as Thomas Harriot had made clear in the 1580s, were just as interested in profiting from North America. But they pursued those profits in a different way.

In contrast to other Europeans, most of the English settlers, including those of the failed Providence Island colony, came to America intending to stay. Especially in the area that came to be known as New England, they arrived in family groups. They re-created European society and family life to an extent not possible in the other colonies, where migrant men found their sexual partners within the Indian or African populations. Among the English colonies, those in the Chesapeake region and on the Caribbean islands most closely resembled colonies founded by other nations with economies, like those of Hispaniola or Brazil, based on large-scale production for the international market by a labor force composed of bonded servants and slaves.

Wherever they settled, the English, like other Europeans, prospered only after they learned to adapt to the alien environment. The first permanent English colonies survived because nearby Indians assisted the newcomers. The settlers had to learn to grow unfamiliar American crops. They also had to develop extensive trading relationships with Native Americans and with colonies established by other European countries. Needing laborers for their fields, they first used English indentured servants, then later began to import African slaves. Thus, the early history of the region that became the United States and the English Caribbean is best understood not as an isolated story of English colonization, but rather as a series of complex interactions among a variety of European, African, and American peoples and environments. ■

New Spain, New France, and New Netherland

Spaniards established the first permanent European settlement within the boundaries of the modern United States, but others initially attempted that feat. Twice in the 1560s, groups of French Protestants (Huguenots) sought to escape from persecution in their homeland by planting colonies on the south Atlantic coast. A passing ship rescued the starving survivors of the first, in present-day South Carolina. The second, near modern Jacksonville, Florida, was destroyed in 1565 by a Spanish expedition under the command of Pedro Menéndez de Avilés. To ensure Spanish domination of the strategically important region (located near sea-lanes used by Spanish treasure ships bound for Europe), Menéndez set up a small fortified outpost, which he named St. Augustine—now the oldest continuously inhabited European settlement in the United States. Franciscan missionaries soon followed, and by the end of the sixteenth century, a chain of Franciscan missions stretched across northern Florida.

More than thirty years after the founding of St. Augustine, in 1598, Juan de Oñate, a Mexican-born adventurer, led a group of about five hundred soldiers and settlers to New Mexico. At first the Pueblos greeted the newcomers cordially.

NEW MEXICO

When the Spaniards began to torture, murder, and rape the villagers to extort food and clothing, however, the residents of Acoma killed several soldiers. The invaders responded ferociously, killing more than eight hundred people and capturing the remainder. Not surprisingly, the other Pueblo villages surrendered.

Because New Mexico held little wealth and was too far from the Pacific coast to assist in protecting Spanish sea-lanes, many of the Spaniards returned to Mexico, and officials considered abandoning the isolated colony. Instead, in 1609, the authorities decided to maintain a small military outpost and a few Christian missions in the area, with the capital at Santa Fe (founded in 1610). Here too, Spanish leaders were granted *encomiendas,* but the absence of mines or fertile agricultural lands made for small profit.

After Spain's destruction of France's Florida settlement in 1565, the French turned their attention northward. In 1608 Samuel de Champlain set up a trading post at an interior site the local Iroquois had called Stadacona; Champlain renamed it Quebec. He had chosen well: Quebec was the most easily defended spot in the entire St. Lawrence River valley and controlled access to the heartland of the continent. In 1642 the French established a second post, Montreal, at the falls of the St. Lawrence (and thus at the end of navigation by oceangoing vessels).

QUEBEC AND MONTREAL

Before the founding of these settlements, fishermen served as the major transporters of North American beaver pelts to France, but the new posts quickly took over control of the lucrative trade in furs (see Table 2.1). In the hope of attracting settlers, the colony's leaders gave land grants along the river to wealthy seigneurs (nobles), who then imported tenants to work their farms. Even so, more than twenty-five years after Quebec's founding, it had just sixty-four resident families, along with traders and soldiers. With respect to territory occupied and farmed, northern New France never grew much beyond the confines of the river valley between Quebec and Montreal (see Map 2.1). Thus, it differed significantly from New Spain, where Europeans resided in widely scattered locations and Spanish men sometimes directly supervised Indian laborers.

Missionaries of the Society of Jesus (Jesuits), a Roman Catholic order dedicated to converting non-

TABLE 2.1

The Founding of Permanent European Colonies in North America, 1565–1640

Colony	Founder(s)	Date	Basis of Economy
Florida	Pedro Menéndez de Avilés	1565	Farming
New Mexico	Juan de Oñate	1598	Livestock
Virginia	Virginia Company	1607	Tobacco
New France	France	1608	Fur trading
New Netherland	Dutch West India Company	1614	Fur trading
Plymouth	Pilgrims	1620	Farming, fishing
Maine	Sir Ferdinando Gorges	1622	Fishing
St. Kitts, Barbados, et al.	European immigrants	1624	Sugar
Massachusetts Bay	Massachusetts Bay Company	1630	Farming, fishing, fur trading
Maryland	Cecilius Calvert	1634	Tobacco
Rhode Island	Roger Williams	1636	Farming
Connecticut	Thomas Hooker	1636	Farming, fur trading
New Haven	Massachusetts migrants	1638	Farming
New Hampshire	Massachusetts migrants	1638	Farming, fishing

JESUIT MISSIONS IN NEW FRANCE

believers to Christianity, also came to New France. First arriving in Quebec in 1625, the Jesuits, whom the Indians called Black Robes, initially tried to persuade indigenous peoples to live near French settlements and adopt European agricultural methods. When that effort failed, the Black Robes learned Indian languages and traveled to remote regions of the interior, where they lived in twos and threes among hundreds of potential converts.

Using a variety of strategies, Jesuits sought to undermine the authority of village shamans (the traditional religious leaders) and to gain the confidence of leaders who could influence others. Trained in rhetoric, they won admirers by their eloquence. Immune to smallpox (for all had survived the disease already), they explained epidemics among the Indians as God's punishment for sin. Perhaps most important, they amazed the villagers by communicating with each other over long distances through marks on paper. The Indians' desire to learn how to harness the extraordinary power of literacy was one of the critical factors making them receptive to the missionaries' spiritual message.

The Jesuits slowly gained thousands of converts, some of whom moved to reserves set aside for Christian Indians. In those communities, the converts replaced their own culture's traditional equal treatment of men and women with notions more congenial to the Europeans' insistence on male dominance and female subordination. They also altered their practice of allowing premarital sexual relationships and easy divorce, customs that Catholic doctrine prohibited.

Online Study Center
Improve Your Grade
Primary Source: Jesuits' Interpretation of Gender Roles

Jesuit missionaries faced little competition from other Europeans for native peoples' souls, but French fur traders had to confront a direct challenge. In 1614, five years after Henry Hudson explored the river that bears his name, his sponsor, the Dutch West India Company, established an outpost (Fort Orange) on that river at the site of present-day Albany, New York. Like the French, the Dutch sought beaver pelts. Because the Dutch were interested primarily in trade rather than colonization,

NEW NETHERLAND

Map 2.1   European Settlements and Indians in Eastern North America, 1650

Note the widely scattered European settlements along the ocean and riverbanks,
while America's native inhabitants controlled the vast interior.

New Netherland remained small. The colony's southern anchor was New Amsterdam (see Map 2.1), a town founded in 1624 on Manhattan Island.

As the Dutch West India Company's colony in North America, New Netherland was an unimportant part of a vast commercial empire. The colony was ruled autocratically, and settlers felt little loyalty to their nominal leaders. Few migrants arrived. Even a company policy of 1629 that offered a large land grant, or patroonship, to anyone who would bring fifty settlers to the province failed to attract takers. As late as the mid-1660s, New Netherland had only about five thousand inhabitants. Some of those were Swedes and Finns, who resided in the former colony of New Sweden (founded in 1638 on the Delaware River), which was taken over by the Dutch in 1655.

The American Indian allies of New France and New Netherland clashed with each other in part because of fur trade rivalries. In the 1640s, the Iroquois, who traded chiefly with the Dutch and lived in modern upstate New York, went to war against the Hurons, who traded primarily with the French and lived in present-day Ontario. Using guns supplied by the Dutch, the Iroquois largely exterminated the Hurons, whose population had already been decimated by a smallpox epidemic. The Iroquois thus established themselves as a major force in the region, one that Europeans could ignore only at their peril. And the European demand for beaver pelts had disastrously affected native communities and their interactions.

The Caribbean

In the Caribbean, France, the Netherlands, and England fought openly in the first half of the seventeenth century. The Spanish concentrated their efforts on colonizing the Greater Antilles: Cuba, Hispaniola, Jamaica, and Puerto Rico. They left many smaller islands alone. But other European nations saw the tiny islands as both bases from which to attack Spanish vessels loaded with American gold and silver and sources of valuable tropical products such as spices, dyes, and fruits.

England was the first northern European nation to establish a permanent foothold in the smaller West Indian islands (the Lesser Antilles). English people settled on St. Christopher (St. Kitts) in 1624, then later on other islands such as Barbados (1627) and

Providence. France colonized Guadeloupe and Martinique, and the Dutch gained control of St. Eustatius (strategically located near St. Kitts). Because of conflict among the European powers, most of the islands were attacked at least once during the course of the century, and some, like Providence, changed hands.

Why did other Europeans devote so much energy to gaining control of these small volcanic islands that Spain had neglected? The primary answer to that question is sugar. Europeans loved sugar; it gave them a quick energy boost and served as a sweetener for two stimulating, addictive, and bitter Asian drinks: coffee and tea.

SUGAR
CULTIVATION

Early in the 1640s, English residents of Barbados discovered that the island's soil and climate were ideally suited for cultivating sugar cane. At the time, a major supplier of the world's sugar was Brazil, where numerous small farmers grew much of the crop and took their cane to central mills. To pay for processing, they turned a large proportion of their crop over to the mill owners, who could not coordinate the actions of the independent farmers. This production method was highly inefficient.

That changed in Barbados. Between 1630 and 1654, the Dutch took control of northeastern Brazil, where they learned Portuguese techniques for growing and processing the crop. Dutch merchants taught those skills to Barbadians, expecting to sell them African slaves and to transport barrels of sugar products to Europe. The results must have exceeded their wildest dreams. In the explosive Barbados sugar boom that began in the 1640s, planters increased the size of their landholdings, adopted large-scale gang labor by bondspeople, and built their own sugar mills that could operate with great efficiency. Planters, slave traders, and Dutch shipping interests alike earned immense profits from introducing economies of scale into sugar production. Sugar remained the most valuable American commodity for more than one hundred years. Yet in the long run, the future economic importance of the Europeans' American colonies lay on the mainland rather than in the Caribbean.

English Interest in Colonization

he failure of Raleigh's Roanoke colony ended English efforts to settle in North America for nearly two decades. When the English decided

Wampum

When Europeans first came to North America, they quickly learned that native peoples highly valued small cylindrical beads made from whelk and quahog shells, known collectively as wampum. The white and purple beads had been strung on fibers for centuries to make necklaces and ornamental belts, but with the Europeans' arrival, wampum changed its character, becoming a currency widely employed by both groups.

The transformation of wampum occurred not only because the Indians prized it and would trade deerskins and beaver pelts to acquire the beads, but also because Dutch and English settlers lacked an equally handy medium of exchange. These settlers had limited access to coins and currency from their homelands, yet they needed to do business with each other and with their native neighbors. Wampum filled a key need, especially in the first decades of settlement.

Whelk (white) and quahog (purple) shells were found primarily along the shores of Long Island Sound. Narragansetts, Montauks, Niantics, and other local peoples had long gathered the shells during the summers; women then fashioned the beads during the long northeastern winters. The shells were hard and brittle, so shaping them into hollow beads was a time-consuming task involving considerable skill. But Europeans' metal tools, including fine drills, allowed a rapid increase in the quantity and quality of wampum. Some villages gave up their hunter-gatherer modes of subsistence and settled permanently in shell-rich areas, where they focused almost exclusively on the manufacture of wampum.

Wampum played a key role in the early economy of both New Netherland and New England. Dutch settlers in Manhattan traded such manufactured goods as guns and kettles, axes, or knives with the wampum makers, then transported wampum up the Hudson River to Fort Orange, where they used it to purchase furs and skins from the Iroquois. In 1627, Isaac de Rasière, a Dutch trader, introduced wampum to the English colonists at Plymouth when he offered it in exchange for corn. Ten years later, the Massachusetts Bay colony made wampum legal tender for the payment of debts under 12 pennies, at a rate of 6 white beads or 3 purple beads (which were rarer) to 1 penny. Wampum beads could be traded in loose handfuls but more often were strung on thin cords in set amounts worth English equivalents. People trading larger sums measured in wampum always feared being shortchanged. In 1660, one resident of New Netherland agreed to accept payment of a substantial debt in wampum only if his wife personally counted all the beads.

Wampum—originally with purely ornamental significance for its Indian makers—became an initial, indispensable link in the commerce between Europe and North America.

Before Europeans arrived in North America, wampum served primarily ceremonial purposes for native peoples, as in this wampum belt depicting the six nations of the Iroquois and the thirteen American colonies. But several decades later, after Dutch and English colonists came to rely on it as a medium of exchange and European tools made it easier to manufacture, wampum became far more utilitarian in design and appearance. (Right: Photo by MPI/Hulton Archives/Getty Images; below: Image #18491 Wampum Beads by Craig Chesek, courtesy the Library, American Museum of Natural History in 1606 to try once more, they again planned colonies that imitated the Spanish model. Yet their success came when they abandoned that model and sent large numbers of men and women to set up agriculturally based colonies on the mainland. Two major developments prompted approximately 200,000 ordinary English men and women to move to North America in the seventeenth century and led their government to encourage their emigration.

The onset of dramatic social and economic change stimulated many English to move to North

SOCIAL CHANGE IN ENGLAND

America. In the 150 years after 1530, largely as a result of the introduction of nutritious American crops into Europe, England's population doubled. All those additional people needed food, clothing, and other goods. The competition for goods led to high inflation, coupled with a fall in real wages as the number of workers increased. The enhanced demand for food and wool for clothing benefited those with sizable landholdings, but drove landless peasants and those with small amounts of land into unremitting poverty.

Well-to-do English people reacted with alarm as they saw landless and homeless people fill the streets and highways. Obsessed with the problem of maintaining order, officials came to believe that England was overcrowded. They concluded that colonies established in North America could siphon off England's "surplus population," thus easing social strains at home. For similar reasons, many English people decided that they could improve their circumstances by migrating to a large, land-rich, apparently empty continent. Such economic considerations were rendered even more significant in light of the second development, a major change in English religious practice.

The sixteenth century witnessed a religious transformation that eventually led large numbers of English

ENGLISH REFORMATION

dissenters to leave their homeland. In 1533 Henry VIII, wanting a male heir and infatuated with Anne Boleyn, sought to annul his marriage to his Spanish-born queen, Catherine of Aragon. When the pope refused to approve the annulment, Henry left the Roman Catholic Church. He founded the Church of England and—with Parliament's concurrence—proclaimed himself its head. At first the reformed Church of England differed little from Catholicism in its practices, but under Henry's

daughter Elizabeth I (the child of his marriage to Anne Boleyn), new currents of religious belief that had originated on the European continent early in the sixteenth century dramatically affected the English church.

This Protestant Reformation was led by Martin Luther, a German monk, and John Calvin, a French cleric and lawyer. Challenging the Catholic doctrine that priests must serve as intermediaries between laypeople and God, Luther and Calvin insisted that people could interpret the Bible for themselves. Both Luther and Calvin rejected Catholic rituals, denying the need for an elaborate church hierarchy. They also asserted that faith in God was the key to salvation, rather than—as Catholic teaching had it—a combination of faith and good works. Calvin went further than Luther, stressing God's omnipotence and emphasizing the need for people to submit totally to God's will.

During her long reign (1558–1603), Elizabeth I tolerated religious diversity as long as her subjects

PURITANS AND SEPARATISTS

acknowledged her authority as head of the Church of England. By the late sixteenth century, many English Calvinists—those who came to be called Puritans because they wanted to purify the Church of England or Separatists because they wanted to leave it entirely—believed that the English Reformation had not gone far enough. Henry had simplified the church hierarchy; they wanted to abolish it altogether. Henry had subordinated the church to the interests of the state; they wanted a church free from political interference. And whereas the Church of England continued to include all English people, Puritans and Separatists wanted to confine church membership to the "saved"—those God had selected for salvation before birth.

Paradoxically a key article of their faith insisted that people could not know for certain if they were "saved" because mortals could not comprehend or affect their predestination to heaven or hell. Thus, pious Puritans and Separatists confronted a serious dilemma: if one was predestined for heaven or hell and could not alter one's fate, why should one attend church or do good works? They resolved this conundrum by reasoning that God gave the elect the ability to accept salvation and to lead a good life. Although piety and good works could not earn a place in heaven, they could indicate one's place in the ranks of the saved.

Elizabeth I's Stuart successors, her cousin James I (1603–1625) and his son Charles I (1625–1649),

THE STUART MONARCHS

were less tolerant of religious dissent. As Scots, they also had little respect for the traditions of representative government that had developed in England. They insisted on the divine right of kings—that a monarch's power came directly from God and that his subjects had a duty to obey him. A king's authority was absolute, they held.

Both James I and Charles I believed that their authority empowered them to enforce religious conformity. Because Puritans and Separatists—and the remaining English Catholics—challenged many important precepts of the English church, the monarchs authorized the removal of dissenting clergymen from their pulpits. In the 1620s and 1630s, a number of English dissenters moved to America, where they hoped to put their religious beliefs into practice unmolested by the Stuarts or the church hierarchy.

Unlike other Europeans, whose governments helped fund their migrations, many of the dissenters and other English people who mi-

JOINT-STOCK COMPANIES

grated to North America and the Caribbean were financed by joint-stock companies. Stock sales funded these forerunners of modern corporations, which had been developed decades earlier to pool the resources of many small investors in trading voyages. They worked well for that purpose: no one risked too much money, and investors usually received quick returns. But joint-stock companies turned out to be a poor way to finance colonies because the early settlements required enormous amounts of capital and, with rare exceptions, failed to return much immediate profit. Colonies founded by joint-stock companies consequently suffered from a chronic lack of capital.

The Founding of Virginia

I n 1606, envisioning the possibility of earning great profits by finding precious metals and opening new trade routes, a group of merchants and wealthy gentry established a joint-stock venture, the Virginia Company, and obtained a charter from King James I. A settlement they financed in present-day Maine soon collapsed, but a second enterprise would become England's first permanent colony in the Western Hemisphere.

In 1607, the Virginia Company sent 104 men and boys to a region near Chesapeake Bay. They arrived in

JAMESTOWN

May and established the settlement called Jamestown. Ill equipped for survival in the unfamiliar environment, the colonists were afflicted by dissension and disease. Moreover, through sheer bad luck, they arrived in the midst of a severe drought (now known to be the worst in the region for 1,700 years). The lack of rainfall not only made it difficult for them to cultivate crops but also polluted their drinking water.

By January 1608, only thirty-eight of the original colonists remained alive. Many of the first immigrants were gentlemen or soldiers who resisted hard labor, tried to maintain traditional social hierarchies, and retained elaborate English dress and casual work habits despite their desperate circumstances. Such attitudes, combined with the effects of chronic malnutrition and epidemic disease, took a terrible toll. Only when Captain John Smith, one of the colony's lower-status founders, imposed military discipline in 1608 was Jamestown saved from collapse. But after Smith's departure the settlement experienced a severe "starving time" (the winter of 1609–1610). Although more settlers (including a few women and children) arrived in 1608 and 1609 and living conditions slowly improved, as late as 1624 only 1,300 of approximately 8,000 English immigrants to Virginia remained alive.

Jamestown owed its survival to a group of six Algonquian tribes known as the Powhatan Confederacy

THE POWHATAN CONFEDERACY

(see Map 2.1). Powhatan was aggressively consolidating his authority over some twenty-five smaller bands when the Europeans arrived. Fortunately for the colonists, Powhatan at first viewed them as potential allies and a reliable source of useful items such as knives and guns. In return, Powhatan's people traded their excess corn and other foodstuffs to the starving settlers. But the initially cordial relationship soon deteriorated. Drought reduced the Indians' crops, and they could no longer exchange food. Suspecting duplicity, English colonists kidnapped Powhatan's daughter, Pocahontas, holding her as a hostage. In captivity, she agreed in 1614 to marry a colonist, John Rolfe, perhaps as a form of diplomacy.

English and Algonquian peoples had much in common: deep religious beliefs, a lifestyle oriented around agriculture, clear political and social hierarchies, and sharply defined gender roles. Yet the two groups focused on their cultural differences. English men regarded Indian men as lazy because they did not cultivate crops and spent much of their time hunting (a sport, not work, in English eyes). Indian men thought English men effeminate because they did "women's work" of cultivation.

ALGONQUIAN AND ENGLISH CULTURAL DIFFERENCES

Other differences between the two cultures caused serious misunderstandings. Among East Coast Algonquians, political power and social status were not necessarily passed down through the male line. Members of the English gentry inherited their position from their fathers, and English leaders tended to rule autocratically. By contrast, the authority of Algonquian leaders rested on consensus. Accustomed to the European concept of powerful kings, the English sought such figures in native villages. Often (for example, when negotiating treaties) they willfully overestimated the ability of chiefs to make independent decisions for their people.

Furthermore, Algonquians and English had very different notions of property ownership. Most Algonquian villages held their land communally. It could not be bought or sold absolutely, although certain rights to use the land (for example, for hunting or fishing) could be transferred. English people, in contrast, were accustomed to individual farms and to buying and selling land. The English also refused to accept Indians' claims to traditional hunting territories, insisting that only land intensively cultivated could be regarded as owned or occupied. Above all, the English settlers believed unwaveringly in the superiority of their civilization.

The spread of tobacco cultivation upset the balance of power in early Virginia. In tobacco, the settlers and the Virginia Company found the salable commodity for which they had been searching. John Rolfe planted the first crop in 1611. By the late 1620s, shipments totaled 1.5 million pounds. The great tobacco boom had begun, fueled by high prices and substantial profits for planters, who were meeting the escalating demand in Europe and Africa. Although the price of tobacco fluctuated wildly from year to year, the crop made Virginia

TOBACCO CULTIVATION

prosper. Soon the once-all-male outpost was an agricultural settlement inhabited by both men and women.

Farmers learned quickly that successful tobacco cultivation required abundant land, since a field could produce only about three satisfactory crops before it had to lie fallow for several years to regain its fertility. Thus, the small English settlements began to expand rapidly: eager applicants asked the Virginia Company for large land grants on both sides of the James River and its tributary streams.

To attract more settlers to the colony, the Virginia Company in 1617 developed the "headright" system: every new arrival paying his or her own way was promised a land grant of fifty acres; those who financed the passage of others received similar headrights for each person. To ordinary English farmers, many of whom owned little or no land, the headright system offered a powerful incentive to move to Virginia. To wealthy gentry, it promised the possibility of establishing vast agricultural enterprises worked by large numbers of laborers. Two years later, the company introduced a second reform, authorizing the landowning men of the major Virginia settlements to elect representatives to an assembly called the House of Burgesses. English landholders had long been accustomed to electing members of Parliament and controlling their own local governments, and they expected the same privilege in the nation's colonies.

VIRGINIA COMPANY POLICIES

Opechancanough, Powhatan's brother and successor, watched the English colonists steadily encroaching on the confederacy's lands and attempting to convert its members to Christianity. Recognizing the danger his brother had overlooked, the war leader launched coordinated attacks all along the James River on March 22, 1622. By the end of the day, 347 colonists (about one-quarter of the total) lay dead. Virginia reeled from the blow but did not collapse, and an uneasy peace prevailed. Two decades later, Opechancanough tried one last time to repel the invaders. He failed, losing his life in the war that ensued. After this defeat and a 1646 treaty subordinating the Powhatan Confederacy to English authority, the Indians' efforts to resist the spread of European settlement ended.

INDIAN UPRISINGS

The 1622 Powhatan uprising that failed to destroy the colony succeeded in killing its parent. The

■ A comparison of the portrait of Sir Walter Raleigh and his son (left), with that of an Algonquian Indian drawn by John White, from Raleigh's Roanoke expedition (right), shows a dramatic difference in standard dress styles that, for many, must have symbolized the apparent cultural gap between Europeans and Americans. Yet that both men (and the young boy) were portrayed in similar stances, with "arms akimbo," demonstrated that all were high-status individuals. In Europe, only aristocrats were represented in such an aggressive pose.   (Left: National Portrait Gallery, London; right: © Trustees of the British Museum)

Virginia Company never made any profits, for internal corruption and the heavy cost of supporting the settlers offset all its earnings. In 1624 James I revoked the charter, transforming Virginia into a royal colony ruled by officials he appointed. James continued the headright policy but abolished the assembly. Virginians protested so vigorously, however, that by 1629 the House of Burgesses was functioning once again. Because Virginians successfully insisted on governing themselves at the local level, the political structure of England's American possessions came to differ from that of New Spain, New France, and New Netherland, all of which were ruled autocratically.

Life in the Chesapeake

y the 1630s, tobacco was firmly established as the staple crop and chief source of revenue in Virginia. It quickly became just as important in the second English colony planted on Chesapeake Bay: Maryland, given by Charles I to George Calvert, first Lord Baltimore, as a personal possession (proprietorship) and settled in 1634. The Calverts intended the colony to serve as a haven for their persecuted fellow Catholics. Cecilius Calvert, second Lord Baltimore, became the first colonizer to offer freedom of religion to all Christian settlers; he understood that protecting the Protestant majority could also ensure Catholics' rights.

In everything but religion, the two Chesapeake colonies resembled each other. In Maryland as in Virginia, tobacco planters spread out along the river banks, establishing isolated farms instead of towns. The region's deep, wide rivers offered dependable water transportation, and each farm or group of farms had its own wharf, where oceangoing vessels could take on or discharge cargo. As a result, Virginia and Maryland had few towns, for their residents did not need commercial centers in which to buy and sell goods.

Online Study Center Improve Your Grade
Interactive Map: Patterns of Settlement in Surry County, Virginia, 1620–1660

Because the planting, cultivation, and harvesting of tobacco were labor intensive, successful Chesapeake tobacco farms required laborers.

DEMAND FOR LABORERS

Nearby Indians, their numbers reduced by war and disease, could not supply the needed workers. Nor were enslaved Africans available: merchants could more easily and profitably sell slaves to Caribbean sugar planters. By 1650 only about three hundred blacks, some of them free, lived in Virginia—a tiny fraction of the population.

Chesapeake tobacco farmers thus looked primarily to England to supply their labor needs. Under the headright system (which Maryland also adopted in 1640), a tobacco farmer anywhere in the Chesapeake could simultaneously obtain both land and labor by importing workers from England. Good management would make the process self-perpetuating: a farmer could use his profits to pay for the passage of more workers and thereby gain title to more land.

Because men did the agricultural work in European societies, colonists assumed that field laborers should be men. Such male laborers, along with a few women, immigrated to America as indentured servants: in return for their passage, they contracted to work for periods ranging from four to seven years. Indentured servants accounted for 75 to 85 percent of the approximately 130,000 English immigrants to Virginia and Maryland during the seventeenth century.

Males between the ages of fifteen and twenty-four composed roughly three-quarters of these servants; only one immigrant in five or six was female. Most of these young men came from farming or laboring families and were what their contemporaries called the "common sort."

For such people, the Chesapeake appeared to offer good prospects. Servants who completed their

CONDITIONS OF SERVITUDE

indentures earned "freedom dues" consisting of clothes, tools, livestock, casks of corn and tobacco, and sometimes even land. Yet immigrants' lives were difficult. Servants typically worked six days a week, ten to fourteen hours a day. Their masters could discipline or sell them, and they faced severe penalties for running away. Even so, the laws did offer them some protection. For example, their masters were supposed to supply them with sufficient food, clothing, and shelter, and cruelly treated servants could turn to the courts for assistance.

Servants and their masters alike contended with epidemic disease. Immigrants first had to survive the process the colonists called "seasoning"—a bout with disease (probably malaria) that usually occurred during their first Chesapeake summer. They then often endured recurrences of malaria, along with dysentery, typhoid fever, and other diseases. Consequently, about 40 percent of male servants did not survive long enough to become freedmen.

For those who survived their indentures, however, the opportunities for advancement were real. Until the last decades of the seventeenth century, former servants often became independent farmers ("freeholders"), living a modest but comfortable existence. Some even assumed positions of political prominence. But after 1670, tobacco prices declined, and good land grew increasingly scarce and expensive, and in 1681 Maryland dropped its legal requirement that servants receive land as part of their freedom dues. By 1700 the Chesapeake was no longer the land of opportunity it once had been.

Life in the early Chesapeake was hard for everyone, regardless of sex or status. Farmers (and sometimes

STANDARD
OF LIVING

their wives) toiled in the fields alongside servants. Most people rose and went to bed with the sun, lived in one- or two-room ramshackle houses, and consumed a filling but not especially nutritious diet based on pork and corn. Colonists devoted their income to improving their farms, buying livestock, and purchasing more laborers rather than to improving their standard of living.

The predominance of males, the incidence of servitude, and the high mortality rates combined to produce unusual patterns of family

CHESAPEAKE
FAMILIES

life. Female servants normally could not marry during their terms of indenture because masters did not want pregnancies to deprive them of workers. Many male ex-servants could not marry at all because of the scarcity of women. In contrast, nearly every adult free woman in the Chesapeake married. Yet because of high infant mortality and because almost all marriages were delayed by servitude or broken by death, Chesapeake women commonly reared only one to three healthy children, in contrast to English women, who normally had at least five.

Thus, Chesapeake families were few, small, and short-lived. Parents often died while their children were still young. In one Virginia county, for example, more than three-quarters of the children had lost at least one parent by the time they either married or reached age twenty-one. Indeed, the large number of orphaned children prompted a legal innovation: the establishment of orphans' courts to oversee the management of orphans' property.

Because of the low rate of natural increase, immigrants composed a majority of the Chesapeake

CHESAPEAKE
POLITICS

population throughout the seventeenth century. Thus, most members of Virginia's House of Burgesses and Maryland's House of Delegates (established in 1635) were immigrants; they also dominated the governor's council, which simultaneously served as each colony's highest court, part of the legislature, and executive adviser to the governor. A native-born ruling elite emerged only in the early eighteenth century. Until then, the Chesapeake's leaders, as immigrants lacking strong ties to one another or to the colonies, made for contentious politics rather than stability.

The Founding of New England

he economic motives that prompted English people to move to the Chesapeake and Caribbean colonies also drew men and women to New England. But because Puritans organized the New England colonies and also because of environmental factors, the northern settlements turned out very differently from those in the South.

Hoping to exert control over a migration that appeared disorderly, royal bureaucrats in late 1634

CONTRASTING
REGIONAL
DEMOGRAPHIC
PATTERNS

ordered port officials in London to collect information on all travelers departing for the colonies. The resulting records for the year 1635 document the departure of 53 vessels in that year alone. On those ships sailed almost 5,000 people, with 2,000 departing for Virginia, about 1,200 for New England, and the rest for island destinations. Nearly three-fifths of all the passengers were between 15 and 24 years old, reflecting the predominance of young male servants among migrants to America. But among those bound for New England, such youths constituted less than one-third of the total; nearly 40 percent were between ages 25 and 50, and another third were aged 14 and below. Whereas women made up just 14 percent of those going to Virginia, they composed almost 40 percent of the passengers to New England. It is therefore evident that New Englanders often traveled in family groups. They also brought more goods and livestock with them and tended to travel with other people from the same regions. In short, although migrants to the Chesapeake and the islands most commonly left friends and families behind, those who moved to New England came in concert with their close associates, which must have made for a more comfortable and less lonely life.

Among Chesapeake migrants, only the Catholics who moved to Maryland seem to have been motivated

CONTRASTING
REGIONAL
RELIGIOUS
PATTERNS

by religious concerns, and neither the Church of England nor the Catholic Church much affected the settlers. Yet religion inspired many of the people who colonized New England, and Puritan congregations quickly became key institutions.

Religion constantly affected the lives of pious Puritans, who regularly reassessed the state of their souls. Many devoted themselves to self-examination and Bible study, and families prayed together each day under the guidance of the husband and father. Yet because even the most pious could never be certain that they were numbered among the elect, anxiety about their spiritual state troubled devout Puritans.

SEPARATISTS — Separatists who thought the Church of England too corrupt to be salvaged were the first to move to New England, hoping to isolate themselves and their children from the corrupting influence of worldly temptations. In 1620, some Separatists, many of whom had earlier migrated to Holland in quest of the right to freely practice their religion, received permission from the Virginia Company to colonize the northern part of its territory. That September more than one hundred people, only thirty of them Separatists, set sail from England on the old and crowded *Mayflower*. Two months later, they landed in America, but farther north than they had intended. Given the lateness of the season, they decided to stay where they were. They established their settlement on a fine harbor and named it Plymouth.

Even before they landed, the Pilgrims had to surmount their first challenge—from the "strangers," or non-Separatists, who sailed with them to America. Because they landed outside the jurisdiction of the Virginia Company, some of the strangers questioned the authority of the colony's leaders. In response, the Mayflower Compact, signed in November 1620 on board the ship, established a "Civil Body Politic" and a rudimentary legal authority for the colony. The male settlers elected a governor and at first made all decisions for the colony at town meetings. Later, after more towns had been founded, Plymouth, like Virginia and Maryland, created an assembly to which the landowning male settlers elected representatives.

INDIAN RELATIONS — Survival also challenged the Pilgrims. Like the Jamestown settlers before them, they were poorly prepared for their new environment. Winter quickly descended, compounding their difficulties. Only half the *Mayflower*'s passengers lived to see spring. But, again like the Virginians, the Pilgrims benefited from the political circumstances of nearby Indians.

The Pokanokets (a branch of the Wampanoags) controlled the area in which the Pilgrims settled and decided to ally with the newcomers to protect themselves from the powerful Narragansetts of the southern New England coast. In the spring of 1621, their leader, Massasoit, signed a treaty with the Pilgrims, and during the colony's first difficult years, the Pokanokets supplied the English with essential foodstuffs. The settlers were also assisted by Squanto, an Indian who had earlier been captured by fishermen and taken to Europe, where he learned to speak English. Squanto became the Pilgrims' interpreter and a major source of information about the unfamiliar environment.

MASSACHUSETTS BAY COMPANY — Before the 1620s ended, a group of Puritan Congregationalists (who hoped to reform the Church of England from within) launched the colonial enterprise that would come to dominate New England. Charles I, who became king in 1625, was more hostile to Puritans than his father had been. In response to Charles's attempts to suppress Puritanism, some Congregationalist merchants, concerned about their long-term prospects in England, sent a body of colonists to Cape Ann (north of Cape Cod) in 1628. The following year the merchants obtained a royal charter, constituting themselves as the Massachusetts Bay Company.

The new joint-stock company quickly attracted the attention of Puritans of the "middling sort," who remained committed to the goal of reforming the Church of England but concluded that they should pursue that aim in America. In a dramatic move, the Congregationalist merchants boldly decided to transfer the Massachusetts Bay Company's headquarters to New England. The settlers would then be answerable to no one in the mother country and would be able to handle their affairs as they pleased.

GOVERNOR JOHN WINTHROP — The most important recruit to the new venture was John Winthrop. In October 1629, the Massachusetts Bay Company elected Winthrop its governor, and he organized the initial segment of the great Puritan migration to America. In 1630 more than one thousand English men and women moved to Massachusetts—most of them to Boston, which soon became the largest town in English North America. By 1643 nearly twenty thousand compatriots had followed them.

■ Some scholars now believe that this 1638 painting by the Dutch artist Adam Willaerts depicts the Plymouth colony about fifteen years after its founding. The shape of the harbor, the wooden gate, and the houses straggling up the hill all coincide with contemporary accounts of the settlement. No one believes that Willaerts himself visited Plymouth, but people returning from the colony to Holland, where the Pilgrims had lived for years before emigrating, could well have described Plymouth to him. (© J. D. Bangs, Courtesy of Leiden American Pilgrim Museum, The Netherlands)

Winthrop's was a transcendent vision. He foresaw in Puritan America a true commonwealth, a community in which each person put the good of the whole ahead of private concerns. "In America we shall be as a city upon a hill," he asserted, "the eyes of all people are upon us." Although, as in England, this society would be characterized by social inequality and clear hierarchies of status and power, Winthrop hoped that its members would live according to the precepts of Christian love. Such an ideal was beyond human reach, but it persisted well into the third and fourth generations of the immigrants' descendants.

The Puritans expressed their communal ideal chiefly in the doctrine of the covenant. They believed

Covenant Ideal

God had made a covenant—that is, an agreement or contract—with them when they were chosen for the special mission to America. In turn,

they covenanted with one another, promising to work together toward their goals. The founders of churches, towns, and even colonies in Anglo-America often drafted formal documents setting forth the principles on which their institutions would be based. The Mayflower Compact was a such a covenant.

The leaders of Massachusetts Bay likewise transformed their original joint-stock company charter into the basis for a covenanted community based on mutual consent. Under pressure from landowning male settlers, they gradually changed the General Court—officially the company's small governing body—into a colonial legislature. They also granted the status of freeman, or voting member of the company, to all property-owning adult male church members. Less than two decades after the first large group of Puritans arrived in Massachusetts Bay, the colony had a functioning system of self-government composed of a governor and a two-house legislature. The General Court also established a judicial system modeled on England's.

The colony's method of distributing land helped further the communal ideal. Groups of men applied

NEW ENGLAND TOWNS

together to the General Court for grants of land on which to establish towns (novel governance units that did not exist in England). The men receiving such a grant determined how the land would be distributed. First they laid out lots for houses and a church. Then they gave each family parcels of land scattered around the town center: a pasture here, a woodlot there, an arable field elsewhere. Every man obtained land, but the best and largest plots went to the most distinguished among them (including the minister).

Thus, New England settlements initially tended to be more compact than those of the Chesapeake. Town centers developed quickly, evolving in three distinctly different ways. Some, chiefly isolated settlements in the interior, tried to sustain Winthrop's vision of harmonious community life based on diversified family farms. A second group, the coastal towns like Boston and Salem, became bustling seaports. The third category, commercialized agricultural towns, grew up in the Connecticut River valley, where easy water transportation enabled farmers to sell surplus goods readily.

When migrants began to move beyond the territorial limits of the Massachusetts Bay colony into

INTERNAL MIGRATION

Connecticut (1636), New Haven (1638), and New Hampshire (1638), the same pattern of land grants persisted. (Only Maine, thinly populated by coastal fishing families, deviated.) The migration to the Connecticut Valley ended the Puritans' relative freedom from clashes with nearby Indians. The first English people in the valley moved there from Massachusetts Bay under the direction of their minister, Thomas Hooker. Although remote from other English towns, the wide river promised ready access to the ocean. The site had just one problem: it fell within the territory controlled by the powerful Pequots.

The Pequots' dominance stemmed from their role as primary middlemen in the trade between New

PEQUOT WAR

England Indians and the Dutch in New Netherland. The arrival of English settlers signaled the end of this power, for previously subordinate bands could now trade directly with Europeans. Pequots and English colonists clashed even before the establishment of settlements in the Connecticut Valley, but their founding tipped the balance toward war. After two English traders were killed (not by Pequots), the English raided a Pequot village. In return, the Pequots attacked the new town of Wethersfield in April 1637, killing nine and capturing two. To retaliate, a Massachusetts Bay expedition the following month attacked and burned the main Pequot town on the Mystic River. The English and their Narragansett allies slaughtered at least four hundred Pequots, mostly women and children.

For the next thirty years, the New England Indians accommodated themselves to the spread of European settlement. They traded with the newcomers and sometimes worked for them, but for the most part they resisted acculturation or incorporation into English society. Native Americans persisted in using traditional farming methods, without plows or fences. The one European practice they adopted was keeping livestock: domesticated animals provided excellent sources of meat now that their hunting territories had been turned into English farms and game had disappeared.

Although the official seal of the Massachusetts Bay colony showed an Indian crying, "Come over and help us," most colonists showed

JOHN ELIOT'S PRAYING TOWNS

little interest in converting the Algonquians to Christianity. Only a few Massachusetts clerics, most notably John Eliot, seriously undertook missionary activities. Eliot insisted that converts reside in towns, farm the land in English fashion, assume English names, wear European-style clothing and shoes, cut their hair, and stop observing a wide range of their own customs. He understandably met with little success. At the peak of Eliot's efforts, only eleven hundred Indians lived in the fourteen "Praying Towns" he established.

The Jesuits' successful missions in New France contrasted sharply with the Puritans' failure to win

MISSIONARY ACTIVITIES COMPARED

many converts. Catholicism had several advantages over Puritanism. The Catholic Church employed beautiful ceremonies, instructed converts that through good works they could help to earn their own salvation, and offered Indian women an inspiring role model: the Virgin Mary. In Montreal and Quebec, communities of nuns taught Indian women and children and ministered to their needs. Furthermore, the few French colonists on the St. Lawrence did not alienate potential converts by encroaching steadily on their lands (as did New Englanders). Perhaps most important, the Jesuits understood that Christian beliefs could be compatible with Native American culture. Unlike Puritans, Jesuits accepted converts who did not wholly adopt European styles of life.

What attracted Indians to these religious ideas? Conversion often alienated new Christians (both Catholic and Puritan) from their relatives and traditions—a likely outcome that must have caused many potential converts to think twice about making such a commitment. But surely many hoped to use the Europeans' religion as a way to cope with the dramatic changes the intruders had wrought. The combination of disease, alcohol, new trading patterns, and loss of territory disrupted customary patterns of life to an unprecedented extent. Shamans had little success in restoring traditional ways. Many Indians must have concluded that the Europeans' own ideas could provide the key to survival in the new circumstances.

Life in New England

*N*ew England's colonizers adopted lifestyles that differed considerably from those of both their Indian neighbors and their counterparts in the Chesapeake. Unlike the Algonquian bands, who usually moved four or five times each year to take full advantage of their environment, English people lived in the same location year-round. And unlike residents of the Chesapeake, New Englanders constructed sturdy dwellings intended to last. They used the same fields again and again, fertilizing with manure rather than clearing new fields every few years. And they fenced their croplands to prevent them from being overrun by the cattle, sheep, and hogs that were their chief sources of meat.

Because Puritans commonly moved to America in family groups, the age range in early New England

NEW ENGLAND FAMILIES

was wide; and because many more women went to New England than to the tobacco colonies, the population could immediately begin to reproduce. Also, New England was

much healthier than the Chesapeake. Once Puritan settlements had survived the difficult first few years, New England proved to be even healthier than the mother country. Adult male migrants to the Chesapeake lost about ten years from their English life expectancy of fifty to fifty-five years; their Massachusetts counterparts gained five or more years. Consequently, while Chesapeake families were few in number and small in size, New England families were numerous and large. If seventeenth-century Chesapeake women could expect to rear one to three healthy children, New England women could anticipate raising five to seven.

The nature of the population had other major implications for family life. New England in effect created grandparents, since in England people rarely lived long enough to know their children's children. And whereas early Chesapeake parents commonly died before their children married, New England parents exercised a good deal of control over their adult offspring. Young men could not marry without acreage to cultivate, and because of the communal land-grant system, they had to depend on their fathers to give them that land. Daughters too needed a dowry of household goods supplied by their parents. Yet parents relied on their children's labor and often seemed reluctant to see them marry and start their own households. These needs at times led to considerable conflict between the generations.

Another important difference lay in the influence of religion on New Englanders' lives. Puritans controlled

IMPACT OF RELIGION

their governments. Congregationalism was the only officially recognized religion; except in Rhode Island, founded by dissenters from Massachusetts, members of other sects had no freedom of worship. Some non-Puritans voted in town meetings, but in Massachusetts Bay and New Haven, church membership was a prerequisite for voting in colony elections. All the early colonies taxed residents to build meetinghouses and pay ministers' salaries, but Puritan colonies in particular attempted to enforce strict codes of moral conduct. Colonists there were frequently tried for drunkenness, card playing, even idleness. Couples who had sex during their engagement—as revealed by the birth of a baby less than nine months after their wedding—were fined and publicly humiliated. More harshly treated were men—and a handful of women—who engaged in behaviors that today would be called homosexual. (The term did not then exist.) Several men who had consenting same-sex relationships were hanged.

Puritans objected to secular interference in religious affairs but at the same time expected the church to influence the conduct of politics and the affairs of society. They also believed that the state was obliged to support and protect the one true church—theirs. As a result, although they came to America seeking freedom to worship as they pleased, they saw no contradiction in refusing to grant that freedom to others.

Roger Williams, a Separatist who immigrated to Massachusetts Bay in 1631, quickly ran afoul of that

ROGER WILLIAMS

Puritan orthodoxy. He told his fellow settlers that the king of England had no right to grant them land already occupied by Indians, that church and state should be kept entirely separate, and that Puritans should not impose their religious beliefs on others. Because Puritan leaders placed a heavy emphasis on achieving consensus in both religion and politics, they could not long tolerate significant dissent.

Banished from Massachusetts, Williams journeyed in early 1636 to the head of Narragansett Bay, where he founded the town of Providence. Because Williams believed that government should not interfere with religion in any way, Providence and other towns in what became Rhode Island adopted a policy of tolerating all religions, including Judaism. Along with Maryland, the tiny colony that Williams founded presaged the religious freedom that eventually became one of the hallmarks of the United States.

A dissenter who presented a more sustained challenge to Massachusetts Bay colony leaders was Mistress

ANNE HUTCHINSON

Anne Marbury Hutchinson. A skilled medical practitioner who was popular with the women of Boston, she greatly admired John Cotton, a minister who stressed the covenant of grace, or God's free gift of salvation to unworthy human beings. By contrast, most Massachusetts clerics emphasized the need for Puritans to engage in good works, study, and reflection in preparation for receiving God's grace. After spreading her ideas for months in the context of childbirth gatherings—when no men were present—Hutchinson began holding women's meetings in her home to discuss Cotton's sermons. She emphasized the covenant of grace more than did Cotton himself, and she even adopted the belief that the

elect could be assured of salvation and communicate directly with God. Such ideas had an immense appeal for Puritans. Anne Hutchinson offered them certainty of salvation instead of a state of constant anxiety.

Hutchinson's ideas posed a dangerous threat to Puritan orthodoxy. So in November 1637, officials charged her with having maligned the colony's ministers. For two days she defended herself cleverly, but then she boldly declared that God had spoken to her directly, explaining that he would curse the Puritans' descendants for generations if they harmed her. That assertion ensured her banishment to Rhode Island in 1638.

The authorities in Massachusetts Bay perceived Anne Hutchinson as doubly dangerous to the existing order: she threatened not only religious orthodoxy but also traditional gender roles. Puritans believed in the equality before God of all souls, including those of women, but they considered actual women (as distinct from their spiritual selves) inferior to men. Christians had long followed Saint Paul's dictum that women should keep silent in church and submit to their husbands. Hutchinson did neither. A minister told her bluntly: "You have stept out of your place, you have rather bine a Husband than a Wife and a preacher than a Hearer; and a Magistrate than a Subject."

The New England authorities' reaction to Anne Hutchinson reveals the depth of their adherence to European gender-role concepts. To them, an orderly society required the submission of wives to husbands as well as the obedience of subjects to rulers.

Summary   *Online Study Center*   **ACE the Test**

*B*y the middle of the seventeenth century, Europeans had come to North America to stay, signaling major changes for the peoples of both hemispheres. Europeans killed Indians with their weapons and diseases and had but limited success in converting them to Christian sects. Contacts with indigenous peoples taught Europeans to eat new foods, speak new languages, and recognize, however reluctantly, the persistence of other cultural patterns. The prosperity and even survival of many of the European colonies depended heavily on the cultivation of American crops (maize and tobacco) and an Asian crop (sugar), thus attesting to the importance of post-Columbian ecological change.

In America, Spaniards reaped the benefits of their South and Central American gold and silver mines, while French people earned their primary profits from Indian trade (in Canada) and cultivating sugar cane (in the Caribbean). Sugar also enriched the Portuguese. The Dutch concentrated on commerce—trading in furs and sugar as well as carrying human cargoes of enslaved Africans to South America and the Caribbean.

Although the English colonies, too, at first sought to rely on trade, they quickly took another road altogether when many English people of the "middling sort" decided to migrate to North America. To a greater extent than their European counterparts, the English transferred the society and politics of their homeland to a new environment. Their sheer numbers, coupled with their need for vast quantities of land on which to grow their crops and raise their livestock, inevitably brought them into conflict with their Indian neighbors. Ultimately New England and the Chesapeake would also be drawn into the increasingly fierce rivalries besetting the European powers. Those rivalries would continue to affect Americans of all races until after the mid-eighteenth century, when France and England fought the greatest war yet known, and the Anglo-American colonies had won their independence.

LEGACY FOR A PEOPLE AND A NATION

The Foxwoods Casino and the Mashantucket Pequot Museum

In 1992 the Mashantucket Pequots opened the enormously successful Foxwoods Resort Casino on their small reservation in southeastern Connecticut. Just six years later, in August 1998, the Pequots proudly inaugurated a new museum (built with some of their substantial profits) presenting their people's story. Both developments surprised many Americans, who did not realize that Native Americans still lived in New England. The existence of the Pequots was particularly startling, because histories had long recorded that the nation was destroyed in the Pequot War of 1637.

Survivors of the Mystic River massacre had regrouped in the Mashantucket swamps, building lives as farmers, laborers, and craftspeople. Some left the area, but a few Pequots remained: the 1910 census, the source today for determining Pequot tribal membership, counted sixty-six residents of a reservation just 213 acres in size. By the 1970s, the residents had been reduced to two, and the state of Connecticut threatened to turn the reservation into a park. But an elder, Elizabeth George, persuaded several hundred people tracing descent from those listed in 1910 to return to live on the reservation. In 1983 the determined Pequots won formal federal recognition, which in turn allowed them to build the profitable casino, a hotel, and several restaurants, and to begin purchasing more land.

Now the museum introduces the history of the Pequots and of eastern Algonquian peoples to hundreds of thousands of visitors each year. At its heart is a re-creation of a Pequot village as it would have looked shortly before Europeans first arrived on Connecticut's shores, complete with sounds and smells controlled by state-of-the-art computers. Exhibits detail the origins of the Pequot War, and a film narrates the tale of the massacre.

The Pequots' success has helped to embolden other eastern Algonquian nations to reassert publicly their long-suppressed Indian identities. The Pequot people's dedication to preserving their culture and reaffirming their history has created a remarkable legacy for the nation.

NORTH AMERICA IN THE ATLANTIC WORLD 1640–1720

The *Seaflower*, Captain Thomas Smith, master, lay at anchor in Boston harbor in early September 1676, awaiting official documents signed by the governors of Massachusetts and Plymouth. Smith expected to sell the cargo in his hold when he got to the West Indies. But that cargo differed from most: it comprised human beings, nearly two hundred "heathen Male-factors—men, women, and Children." The certificates from the governors explained "To all People" the origins of Captain Smith's human cargo: "Philip an heathen Sachem . . . with others his wicked complices and abettors have treacherously and perfidiously rebelled against" these colonies. "By due and legall procedure," the captives on board the *Seaflower* were "Sentenced & condemned to perpetuall Servitude." The Pokanoket leader, King Philip (called Metacom at birth and later renamed "Philip" by New Englanders), had been killed a month earlier in the war that bore his name. His young son seems to have been sold into slavery, along with many shiploads of Philip's followers.

Only one prominent New Englander objected on moral grounds to the policy of selling the vanquished Algonquians into West Indian slavery. The Reverend John Eliot reminded the authorities that the colonists had a solemn duty to "inlarge the kingdom of Jesus Christ"; "to sell [the Indians] away for slaves, is to hinder the inlargement of his kingdom." If the Indians deserved to die, then "godly governors" should ensure that they died "penitently," rather than depriving them of "all meanes of grace" by selling them as slaves. It was the subversion of God's plan for Massachusetts, not enslavement itself, that concerned Eliot.

The tale of Thomas Smith and the *Seaflower*'s human cargo illustrates not only the English colonists' willingness to enslave "heathen" peoples and their increasingly contentious relationship with Native Americans, but also the participation of the mainland colonies in a growing international network. North America, like England itself, was becoming embedded in a worldwide matrix of trade and warfare. The web woven by oceangoing

Growth of Anglo-American Settlements

A Decade of Imperial Crises: The 1670s

African Slavery on the Mainland

The Web of Empire and the Atlantic Slave Trade

LINKS TO THE WORLD
International Piracy

Enslavement of Africans and Indians

Imperial Reorganization and the Witchcraft Crisis

LEGACY FOR A PEOPLE AND A NATION
Americans of African Descent

Online Study Center
This icon will direct you to interactive map and primary source activities on the website
http://college.hmco.com/pic/nortonbrief7e

C H R O N O L O G Y

1642–46 • English Civil War

1649 • Charles I executed

1651 • First Navigation Act passed to regulate colonial trade

1660 • Stuarts restored to throne
• Charles II becomes king

1663 • Carolina chartered

1664 • English conquer New Netherland
• New York founded
• New Jersey established

1670s • Marquette, Jolliet, and La Salle explore the Great Lakes and Mississippi valley for France

1675–76 • King Philip's War devastates New England

1676 • Bacon's Rebellion disrupts Virginia government
• Jamestown destroyed

1680–1700 • Pueblo revolt temporarily drives Spaniards from New Mexico

1681 • Pennsylvania chartered

1685 • James II becomes king

1686–89 • Dominion of New England established, superseding all charters of colonies from Maine to New Jersey

1688–89 • James II deposed in Glorious Revolution
• William and Mary ascend throne

1688–99 • King William's War fought on northern New England frontier

1692 • Witchcraft crisis in Salem; nineteen executions result

1696 • Board of Trade and Plantations established to coordinate English colonial administration

1701 • Iroquois adopt neutrality policy toward France and England

1702–13 • Queen Anne's War fought by French and English

1711–13 • Tuscarora War (North Carolina) leads to capture or migration of most Tuscaroras

1715 • Yamasee War nearly destroys South Carolina

1718 • New Orleans founded in French Louisiana

vessels now crisscrossed the globe, carrying European goods to America and Africa, West Indian sugar to New England and Europe, Africans to the Americas, and New England fish and wood products—and occasionally Indian slaves—to the Caribbean.

Three developments shaped life in the mainland English colonies between 1640 and 1720: the expansion of slavery, changes in the colonies' political and economic relationships with England, and escalating conflicts with Indians and other European colonies in North America.

The explosive growth of the slave trade significantly altered the Anglo-American economy. Carrying human cargoes paid off handsomely. At first primarily encompassing Indians and already enslaved Africans from the Caribbean, the trade soon came to focus on cargoes brought to the Americas directly from Africa. The arrival of large numbers of West African peoples dramatically reshaped colonial society and fueled the international trading system. Moreover, the burgeoning North American economy attracted new attention from colonial administrators in London, who attempted to supervise the American settlements more effectively to ensure that the mother country benefited from their economic growth.

Neither English colonists nor London administrators could ignore other peoples living on the North American continent. As the English settlements expanded, they came into violent conflict not only with powerful Indian nations but also with the Dutch, the Spanish, and especially the French. By 1720, war had become an all-too-familiar feature of American life. No longer isolated from each other or from Europe, the people and products of the North American colonies had become integral to the world trading system and inextricably enmeshed in its conflicts. ■

Growth of Anglo-American Settlements

*B*etween 1642 and 1646, civil war between supporters of King Charles I and the Puritan-dominated Parliament engulfed the colonists' English homeland. Parliament triumphed, leading to the execution of the king in 1649 and interim rule by the parliamentary army's leader, Oliver Cromwell. But after Cromwell's death, Parliament decided to restore the monarchy if Charles I's son and heir agreed to restrictions on his authority. Charles II did so, and the Stuarts returned to the throne in 1660. The new king subsequently rewarded nobles and others who had supported him during the Civil War with huge tracts of land on the North American mainland. The colonies so established made up six of the thirteen polities that eventually would form the American nation: New York, New Jersey, Pennsylvania (including Delaware), and North and South Carolina. Collectively, these became known as the Restoration colonies because they were created by the restored Stuart monarchy. All were proprietorships; in each of them, as in Maryland, one man or several men held title to the soil and controlled the government.

In 1664, Charles II gave his younger brother James, the duke of York, the region between the

NEW YORK

Connecticut and Delaware Rivers, including the Hudson valley and Long Island. James immediately organized an invasion fleet. In August James's warships anchored off Manhattan Island and demanded New Netherland's surrender. The colony complied without resistance.

Thus James acquired a heterogeneous possession, which he renamed New York (see Table 3.1). An appreciable minority of English people already lived there, along with sizable numbers of Indians, Africans, and Germans and a smattering of other European peoples. The Dutch West India Company had actively imported slaves into the colony. Indeed, almost one-fifth of Manhattan's approximately fifteen hundred inhabitants were of African descent.

Recognizing the population's diversity, James's representatives moved cautiously in their efforts to establish English authority. The Duke's Laws, a legal code proclaimed in 1665, applied solely to the English settlements on Long Island, only later being extended to the rest of the colony. James's policies initially maintained Dutch forms of local government, confirmed Dutch land titles, and allowed Dutch residents to maintain customary legal practices. Each town was permitted to decide which church (Dutch Reformed, Congregational, or Church of England) to support with its tax revenues. Much to the dismay of English residents, the Duke's Laws made no provision for a representative assembly. Like other Stuarts, James distrusted legislative bodies, and not until 1683 did he agree to the colonists' requests for an elected legislature. The English takeover thus had little immediate effect on the colony. Its population grew slowly, barely reaching eighteen thousand by the time of the first English census in 1698.

A primary reason for New York's slow growth was that in 1664 the duke of York regranted the land

NEW JERSEY

between the Hudson and Delaware Rivers—East and West Jersey—to his friends Sir George Carteret and John Lord Berkeley. That grant deprived New York of much fertile land and hindered its economic growth. Meanwhile, the Jersey proprietors acted rapidly to attract settlers, promising generous land grants, limited freedom of religion, and—without authorization from the Crown—a representative assembly. As a result, New Jersey grew quickly; in 1726, at the time of its first census as a united colony, it had 32,500 inhabitants, only 8,000 fewer than New York.

Within twenty years, Berkeley and Carteret sold their interests in the Jerseys to separate groups of investors. The purchasers of all of Carteret's share (West Jersey) and portions of Berkeley's (East Jersey) were members of the Society of Friends, also called Quakers, who rejected earthly and religious hierarchies. Quakers believed that anyone could be saved by directly receiving God's "inner light" and that all people

TABLE 3.2

The Founding of English Colonies in North America, 1664–1681

Colony	Founder(s)	Date	Basis of Economy
New York (formerly New Netherland)	James, duke of York	1664	Farming, fur trading
New Jersey	Sir George Carteret John Lord Berkeley	1664	Farming
North Carolina	Carolina proprietors	1665	Tobacco, forest products
South Carolina	Carolina proprietors	1670	Rice, indigo
Pennsylvania (incl. Delaware)	William Penn	1681	Farming

were equal in God's sight. With no formally trained clergy, Quakers allowed anyone, male or female, to speak in meetings or spread God's word. The Quaker message of radical egalitarianism was unwelcome in the hierarchical society of England and the colonies, and Quakers encountered persecution everywhere.

The Quakers obtained their own colony in 1681, when Charles II granted the region between Maryland

PENNSYLVANIA and New York to his close friend William Penn, a prominent member of the sect. Although Penn held the colony as a personal proprietorship, he saw his province not merely as a source of revenue but also as a haven for persecuted coreligionists. Penn offered land to all comers on liberal terms, promised toleration of all religions (although only Christians were given the vote), guaranteed English liberties such as the right to bail and trial by jury, and pledged to establish a representative assembly. He also publicized the ready availability of land in Pennsylvania throughout Europe.

Penn's activities and the Quakers' attraction to his lands gave rise to a migration rivaling the Puritan exodus to New England in the 1630s. By mid-1683, more than three thousand people—among them Welsh, Irish, Dutch, and Germans—had moved to Pennsylvania, and within five years the population reached twelve thousand. Philadelphia, carefully planned on the navigable Delaware River to be the major city in the province, drew merchants and artisans from throughout the English-speaking world. Pennsylvania's plentiful and fertile lands soon enabled its residents to begin exporting surplus flour and other foodstuffs to the West Indies. Practically

overnight Philadelphia acquired more than two thousand citizens and started to challenge Boston's commercial dominance.

A pacifist with egalitarian principles, Penn attempted to treat native peoples fairly. He learned to speak the language of the Delawares (or Lenapes), from whom he purchased tracts of land to sell to European settlers. Penn also established strict regulations for trade and forbade the sale of alcohol to Indians. His policies attracted native peoples, who moved to Pennsylvania near the end of the seventeenth century to escape repeated clashes with English colonists in other colonies. Most important were the Tuscaroras, Shawnees, and Miamis. By a supreme irony, however, the same toleration that attracted Native Americans also brought non-Quaker Europeans, who showed little respect for Indian claims. In effect, Penn's policy was so successful that it caused its own downfall.

The southernmost proprietary colony, granted by Charles II in 1663, encompassed a huge tract of land

CAROLINA stretching from the southern boundary of Virginia to Spanish Florida. The area had great strategic importance: a successful English settlement there would prevent the Spaniards from pushing farther north. The proprietors named their new province Carolina in honor of Charles (*Carolus* in Latin). The "Fundamental Constitutions of Carolina," which they asked the political philosopher John Locke to draft for them, set forth an elaborate plan for a colony governed by a hierarchy of landholding aristocrats, with a carefully structured distribution of political and economic power.

However, Carolina quickly developed two distinct population centers, which in 1729 split into separate colonies. Virginia planters settled the Albemarle region that became North Carolina. They established a society much like their own, with an economy based on cultivating tobacco and exporting such forest products as pitch, tar, and timber. Because North Carolina lacked a satisfactory harbor, its planters relied on Virginia's ports and merchants to conduct their trade, and the colonies remained tightly linked. The other population center, which eventually formed the core of South Carolina, developed at Charles Town, founded in 1670 near the juncture of the Ashley and Cooper Rivers. Many of its early residents had migrated from Barbados and expected to establish plantation agriculture.

But after unsuccessfully attempting to grow tropical plants (including sugar), the Carolinians began to raise corn and herds of cattle, which they sold to Caribbean sugar planters hungry for foodstuffs. They also depended on trade with nearby Indians to supply commodities they could sell elsewhere: deerskins, almost as valuable as beaver pelts, and Indian slaves. During the first decade of the eighteenth century, Carolinians exported an average of 54,000 skins annually. Before 1715 they exported an estimated 30,000 to 50,000 Indian slaves.

THE CHESAPEAKE AND NEW ENGLAND The English Civil War also affected the earlier English settlements, retarding their development. In the Chesapeake, struggles between supporters of the king and of Parliament caused military clashes in Maryland and political upheavals in Virginia. But once the war ended and immigration resumed, the colonies expanded once again. Wealthy Chesapeake tobacco growers imported increasing numbers of English indentured servants to work on what were developing into large plantations.

In New England, migration essentially ceased after the Civil War began in 1642, and few Puritans migrated after the Restoration. Yet the Puritan colonies' population continued to grow dramatically because of natural increase. By the 1670s, New England's population had more than tripled, reaching approximately seventy thousand. Such a rapid expansion placed great pressure on available land. Many members of the third and fourth generations had to migrate—north to New Hampshire or Maine, south to New York or New Jersey, west beyond the Connecticut River—to find sufficient farmland. Others abandoned agriculture and learned such skills as blacksmithing or carpentry to support themselves in the growing towns.

Online Study Center **Improve Your Grade**
Interactive Map: English Migration, 1610–1660

WITCHCRAFT The people who remained behind in the small yet densely populated New England communities experienced a new phenomenon after approximately 1650: burgeoning witchcraft accusations and trials.

Most people in the seventeenth century believed that witches existed. These allies of the Devil were thought to harness invisible spirits for good or evil purposes. For example, a witch might engage in fortunetelling or cause the death of a child or valuable animals. Yet among English mainland colonies, only New England witnessed many trials of accused witches (about one hundred in all before 1690). Most, though not all, of the accused were middle-aged women who had angered their neighbors. Historians have concluded that day-to-day interaction in the closely knit communities bred long-standing quarrels that led to such accusations. Even so, only a few of the accused were convicted, and fewer still were executed.

COLONIAL POLITICAL STRUCTURES That New England courts halted questionable prosecutions suggests that well-established political and judicial structures were present in almost all the Anglo-American colonies by the last quarter of the seventeenth century. In New England, property-holding men or the legislature elected the governors; in other regions, the king or the proprietor appointed such leaders. A council, either elected or appointed, advised the governor on matters of policy and served as the upper house of the legislature. Each colony had a judiciary with local justices of the peace, county courts, and, usually, an appeals court composed of the councilors.

Local political institutions also developed. In New England, elected selectmen initially governed the towns, but by the end of the seventeenth century, town meetings, held at least annually and attended by most free adult male residents, handled matters of local concern. In the Chesapeake colonies and both of the Carolinas, appointed magistrates ran local governments. At first, the same was true in Pennsylvania, but by the early eighteenth century, elected county officials began to take over some government functions. And in New York, local elections were the rule even before the establishment of the colonial assembly in 1683.

A Decade of Imperial Crises: The 1670s

*a*s the Restoration colonies were extending the range of English settlement in North America, the first English colonies and French and Spanish settlements faced new crises caused primarily by their changing relationships with indigenous peoples. Between 1670 and 1680, New England, Virginia, New France, and New Mexico experienced bitter conflicts as their interests collided with those of America's original inhabitants.

In the mid-1670s, Louis de Buade de Frontenac, the governor-general of Canada, decided to expand

New France and the Iroquois

New France's reach to the south and west, hoping to establish a trade route to Mexico and gain direct control of the valuable fur trade on which the colony's prosperity rested. Accordingly, he encouraged the explorations of Father Jacques Marquette, Louis Jolliet, and Robert Cavelier de La Salle in the Great Lakes and Mississippi valley regions. His goal, however, brought him into conflict with the powerful Iroquois Confederacy, comprising five Indian nations: the Mohawks, Oneidas, Onondagas, Cayugas, and Senecas. (In 1722 the Tuscaroras became the sixth.)

Under the terms of a unique defensive alliance forged early in the sixteenth century, a representative council made decisions of war and peace for the entire Iroquois Confederacy, although each nation still retained some autonomy and could not be forced to comply with a council directive. Before the arrival of Europeans, the Iroquois waged wars primarily to acquire captives to replenish their population. The Europeans' presence created an economic motive: the desire to dominate the fur trade and gain unimpeded access to European goods. The war with the Hurons in the 1640s initiated a series of conflicts with other Indians known as the Beaver Wars, in which the Iro-

■ Contemporary engraving of John Verelst's 1710 portrait of the Mohawk chief known as Hendrick to Europeans (his Indian name was rendered as "Dyionoagon" or "Tee Yee Neen Ho Ga Row"). Hendrick and three other Iroquois leaders visited London in 1710, symbolically cementing the Covenant Chain negotiated in 1677. His primarily European dress and the wampum belt in his hand accentuate his identity as a cross-cultural diplomatic emissary.
(Anne S. K. Brown Military Collection, Brown University Library)

quois fought to achieve control of the lucrative peltry trade.

In the mid-1670s, as Iroquois dominance grew, the French intervened, for an Iroquois triumph would have destroyed France's plans to trade directly with western Indians. Over the next twenty years, the French launched repeated attacks on Iroquois villages. The English offered little assistance other than weapons to their trading partners. Its people and resources depleted by constant warfare, the confederacy in 1701 negotiated a neutrality treaty with France and other Indians. For the next half-century, the Iroquois nations maintained their power through trade and skillful diplomacy rather than warfare.

The wars against the Iroquois were crucial components of French Canada's plan to penetrate the heartland of North America. Unlike the Spaniards, French adventurers did not attempt to subjugate the Indians they encountered or formally claim large territories for France. And by tolerating the French presence, Indians gained access to European goods.

FRENCH
EXPANSION

When France decided to strengthen its presence near the Gulf of Mexico by founding New Orleans in 1718—to counter westward thrusts of the English colonies and eastward moves of the Spanish—the Mississippi posts became the glue of empire. *Coureurs de bois* (literally, "forest runners") traveled regularly between Quebec and Louisiana, using the rivers and lakes of the interior to carry trade goods to French outposts. At most such sites lived a small military garrison and a priest, surrounded by powerful nations such as the Choctaws, Chickasaws, and Osages. In all the French outposts, the shortage of European women led to unions between French men and Indian women and to the creation of mixed-race people known as *métis*.

In New Mexico, too, a crisis in the 1670s led to long-term consequences. Under Spanish domination, the Pueblo peoples had added Christianity to their religious beliefs while retaining traditional rituals. But as decades passed, Franciscans adopted increasingly brutal tactics to erase all traces of the native religion. Those who held *encomiendas* also placed heavy labor demands on the population. In 1680, Pueblos under the leadership of Popé, a respected shaman, successfully revolted, driving the Spaniards out of New Mexico. Spanish authority was restored by 1700, but Spanish governors no longer attempted to reduce the Pueblos to bondage or to violate their cultural integrity. The Pueblo revolt was the most successful and sustained Indian resistance movement in colonial North America.

POPÉ AND THE
PUEBLO REVOLT

When the Spanish expanded their territorial claims to the east and north, they followed the same strategy they had adopted in New Mexico, establishing their presence through military outposts and Franciscan missions. The army maintained order among the subject Indians and guarded the boundaries of New Spain. The friars concentrated on conversions. By the late eighteenth century, Spain claimed a vast territory that stretched from California (first colonized in 1769) through Texas (settled after 1700) to the Gulf Coast.

SPAIN'S NORTH
AMERICAN
POSSESSIONS

In the more densely settled English colonies, hostilities developed in the 1670s over land. In both New England and Virginia—though for different reasons—settlers began to encroach on territories that until then had remained in the hands of Native Americans.

By the early 1670s, the growing settlements in southern New England surrounded Wampanoag ancestral lands on Narragansett Bay. The local chief, King Philip, troubled by the loss of territory and concerned about the impact of European culture and Christianity on his people, led his warriors in attacks on nearby communities in June 1675. Other Algonquian peoples, among them Nipmucks and Narragansetts, soon joined King Philip's forces. In the fall, the Indian nations jointly attacked settlements in the northern Connecticut River valley, and the war spread to Maine when the Abenakis entered the conflict. In early 1676, the Indians devastated well-established villages and even attacked Plymouth and Providence. Altogether, the alliance wholly or partially destroyed twenty-five of ninety-two northern towns and attacked forty others.

KING PHILIP'S
WAR

The tide turned in southern New England in the summer of 1676. The Indian coalition ran short of food and ammunition, and after King Philip was killed that August, the southern alliance crumbled. Nevertheless, fighting continued on the Maine frontier for another two years until both sides agreed to end the conflict. Many surviving Pokanokets, Nipmucks, and Narragansetts were captured and sold into slavery, and still more died of starvation and disease. New Englanders had broken the power of the southern coastal native peoples. Thereafter, the Indians lived in small clusters, subordinated to the colonists and often working as servants or sailors. But the settlers had paid a terrible price for their victory: an estimated one-tenth of the able-bodied adult male population was killed or wounded. Proportional to population, it was the most costly conflict in American history.

Not coincidentally, conflict with Indians simultaneously wracked Virginia. In the early 1670s, Virginians avidly eyed the rich lands north of the York River reserved for native peoples by early treaties. When some Doeg Indians killed an English servant in July 1675, settlers attacked not only the Doegs but also the powerful Susquehannocks. In retaliation, Susquehannock bands raided outlying farms early in 1676. When Governor William Berkeley resisted starting a major war, dissatisfied land-hungry colonists rallied behind the leadership of a recent immigrant, the wealthy Nathaniel Bacon, who like other new arrivals had found all the desirable land in settled areas already occupied.

BACON'S REBELLION

After Bacon held members of the House of Burgesses hostage until they authorized him to attack the Indians, Berkeley declared Bacon and his men to be in rebellion. As the chaotic summer of 1676 wore on, Bacon alternately pursued Indians and battled the governor's supporters. In September he marched on Jamestown itself, burning the capital to the ground. But when Bacon died the following month, the rebellion began to collapse. Even so, a new treaty signed in 1677 opened much of the disputed territory to English settlement.

The war, a turning point in Virginia's relationship with nearby Indians, also marked a turning point in the colony's internal race relations. After Bacon's Rebellion, Virginia landowners for the first time began to purchase large numbers of imported African slaves. By 1700 Anglo-Americans in the Chesapeake had irrevocably altered the racial composition of their labor force.

African Slavery on the Mainland

*I*n the 1670s and 1680s, the prosperity of the Chesapeake rested on tobacco, and successful tobacco cultivation depended on an ample labor supply. But fewer and fewer English men and women proved willing to indenture themselves for long terms of service in Maryland and Virginia. To obtain the workers they needed, wealthy Chesapeake tobacco growers looked to the Caribbean sugar islands, where planters had eagerly purchased African slaves since the 1640s.

Slavery had been practiced in Europe (although not in England) for centuries. European Christians, both Catholics and Protestants, believed that enslaving heathen peoples was justifiable in religious terms. Consequently, when Portuguese mariners reached the sub-Saharan African coast and encountered non-Christian societies holding slaves, they purchased bondspeople as part of the exchange of many items.

WHY AFRICAN SLAVERY?

Some slaves were taken to the Iberian Peninsula; others to the Wine Islands. Iberians then exported African slavery to their American possessions, New Spain and Brazil. Because the Catholic Church prevented the formal enslavement of Indians in those domains and free laborers could find better work than enduring the mines or sugar plantations, African bondspeople became mainstays of the Caribbean and Brazilian economies. Sugar planters on English islands, who had the same problems of labor supply, also purchased slaves.

The slave system that was well established in the Caribbean by the mid-1650s did not immediately take root in the English mainland colonies. Before the 1660s, the few residents of African descent on the mainland varied in status: some were free, some indentured, some enslaved. All came from a population that the historian Ira Berlin has termed Atlantic creoles. Often of mixed race, many came to the English colonies from elsewhere in the Americas. Already familiar with Europeans, the Atlantic creoles fit easily into established niches in the hierarchical social structures of the early colonies. Berlin has characterized all the early mainland colonies as "societies with slaves": some people were held in perpetual bondage, but the societies did not rely wholly on slave labor. He usefully contrasts such communities with "slave societies," in which slavery served as the fundamental basis of the economy.

ATLANTIC CREOLES IN SOCIETIES WITH SLAVES

The many ambiguities of status in societies with slaves are evident in early laws in which Virginians and Marylanders revealed initial difficulty in developing a definition of enslavement. Several Virginia statutes used the term *Christian* to mean "free person"; when at least one slave converted and therefore claimed freedom, the House of Burgesses provided (in 1667) that "the blessed sacrament of baptism" would not liberate bondspeople from perpetual servitude. And in 1670 the House of Burgesses declared that "all servants not being christians imported into this colony by shipping shalbe slaves for their lives," but similar servants that "shall come by land" would serve only for a term of years. The awkward phrases attempted to differentiate Africans from Indians; Virginians saw both groups as distinguishable from English people, but expressed those distinctions in terms of religion and geography rather than race.

Just a few years later, Chesapeake legislators started to employ racial terminology, as increasing numbers of slaves arrived each year, MAINLAND SLAVE SOCIETIES first from the Caribbean and then directly from Africa. Virginia in 1682 altered its definition of who could be enslaved, declaring bluntly that "Negroes, Moors, Mollatoes or Indians" arriving "by sea or land" could all be held in bondage for life if their "parentage and native country are not christian." Most of the English colonies, even those without many bondspeople, adopted detailed codes to govern slaves' behavior. By 1700 African slavery was firmly established as the basis of the economy in the Chesapeake and South Carolina as well as in the Caribbean. Under Berlin's definition, those colonies had become "slave societies."

English enslavers evidently had few moral qualms about these actions. Few at the time questioned the decision to hold Africans and their descendants in perpetual bondage. Initially the colonists lacked clear conceptual categories defining both "race" and "slave." They developed such categories and their meanings over time, through their experience with the institution of African (and Indian) slavery, originally adopted for economic reasons.

Between 1492 and 1770 more Africans than Europeans came to the Americas. Most went to Brazil or the Caribbean: of at least 10 million enslaved people brought to the Americas during the existence of slavery, only about 260,000 by 1775 were imported into what would become the United States. This massive trade in human beings is best understood within the context of the Atlantic trading system that developed during the middle years of the seventeenth century.

The Web of Empire and the Atlantic Slave Trade

*T*he elaborate Atlantic economic system is commonly called the triangular trade, with the slave traffic viewed as the triangle's middle leg and therefore called the middle passage. But *triangular trade* fails to convey the complexities of the Atlantic world's late-seventeenth-century commercial relationships. Trade involving Europe, Africa, and the Americas moved across the ocean not in easily diagrammed patterns but in a complicated and inextricably linked web of people and products (see Map 3.1).

Although slavery had long been practiced, the oceanic slave trade was entirely new and was the linchpin of the Atlantic system. The ATLANTIC TRADING SYSTEM expanding network of commerce between Europe and its colonies was fueled by the sale and transport of slaves, the exchange of commodities produced by slave labor, and the need to feed and clothe so many bound laborers. The profits from Chesapeake tobacco and Caribbean and Brazilian sugar sold in Europe paid for both the African laborers who grew these crops and European manufactured goods. Europeans purchased slaves from African coastal rulers for resale in their colonies and acquired sugar and tobacco from America for sale in Europe, in exchange dispatching their manufactures everywhere.

New England had the most complex relationship to the trading system. The region produced only one item England wanted: tall trees to NEW ENGLAND AND THE CARIBBEAN serve as masts for sailing vessels. To buy English manufactures, New Englanders therefore needed profits earned elsewhere: the Wine Islands and the Caribbean. Those islands lacked precisely the items that New England could produce in abundance: cheap food (corn and salt fish) to feed the slaves and wood for barrels to hold wine, sugar, and molasses. By the late 1640s, New England's economy rested on consumption by slaves and their owners. After the founding of Pennsylvania, New York, and New Jersey, those colonies too participated in the lucrative West Indian trade.

Shopkeepers in the interior of New England and the middle colonies bartered with local farmers for grains, livestock, and barrel staves, then traded those

International Piracy

The web of commerce across the Atlantic drove trade—and theft—to new levels. The last decades of the seventeenth century were the heyday of pirates, who, from bases in North America and the Caribbean, ranged the world. In New York and Charles Town, merchants asked few questions about the origins of valuable goods, and the solitary ocean voyages of merchant and slaving vessels were easy prey for resourceful marauders. The cargoes of precious metals, slaves, and luxury goods such as fine wines and silks made the return worth the risk.

As early as the sixteenth century, European kingdoms encouraged attacks on the commerce of rivals. Queen Elizabeth knighted Francis Drake for the treasure he stole from Spain. Though in wartime, letters of marque could transform law-breaking pirates into legal privateers, authorized to prey on the enemy, the line between pirates and privateers was easily breached. Privateers could keep most of their booty, and the crews, with sailors of many nations, were loyal primarily to themselves.

The infamous Captain William Kidd (c. 1645–1701) was both pirate and privateer. Probably Scots by birth, he plundered in the Caribbean before settling in New York, where he married a rich widow and cultivated local politicians. In 1696 he returned to sea with new privateering credentials, issued in London. With a crew recruited in England and New York, he sailed to the Indian Ocean, picking up other mariners along the way. Kidd encountered no vessels he could legally capture, and his crew, composed largely of pirates, became restive, so he resumed marauding. Over the next months, Kidd and his men seized Dutch and Portuguese ships and eventually a freighter sailing from India to the Moluccas. In late 1698, they headed for the Americas with a booty of valuable textiles. But in Boston, Kidd was arrested for piracy and murder. The English and colonial governments, he discovered, were newly committed to stamping out piracy. Sent to London for trial, he was convicted and hanged in May 1701.

Captain Kidd's exploits were a product of his time and place. In the 1690s, international crews of buccaneers sailed from the Americas to wherever in the world they thought they would find rich prizes. The rapidly developing web of international commerce that linked the Western Hemisphere to Africa, Asia, and Europe also spawned the legendary thieves who preyed on it.

The sorts of valuable, exotic items pictured here were among the cargoes pirates sought. Fine ceramics and textiles from Asia commanded high prices from American and European purchasers who did not concern themselves with the origins of these desirable consumer goods.   (Left: V&A Image, The Victoria and Albert Museum, London; right: The Metropolitan Museum of Art, purchased by subscription, 1879. [79.2.311] Photograph © 1995 The Metropolitan Museum of Art)

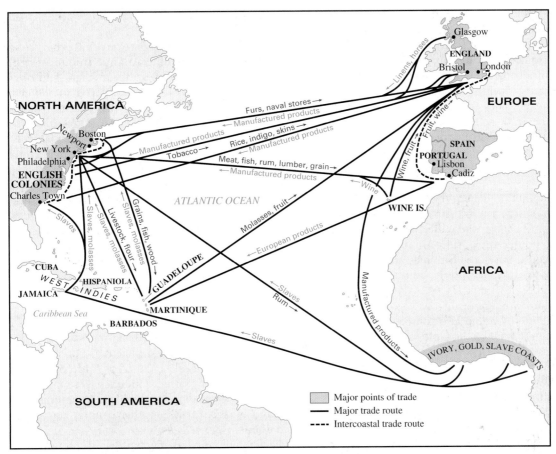

Map 3.1   Atlantic Trade Routes

By the late seventeenth century, an elaborate trade network linked the countries and colonies bordering the Atlantic Ocean. The most valuable commodities exchanged were enslaved people and the products of slave labor.

items to merchants in port towns. Such merchants dispatched ships to the Caribbean, where they sailed from island to island, exchanging their cargoes for molasses, fruit, spices, and slaves. Once they had a full load, the ships returned to Boston, Newport, New York, or Philadelphia to dispose of their cargoes. Americans began to distill molasses into rum, which was shipped to Africa and traded for slaves.

Tying the system together was the voyage that brought Africans to the Americas. That voyage was always traumatic and sometimes fatal. An average of 10 to 20 percent of the newly enslaved died en route. In addition, another 20 percent or so of slaves died ei-

ther before the ships left Africa or shortly after their arrival in the Americas. Their European captors also died at high rates, chiefly of diseases endemic to Africa. Just 10 percent of the men sent to run the Royal African Company's forts in Lower Guinea lived to return home to England.

Most of the enslaved people carried to North America originated in West Africa. Certain coastal

*WEST AFRICA
AND THE
SLAVE TRADE*

rulers served as middlemen, allowing the establishment of permanent slave-trading posts in their territories and supplying resident Europeans with slaves to fill their ships.

Such rulers controlled both European traders' access to slaves and inland peoples' access to desirable European goods. The slave trade had varying political and economic consequences for the nations of West Africa. The trade's centralizing tendencies helped create such powerful eighteenth-century kingdoms as Dahomey and Asante. Furthermore, the extent of nations' participation in the trade varied according to their involvement in warfare. And because prisoners of war constituted the bulk of the slaves shipped to the Americas, the most active traders were also the most successful in battle.

The trade in human beings did not uniformly depopulate West Africa, a fertile and densely inhabited region. Instead, the slave trade affected African societies unevenly. For example, rulers in parts of Upper Guinea, especially modern Gambia and Senegal, largely resisted involvement with the trade. Despite planters' preference for male slaves, women predominated in cargoes originating in the Bight of Biafra (modern Cameroon, Gabon, and southeastern Nigeria). And in such regions as the Gold Coast, the trade had a significant impact on the sex ratio of the remaining population. There, a relative shortage of men increased work demands on women, encouraged polygyny, and opened new avenues for advancement to women and their children.

By the late seventeenth century, the Atlantic commerce in slaves and the products of slave labor

EUROPEAN RIVALRIES AND THE SLAVE TRADE

constituted the basis of the European economic system, previously oriented toward the Mediterranean and Asia. Thus Columbus, seeking the wealth of Asia, instead found the lands that—along with Africa—ultimately replaced Asia as the source of European prosperity.

European nations fought bitterly to control the slave trade. The Portuguese, who at first dominated the trade, were supplanted by the Dutch in the 1630s. The Dutch, in turn, lost out to the English, who by the 1670s controlled the trade through the Royal African Company. Holding a monopoly on all English trade with sub-Saharan Africa, this company transported about 100,000 slaves to England's Caribbean colonies. Yet even before the company's monopoly expired in 1712, many individual English traders had illegally entered the market for slaves, and by the early eighteenth century they carried most of the Africans imported into the colonies, earning huge profits from successful voyages.

English officials decided to tap into the profits produced by the expanding Atlantic trading system. Chesapeake tobacco and Caribbean sugar had obvious value, but other colonial products also had considerable potential. Additional tax revenues could put England back on a sound financial footing after the disruptions of the Civil War, and English merchants wanted to ensure that they—not their Dutch rivals—reaped the benefits of trading with English colonies. Parliament accordingly began to draft laws designed to confine the proceeds of the English imperial web of trade primarily to the mother country.

Like other European nations, England based its commercial policy on a series of assumptions about

MERCANTILISM

the world's economic system. Collectively called mercantilism, these assumptions viewed the economic world as a collection of national states, whose governments competed for shares of a finite amount of wealth. Each nation sought to become as economically self-sufficient as possible while maintaining a favorable balance of trade by exporting more than it imported. Colonies were important because they could supply valuable raw materials and serve as a market for the mother country's manufactured goods.

Parliament applied mercantilist thinking to the American colonies in laws known as the Navigation

NAVIGATION ACTS

Acts. The major acts—passed between 1651 and 1673—established three main principles. First, only English or colonial merchants and ships could engage in trade in the colonies. Second, certain valuable American products could be sold only in England or in English colonies. At first, these "enumerated" goods included wool, sugar, tobacco, indigo, ginger, and dyes; later acts added rice, naval stores (spars, pitch, tar, and turpentine), copper, and furs to the list. Third, all foreign goods destined for sale in the colonies had to be shipped by way of England and English import duties paid. Some years later, a new series of laws established a fourth principle: the colonies could not export items (such as wool clothing, hats, or iron) that competed with English products.

The Navigation Acts aimed at forcing American trade to center on England. The mother country would benefit from both colonial imports and exports. The laws adversely affected some colonies, like those in the Caribbean and the Chesapeake, because planters there could not seek new markets for their staple crops. In others, the impact was minimal or even positive. Builders and owners of ships benefited from the monopoly on American trade given to English and colonial merchants. And the northern and middle colonies produced many unenumerated goods (fish and flour, for example) that could be traded directly to foreign buyers as long as the goods were carried in English or American ships.

The English authorities soon learned that writing mercantilist legislation was far easier than enforcing it. The many harbors of the American coast provided ready havens for smugglers, and colonial officials often looked the other way when illegally imported goods were offered for sale. Consequently, Parliament in 1696 enacted another Navigation Act, establishing in America a number of vice-admiralty courts, which operated without juries. Because American juries tended to favor local smugglers over customs officers, Parliament decided to remove Navigation Act cases from the regular colonial courts.

Enslavement of Africans and Indians

Following Bacon's Rebellion, so many Africans were imported into Virginia and Maryland so rapidly that by 1710, people of African descent composed one-fifth of the region's population. Even so, a decade later, American-born slaves already outnumbered their African-born counterparts in the Chesapeake, and the native-born proportion continued to grow.

Slaves brought from Africa tended to be assigned to outlying parts of the plantations (called quarters),

AFRICAN ENSLAVEMENT IN THE CHESAPEAKE

at least until they learned some English and the routines of tobacco cultivation. Mostly men, they often lived in quarters of ten to fifteen workers housed together in one or two buildings and supervised by an Anglo-American overseer. Each man was expected to cultivate about two acres of tobacco a year. Planters allowed them Sunday off. Many used that time to cultivate their own gardens or to hunt or fish to supplement their meager diets. Only rarely could they form families because there were so few women among newly imported Africans.

Slaves usually cost about two and a half times as much as indentured servants, but they repaid the greater investment with a lifetime of service. Planters with enough money could acquire slaves, accumulate wealth, and establish large plantations. Other planters could afford neither slaves nor indentured servants, whose cost had risen because of their scarcity. Anglo-American society in the Chesapeake thus became more and more stratified—that is, the gap between rich and poor steadily widened. The introduction of large numbers of African slaves contributed to this outcome.

Africans who had lived in the Caribbean came with their masters to South Carolina from Barbados

AFRICAN ENSLAVEMENT IN SOUTH CAROLINA

in 1670, composing one-quarter to one-third of the early population. The Barbadian slaveowners quickly discovered that African-born slaves had a variety of skills well suited to South Carolina. African-style dugout canoes became the chief means of transportation in the colony, which was crossed by rivers and included large islands just offshore. Fishing nets copied from African models proved more efficient than those of English origin. Africans' skill at killing crocodiles in their native country equipped them to handle alligators in America. Finally, Africans adapted their traditional techniques of cattle herding for use in America. Since meat and hides numbered among the colony's chief exports in its earliest years, Africans contributed significantly to South Carolina's prosperity.

After 1700, South Carolinians began to import slaves directly from Africa. From 1710 to midcentury, African-born slaves constituted a majority of the slave population there, which, coupled with the similarity of the semitropical South Carolinian and West African environments, ensured that more aspects of West African culture survived in that colony than elsewhere on the North American mainland. Only in South Carolina did enslaved parents continue to give their children African names; only there did a dialect develop that combined English words with African terms. (Known as Gullah, it has survived to the present day in isolated areas.) African skills remained useful, so techniques lost in other regions when the migrant generation died were passed down to the migrants' children. And in South Carolina African women became the primary petty traders, dominating the markets of Charles Town as they did those of Guinea.

The importation of large numbers of Africans coincided with the successful introduction of rice in

RICE AND INDIGO

South Carolina. English people knew little about the techniques of growing and processing rice, but people from Africa's Rice Coast had spent their lives working with the crop. The Africans almost certainly assisted their English masters in cultivating the crop profitably. Every slave on a rice plantation was expected to cultivate three to four acres of rice a year and to grow part of their own food. In a universally adopted system of predefined work assignments, after bondspeople had finished their set "tasks" for the day, they could rest or work in their own garden plots or on other projects. Experienced slaves could often complete their tasks by early afternoon; after that, as on Sundays, their masters had no legitimate claim on their time.

Developers of South Carolina's second cash crop also used the task system and drew on slaves' specialized skills. Indigo, the only source of blue dye for England's textile industry, was much prized. In the early 1740s, Eliza Lucas, a young woman managing her father's plantations, began to experiment with indigo cultivation. Drawing on the knowledge of slaves and overseers from the Caribbean, she developed the planting and processing techniques later adopted throughout the colony. Indigo grew on high ground, and rice was planted in low-lying swamps; rice and indigo also had different growing seasons. Thus, the two crops complemented each other.

Among the people held in slavery in both Carolinas were Indian captives who had been retained

INDIAN ENSLAVEMENT IN NORTH AND SOUTH CAROLINA

rather than exported. In 1708, enslaved Indians composed as much as 14 percent of the South Carolina population. The widespread traffic in Indian slaves significantly affected South Carolina's relationship with its indigenous neighbors. Native Americans used the ready market for captive enemies to rid themselves of real or potential rivals. Yet native groups soon learned that Carolinians could not be trusted. As settlers and

traders shifted their priorities, first one set of former allies and then another found themselves the enslaved rather than the enslavers.

At first the Carolinians themselves did not engage directly in conflicts with neighboring native groups. But in 1711 the Tuscaroras, an Iroquoian people, attacked a Swiss-German settlement at New Bern that had expropriated their lands. South Carolinians and their Indian allies then combined to defeat the Tuscaroras in a bloody war in 1713. Afterward, more than a thousand Tuscaroras were enslaved, and the remnants of the group drifted northward, where they joined the Iroquois Confederacy.

Four years later, the Yamasees, who had helped overcome the Tuscaroras, turned on their English allies. In what seems to have been long-planned retaliation for multiple abuses by traders as well as threats to their own lands, the Yamasees enlisted the Creeks and other Muskogean peoples in coordinated attacks on outlying English settlements. In the spring and summer of 1715, English and African refugees by the hundreds streamed into Charles Town. The Creek-Yamasee offensive was eventually thwarted when reinforcements arrived from the north, colonists hastily armed their African slaves, and Cherokees joined the fight against the Creeks, their ancient foes. After the war, Carolinian involvement in the Indian slave trade essentially ceased, for all their native neighbors moved away for self-protection: Creeks migrated west, Yamasees went south, and other groups moved north.

Indian or African slavery was never of great importance to Spain's North American territories,

SLAVES IN SPANISH AND FRENCH NORTH AMERICA

which had no plantations or cash crops. As slavery took deeper root in South Carolina, Florida officials in 1693 offered freedom to fugitives who would convert to Catholicism. Hundreds of South Carolina runaways took advantage of the offer. Many settled in a town founded for them near St. Augustine, Gracia Real de Santa Teresa de Mose, headed by a former slave and militia captain.

In early Louisiana, too, slaves—some Indians, some Atlantic creoles—at first composed only a tiny proportion of the residents. But a growing European population demanded that the French government supply them with slaves, and in 1719 officials finally acquiesced, dispatching more than six thousand Africans (most from Senegal) over the next decade.

The residents failed to develop a successful plantation economy, but they did anger the Natchez Indians, whose lands they had usurped. In 1729 the Natchez, assisted by newly arrived slaves, attacked northern reaches of the colony, killing more than 10 percent of its European people. The French struck back, slaughtering the Natchez and their enslaved allies.

Atlantic creoles from the Caribbean and Indians from the Carolinas and Florida composed almost all the bondspeople in the northern mainland colonies. Some bondspeople resided in urban areas, especially New York, which in 1700 had a larger black population than any other mainland city. Women tended to work as domestic servants, men as unskilled laborers. Yet most bondspeople worked in rural agriculture. Some slaves also worked for iron-masters at forges and foundries. Although relatively few northern colonists owned slaves, those who did relied heavily on their labor and had good reason to want to preserve the institution.

ENSLAVEMENT IN THE NORTH

Imperial Reorganization and the Witchcraft Crisis

In the early 1680s, London administrators confronted a bewildering array of colonial governments. Massachusetts Bay (including Maine) functioned under its original charter. Neighboring Connecticut (having absorbed New Haven) and Rhode Island were granted charters by Charles II in 1662 and 1663, respectively, but Plymouth remained autonomous. Virginia, a royal colony, was joined in that status by New Hampshire in 1679 and New York in 1685 when its proprietor ascended the throne as James II. All the other mainland settlements were proprietorships.

By the 1670s, these colonial governments and their residents had become accustomed to considerable local political autonomy. Free adult men who owned more than a minimum amount of property (which varied from place to place) expected to have an influential voice in their governments, especially in decisions concerning taxation. After James II became king in 1685, such expectations clashed with those of the

COLONIAL AUTONOMY CHALLENGED

monarch. James and his successors sought to bring more order to colonial administration by tightening the reins of government and reducing the colonies' political autonomy. Administrators began to chip away at the privileges granted in colonial charters and to reclaim proprietorships for the Crown. Massachusetts (1691), New Jersey (1702), and the Carolinas (1729) all became royal colonies. The charters of Rhode Island, Connecticut, Maryland, and Pennsylvania were temporarily suspended but ultimately restored to their original status.

The most drastic reordering of colonial administration targeted Puritan New England, which English officials saw as a hotbed of smuggling. Moreover, Puritans refused to allow freedom of religion to non-Congregationalists and insisted on maintaining laws incompatible with English practice. New England thus seemed an appropriate place to exert English authority with greater vigor. The Crown revoked the charters of all the colonies from New Jersey to Maine and established the Dominion of New England in 1686. Sir Edmund Andros, the governor, had immense power: Parliament dissolved all the assemblies, and Andros needed only the consent of an appointed council to make laws and levy taxes.

DOMINION OF NEW ENGLAND

New Englanders endured Andros's autocratic rule for more than two years. Then they learned that James II's hold on power was crumbling amid anger at taxes he had levied without parliamentary approval and his announcement that he had converted to Catholicism. In April 1689, Boston's leaders jailed Andros and his associates. The following month they received definite news that in 1688, Parliament had deposed James and offered the throne to his daughter Mary and her husband, the Dutch prince William of Orange, both Protestants. Called the Glorious Revolution, this bloodless coup affirmed the supremacy of both Parliament and Protestantism.

GLORIOUS REVOLUTION IN AMERICA

Bostonians quickly proclaimed their loyalty to William and Mary, writing to England for instructions about the form of government they should now adopt. In other colonies, too, the Glorious Revolution emboldened people for revolt. In Maryland the Protestant Association overturned the government of the Catholic proprietor, and in New York a militia officer of German origin, Jacob Leisler, assumed control of the government. Like the New Englanders, the Maryland and New York rebels supported William and Mary and saw themselves as carrying out the colonial phase of the English revolt against Stuart absolutism.

But, like James II, William and Mary believed that England should exercise tighter control over its unruly American possessions. Consequently, only the Maryland rebellion received royal sanction, primarily because of its anti-Catholic thrust. In New York, Jacob Leisler was hanged for treason, and Massachusetts (including the formerly independent jurisdiction of Plymouth) became a royal colony with an appointed governor. The province retained its town meeting system of local government and continued to elect its council, but the new 1691 charter eliminated the traditional religious test for voting and office-holding. A parish of the Church of England appeared in the heart of Boston.

A war with the French and their Algonquian allies compounded New England's difficulties. King

_____
KING WILLIAM'S WAR

Louis XIV of France allied himself with the deposed James II, and England declared war on France in 1689. In Europe, this conflict was known as the War of the League of Augsburg, but the colonists called it King William's War. Indian attacks wholly or partially destroyed several English settlements in New York, Maine, and New Hampshire. Even the Peace of Ryswick (1697), which formally ended the war in Europe, failed to bring much of a respite from warfare to the northern frontiers. Maine could not be fully resettled for several decades because of the continuing conflict.

During the hostilities, New Englanders understandably feared a repetition of the devastation of King Philip's War. For eight months

_____
THE 1692 WITCHCRAFT CRISIS

in 1692, witchcraft accusations spread like wildfire through the rural communities of Essex County, Massachusetts—precisely the area most threatened by the Indian attacks in southern Maine and New Hampshire. Earlier incidents in which personal disputes occasionally led to isolated witchcraft charges bore little relationship to the witch fears that convulsed the region in 1692. Before the crisis ended, 14 women and 5 men were hanged, 1 man was pressed to death with heavy

stones, 54 people confessed to being witches, and more than 140 people were jailed, some for many months.

The crisis began in late February 1692 when several young women in Salem Village (an outlying precinct of the bustling port of Salem) formally charged some older female neighbors with having tortured them in spectral form. Soon other accusers and confessors chimed in, some of them female domestic servants who had been orphaned in the Indian attacks on Maine. One had lost her grandparents in King Philip's War and her parents in King William's War. These young women, perhaps the most powerless people in a region apparently powerless to affect its fate, offered their fellow New Englanders a compelling explanation for the seemingly endless chain of troubles afflicting them: their province was under direct attack not only by the Indians but also by the Devil and his allied witches. The so-called afflicted girls accused not just the older women, but also prominent men from the Maine frontier who had traded with or failed to defeat the Indians. The colony's magistrates, who were also its political and military leaders, were all too willing to believe such accusations, because if the Devil had caused New England's current troubles, they personally bore no responsibility.

In October, the worst phase of the crisis ended when the governor, supported by several prominent clergymen, dissolved the special court established to try the suspects. Most critics of the trials did not think the girls were faking, nor did they conclude that witches did not exist or that confessions were false. Rather, they questioned whether the guilt of the accused could be legally established by the evidence presented in court. During the final trials in regular courts, almost all the defendants were acquitted, and the governor reprieved the few found guilty.

Online Study Center
Improve Your Grade
Primary Source: Ann Putnam's Deposition

In 1696, England took a major step in colonial administration by creating the fifteen-member Board

_____
NEW IMPERIAL MEASURES

of Trade and Plantations, which thereafter served as the chief organ of government concerned with the American colonies. Previously, no single body had that responsibility. The board gathered information, reviewed Crown

The Wonders of the Invisible World.

OBSERVATIONS

As well *Historical* as *Theological*, upon the NATURE, the NUMBER, and the OPERATIONS of the

DEVILS.

Accompany'd with,

I. Some Accounts of the Grievous Molestations, by DÆ-MONS and WITCHCRAFTS, which have lately annoy'd the Countrey; and the Trials of some eminent *Malefactors* Executed upon occasion thereof: with several Remarkable *Curiosities* therein occurring.

II. Some Counsils, Directing a due Improvement of the terrible things, lately done, by the Unusual & Amazing Range of EVIL SPIRITS, in Our Neighbourhood: & the methods to prevent the *Wrongs* which those *Evil Angels* may intend against all sorts of people among us; especially in Accusations of the Innocent.

III. Some Conjectures upon the great EVENTS, likely to befall, the WORLD in General, and NEW-ENGLAND in Particular; as also upon the Advances of the TIME, when we shall see BETTER DAYES.

IV A short Narrative of a late Outrage committed by a knot of WITCHES in *Sweden*, very much Resembling, and so far Explaining, *That* under which our parts of *America* have laboured!

V. THE DEVIL DISCOVERED: In a Brief Discourse upon those TEMPTATIONS, which are the more Ordinary *Devices* of the Wicked One.

By **Cotton Mather.**

Boston Printed by *Benj. Harris* for *Sam. Phillips.* 1693.

■ The Reverend Cotton Mather of Boston, twenty-nine years old in 1692 at the time of the Salem witchcraft crisis, rushed this book—*The Wonders of the Invisible World*—into print shortly after the trials ended. He tried to explain to his fellow New Englanders the "Grievous Molestations, by Daemons and Witchcrafts, which have lately annoy'd the Countrey" by providing both brief trial narratives and examples of similar recent occurrences elsewhere, most notably in Mohra, Sweden.   (Image courtesy of The Massachusetts Historical Society)

appointments in America, scrutinized legislation passed by colonial assemblies, supervised trade policies, and advised successive ministries on colonial issues. Still, the Board of Trade did not have any direct powers of enforcement. It also shared jurisdiction over American affairs not only with the customs service but also with a member of the ministry. In short, supervision of the American provinces remained decentralized and haphazard.

That surely made it easier for Massachusetts and the rest of the English colonies in America to accommodate themselves to the new imperial order. Most colonists resented alien officials who arrived in America determined to implement the policies of king and Parliament, but they adjusted to their demands and to the trade restrictions imposed by the Navigation Acts. They fought another of Europe's wars—the War of the Spanish Succession, or Queen Anne's War in the colonies—from 1702 to 1713 without enduring the stresses of the first. Colonists who allied themselves with royal government received patronage in the form of offices and land grants and composed "court parties" that supported English officials. Others, who were either less fortunate in their friends or more principled in defense of colonial autonomy, made up the opposition, or "country" interest. By the end of the first quarter of the eighteenth century, most men in both groups had been born in America and were members of elite families.

Summary   *Online Study Center*   **ACE the Test**

The eighty years from 1640 to 1720 established the basic economic and political patterns that were to structure mainland colonial society. By 1720, nearly the entire east coast of North America was in English hands, and Indian control east of the Appalachian Mountains had largely been broken. What had been an immigrant population was now mostly American-born, except for the many African-born people in South Carolina; economies originally based on trade in fur and skins had become far more complex and more closely linked with the mother country; and a wide variety of political structures had been reshaped into a more uniform pattern. Yet at the same time, the introduction of large-scale slavery into the Chesapeake and the Carolinas differentiated their societies from those of the colonies to the north. They had become true slave societies, heavily reliant on a system of perpetual servitude. Although the northern colonies were not slave societies, their economies rested on profits derived from the Atlantic trading system, the key element of which was traffic in enslaved humans.

Meanwhile, from a small outpost in Santa Fe, New Mexico, and missions in Florida, the Spanish had expanded their influence throughout the Gulf Coast region and as far north as California. The French had come to dominate the length of the Mississippi River and the entire Great Lakes region. Both groups of colonists lived near Indian nations and depended on the indigenous people's labor and goodwill. The extensive Spanish and French presence to the south and west of the English settlements made future conflicts among the European powers in North America nearly inevitable.

By 1720, the essential elements of the imperial administrative structure that would govern the English colonies until 1775 had been put firmly in place. The regional economic systems originating in the late seventeenth and early eighteenth centuries also continued to dominate North American life until after independence. And Anglo-Americans had developed the commitment to autonomous local government that later would lead them into conflict with Parliament and the king.

LEGACY FOR A PEOPLE AND A NATION
Americans of African Descent

After the 1670s, the rise of southern economies based largely on the enslavement of Africans, and the widespread employment of enslaved Africans in northern colonies, dramatically altered the American population. By 1775, more than a quarter million Africans had been imported into the territory that later became the United States, constituting about 20 percent of the population at the time of the Revolution.

According to the 2000 census, 12.5 percent of the American people now claim descent from African ancestors. Because the legal importation of African slaves ended in 1808 and the United States attracted relatively few voluntary migrants of African descent until the late twentieth century, most of today's African Americans have colonial ancestors, a claim few Americans of European descent can make.

The modern African American population reflects the large number of interracial sexual relationships (both coerced and voluntary) during the long African residence in mainland North America. African Americans, both free and enslaved, have had children with both Europeans and Indians since the colonial period; more recently, they have intermarried with Asian immigrants. In large part the mingling of different peoples of color resulted from state miscegenation laws, which from the early years of the American republic until 1967—when the Supreme Court struck them down—forbade legal marriages between people of European descent and those of other races. That forced the non-European groups to seek partners only among themselves. And other state and federal laws then defined people with any appreciable African ancestry as "black."

Recently, increasing numbers of interracial unions have produced multiracial children. The 2000 census for the first time allowed Americans to define themselves as members of more than one race. Opposition to this change came largely from leaders of the African American community, and on census forms, people of African descent proved less willing to define themselves as multiracial than did people with other origins. The racial self-definition of this large component of the American people thus continues to be influenced by a legacy of discrimination.

*a*MERICAN SOCIETY TRANSFORMED 1720–1770

"*as* I in that Country I would not Stay one day longer in it," Alexander McAllister wrote to his cousin in Scotland in late 1770. "If god Spers [spares] you in this Cuntrie but a few years you will blis [bless] the day you left." As a youth, McAllister had moved from the Scottish Highlands to North Carolina with his parents. In many letters to friends and family back in Argyleshire, he elaborated on the attractions of his adopted home at Cross Creek. Anyone could easily grow corn, wheat, barley, rye, oats, potatoes, and tobacco, he wrote: "In truth it is the Best poor mans Cuntry I Ever heard of." McAllister assured his correspondents that all immigrants were doing well, insisting that "ther is non but what is in a good way."

One historian has estimated that McAllister's network of correspondence brought about five thousand of his countrymen to North America in the two decades after the mid-1750s. When Scots arrived in North Carolina with letters of introduction from people McAllister knew, he helped them find land and supplies. Although he understood that, as he told one correspondent, "the best [land] is taken up many years ago," and that newcomers' first few years would be hard, he never altered his recommendations. Certainly McAllister himself thrived in his new homeland; by the late 1780s, having fathered numerous children by two wives, he owned forty slaves and more than 2,500 acres of land. He served as an elder of the Presbyterian church, a member of the colonial assembly, and a state senator after independence was won. Although he was more successful than most migrants, his prosperity showed what some could achieve.

Alexander McAllister and other Highland Scots took part in a massive eighteenth-century migration of European and African peoples that by 1770 had changed the nature of the American population and the look of the American landscape. Ethnic diversity was especially pronounced in the small colonial cities, but the countryside too attracted settlers from many European nations. The British colonies south of New England drew by far the largest number of newcomers. Their arrival not only swelled the population but also

Population Growth and Ethnic Diversity

Economic Growth and Development

Colonial Cultures

LINKS TO THE WORLD
Exotic Beverages

Colonial Families

Politics: Stability and Crisis in British America

A Crisis in Religion

LEGACY FOR A PEOPLE AND A NATION
"Self-Made Men"

Online Study Center
This icon will direct you to interactive map and primary source activities on the website
http://college.hmco.com/pic/nortonbrief7e

CHRONOLOGY

1691 • Locke's *Two Treatises of Government* published, a key example of Enlightenment political thought

1732 • Founding of Georgia

1739 • Stono Rebellion (South Carolina) leads to increased white fears of slave revolts
  • George Whitefield arrives in America; Great Awakening broadens

1739–48 • King George's War disrupts American economy

1740s • Black population of the Chesapeake begins to grow by natural increase, contributing to rise of large plantations

1741 • New York City "conspiracy" reflects whites' continuing fears of slave revolts

1760s • Baptist congregations take root in Virginia

1760–75 • Peak of eighteenth-century European and African migration to English colonies

1765–66 • Hudson River land riots pit tenants and squatters against large landlords

1767–69 • Regulator movement (South Carolina) tries to establish order in backcountry

1771 • North Carolina Regulators defeated by eastern militia at Battle of Alamance

---

altered political balances and affected the religious climate by introducing new sects.

Along with population growth and the new ethnic diversity, several other key themes marked colonial development in the mid-eighteenth century: the increasing importance of colonial urban centers, the creation of a prosperous urban elite, rising levels of consumption for all social ranks, and the new significance of internal markets. In the French and British mainland colonies, exports continued to dominate the economy in an international commercial system that fluctuated wildly. Yet expanding local populations demanded greater quantities and types of goods, and Europe could not supply all those needs. Therefore, colonists came to depend more on exploiting and consuming their own resources.

Intermarried networks of wealthy families developed in each of Europe's American possessions by the 1760s. These well-off, educated colonists participated in transatlantic intellectual life, such as the movement known as the Enlightenment, whereas many colonists of the "lesser sort" could neither read nor write. The elites lived in comfortable houses and enjoyed leisure-time activities. Most colonists, whether free or enslaved, worked with their hands from dawn to dark. Such divisions were most pronounced in British America, where the social and economic distance among different ranks of Anglo-Americans had widened noticeably by 1750.

In 1720, much of North America was still under Indian control. By 1770, settlements of Europeans and Africans ruled by Great Britain filled almost all of the region between the Appalachian Mountains and the Atlantic Ocean; and the British, as discussed in the next chapter, had come to dominate the extensive system of rivers and lakes running through the heart of the continent. Spanish missions extended in a great arc from present-day northern California to the Gulf Coast. Immigration, population growth, geographical expansion, new economic activity, and social change had transformed the character of Europe's North American possessions. ■

Population Growth and Ethnic Diversity

*O*nly about 250,000 European and African Americans resided in the colonies in 1700; by 1775, 2.5 million lived there. Such rapid expansion appears even more remarkable when it is compared with the modest changes that occurred in French and Spanish North America. At the end of the eighteenth century, Texas had only about 2,500 Spanish residents and California even fewer; the largest Spanish colony, New Mexico, included just 20,000 or so. The total European population of New France was about 70,000 in the 1760s.

Although migration accounted for a considerable share, most of the growth in Anglo America resulted from natural increase. Once the difficult early decades of settlement had passed and the sex ratio evened out in the South (after 1700), the American population doubled approximately every twenty-five years. Such a rate of growth, unparalleled in human history until very recent times, had a variety of causes, chief among them women's youthful age at the onset of childbearing, from late teens to early twenties. Since married women became pregnant every two or three years, women normally bore five to ten children. Because the colonies were relatively healthful places to live, especially north of Virginia, a large proportion of children who survived infancy reached maturity and began families of their own. Consequently, about half of the American population was under sixteen years old in 1775.

The height of the slave trade occurred in the eighteenth century, when about two-thirds of all slaves

INVOLUNTARY MIGRANTS FROM AFRICA

were carried across the Atlantic as rice, indigo, tobacco, and sugar plantations expanded rapidly. In the slaveholding societies of South America and the Caribbean, a surplus of males over females and appallingly high mortality rates meant that only a large, continuing influx of slaves could maintain the work force. South Carolina, where rice cultivation was difficult and unhealthful and planters preferred to purchase men, also required an inflow of Africans. But in the Chesapeake the number of bondspeople grew especially rapidly because imports were added to an enslaved population that, with tobacco's easier work

routines and a roughly equal sex ratio, began to sustain itself through natural increase after 1740.

The involuntary migrants came from many different ethnic groups and regions of Africa (see Map 4.1), and people from the same area (enemies as well as allies) tended to be taken to the Americas together. That tendency was heightened by planter partiality for slaves of particular ethnic groups. Virginians, for example, evidently preferred to purchase Igbos from the Bight of Biafra (modern Cameroon, Gabon, and southeastern Nigeria), whereas South Carolinians and Georgians selected Senegambians and people from West Central Africa (modern Congo and Angola). Rice planters' desire to purchase Senegambians, who had cultivated rice in their homeland, is easily explained, but historians disagree about the reasons for the other preferences.

Thousands, possibly tens of thousands, of these enslaved Africans were Muslims. Some were literate in Arabic, and several came from aristocratic families. The discovery of noble birth could lead to a slave's being freed to return home. Job Ben Solomon, for example, arrived in Maryland in 1732. Himself a slave trader from Senegal, he had been captured by raiders while selling bondspeople in Gambia. A letter he wrote in Arabic so impressed his owners that he was liberated the next year.

Despite the approximately 280,000 slaves brought to the mainland, American-born people of African descent soon numerically dominated the enslaved population because of high natural increase. A planter who owned adult female slaves could watch the size of his labor force expand steadily. The slaveholder Thomas Jefferson indicated that he fully understood the connections when he observed, "I consider a woman who brings a child every two years more profitable than the best man of the farm. What she produces is an addition to the capital, while his labors disappear in mere consumption."

In addition to the new group of Africans, about 585,000 Europeans moved to North America during

NEWCOMERS FROM EUROPE

the eighteenth century, most of them after 1730. Late in the seventeenth century, English officials decided to recruit German and French Protestants to prevent further large-scale emigration from England itself. Influenced by mercantilist thought, they had come to regard a large, industrious population at home as an asset rather

Map 4.1 Major Origins and Destinations of Africans Enslaved in the Americas

Enslaved Africans were drawn from many regions of western Africa (with some coming from the interior of the continent) and were shipped to areas throughout the Americas.

than a liability. Thus, they deported to the colonies "undesirables"—convicts and Jacobite rebels (supporters of the deposed Stuart monarchs)—but otherwise discouraged emigration. They offered foreign Protestants free lands and religious toleration.

The patterns evident in the chapter-opening vignette applied generally to all the voluntary eighteenth-century European migrants. Early arrivals wrote home, starting chains of migration from particular regions. The most successful migrants came well prepared, having learned from their American correspondents that land and resources were abundant, especially in the backcountry, but that they would need capital to take full advantage of the new opportunities. People who arrived penniless did less well.

Online Study Center **Improve Your Grade**
Interactive Map: Immigration and Frontier
   Expansion to 1755

One of the largest groups of immigrants—nearly 150,000—came from Ireland or Scotland. About

*SCOTS-IRISH,
GERMANS,
AND SCOTS*

66,000 Scots-Irish descendants of Presbyterian Scots who had settled in the north of Ireland during the seventeenth century joined some 35,000 people who came directly to America from Scotland. Another 43,000 migrated from southern Ireland. High rents, poor harvests, and religious discrimination (in Ireland) combined to push people toward North America. Vessels engaged in the linen trade with Pennsylvania regularly left Ireland with plenty of room for passengers. By the 1720s, the migration route was well established, fueled by positive reports of prospects for advancement in North America.

Such immigrants usually landed in Philadelphia or New Castle, Delaware. They moved into the backcountry of western Pennsylvania along the Susquehanna River, where the colonial government created a county named Donegal for them. Later migrants moved farther west and south, to the backcountry of Maryland, Virginia, and the Carolinas. Frequently unable to afford any acreage, they settled illegally on land belonging to Indians, land speculators, or colonial governments. In the frontier setting, they gained a reputation for lawlessness, hard drinking, and ferocious fighting.

Migrants from Germany numbered about 85,000. Most emigrated between 1730 and 1755, also usually arriving in Philadelphia. Late in the century, they and their descendants accounted for one-third of Pennsylvania's residents. But many Germans moved west and then south into the backcountry of Maryland and Virginia. Others landed in Charles Town and settled in the southern interior. The Germans belonged to a wide variety of Protestant sects and in Pennsylvania added to the colony's substantial religious diversity.

The most concentrated period of immigration to the colonies fell between 1760 and 1775. Tough economic times in Germany and the British Isles led many to seek a better life in America; simultaneously, the slave trade burgeoned. In those fifteen years more than 220,000 persons arrived—nearly 10 percent of the entire population of British North America in 1775. Late-arriving free immigrants had little choice but to remain in the cities or move to the edges of settlement; land elsewhere was fully occupied.

Because of these migration patterns and the concentration of slaveholding in the South, half the

*MAINTAINING
ETHNIC AND
RELIGIOUS
IDENTITIES*

colonial population south of New England had non-English origins by 1775. Whether the migrants assimilated readily into Anglo-American culture depended on patterns of settlement, the size of the group, and the strength of the migrants' ties to their common culture. For example, the Huguenots—French Protestants who fled religious persecution in their homeland after 1685—settled in tiny enclaves in American cities but were unable to sustain either their language or their religious practices. By contrast, the colonial Jews, an equally small group, maintained a distinct identity. In places like New York and Newport, Rhode Island, they established synagogues and worked actively to preserve their religion. As a general rule, members of the larger groups of migrants (Germans, Irish, and Scots) found it easier to sustain their Old World ways.

Where migrants from different countries settled in the same region, ethnic antagonisms often surfaced. Anglo-American elites fostered such antagonisms to maintain their political and economic power, and they frequently subverted the colonies' generous naturalization laws, thus depriving even long-resident immigrants of a voice in government. The elites probably would have preferred to ignore the English colonies' growing racial and ethnic diversity, but ultimately they could not do so. When they moved toward revolution in the 1770s, they recognized that they needed the support of non-English Americans. Quite deliberately, they began to speak of "the rights of man," rather than "English liberties," when they sought recruits for their cause.

Economic Growth and Development

*T*he dramatic increase in the population of Anglo America served as one of the few sources of stability for the colonial economy, which was driven primarily by the vagaries of international markets. A comparison to French and Spanish America reveals significant differences. The population and economy of New Spain's Borderlands stagnated. The isolated settlements produced few items for export. French Canada exported large quantities of furs and fish, but monopolistic trade practices ensured that most of the profits ended up in the home country. The Louisiana colony required substantial government subsidies to survive. Of France's American possessions, only the Caribbean islands flourished economically.

In British North America, by contrast, the rising population generated ever-greater demands for goods and services, leading to the development of small-scale colonial manufacturing and a complex network of internal trade. Roads, bridges, mills, and stores were built to serve the many new settlements. A lively coastal trade developed, and its ships not only collected goods for export and distributed imports but also sold items made in America. The colonies thus began to move away from their earlier pattern of dependence on European manufactured goods. Iron making became the largest indigenous industry; by 1775, Anglo America's iron production surpassed England's.

OVERVIEW OF THE ANGLO-AMERICAN ECONOMY

The major energizing, yet destabilizing, influence on the colonial economy nevertheless remained foreign trade. Colonial prosperity still depended heavily on overseas demand for American products like tobacco, rice, indigo, fish, and barrel staves, which earned the colonists the credit they needed to purchase English and European imports. If demand for American exports slowed, the colonists' income dropped, as did their ability to buy imported goods.

Despite fluctuations, the economy slowly grew during the eighteenth century. That growth produced better standards of living for all property-owning Americans. Early in the century, households began to acquire amenities such as chairs and earthenware dishes. Diet also improved as trading networks brought access to more varied foods. Thus, the colonists became consumers, in the sense that for the first time they could make choices among a variety of products and could afford to buy items not essential for subsistence.

WEALTH AND POVERTY

Yet the benefits of economic growth were unevenly distributed: wealthy Americans improved their position relative to other colonists. The native-born elite families who dominated American political, economic, and social life by 1750 had begun the century with sufficient capital to take advantage of the changes caused by population growth. They were the urban merchants, the large landowners, the slave traders, and the owners of rum distilleries. Their rise helped make the social and economic structure of mid-eighteenth-century America more stratified than before.

New arrivals did not have the opportunities for advancement that had greeted their predecessors. Even so, few free settlers in rural areas (where about 95 percent of colonists lived) appear to have been truly poor. But in the cities, families of urban laborers lived on the edge of destitution. In Philadelphia, for instance, a male laborer's average annual earnings fell short of the amount needed to supply his family with the bare necessities. Even in a good year, his wife or children had to do wage work; a bad year could reduce the family to beggary. By the 1760s, applicants for assistance overwhelmed public urban poor-relief systems, and some cities began to build workhouses or almshouses to shelter the growing number of poor people.

Within this overall picture were different regional patterns: New England, the middle colonies (Pennsylvania, New York, and New Jersey), the Chesapeake (including North Carolina), and the Lower South (South Carolina and Georgia) each had its own economic rhythm derived from the nature of its export trade.

In New England, three elements combined to influence economic development: the nature of the landscape, New England's leadership in shipping, and the impact of imperial wars. Wood products constituted important salable commodities because farms did not produce surpluses other than livestock. They were worked primarily by family members; the region had relatively few hired laborers. It also had the lowest average wealth per freeholder in the colonies. But New England had many wealthy merchants and professionals who profited substantially from trade with the Caribbean.

NEW ENGLAND AND KING GEORGE'S WAR

Boston, by the 1730s a major shipbuilding center, soon felt the impact when warfare between European powers resumed in 1739. British vessels clashed with Spanish ships in the Caribbean, sparking a conflict known in America as King George's War (called the War of the Austrian Succession in Europe). The war initially energized Boston's economy. New England privateers seized enemy shipping, and area merchants profited from military supply contracts. But then New Englanders suffered major losses in Caribbean battles and forays against Canada. In 1745 a New England expedition captured the French fortress of Louisbourg (in modern Nova Scotia), but the expensive victory led to heavy taxation of Massachusetts residents, and after the war, unprecedented numbers of widows and children crowded Boston's relief rolls. The shipbuilding boom ended when the war did, the economy stagnated, and taxes remained high. Britain even returned Louisbourg to France in the Treaty of Aix-la-Chapelle (1748).

MIDDLE COLONIES AND THE CHESAPEAKE

King George's War and its aftermath affected the middle colonies more positively because of the greater fertility of the soil in those regions, where commercial farming prevailed. With the outbreak of hostilities, the middle colonies were able to profit from the wartime demand for grain and flour, especially in the Caribbean. After the war, poor grain harvests in Europe caused flour prices to rise rapidly. Philadelphia and New York became leaders in the foodstuffs trade.

Increased European demand for grain had a significant impact on the Chesapeake as well. After 1745, some Chesapeake planters began to convert tobacco fields to wheat and corn. By diversifying their crops, they could avoid dependency on one product for their income. Tobacco still ruled, but the conversion to grain brought about the first significant change in Chesapeake settlement patterns by encouraging the development of port towns (like Baltimore) to house the merchants who marketed the new products.

THE LOWER SOUTH

The Lower South too depended on staple crops and an enslaved labor force, but after Parliament in 1730 removed rice from the list of enumerated products, South Carolinians could trade directly with continental Europe. Rice prices thereafter climbed steeply, doubling by the late 1730s. Dependence on European sales had its drawbacks, however. King George's War in 1739 disrupted trade, causing a decade-long depression in South Carolina. Still, prosperity returned by the 1760s. Indeed, the Lower South experienced more rapid economic growth in that period than did the other colonial regions. Partly as a result, it had the highest average wealth per freeholder in Anglo America by the time of the American Revolution.

GEORGIA

Closely linked to South Carolina geographically, demographically, and economically was the mainland's newest colony, Georgia, chartered in 1732 as a haven for English debtors released from confinement to settle the colony. Its founder, James Oglethorpe, envisioned Georgia as a garrison province peopled by sturdy farmers who would defend the southern flank of English settlement against Spanish Florida. Thus, its charter prohibited slavery. But Carolina rice planters won removal of the restriction in 1751. Thereafter, they essentially invaded Georgia, which—despite remaining politically independent and becoming a royal colony in 1752—developed into a rice-planting slave society resembling South Carolina.

The differing economic impacts of King George's War on the British mainland colonies highlight a crucial fact: those colonies did not compose a unified whole. Although linked economically into regions, they had few political or social ties beyond or even within those regions. Despite the growing coastal trade, the individual colonies' economic fortunes depended not on their neighbors in America but rather on the shifting markets of Europe and the Caribbean.

Colonial Cultures

a seventeenth-century resident of England's American possessions miraculously transported to 1750 would have been surprised by what one historian has termed "the refinement of America." Native-born colonial elites sought to distinguish themselves from ordinary folk in a variety of ways as they consolidated their hold on the local economy and political power.

Wealthy colonists spent their money ostentatiously. Most notably, they built large houses with rooms specifically designed for such forms of socializing as dancing, card playing, or drinking tea. Sufficiently well-off to enjoy "leisure" time, they attended concerts and the theater, gambled at horse races, and played billiards and other games. They also cultivated polite manners. Elite families in New Mexico, Louisiana, and Quebec also set themselves off from the "lesser sort."

GENTEEL CULTURE

Online Study Center
Improve Your Grade
Primary Source: Virginia Gentleman Weighs "a Frail Woman's" Class

Men from such families prided themselves not only on their possessions and positions, but also on their level of education and their intellectual connections to Europe. Many had been tutored by private teachers; some even attended college in Europe or America. (Harvard, the first colonial college, was founded in 1636.) From a seventeenth-century focus on ancient languages and theology, colleges by the mid-eighteenth century broadened their curricula to include courses on mathematics, the natural sciences, law, and medicine. Accordingly, a very few young men from elite or upwardly mobile families enrolled in college to study for careers other than the ministry. American women were mostly excluded from advanced education.

The intellectual current known as the Enlightenment deeply affected the learned clergymen who headed colonial colleges and their students. In the mid-seventeenth century, some European thinkers began to analyze nature in an effort to determine the laws that govern the universe. They employed experimentation and

THE ENLIGHTENMENT

■ Elizabeth Murray, the subject of this 1769 painting by John Singleton Copley, was the wife of James Smith, a wealthy rum distiller. Her fashionable dress and pose would seem to mark her as a lady of leisure, yet both before and during her marriage, this Scottish immigrant ran a successful dry goods shop in Boston. She thus simultaneously catered to and participated in the new culture of consumption.   (Gift of Joseph W. R. Rogers and Mary C. Rogers. Museum of Fine Arts, Boston. Reproduced with permission. © Museum of Fine Arts, Boston)

abstract reasoning to discover general principles behind phenomena such as the motions of planets and stars and the characteristics of light and sound. Above all, Enlightenment philosophers emphasized acquiring knowledge through reason. Belief in such phenomena as witchcraft and astrology thus came under attack.

The Enlightenment supplied educated, well-to-do people in Europe and America with a common vocabulary and a unified view of the world, through which they endeavored to make sense of God's orderly creation. American naturalists like John and William Bartram supplied European scientists with information about New World plants and animals so that they could be included in universal classification systems. A notable American participant in the Enlightenment was Benjamin Franklin, who retired from a successful printing business in 1748 when he was just forty-two, thereafter devoting himself to scientific experimentation and public service. His *Experiments and Observations on Electricity* (1751) established the terminology and basic theory of electricity still used today.

The Enlightenment spirit of experimentation affected the lives of ordinary Americans most dramatically through advances in medicine—specifically, the treatment of smallpox. The Reverend Cotton Mather, a prominent Puritan cleric, learned from his African-born slave about inoculation (deliberately infecting a person with a mild case of a disease) as a protection against smallpox. When Boston in 1720–1721 suffered a major smallpox epidemic, Mather urged the adoption of inoculation despite fierce opposition from the city's leading physician. Mortality rates eventually supported Mather: of those inoculated, just 3 percent died; of others, 15 percent.

Enlightenment rationalism affected politics as well as science. John Locke's *Two Treatises of Government* (1691) challenged previous concepts of a divinely sanctioned political order. Men created governments and so could alter them, Locke declared. A ruler who broke his contract with the people and failed to protect their rights could legitimately be ousted from power by peaceful—or even violent—means. A proper political order could prevent the rise of tyrants; God's natural laws governed even the power of monarchs.

The world in which such ideas were discussed was that of the few, not the many. Most residents of

ORAL CULTURES

North America did not know how to read or write, and books were scarce and expensive. No colony required children to attend school; European American youngsters who learned to read usually did so in their own homes. A few months at a private "dame school" run by a literate local widow might teach them the basics of writing and simple arithmetic. Few Americans tried to instruct enslaved children. And only the most zealous Indian converts learned Europeans' literacy skills.

Thus, the cultures of colonial North America were primarily oral, communal, and—at least through the first half of the eighteenth century—intensely local. Different areas developed divergent cultural traditions, and racial and ethnic variations heightened those differences. Public rituals served as the chief means through which the colonists forged their cultural identities.

Attendance at church was perhaps the most important such ritual. In Congregational (Puritan)

RELIGIOUS AND CIVIC RITUALS

churches, church leaders assigned seating to reflect position in the community. By the mid-eighteenth century, wealthy men and their wives sat in privately owned pews; their children and servants, and the less fortunate members of the community, sat in sex-segregated fashion at the rear or sides of the church. In eighteenth-century Virginia, seating in Church of England parishes also conformed to the local status hierarchy. In Quebec city, formal processions of men into the parish church celebrated Catholic feast days; each participant's rank determined his placement in the procession. By contrast, Quaker meetinghouses in Pennsylvania and elsewhere used an egalitarian, though also sex-segregated, seating system.

Communal culture also centered on the civic sphere. In New England, colonial governments proclaimed official days of thanksgiving and days of fasting and prayer. Everyone was expected to participate in the public rituals held in churches on such occasions. Monthly militia musters of all able-bodied men (known as training days) also brought the community together. In the Chesapeake, important cultural rituals occurred on court and election days. When the county court met, men came from miles around to file suits, appear as witnesses, or serve as jurors. Attendance at court functioned as a method of civic education; from watching the proceedings, men learned what behavior their neighbors expected of them.

Everywhere in colonial North America, the public punishment of criminals, including hangings and whippings, served not just to humiliate the offender and express community outrage but also to remind the community of proper standards of behavior. Penalties often shamed miscreants in especially appropriate ways. When a New Mexico man assaulted his father-in-law, he was directed to kneel before him and beg his forgiveness in front of the entire community.

The wide availability of consumer goods after the early years of the eighteenth century fostered new

Exotic Beverages

As colonists became consumers, they developed a taste not only for tea (from China) but for coffee (from Arabia), chocolate (from Mesoamerica), and rum (distilled from sugar, which also sweetened the bitter taste of the other three). The demand for these once-exotic beverages in America and Europe helped reshape the world economy after the mid-seventeenth century. Indeed, one historian has estimated that approximately two-thirds of the people who migrated across the Atlantic before 1776 were involved in one way or another, primarily as slaves, in the production of tobacco, calico, and these four drinks for the world market. The exotic beverages had a profound impact, too, on custom and culture, as they moved swiftly from luxury to necessity.

Each beverage had its own pattern of consumption. Chocolate, brought to Spain from Mexico and enjoyed there for a century before spreading more widely throughout Europe, became the preferred drink of aristocrats, consumed hot at intimate gatherings in palaces and mansions. Coffee, by contrast, became the preeminent morning beverage of English and colonial businessmen, who praised its caffeine for keeping drinkers sober and focused. Coffee was served in new public coffeehouses, patronized only by men, where politics and business were the topics of conversation. The first coffeehouse opened in London in the late 1660s; Boston had several by the 1690s. By the mid-eighteenth century, though, tea had supplanted coffee as the preferred hot, caffeinated beverage in England and America. It was consumed in the afternoons, in private homes at tea tables presided over by women. Tea embodied genteel status and polite conversation. In contrast, rum was the drink of the masses. This inexpensive, potent distilled spirit, made possible by new technology and the increasing production of sugar, was devoured by free working people everywhere in the Atlantic world.

The American colonies played a vital role in the production, distribution, and consumption of each of these beverages. Chocolate, most obviously, originated in America, and cacao plantations in the South American tropics multiplied in size and number to meet the rising demand. Coffee and tea (particularly the latter) were as avidly consumed in the colonies as in England. And rum involved Americans in every phase of its production and consumption. The sugar grown on French and English Caribbean plantations was transported to the mainland in barrels and ships made from North American wood. There the syrup was turned into rum at 140 distilleries. The Americans themselves drank a substantial share of the distilleries' output—an estimated four gallons per person annually—but exported much of it to Africa. There the rum purchased more slaves to produce more sugar to make still more rum, and the cycle began again.

Thus new tastes and customs connected to four different beverages linked the colonies to the rest of the world and altered their economic and social development.

The frontispiece of Peter Muguet, *Tractatus De Poto Caphe, Chinesium The et de Chocolata,* 1685. Muguet's treatise visually linked the three hot, exotic beverages recently introduced to Europeans. The drinks are being consumed by representatives of the cultures in which they originated: a turbaned Turk (with coffeepot in the foreground), a Chinese man (with teapot on the table), and an Indian drinking from a hollowed, handled gourd (with a chocolate pot and ladle on the floor in front of him). (Library of Congress)

rituals centered on consumption. First came the acquisition of desirable items. By 1750 specialized shops selling nonessentials had proliferated in cities such as Boston, New York, Philadelphia, and New Orleans, and even small and medium-size towns had one or two retail establishments. A colonist with money to spend would set aside time to "go shopping," a novel and pleasurable activity. The purchase of a desired object—for example, a ceramic bowl or a mirror—marked only the beginning of consumption rituals.

Consumers would then deploy their purchases in an appropriate manner: hanging the mirror prominently on a wall, displaying the bowl on a table or sideboard. Individual colonists took pleasure in owning lovely objects, but they also proudly displayed their acquisitions publicly for kin and neighbors to admire.

Tea drinking, a consumption ritual dominated and controlled by women, played an especially important role in Anglo-American consumption rituals. From early in the eighteenth century, households with aspirations to genteel status sought to acquire proper tea accouterments: not just pots and cups but also strainers, sugar tongs, bowls, and even special tables. Because of its cost, tea served as a crucial marker of status. Although poor households also consumed tea, they could not afford the fancy equipment that their better-off neighbors used.

Other sorts of rituals allowed the disparate cultures of colonial North America to interact with one another. Particularly important

rituals developed on what the historian Richard White has termed the "middle ground"—that is, the psychological and geographical space in which Indians and Europeans encountered each other.

When Europeans sought to trade with Indians, they encountered an indigenous system of exchange that stressed gift giving rather than formalized buying and selling. Although French and English traders complained constantly about the need to present Indians with gifts prior to negotiating for pelts and skins, successful bargaining required such a step. Over time, an appropriate ritual developed. A European trader arriving at a village would give gifts (cloth, rum, gunpowder, and other items) to Indian

hunters. Eventually those gifts would be reciprocated, and formal trading could begin. To the detriment of Indian societies, rum became a crucial component of these intercultural trading rituals. Traders soon concluded that drunken Indians would sell their furs more cheaply.

Intercultural rituals also developed to deal with murders. Europeans sought to identify and punish a murderer. To Indians, such "eye for an eye" revenge was just one of many possible responses to murder. Compensation could also be accomplished by capturing an Indian or colonist who could take the dead person's place or by "covering the dead"—providing the family of the deceased with compensatory goods. Eventually, the French and the Algonquians evolved an elaborate ritual that encompassed elements of both societies' traditions: murders were investigated and murderers identified, but by mutual agreement deaths were usually "covered" by trade goods rather than by blood revenge.

Colonial Families

Families (rather than individuals) constituted the basic units of colonial society. People living together as families, commonly under the direction of a marital pair, were everywhere the chief mechanisms for both production and consumption. Yet family forms and structures varied widely in the mainland colonies, and not all were headed by couples.

As Europeans consolidated their hold on North America during the first three-quarters of the eighteenth

century, Native Americans had to adapt. Bands reduced in numbers by disease and warfare recombined into new units; for example, the group later known as the Catawbas emerged in the 1730s in the western Carolinas from the fragmentary remains of several earlier Indian nations. Likewise, pressure from European secular and religious authorities reshaped Indian family forms. Whereas many Indian societies had permitted easy divorce, Christian missionaries frowned on such practices; and societies that had allowed polygynous marriages (including New England Algonquians) redefined such relationships, designating one wife as "legitimate" and others as "concubines."

Continued high mortality rates created Indian societies in which extended kin took on new importance, for when parents died, relatives assumed child-rearing responsibilities. Furthermore, European dominance in a region meant that Indians could no longer pursue traditional modes of subsistence. That in turn altered family life. In New England, for instance, Algonquian husbands and wives often could not live together, for adults supported themselves by working separately (perhaps wives as domestic servants, husbands as sailors). And in New Mexico, detribalized Navajos, Pueblos, and Apaches employed as servants by Spanish settlers clustered in the small towns of the Borderlands. Known collectively as *genizaros*, they lost contact with Indian cultures.

Wherever the population contained relatively few European women, sexual liaisons occurred between

MIXED-RACE FAMILIES

European men and Indian women. The resulting mixed-race population of *mestizos* and *métis* worked as a familial "middle ground" to ease other cultural interactions. In New France and the Anglo-American backcountry, such families frequently resided in Indian villages and were enmeshed in trading networks; often, children of these unions became prominent leaders of Native American societies. By contrast, in the Spanish Borderlands, the offspring of Europeans and *genizaros* were treated as degraded individuals.

Eighteenth-century Anglo-Americans used the word *family* to mean all the people who occupied one

EUROPEAN AMERICAN FAMILIES

household (including any resident servants or slaves). European migrants to North America had far more stable family lives than did Indian and *mestizo* peoples. European men or their widows headed households considerably larger than American families today. Typical households were nuclear—that is, they included only parents and children. The head of the household represented it to the outside world, managing the finances and holding legal authority over the rest of the family, including his servants or slaves.

In English, French, and Spanish America alike, the vast majority of European families supported themselves through agriculture. The scale and nature of the work varied: the production of indigo in Louisiana required different sorts of labor from subsistence farming in New England or cattle ranching in Texas. As in other societies, household tasks were allocated by sex.

The mistress took responsibility for what Anglo-Americans called "indoor affairs." She and her female helpers prepared food, cleaned the house, did laundry, and often made clothing. Preparing food alone involved planting and cultivating a garden, harvesting and preserving fruits and vegetables, salting and smoking meat, milking cows and making butter and cheese, not to mention cooking and baking. The head of the household and his male helpers were responsible for "outdoor affairs." They planted and cultivated the fields, built fences, chopped wood for the fireplace, harvested and marketed crops, cared for livestock, and butchered cattle and hogs to provide meat.

Most African American families lived as components of European American households. More than

AFRICAN AMERICAN FAMILIES

95 percent of colonial African Americans were held in perpetual bondage. Although many African Americans lived on farms with only one or two other slaves, others had the experience of living and working in a largely black setting. In South Carolina, a majority of the population was of African origin; in Georgia, about half; and in the Chesapeake, 40 percent.

The setting in which African Americans lived determined the shape of their family lives, yet wherever possible, slaves established strong family structures in which youngsters carried relatives' names. In the North, the scarcity of other blacks often made it difficult for bondspeople to form stable households. In the Chesapeake, men and women who regarded themselves as married (slaves could not legally wed) frequently lived in different quarters or even on different plantations. Children generally resided with their mothers, seeing their fathers only on Sundays. On large Carolina and Georgia rice plantations, however, enslaved couples usually lived together with their children.

Because all the English colonies legally permitted slavery, bondspeople had few options for escape.

FORMS OF RESISTANCE

Some recently arrived Africans stole boats to try to return home or ran off in groups to frontier regions to join the Indians or establish independent communities. Among American-born slaves, family ties strongly affected such decisions. South Carolina planters soon learned, as one wrote, that slaves "love their families dearly and none runs away from the other." Thus, many owners sought to keep families together for purely practical reasons.

Although colonial slaves rarely rebelled collectively, they often resisted enslavement in other ways. Bondspeople uniformly rejected attempts by their owners to commandeer their labor on Sundays without compensation. Extended-kin groups protested excessive punishment of relatives and sought to live near each other. Among African American families who had lived on the same plantation for several generations, relatives could help with child rearing and similar tasks, providing a kind of insurance if parents and children were separated by sale. Among African Americans, just as among Indians, the extended family served a more important function than it did among European Americans.

Most slave families managed to carve out a small measure of autonomy, especially in their working and spiritual lives. Enslaved Muslims often clung to their faith. Some African Americans preserved traditional beliefs; others converted to Christianity (often retaining some African elements), finding comfort in the assurance that all people would be free and equal in heaven. South Carolina and Georgia slaves jealously guarded their customary ability to control their own time after the completion of their "tasks." Late in the century, some Chesapeake planters with a surplus of laborers began to hire out slaves to others, often allowing the workers to keep a small part of their earnings. Such accumulated property could buy desired goods or serve as a legacy for children.

Just as African and European Americans lived together on plantations, so too they lived in unsegregated urban neighborhoods. In 1760s Philadelphia, one-fifth of the work force was enslaved, and by 1775, blacks composed nearly 15 percent of the population of New York City. Such cities were nothing but large towns by today's standards. In 1750, the largest, Boston, had just seventeen thousand inhabitants. Life in the cities nonetheless differed considerably from that in rural areas. City dwellers everywhere purchased food and wood at markets. They also had much more contact with the world beyond their own homes than did their rural counterparts.

By the 1750s, most major cities had at least one weekly newspaper that printed the latest "advices

LIFE IN THE CITIES

from London," news from other English colonies, and local reports. Newspapers were available at taverns and inns, so people who could not afford to buy them could catch up on the news. Even illiterates could do so, since literate customers often read the papers aloud. Contact with the outside world, however, had its drawbacks. Sailors sometimes brought deadly diseases into port.

Politics: Stability and Crisis in British America

*E*arly in the eighteenth century, Anglo-American political life exhibited a new stability. By then, most residents had been born in America. Men from genteel families dominated the political structures in each province, for voters (free male property holders) tended to defer to their well-educated "betters."

Throughout the Anglo-American colonies, political leaders sought to increase the powers of elected assemblies. Assemblies began to claim privileges associated with the British House of Commons, such as the rights to initiate all tax legislation and to control the militia. The assemblies also developed ways to influence British appointees, especially by threatening to withhold their salaries. In some colonies (Virginia and South Carolina, for example), elite members of the assemblies usually presented a united front to royal officials, but in others (such as New York), they fought among themselves long and bitterly. To win hotly contested elections, New York's genteel leaders began to appeal to "the people" and compete openly for their votes. Yet in 1733, that same New York government imprisoned a newspaper editor, John Peter Zenger, who had too vigorously criticized its actions. Defending Zenger against the charge of "seditious libel," his lawyer argued that the truth could not be defamatory, thus helping to establish a free-press principle now found in American law.

RISE OF THE ASSEMBLIES

Much of the business of colonial assemblies would today be termed administrative. Only rarely did they formulate new policies or pass significant laws. Assemblymen saw themselves as acting defensively to prevent encroachments on the colonists' liberties— for example, by preventing governors from imposing oppressive taxes. By midcentury, they were comparing the structure of their governments to Britain's balanced combination of monarchy, aristocracy, and democracy. Drawing rough analogies, political leaders equated their governors with the monarch, their councils with the aristocracy, and their assemblies with the House of Commons. All three elements were believed essential to good government, but Anglo-Americans viewed governors and appointed councils as potential threats to customary colonial ways of life, since they primarily represented Britain. Many colonists saw the assemblies, however, as the people's representatives and protectors.

Yet the colonial ideal of the assembly as the defender of the people's liberties differed from the colonial reality. The assemblies, firmly controlled by dominant families, rarely responded to the concerns of their poorer constituents. Although settlements continually expanded, assemblies failed to reapportion themselves to provide adequate representation for newer communities, leading to serious grievances among frontier dwellers. In reality, the assemblies most dearly defended wealthy colonists, particularly the assembly members themselves.

At midcentury, the political structures that had stabilized in a period of relative calm confronted a series of crises. The crises of various descriptions exposed the internal tensions building in the pluralistic American society. Most important, they demonstrated that the political accommodations arrived at in the aftermath of the Glorious Revolution were no longer adequate to govern Britain's American empire.

One of the first and greatest crises occurred in South Carolina. Early one morning in September 1739, about twenty South Carolina slaves gathered near the Stono River south of Charles Town. Seizing guns and ammunition from a store, they killed the storekeepers and some nearby planter families. Then, joined by other local slaves, they headed toward Florida in hopes of finding refuge. Later that day, however, a troop of militia attacked the fugitives, who then numbered about a hundred, killing some and dispersing the rest. More than a week later, most of the remaining conspirators were captured. Those not killed on the spot were later executed.

The Stono Rebellion shocked residents of other colonies as well as South Carolinians. Throughout

STONO REBELLION

British America, laws governing the behavior of African Americans were stiffened. In New York City, the news from the South, coupled with fears of Spain generated by the outbreak of King George's War, set off a reign of terror in the summer of 1741. Hysterical whites suspected a biracial gang of conspiring to foment a slave uprising under the guidance of a supposed priest in the pay of Spain. By summer's end, thirty-one blacks and four whites had been executed for participating in the alleged plot. The Stono Rebellion and the New York "conspiracy" not only exposed and confirmed Anglo-Americans' deepest fears about the dangers of slaveholding but also revealed the assemblies' inability to prevent serious internal disorder. Events of the next two decades confirmed that pattern.

NEW YORK CONSPIRACY

By midcentury most of the fertile land east of the Appalachians had been purchased or occupied. Consequently, conflicts over land titles and conditions of landholding multiplied. In 1746, for example, some New Jersey farmers clashed violently with agents of the East Jersey proprietors, who claimed the farmers' land as theirs and demanded annual payments, called quit-rents, for the use of the property.

LAND RIOTS

The most serious land riots of the period took place in the lower Hudson River valley in 1765–1766. Late in the seventeenth century, the governor of New York had granted huge tracts there to prominent colonial families. The proprietors divided these estates into small farms, which they rented chiefly to poor Dutch and German migrants. After 1740, though, increasing numbers of migrants from New England resisted tenancy on the great New York estates. Many squatted on vacant portions of the manors, and they rebelled violently when proprietors tried to evict them in the mid-1760s, resisting successfully until British troops finally captured their leaders.

Violent conflicts of a different sort erupted in the late 1760s in South Carolina and the early 1770s in North Carolina, pitting backcountry farmers against wealthy eastern planters who controlled the provincial governments. Frontier dwellers, most of Scots-Irish origin, protested their lack of an adequate voice in colonial political affairs. South Carolinians for months policed the coun-

REGULATORS IN THE CAROLINAS

tryside in vigilante bands known as Regulators, complaining of lax and biased law enforcement. North Carolina Regulators, who primarily objected to heavy taxation, fought and lost a battle with eastern militiamen at Alamance in 1771.

A Crisis in Religion

*T*he most widespread crisis of this period was religious. From the mid-1730s through the 1760s, waves of religious revivalism—today known collectively as the First Great Awakening—swept over various colonies, primarily New England (1735–1745) and Virginia (1750s and 1760s). Orthodox Calvinists sought to combat Enlightenment rationalism, which denied innate human depravity. In addition, many recent immigrants and residents of the backcountry had no prior religious affiliation and were potential converts for evangelists.

The Great Awakening began in New England, where descendants of the Puritan founding generation still composed the membership of Congregational churches. During 1734 and 1735, Reverend Jonathan Edwards, a noted preacher and theologian, noticed a remarkable reaction among the youthful members of his church in Northampton, Massachusetts, to a message based squarely on Calvinist principles. Individuals could attain salvation, Edwards contended, only through recognition of their own depraved natures and the need to surrender completely to God's will. Such intensely emotional surrender came to be seen as a single identifiable moment of conversion.

The effects of such conversions remained isolated until 1739, when George Whitefield, a Church of England clergyman, arrived in America. For fifteen months, he toured the British colonies preaching to large audiences from Georgia to New England. A gripping orator, Whitefield in effect generated the Great Awakening. Everywhere he traveled, his fame preceded him. Thousands of free and enslaved folk turned out to listen and to experience conversion. Regular clerics initially welcomed Whitefield and the American-born itinerant evangelist preachers, who quickly imitated him. Soon, however, many clergymen began to realize that although "revived" religion filled their churches,

GEORGE WHITEFIELD

it ran counter to their own approach to doctrine and matters of faith. They disliked the emotional style of the itinerant revivalists and the disruption of normal church attendance patterns. Particularly troublesome were female exhorters who proclaimed their right to expound God's word.

Opposition to the Awakening heightened rapidly, causing congregations to splinter. "Old Lights"—traditional clerics and their followers—engaged in bitter disputes with the "New Light" evangelicals. Already characterized by numerous sects, American Protestantism fragmented further as the major denominations split into Old Light and New Light factions and as new evangelical sects—Methodists and Baptists—gained adherents. Paradoxically, the angry fights and the rapid rise in the number of distinct denominations eventually led to an American willingness to tolerate religious diversity.

IMPACT OF THE AWAKENING

Most significant, the Awakening challenged traditional modes of thought, for the revivalists' message directly contested the colonial tradition of deference. Itinerant preachers, only a few of whom were ordained clergymen, claimed they understood the will of God better than did elite college-educated clerics. The Awakening's emphasis on emotion rather than learning undermined the validity of received wisdom, and New Lights questioned not only religious but also social and political orthodoxy.

Nowhere was this trend more evident than in Virginia, where taxes supported the established Church of England. By the 1760s, Baptists had gained a secure foothold in Virginia; inevitably, their beliefs and behavior clashed with the way most genteel families lived. They rejected as sinful the horseracing, gambling, and dancing that occupied much of the gentry's leisure time. They addressed one another as "Brother" and "Sister" regardless of social status, and they elected the leaders of their congregations.

VIRGINIA BAPTISTS

Strikingly, almost all the Virginia Baptist congregations included both free and slave members. Church rules applied equally to all members; interracial sexual relationships, divorce, and adultery were forbidden to all. In addition, congregations forbade masters from breaking up slave couples through sale. Biracial committees investigated complaints about church members' misbehavior. Churches excommunicated slaves for stealing from their masters, but they also excommunicated masters for physically abusing their slaves. Some Baptists decided that owning slaves was "unrighteous" and freed their bondspeople.

Summary   *Online Study Center*   ACE the Test

*T*he Great Awakening injected an egalitarian strain into Anglo-American life at midcentury. Although primarily a religious movement, the Awakening had important social and political consequences, calling into question habitual modes of behavior in the secular as well as the religious realm. In short, the Great Awakening helped break Anglo-Americans' ties to their seventeenth-century origins. So too did the newcomers from Germany, Scotland, Ireland, and Africa, who brought with them their languages, customs, and religions.

The economic life of all Europe's North American colonies proceeded simultaneously on two levels. On the farms, plantations, and ranches on which most colonists resided, chores dominated people's lives while providing the goods consumed by households and sold in the markets. Simultaneously, an intricate international trade network affected the economies of the European colonies. The bitter wars fought by European nations during the eighteenth century inevitably involved the colonists by creating new opportunities for overseas sales or by disrupting their traditional markets. The volatile colonial economy fluctuated for reasons beyond Americans' control.

A century and a half after European peoples first settled in North America, the colonies mixed diverse European, American, and African traditions into a novel cultural blend that owed much to Europe but just as much to North America itself. Europeans who interacted regularly with peoples of African and American origin—and with Europeans who came from nations other than their own—had to develop new identities and new methods of accommodating intercultural differences in addition to creating ties within their own potentially fragmenting communities. Yet at the same time, the dominant colonists continued to identify themselves as French, Spanish, or British rather than as Americans. In the 1760s, however, some Anglo-Americans began to realize that their interests did not necessarily coincide with those of Great Britain or its monarch. For the first time, they offered a direct challenge to British authority.

LEGACY FOR A PEOPLE AND A NATION
"Self-Made Men"

One of the most common American themes celebrates the "self-made man" (always someone explicitly male) of humble origins who gains wealth and/or prominence through his own extraordinary effort and talent. The initial exemplars of this tradition lived in eighteenth-century America and the wider Atlantic world. Benjamin Franklin's *Autobiography* chronicled his method for achieving success as a printer after beginning life as the seventeenth child of a Boston candlemaker. From such humble origins, Franklin became a wealthy, influential man.

Franklin's tale is rivaled by that of a man apparently born a slave in South Carolina. Having worked for years as a sailor, he purchased his freedom, learned to read and write, held an important administrative post, married a wealthy young English woman, became an influential abolitionist, and eventually published a popular autobiography. His first master called him Gustavus Vassa, but when publishing his *Interesting Narrative* in 1789, he called himself Olaudah Equiano.

In that *Narrative*, Equiano claimed to have been born in Africa in 1745, kidnapped at the age of eleven, and carried first to Barbados, then to Virginia, where a British naval officer purchased him and introduced him to a maritime life. For years, scholars and students have relied on that account for its insights into the middle passage. But evidence recently uncovered by Vincent Carretta, while confirming the accuracy of much of Equiano's autobiography, shows that Equiano twice publicly identified his birthplace as Carolina. Why would Equiano conceal his origins? Carretta speculates that the *Narrative* gained part of its credibility from Equiano's African birth.

Equiano, or Vassa, thus truly "made himself." Equiano used information undoubtedly gleaned from acquaintances who *had* experienced the middle passage to accurately depict the horrors of the slave trade. In the process he became one of the first Americans to explicitly reinvent himself.

SEVERING THE BONDS OF EMPIRE 1754–1774

The two men must have found the occasion remarkable. The artist customarily painted portraits of the wealthy and high born, not of artisans. Moreover, the political sympathies of the artist, John Singleton Copley, lay primarily with Boston's conservatives, whereas the sitter, Paul Revere, was a noted leader of resistance to British policies. Yet sometime in 1768, Revere commissioned Copley to paint his portrait, and the result is one of the greatest works of American art.

Copley portrayed Revere, a silversmith, surrounded by the tools of his trade and contemplating a teapot he was crafting. Revere's pose and apparel convey an impression of thoughtfulness, virtuous labor, and solidity. The teapot too carries a message, especially in the year 1768. Simultaneously a reflection of a craftsman's skills and a prominent emblem of the new "empire of goods" in British America, it resonated with symbolism because, as shall be seen later in this chapter, tea boycotts were an important component of colonial resistance to Great Britain.

In retrospect, John Adams identified the years between 1760 and 1775 as the era of the true American Revolution. The Revolution, Adams declared, ended before the fighting started, for it was "in the Minds of the people," involving not the actual winning of independence but a fundamental shift of allegiance from Britain to America. Today, not all historians would concur that the shift Adams identified constituted the Revolution. But none would deny the importance of those crucial years.

The story of the 1760s and early 1770s describes an ever-widening split between Great Britain and Anglo America. In the long history of British settlement in the Western Hemisphere, considerable tension had occasionally marred the relationship between individual provinces and the mother country. Still, that tension had rarely persisted for long and had not been widespread, except during the crisis following the Glorious Revolution in 1689. In the 1750s, however, a series of events caused the colonists to examine

Renewed Warfare Among Europeans and Indians

LINKS TO THE WORLD
The First Worldwide War

1763: A Turning Point

The Stamp Act Crisis

Resistance to the Townshend Acts

Confrontations in Boston

Tea and Turmoil

LEGACY FOR A PEOPLE AND A NATION
The Census and Reapportionment

Online Study Center
This icon will direct you to interactive map and primary source activities on the website
http://college.hmco.com/pic/nortonbrief7e

CHRONOLOGY

1754 • Albany Congress meets to try to forge colonial unity
   • Fighting breaks out with Washington's defeat at Fort Necessity

1756 • Britain declares war on France; Seven Years War officially begins

1759 • British forces take Quebec

1760 • American phase of war ends with fall of Montreal to British troops
   • George III becomes king

1763 • Treaty of Paris ends Seven Years War
   • Pontiac's allies attack British forts in West
   • Proclamation of 1763 attempts to close land west of Appalachians to English settlement

1764 • Sugar Act lays new duties on molasses, tightens customs regulations
   • Currency Act outlaws paper money issued by the colonies

1765 • Stamp Act requires stamps on all printed materials in colonies
   • Sons of Liberty formed

1766 • Stamp Act repealed
   • Declaratory Act insists that Parliament can tax the colonies

1767 • Townshend Acts lay duties on trade within the empire, send new officials to America

1768–70 • Townshend duties resisted; boycotts and public demonstrations divide merchants and urban artisans

1770 • Lord North becomes prime minister
   • Townshend duties repealed, except for tea tax
   • Boston Massacre kills five colonial rioters

1772 • Boston Committee of Correspondence formed

1773 • Tea Act aids East India Company
   • Boston Tea Party protests the Tea Act

1774 • Coercive Acts punish Boston and Massachusetts as a whole
   • Quebec Act reforms government of Quebec
   • First Continental Congress called

their relations with Great Britain. It all started with the Seven Years War.

Britain's overwhelming victory in that war, confirmed by treaty in 1763, forever altered the balance of power in North America. France was ousted from the continent and Spain from Florida, events with major consequences for both the indigenous peoples of the interior and the residents of the British colonies. Indians could no longer play off European powers against one another and so lost one of their major diplomatic tools. Anglo-Americans no longer had to fear the French threat on their northern and western borders or the Spanish in the Southeast.

The British victory in 1763 had a significant impact on Great Britain. Britain's massive war-related debt needed to be paid, and so Parliament for the first time imposed revenue-raising taxes on the colonies in addition to the customs duties that had long regulated trade. That decision exposed differences in the political thinking of Americans and Britons.

During the 1760s and early 1770s, a broad coalition of the residents of Anglo America resisted new tax levies and attempts by British officials to tighten control over provincial governments. The colonies' elected leaders became ever more suspicious of Britain's motives as the years passed. They laid aside old antagonisms to coordinate their responses to the new measures, and they slowly began to reorient their political thinking. As late as the summer of 1774, though, few harbored thoughts of independence. ■

Renewed Warfare Among Europeans and Indians

*I*n the mid-eighteenth century, the English colonies along the Atlantic seaboard were surrounded by hostile, or potentially hostile, neighbors: Indians everywhere, the Spanish in Florida and along the coast of the Gulf of Mexico, the French along the great inland system of rivers and lakes that stretched from the St. Lawrence to the Mississippi. The Spanish outposts posed little direct threat, for Spain's days as a major power had passed. But the long chain of French forts and settlements dominated the North American interior, facilitating trading partnerships and alliances with the Indians. In none of the three wars fought between 1689 and 1748 was England able to shake France's hold on the American frontier, although the Peace of Utrecht, which ended Queen Anne's War in 1713, gave the English control of such peripheral northern areas as Newfoundland, Hudson's Bay, and Acadia (Nova Scotia) (see Table 5.1).

During both Queen Anne's War and King George's War, the Iroquois Confederacy maintained the policy of neutrality it had first developed in 1701, skillfully manipulating the Europeans while refusing to commit warriors fully to either side. The Iroquois continued a long-standing conflict with Cherokees and Catawbas in the South, thus giving their young warriors combat experience and acquiring new captives to replace population losses. They also cultivated peaceful relationships with Pennsylvania and Virginia, in part so the colonists would endorse their domination of the Shawnees and Delawares. And they forged friendly ties with Algonquians of the Great Lakes region, thereby avoiding potential assaults from those allies of the French and also making themselves indispensable middlemen for commerce and communication between the Atlantic coast and the West. Thus, the Iroquois consolidated their control over the entire American interior north of Virginia and south of the Great Lakes.

IROQUOIS NEUTRALITY

But even the Iroquois could not prevent the region inhabited by the Shawnees and Delawares (now western Pennsylvania and eastern Ohio) from providing the spark that set off a major war. That conflict spread from America to Europe, decisively resolving the contest for North America. Trouble began in the mid-1740s, when Iroquois negotiators, claiming to speak for Delawares and Shawnees, ceded large tracts of the subordinate tribes' land to English colonists. Disgruntled Delawares and Shawnees migrated west, and Virginia land speculators began pressing to develop the ceded territory, focusing first on the area where the Allegheny and Monongahela Rivers join to form the Ohio (see Map 5.1).

That region, also claimed by Pennsylvania, was vital to the French, for the Ohio River offered direct access to French posts on the Mississippi. A permanent British presence in the Ohio country would threaten France's control of the western fur trade and its prominence in the Mississippi valley. A devastating 1752 raid by the French and Indians on a trading outpost at the site of modern Cleveland rid the region of Pennsylvanians, but the speculators of Virginia posed a more serious challenge. Accordingly, in 1753, the French pushed southward from Lake Erie, building fortified outposts at strategic points.

In response to the French threat, delegates from seven northern and middle colonies gathered in Albany, New York, in June 1754. Backed by administrators in London, they sought two goals: to persuade the Iroquois to abandon their traditional neutrality and to coordinate the defenses of the colonies. They succeeded in neither. The Iroquois saw no reason to change a policy that had served them well for half a century. And although the Albany Congress delegates adopted a Plan of Union (which would have established an elected intercolonial legislature with the power to tax), their provincial governments uniformly rejected the plan—primarily because those governments feared a loss of autonomy.

ALBANY CONGRESS

While the Albany Congress delegates deliberated, the war they sought to prepare for was already beginning. The governor of Virginia sent a small militia troop to the forks of the Ohio, then later dispatched reinforcements. When a substantial French force arrived at the forks, the first contingent of Virginia militia surrendered peacefully, and the French then began to construct Fort Duquesne. Learning of the confrontation, the inexperienced young officer leading the Virginia reinforcements pressed onward, attacked a French detachment, and then allowed himself to be trapped in his crudely built Fort Necessity at Great

TABLE 5.1

The Colonial Wars, 1689–1763

American Name	European Name	Dates	Participants	American Sites	Dispute
King William's War	War of the League of Augsburg	1689–97	England, Holland versus France, Spain	New England, New York, Canada	French power
Queen Anne's War	War of Spanish Succession	1702–13	England, Holland, Austria versus France, Spain	Florida, New England	Throne of Spain
King George's War	War of Austrian Succession	1739–48	England, Holland, Austria versus France, Spain, Prussia	West Indies, New England, Canada	Throne of Austria
French and Indian War	Seven Years War	1756–63	England versus France, Spain	Ohio country, Canada	Possession of Ohio country

Meadows, Pennsylvania. After a day-long battle (on July 3, 1754), during which more than one-third of his men were killed or wounded, twenty-two-year-old George Washington surrendered. He and his men were allowed to return to Virginia.

Washington's grievous blunder helped ignite a war that eventually would encompass nearly the entire world. He also ensured that the Ohio Indians would support France. In July 1755, a few miles south of Fort Duquesne, a combined force of French and Indians ambushed British and colonial troops led by General Edward Braddock, killing Braddock and demoralizing his surviving soldiers. After news of the debacle reached London, Britain declared war on France in 1756, formally beginning the conflict known as the Seven Years War.

SEVEN YEARS WAR

For three more years, one British disaster followed another. British officers tried, without much success, to coerce the colonies into supplying men and materiel to the army. The war went so badly that Britain began to fear France would try to retake Nova Scotia. Afraid the approximately twelve thousand French residents of Nova Scotia might break their pledges of neutrality, Britain forced about half of them from their homeland—the first large-scale modern deportation. Ships crammed with Acadians sailed to each of the mainland colonies, where the dispirited exiles encountered hostility and discrimination.

In 1757, William Pitt, a civilian official, was placed in charge of the war effort. Pitt agreed to reimburse the colonies for their wartime expenditures and placed troop recruitment wholly in local hands, thereby gaining greater American support for the war. In July 1758, British forces recaptured the fortress at Louisbourg controlling the entrance to the St. Lawrence River, thus cutting the major French supply route. Then, in September 1759, General James Wolfe's troops took Quebec. Sensing a British victory, the Iroquois abandoned their traditional neutrality and allied with Britain. A year later, the British captured Montreal, and the American phase of the war ended.

In the Treaty of Paris (1763), France ceded its major North American holdings to Britain. Spain, an ally of France toward the end of the war, gave Florida to the victors. France, meanwhile, ceded Louisiana west of the Mississippi to its ally Spain. The British thus gained control of the continent's fur trade. No longer would the English seacoast colonies have to worry about the threat to their existence posed by the French presence.

Map 5.1   European Settlements and Indians, 1754

By 1754, Europeans had expanded the limits of the English colonies to the
eastern slopes of the Appalachian Mountains.

The First Worldwide War

Today we call two twentieth-century conflicts "world wars," but the first worldwide war predated them by more than a century. The contest began in the backwoods of southwestern Pennsylvania in the spring of 1754, over a seemingly local quarrel: whether Britain or France would build a fort at the forks of the Ohio. That it eventually involved combatants around the world attests not only to the growing importance of European nations' overseas empires but also to the increasing centrality of North America in their struggles for dominance.

Previous wars among Europeans had taken place mostly in Europe, though overseas colonies occasionally got involved. But the contest at the forks of the Ohio helped to reinvigorate a conflict between Austria and Prussia that sent the nations of Europe scrambling for allies. Eventually England, Hanover, and Prussia lined up against France, Austria, and Russia, joined by Sweden, Saxony, and, later, Spain. The war in Europe would last seven years. In 1763 these nations signed a peace treaty that returned the continent to the status quo before the war, but elsewhere, in the rest of the world, Britain had decisively vanquished both France and Spain.

"Elsewhere" included a mind-boggling list of battles. In the Caribbean, Britain seized the French islands of Guadeloupe and Martinique and took Havana, Cuba, from Spain. In North America, the British recaptured the French fortress of Louisbourg and conquered the capital of New France, Quebec. In Africa, the British overwhelmed France's slave-trading posts in Senegambia. In India, British forces won control of Bengal by defeating both a local ruler and French soldiers stationed there. Three years later, the British beat a French army at Pondicherry. So four months after France lost Canada, its influence in India was also extinguished. At the very end of the war, a British expedition took Manila in the Philippines from Spain. The commander there had not yet learned that his nation had declared war on Britain, so the assault caught him unaware.

Thus, the war that started in the American backcountry revealed the steadily growing links between North America and the rest of the world. And the aftermath exposed an unexpected further link. Both winners and losers had to pay for this first worldwide war. Financial struggles in Britain and France, though separate, ultimately produced similar outcomes: revolutions abroad (for Britain, in America) and at home (for France).

In 1771 the artist Dominic Serres, the Elder, depicted British naval vessels attacking the French fortress at Chandernagore in India in 1757 (at left in background). Cannon fire from the warships was critical to the British victory, one of the keys to the conquest of India during the Seven Years War.
(National Maritime Museum, London)

Online Study Center **Improve Your Grade**
Interactive Map: European Claims in North America

The overwhelming British triumph stimulated some Americans to think expansively. People like the Philadelphia printer Benjamin Franklin, who had long touted the colonies' wealth and potential, predicted a glorious new future for British North America. Such individuals uniformly opposed any laws that would retard America's growth and persistently supported steps to increase Americans' control over their own destiny. Many of them also invested heavily in western land speculations.

1763: A Turning Point

The great victory over France had an irreversible impact on North America, felt first by the indigenous peoples of the interior. With France excluded from the continent altogether and Spanish territory confined to west of the Mississippi, the diplomatic strategy that had served the Indians well for so long was now obsolete. The consequences were immediate and devastating.

Even before the Treaty of Paris, British advances in the American war in 1758 denied the Creeks and Cherokees in the South of their ability to force concessions by threatening to turn instead to France or Spain. In desperation, and in retaliation for British atrocities, Cherokees attacked the Carolina and Virginia frontiers in 1760. The Indians were defeated the following year and late in 1761 agreed to a treaty allowing the construction of British forts in their territories and opening a large tract of land to European settlement.

In the Ohio country, the Ottawas, Chippewas, and Potawatomis reacted angrily when Great Britain,

NEOLIN AND PONTIAC

no longer facing French competition, raised the price of trade goods and ended traditional gift-giving practices. Settlers rapidly moved into the Monongahela and Susquehanna valleys. A shaman named Neolin (also known as the Delaware Prophet) urged Indians to both resist British incursions and throw off dependence on European goods (especially alcohol). If all Indians west of the mountains united to reject the invaders, Neolin declared, the Master of Life would replenish the depleted

Benjamin West, the first well-known American artist, engraved this picture of a prisoner exchange at the end of Pontiac's Uprising, showing the return of settlers abducted during the war. In the foreground, a child resists leaving the Indian parents he had grown to love. Many colonists were fascinated by the phenomenon West depicted: the reluctance of captives to abandon their adoptive Indian families. (Ohio Historical Society)

deer herds and once again look kindly on his people. Yet ironically, Neolin's call for a return to native traditions, in its reference to a single Master of Life, itself showed the influence of Europeans' Christianity.

Pontiac, the war chief of an Ottawa village near Detroit, became the leader of a movement based on Neolin's precepts. In the spring of 1763, Pontiac forged an unprecedented alliance among many Indian nations. He then laid siege to Fort Detroit while war parties attacked other British outposts in the Great Lakes. Detroit withstood the siege, but by late June, all the other forts west of Niagara and north of Fort Pitt (formerly Fort Duquesne) had fallen to the alliance. Indians then raided the Virginia and Pennsylvania frontiers at will throughout the summer, killing at least two thousand settlers. Still, they failed to take the strongholds of Niagara, Fort Pitt, or Detroit. In early August, colonial militiamen soundly defeated a combined Indian force at Bushy Run, Pennsylvania. A treaty ending the war was finally negotiated three years later.

The uprising showed that the huge territory Britain had acquired from France would be difficult to govern. In October, the govern-

PROCLAMATION OF 1763

ing ministry issued the Proclamation of 1763, which designated the headwaters of rivers flowing into the Atlantic from the Appalachian Mountains as the temporary western boundary for colonial settlement (see Map 5.1). Its promulgators expected the proclamation to prevent clashes by keeping colonists off Indian lands until tribes had given up their territory by treaty. But it infuriated those who had already squatted on lands west of the line, as well as land speculation companies from Pennsylvania and Virginia. Though the latter group negotiated with the Iroquois to push the boundary farther west and south, they could not convince administrators in London to validate their speculations. Significant western expansion, the British realized, would require the expenditure of funds they did not have.

The hard-won victory in the Seven Years War had cost Britain millions of pounds and created an

GEORGE III

immense war debt. The problem of paying this debt and funding the defense of the newly acquired territories bedeviled George III, who in 1760 had succeeded his grandfather, George II. The twenty-two-year-old king, an intelligent, passionate man with a mediocre education, was an erratic judge of character. During the crucial years between 1763 and 1770, when the rift with the colonies grew ever wider and a series of political crises beset England, the king replaced ministers with bewildering rapidity. Determined to assert the monarchy's power, but immature and unsure of himself, he often substituted stubbornness for cleverness, and he regarded adherence to the status quo as the hallmark of patriotism.

The man he selected as prime minister in 1763, George Grenville, confronted a financial crisis: England's burden of indebtedness had nearly doubled since 1754. Grenville's ministry had to find new sources of funds, and the British people themselves were already heavily taxed. Since the colonists had benefited greatly from the wartime expenditures, Grenville concluded that Anglo-Americans should be asked to pay a larger share of the cost of running the empire.

Grenville did not question Great Britain's right to levy taxes on the colonies. Like all his countrymen, he

THEORIES OF REPRESENTATION

believed that the government's legitimacy derived ultimately from the consent of the people, but he defined consent differently from the colonists. Americans had come to believe that they could be represented only by men who lived nearby and for whom they or their property-holding neighbors had voted. Grenville and his English contemporaries, however, believed that Parliament—king, lords, and commons acting together—by definition represented all British subjects, even colonists, who could not vote.

Parliament saw itself as collectively representing the entire nation; the particular constituency that chose a member of the House of Commons had no special claim on that member's vote, nor did he have to live near his constituents. According to this theory of government, called *virtual representation,* the colonists were seen as virtually, if not actually, represented in Parliament. Thus, their consent to acts of Parliament could be presumed. In the colonies, by contrast, members of the lower houses of the assemblies were viewed as specifically representing the regions that had elected them. Before Grenville proposed to tax the colonists, the two notions had coexisted because no conflict exposed the central contradiction.

Events in the 1760s threw into sharp relief Americans' attitudes toward political power. The colonists had become accustomed to a central

REAL WHIGS

government that wielded only limited authority over them, affecting their daily lives very little. Consequently, they believed that a good government was one that largely left them alone, a view in keeping with the theories of a group of British writers known as the Real Whigs. These writers stressed the danger inherent in a powerful government, particularly one headed by a monarch. They warned the people to guard constantly against government attempts to encroach on their liberty and seize their property. Political power, they wrote, was always to be feared. Only perpetual vigilance could preserve the people's precious yet fragile liberty, which was closely tied to their right to private property.

Britain's attempts to tighten the reins of government and raise revenues from the colonies convinced many Americans to interpret British measures in light of the Real Whigs' warnings, especially because of the link between liberty and property rights. Excessive and unjust taxation, they believed, could destroy their freedoms. In time they began to see oppressive designs behind the actions of Grenville and his successors. In the mid-1760s, however, colonial leaders did not immediately accuse Grenville of conspiring to oppress them. They at first merely questioned the wisdom of the laws he proposed.

Parliament passed the first such measures, the Sugar and Currency Acts, in 1764. The Sugar Act revised existing customs regulations and laid new duties on some foreign imports into the colonies. Its most important provisions, strongly advocated by influential planters of the British Caribbean wishing to increase demand for their sugar, aimed to discourage American rum distillers from smuggling French West Indian molasses. It also established a vice-admiralty court at Halifax, Nova Scotia. (Vice-admiralty courts operated without juries.) Although the Sugar Act appeared to resemble the Navigation Acts, which the colonies had long accepted as legitimate, it broke with tradition in being explicitly designed to raise revenue, not to channel American trade through Britain. The Currency Act effectively outlawed colonial issues of paper money because British merchants had long complained that Americans were paying their debts in inflated local currencies. Americans could accumulate little sterling, since they imported more than they exported; thus, the act seemed to the colonists to deprive them of a useful medium of exchange.

SUGAR AND CURRENCY ACTS

The Sugar and Currency Acts were imposed on an economy already hit hard by a depression that followed when the Seven Years War shifted overseas. Individual American essayists and incensed colonial governments protested the new policies. But, lacking any precedent for a united campaign against acts of Parliament, Americans in 1764 took only hesitant and uncoordinated steps. Eight colonial legislatures sent separate petitions to Parliament requesting the Sugar Act's repeal, arguing that its commercial restrictions would hurt Britain as well as the colonies and that they had not consented to its passage. The protests had no effect, and Grenville proceeded with another revenue plan.

The Stamp Act Crisis

The Stamp Act (1765), Grenville's most important proposal, was modeled on a law that had been in effect in Great Britain for almost a century. It touched nearly every colonist by requiring tax stamps on most printed materials, but it fell heaviest on merchants and others of the colonial elite, who used printed matter more frequently than did ordinary folk. Anyone who purchased a newspaper, made a will, transferred land, bought dice or playing cards, applied for a liquor license, or borrowed money would have to pay the tax. The act also required that tax stamps be paid for with scarce sterling and that violators be tried in vice-admiralty courts. Finally, such a law would break decisively with the colonial tradition of self-imposed taxation.

The most important colonial pamphlet protesting the Sugar Act and the proposed Stamp Act was *The Rights of the British Colonies Asserted and Proved*, by James Otis Jr., a brilliant young Massachusetts attorney. Otis starkly exposed the ideological dilemma that confounded the colonists for the next decade. How could they justify their opposition to certain acts of Parliament without questioning Parliament's authority over them? On the one hand, Otis asserted, Americans were "entitled to all the natural, essential, inherent, and inseparable rights" of Britons, including the right not to be taxed without their consent. On the other hand, Otis admitted that under the British system, "the power of parliament is uncontrollable but by themselves, and we must obey."

JAMES OTIS'S RIGHTS OF THE BRITISH COLONIES

Otis's first contention implied that Parliament could not constitutionally tax the colonies because Americans were not represented in its ranks. Yet his second point both acknowledged political reality and accepted the prevailing theory of British government: that Parliament was the sole, supreme authority in the empire. Even unconstitutional laws enacted by Parliament had to be obeyed until Parliament decided to repeal them. Otis tried to find a middle ground by proposing colonial representation in Parliament, but his idea was never taken seriously on either side of the Atlantic. The British believed that the colonists were already virtually represented in Parliament, and Anglo-Americans quickly realized that a handful of colonial delegates to London would simply be outvoted.

Otis published his pamphlet before the Stamp Act was passed. When Americans first learned of the act's adoption in the spring of 1765, they reacted indecisively. Few colonists publicly favored the law, but colonial petitions had already failed to prevent its adoption, and further lobbying appeared futile. Perhaps Otis was correct: the only course open to Americans was to pay the stamp tax, reluctantly but loyally.

Not all the colonists shared Otis's view. One twenty-nine-year-old lawyer serving his first term in

PATRICK HENRY AND THE VIRGINIA STAMP ACT RESOLVES

the Virginia House of Burgesses was appalled by his fellow legislators' unwillingness to oppose the Stamp Act. "Alone, unadvised, and unassisted," Patrick Henry decided to act. "On a blank leaf of an old law book," he wrote the Virginia Stamp Act Resolves.

Henry introduced his seven proposals near the end of the 1765 legislative session, when many burgesses had already departed for home. His fiery speech led the Speaker of the House to accuse him of treason. (Henry denied the charge, contrary to the nineteenth-century myth that he exclaimed, "If this be treason, make the most of it!") The few burgesses remaining adopted five of Henry's resolutions by a bare majority. Although they repealed the most radical of the five the next day, their action had far-reaching effects.

The four propositions that the burgesses adopted repeated Otis's arguments, asserting that the colonists had never forfeited the rights of British subjects, among which was consent to taxation. The other three resolutions went much further. The one that was repealed claimed for the burgesses "the only exclusive right" to tax Virginians, and the final two (those never considered) asserted that residents of Virginia need not obey tax laws passed by other legislative bodies (namely, Parliament).

The burgesses' decision to accept only the first four of Henry's resolutions anticipated the position

CONTINUING LOYALTY TO BRITAIN

most Americans would adopt throughout the following decade. Though willing to contend for their rights, the colonists did not seek independence. Rather, they wanted some measure of self-government. Accordingly, they backed away from the assertions that they owed Parliament no obedience and that only their own assemblies could tax them.

Over the next ten years, America's political leaders searched for a formula that would enable them to control their internal affairs, especially taxation, but remain under British rule. The chief difficulty lay in British officials' inability to compromise on the issue of parliamentary power. The notion that Parliament could exercise absolute authority over all colonial possessions was inherent in the British theory of government. In effect, the Americans wanted British leaders to revise their fundamental understanding of the workings of their government. And that was simply too much to expect.

The ultimate effectiveness of Americans' opposition to the Stamp Act derived not from ideological arguments over parliamentary power but from the decisive and inventive actions of some colonists. In August 1765 the Loyal Nine, a Boston social club of printers, distillers, and other artisans, organized a demonstration against the Stamp Act. Hoping to show that people of all ranks opposed the act, they approached the leaders of the city's rival laborers' associations, based in Boston's North End and South End neighborhoods. The two gangs often clashed, but the Loyal Nine convinced them to lay aside their differences to participate in the demonstration.

Early on August 14, the demonstrators hung an effigy of Andrew Oliver, the province's stamp distributor,

ANTI–STAMP ACT DEMONSTRATIONS

from a tree on Boston Common. That night a large crowd led by a group of about fifty well-dressed tradesmen paraded the effigy around the city and threw stones at officials who tried to disperse them. In the midst of the melee, the North End and South End leaders drank a toast to their successful union. Oliver publicly promised not to fulfill the duties of his office. Twelve days later, a mob reportedly led by the South End leader Ebenezer MacIntosh attacked the homes of several customs officers. The crowd then destroyed Lieutenant Governor Thomas Hutchinson's elaborately furnished townhouse, an action that drew no praise from Boston's respectable citizens.

The differences between the two Boston mobs of August 1765 exposed divisions that would continue to characterize colonial protests. Few residents of the colonies sided with Great Britain during the 1760s, but various colonial groups had divergent goals. The skilled craftsmen who composed the Loyal Nine and merchants, lawyers, and others of the educated elite preferred orderly demonstrations confined to political issues. For the city's laborers, by contrast, economic grievances may have been paramount. Certainly, their wrecking of Hutchinson's house suggests resentment against the lieutenant governor's ostentatious display of wealth.

AMERICANS' DIVERGENT INTERESTS

Colonists, like Britons, had a long tradition of crowd action in which disfranchised people took to the streets to redress deeply felt local grievances. But the Stamp Act controversy drew ordinary urban folk into the vortex of transatlantic politics for the first time. Matters that previously had been of concern only to the gentry or to members of colonial legislatures were now discussed on every street corner.

The entry of unskilled workers, slaves, and women into imperial politics both threatened and aided the elite men who wanted to mount effective opposition to British measures. To be sure, crowd action could have a stunning impact. Anti–Stamp Act demonstrations occurred in cities and towns stretching from Halifax in the north to the Caribbean island of Antigua in the south, and by November 1, when the law was scheduled to take effect, not one stamp distributor was willing to carry out his duties. Thus, the act could not be enforced. But wealthy men also recognized that mobs composed of the formerly powerless could endanger their own dominance. What would happen, they wondered, if the crowd turned against them?

Elite men therefore attempted to channel resistance into acceptable forms by creating an intercolonial association, the Sons of Liberty. New Yorkers organized the first such group in early November, and branches spread rapidly through the coastal cities. Composed of merchants, lawyers, and prosperous tradesmen, the Sons of Liberty by early 1766 linked protest leaders from Charleston, South Carolina, to Portsmouth, New Hampshire.

SONS OF LIBERTY

The Sons of Liberty could influence events but could not control them. In Charleston in October 1765, an informally organized crowd forced the resignation of the South Carolina stamp distributor. But the new Charleston chapter of the Sons of Liberty was horrified when in January 1766, local slaves paraded through the streets crying, "Liberty!" Freedom from slavery was not the sort of liberty elite slaveowners had in mind.

In Philadelphia, too, resistance leaders were dismayed when an angry mob threatened to attack Benjamin Franklin's house. The city's laborers believed Franklin was partly responsible for the Stamp Act, since he had obtained the post of stamp distributor for a close friend. But Philadelphia's artisans—the backbone of the opposition movement there and elsewhere—were fiercely loyal to Franklin and gathered to protect his home and family from the crowd. The resulting split between the better-off tradesmen and the common laborers prevented the establishment of a successful workingmen's alliance like that of Boston.

During the fall and winter of 1765–1766, opposition to the Stamp Act proceeded on three separate fronts. Colonial legislatures petitioned Parliament to repeal the hated law, and courts closed because they could not obtain the stamps now required for all legal documents. In October nine colonies sent delegates to a general congress. The Stamp Act Congress met in New York to draft a unified but conservative statement of protest, stressing economic considerations rather than issues of American rights. At the same time, the Sons of Liberty held mass meetings to rally public support for resistance. Finally, American merchants organized nonimportation associations to pressure British exporters. By the 1760s, one-quarter of all British exports went to the colonies, and American merchants reasoned that London merchants whose sales suffered severely would lobby for repeal. Since times were bad, American merchants believed that nonimportation would also help reduce their bloated inventories.

OPPOSITION AND REPEAL

In March 1766, Parliament repealed the Stamp Act. The nonimportation agreements had had the anticipated effect among wealthy London merchants. But boycotts, formal protests, and crowd actions were less important in winning repeal than was the appointment of a new prime minister. Lord Rockingham, who replaced Grenville in the summer of 1765, had opposed the Stamp Act, not because he believed Parliament lacked the power to tax the colonies but because he thought the law unwise and divisive. Thus, although Rockingham proposed repeal, he linked it to passage of a Declaratory Act, which asserted Parliament's authority to tax and legislate for Britain's American possessions "in all cases whatsoever." Colonists welcomed the Stamp Act's repeal with celebrations stressing their unwavering loyalty to Great Britain; few of them saw the implications of the Declaratory Act.

Resistance to the Townshend Acts

Zn the summer of 1766, another change in the ministry in London revealed how fragile the colonists' victory had been. The new prime minister, William Pitt, was often ill, and another minister, Charles Townshend, became the dominant force in the ministry. An ally of Grenville, Townshend decided to renew the attempt to obtain additional funds from Britain's American possessions.

The duties Townshend proposed in 1767, to be levied on trade goods like paper, glass, and tea, seemed to be nothing more than extensions of the existing Navigation Acts. But the Townshend duties differed from previous customs levies in two ways. First, they applied to items imported into the colonies from Britain, not from foreign countries. Thus, they violated mercantilist theory (see Chapter 3). Second, the revenues were to fund the salaries of some royal officials in the colonies. Previously those men were paid from local taxation, and assemblies could ensure their cooperation by threatening to withhold their salaries. Now assemblies would lose some of that leverage. In addition, Townshend's scheme would create an American Board of Customs Commissioners and vice-admiralty courts at Boston, Philadelphia, and Charleston. These moves angered merchants because more vigorous enforcement of the Navigation Acts would threaten their profits.

Online Study Center **Improve Your Grade**
Primary Source: William Shepherd Attempts to Collect Customs Duties

The passage of the Townshend Acts drew a quick response. One series of essays in particular, *Letters*

JOHN DICKINSON'S FARMER'S LETTERS

from a Farmer in Pennsylvania, by the prominent lawyer John Dickinson, expressed a broad consensus. Dickinson contended that Parliament could regulate colonial trade but could not exercise that power to raise revenue. By distinguishing between trade regulation and unacceptable commercial taxation, Dickinson avoided the sticky issue of consent and how it affected colonial subordination to Parliament. But his argument created a different, and equally knotty, problem. In effect, it obligated the colonies to assess Parliament's motives in passing any law pertaining to trade before deciding whether to obey it. That was an unworkable position in the long run.

The Massachusetts assembly responded to the Townshend Acts by drafting a letter to circulate among the other colonial legislatures, calling for unity and suggesting a joint petition of protest. Not the letter itself but the ministry's reaction to it united the colonies. When Lord Hillsborough, the first secretary of state for America, learned of the circular letter, he ordered Governor Francis Bernard of Massachusetts to insist that the assembly recall it. He also directed other governors to prevent their assemblies from discussing the letter. Hillsborough's order gave colonial assemblies the incentive to join forces against this new threat to their prerogatives. In late 1768 the Massachusetts legislature met, debated, and resoundingly rejected recall. Bernard immediately dissolved the assembly, and other governors followed suit when their legislatures debated the circular letter.

Like other formal assertions of colonial rights, the vote against recalling the circular letter provided a symbol to be commemorated in the public rituals organized by supporters of the resistance. Such rituals, as when legislators drank mass public toasts or Boston's Sons of Liberty invited hundreds to dine with them, served important educational and unifying functions. As pamphlets did for the literate, public processions, celebrations, and song fests taught illiterate Americans about the reasons for resistance and encouraged their commitment to the cause.

During the campaign against the Townshend duties, the Sons of Liberty and other American leaders stepped up the deliberate effort to involve ordinary folk in the resistance movement. Most important, they urged colonists of all ranks and both sexes to sign agreements not to purchase or consume British products. The new consumerism that previously had linked the colonists economically now linked them politically as well, offering a ready method of displaying their allegiance.

As the primary purchasers of textiles and household goods, women played a central role in the nonconsumption movement and introduced public rituals of their own. In Boston more than three hundred matrons publicly promised not to buy or drink tea, "Sickness excepted." The women of Wilmington, North Carolina, burned their tea after walking through town in a solemn procession. The best known of the protests, the so-called Edenton Ladies Tea Party, actually was a meeting of prominent North Carolina women who pledged formally to work for the public good and support resistance to British measures.

DAUGHTERS OF LIBERTY

Women also encouraged home manufacturing. In many towns, young women calling themselves Daughters of Liberty met to spin in public in an effort to persuade other women to make homespun, thereby ending the colonies' dependence on British cloth. When young ladies from well-to-do families sat publicly at spinning wheels all day, eating only American food and drinking local herbal tea, they were serving as political instructors. Many women took great satisfaction in their newfound role.

But the colonists were by no means united in support of nonimportation and nonconsumption. If the Stamp Act protests had occasionally revealed a division between artisans and merchants on one side and common laborers on the other, resistance to the Townshend Acts exposed new splits in American ranks. The most significant—which arose from a change in economic circumstances—divided urban artisans and merchants, allies in 1765 and 1766.

DIVIDED OPINION OVER BOYCOTTS

The Stamp Act boycotts had helped revive a depressed economy by creating a demand for local products and reducing merchants' inventories. But in 1768 and 1769, merchants were enjoying boom times and had no financial incentive to support a boycott. They signed the agreements only reluctantly. In contrast, artisans supported nonimportation enthusiastically, recognizing that the absence of British goods would create a ready market for their own manufactures. Tradesmen also used coercion, sometimes destroying property, to enforce boycotts.

Such tactics were effective: colonial imports from England dropped dramatically in 1769. But they also aroused heated opposition. Some Americans who supported resistance to British measures began to question the use of violence to force others to join the boycott. In addition, wealthier and more conservative colonists were frightened by the threat to private property inherent in the campaign. Political activism by ordinary colonists challenged the ruling elite's domination.

Americans were relieved when news arrived in April 1770 that the Townshend duties had been repealed, with the exception of the tea tax. A new prime minister, Lord North, persuaded Parliament that duties on trade within the empire were ill advised. Although some colonial leaders argued that nonimportation should continue until the tea tax was repealed, merchants quickly resumed importing. The rest of the Townshend Acts remained in force, but repealing the duties made the other provisions appear less objectionable.

TOWNSHEND DUTIES REPEALED

Confrontations in Boston

*O*n the very day Lord North proposed repeal of the Townshend duties, a confrontation between civilians and soldiers in Boston led to the death of five Americans. The origins of the event that patriots called the Boston Massacre lay in repeated clashes between customs officers and the people of Massachusetts. The decision to base the American Board of Customs Commissioners in Boston was the source of the problem.

Mobs targeted the customs commissioners from the day they arrived in November 1767. In June 1768 their seizure of the patriot leader John Hancock's sloop *Liberty* on suspicion of smuggling caused a riot in which customs officers' property was destroyed. The riot in turn helped convince the British that troops were needed to maintain order in the unruly port. The troops constantly reminded Bostonians of the oppressive potential of British power. Redcoat patrols roamed the city day and night, questioning and sometimes harassing passersby. Parents began to fear for the safety of their daughters, who were subjected to soldiers' coarse sexual insults. But the greatest potential for violence lay in the uneasy relationship between the soldiers, many of whom competed for unskilled jobs in their off-duty hours, and Boston laborers. The two groups brawled repeatedly.

Early on the evening of March 5, 1770, a crowd of laborers began throwing hard-packed snowballs at soldiers guarding the Customs House. Goaded beyond endurance, the sentries acted against express orders and fired on the crowd, kill-

BOSTON MASSACRE

ing four and wounding eight, one mortally. Resistance leaders idealized the dead rioters as martyrs for the cause of liberty, holding a solemn funeral and later commemorating March 5 annually with patriotic orations.

Leading patriots wanted to ensure that the soldiers did not become martyrs as well. Thus, when the soldiers were tried for the killings in November, John Adams and Josiah Quincy Jr., both unwavering patriots, acted as their defense attorneys and won

■ Shortly after the Boston Massacre, Paul Revere printed this illustration of the confrontation near the Customs House on March 5, 1770. Offering visual support for the patriots' version of events, it showed the British soldiers firing on an unresisting crowd (instead of the aggressive mob described at the soldiers' trial) and—even worse—a gun firing from the building itself, which has been labeled "Butcher's Hall."   (Photo: Anne S. K. Brown Military Collection, Brown University Library)

acquittal of all but two, who were released after be-ing branded on the thumb. Undoubtedly the favor-able outcome of the trials persuaded London officials not to retaliate against the city.

For the next few years, amid a superficial calm, the most outspoken colonial newspapers published

A BRITISH PLOT? essays drawing on Real Whig ideol-ogy and accusing Great Britain of deliberately scheming to oppress the colonies. After the Stamp Act's re-peal, the patriots had praised Parliament; following repeal of the Townshend duties, they warned of im-pending tyranny. Formerly viewed as an isolated mis-take, the stamp tax now appeared to be part of a plot against American liberties. Essayists pointed to the stationing of troops in Boston and the growing num-ber of vice-admiralty courts as evidence of plans to "enslave" the colonists.

Still, no one yet advocated complete independence from the mother country. Although the patriots were becoming increasingly convinced that they should seek freedom from parliamentary authority, they continued to acknowledge their British identity and their alle-giance to George III. They therefore began to envision a system that would enable them to be ruled by their own elected legislatures while remaining loyal to the king. But any such scheme violated Britons' conception of Parliament's sole undivided sovereignty over the empire.

Then, in the fall of 1772, the North ministry began to implement the Townshend Act that provided for governors and judges to be paid from customs rev-enues. In early November, voters at a Boston town meeting established a Committee of Correspondence to publicize the decision by exchanging letters with other Massachusetts towns. Heading the committee was the man who had proposed its formation, Samuel Adams.

Fifty-one in 1772, Samuel Adams had been a Boston tax collector, a member and clerk of the

SAMUEL ADAMS AND COMMITTEES OF CORRESPONDENCE Massachusetts assembly, an ally of the Loyal Nine, and a member of the Sons of Liberty. An experi-enced political organizer, he con-tinually stressed the need for prudent collective action. His Committee of Correspondence thus undertook the task of creating an informed consensus among all the residents of Massachusetts.

Such committees, which were eventually estab-lished throughout the colonies, represented the next logical step in the organization of American resis-tance. Until 1772, the protest movement was largely confined to the seacoast and primarily to major cities and towns. Adams realized that the time had come to involve more colonists in the struggle. Accordingly, the Boston town meeting directed the Committee of Correspondence "to state the Rights of the Colonists and of this Province in particular," to list "the In-fringements and Violations thereof that have been, or from time to time may be made," and to send copies to the other towns throughout the province.

The statement of colonial rights declared that Amer-icans had absolute rights to life, liberty, and property. The idea that "a British house of commons, should have a right, at pleasure, to give and grant the property of the colonists" was "irreconcileable" with "the first principles of natural law and Justice . . . and of the British Constitution in particular." The list of griev-ances complained of taxation without representation, the presence of unnecessary troops and customs officers on American soil, the use of imperial revenues to pay colonial officials, the expanded jurisdiction of vice-admiralty courts, and even the nature of the instruc-tions given to American governors by their superiors in London. No mention was made of obedience to Parlia-ment. Patriots—at least in Boston—placed American rights first, loyalty to Great Britain a distant second.

In their response, most towns aligned themselves with the city. From Braintree came the assertion that "all civil officers are or ought to be Servants to the people and dependent upon them for their official Support, and every instance to the Contrary from the Governor downwards tends to crush and destroy civil liberty." The town of Holden declared that "the People of New England have never given the People of Britain any Right of Jurisdiction over us." And the citizens of Petersham commented that resistance to tyranny was "the first and highest social Duty of this people." Beliefs like these made the next crisis in Anglo-American affairs the final one.

Tea and Turmoil

*T*he tea tax was the only Townshend duty still in effect by 1773. In the years after 1770, some Americans continued to boycott English tea, while others resumed drinking it. Tea figured prominently in the colonists' social lives, so observing the boycott required them not only to forgo a favorite beverage but also to alter habitual forms of socializing. Tea thus retained an explosively symbolic character even though the boycott began to fall apart after 1770.

In May 1773, Parliament passed an act designed to save the East India Company from bankruptcy.

TEA ACT

The company, which held a monopoly on British trade with the East Indies, was critically important to the British economy. According to the Tea Act, legal tea would henceforth be sold in America only by the East India Company's designated agents, which would enable the company to avoid middlemen in both England and the colonies and to price its product competitively with smuggled tea. The net result would be cheaper tea for American consumers, but tea that still would be taxed under the Townshend law. Resistance leaders interpreted the new measure as a pernicious device to make them admit Parliament's right to tax them. Others saw the Tea Act as the first step in establishing an East India Company monopoly of all colonial trade. Residents of the four cities designated to receive the first shipments of tea prepared to respond to what they perceived as a new threat to their freedom.

In New York City, the tea ships failed to arrive on schedule. In Philadelphia, Pennsylvania's governor persuaded the captain to turn around and sail back to Britain. In Charleston, the tea was unloaded and stored; some was destroyed and the rest sold in 1776 by the new state government. The only confrontation occurred in Boston, where both the town meeting and Governor Thomas Hutchinson rejected compromise.

The first of three tea ships entered Boston harbor on November 28. After a series of mass meetings,

THE BOSTON TEA PARTY

Bostonians voted to post guards on the wharf to prevent the tea from being unloaded. Hutchinson refused to permit the vessels to leave the harbor.

On December 16, more than five thousand people (nearly a third of the city's population) crowded into Old South Church. The meeting, chaired by Samuel Adams, made a final attempt to persuade Hutchinson to send the tea back to England. But the governor remained adamant. In the early evening, Adams reportedly announced "that he could think of nothing further to be done—that they had now done all they

could for the Salvation of their Country." Cries then rang out from the back of the crowd: "Boston harbor a tea-pot tonight! The Mohawks are come!" Within a few minutes, about sixty men of all social ranks crudely disguised as Indians assembled at the wharf, boarded the three ships, and dumped the cargo into the harbor. By 9:00 P.M. their work was done: 342 chests of tea worth approximately £10,000 floated in splinters on the water.

While resistance leaders rejoiced, the North administration reacted with considerably less enthusiasm. In

COERCIVE AND QUEBEC ACTS

March 1774, Parliament adopted the first of four laws that became known as the Coercive, or Intolerable, Acts. It ordered the port of Boston closed until the tea was paid for, prohibiting all but coastal trade in food and firewood. Passed later in the spring, the Massachusetts Government Act altered the province's charter, substituting an appointed council for the elected one, increasing the governor's powers, and forbidding most town meetings; the Justice Act provided that a person accused of committing murder while suppressing a riot or enforcing the laws could be tried outside the colony where the incident occurred; and the Quartering Act allowed military officers to commandeer privately owned buildings to house their troops. Thus, the Coercive Acts punished not just Boston but all of Massachusetts, alerting other colonies that their residents too could be subject to retaliation if they opposed British authority.

After passing the last of the Coercive Acts, Parliament turned its attention to reforming the government of Quebec. The 1774 Quebec Act granted greater religious freedom to Catholics—alarming Protestant colonists—and reinstated French civil law. Most important, the act annexed to Quebec the area east of the Mississippi River and north of the Ohio River. It thus removed that region from the jurisdiction of seacoast colonies that claimed parts of it—and made the task of wealthy colonists who hoped to develop the Ohio country much more difficult.

Members of Parliament who voted for the punitive legislation believed that the acts would be obeyed. But to patriots, the Coercive Acts and the Quebec Act proved what they had feared since 1768: that Great Britain had embarked on a deliberate plan to oppress them. If the port of Boston could be closed, why not the ports of Philadelphia or New York? If the royal charter of Massachusetts could be changed, why not the charter of South Carolina? If troops could be forcibly quartered in private houses, did not that action pave the way for the occupation of all of America?

The Boston Committee of Correspondence urged all the colonies to join in an immediate boycott of British goods. But the other provinces hesitated. Rhode Island, Virginia, and Pennsylvania each suggested that another intercolonial congress be convened to consider an appropriate response. Few people wanted to take hasty action; even the most ardent patriots remained loyal to Britain and hoped for reconciliation with its leaders. So the colonies agreed to send delegates to Philadelphia in September to attend a Continental Congress.

Summary   *Online Study Center* ACE the Test

*J*ust twenty years earlier, at the outbreak of the Seven Years War in the wilderness of western Pennsylvania, no one could have predicted that the future would bring such swift and dramatic change to Britain's mainland colonies. Yet that conflict—which simultaneously removed France from North America and created a huge war debt Britain had to find ways to pay—set in motion the process leading to the convening of the First Continental Congress.

In the years after the war ended in 1763, momentous changes occurred in the ways colonists thought about themselves and their allegiances. Once linked unquestioningly to Great Britain, they began to develop a sense of their own identity as Americans, including a recognition of the cultural and social gulf that separated them from Britons. They started to realize that their concept of the political process differed from that held by people in the mother country. They also came to understand that their economic interests did not necessarily coincide with those of Great Britain. Colonial political leaders reached such conclusions only after a long train of events.

By the late summer of 1774, Americans were committed to resistance but not to independence. Even so, they had started to sever the bonds of empire. During the next decade, they would forge the bonds of a new American nationality to replace those rejected Anglo-American ties.

LEGACY FOR A PEOPLE AND A NATION
The Census and Reapportionment

When in the prerevolutionary years American colonists argued that "they were not represented in" Parliament, they developed a definition of *representation* very different from the understanding traditionally accepted in Great Britain. There, numbers did not matter: the entire British population was seen as being "virtually" represented in Parliament.

Americans, by contrast, placed great emphasis on being represented in government by someone for whom they—or at least their better-off male neighbors—had actually voted. And that carried with it the related desire for election districts that were regularly reapportioned in accordance with the movements and increase of the population. Article 1, Section 2, of the U.S. Constitution thus provides for an "actual enumeration" of the nation's residents every ten years so that "representatives . . . shall be apportioned among the several States . . . according to their respective numbers." Each decade, from 1790 to 2000, the government has tried to count the nation's residents accurately—although, according to historians and demographers, it has often failed to achieve that goal.

The 2000 census, the planning for which Congress debated heatedly, turned out to be the most accurate in recent decades. It also led to two Supreme Court decisions: one outlining appropriate techniques for conducting the mandated "actual enumeration" of the American population, and another rejecting Utah's challenge to the final count. (Utah, which has only one member of the House and hoped to obtain a second, charged that the Census Bureau had improperly awarded a seat to North Carolina.) In other years too, especially

1920, near the close of an era of dramatic demographic change, planning and conducting the census proved extremely contentious. The commonly unacknowledged origin of such contests lies in Americans' prerevolutionary experience.

Thus, every ten years, the nation must still wrestle with an enduring legacy of the colonial period: the need to enumerate the American people and alter the boundaries of electoral districts according to the results.

A REVOLUTION, INDEED 1774–1783

*T*he Shawnee chief Blackfish named his new captive Sheltowee, or Big Turtle, and adopted him as his son. Blackfish's warriors had easily caught the lone hunter, who was returning with a slaughtered buffalo to an encampment of men. The captive then persuaded his fellow frontiersmen to surrender. It was February 1778. The hunter was Daniel Boone, who recently had moved his family from North Carolina to the western region of Virginia known as Kentucky. Some historians have wondered about Boone's allegiance during the American Revolution, for he moved to the frontier just as the war began. His encounter with the Shawnees highlights many ambiguities of revolutionary era loyalties.

The Shawnees were seeking captives to compensate for the death of their chief Cornstalk. Of the twenty-six men taken with Boone, about half were adopted into Shawnee families; the others were dispatched as prisoners to the Shawnees' British allies. Boone, who assured Blackfish that he would later negotiate the surrender of the women and children remaining at his home settlement of Boonesborough, watched and waited. In June 1778 he escaped, hurrying home to warn the Kentuckians of impending attack. When Blackfish's Shawnees and their British allies appeared outside the Boonesborough stockade in mid-September, Boone proved amenable to negotiations. Fragmentary evidence suggests the settlers agreed to swear allegiance to the British in order to avert a bloody battle. But the discussions dissolved into a melee, and the Indians then besieged the fort for a week before withdrawing. With that threat gone, Boone was charged with treason and court-martialed by Kentucky militia. Although he was cleared, questions haunted him for the rest of his life.

Where did Daniel Boone's loyalties lie? Had he betrayed the settlers to the Shawnees and sought to establish British authority in Kentucky? Had he—as he later claimed—deceived the Shawnees? Or had he made the survival of the fragile settlements his highest priority?

Online Study Center
This icon will direct you to interactive map and primary source activities on the website http://college.hmco.com/pic/nortonbrief7e

C H R O N O L O G Y

1774 • First Continental Congress meets in Philadelphia, adopts Declaration of Rights and Grievances
- Continental Association implements economic boycott of Britain; committees of observation established to oversee boycott

1774–75 • Provincial conventions replace collapsing colonial governments

1775 • Battles of Lexington and Concord; first shots of war fired
- Second Continental Congress begins
- Washington named commander-in-chief
- Dunmore's proclamation offers freedom to patriots' slaves who join British forces

1776 • Paine publishes *Common Sense,* advocating independence

- British evacuate Boston
- Declaration of Independence adopted
- New York City falls to British

1777 • British take Philadelphia
- Burgoyne surrenders at Saratoga

1778 • French alliance brings vital assistance to the United States
- British evacuate Philadelphia

1779 • Sullivan expedition destroys Iroquois villages

1780 • British take Charleston

1781 • Cornwallis surrenders at Yorktown

1782 • Peace negotiations begin

1783 • Treaty of Paris signed, granting independence to the United States

Daniel Boone was not the only American of uncertain or shifting allegiance in the 1770s. As a civil war, the American Revolution uprooted thousands of families, disrupted the economy, and forced many colonists into permanent exile; it also led Americans to develop new conceptions of politics, and it created a nation from thirteen separate colonies.

The struggle for independence required revolutionary leaders to accomplish three separate but closely related tasks. The first was political and ideological: transforming a consensus favoring loyal resistance into a coalition supporting independence, a task the colonies' leaders pursued using various measures, from persuasion to coercion.

The second involved foreign relations. To win independence, patriot leaders knew they needed international recognition and aid, particularly from France. Thus, they dispatched to Paris the most experienced American diplomat, Benjamin Franklin.

Only the third task directly involved the British. George Washington, commander-in-chief of the American army, soon recognized that his primary goal should be not to win battles but to avoid losing them decisively. The outcome of any one battle was less important than ensuring that his army survived to fight another day. The American war effort was aided by Britain's focus on military victories rather than on the primary goal of retaining the colonies' allegiance. In the end, British mistakes and American endurance, more than military prowess, decided the outcome. ■

Government by Congress and Committee

*W*hen the fifty-five delegates to the First Continental Congress convened in Philadelphia in September 1774, they knew that many Americans would support any measures they adopted. That summer, open meetings held throughout the colonies had endorsed the idea of another nonimportation pact. Committees of correspondence publicized these meetings so effectively that Americans everywhere knew about them. Most of the congressional delegates were selected by extralegal provincial conventions, since governors had forbidden regular assemblies to conduct formal elections. Thus, the very act of designating delegates to attend the Congress involved Americans in open defiance of British authority.

The colonies' leading political figures—most of them lawyers, merchants, and planters—attended the

FIRST CONTINENTAL CONGRESS

Philadelphia Congress, representing every colony but Georgia. The Massachusetts delegation included both Samuel Adams and his younger cousin John, an ambitious lawyer. Among others, New York sent John Jay, a talented young attorney. From Pennsylvania came the conservative Joseph Galloway and his longtime rival, John Dickinson. Virginia elected patriot zealots Richard Henry Lee and Patrick Henry, as well as George Washington.

The congressmen faced three tasks when they convened on September 5, 1774. The first two were explicit: defining American grievances and developing a plan for resistance. The third—articulating their constitutional relationship with Great Britain—proved troublesome. The most radical congressmen, like Lee of Virginia, argued that the colonists owed allegiance only to George III and that Parliament was nothing more than a legislature for Britain, with no authority over the colonies. The conservatives—Joseph Galloway and his allies—proposed a formal plan of union that would have required Parliament and a new American legislature to consent jointly to all laws pertaining to the colonies. The delegates narrowly rejected Galloway's proposal but also refused to embrace the radicals' position.

Finally, they accepted a compromise position worked out by John Adams. The crucial clauses in the Congress's Declaration of Rights and Grievances declared that Americans would obey Parliament, but only because that action was in everyone's best interest, and asserted that colonists would resist all taxes in disguise, like the Townshend duties. Remarkably, such a position—which only a few years before would have been regarded as extreme—represented a compromise in the fall of 1774.

With the constitutional issue resolved, the delegates readily agreed on the laws they wanted repealed

CONTINENTAL ASSOCIATION

(notably the Coercive Acts) and decided to implement an economic boycott while petitioning the king for relief. They adopted the Continental Association, which called for nonimportation of British goods (effective December 1, 1774), nonconsumption of British products (effective March 1, 1775), and nonexportation of American goods to Britain and the British West Indies (effective September 10, 1775).

The provisions of the Association were carefully designed to appeal to different groups and regions. For example, the delay of the nonconsumption agreement until three months after nonimportation took effect would allow northern urban merchants to sell items they already had. And the postponement of nonexportation for nearly a year gave small farmers in Virginia time to dry and cure their tobacco crop and northern exporters of wood products and foodstuffs to the Caribbean a final season of sales before the embargo began.

To enforce the Continental Association, Congress recommended the election of local committees

COMMITTEES OF OBSERVATION

of observation and inspection. By specifying that committee members be chosen by all men qualified to vote for members of the lower house of the colonial legislatures, Congress guaranteed the committees a broad popular base. The seven to eight thousand committeemen became the local leaders of American resistance.

Though officially charged only with overseeing implementation of the boycott, the committees soon became de facto governments. They examined merchants' records and published the names of those who continued to import British goods. They promoted home manufactures, encouraging Americans to adopt simple modes of dress and behavior to symbolize their commitment to liberty and virtuous conduct. Since expensive leisure-time activities were believed to reflect vice and corruption, Congress urged Americans to forgo dancing, gambling, horseracing, cockfighting, and other forms of "extravagance and dissipation." Thus, private activities acquired public significance.

The committees gradually extended their authority over many aspects of American life. They attempted to identify opponents of American resistance, developing elaborate spy networks and investigating reports of questionable remarks and activities. Suspected dissenters were urged to support the colonial cause; if they refused, the committees had them watched, restricted their movements, or tried to force them to leave the area. People engaging in casual political exchanges with friends one day could find themselves charged with "treasonable conversation" the next.

PROVINCIAL CONVENTIONS

While the committees of observation were expanding their power during the winter and early spring of 1775, the regular colonial governments were collapsing. Only a few legislatures continued to meet without encountering patriot challenges to their authority. In most colonies, popularly elected provincial conventions took over the task of running the government. In late 1774 and early 1775, these conventions approved the Continental Association, elected delegates to the Second Continental Congress (scheduled for May), organized militia units, and gathered arms and ammunition.

Unable to stem the tide of resistance, the British-appointed governors and councils watched helplessly as their authority crumbled. Courts were prevented from holding sessions, taxes were paid to the conventions' agents rather than to provincial tax collectors, sheriffs' powers were challenged, and militiamen would muster only when committees ordered. In short, during the six months preceding the battles at Lexington and Concord, independence was being won at the local level. Not many Americans fully realized what was happening. The vast majority still proclaimed their loyalty to Great Britain, denying that they sought to leave the empire.

Contest in the Backcountry

*A*fter the mid-1760s, land-hungry folk, ignoring the Proclamation of 1763, pronouncements by colonial governors, and the threat of Indian attacks, swarmed onto lands along the Ohio River and its tributaries. Sometimes they purchased property from opportunistic speculators; often they simply squatted on land in hopes that their titles would eventually be honored. By late 1775, thousands of new homesteads dotted the backcountry from western Pennsylvania south through Virginia and eastern Kentucky into western North Carolina.

DISTRUST AND WARFARE

Few of the backcountry folk saw the region's native peoples in a positive light. The frontier dwellers had little interest in the small-scale trade that had once helped to sustain an uneasy peace in the region; they only wanted land on which to grow crops and pasture their livestock. They interpreted Pontiac's uprising as a sign that no Indian—regardless of religion or tribal affiliation—could be trusted. That widely held opinion was first publicly exhibited in December 1763 when a group of fifty Scots-Irish men from Paxton Township, Pennsylvania, massacred twenty peaceful Christian Conestoga Indians.

In 1774, Virginia, headed by a new governor, Lord Dunmore, moved vigorously to assert its title to the rapidly developing backcountry. During the spring and early summer, tensions mounted as Virginians surveyed land in Kentucky in territory still claimed by the Shawnees. "Lord Dunmore's war" consisted of one large-scale confrontation between Virginia militia and some Shawnee warriors. Neither side won a clear-cut victory, but in the immediate aftermath, thousands of settlers—including Daniel Boone and his associates—flooded across the mountains.

When the Revolutionary War began just as large numbers of people were migrating into Kentucky, the loyalties of all Indians and settlers in the backcountry remained, like Boone's, fluid and uncertain. They were more or less at war with each other, and which side each would take in the imperial struggle might well depend on which could better serve their interests. Understanding that, the Continental Congress moved to establish garrisons in the Ohio country. Relying on such protection, as many as twenty thousand settlers poured into Kentucky by 1780. Yet frontier affiliations were not clear: the growing town of Pittsburgh, for example, harbored many active loyalists.

INDIANS' CHOICES

The native peoples' grievances against the European American newcomers predisposed many toward an alliance with Great Britain. Yet some chiefs urged caution: after all, the failure to enforce the Proclamation of 1763 suggested that Britain lacked the will and ability to protect them in the future. Furthermore, British officials hesitated to make use of their potential native allies, realizing that neither the Indians' style of fighting nor their war aims necessarily coincided with British goals and methods. Accordingly, they at first sought from Indians only a promise of neutrality.

Recognizing that their standing with native peoples was poor, the patriots also sought the Indians' neutrality. In 1775, the Second Continental Congress sent a general message to Indian communities describing the war as "a family quarrel between us and Old England" and requesting that they "not join on either side." A group of Cherokees led by Chief Dragging Canoe nevertheless decided to take advantage of the "family quarrel" to regain some land. They attacked settlements along the western borders of the Carolinas and Virginia in the summer of 1776. But a militia campaign destroyed many Cherokee towns. Dragging Canoe and his diehard followers fled to the west; the rest of the Cherokees agreed to a treaty that ceded still more of their land.

Bands of Shawnees and Cherokees continued to attack frontier settlements in the backcountry

INDIANS DURING THE REVOLUTION

throughout the war, but dissent in their own ranks crippled their efforts. The British victory over France had destroyed the Indian nations' most effective means of maintaining their independence: playing European powers off against one another. Successful strategies were difficult to envision under these new circumstances, and Indian communities split asunder as older and younger men, or civil and war leaders, disagreed vehemently over what policy to adopt. Only a few communities unwaveringly supported the American revolt; most other native villages either tried to remain neutral or hesitantly aligned with the British. And the settlers fought back: in 1778 and early 1779, a frontier militia force under George Rogers Clark captured British posts in modern Illinois (Kaskaskia) and Indiana (Vincennes), but the Anglo-Americans could never take the redcoats' major stronghold at Detroit.

Warfare between settlers and Indian bands persisted in the backcountry long after fighting between the patriots and redcoats had ceased. Indeed, the Revolutionary War itself constituted a brief chapter in the ongoing struggle for control of the region west of the Appalachians that began in 1763 and continued into the next century.

Choosing Sides

In 1765, protests against the Stamp Act had won the support of most colonists in the Caribbean and Nova Scotia as well as in the future United States. Demonstrations occurred in Halifax and Britain's Caribbean possessions as well as in Boston, New York, and Charleston. When the act went into effect, though, islanders loyally paid the stamp duties until repeal. And eventually a significant number of colonists in North America and the West Indies began to question both the aims and the tactics of the resistance movement. Doubts arose with particular urgency in Nova Scotia and the Caribbean.

Both the northern mainland and southern island colonies depended heavily on Great Britain militarily

NOVA SCOTIA AND THE CARIBBEAN

and economically. Despite the overwhelming British victory in the Seven Years War, they believed themselves vulnerable to French counterattack and were eager to have regular troops and naval vessels stationed within their borders. Additionally, sugar planters—on some islands outnumbered by their bondspeople twenty-five to one—feared the potential for slave revolts in the absence of British troops.

Economically, Nova Scotians and West Indians had major reasons for choosing to support the mother country. In the mid-1770s, the northerners began to reduce New England's domination of the Caribbean and northern coastal trade, and once the shooting started, they benefited greatly from Britain's retaliatory measures against the rebels' commerce. British sugar producers relied for their profits primarily on their monopoly of trade within the empire, for more efficient French planters were able to sell their sugar for one-third less. Neither islanders nor Nova Scotians had reason to believe that they would be better off independent.

In the thirteen colonies, active revolutionaries accounted for about two-fifths of the European

PATRIOTS

American population. Among them were yeoman farmers, members of dominant Protestant sects, Chesapeake gentry, merchants dealing mainly in American commodities, city artisans, elected officeholders, and people of English descent. Wives usually, but not always, adopted their husbands' political beliefs. Although all these patriots supported the

Revolution, they pursued divergent goals within the broader coalition, as they had in the 1760s. Some sought limited political reform, others extensive political change, and still others social and economic reforms.

Some colonists, though, found that they could not in good conscience endorse independence. Most objected to parliamentary policies, but they preferred the remedy of imperial constitutional reform. Their objections to violent protest, their desire to uphold legally constituted government, and their fears of anarchy combined to make them sensitive to the dangers of resistance.

About one-fifth of the European American population remained loyal to Great Britain, firmly rejecting independence. Most loyalists had
LOYALISTS   long opposed the men who became patriot leaders, though for varying reasons. British-appointed government officials; Anglican clergy everywhere and lay Anglicans in the North, where they were in the minority; tenant farmers, particularly those with patriot landlords; members of persecuted religious sects; many veterans of backcountry southern rebellion against eastern rule; and non-English ethnic minorities, especially Scots: past experience led all these groups to fear the power wielded by those who controlled the colonial assemblies. Joined by merchants whose trade depended on imperial connections and by former British soldiers who had settled in America after 1763, they formed a loyalist core. As the British army evacuated American posts during and after the war, many loyalists followed and scattered to different parts of the British Empire—Britain, the Bahamas, and especially Canada. All told, perhaps as many as 100,000 Americans preferred exile to life in a nation independent of British rule.

Between the patriots and the loyalists, perhaps two-fifths of European Americans tried to avoid taking sides. Some were sincere
NEUTRALS   pacifists, such as Quakers. Others opportunistically shifted their allegiance to whatever side happened to be winning currently. Still others simply wanted to be left alone. The last group included large numbers in the southern backcountry (including Boone's Kentucky), where Scots-Irish settlers had little love for either the patriot gentry or the English authorities.

To patriots, apathy or neutrality was as heinous as loyalism. By the winter of 1775–1776, the Second Continental Congress was recommending that all "disaffected" persons be disarmed and arrested. State legislatures passed laws severely penalizing suspected loyalists or neutrals. Many began to require all voters (or, in some cases, all free adult men) to take oaths of allegiance; the penalty for refusal was usually banishment to England or extra taxes. After 1777, many states confiscated the property of banished persons, using the proceeds for the war effort.

Online Study Center   **Improve Your Grade**
Primary Source:
Pennsylvania Radicals Attack Loyalism

The patriots' policies helped ensure that their scattered and persecuted opponents could not band together to threaten the revolution-
SLAVERY AND   ary cause. But loyalists and neutrals
REVOLUTIONARY were not the patriots' only worry,
FERVOR   for revolutionaries could not assume that their slaves would support them.

In New England, with few resident bondspeople, revolutionary fervor was widespread, and free African Americans enlisted in local patriot militias. The middle colonies and Virginia and Maryland were more divided but still largely revolutionary. In contrast, South Carolina and Georgia, where slaves composed more than half the population, were noticeably less enthusiastic about resistance. Georgia sent no delegates to the First Continental Congress and reminded its representatives at the second one to consider its circumstances, "with our blacks and tories [loyalists] within us," when voting on the question of independence. On the mainland as well as in the Caribbean islands, colonists feared the potential enemy in their midst.

Bondspeople faced a dilemma. Their goal was *personal* independence. But how best could they escape from slavery? Should they fight with
SLAVES'   or against their masters? African
DILEMMA   Americans made different decisions, but to most slaves, supporting the British appeared the more promising choice. In late 1774 and early 1775, groups of slaves began to offer to assist the British army in return for freedom. Some bondspeople futilely petitioned General Thomas Gage, who commanded British forces in Boston, promising to fight for the redcoats if he would liberate them. The most serious incident occurred in

New Nations

In northern North America before the Revolution, only Nova Scotia had a sizable number of English-speaking settlers. During and after the Revolution, however, many loyalist families, especially those from the northern and middle colonies, moved to the region that is now Canada, which remained under British rule. The provinces of New Brunswick and Upper Canada (later Ontario) were established to accommodate them, and some exiles settled in Quebec as well, laying the foundation of the modern bilingual (but majority English-speaking) Canadian nation.

Sierra Leone too was founded by colonial exiles: African Americans who had fled to the British army during the war, many of whom ended up in London. Seeing the refugees' poverty, a group of charitable merchants—calling themselves the Committee to Aid the Black Poor—developed a plan to resettle the African Americans elsewhere. The refugees concurred in a scheme to return them to the land of their ancestors. In early 1787, vessels carrying about four hundred settlers reached Sierra Leone in West Africa. In 1792, they were joined by several thousand other loyalist African Americans who had originally moved to Nova Scotia. The influx ensured the colony's survival; it remained part of the British Empire until achieving its independence in 1961.

While the Sierra Leone migrants were preparing to sail from London in late 1786, the first prison ships were simultaneously being readied for Australia. Unable to use the United States as a dumping ground for convicts, as it had the colonies throughout the eighteenth century, the British needed another destination for convicts sentenced to transportation for crimes such as theft, assault, and manslaughter. It decided to send them halfway around the world, to the continent Captain James Cook had explored and claimed in 1770. Long before 1868, when Britain stopped sending convicts to Australia, voluntary migrants had begun to arrive. The modern nation was created on January 1, 1901.

Thus, the founding event in the history of the United States links the nation to the formation of its northern neighbor and to new nations in West Africa and the Asian Pacific.

An early view of the settlement of black loyalists in West Africa, the foundation of the modern nation of Sierra Leone. (Manuscripts, Archives and Rare Books Division, Schomburg Center for Research in Black Culture, The New York Public Library, Astor, Lenox and Tilden Foundations.)

Thomas Rowlandson, an English artist, sketched the boatloads of male and female convicts as they were being ferried to the ships that would take them to their new lives in the prison colony of Australia. Note the gibbet on the shore with two hanging bodies—symbolizing the fate these people were escaping. (By permission of the National Library of Australia)

1775 in Charleston, where Thomas Jeremiah, a free black harbor pilot, was brutally executed after being convicted of attempting to foment a slave revolt.

The slaveowners' worst fears were realized in November 1775, when Virginia's royal governor, Lord Dunmore, offered to free any slaves and indentured servants who would leave their patriot masters to join the British forces. In addition to obtaining added manpower, Dunmore hoped to disrupt the economy by depriving planters of their labor force. But only about one thousand African Americans rallied to the British standard. Even so, Dunmore's proclamation led Congress in January 1776 to modify a policy that had prohibited the enlistment of African Americans in the regular American army.

The patriots sometimes turned rumors of slave uprisings to their own advantage. In South Carolina, resistance leaders argued that unity under the Continental Association would protect masters from their slaves at a time when royal government was unable to muster adequate defense forces. The strategy drew many fearful whites into the patriot camp.

Patriots could never completely ignore the threats posed by loyalists, neutrals, slaves, and Indians, but fear of these groups rarely hampered the revolutionary movement. In general, the practical impossibility of a large-scale slave revolt, the dissension in Indian communities, and the patriots' successful campaign to disarm and neutralize loyalists ensured that the revolutionaries would by and large remain firmly in control of the countryside.

War and Independence

*O*n January 27, 1775, Lord Dartmouth, secretary of state for America, addressed a fateful letter to General Thomas Gage in Boston, urging him to take a decisive step. Opposition could not be "very formidable," Dartmouth wrote, and it would be better to bring on conflict now than "in a riper state of Rebellion."

After Gage received Dartmouth's letter on April 14, he sent an expedition to confiscate colonial military supplies stockpiled at Concord, some 20 miles away. Bostonians dispatched two messengers, William Dawes and Paul Revere (later joined by Dr. Samuel Prescott), to rouse

BATTLES OF LEXINGTON AND CONCORD

the countryside. So when the British vanguard of several hundred men approached Lexington at dawn on April 19, they found a ragtag group of seventy militiamen. The Americans' commander ordered his men to withdraw, realizing they could not halt the redcoats. But as they began to disperse, a shot rang out; the British soldiers then fired several volleys. When they stopped, eight Americans lay dead. The British moved on to Concord, 5 miles away.

There the contingents of militia were larger. An exchange of gunfire at the North Bridge left three redcoats dead. Thousands of militiamen then fired from houses and from behind trees and bushes as the British retreated to Boston. By the end of the day, the redcoats had suffered 272 casualties, including 70 deaths. The patriots suffered just 93 casualties.

By the evening of April 20, perhaps twenty thousand American militiamen had gathered around Boston. Many, needed at home for spring planting, did not stay long, but those who remained dug in along siege lines encircling the city. For nearly a year, the two armies sat and stared at each other. The redcoats attacked their besiegers only once, on June 17, when they advanced against trenches atop Breed's Hill in Charlestown. In that misnamed Battle of Bunker Hill, the British incurred their greatest losses of the entire war: over 800 wounded and 228 killed. The Americans, though forced to abandon their position, lost less than half that number.

FIRST YEAR OF WAR

During the same eleven-month period, patriots captured Fort Ticonderoga, a British fort on Lake Champlain, acquiring much-needed cannon. Trying to bring Canada into the war on the American side, they also mounted a northern campaign that ended in disaster, with their troops ravaged by smallpox, at Quebec in early 1776. Most significant, the lull in the fighting at Boston gave both sides a chance to regroup, organize, and plan their strategies.

Online Study Center **Improve Your Grade**
Interactive Map:
The First Battles in the War for Independence, 1775

Lord North and his new American secretary, Lord George Germain, made three central assumptions about the war they faced. First, they concluded that patriot forces could not withstand the assaults of trained

BRITISH STRATEGY

British regulars. Accordingly, they dispatched to America the largest force Great Britain had ever assembled anywhere: 32,000 troops, accompanied by tons of supplies and supporting naval vessels and sailors. Such an extraordinary effort, they thought, would ensure a quick victory. In a common eighteenth-century practice, included among the troops were mercenaries from the German state of Hesse.

Second, British officials and army officers treated this war as comparable to wars in Europe. They adopted a conventional strategy of capturing major American cities and defeating the rebel army decisively without suffering serious casualties themselves. Third, they assumed that a clear-cut military victory would automatically restore the colonies' allegiance.

All these assumptions proved false. North and Germain vastly underestimated Americans' commitment to armed resistance. Battlefield defeats did not lead patriots to sue for peace. London officials also failed to recognize the significance of the American population's dispersal over an area 1,500 miles long. Although Britain would control each of the largest American ports at some time during the war, less than 5 percent of the population lived in those cities. Furthermore, the coast offered so many excellent harbors that essential commerce was easily rerouted.

Most of all, British officials did not at first understand that military triumph would not necessarily lead to political victory. Securing the colonies permanently would require hundreds of thousands of Americans to return to their original allegiance. After 1778, the ministry adopted a strategy designed to achieve that goal through the expanded use of loyalist forces and the restoration of civilian authority in occupied areas. But the new policy came too late. Britain's leaders never fully realized that they were fighting an entirely new kind of conflict: the first modern war of national liberation.

Great Britain at least had a bureaucracy ready to supervise the war effort. The Americans had only the Second Continental Congress, originally intended simply to consider the ministry's response to the Continental Association. Instead, the delegates who convened in Philadelphia on May 10, 1775, had to assume the mantle of intercolonial government. As the summer passed, Congress authorized the printing of money, established a committee to supervise relations

SECOND CONTINENTAL CONGRESS

with foreign countries, and took steps to strengthen the militia. Most important, it created the Continental Army and appointed its generals.

Until Congress met, the Massachusetts provincial congress had taken responsibility for organizing the militiamen encamped at Boston. However, the cost of maintaining that army was a burden, so Massachusetts asked the Continental Congress to assume the task of directing it. As a first step, Congress had to choose a commander-in-chief, and many delegates recognized the importance of naming someone who was not a New Englander. John Adams proposed the appointment of a Virginian whose military experience and excellent character "would command the Approbation of all America": George Washington. The Congress unanimously concurred.

Washington was no fiery radical and had not played a prominent role in the prerevolutionary agitation. Devoted to the American cause, he was dignified, conservative, and respectable—a man of unimpeachable integrity. Though unmistakably an aristocrat, he was unswervingly committed to representative government. His stamina was remarkable, and he both looked and acted like a leader.

WASHINGTON AS LEADER

Washington needed all the coolness and caution he could muster when he took command of the army outside Boston in July 1775. It took him months, but he imposed hierarchy and discipline on the unruly troops and brought order to the supply system. In March 1776, the arrival of cannon from Ticonderoga finally enabled him to put direct pressure on the redcoats in the city. Sir William Howe, who had replaced Gage, wanted to transfer his troops to New York City anyway, and the patriots' new cannon decided the matter. On March 17, the British and more than a thousand of their loyalist allies abandoned Boston forever.

BRITISH EVACUATION OF BOSTON

That spring of 1776, as the British fleet left Boston for the temporary haven of Halifax, the colonies were moving inexorably toward a declaration of independence. Even months after fighting began, American leaders had still denied seeking a break with Great Britain until a pamphlet published in January 1776 advocated such a step.

Thomas Paine's *Common Sense* exploded on the American scene, quickly selling tens of thousands of

■ George Washington at Princeton, 1779, by Charles Willson Peale. Two years after the battle, Peale created this heroic image of the Continental Army's commander, intended (as were all his portraits of revolutionary leaders) to instill patriotic sentiments and pride in its viewers. (Courtesy of the Pennsylvania Academy of the Fine Arts, Philadelphia. Gift of Maria McKean Allen and Phoebe Warren Downes through the bequest of their mother, Elizabeth Wharton McKean)

that only a balance of monarchy, aristocracy, and democracy could preserve freedom, he advocated establishing a republic, a government by the people with no king or nobility. Instead of acknowledging the benefits of links to the mother country, Paine insisted that Britain had exploited the colonies unmercifully. And for the frequently heard assertion that an independent America would be weak and divided, he substituted an unlimited confidence in America's strength once freed from European control.

It is unclear how many people were converted to the cause of independence by reading *Common Sense*. But by late spring, independence had become inevitable. On May 10, the Second Continental Congress formally recommended that individual colonies form new governments, replacing their colonial charters with state constitutions.

Then on June 7, Richard Henry Lee of Virginia, seconded by John Adams of Massachusetts, introduced the crucial resolution: "that these United Colonies are, and of right ought to be, free and independent States, . . . absolved of all allegiance to the British Crown." Congress debated Lee's resolution but postponed a vote on adopting it until early July and appointed a five-man committee—including Thomas Jefferson, John Adams, and Benjamin Franklin—to draft a declaration of independence. The committee assigned primary responsibility for writing the declaration to Jefferson, who was well known for his eloquent style.

The thirty-four-year-old Thomas Jefferson, a Virginia lawyer and member of the House of Burgesses, had read widely in history and political theory. That broad knowledge was evident in both the declaration and his draft of the Virginia state constitution, completed a few days before his appointment to the committee.

JEFFERSON AND
THE DECLARATION
OF INDEPENDENCE

The draft of the declaration was laid before Congress on June 28, 1776. The delegates officially voted for independence four days later, then debated the wording of the declaration for two more days, adopting it with some changes on July 4. Since Americans had long ago ceased to see themselves as legitimate subjects of Parliament, the Declaration of Independence concentrated on George III (see the appendix). The document accused the king of attempting to destroy representative government in the colonies and

COMMON SENSE copies. The author, a radical English printer who had lived in America only since 1774, called stridently for independence. Paine also challenged many common American assumptions. Rejecting the notion of oppressing Americans through the unjustified use of excessive force.

The declaration's chief long-term importance, however, did not lie in its lengthy catalogue of grievances against George III. It lay in the ringing statements of principle that have served ever since as the ideal to which Americans aspire: "We hold these truths to be self-evident: That all men are created equal; that they are endowed by their Creator with certain unalienable rights; that among these are life, liberty and the pursuit of happiness; that, to secure these rights, governments are instituted among men, deriving their just powers from the consent of the governed." These phrases have echoed down through American history like no others.

When the delegates in Philadelphia adopted the declaration, they were committing treason. Therefore, when they concluded the declaration with the assertion that they "mutually pledge[d] to each other our lives, our fortunes, and our sacred honor," they spoke no less than the truth. The real struggle still lay ahead.

Map 6.1   The War in the North, 1775–1777

The early phase of the Revolutionary War was dominated by British troop movements in the Boston area, the redcoats' evacuation to Nova Scotia in the spring of 1776, and the subsequent British invasion of New York and New Jersey.

The Struggle in the North

*O*n July 2, the day Congress voted for independence, redcoats landed on Staten Island, having returned south from Halifax (see Map 6.1). Washington marched his army of seventeen thousand from Boston to defend Manhattan. Because Sir William Howe waited until more troops arrived from England before attacking, the American army was able to prepare defenses.

But Washington and his men, still inexperienced in fighting and maneuvering, made major mistakes, losing battles at Brooklyn Heights and on Manhattan Island. The city fell to the British, who captured nearly three thousand American soldiers. Washington then slowly retreated across New Jersey, and British forces took control behind him. Occupying troops met little opposition; the revolutionary cause appeared to be in disarray. "These are the times that try men's souls," wrote Thomas Paine in his pamphlet *The Crisis*.

NEW YORK AND NEW JERSEY

The British forfeited their advantage, however, as redcoats stationed in New Jersey went on a rampage of rape and plunder. Washington determined to strike back. Moving quickly under cover of a nasty winter storm, he crossed the ice-choked Delaware River at night to attack a Hessian encampment at Trenton early on the morning of December 26. The patriots captured more than nine hundred Hessians and killed thirty; only three Americans were wounded. A few days later, Washington attacked again at Princeton. Having gained command of the field and buoyed American spirits, he set up winter quarters at Morristown, New Jersey.

British strategy for 1777, sketched in London over the winter, aimed to cut New England off from the other colonies. General John Burgoyne, a subordinate of Howe and one of the planners, would lead an invading force of redcoats and Indians down the Hudson River from Canada to rendezvous near Albany with a similar force that would move east along the Mohawk River valley. The combined forces would then presumably link up with Howe's troops in New York City. But in New York, Howe simultaneously prepared his own

CAMPAIGN OF 1777

plan to capture Philadelphia. Consequently, in 1777, the British armies in America would operate independently. The result would be disaster.

Howe took Philadelphia, but inexplicably he spent six weeks transporting his troops by sea instead of marching them overland and ended up only 40 miles closer to his goal than when he started. By the time he advanced on the city, Washington had had time to prepare its defenses. Twice, at Brandywine Creek and again at Germantown, the two armies clashed near the patriot capital. Although the British won both engagements, the Americans handled themselves well. The redcoats took Philadelphia in late September, but to little effect. The campaign season was nearly over, and far to the north Burgoyne was going down to defeat.

Burgoyne and his men had set out from Montreal in mid-June, traveling first by boat on Lake Champlain, then later marching slowly overland toward the Hudson, forced as they went to clear giant trees felled across their path by patriot militiamen. An easy triumph at Fort Ticonderoga in July was followed in August by two setbacks—the redcoats and Indians marching east along the Mohawk River turned back after a battle at Oriskany, New York; and in a clash near Bennington, Vermont, American militiamen nearly wiped out eight hundred of Burgoyne's German mercenaries. Then, after several skirmishes with an American army commanded by General Horatio Gates, Burgoyne was surrounded near Saratoga, New York. On October 17, 1777, he surrendered his entire force of more than six thousand men.

The August 1777 battle at Oriskany divided the Iroquois Confederacy. The Six Nations had formally pledged to remain neutral in the war. But two influential Mohawk leaders, the siblings Mary and Joseph Brant, believed that the Iroquois should ally with the British to protect their territory from land-hungry colonists. The Brants won over to the British the Senecas, Cayugas, and Mohawks. But the Oneidas preferred the American side and brought the Tuscaroras with them. The Onondagas split into three factions, one on each side and one supporting neutrality. The wartime division shattered the Iroquois' three-hundred-year league of friendship.

IROQUOIS CONFEDERACY SPLINTERS

Disunion and the confederacy's abandonment of neutrality had significant consequences. In 1778 Iroquois warriors allied with the British raided frontier villages in Pennsylvania and New York. To retaliate, an American expedition under General John Sullivan burned Iroquois crops, orchards, and settlements. The resulting devastation led many bands to seek food and shelter north of the Great Lakes. A large number of Iroquois settled permanently in Canada. Burgoyne's surrender at Saratoga brought joy to patriots, discouragement to loyalists and Britons. It also prompted Lord North to authorize a peace commission to offer the Americans what they had requested in 1774—in effect, a return to the imperial system of 1763. That proposal came far too late: the patriots rejected the overture.

Most important, the American victory at Saratoga drew France formally into the conflict. Ever since 1763, the French had sought to avenge their defeat in the Seven Years War, and the American Revolution gave them that opportunity. Even before Benjamin Franklin arrived in Paris in late 1776, France covertly supplied the revolutionaries with military necessities.

Franklin worked tirelessly to strengthen ties between the two nations. Adopting a plain style of dress and presenting himself as a representative of American simplicity, he played on the French image of Americans as virtuous farmers.

FRANCO-AMERICAN ALLIANCE OF 1778

His efforts culminated in 1778 when the countries signed two treaties. In the Treaty of Amity and Commerce, France recognized American independence, establishing trade ties with the new nation. In the Treaty of Alliance, France and the United States promised—assuming that France would declare war on Britain, which it soon did—that neither would negotiate peace without consulting the other. France also formally abandoned any claim to Canada and to North American territory east of the Mississippi River.

The French alliance had two major benefits for the patriot cause. First, France began to aid the Americans openly, sending troops and naval vessels in addition to arms, ammunition, clothing, and blankets. Second, Britain could no longer focus solely on the American mainland, for it had to fight France in the Caribbean and elsewhere. Spain's entry into the war in 1779 as an ally of France (but not of the United States) further magnified Britain's problems, for the Revolution then became a global war.

Life in the Army and on the Home Front

*O*nly in the first months of the war was the revolutionaries' army manned primarily by the semi-mythical "citizen soldier" militiaman. After a few months or at most a year, the early arrivals went home. They reenlisted, if at all, only briefly and only if the contending armies came close to their farms and towns.

After 1776 the ranks of the Continental Army—those who enlisted for long periods or for the war's duration—were filled primarily by young, single, or propertyless men who signed up to earn monetary bonuses or allotments of land after the war. As the fighting dragged on, those bonuses and land grants grew larger. To meet their quotas of enlistees, towns and states eagerly signed up everyone they could, including slaves and indentured servants (who were promised freedom after the war) and recent immigrants.

DIVERSITY IN THE RANKS

Recruiters in northern states turned increasingly to African Americans, both slave and free. Southern states initially resisted the trend, but later all but Georgia and South Carolina also enlisted black soldiers. Approximately five thousand African Americans eventually served in the Continental Army, most winning their freedom as a result. They commonly served in racially integrated units but were assigned tasks that others shunned, such as cooking and driving wagons.

Also attached to the American forces were a number of women, the wives and widows of poor soldiers, who came to the army with their menfolk because they were too impoverished to survive alone. Such camp followers—estimated overall to be about 3 percent of the number of troops—worked as cooks, nurses, and launderers in return for rations and low wages.

The officers of the Continental Army developed an intense sense of pride and commitment to the revolutionary cause that helped to forge an esprit de corps that outlasted the war. The realities of warfare were often dirty, messy, and corrupt, but the officers drew strength from a developing image of themselves as professionals who sacrificed personal gain for the good of the entire nation.

OFFICER CORPS

■ Barzillai Lew, a free African American born in Groton, Massachusetts, in 1743, served in the Seven Years War before enlisting with patriot troops in the American Revolution. An accomplished fifer, Lew fought at the Battle of Bunker Hill. Like other freemen in the North, he cast his lot with the revolutionaries, in contrast to southern bondspeople, who tended to favor the British.   (Courtesy of Mae Theresa Bonitto)

The officers' wives too prided themselves on their and their husbands' service to the nation. Unlike poor women, they did not travel with the army but instead came for extended visits while the troops were in camp. They brought with them food, clothing, and household furnishings to make their stay more comfortable, and they entertained each other and their menfolk at teas, dinners, and dances. Socializing and discussing current events created friendships later renewed in civilian life when some of their husbands became the new nation's leaders.

Life in the American army was difficult for everyone, although ordinary soldiers endured more hardships than their officers. Wages, even when paid, were small. Rations (a daily standard allotment of bread, meat, vegetables, milk, and beer) did not always appear, and men had to forage for their food. Clothing and shoes the army supplied were often of poor quality; soldiers had to make do or find their own. When conditions deteriorated, troops threatened mutiny (though only a few carried out that threat) or, more often, simply deserted.

HARDSHIP AND DISEASE

Endemic disease in the camps—especially dysentery, various fevers, and, early in the war, smallpox—made matters worse. Unlike British soldiers, most native-born colonists had not been exposed to smallpox, so soldiers and civilians were vulnerable when smallpox spread through the northern countryside after the early months of 1774.

Washington recognized that smallpox could potentially decimate the revolutionaries' ranks, especially after it helped cause the failure of the 1775 Quebec expedition. Thus, in Morristown in early 1777, he ordered that the entire regular army and all new recruits be inoculated, although some would die from the risky procedure and survivors would be incapacitated for weeks. Washington's dramatic measures helped protect Continental soldiers later in the war, contributing significantly to the eventual American victory.

Men who enlisted in the army or served in Congress were away from home for long periods of time. In their absence, their womenfolk, who previously had handled only the "indoor affairs" of the household, shouldered the responsibility for "outdoor affairs" as well. John and Abigail Adams took great pride in Abigail's developing skills as a "farmeress." Like other female contemporaries, Abigail Adams stopped calling the farm "yours" in letters to her husband and began referring to it as "ours." Most women did not work in the fields themselves, but they supervised field workers and managed their families' resources.

HOME FRONT

Wartime disruptions affected all Americans. Even far from the battlefields, people suffered from shortages of necessities like salt, soap, and flour. Small luxuries like new clothing or even ribbons or gloves were essentially unavailable. Severe inflation added to the country's woes. For those who lived near the armies' camps or lines of march, difficulties were compounded. Soldiers of both sides plundered farms and houses, looking for food or salable items—and they carried disease with them wherever they went.

Victory in the South

In the aftermath of the Saratoga disaster, Lord George Germain and British military officials reassessed their strategy. Loyalist exiles in London persuaded them to shift the field of battle southward, contending that loyal southerners would welcome the redcoat army as liberators.

Sir Henry Clinton, Howe's replacement, oversaw the regrouping of British forces in America. In 1778 he sent a convoy that successfully captured the French Caribbean island of St. Lucia, which thereafter served as a key base for Britain. In late 1779, Clinton sailed down the coast from New York to besiege Charleston (formerly Charles Town), the most important city in the South (see Map 6.2). The Americans held out for months, but on May 12, 1780, General Benjamin Lincoln surrendered the entire southern army. The redcoats then spread throughout South Carolina, organizing loyalist regiments.

SOUTH CAROLINA AND THE CARIBBEAN

Yet the triumph was less complete than it appeared. The success of the southern campaign depended on control of the seas, so that the widely dispersed British armies could coordinate their efforts. For the moment, the Royal Navy safely dominated the American coastline, but French naval power posed a threat to the entire southern enterprise. American privateers infested Caribbean waters, seizing valuable cargoes bound to and from the British West Indies. And after late 1778, France picked off British islands one by one.

Then, too, the redcoats never managed to establish full control of the areas they seized in South Carolina. Patriot bands operated freely, and loyalists could not be protected. In fact, the fall of Charleston spurred the patriots to greater exertions. The outcome was vicious guerrilla warfare.

Nevertheless, the war in South Carolina went badly for the patriots throughout most of 1780. At

Map 6.2 The War in the South

The southern war—after the British invasion of Georgia in late 1778—was characterized by a series of British thrusts into the interior, leading to battles with American defenders in both North and South Carolina. Finally, after promising beginnings, Cornwallis's foray into Virginia ended with disaster at Yorktown in October 1781.

Camden in August, forces under Lord Cornwallis, the new British commander in the South, crushed a reorganized southern army led by Horatio Gates. Thousands of enslaved African Americans joined the redcoats, seeking promised freedom. Their actions disrupted planting and harvesting in the Carolinas, as the British had hoped.

After the Camden defeat, Washington appointed General Nathanael Greene to command the southern campaign. In the dire circumstances that he faced, Greene recognized that the patriots could win only by convincing the populace that they could bring stability to the region.

GREENE AND THE SOUTHERN CAMPAIGN

He adopted a conciliatory policy toward loyalists and neutrals, persuading South Carolina to pardon those who had fought for the British if they would now join patriot militias. He also ordered his troops to treat captives fairly and not to loot loyalist property.

Since he had so few regulars (only sixteen hundred when he took command), Greene had to rely on western volunteers and could not afford to have frontier militia companies occupied in defending their homes from Indian attack. He accordingly pursued diplomacy aimed at keeping the Indians out of the war. His policy worked: by war's end, only the Creeks remained allied with Great Britain.

Even before Greene took command of the southern army in December 1780, the tide had begun to turn. In October, at King's Mountain, a force from the backcountry defeated a large party of redcoats and loyalists. Then in January 1781, Greene's trusted aide Daniel Morgan brilliantly routed the crack British regiment Tarleton's Legion at Cowpens. Greene himself confronted the main body of British troops under Lord Cornwallis at Guilford Court House, North Carolina, in March. Although Cornwallis controlled the field at the end of the day, most of his army had been destroyed. He had to retreat to the coast to receive supplies and fresh troops from New York.

Surrender at Yorktown

Cornwallis headed north into Virginia, where he joined forces with a detachment of redcoats commanded by the American traitor Benedict Arnold. Instead of acting decisively with his new army of 7,200 men, Cornwallis withdrew to the peninsula between the York and James Rivers, where he fortified Yorktown and awaited supplies and reinforcements. Seizing the opportunity, Washington quickly moved more than 7,000 troops south from New York City. When a French fleet defeated the Royal Navy vessels sent to relieve Cornwallis, the British general was trapped. On October 19, 1781, Cornwallis surrendered. When news of the defeat reached London, Lord North's ministry fell. Parliament voted to cease offensive operations in America, authorizing peace negotiations. Washington returned with the main army to the environs of New York, where his underpaid—and, they thought, underappreciated—

officers grew restive; in March 1783, they threatened to mutiny unless Congress compensated them adequately. Washington, warned in advance of the so-called Newburgh Conspiracy, met the challenge brilliantly. Summoning his officers, he defused the crisis with a well-reasoned but emotional speech drawing on their patriotism. When, fumbling for glasses, he remarked that "I have grown gray in your service and now find myself growing blind," eyewitnesses reported that many of the rebellious officers began to cry. At the end of the year, Washington stood before Congress and formally resigned his commission as commander-in-chief. Through this action, Washington established an enduring precedent: civilian control of the American military.

The war had been won, but at terrible cost. More than twenty-five thousand American men had died.

THE COST OF VICTORY
In the South, years of guerrilla warfare and the loss of thousands of runaway slaves shattered the economy. Indebtedness soared, and local governments were crippled for lack of funds, since few people could afford to pay their taxes.

Americans rejoiced when they learned of the preliminary peace treaty signed at Paris in November 1782. The American diplomats—

TREATY OF PARIS
Benjamin Franklin, John Jay, and John Adams—ignored their instructions from Congress to be guided by France and instead negotiated directly with Great Britain. Their instincts were sound: the French government was more an enemy to Britain than a friend to the United States. In fact, French ministers worked secretly behind the scenes to try to prevent the establishment of a strong and unified government in America. But the American delegates proved adept at power politics, and, weary of war, the new British ministry, headed by Lord Shelburne, made numerous concessions.

The treaty, signed formally on September 3, 1783, granted the Americans unconditional independence. Generous boundaries delineated the new nation: to the north, approximately the present-day boundary with Canada; to the south, the 31st parallel (about the modern northern border of Florida); to the west, the Mississippi River. Florida, which Britain had acquired in 1763, reverted to Spain. The Americans also gained unlimited fishing rights off Newfoundland. In ceding so much land to the United States, Great Britain ignored the territorial rights of its Indian allies. British diplomats also poorly served loyalists and British merchants. The treaty's ambiguously worded clauses pertaining to the payment of prewar debts and the postwar treatment of loyalists caused trouble for years to come.

Summary *Online Study Center* **ACE the Test**

The long war finally over, the victorious Americans could look back on their achievement with satisfaction and awe. They had taken on the greatest military power in the world and won. In the process, they reshaped the physical and mental landscapes in which they lived. They abandoned the British identity once so important to them and began creating loyalty to a new nation. They also laid claim to most of the territory east of the Mississippi River and south of the Great Lakes, thereby greatly expanding the land potentially open to their settlements and threatening Indian dominance of the interior.

In achieving independence, Americans surmounted formidable challenges. But in the future they faced perhaps even greater ones: establishing stable republican governments at the state and national levels and ensuring their government's continued existence in a world of bitter rivalries among the major powers—Britain, France, and Spain.

LEGACY FOR A PEOPLE AND A NATION
Revolutionary Origins

The United States was created in an event termed the "American Revolution." Yet many historians would contend today that it was not truly "revolutionary," if a revolution means overturning an earlier power structure. The nation won its independence and established a republic, but essentially the same men who had led the colonies also led the new country (with the exception of British officials and appointees). In sharp contrast, the French Revolution witnessed the execution of the monarch and many aristocrats, and a consequent redistribution of authority. So the legacy of the "American Revolution" appears ambiguous.

Since the "revolution," groups of widely varying political views, from far left to far right, have claimed to represent its true meaning. Acting "in the spirit of the Revolution," people protesting discriminatory policies against women and minorities (usually "liberals") invoke the "created equal" language of the Declaration of Independence; left-wing organizations rail against concentrations of wealth and power in the hands of a few. Those protesting higher taxes (usually "conservatives" wanting a reduced role for government) often adopt the symbolism of the Boston Tea Party. Right-wing militias arm themselves against what they believe is a malevolent government, just as they believe the minutemen did in 1775. The message of the Revolution can be evoked to support extralegal demonstrations of any description, from invasions of military bases by antiwar protesters to demonstrations outside abortion clinics, all of which may be analogized to the demonstrations against British policies in the 1760s. But the Revolution can also be evoked to oppose such street protests, because—some would argue—in a republic change should come peacefully, via the ballot box, not the streets.

Just as Americans in the eighteenth century disagreed over the meaning of their struggle against the mother country, so the legacy of revolution remains contested in the first decade of the twenty-first century, for both the nation and today's American people.

*F*ORGING A NATIONAL REPUBLIC 1776–1789

*O*n December 26, 1787, a group of Federalists— supporters of the proposed Constitution—gathered in Carlisle, a town on the Pennsylvania frontier. The men planned to fire a cannon to celebrate their state convention's ratification vote two weeks earlier, but a large crowd of Antifederalists prevented them from doing so. After forcing the Federalists to flee, the angry Antis publicly burned a copy of the Constitution.

The next day, the Federalists returned in force to fire their cannon and read the convention's ratification proclamation. Deciding against another violent confrontation, Antifederalists instead paraded around the town effigies of two supporters of the Constitution, then burned them. When Federalist officials later arrested several Antifederalists on riot charges, the Antifederalist-dominated militia mustered to break the men out of jail. Only a flaw in the warrant—which freed the arrestees legally—prevented another bloody brawl.

The Carlisle riots presaged violent disputes over the new Constitution in Albany (New York), Providence (Rhode Island), and other cities. These incidents manifested an ongoing struggle that began in 1775 and continued until the end of the century. In that contest, Americans argued continually over how to implement republican principles and who represented the people's will. Easterners debated with westerners; elites contended with ordinary folk. Public celebrations played an important part in the struggle, because in a world in which only relatively few property-holding men had the right to vote, other people expressed their political opinions in the streets.

Republicanism—the idea that governments should be based wholly on the consent of the people—originated with political theorists in ancient Greece and Rome. Republics, theorists declared, were desirable yet fragile forms of government. Unless their citizens were especially virtuous—that is, sober, moral, and industrious—and largely in agreement on key issues, republics were doomed to failure. When Americans left the British Empire, they abandoned the idea that the best system of government required participation by

Online Study Center
This icon will direct you to interactive map and primary source activities on the website
http://college.hmco.com/pic/nortonbrief7e

CHRONOLOGY

1776 • Second Continental Congress directs states to draft constitutions

1777 • Articles of Confederation sent to states for ratification
• Vermont becomes first state to abolish slavery

1781 • Articles of Confederation ratified

1786 • Annapolis Convention meets, discusses reforming government

1786–87 • Shays's Rebellion in western Massachusetts raises questions about future of the republic

1787 • Northwest Ordinance organizes territory north of Ohio River and east of Mississippi River
• Constitutional Convention

1788 • Hamilton, Jay, and Madison write *The Federalist*
• Constitution ratified

1794 • Wayne defeats Miami Confederacy at Fallen Timbers

1795 • Treaty of Greenville opens Ohio to settlement

1800 • Weems publishes his *Life of Washington*

a king, the nobility, and the people. They substituted a belief in the superiority of republicanism, in which the people, not Parliament, were sovereign. That decision raised several interrelated questions. How could Americans ensure political stability? How could they foster consensus among the populace? How could they create and sustain a virtuous republic?

America's political and intellectual leaders worked hard to inculcate virtue in their fellow countrymen and countrywomen. After 1776, American literature, theater, art, architecture, and education all pursued explicitly moral goals. The education of women was considered particularly important, for as the mothers of the republic's children, they were primarily responsible for ensuring the nation's future. On such matters, Americans could agree, but they disagreed on many other critical issues. Almost all white men assumed that women, Indians, and African Americans should have no formal role in politics, but they found it difficult to reach a consensus on how many of their own number should be included, how often elections should be held, or how their new governments should be structured.

Especially troublesome were Thomas Jefferson's words in the Declaration of Independence: "all men

are created equal." Given that bold statement of principle, how could white republicans justify holding African Americans in perpetual bondage? Some answered that question by freeing their slaves or by voting for state laws that abolished slavery. Others responded by denying that blacks were "men" in the same sense as whites.

The most important task facing Americans in these years was the construction of a genuinely national government. Before 1765 the British mainland colonies had rarely cooperated on common endeavors, but fighting the Revolutionary War brought them together and created a new nationalistic spirit. During the war, Americans began the process of replacing loyalties to state and region with loyalties to the nation.

Still, forging a national republic was neither easy nor simple. America's first such government, under the Articles of Confederation, proved too weak and decentralized. But some of the nation's political leaders learned from their experiences and tried another approach when they drafted the Constitution in 1787. Although some historians have argued that the Constitution represents an "aristocratic" counterrevolution against the "democratic" Articles, the two documents are more accurately viewed as successive attempts to solve the same problems—for instance, the relationship of states and nation and the extent to which authority should be centralized. ■

Creating a Virtuous Republic

*W*hen the colonies declared their independence from Great Britain, John Dickinson recalled many years later, "there was no question concerning forms of Government, no enquiry whether a Republic or a limited Monarchy was best. . . . We knew that the people of this country must unite themselves under some form of Government and that this could be no other than the republican form." But how should that goal be implemented?

Three different definitions of republicanism emerged in the new United States. Ancient history and political theory informed the first, held chiefly by members of the educated elite. The histories of popular governments in Greece and Rome suggested that republics could succeed only if they were small in size and homogeneous in population. Unless a republic's citizens were willing to sacrifice their own private interests for the good of the whole, the government would collapse. In return for sacrifices, though, a republic offered its citizens equality of opportunity. A republic's government would be in the hands of a "natural aristocracy" of men whose rank had been attained by merit rather than inheritance.

VARIETIES OF
REPUBLICANISM

A second definition, advanced by other members of the elite but also by some skilled craftsmen, drew more on economic theory than on political thought. Instead of perceiving the nation as an organic whole composed of people nobly sacrificing for the common good, this version of republicanism followed the Scottish theorist Adam Smith in emphasizing individuals' pursuit of rational self-interest. When republican men sought to improve their own economic and social circumstances, the entire nation would benefit. Republican virtue would be achieved through the pursuit of private interests rather than through subordination to some communal ideal.

The third notion of republicanism was less influential but more egalitarian than the other two. Many of its illiterate or barely literate proponents could write little to promote their beliefs. Men who advanced the third version of republicanism called for widening men's participation in the political process. They also wanted government to respond directly to the needs of ordinary folk, rejecting any notion that the "lesser sort" should automatically defer to their "betters." They were indeed democrats in more or less the modern sense.

Despite their differences, the three strands of republicanism shared many of the same assumptions. All three contrasted the industrious virtue of America to the corruption of Britain and Europe. In the first version, that virtue manifested itself in frugality and self-sacrifice; in the second, it would prevent self-interest from becoming vice; in the third, it justified including even propertyless free men in the ranks of voters.

As citizens of the United States set out to construct their republic, they believed they were embarking on an unprecedented enterprise. With great pride in their new nation, they expected to replace the vices of monarchical Europe—immorality, selfishness, and lack of public spirit—with the sober virtues of republican America. They wanted to embody republican principles not only in their governments but also in their society and culture. They looked to painting, literature, drama, and architecture to convey messages of nationalism and virtue to the public.

VIRTUE AND
THE ARTS

Americans faced a crucial contradiction at the very outset of their efforts. To some republicans, the fine arts themselves represented vice. What need did a frugal yeoman have for a painting—or, worse yet, a novel? The first American artists, playwrights, and authors thus confronted an impossible dilemma: they wanted to produce works embodying virtue, but those very works were viewed by many as corrupting.

Still, they tried. William Hill Brown's *The Power of Sympathy* (1789), the first novel written in the United States, was a lurid tale of seduction intended as a warning to young women. In Royall Tyler's *The Contrast* (1787), the first successful American play, the virtuous conduct of Colonel Manly was "contrasted" with the reprehensible behavior of the fop Billy Dimple. The most popular book of the era, Mason Locke Weems's *Life of Washington* (1800), was intended by its author to "hold up his great Virtues . . . to the imitation of Our Youth."

Painting and architecture, too, were expected to embody high moral standards. Two of the most prominent artists of the period, Gilbert Stuart and Charles Willson Peale, painted innumerable portraits of upstanding republican citizens. John Trumbull's vast canvases depicting milestones of American history such as Cornwallis's capitulation at Yorktown were intended to instill patriotic sentiments in their viewers. Architects likewise hoped to convey in their buildings a sense of the young republic's ideals. When the Virginia government asked Thomas Jefferson for advice on the design of the state capitol in Richmond, Jefferson unhesitatingly recommended copying a Roman building. Jefferson set forth ideals that would guide American architecture for a generation to come: simplicity of line, harmonious proportions, a feeling of grandeur.

Despite the artists' efforts, some Americans began to detect signs of luxury and corruption by the mid-1780s. The resumption of European trade after the war brought a return to fashionable clothing and abandonment of the simpler homespun garments patriots had once worn with pride. Elite families again attended balls and concerts. Parties no longer seemed complete without gambling and cardplaying. Especially alarming to fervent republicans was the establishment in 1783 of the Society of the Cincinnati, a hereditary association for Revolutionary War officers and their male descendants. Opponents feared the group would become the nucleus of a native-born aristocracy.

Americans' deep-seated concern for the future of the republic focused their attention on their children, the "rising generation." Education had previously been seen as a private means to personal advancement, a concern only for individual families. Now, schooling would serve a public purpose. If young people were to become useful citizens prepared for self-government, they would need a good education. The very survival of the nation depended on it. The 1780s and 1790s thus witnessed two major changes in educational practice.

EDUCATIONAL REFORM

First, some northern states began to use tax money to support public elementary schools. In 1789 Massachusetts became one of the first states to require towns to offer free public elementary education. Second, schooling for girls was improved. Americans realized that mothers would have to be properly educated if they were to instruct their children adequately for republican citizenship. Therefore, Massa-chusetts insisted in its 1789 law that town elementary schools be open to girls as well as boys. Throughout the United States, private academies were founded to give teenage girls from well-to-do families an opportunity for advanced schooling. No one yet proposed opening colleges to women, but a few fortunate girls could study history, geography, rhetoric, and mathematics.

The chief theorist of women's education in the early republic was Judith Sargent Murray of Massa-chusetts. In a series of essays published in the 1780s and 1790s, Murray argued that women and men had equal intellectual capacities,

JUDITH SARGENT MURRAY

■ Judith Sargent Stevens (later Murray), by John Singleton Copley, c. 1770–1772. The eventual author of tracts advocating improvements in women's education sat for this portrait two decades earlier, during her first marriage. Her clear-eyed gaze suggests both her intelligence and her seriousness of purpose.   (Terra Foundation for the American Art, Chicago/Art Resource, NY)

Novels

The citizens of the United States, fiercely patriotic and proud of achieving political independence from Great Britain, also sought intellectual and cultural independence. In novels, poems, paintings, plays, and histories, they explored aspects of their new national identity. Ironically, though, the standards against which they measured themselves and the models they followed were European, primarily British.

That was especially true of the most widely read form of literature in the new United States, the novel. Susanna Haswell Rowson's *Charlotte: A Tale of Truth,* the most popular early "American" novel, was actually composed in England, where the novel, as a literary form, originated. In the mid-eighteenth century Samuel Richardson had composed the first works of fiction that today are called novels, the very name revealing their "newness," or novelty. Written in epistolary style (that is, through letters drafted by the various characters), Richardson's novels—*Pamela* (1740), *Clarissa* (1748), and *Sir Charles Grandison* (1753)—all revolved around the courtship and sexual relationships of young adults. The same themes permeated *Charlotte* and Richardson's other American imitators, and for good reason. Changing social mores in the late eighteenth century largely freed English and American young people from parental supervision of their marital decisions. While giving them greater individual choice, that freedom also rendered girls particularly vulnerable to new dangers of deception and seduction by unscrupulous suitors. And these same young women, as a group, were the most avid readers of novels, especially as expanded women's education increased female literacy rates.

William Hill Brown's *Power of Sympathy* (1789) and Hannah Foster's *Coquette* (1797), fictional versions of true "seduction and abandonment" tales, had avid readerships, but neither matched the sales of *Charlotte,* which despite its subtitle, *A Tale of Truth,* had no known factual basis. Rowson, born in England but raised in Massachusetts as the daughter of a customs officer in the British service, lived with her family in England during the Revolution but permanently returned to the United States in 1793. Her popular novel, first published in London in 1791, was reprinted in Philadelphia three years later and eventually went through more than 160 editions. *Charlotte* (later titled *Charlotte Temple*) narrates the story of a naive young woman who elopes, pregnant and unmarried, with her seducer, only to be deserted when a beautiful, rich, and virtuous rival appears on the scene. After giving birth to her baby, Charlotte dies in her father's arms, with her last breath directing him to care for the child. "Oh my dear girls," Rowson cautions her readers, "pray for fortitude to resist the impulses of inclination, when it runs counter to the precepts of religion and virtue."

Generations of young American women sobbed over Charlotte's fate, visiting Trinity churchyard in lower Manhattan, where a real-life counterpart of the fictional heroine was reputed to be buried. Their tears and women's preference on both sides of the Atlantic for such sentimental novels linked the young readers and their nation to the former mother country from which they were nominally so eager to separate.

This "Eighth American Edition" (such statements on the title pages of early novels can rarely be trusted because some printings were pirated) of Susanna Rowson's *Charlotte Temple* included a "portrait" of its entirely fictional heroine. That engraving thus reinforced the subtitle, *A Tale of Truth.* *(AC7.R7997.791c 1809, Houghton Library, Harvard College Library)*

that boys and girls should be offered equivalent scholastic training, and that girls should be taught to support themselves by their own efforts.

Murray's theories were part of a general rethinking of women's position that occurred as a result of the Revolution. Both men and women realized that female patriots had made vital contributions to winning the war through their work at home and that their notions of proper gender roles had to be rethought. Americans began to develop new ideas about the role women should play in a republican society.

The best-known expression of those new ideas appears in a letter Abigail Adams addressed to her

WOMEN AND THE REPUBLIC

husband, John, in March 1776. "In the new Code of Laws which I suppose it will be necessary for you to make I desire you would Remember the Ladies," she wrote. "If perticuliar care and attention is not paid to the Laidies we are determined to foment a Rebelion, and will not hold ourselves bound by any Laws in which we have no voice, or Representation." With these words, Abigail Adams took a step soon to be duplicated by other disfranchised Americans: she deliberately applied the ideology developed to combat parliamentary supremacy to purposes that revolutionary leaders had never intended.

Abigail Adams did not ask that women be allowed to vote, but others claimed that right. The men who drafted the New Jersey state constitution in 1776 defined voters carelessly as "all free inhabitants" who met certain property qualifications. They thereby unintentionally gave the vote to property-holding white spinsters and widows, as well as free black landowners. Qualified women and African Americans regularly voted in New Jersey's local and congressional elections until 1807, when the state legislature disfranchised them. Yet that women voted at all was evidence of their altered perception of their place in the country's political life.

Such dramatic episodes were unusual. After the war, European Americans continued to believe that a woman's primary function was to be a good wife, mother, and mistress of the household. They perceived significant differences between the male and female characters. That distinction eventually enabled Americans to resolve the conflict between the two most influential strands of republican thought. Because wives could not own property or participate directly in economic life, women in general came to be seen as the

embodiment of self-sacrificing, disinterested republicanism. Through new female-run charitable associations founded after the war, better-off women assumed public responsibilities, in particular by caring for poor widows and orphaned children. This freed men to pursue economic self-interest (that other republican virtue), secure in the knowledge that their wives and daughters were fulfilling the family's obligation to the common good. The ideal republican man therefore was an individualist, seeking advancement for himself and his family. The ideal republican woman, by contrast, always put the well-being of others ahead of her own.

Together European American men and women established the context for the creation of a virtuous republic. But how did approximately 700,000 African Americans fit into the developing national plan?

The First Emancipation and the Growth of Racism

*R*evolutionary ideology exposed one of the primary contradictions in American society. Both European and African Americans saw the irony in slaveholders' claims that they sought to prevent Britain from "enslaving" them. In 1773 Dr. Benjamin Rush of Philadelphia, an ardent patriot, warned that liberty "cannot thrive long in the neighborhood of slavery."

African Americans did not need revolutionary ideology to tell them that slavery was wrong, but they quickly took advantage of that ideology. In 1779 a group of slaves from Portsmouth, New Hampshire, asked the state legislature "from what authority [our masters] assume to dispose of our lives, freedom and property." The same year several bondspeople in Fairfield, Connecticut, petitioned the legislature for their freedom, characterizing slavery as a "dreadful Evil" and "flagrant Injustice."

Both legislatures responded negatively, but the postwar years witnessed the gradual abolition of

EMANCIPATION AND MANUMISSION

slavery in the North, a process that has become known as "the first emancipation." Vermont banned slavery in its 1777 constitution. Massachusetts courts decided in the 1780s that a clause in the state constitution prohibited slavery. Most of the other states north of Maryland adopted gradual emancipation laws between 1780 (Pennsylvania) and 1804 (New Jersey). No southern state adopted similar general emancipation laws, but the legislatures of Virginia (1782), Delaware (1787), and Maryland (1790 and 1796) altered laws that had restricted slaveowners' ability to free their bondspeople. South Carolina and Georgia never considered adopting such acts, and North Carolina insisted that all manumissions (emancipations of individual slaves) be approved by county courts.

Revolutionary ideology thus had limited impact on the well-entrenched economic interests of large slaveholders. Only in the North, where slaves were relatively few, could state legislatures vote to abolish slavery. Even there, legislators' concern for property rights led them to favor gradual emancipation. For example, New York's law freed children born into slavery after July 4, 1799, but only after they had reached their mid-twenties (and provided their masters with labor until then). Thus, the owners' current human property remained largely intact. For decades, then, African Americans in the North lived in an intermediate stage between slavery and freedom. Although the emancipation laws forbade the sale of slaves to jurisdictions in which the institution remained legal, slaveowners regularly circumvented such provisions. The 1840 census still recorded the presence of slaves in several northern states; not until later that decade did Rhode Island and Connecticut, for instance, abolish all vestiges of slavery.

Despite the slow progress of abolition, the ranks of free people of African descent in the United States, few in number before the war, grew

GROWTH OF FREE BLACK POPULATION

dramatically in the first years after the Revolution. Wartime disruptions radically augmented the freed population, adding slaves who had escaped from plantations during the war, others who had served in the American army, and still others who had been emancipated by their owners or by state laws. By 1790 nearly 60,000 free people of color lived in the United States; ten years later, they numbered more than 108,000, nearly 11 percent of the total African American population.

In the Chesapeake, economic changes and the rising influence of antislavery Baptists and Methodists accelerated manumissions. With declining soil fertility and the shift from tobacco growing to less labor-intensive grain cultivation, planters began to complain about "excess" slaves. They occasionally solved that problem by freeing some of their less productive or more favored bondspeople or agreeing to allow slaves to work independently and purchase their freedom.

In the 1780s and thereafter, freed people from rural areas often made their way to northern port cities.

MIGRATION TO NORTHERN CITIES

Boston and Philadelphia, where slavery was abolished sooner than in New York City, were popular destinations. Women outnumbered men among the migrants by a margin of three to two, for they had better employment opportunities in the cities, especially in domestic service. Some freedmen also worked in domestic service, but larger numbers were employed as unskilled laborers and sailors. A few women and a sizable proportion of men were skilled workers or retailers. As soon as possible, freed people established independent two-parent nuclear families instead of continuing to live in their employers' households. They also began to occupy distinct neighborhoods, probably as a result of discrimination.

Both communities and laws discriminated against freed people as against slaves. South Carolina, for example, did not permit free blacks to testify against whites in court. New Englanders tried to use indenture contracts to control freed youths. Public schools often refused to educate children of color. Freedmen found it difficult to purchase property and find good jobs. And though in many areas African Americans were accepted as members—even ministers—of evangelical churches, they were rarely allowed an equal voice in church affairs.

Gradually freed people developed their own institutions. In Charleston mulattos formed the Brown Fellowship Society, which provided

FREED PEOPLE'S INSTITUTIONS

insurance coverage for its members, financed a school, and helped support orphans. In 1794 former slaves in Philadelphia and Baltimore founded societies that eventually became the African Methodist Episcopal (AME) denomination. AME churches later sponsored schools in a number of cities and, along with African Baptist, African Episcopal, and African Presbyterian churches, became cultural centers of the free black community.

Their endeavors were all the more important because in the postrevolutionary years, a formal racist

DEVELOPMENT OF RACIST THEORY — theory developed in the United States. European Americans had long regarded their slaves as inferior, but the most influential writers had argued that African slaves' seemingly debased character derived from their enslavement, rather than enslavement being the consequence of inherited inferiority. In the Revolution's aftermath, though, slaveowners needed to defend holding other human beings in bondage against the notion that "all men are created equal." Consequently, they began to argue that people of African descent were less than fully human and that the principles of republican equality applied only to European Americans. To avoid having to confront the contradiction between their practice and the egalitarian implications of revolutionary theory, they redefined the theory.

Simultaneously, the notion of "race" appeared in coherent form, applied to groups defined by skin color as "whites" and "blacks." The rise of egalitarian thinking among European Americans both downplayed status distinctions within their own group and differentiated all "whites" from people of color. (That differentiation soon manifested itself in new miscegenation laws adopted in both northern and southern states to forbid intermarriage among whites and blacks or Indians.) Meanwhile, a generation or two as slaves on American soil forged the identity "African" or "black" from the various ethnic and national affiliations of people who had survived the transatlantic crossing. Strikingly, among the first to term themselves "Africans" were oceanic sailors: men whose wide-ranging contacts with Europeans caused them to construct a separate, unified identity. Thus, in the revolutionary era, *whiteness* and *blackness*—along with the superiority of the former—developed as contrasting terms in tandem with each other.

Such racism had several intertwined elements. First came the assertion that, as Thomas Jefferson insisted in 1781, blacks were "inferior to the whites in the endowments both of body and mind." There followed the belief that blacks were congenitally lazy and disorderly, even though owners had often argued, conversely, that slaves were "natural" workers. Third was the notion that all blacks were sexually promiscuous and that African American men lusted after European American women. The specter of interracial sexual intercourse involving black men and white women haunted early American racist thought. Significantly, the more common reverse circumstance—the sexual exploitation of enslaved women by their masters—aroused little comment or concern.

African Americans did not allow these developing racist notions to go unchallenged. Benjamin Banneker, a free black surveyor, astronomer, and mathematical genius, directly disputed Thomas Jefferson's belief in Africans' intellectual inferiority. In 1791 Banneker sent Jefferson a copy of his latest almanac (which included his astronomical calculations) as an example of blacks' mental powers. Jefferson's response admitted Banneker's intelligence but indicated that he regarded Banneker as an exception.

At its birth, then, the republic was defined by its leaders as an exclusively white male enterprise. Indeed, **A REPUBLIC FOR WHITE MEN ONLY** some historians have argued that the subjugation of blacks and women was necessary for theoretical equality among white men. They suggest that identifying a common racial antagonist helped create white solidarity and lessen the threat to gentry power posed by the enfranchisement of poorer white men. Some scholars have pointed out that it was less dangerous to allow white men with little property to participate formally in politics than to open the possibility that they might join with former slaves to question the rule of elites. That was perhaps one reason why after the Revolution, the division of American society between slave and free was transformed into a division between blacks—some of whom were free—and whites. The white males wielding power ensured their continued dominance in part by substituting race for enslavement as the primary determinant of African Americans' status.

Designing Republican Governments

In May 1776, the Second Continental Congress directed states to devise new republican governments to replace the provincial congresses and committees that had met since 1774. Thus, American men initially concentrated on drafting state constitutions and devoted little attention to their national government.

They immediately faced the problem of defining a "constitution." Americans wanted to create tangible documents specifying the fundamental structures of government. Beginning with Vermont in 1777 and Massachusetts in 1780, the states decided that specially elected conventions—not their regular legislative bodies—should draft the constitutions. Then, seeking direct authorization from the people—the theoretical sovereigns in a republic—delegates submitted the new constitutions to voters for ratification.

STATE CONSTITUTIONS

The framers of state constitutions concerned themselves primarily with outlining the distribution of and limitations on government power. Through their experience under British rule, Americans had learned to fear the power of the governor and see the legislature as their defender. Accordingly, the first state constitutions typically provided for the governor to be elected annually (commonly by the legislature), limited the number of terms he could serve, and gave him little independent authority. Simultaneously, the constitutions expanded the legislature's powers. Every state except Pennsylvania and Vermont retained a two-house structure, with members of the upper house having longer terms and being required to meet higher property-holding standards. But they also redrew electoral districts to reflect population patterns more accurately, and they increased the number of members in both houses. Finally, most states lowered property qualifications for voting. Thus, the revolutionary era witnessed the first deliberate attempt to broaden the base of American government, a process that has continued into our own day.

LIMITING STATE GOVERNMENTS

The constitutions also included explicit limitations on government authority. To protect what their authors regarded as the inalienable rights of individual citizens, seven of the constitutions contained formal bills of rights, and the others had similar clauses. Most guaranteed citizens freedom of the press, the right to a fair trial, the right of consent to taxation, and protection against general search warrants. An independent judiciary was charged with upholding such rights. Most states also guaranteed freedom of religion, but with restrictions. For example, seven states required that all officeholders be Christians, and some continued to support churches with tax money.

In general, the constitution makers put far greater emphasis on preventing state governments from becoming tyrannical than on making them effective in wielding political authority. This approach to shaping governments was understandable, given the American experience with Great Britain. But establishing such weak political units, especially in wartime, practically ensured that the constitutions soon would need revision.

REVISING THE STATE CONSTITUTIONS

Invariably, the revised versions increased the powers of the governor and reduced the legislature's authority. In the mid-1780s, some American political leaders started to develop a theory of checks and balances. To control government power, they sought to balance the powers of the legislative, executive, and judicial branches against one another.

The constitutional theories Americans applied at the state level did not at first influence their conception of national government. Since American officials initially focused on organizing the military struggle against Britain, the powers and structure of the Continental Congress evolved by default early in the war. Not until late 1777 did Congress send the Articles of Confederation to the states for ratification.

ARTICLES OF CONFEDERATION

The chief organ of national government was a unicameral (one-house) legislature in which each state had one vote. Its powers included conducting foreign relations, mediating disputes between states, controlling maritime affairs, regulating Indian trade, and valuing state and national coinage. The Articles did not give the national government the ability to raise revenue effectively to enforce a uniform commercial policy. The United States of America was described as "a firm league of friendship" in which each state "retains its sovereignty, freedom and independence, and every Power, Jurisdiction and right, which is not by this confederation expressly delegated to the United States, in Congress assembled."

The Articles required unanimous consent of state legislatures for ratification or amendment, and a clause concerning western lands proved troublesome. The draft accepted by Congress allowed states to retain all land claims derived from their original charters. Maryland, whose charter specified no western land claims, feared being overpowered by states that could

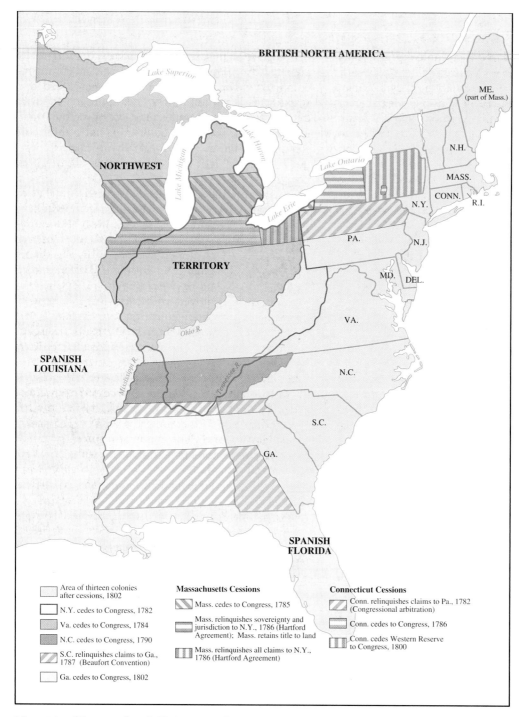

Area of thirteen colonies after cessions, 1802

N.Y. cedes to Congress, 1782

Va. cedes to Congress, 1784

N.C. cedes to Congress, 1790

S.C. relinquishes claims to Ga., 1787 (Beaufort Convention)

Ga. cedes to Congress, 1802

Massachusetts Cessions

Mass. cedes to Congress, 1785

Mass. relinquishes sovereignty and jurisdiction to N.Y., 1786 (Hartford Agreement); Mass. retains title to land

Mass. relinquishes all claims to N.Y., 1786 (Hartford Agreement)

Connecticut Cessions

Conn. relinquishes claims to Pa., 1782 (Congressional arbitration)

Conn. cedes to Congress, 1786

Conn. cedes Western Reserve to Congress, 1800

Map 7.1   Western Land Claims and Cessions, 1782–1802

After the United States achieved independence, states competed with each other for control of valuable lands to which they had possible claims under their original charters. That competition led to a series of compromises among the states or between individual states and the new nation, which are indicated on this map.

grow in size and power through land claims beyond the Appalachians. It therefore refused to accept the Articles until 1781, when Virginia finally promised to surrender its western holdings to national jurisdiction (see Map 7.1). Other states followed suit, establishing the principle that unorganized lands would be held by the nation as a whole.

The capacity of a single state to delay ratification for three years portended the fate of American government under the Articles of Confederation. The Articles' authors had not given adequate thought to the distribution of power within the national government or to the relationship between the Confederation and the states. The Congress they created was simultaneously a legislative body and a collective executive (there was no judiciary), but it had no independent income and no authority to compel the states to accept its rulings.

Trials of the Confederation

inance posed the most persistent problem that both state and national governments faced. Because legislators at all levels levied taxes only reluctantly, both Congress and the states at first tried to finance the war simply by printing currency. Although the money was backed by nothing but good faith, it circulated freely and without excessive depreciation during 1775 and most of 1776.

But in late 1776, as the American army suffered reverses in New York and New Jersey, prices began to rise, and inflation set in. The cur-

FINANCIAL AFFAIRS

rency's value rested on Americans' faith in their government, a faith that was sorely tested during the dark days of early British triumphs in the South (1779 and 1780). By early 1780, it took forty paper dollars to purchase one silver dollar. Soon, Continental currency was worthless.

In 1781, faced with total collapse of the monetary system, the congressmen undertook ambitious reforms. After establishing a department of finance under the wealthy Philadelphia merchant Robert Morris, they asked the states to amend the Articles of Confederation to allow Congress to levy a duty of 5 percent on imported goods. Morris put national finances on a solid footing, but the customs duty was never adopted. First Rhode Island and then New York refused to agree to the tax. The states' resistance reflected fear of a too-powerful central government.

Because the Articles denied Congress the power to establish a national commercial policy, the realm

FOREIGN AFFAIRS

of foreign trade also exposed the new government's weaknesses. Immediately after the war, Britain, France, and Spain restricted American trade with their colonies. Congress watched helplessly as British manufactured goods flooded the United States while American produce could no longer be sold in the British West Indies, once its prime market. Although Americans reopened commerce with other European countries and started a profitable trade with China in 1784, neither substituted for access to closer and larger markets.

Congress furthermore had difficulty dealing with the Spanish presence on the nation's southern and western borders. Determined to prevent the republic's expansion, Spain in 1784 closed the Mississippi River to American navigation, thereby depriving the growing settlements west of the Appalachians of their access to the Gulf of Mexico. Congress opened negotiations with Spain in 1785, but the talks collapsed the following year after Congress divided sharply: southerners and westerners insisted on navigation rights on the Mississippi, whereas northerners were willing to abandon that claim in order to win commercial concessions in the West Indies. To some congressmen, a national consensus on foreign affairs seemed unreachable.

Two provisions of the 1783 Treaty of Paris also aroused considerable opposition: Article Four, which

PEACE TREATY PROVISIONS

promised the repayment of prewar debts (most of them owed by Americans to British merchants), and Article Five, which recommended that states allow loyalists to recover their confiscated property. States passed laws denying British subjects the right to sue for recovery of debts or property in American courts, and town meetings decried the loyalists' return.

Online Study Center **Improve Your Grade** Primary Source: Loyalist Widow Decries the Fate of Tory Exiles in Canada

The refusal of state and local governments to comply with Articles Four and Five gave Britain an excuse to maintain military posts on the Great Lakes long after its troops were supposed to have withdrawn. Furthermore, Congress's inability to convince the states to implement the treaty disclosed its lack of power. Concerned nationalists argued publicly that enforcement of the treaty, however unpopular, was a crucial test of the republic's credibility in foreign affairs.

Order and Disorder in the West

Congressmen also confronted knotty problems when they considered the status of land beyond the Appalachians. Although British and American diplomats did not discuss tribal claims, the United States assumed that the Treaty of Paris cleared its title to all land east of the Mississippi except the area still held by Spain. Still, recognizing that land cessions should be obtained from the most powerful tribes, Congress initiated negotiations with both northern and southern Indians.

At Fort Stanwix, New York, in 1784, American diplomats negotiated a treaty with chiefs who said

INDIAN RELATIONS

they represented the Iroquois; and at Hopewell, South Carolina, in late 1785 and early 1786, they did the same with emissaries from the Choctaw, Chickasaw, and Cherokee nations. In 1786 the Iroquois formally repudiated the Fort Stanwix treaty, denying that the men who attended the negotiations had been authorized to speak for the Six Nations. The confederacy threatened new attacks on frontier settlements, but everyone knew the threat was empty; the flawed treaty stood by default. Thereafter, New York State purchased large tracts of land from individual Iroquois nations, and by 1790 the once-dominant confederacy was confined to a few scattered reservations. In the South too, the United States took the treaties as confirmation of its sovereignty, authorizing settlers to move onto the territories in question. European Americans poured over the southern Appalachians, provoking the Creeks—who had not agreed to the Hopewell treaties—to defend their territory by declaring war. Only in 1790 did they come to terms with the United States.

After the collapse of Iroquois power, once-subordinate western nations such as the Shawnees, Chippewas, Ottawas, and Potawatomis formed their own confederacy and demanded direct negotiations with the United States. They intended to present a united front so as to avoid the piecemeal surrender of land by individual bands and villages.

At first the national government ignored the western confederacy. Shortly after state land cessions

ORDINANCES OF 1784 AND 1785

were completed, Congress began to organize the Northwest Territory, bounded by the Mississippi River, the Great Lakes, and the Ohio River. Ordinances passed in 1784, 1785, and 1787 outlined the process through which the land could be sold to settlers and formal governments organized.

In 1785, Congress directed that the land be surveyed into townships 6 miles square, each divided into thirty-six sections of 640 acres (1 square mile). Revenue from the sale of the sixteenth section of each township was to be reserved for the support of public schools—the first instance of federal aid to education in American history. One dollar was the minimum price per acre; the minimum sale was one section. The resulting $640 minimum outlay was beyond the reach of ordinary Americans. Proceeds from western land sales constituted the first independent revenues available to the national government.

The most important of the three land policies—the Northwest Ordinance of 1787—contained a bill

NORTHWEST ORDINANCE

of rights guaranteeing settlers freedom of religion and the right to a jury trial, forbidding cruel and unusual punishments, and nominally prohibiting slavery. Eventually that prohibition became an important symbol for antislavery northerners, but at the time it had little effect. Some residents of the territory already had slaves, and Congress did not intend to deprive them of their property. Moreover, the ordinance allowed slaveowners to "lawfully reclaim" runaway bondspeople who took refuge in the territory—the first national fugitive slave law. Not until 1848 was enslavement abolished throughout the region, now known as the Old Northwest. And by omission Congress implied that slavery would be legal in the territories south of the Ohio River.

The ordinance of 1787 also specified the process by which residents of the territory could organize state governments and seek admission to the Union "on an equal footing with the original States." Early in the nation's history, therefore, Congress laid down

■ The two chief antagonists at the Battle of Fallen Timbers and negotiators of the Treaty of Greenville (1795). On the left, Little Turtle, the leader of the Miami Confederacy; on the right, General Anthony Wayne. Little Turtle, in a copy of a portrait painted two years later, appears to be wearing a miniature of Wayne on a bear-claw necklace.
(Left: Chicago Historical Society/Neg #ICHi–35980/Painter—Ralph Dille; right: Independence National Historic Park)

a policy of admitting new states and ensuring their residents the same rights held by citizens of the original states.

In a sense, though, in 1787 the ordinance was purely theoretical. Miamis, Shawnees, and Delawares refused to acknowledge American sovereignty and attacked unwary pioneers who ventured too far north of the Ohio River. In 1788 the Ohio Company, to which Congress had sold a large tract of land at reduced rates, established the town of Marietta at the juncture of the Ohio and Muskingum Rivers. But Indians prevented the company from extending settlement very far into the interior. After General Arthur St. Clair, the Northwest Territory's first governor, failed to negotiate a meaningful treaty with the Indians in early 1789, the United States could not avoid clashing with the Miami-led western confederacy.

Little Turtle, the able war chief of the Miami Confederacy, defeated first General Josiah Harmar (1790) and then St. Clair himself (1791) in major battles near the present border between Indiana and Ohio. More than six hundred of St. Clair's men died, and scores more were wounded, in the United States's worst defeat in the entire history of the American frontier. In 1793 the Miami Confederacy declared that peace could be achieved only if the United States recognized the Ohio River as its northwestern boundary. But the national government refused, and a new army under General Anthony Wayne, a Revolutionary War hero, attacked and defeated the confederacy in August 1794 at the Battle of Fallen Timbers. Peace negotiations began after the victory.

WAR IN THE OLD NORTHWEST

The Treaty of Greenville (1795) gave each side a portion of what it wanted. The United States gained the right to settle much of what was to become Ohio, and Indians received the acknowledgment they had long sought. At Greenville, the United States formally accepted the principle of Indian sovereignty, by virtue of residence, over all lands the native peoples had not ceded. Never again would the U.S. government claim that it had acquired Indian territory solely through negotiation with a European or North American country.

The problems the United States encountered in ensuring safe settlement of the Northwest Territory revealed the basic weakness of the Confederation government. Not until after the Articles of Confederation were replaced with a new constitution could the United States muster sufficient force to implement the Northwest Ordinance.

From Crisis to the Constitution

*T*he most obvious deficiencies of the Articles concerned finance, overseas trade, and foreign affairs. Congress could not levy taxes or impose its will on the states to establish a uniform commercial policy or ensure the enforcement of treaties. Partly as a result, the American economy slid into a depression less than a year after war's end. Exporters of staple crops (especially tobacco and rice) and importers of manufactured goods suffered from the postwar restrictions European powers imposed on American commerce. Although recovery began by 1786, the war's effects proved impossible to erase.

The war wrought permanent change in the American economy. The near total cessation of foreign commerce in nonmilitary items during the war stimulated domestic manufacturing. Consequently, despite the influx of European goods after 1783, the postwar period witnessed the stirrings of American industrial development. For example, the first American textile mill began production in Pawtucket, Rhode Island, in 1793. Moreover, foreign trade patterns continued to shift from Europe toward the West Indies. Foodstuffs shipped to the French and Dutch Caribbean islands became America's largest single export.

Recognizing the Confederation Congress's inability to deal with commercial matters, representatives of

ECONOMIC CHANGE AND COMMERCIAL REFORM

Virginia and Maryland met in March 1785 to negotiate an agreement about trade on the Potomac River, which formed part of their border. The successful meeting led to an invitation to other states to discuss trade policy at a convention in Annapolis, Maryland. Although nine states named representatives to the meeting in September 1786, only five delegations attended, too few to have any significant impact on the political system. Those present issued a call for another convention, to be held in Philadelphia nine months later, "to devise such further provisions as shall . . . appear necessary to render the constitution of the federal government adequate to the exigencies of the Union."

The other states did not respond immediately. But then an armed rebellion in Massachusetts convinced doubters that reform was needed. Farmers from the western part of the state, many of them veterans, violently opposed the high taxes levied by the eastern-dominated legislature to pay off war debts. Courts had also begun to foreclose on the lands of tax defaulters. On January 25, 1787, about 1,500 men nominally led by Daniel Shays, a former officer in the Continental Army, assaulted the federal armory at Springfield. The militiamen mustered to defend the armory fired on their former comrades in arms, who then withdrew. But in challenging the legitimacy of a government controlled by eastern merchants, the westerners termed Massachusetts "tyrannical" and insisted that "whenever any encroachments are made either upon the liberties or properties of the people, if redress cannot be had without, it is virtue in them to disturb government." They thereby explicitly linked their rebellion to the earlier independence struggle.

SHAYS'S REBELLION

To some, the rebellion confirmed the need for a much stronger federal government. After most of the states had already appointed delegates, the Confederation Congress belatedly endorsed the proposed convention, "for the sole and express purpose of revising the Articles of Confederation." In mid-May 1787, fifty-five men, representing all the states but Rhode Island, assembled in Philadelphia.

CONSTITUTIONAL CONVENTION

The vast majority of delegates to the Constitutional Convention were men of property and substance. Their ranks included merchants, planters, physicians, generals, governors, and especially lawyers—twenty-three had studied the law. Most had been born in America. Most were Congregationalists, Presbyterians, or Anglicans. In an era when only a tiny proportion of the population had any advanced education, more than half of the delegates had attended college. A few had been educated in Britain, but most had graduated from American institutions. The youngest delegate was twenty-six, the oldest—Benjamin Franklin—eighty-one. Like George Washington, whom they elected their presiding officer, most were in their vigorous middle years. A dozen men did the bulk of the convention's work. Of these, James Madison of Virginia was by far the most important; he deserves the title "Father of the Constitution."

Madison stood out among the delegates for his systematic preparation for the Philadelphia meeting.

MADISON AND THE CONSTITUTION
Through Jefferson in Paris, he bought more than two hundred books on history and government, carefully analyzing their accounts of past confederacies and republics. A month before the Constitutional Convention began, he summed up the results of his research in a lengthy paper entitled "Vices of the Political System of the United States." In this paper, Madison set forth the principle of checks and balances. The government, he believed, had to be constructed in such a way that it could not become tyrannical or fall wholly under the influence of a particular faction. He regarded the large size of a potential national republic as an advantage in that respect, rejecting the common assertion that republics had to be small to survive. Because the large, diverse nation would include many different factions, no one of them would be able to control the government. Political stability would result from compromises among the contending parties.

The so-called Virginia Plan, introduced on May 29 by Edmund Randolph, embodied Madison's conception of national government.

VIRGINIA AND NEW JERSEY PLANS
The plan provided for a two-house legislature, the lower house elected directly by the people and the upper house selected by the lower; representation in both houses proportional to property or population; an executive elected by Congress; a national judiciary; and congressional veto over state laws. The Virginia Plan gave Congress the broad power to legislate "in all cases to which the separate states are incompetent." Had it been adopted intact, it would have created a government in which national authority reigned unchallenged and state power was greatly diminished. Proportional representation in both houses would also have given large states a dominant voice in the national government.

The convention included many delegates who recognized the need for change but believed the Virginia Plan went too far in the direction of national consolidation. Disaffected delegates—particularly those from small states—united under the leadership of William Paterson of New Jersey, who presented an alternative scheme; the New Jersey Plan called for strengthening the Articles rather than completely overhauling the government. Although the convention initially rejected Paterson's position, he and his allies won a number of victories in the months that followed.

The delegates began their work by discussing the structure and functions of Congress. They readily agreed that the new national government should have a two-house (bicameral) legislature. But they discovered that they differed widely in their answers to three key questions: Should representation in *both* houses of Congress be proportional to population? How was representation in either or both houses to be apportioned among the states? And, finally, how were the members of the two houses to be elected?

DEBATES OVER CONGRESS

The last issue proved the easiest to resolve. To quote John Dickinson, the delegates thought it "essential" that members of the lower branch of Congress be elected directly by the people and "expedient" that members of the upper house be chosen by state legislatures. Since legislatures had selected delegates to the Confederation Congress, they would expect a similar privilege in the new government. Disappointing them might create significant opposition to the Constitution among state political leaders.

The method of representation in the Senate caused considerably greater disagreement. The delegates accepted without much debate the principle of proportional representation in the House of Representatives. But small states argued for equal representation in the Senate, while large states supported a proportional plan for the upper house. For weeks the convention deadlocked. A committee appointed to work out a compromise recommended equal representation in the Senate, coupled with a proviso that all appropriation bills originate in the lower house.

But not until the convention accepted a suggestion that a state's two senators vote as individuals rather than as a unit was a breakdown averted.

One critical question remained: How was representation in the lower house to be apportioned

SLAVERY AND THE CONSTITUTION

among states? Delegates concurred that a census should be conducted every ten years to determine the nation's actual population, and they agreed that Indians who paid no taxes should be excluded for purposes of representation. Delegates from states with large numbers of slaves wanted African and European inhabitants to be counted equally; delegates from states with few slaves wanted only free people to be counted. The convention resolved the dispute by using a formula developed by the Confederation Congress in 1783 to allocate financial assessments among states: three-fifths of slaves would be included in population totals. (The formula reflected the delegates' judgment that slaves were less efficient producers of wealth than free people, not that they were 60 percent human and 40 percent property.) The three-fifths compromise on representation won unanimous approval.

Although the words *slave* and *slavery* do not appear in the Constitution (the framers used euphemisms such as "other persons"), the document contained both direct and indirect protections for slavery. The three-fifths clause, for example, ensured white southern male voters not only congressional representation out of proportion to their numbers but also a disproportionate influence on the selection of the president, since the number of each state's electoral votes was determined by the size of its congressional delegation. The Constitution prohibited Congress from outlawing the slave trade for at least twenty years, and the fugitive slave clause required all states to return runaways to their masters. By guaranteeing that the national government would aid any states threatened with "domestic violence," the Constitution promised aid in putting down future slave revolts.

Once delegates reached agreement on the problems of slavery and representation, they readily

CONGRESSIONAL AND PRESIDENTIAL POWERS

achieved consensus on the other issues. All agreed that the national government needed the authority to tax and regulate commerce. And while delegates enumerated congressional powers, they then provided for flexibility by granting Congress all authority "necessary and proper" to carry out those powers. They further provided that the Constitution plus national laws and treaties would constitute "the supreme law of the land; and the judges in every state shall be bound thereby." As another means of circumscribing state powers, delegates drafted a long list of actions forbidden to states. The also provided that religious tests could never be required of U.S. officeholders. Finally, the convention established the electoral college and a four-year term for the chief executive, who could seek reelection. Foreign affairs were placed in the hands of the president, who was also made the commander-in-chief of the armed forces. (The text of the Constitution appears in the appendix.)

The key to the Constitution was the distribution of political authority—that is, separation of powers among executive, legislative, and judicial branches of the national government and division of powers between states and nation. The systems of checks and balances would make it difficult for the government to become tyrannical. At the same time, though, the elaborate system would sometimes prevent the government from acting quickly and decisively. Furthermore, the Constitution drew such a vague line between state and national powers that the United States fought a civil war in the next century over that very issue.

The convention held its last session on September 17, 1787. Of the forty-two delegates still present, only three refused to sign the Constitution, two of them in part because of the lack of a bill of rights. Although the delegates had accepted the Constitution, a key question remained: Would the states ratify it?

Opposition and Ratification

*T*he ratification clause provided for the new system to take effect once it was approved by special conventions in at least nine states, with delegates being elected by qualified voters. Thus, the national Constitution, unlike the Articles of Confederation, would rest directly on popular authority.

As states began to elect delegates to the special conventions, discussion of the proposed government grew more heated. Newspaper essays and pamphlets vigorously defended or attacked the Philadelphia convention's decisions. The extent of the debate was unprecedented, and it quickly became apparent that disputes within the Constitutional Convention had been mild compared to the divisions of opinion within the populace as a whole.

Those supporting the proposed Constitution called themselves Federalists. They argued that the

FEDERALISTS AND ANTIFEDERALISTS

carefully structured government would preclude the possibility of tyranny. A republic could be large, they declared, if the government's design prevented any one group from controlling it. The separation of powers, and the division of powers between states and nation, would accomplish that goal. People did not need to be protected from the powers of the new government in a formal way. Instead, their liberties would be guarded by elected officials of the "better sort" whose only goal (said George Washington) was "to merit the approbation of good and virtuous men."

The Federalists termed those who opposed the Constitution Antifederalists. Antifederalists feared a too-powerful central government. They saw the states as the chief protectors of individual rights; consequently, weakening the states could bring the onset of arbitrary power. Heirs of the Real Whig ideology of the late 1760s and early 1770s, Antifederalists stressed the need for constant popular vigilance to avert oppression. Indeed, some of them had originally promulgated those ideas—Samuel Adams, Patrick Henry, and Richard Henry Lee led the opposition to the Constitution. Joining them were small farmers preoccupied with guarding their property against excessive taxation, backcountry Baptists and Presbyterians, and ambitious, upwardly mobile men who would benefit from an economic and political system less tightly controlled than that the Constitution envisioned. Federalists denigrated such men as disorderly, licentious, and even "unmanly" and "boyish" because they would not follow the elites' lead in supporting the Constitution.

Online Study Center **Improve Your Grade**
Interactive Map: Federalist and Antifederalist Strongholds, 1787–1790

As public debate continued, Antifederalists focused on the Constitution's lack of a bill of rights.

BILL OF RIGHTS

Even if the new system weakened the states, critics believed, specific guarantees of rights could still pro-tect people from tyranny. *Letters of a Federal Farmer,* perhaps the most widely read Antifederalist pamphlet, listed the rights that should be protected: freedom of the press and religion, trial by jury, and guarantees against unreasonable searches.

As state conventions considered ratification, the lack of a bill of rights loomed ever larger. Four of the

RATIFICATION

first five states to ratify did so unanimously, but serious disagreements then surfaced. Massachusetts, in which Antifederalist forces had been bolstered by a backlash against the state government's heavy-handed treatment of the Shays rebels, ratified by a majority of only 19 votes out of 355 cast. In June 1788, when New Hampshire ratified, the requirement of nine states was satisfied. But New York and Virginia had not yet voted, and everyone realized the new Constitution could not succeed unless those key states accepted it.

Despite a valiant effort by the Antifederalist Patrick Henry, pro-Constitution forces won by 10 votes in the Virginia convention. In New York, James Madison, John Jay, and Alexander Hamilton campaigned for ratification by publishing *The Federalist,* a political tract that explained the theory behind the Constitution and masterfully answered its critics. Their reasoned arguments, coupled with Federalists' promise to add a bill of rights to the Constitution, helped win the battle. On July 26, 1788, New York ratified the Constitution by the slim margin of 3 votes. Although the last states—North Carolina and Rhode Island—did not join the Union until November 1789 and May 1790, respectively, the new government was a reality.

Americans in many cities celebrated ratification (somewhat prematurely) with a series of parades on

CELEBRATING RATIFICATION

July 4, 1788. The carefully planned processions dramatized the history and symbolized the unity of the new nation, seeking to counteract memories of the dissent that had so recently engulfed such towns as Carlisle, Pennsylvania. Like pre-Revolution protest meetings, the parades served as political lessons for literate and illiterate Americans alike. The processions aimed to educate men and women about the significance of the new Constitution and instruct them about political leaders' hopes for industry and frugality on the part of a virtuous American public.

Summary   *Online Study Center* ACE the Test

During the 1770s and 1780s, the nation took shape as a political union. It began to develop an economy independent of the British Empire and attempted to chart its own course in the world to protect the national interest. Some Americans outlined cultural and intellectual goals for a properly virtuous republic. An integral part of the formation of the Union was the systematic formulation of American racist thought. Emphasizing race as a determinant of African Americans' standing in the nation, and defining women as nonpolitical, allowed men who now termed themselves "white" to define *republicanism* to exclude all people but themselves and ensure their control of the country.

The experience of fighting a war and struggling for survival as an independent nation altered the political context of American life in the 1780s. At the outset of the war, most Americans believed that "that government which governs best governs least," but by the late 1780s, many had changed their minds. They were the drafters and supporters of the Constitution, who concluded from the republic's vicissitudes under the Articles of Confederation that a more powerful central government was needed. During ratification debates, they contended that their proposals were just as "republican" in conception as the Articles (if not more so). Ratification created the constitutional republic; the decade of the 1790s would witness the first hesitant steps toward the creation of a true nation, the United States of America.

LEGACY FOR A PEOPLE AND A NATION
Women's Education

Women today constitute a majority of students enrolled in U.S. colleges and universities. Because women were denied all access to collegiate education in this country until the mid-nineteenth century, that is a remarkable development. Moreover, it differentiates the United States from other nations, where the majority of university students are male. The origins of women's higher education lie deep, in the republican ideology of the 1770s and 1780s.

Once the United States had established republican forms of government, its citizens began to worry about sustaining those governments. The future, everyone knew, lay in the hands of the nation's children, especially its sons. And theorists concluded that those sons could successfully perpetuate the republic only if they learned the lessons of patriotism from their mothers. Male and female reformers therefore began to argue that women in the United States should be better educated than those who lived under other forms of government.

Some American reformers founded private academies (roughly equivalent to modern high schools) to teach young women from leading families such subjects as history, geography, mathematics, and languages. Some of the women who attended those academies later started educational establishments of their own—including Mary Lyon, who in 1837 founded Mt. Holyoke College in western Massachusetts, the first institution of higher education for women in the United States. A few years later, some colleges for men (such as Oberlin, in Ohio) and state universities (for example, Michigan) admitted women, and a number of women's colleges were established. Not until the second half of the twentieth century, however, did American women gain truly equal access to higher education. In the 1970s, such Ivy League universities as Yale and Princeton finally opened their doors to women students, and others (such as Cornell) that had restricted women's enrollment through quotas removed all constraints. Along with the existence of the nation itself, increased educational opportunity for women is therefore one of the most important legacies of the revolutionary era for the American people.

The Early Republic: Conflicts at Home and Abroad 1789–1800

*I*n the last months of 1798, the wealthy Philadelphia matron Deborah Norris Logan met with widespread public criticism. Her husband, the Jefferson supporter Dr. George Logan, had undertaken a personal peace mission to France, fearing the prospect of war between the United States and its former ally. In his absence, his wife loyally defended her husband's actions, and she in turn had to endure a campaign unlike any an American woman had ever experienced. That such an episode could occur suggested the political symbolism now embodied by women, the growing division between the factions known as Federalists and Democratic-Republicans, and the significance of foreign affairs in the early republic.

First to attack was "Peter Porcupine," the Federalist newspaper editor William Cobbett, who observed with sly sexual innuendo in his *Porcupine's Gazette* in July that "it is said that JEFFERSON went to his friend Doctor Logan's farm and spent three days there, soon after the Doctor's departure for France. *Query:* What did he do there? Was it to arrange the Doctor's *valuable manuscripts?*" Later Cobbett suggested that both George and Deborah Logan should be pilloried for their actions—him, presumably, for treason and her, Cobbett implied, for adultery. Understanding the symbolic significance of women's virtuous conduct in the fragile young republic, Democratic-Republican newspapers leaped to Deborah's defense, attacking Cobbett's vulgarity and insisting that not even a corrupt Londoner could have written "a greater libel upon public virtue or national morals."

Deborah Logan remained resolute. As reports emerged that her husband had had some success in quelling hostilities, she reveled in the praise subsequently showered on him. George Logan was enthusiastically welcomed home, at least by Jeffersonian partisans. Congress, controlled by Federalists, was less impressed. In January 1799 it adopted the so-called Logan Act, still

CHRONOLOGY

1789 • Washington inaugurated as first president
     • Judiciary Act of 1789 organizes federal court system
     • French Revolution begins

1790 • Hamilton's *Report on Public Credit* proposes assumption of state debts

1791 • First ten amendments (Bill of Rights) ratified
     • First national bank chartered

1793 • France declares war on Britain, Spain, and the Netherlands
     • Washington's neutrality proclamation
     • Democratic-Republican societies founded

1794 • Whiskey Rebellion in western Pennsylvania

1795 • Jay Treaty with England
     • Pinckney's Treaty with Spain

1796 • First contested presidential election: Adams elected president, Jefferson vice president

1798 • XYZ affair
     • Sedition Act penalizes dissent
     • Virginia and Kentucky resolutions

1798–99 • Quasi-War with France

1800 • Franco-American Convention
     • Gabriel's Rebellion

in effect, which forbids private citizens from undertaking diplomatic missions.

The controversy caused by the Logans' actions was but one of many such battles in the 1790s. The fight over ratifying the Constitution turned out to presage an even wider division over the major political, economic, and diplomatic questions confronting the young republic: the extent to which authority should be centralized in the national government; the relationship of national power and states' rights; the formulation of foreign policy in an era of continual warfare in Europe; and the limits of dissent. Americans did not anticipate the acrimonious disagreements that rocked the 1790s. And no one predicted the difficulties that would develop as the United States attempted to deal with Indian nations now wholly encompassed within its borders.

Most important of all, perhaps, Americans could not understand or fully accept the division of the country's political leaders into two factions (not yet political parties), believing that only monarchies should experience such factional disputes. In republics, they believed, the rise of factions signified decay and corruption. ■

Building a Workable Government

The nationalistic spirit expressed in the processions celebrating ratification of the Constitution carried over to the first session of Congress. Only a few Antifederalists ran for office in the congressional elections held late in 1788, and even fewer were elected. Thus, the First Congress consisted chiefly of men who supported a strong national government. The drafters of the Constitution had deliberately left many key issues undecided, so the nationalists' domination of Congress meant that their views on those points quickly prevailed.

Congress faced four immediate tasks when it convened in April 1789: raising revenue to support the new government, responding to states' calls for a bill of rights, setting up executive departments, and organizing the federal judiciary. The last task was especially important. The Constitution had established a Supreme Court but left it to Congress to decide whether to have other federal courts as well.

FIRST CONGRESS

James Madison, who had been elected to the House of Representatives, soon became as influential in Congress as he had been at the Constitutional Convention. A few months into the first session, he persuaded Congress to adopt the Revenue Act of 1789, imposing a 5 percent tariff on certain imports. Thus, the First Congress quickly achieved what the Confederation Congress never had: an effective national tax law. The new government would have problems in its first years, but lack of revenue was not one of them.

Madison also took the lead with respect to constitutional amendments. He placed nineteen proposed

BILL OF RIGHTS

amendments before the House. The states soon ratified ten, which officially became part of the Constitution on December 15, 1791. Their adoption defused Antifederalist opposition and rallied support for the new government.

The First Amendment specifically prohibited Congress from passing any law restricting the right to freedom of religion, speech, press, peaceable assembly, or petition. The Second Amendment guaranteed the right "to keep and bear arms" because of the need for a "well-regulated Militia." Thus, the constitutional right to bear arms was based on the expectation that most able-bodied men would serve the nation as citizen-soldiers, and there would be little need for a standing army, which former colonists feared as a threat to freedom. The Third Amendment limited the conditions under which troops could be quartered in private homes. The Fourth Amendment prohibited "unreasonable searches and seizures"; the Fifth and Sixth established the rights of accused persons; the Seventh specified the conditions for jury trials in civil (as opposed to criminal) cases; and the Eighth forbade "cruel and unusual punishments." The Ninth and Tenth Amendments reserved to the people and the states other unspecified rights and powers. In short, the amendments' authors made it clear that in listing some rights, they did not mean to preclude the exercise of others.

Congress also considered the organization of the executive branch. It readily agreed to continue the

EXECUTIVE AND JUDICIARY

three administrative departments established under the Articles of Confederation: War, Foreign Affairs (renamed State), and Treasury. Congress instituted two lesser posts: the attorney general—the nation's official lawyer—and the postmaster general. And by agreeing that the president alone could dismiss officials he had originally appointed with the consent of the Senate, Congress established the principle that the heads of

executive departments are accountable solely to the president. Aside from constitutional amendments, the most far-reaching piece of legislation enacted by the First Congress was the Judiciary Act of 1789, which defined the jurisdiction of the federal judiciary and established a six-member Supreme Court, thirteen district courts, and three circuit courts of appeal. Its most important provision, Section 25, allowed appeals from state courts to federal courts when cases raised certain types of constitutional issues. Section 25 thus implemented Article VI of the Constitution, which stated that federal laws and treaties were to be "the supreme Law of the Land." The Judiciary Act of 1789 presumed that the wording of Article VI implied the right of appeal from state to federal courts, although the Constitution did not explicitly permit such action. Nineteenth-century states' rights advocates would challenge this interpretation.

In a significant 1796 decision, *Ware v. Hylton,* the Court for the first time declared a state law unconstitutional. That same year it also reviewed the constitutionality of an act of Congress, upholding it in the case of *Hylton v. U.S.* The most important case of the decade, *Chisholm v. Georgia* (1793), established that states could be sued in federal courts by citizens of other states. The Eleventh Amendment to the Constitution overruled this decision, which was unpopular with state governments, five years later.

In early 1790, three groups of Quakers petitioned Congress to end the foreign slave trade, despite the

DEBATE OVER SLAVERY

constitutional provisions forbidding such action before 1808. The ensuing debates directly addressed the questions suppressed in euphemisms in the Constitution itself. Southerners vigorously asserted that Congress not only should reject the petitions but should not even discuss them seriously. The legislators went on to develop a positive defense of slavery, insisting that abolition would cause more problems than it solved, primarily by confronting the nation with how to deal with a sizable population of freed people. Some northern congressmen contested the southerners' position, but a consensus soon emerged to quash such discussions in the future. Congress accepted a committee report denying it the power to halt the slave trade before 1808 or effect the emancipation of any slaves at any time, that authority "remaining with the several States alone."

Domestic Policy Under Washington and Hamilton

*I*n 1783 George Washington returned to Mount Vernon eager for the peaceful life of a Virginia planter. But his fellow countrymen never regarded Washington as just another private citizen. When the new Constitution was adopted, Americans concurred that only George Washington had sufficient stature to serve as the republic's first president. The unanimous vote of the electoral college merely formalized that consensus.

Washington acted cautiously during his first months in office in 1789, knowing that whatever he did would set precedents for the future. When the title by which he should be addressed aroused controversy, Washington said nothing. The accepted title soon became a plain "Mr. President." By using the heads of the executive departments collectively as his chief advisers, he created the cabinet. As the Constitution required, he sent Congress an annual State of the Union message. Washington also concluded that he should exercise his veto power over congressional legislation very sparingly—only, indeed, if he became convinced a bill was unconstitutional.

WASHINGTON'S FIRST STEPS

Early in his term, Washington undertook elaborately organized journeys to all the states. At each stop, he was ritually welcomed by uniformed militia units, young women strewing flowers in his path, local leaders, groups of Revolutionary War veterans, and respectable citizens who gave formal addresses reaffirming their loyalty to the United States. The president thus personally came to embody national unity, simultaneously drawing ordinary folk into the sphere of national politics.

Washington's first major task as president was to choose the heads of the executive departments. For the War Department he selected Henry Knox of Massachusetts, his reliable general of artillery during the Revolution. His choice for the State Department was his fellow Virginian Thomas Jefferson, just returned from his post as minister to France. And for the crucial position of secretary of the treasury, the president chose the brilliant, intensely ambitious Alexander Hamilton.

Two traits distinguished Hamilton from most of his contemporaries. First, he displayed an undivided

ALEXANDER HAMILTON

loyalty to the nation as a whole. The illegitimate son of an aristocrat, Hamilton had grown up in poverty in the West Indies and had lived on the mainland only briefly before the war. He had no ties to a particular state, and he showed little sympathy for, or understanding of, demands for local autonomy. Thus, the aim of his fiscal policies was always to consolidate power at the national level. Furthermore, he never feared the exercise of centralized executive authority, as did older counterparts who had clashed repeatedly with colonial governors, and he was not afraid of maintaining close political and economic ties with Britain.

Second, Hamilton regarded his fellow human beings with unvarnished cynicism. Perhaps because of his difficult early life and his own overriding ambition, Hamilton believed people are motivated primarily by self-interest—particularly economic self-interest. He placed no reliance on people's capacity for virtuous and self-sacrificing behavior and could not envision that public-spirited citizens would pursue the common good rather than their own private advantage.

In 1789, Congress ordered the new secretary of the treasury to assess the public debt and submit recommendations for supporting the government's credit. Hamilton found that the country's remaining war debts fell into three categories: those owed by the nation to foreign governments and investors, mostly to France (about $11 million); those owed by the national government to merchants, former soldiers, holders of revolutionary bonds, and the like (about $27 million); and, finally, similar debts owed by state governments (roughly $25 million). With respect to the national debt, few disagreed: Americans recognized that if their new government was to succeed, it would have to repay at full face value those financial obligations incurred by the nation while winning independence.

NATIONAL AND STATE DEBTS

The state debts were another matter. Some states—notably Virginia, Maryland, North Carolina, and Georgia—already had paid off most of their war debts. They would oppose the national government's assumption of responsibility for other states' debts. Massachusetts, Connecticut, and South Carolina, by contrast, still had sizable unpaid debts and would welcome a system of national assumption. The possible assumption of state debts also had political implications. Consolidating the debt in the hands of the national government would help to concentrate economic and political power at the national level. A contrary policy would reserve greater independence of action for the states.

Hamilton's first *Report on Public Credit,* sent to Congress in January 1790, proposed that Congress

HAMILTON'S FINANCIAL PLAN

assume outstanding state debts, combine them with national obligations, and issue new securities covering both principal and accumulated unpaid interest. Hamilton thereby hoped to ensure that holders of the public debt—many of them wealthy merchants and speculators—had a significant financial stake in the new government's survival. The opposition coalesced around James Madison, who was against the assumption of state debts for two reasons: first, his state had already paid off most of its obligations, and second, he wanted to avoid rewarding wealthy speculators who had purchased debt certificates at a small fraction of their face value from needy veterans and farmers.

The House initially rejected the assumption of state debts. The Senate, however, adopted Hamilton's plan largely intact. A series of compromises followed, in which the assumption bill became linked with another controversial issue: the location of the permanent national capital. Several related political deals were struck. A southern site—on the Potomac River—was selected for the capital, and the first part of Hamilton's financial program became law in August 1790.

Four months later, Hamilton submitted to Congress a second report on public credit, recommending

FIRST BANK OF THE UNITED STATES

the chartering of a national bank. The Bank of the United States, to be chartered for twenty years, was to be capitalized at $10 million. Just $2 million would come from public funds. Private investors would supply the rest. The bank would also act as collecting and disbursing agent for the Treasury, and its notes would circulate as the nation's currency, providing a dependable medium of exchange. Most political leaders recognized that such an institution would be beneficial, but asked whether the Constitution gave Congress the power to establish such a bank.

James Madison answered that question with a resounding no. He pointed out that Constitutional

INTERPRETING THE CONSTITUTION

Convention delegates had specifically rejected a clause authorizing Congress to issue corporate charters. Consequently, he argued, the power to do so could not be inferred from other parts of the Constitution. Thomas Jefferson, the secretary of state, agreed with Madison. Jefferson referred to Article I, Section 8, of the Constitution, which gave Congress the power "to make all Laws which shall be necessary and proper for carrying into Execution the foregoing Powers." The key word, Jefferson argued, was *necessary:* Congress could do what was needed, but without specific constitutional authorization, it could not do what was merely desirable. Thus, Jefferson formulated the strict-constructionist interpretation of the Constitution.

Washington asked Hamilton to reply to the negative assessments of his proposal. Hamilton's *Defense of the Constitutionality of the Bank* (1791) brilliantly expounded a broad-constructionist view of the Constitution. Hamilton argued forcefully that Congress could choose any means not specifically prohibited by the Constitution to achieve a constitutional end. He reasoned thus: if the end was constitutional and the means was not unconstitutional, then the means was constitutional. Washington concurred, and the bill became law. Both the bank and the debt-funding scheme proved successful. The new nation's securities became desirable investments, and the capital they attracted contributed to a new prosperity.

In December 1791, Hamilton presented to Congress his *Report on Manufactures,* outlining an

HAMILTON'S REPORT ON MANUFACTURES

ambitious plan for encouraging and protecting the United States's infant industries. Hamilton argued that the nation could never be truly independent as long as it relied heavily on Europe for manufactured goods. He thus urged Congress to promote the immigration of technicians and laborers and to support industrial development through a limited use of protective tariffs. Many of Hamilton's ideas were implemented in later decades, but in 1791 most congressmen firmly believed that America's future lay in agriculture and the carrying trade and that the mainstay of the republic was the virtuous small farmer. Therefore, Congress rejected the report.

That same year, Congress accepted Hamilton's proposed tax on whiskey produced within the United

States. Although proceeds from the Revenue Act of 1789 covered the interest on the national debt, the decision to fund state debts meant that the national government required additional income. A tax on whiskey affected relatively few farmers—those west of the mountains who sold their grain in the form of distilled spirits to avoid the high cost of transportation. Moreover, Hamilton knew that those western farmers were Jefferson's supporters, and he saw the benefits of taxing them rather than the merchants who supported his own policies.

News of the tax set off protests in frontier areas of Pennsylvania. Unrest continued for two years on

WHISKEY REBELLION

the frontiers of Pennsylvania, Maryland, and Virginia. President Washington responded with restraint until violence erupted in July 1794, when western Pennsylvania farmers resisted a federal marshal and a tax collector trying to enforce the law. Three rioters were killed and several militiamen wounded. About seven thousand rebels convened on August 1 to plot the destruction of Pittsburgh but decided not to face the heavy guns of the fort guarding the town. Washington then took decisive action to prevent a crisis reminiscent of Shays's Rebellion. On August 7, he called on the insurgents to disperse and summoned almost thirteen thousand militia from Pennsylvania and neighboring states. By the time federal forces marched westward in October and November, the disturbances had ceased.

The chief importance of the Whiskey Rebellion's suppression lay in the message it conveyed to the American people. The national government, Washington had demonstrated, would not allow violent resistance to its laws. In the republic, change would be effected peacefully, by legal means.

The French Revolution and the Development of Partisan Politics

By 1794, some Americans were already beginning to seek change systematically through electoral politics, even though traditional political theory regarded organized opposition as illegitimate. In a republic, serious and sustained disagreement was taken as a sign of corruption and subversion.

Jefferson and Madison became convinced as early as 1792 that Hamilton's policy of favoring

DEMOCRATIC- REPUBLICANS AND FEDERALISTS

wealthy commercial interests at the expense of agriculture aimed at imposing a corrupt, aristocratic government on the United States. Characterizing themselves as the true heirs of the Revolution, Jefferson, Madison, and their followers in Congress began calling themselves Democratic-Republicans. Hamilton likewise accused Jefferson and Madison of plot-

■ A Federalist political cartoon from the 1790s shows "Mad Tom" Paine "in a rage," trying to destroy the federal government as carefully constructed (in classical style) by President Washington and Vice President Adams. That Paine is being aided by the Devil underscores the hostility to partisanship common in the era.   (The Huntington Library, Art Collections, and Botanical Gardens, San Marino, California/Superstock)

ting to destroy the republic. He and his supporters began calling themselves Federalists, to legitimize their claims and link themselves with the Constitution. Each group accused the other of being an illicit faction working to sabotage the republican principles of the Revolution. (By traditional definition, a faction was opposed to the public good.) Newspapers aligned with the two sides fueled partisanship, publishing virulent attacks on their political opponents.

At first, President Washington tried to remain aloof from the political dispute that divided Hamilton and Jefferson, his chief advisers. Yet the growing controversy helped persuade him to seek a second term of office in 1792 in hopes of promoting political unity. But in 1793 and thereafter, developments in foreign affairs magnified the disagreements.

In 1789 Americans welcomed the news of the French Revolution and France's move toward republicanism. But by the early 1790s, the reports from France were disquieting. Outbreaks of violence continued, ministries succeeded each other with bewildering rapidity, and executions mounted—the king himself was beheaded. Although many Americans, including Jefferson and Madison, retained a sympathetic view of the revolution, Hamilton and others began to cite France as a prime example of the perversion of republicanism.

THE FRENCH REVOLUTION

Debates within the United States intensified when the newly republican France, fearing that neighboring monarchies would crush the revolution and seeking to spread republicanism throughout the continent, declared war first on Austria and then, in 1793, on Britain, Spain, and Holland. Americans faced a dilemma. The 1778 Treaty of Alliance with France bound them to that nation "forever," and a mutual commitment to republicanism created ideological bonds. Yet the United States was connected to Great Britain as well. Beyond the shared history and language, Great Britain was America's most important trading partner. Indeed, the financial system of the United States depended heavily on import tariffs levied on goods from the former mother country.

The political and diplomatic climate grew even more complicated in April 1793, when Citizen Edmond Genêt, a representative of the French government, landed in Charleston, South Carolina. As Genêt made his way north to New York City, he re-

CITIZEN GENÊT

cruited Americans for expeditions against British and Spanish colonies in the Western Hemisphere, freely distributing privateering commissions. Genêt's arrival raised troubling questions for President Washington. Should he receive Genêt, thus officially recognizing the French revolutionary government? Should he acknowledge an obligation to aid France under the terms of the 1778 Treaty of Alliance? Or should he proclaim American neutrality?

For once, Hamilton and Jefferson saw eye to eye. Both told Washington that the United States could not afford to ally itself with either side. Washington concurred. He received Genêt but also issued a proclamation informing the world that the United States would adopt "a conduct friendly and impartial toward the belligerent powers."

Genêt himself disappeared from the diplomatic scene when his faction fell from power in Paris, but the domestic divisions he helped to widen were perpetuated by clubs called Democratic-Republican societies. These activist organizations were formed by Americans sympathetic to the French Revolution and worried about the policies of the Washington administration.

More than forty Democratic-Republican societies were organized between 1793 and 1800. Their members saw themselves as heirs of the Sons of Liberty, seeking the same goal as their predecessors: protection of people's liberties against encroachments by corrupt and self-serving rulers. To that end, they publicly protested the Washington administration's fiscal and foreign policy and repeatedly proclaimed their belief in the rights to free speech, free press, and assembly. Like the Sons of Liberty, the Democratic-Republican societies chiefly comprised artisans and craftsmen, although professionals, farmers, and merchants also joined.

DEMOCRATIC-REPUBLICAN SOCIETIES

The rapid growth of such groups deeply disturbed Hamilton and eventually Washington himself. Some newspapers charged that the societies were subversive agents of a foreign power. The counterattack climaxed in the fall of 1794, when Washington accused the societies of having fomented the Whiskey Rebellion.

In retrospect, Washington and Hamilton's reaction to the Democratic-Republican societies seems disproportionately hostile. But at the time, factions were seen as dangerous, and the idea that a loyal opposition was part of a free government had not yet been accepted.

Partisan Politics and Relations with Great Britain

In 1794 George Washington dispatched Chief Justice John Jay to London to negotiate four unresolved questions in Anglo-American relations. The first point at issue was recent British seizures of American merchant ships trading in the French West Indies. The United States wanted to establish the principle of freedom of the seas and assert its right, as a neutral nation, to trade freely with both combatants. Second, in violation of the 1783 peace treaty, Great Britain had not yet evacuated its posts in the American Northwest. The Americans also hoped for a commercial treaty and sought compensation for the slaves who left with the British army at the end of the war.

The negotiations in London proved difficult, since Jay had little to offer in exchange for the concessions he sought. Britain did agree to evacuate the western forts and ease restrictions on American trade with England and the West Indies. The treaty established two arbitration commissions—one to deal with prewar debts Americans owed to British creditors and the other to hear claims for captured American merchant ships—but Britain adamantly refused to compensate slaveowners for their lost bondspeople. Under the circumstances, Jay did remarkably well: the treaty averted a war with England that the United States could not have won at the time. Nevertheless, most Americans, including the president, were dissatisfied.

JAY TREATY

The Senate debated the Jay Treaty in secret, so members of the public did not learn its provisions until after Senate ratification in June 1795. The Democratic-Republican societies led protests against the treaty. Especially vehement opposition arose in the South over the failure to obtain compensation for runaway slaves and against the commission on prewar debts, which might require planters to pay off sizable obligations to British merchants. Once President Washington had signed the treaty, though, there seemed little the Democratic-Republicans could do to prevent it from taking effect. Just one opportunity remained: Congress had to appropriate funds to carry out the treaty provisions.

When the House debated the issue in March 1796, members opposing the treaty tried to prevent approval of the appropriations. To that end, they asked Washington to submit to the House all documents pertinent to the negotiations. In successfully resisting the House's request, Washington established the doctrine of executive privilege: the power of the president to withhold information from Congress if he believes circumstances warrant doing so.

In the end, the House appropriated the money for the Jay Treaty. In 1795 Thomas Pinckney of South Carolina had negotiated a treaty with Spain giving the United States navigation privileges on the Mississippi River, a boon to the South and West. Regional interests and the popularity of Pinckney's Treaty helped overcome opposition to the Jay Treaty.

Analysis of the vote reveals both the regional nature of divisions and the growing cohesion of the Democratic-Republican and Federalist factions in Congress. Voting for the appropriations were 44 Federalists and 7 Democratic-Republicans; voting against were 45 Democratic-Republicans and 3 Federalists. The final tally also divided by region: southerners cast the vast majority of votes against the bill.

PARTISAN DIVISIONS IN CONGRESS

The small number of defectors on both sides reveals a new force at work in American politics: partisanship. Voting statistics from the first four Congresses show the ever-increasing tendency of members of the House of Representatives to vote as cohesive groups rather than as individuals. The growing division cannot be explained in the terms used by Jefferson and Madison (aristocrats versus the people) or by Hamilton and Washington (true patriots versus subversive rabble). Simple economic differences between agrarian and commercial interests do not provide the answer either.

Nevertheless, certain distinctions can be made. Democratic-Republicans, especially prominent in the southern and middle states, tended to be self-assured, confident, and optimistic about both politics and the economy. Southern planters, firmly in control of their region and of a class of enslaved laborers, foresaw a prosperous future

BASES OF PARTISANSHIP

based partly on continued westward expansion, a movement they expected to dominate. Democratic-Republicans employed democratic rhetoric to win the allegiance of small farmers south of New England. Members of non-English ethnic groups—especially Irish, Scots, and Germans—found Democratic-Republicans' words attractive. Democratic-Republicans of all descriptions emphasized developing America's own resources, worrying less than Federalists did about the nation's place in the world. Democratic-Republicans also remained sympathetic to France in international affairs.

By contrast, Federalists, concentrated in New England, came mostly from English stock. Insecure and uncertain of the future, they stressed the need for order, authority, and regularity in the political world. Federalists had no grassroots political organization and put little emphasis on involving ordinary people in government. Wealthy New England merchants aligned themselves with the Federalists, but so too did the region's farmers who, prevented from expanding agricultural production because of New England's poor soil, gravitated toward the more conservative party. Federalists, like Democratic-Republicans, assumed that southern and middle-state interests would dominate the land west of the mountains, so they had little incentive to work actively to develop that potentially rich territory. In Federalist eyes, potential enemies—both internal and external—perpetually threatened the nation, which required a continuing alliance with Great Britain for its own protection. Overall, their vision proved narrow and unattractive, holding out little hope for a better future for residents of any particular region.

The presence of the two organized groups made the presidential election of 1796 the first serious contest for the position. Wearied by criticism, George Washington decided to retire. In September Washington published his Farewell Address. In it he outlined two principles that guided American foreign policy at least until the late 1940s: to maintain commercial but not political ties to other nations and to enter no permanent alliances. He thus encouraged the nation to follow the path of independent action in foreign affairs, today called unilateralism.

WASHINGTON'S FAREWELL ADDRESS

Washington also lamented the existence of factional divisions, and historians have often interpreted

this as a call to end partisanship for the good of the whole. But in the context of the impending presidential election, the Farewell Address appears rather as an attack on the legitimacy of the Democratic-Republican opposition. Washington advocated unity behind the Federalist banner, while both sides perceived their opponents as misguided, unpatriotic troublemakers who sought to undermine revolutionary ideals.

Online Study Center   **Improve Your Grade**
Primary Source: Washington's Farewell Address

To succeed Washington, the Federalists in Congress put forward Vice President John Adams, with the diplomat Thomas Pinckney as his running mate. Congressional Democratic-Republicans chose Thomas Jefferson as their presidential candidate; Aaron Burr of New York agreed to run for vice president.

ELECTION OF 1796

That the election was contested does not mean that the people decided its outcome. Voters could cast their ballots only for electors, not for the candidates themselves, and not all electors publicly declared their preferences. State legislatures, not a popular vote, selected more than 40 percent of the members of the electoral college. Moreover, the Constitution's drafters had not foreseen the development of competing national political organizations, so the Constitution provided no way to express support for one person for president and another for vice president. The electors simply voted for two people. The man with the highest total became president; the one with the second highest, vice president. Thus, Adams, the Federalist, won the presidency with 71 votes, and Jefferson, the Democratic-Republican, with 68 votes, became the vice president.

Adams-Federalist
Jefferson-Demo-Repub

John Adams and Political Dissent

John Adams took over the presidency peculiarly blind to the partisan developments of the previous four years. As president, he never abandoned an outdated notion discarded by George Washington as early as 1794: that the president should be above politics, an independent and dignified

■ John Adams, painted in 1798 by the English artist William Winstanley. Adams wears the same suit and sword he donned for his inauguration as the second president in March 1797. The open books and quill pen on the table suggest his lifelong love of reading and writing.   (U.S. Department of the Interior, National Park Service, Adams National Historic Site)

figure. Thus, Adams kept Washington's cabinet intact, despite its key members' allegiance to his chief rival, Alexander Hamilton. Adams often adopted a passive posture, letting others (usually Hamilton) take the lead when he as president should have acted decisively. As a result, his administration gained a reputation for inconsistency. When Adams's term ended, the Federalists were severely divided. But Adams's detachment from Hamilton's maneuverings did enable him to weather the greatest international crisis the republic had yet faced: the Quasi-War with France.

The Jay Treaty improved America's relationship with Great Britain, but it provoked the French

XYZ Affair

government to retaliate by ordering its ships to seize American vessels carrying British goods. In response, Congress increased military spending, and President Adams sent three commissioners to Paris to negotiate a settlement. For months, the American commissioners sought talks with Talleyrand, the French foreign minister, but Talleyrand's agents demanded a bribe of $250,000 before negotiations could begin. The Americans reported the incident in dispatches that the president received in early March 1798. Adams informed Congress of the impasse and recommended further increases in defense appropriations.

Convinced that Adams had deliberately sabotaged the negotiations, congressional Democratic-Republicans insisted that the dispatches be turned over to Congress. Adams complied, aware that releasing the reports would work to his advantage. He withheld only the names of the French agents, referring to them as X, Y, and Z. The revelation that the Americans had been treated with contempt stimulated a wave of anti-French sentiment. Cries for war filled the air. Congress formally abrogated the Treaty of Alliance and authorized American ships to seize French vessels.

Thus began an undeclared war with France. U.S. warships and French privateers seeking to capture

Quasi-War with France

American merchant vessels fought the Quasi-War in Caribbean waters. Although Americans initially suffered heavy losses of merchant shipping, by early 1799 the U.S. Navy had established its superiority in the West Indies, easing the threat to America's vital trade in that region.

The Democratic-Republicans, who opposed war and continued to sympathize with France, could do

Alien and Sedition Acts

little to stem the tide of anti-French feelings. Since Agent Y had boasted of the existence of a "French party in America," Federalists flatly accused Democratic-Republicans (including George Logan) of traitorous designs. And Federalists saw the climate of opinion as an opportunity to deal a death blow to their opponents. Now that the country seemed to see the truth of what they had been saying ever since the Whiskey Rebellion in 1794—that Democratic-Republicans were subversive foreign agents—Federalists sought to codify that belief into law. In 1798 the Federalist-controlled Congress adopted a set of four laws known as the Alien and Sedition Acts, intended to suppress dissent and prevent further growth of the Democratic-Republican faction.

Three of the acts targeted recently arrived immigrants, whom Federalists accurately suspected of being Democratic-Republican in their sympathies. The Naturalization Act lengthened the residency period required for citizenship and ordered all resident aliens to register with the federal government. The two Alien Acts, though not immediately implemented, provided for the detention of enemy aliens in time of war and gave the president authority to deport any alien he deemed dangerous to the nation's security.

The fourth statute, the Sedition Act, sought to control both citizens and aliens. It outlawed conspiracies to prevent the enforcement of federal laws, setting the maximum punishment for such offenses at five years in prison and a $5,000 fine. The act also tried to control speech. Writing, printing, or uttering "false, scandalous and malicious" statements against the government or the president became a crime punishable by as much as two years' imprisonment and a fine of $2,000.

The Sedition Act led to fifteen indictments and ten convictions. Most of the accused were outspoken Democratic-Republican newspaper editors. But the first victim was a hot-tempered Democratic-Republican congressman from Vermont, Matthew Lyon. The Irish-born Lyon was convicted, fined $1,000, and sent to prison for four months for declaring in print that John Adams had displayed "a continual grasp for power" and "an unbounded thirst for ridiculous pomp, foolish adulation, and selfish avarice." Lyon was reelected while serving his jail term.

Faced with prosecutions of their supporters, Jefferson and Madison sought an effective way to combat the acts. In doing so, they

VIRGINIA AND KENTUCKY RESOLUTIONS

turned to the state legislatures. Carefully concealing their own role to avoid being indicted for sedition, Jefferson and Madison each drafted a set of resolutions that were introduced into the Kentucky and Virginia legislatures, respectively, in the fall of 1798. Since a compact among the states created the Constitution, they contended, people speaking through their states had a legitimate right to judge the constitutionality of actions taken by the federal government. Both sets of resolutions pronounced the Alien and Sedition Acts unconstitutional and asked other states to join in a concerted protest against them.

Although no other state endorsed them, the Virginia and Kentucky resolutions nevertheless had considerable influence. First, they constituted superb political propaganda, rallying Democratic-Republican opinion throughout the country and placing the party in the revolutionary tradition of resistance to tyrannical authority. Second, the theory of union they proposed inspired southern states' rights advocates in the 1830s and thereafter. Jefferson and Madison had identified a key constitutional issue: How far could states go in opposing the national government? How could a conflict between the two be resolved?

Meanwhile, the Federalists split over the course of action the United States should take toward

CONVENTION OF 1800

France. Hamilton and his supporters called for a declaration legitimizing the undeclared naval war. But Adams received a number of private signals, among them Logan's report, that the French government regretted its treatment of the American commissioners. Acting on such assurances, he dispatched the envoy William Vans Murray to Paris to negotiate with Napoleon Bonaparte, France's new leader. The United States sought two goals: compensation for ships the French had seized since 1793 and abrogation of the treaty of 1778. The Franco-American Convention of 1800, which ended the Quasi-War, provided for the latter but not the former. The results of the negotiations did not become known in the United States until after the presidential election of 1800. By then, divisions within the Federalist party had already cost Adams the election.

Indians and African Americans at the End of the Century

By the end of the eighteenth century, the nation had added three states (Vermont, Kentucky, and Tennessee) to the original thirteen and more than 1 million people to the nearly 4 million counted by the 1790 census. Nine-tenths of the approximately 1 million resident African Americans—most still enslaved—lived in the Chesapeake or the

Haitian Refugees

Although many European Americans initially welcomed the news of the French Revolution in 1789, few expressed similar sentiments about the slave rebellion that broke out soon after in the French colony of St. Domingue (later Haiti), which shared the island of Hispaniola with Spanish Santo Domingo. The large number of refugees who soon flowed into the new United States from that nearby revolt brought with them consequences deemed undesirable by most political leaders. Less than a decade after winning independence, the new nation confronted its first immigration crisis.

Among the approximately 600,000 residents of St. Domingue in the early 1790s were about 100,000 free people, almost all of them slaveowners; half were whites, the rest mulattos. When, in the wake of the French Revolution, those free mulattos split the slaveholding population by seeking greater social and political equality, the slaves seized the opportunity to revolt. By 1793, they had triumphed under the leadership of a former slave, Toussaint L'Ouverture, and in 1804 they finally ousted the French, thereafter establishing the republic of Haiti. Thousands of whites and mulattos, accompanied by as many slaves as they could readily transport, sought asylum in the United States during those turbulent years.

Although willing to offer shelter to refugees from the violence, American political leaders nonetheless feared the consequences of their arrival. Southern plantation owners shuddered at the thought that slaves so familiar with ideas of freedom and equality would mingle with their own bondspeople. Many were uncomfortable with the immigration of numerous free people of color, even though the immigrants were part of the slaveholding class. Most of the southern states adopted laws forbidding the entry of Haitian slaves and free mulattos, but the laws were difficult, if not impossible, to enforce, as was a later congressional act to the same effect. And so more than 15,000 refugees—white, black, and of mixed race origins—flooded into the United States and Spanish Louisiana. Many ended up in Virginia (which did not pass an exclusion law) or the cities of Charleston, Savannah, and New Orleans.

There they had a considerable impact on the existing population. In both New Orleans and Charleston, the influx of mulattos gave rise to heightened color consciousness that placed light-skinned people at the top of a hierarchy of people of color. Not coincidentally, the Charleston Brown Fellowship Society, composed exclusively of free mulattos, was founded in 1793. After the United States purchased Louisiana in 1803, the number of free people of color in the territory almost doubled in three years, largely because of a final surge of immigration from the new Haitian republic. And in Virginia, stories of the successful revolt helped to inspire local slaves in 1800 when they planned the action that has become known as Gabriel's Rebellion.

The Haitian refugees thus linked both European and African Americans to current events in the West Indies, indelibly affecting both groups of people.

A free woman of color in Louisiana early in the nineteenth century, possibly one of the refugees from Haiti. Esteban Rodriguez Miró, named governor of Spanish Louisiana in 1782, ordered all slave and free black women to wear head wraps rather than hats—which were reserved for whites—but this woman and many others subverted his order by nominally complying, but nevertheless creating elaborate headdresses.
(Louisiana State Museum)

Lower South. And by 1800, all the Indian nations residing in U.S. territory east of the Mississippi River had made peace with the republic.

The new nation's policymakers, all of European American descent, could not ignore such large proportions of the population. How should the republic deal with eastern Indians, who no longer posed a military threat to the country? Did the growing population of bondspeople present new hazards? The second question took on added significance after 1793, when a bloody revolt of mulattos and blacks led by Toussaint L'Ouverture overthrew French rule in St. Domingue (Haiti).

In 1789 Secretary of War Knox proposed that the new national government assume the task of "civilizing" America's indigenous population. The first step in such a project, Knox suggested, should be to introduce to Indian peoples "a love for exclusive property"; to that end, he proposed that the government give livestock to individual Indians. Four years later, the Indian Trade and Intercourse Act of 1793 codified Knox's plan, promising Indians federally supplied animals, agricultural implements, and instructors.

"CIVILIZING" THE INDIANS

This well-intentioned plan reflected federal officials' blindness to the realities of native peoples' lives. It ignored both the Indians' traditional commitment to communal notions of landowning and the centuries-long agricultural experience of eastern Indian peoples. The policymakers focused only on Indian men: since they hunted, male Indians were "savages" who had to be "civilized" by being taught to farm. That in these societies women traditionally did the farming was irrelevant because in the eyes of the officials, Indian women—like those of European descent—should properly confine themselves to child rearing, household chores, and home manufacturing.

Indian nations at first responded cautiously to the "civilizing" plan. In the 1790s, people of the Iroquois Confederacy lived in what one historian has called "slums in the wilderness," restricted to small reservations amid expanding Anglo-American farmlands and no longer able to hunt. Quaker missionaries started a demonstration farm among the Senecas, intending to teach men to plow, but women showed greater interest in their message. The same was true among the Chero-

IROQUOIS AND CHEROKEES

kees of Georgia. As their southern hunting territories were reduced, Cherokee men did begin to raise cattle and hogs, but they startled the reformers by treating livestock like wild game, allowing the animals to run free in the woods and simply shooting them when needed. Men also started to plow the fields, although Cherokee women continued to bear primary responsibility for cultivation and harvest.

Iroquois men became more receptive to the Quakers' lessons after the spring of 1799, when a Seneca named Handsome Lake experienced a remarkable series of visions. Like other prophets stretching back to Neolin (see Chapter 5), Handsome Lake preached that Indian peoples should renounce alcohol, gambling, and other destructive European customs. He directed his followers to heed the Quakers' lessons, but in doing so, he aimed above all to preserve Iroquois culture. Handsome Lake recognized that since men could no longer hunt to obtain meat, only by adopting the European sexual division of labor could the Iroquois retain an autonomous existence.

Online Study Center **Improve Your Grade**
Interactive Map: African American Population, 1790

African Americans had long been forced to conform to European American notions of proper gender roles and had embraced Christianity. Yet just as Cherokees and Iroquois adapted the reformers' plans to their own purposes, so too enslaved blacks found new meanings in the dominant society's ideas. African Americans (both slave and free) became familiar with concepts of liberty and equality during the Revolution. They also witnessed the benefits of fighting collectively for freedom rather than resisting individually or running away. And as white evangelicals by the end of the century began to back away from their earlier racial egalitarianism, African Americans increasingly formed their own separate Baptist and Methodist congregations.

Such congregations near Richmond became the seedbeds of revolt. Gabriel, an enslaved blacksmith who argued that African Americans should fight for their freedom, carefully planned a large-scale rebellion. Often accompanied by his brother Martin, a preacher, he visited Sunday church services, where blacks gathered outside the watchful eyes of their owners. Gabriel first recruited to his cause other skilled African Americans

GABRIEL'S REBELLION

who like himself lived in semifreedom under minimal supervision. Next he enlisted rural slaves. The conspirators planned to attack Richmond on the night of August 30, 1800, set fire to the city, seize the state capitol, and capture the governor. At that point, Gabriel believed, other slaves and sympathetic poor whites would join in.

The plan showed considerable political sophistication, but heavy rain forced a postponement. Several planters then learned of the plan from slave informers and spread the alarm. Gabriel avoided arrest for some weeks, but militia troops quickly apprehended and interrogated most of the other leaders of the rebellion. Twenty-six conspirators, including Gabriel himself, were hanged, but that did not end the unrest among Virginia's slaves.

At his trial, one of Gabriel's followers made explicit the links that so frightened Chesapeake slaveholders. He told his judges that, like George Washington, "I have adventured my life in endeavouring to obtain the liberty of my countrymen, and am a willing sacrifice in their cause." Southern state legislatures responded to such claims by increasing the severity of the laws regulating slavery. Before long, all talk of emancipation ceased in the South, and slavery became even more firmly entrenched as an economic institution and way of life.

Summary ⟨Online Study Center⟩ ACE the Test

*A*s the nineteenth century began, inhabitants of the United States faced changed lives in the new republic. Indian peoples east of the Mississippi River found that they had to give up some parts of their traditional culture to preserve others. Some African Americans struggled unsuccessfully to free themselves from the inhuman bonds of slavery, then subsequently confronted more constraints than ever before because of increasingly restrictive laws.

European Americans too adjusted to changed circumstances. The first eleven years of government under the Constitution established many enduring precedents for congressional, presidential, and judicial action—among them the establishment of the cabinet, interpretations of key clauses of the Constitution, and the stirrings of judicial review of state and federal legislation. Building on successful negotiations with Spain, Britain, and France, the United States de-

veloped its diplomatic independence, striving to avoid entanglement with European countries and their wars. The 1790s also spawned vigorous debates over foreign and domestic policy and saw the beginnings of a system of organized political factionalism.

At the end of the 1790s, after more than a decade of struggle, the Jeffersonian view of the future of republicanism prevailed over Hamilton's vision. For decades to come, the country would be characterized by a decentralized economy, minimal government, and maximum freedom of action and mobility for individual white men. Jeffersonians failed to extend to white women, Indian peoples, and African Americans the freedom and individuality they recognized as essential for themselves.

LEGACY FOR A PEOPLE AND A NATION
Dissent During Wartime

The Quasi-War with France in 1798 and 1799, the nation's first overseas conflict, brought the first attempt to suppress dissent. The Sedition Act of 1798 tried to quiet the Democratic-Republicans' criticism of the war and President John Adams. Ten men were fined and jailed after being convicted under the statute's provisions.

Americans might assume that their right to free speech under the First Amendment, more fully accepted now than it was two hundred years ago, today protects dissenters during war, but the history of the nation suggests otherwise. Each major conflict fought under the Constitution—the Civil War, World War I, World War II, and Vietnam—has stimulated efforts by both government and individual citizens to suppress dissenting voices. For example, during the Civil War, the Union jailed civilian Confederate sympathizers, holding them under martial law for long periods. During World War I, a Sedition Act allowed the government to deport immigrant aliens who too vocally criticized the war effort. Moreover, citizens who objected to government policies endured a variety of formal and informal sanctions by their neighbors. During World War II, those who had opposed American entry into the war were denied public outlets for their ideas. The divisions over antiwar protests in the Vietnam era still affect the nation today. Although during the first Persian Gulf war (1991) and the Afghanistan campaign (2001), military officials restricted reporters' access to the battlefront, that policy was reversed during the war against Iraq (2003), with mixed results.

Freedom of speech is never easy to maintain, and wartime conditions make it much more difficult. When the nation comes under attack, many patriotic Americans argue that the time for dissent has ceased. Others contend that if freedom in the nation is to mean anything, people must have the right to speak their minds freely at all times. Events in the United States since the attacks of September 11, 2001, suggest that this legacy remains extremely contentious for the American people.

PARTISAN POLITICS AND WAR: THE DEMOCRATIC-REPUBLICANS IN POWER 1801–1815

John Foss, captured by "pirates" off the Barbary Coast of North Africa in the 1790s, wrote of the "hellish tortures and punishments" inflicted "on the unfortunate Christians." Marched through Algiers, the party of nine ragged sailors heard shouts from the Islamic crowds praising victories over "Christian dogs," and in prison they learned of ten other American vessels recently captured. In Algiers they became white slaves under African masters.

In the nineteenth century, the dramatic Barbary captivity stories, in telling of captives beaten as Christians and humiliated as Americans and of white slaves with black masters, turned American assumptions on their heads. Firsthand descriptions of Africa projected images of a despotic, depraved people, so very different from Americans. In the end, the Americans—at least those who survived to tell their stories—prevailed, and so the stories became epic affirmations of western culture over "barbarians."

In reality, the "pirates"—from what Europeans called the Barbary states and Africans the Maghreb—had challenged the United States in a most fundamental way: was this new nation an independent, sovereign state that could protect its citizens and commerce abroad?

The issue was money. In 1801 the *bashaw* of Tripoli, angry over the young nation's refusal to pay tribute for safe passage of its ships through the Mediterranean, declared war on the United States. President Thomas Jefferson responded by sending a naval squadron to protect American ships in the area. After two years of stalemate, Jefferson ordered a blockade of Tripoli, but the American frigate *Philadelphia* ran aground in its harbor, and three hundred American officers and sailors were captured. Jefferson refused to

Online Study Center
This icon will direct you to interactive map and primary source activities on the website
http://college.hmco.com/pic/nortonbrief7e

ransom them. With the blockade still in place, seven marines and four hundred soldiers of fortune marched overland from Egypt to seize the port of Derne, on the shores of Tripoli. Finally, by treaty with Tripoli in 1805, the United States paid $60,000 to free the *Philadelphia* prisoners, and the war was over. But the United States continued to pay tribute to the other three Barbary states until 1815. The question of U.S. independence and sovereignty still rankled.

In replacing John Adams as president, Thomas Jefferson piloted the young nation in new directions at home as well as abroad. In the tradition of the Revolution, Jefferson and his Democratic-Republican successor presidents sought to restrain the national government, believing that limited government would foster republican virtue. The Federalists advocated a strong national government with centralized authority to promote economic development. In addition to politics, divisions along lines of class, race, ethnicity, gender, religion, and region contributed to factionalism. As the factions competed for popular support, they laid the basis for a national political culture.

Events abroad and in the West both encouraged and threatened Americans. Seizing one opportunity, the United States purchased the Louisiana Territory. But as American interests turned westward, events in Europe and at sea on the Atlantic forced an about-face. Caught between the warring British and French, the United States found its ships seized, its foreign commerce interrupted, its sailors forcibly drafted, and its rights as a neutral and independent nation violated. In what some have called the second war for independence, the United States fought Great Britain to a standoff, while on another front shattering Native American unity and resistance. A peace treaty restored the prewar status quo, but the war and the treaty reaffirmed U.S. sovereignty and strengthened America's determination to steer clear of further European conflicts. The war also stimulated industry and nationalism. ■

The Jefferson Presidency and Marshall Court

*I*n later years, Thomas Jefferson would always refer to his winning the presidency as the "Revolution of 1800." The Democratic-Republicans, he believed, would restore government to its limited role, restrained and frugal. He stressed the republican virtues of independence, self-reliance, and equality, in contrast to the monarchical ambitions of the Federalists. To counter Federalist formality, Jefferson and his fellow Democratic-Republicans promoted simplicity, even in dress. They wore plain trousers instead of the wigs and knee breeches favored by George Washington and John Adams.

Yet in his inaugural address in March 1801, Jefferson reached out to his opponents. Standing in the

JEFFERSON'S INAUGURAL

Senate chamber, he appealed to the electorate not as party members but as citizens sharing common beliefs. "We are all republicans, we are all federalists," Jefferson offered, laying out his vision of a restored republicanism: "A wise and frugal government, which shall restrain men from injuring one another, which shall leave them free to regulate their pursuits of industry and improvement, and shall not take from the mouth of labor the bread it has earned."

But outgoing president John Adams was not there to hear Jefferson's call for unity. He had left Washington before dawn to avoid the Democratic-Republican takeover. He and Jefferson, once close friends, now disliked each other intensely. Despite the spirit of Jefferson's inaugural address, the Democratic-Republicans and Federalists remained bitter opponents.

To implement the restoration of republican values, Jefferson aggressively extended the Democratic-

DEMOCRATIC-REPUBLICAN ASCENDANCY

Republicans' grasp on the national government. Virtually all of the six hundred or so officials appointed during the administrations of Washington and Adams had been loyal Federalists. To bring into his administration men who shared his vision of an agrarian republic and individual liberty, Jefferson refused to recognize appointments Adams had made in the last days of his presidency and dismissed Federalist customs collectors from New England ports. He awarded vacant treasury and judicial offices to Democratic-Republicans. By July 1803, Federalists held only 130 of 316 presidentially controlled offices.

The Democratic-Republican Congress proceeded to affirm its belief in limited government. Albert Gallatin, secretary of the treasury, and Representative John Randolph of Virginia translated ideology into policy, putting the federal government on a diet. Congress repealed all internal taxes, including the whiskey tax. Gallatin cut the army budget in half and reduced the 1802 navy budget by two-thirds. He then moved to reduce the national debt from $83 million to $57 million as part of a plan to retire it altogether by 1817.

More than frugality, however, distinguished Democratic-Republicans from Federalists. Before Jefferson's election, opposition to the Alien and Sedition Acts of 1798 had helped unite Democratic-Republicans. Jefferson now declined to use the acts against his opponents, and Congress let them expire in 1801 and 1802. Congress also repealed the Naturalization Act of 1798, which had required fourteen years of residency for citizenship. The 1802 act that replaced it required only five years of residency, loyalty to the Constitution, and the forsaking of foreign allegiance and titles.

The Democratic-Republicans turned next to the judiciary, the last stronghold of Federalist power.

WAR ON THE JUDICIARY

During the 1790s, not a single Democratic-Republican had occupied the federal bench; thus, the judiciary became a battlefield following the revolution of 1800. The first skirmish erupted over repeal of the Judiciary Act of 1801, which had been passed in the final days of the Adams administration. The act created fifteen new judgeships, which Adams filled by signing "midnight" appointments until his term was just hours from expiring. The act also reduced by attrition the number of justices on the Supreme Court from six to five. Since that reduction would have denied Jefferson a Supreme Court appointment until two vacancies occurred, the new Congress, dominated by the Democratic-Republicans, repealed the 1801 act.

Partisan Democratic-Republicans next targeted opposition judges for removal. Democratic-Republicans were especially infuriated with the Federalist judges who had refused to review the Sedition Act, under which Federalists had prosecuted critics of the Adams administration. At Jefferson's prompting, the House impeached (indicted) Federal District Judge John Pickering of New Hampshire, an emotionally disturbed alcoholic. In 1805 the Senate convicted him, removing him from office.

The day Pickering was ousted, the House impeached Supreme Court Justice Samuel Chase for judicial misconduct. A staunch Federalist, Chase had repeatedly denounced Jefferson's administration from the bench. The Democratic-Republicans, however, failed to muster the two-thirds majority of senators necessary to convict him. Chase's acquittal preserved the Court's independence and established the precedent that criminal actions, not political disagreements, were the only proper grounds for impeachment. In his tenure as president, Jefferson appointed three new Supreme Court justices. Nonetheless, under Chief Justice John Marshall, the Court remained a Federalist stronghold.

In his last weeks as a lame-duck president, Adams, in an act especially galling to Jefferson, appointed Marshall as chief justice. A Virginia Federalist, Marshall was an autocrat by nature but possessed a grace and openness of manner that complemented the new Republican political style. Under Marshall's domination, the Supreme Court retained a Federalist outlook even after Democratic-Republican justices achieved a majority in 1811. Throughout his tenure (1801–1835), the Court consistently upheld federal supremacy over the states and protected the interests of commerce and capital.

JOHN MARSHALL

Marshall made the Court an equal branch of government in practice as well as theory. Judicial service, previously regarded lightly, became a coveted honor for ambitious and talented men. Marshall also

This portrait of President Thomas Jefferson was painted by Rembrandt Peale in 1805. Charles Willson Peale (Rembrandt's father) and his five sons helped establish the reputation of American art in the new nation. Rembrandt Peale achieved fame for his presidential portraits; here he has captured Jefferson in a noble pose without the usual symbols of office or power, befitting the Republican age.   (© Collection of The New York Historical Society)

unified the Court, influencing the justices to issue joint majority opinions rather than a host of individual concurring judgments. Marshall himself became the voice of the majority: from 1801 through 1810, he wrote 85 percent of the opinions, including every important one.

Marshall significantly increased the Supreme Court's power in the landmark case of *Marbury v. Madison* (1803). William Marbury, one of Adams's midnight appointees, had been named a justice of the peace in the District of Columbia.

MARBURY V. MADISON

James Madison, Jefferson's new secretary of state, declined to certify Marbury's appointment so that the president could instead appoint a Democratic-Republican. Marbury sued, requesting a writ of mandamus (a court order forcing the president to appoint him). The case presented a political dilemma. If the Supreme Court ruled in favor of Marbury and issued a writ, the president probably would not comply with it, and the Court had no way to force him to do so. But if the Federalist-dominated bench refused to issue the writ, it would be handing the Democratic-Republicans a victory.

Marshall brilliantly avoided both pitfalls. Speaking for the Court, he ruled that Marbury had a right to his appointment but that the Supreme Court could not compel Madison to honor the appointment because the Constitution did not grant the Court power to issue a writ of mandamus. In the absence of any specific mention in the Constitution, Marshall ruled, the section of the Judiciary Act of 1789 that authorized the Court to issue such writs was unconstitutional. In *Marbury v. Madison,* the Supreme Court denied itself the power to issue writs of mandamus but established its far greater power to judge the constitutionality of laws passed by Congress.

In succeeding years Marshall fashioned the theory of judicial review, the power of the Supreme Court to decide the constitutionality of legislation and presidential acts. Since the Constitution was the supreme law, he reasoned, any federal or state act contrary to the Constitution must be null and void. The Supreme Court, whose duty it was to uphold the law, would decide whether a legislative act contradicted the Constitution. The power of judicial review established in *Marbury v. Madison* permanently enhanced the independence of the judiciary.

Louisiana and Lewis and Clark

Democratic-Republicans and Federalists divided sharply over other issues; the acquisition of the Louisiana Territory in 1803 was another point of contention. Jefferson shared with many other Americans the belief that the United States was destined to expand its "empire of liberty."

By 1800 hundreds of thousands of Americans had settled in the rich Mississippi and Ohio River val-

leys, intruding on Indian lands. These settlers floated their farm goods down the Ohio and Mississippi Rivers to New Orleans for export. Whoever controlled the port of New Orleans had a hand on the throat of the American economy. Spain had owned Louisiana since acquiring it from France at the end of the Seven Years War in 1763. Americans preferred Spanish control to control by France, a much stronger power.

In secret pacts with Spain in 1800 and 1801, however, France had reacquired the territory. The United States learned of the transfer only in 1802, when Napoleon seemed poised to rebuild a French empire in the New World. Then, on the eve of ceding control to the French, Spain violated Pinckney's Treaty by denying Americans the privilege of storing their products at New Orleans prior to transshipment to foreign markets. Western farmers and eastern merchants thought a devious Napoleon had closed the port; they grumbled and talked war.

Jefferson personally took charge. To relieve the pressure for war and win western farm support, he prepared for war while sending Virginia governor James Monroe as his personal envoy to join Robert Livingston, the American minister in France. Their mission: to buy the port of New Orleans and as much of the Mississippi valley as possible. Meanwhile, Congress authorized the call-up of eighty thousand militiamen in case war became necessary. Arriving in Paris in April 1803, Monroe was astonished to learn that France already had offered to sell all 827,000 square miles of Louisiana to the United States for a mere $15 million. Napoleon had lost interest in the New World. On April 30 Monroe and Livingston signed a treaty buying the vast territory, whose exact borders and land were uncharted (see Map 9.1).

The Louisiana Purchase doubled the size of the nation and opened the way for continental expansion. But was this most popular achievement of Jefferson's presidency constitutional? The Constitution nowhere authorized the president to acquire new territory and incorporate it into the nation. But Jefferson believed that the president's implied powers to protect the nation justified the purchase. His long-standing interest in Louisiana and the West also allayed his constitutional concerns. As a naturalist and scientist, Jefferson seemed obsessed with the West—its geography, people,

LOUISIANA
PURCHASE

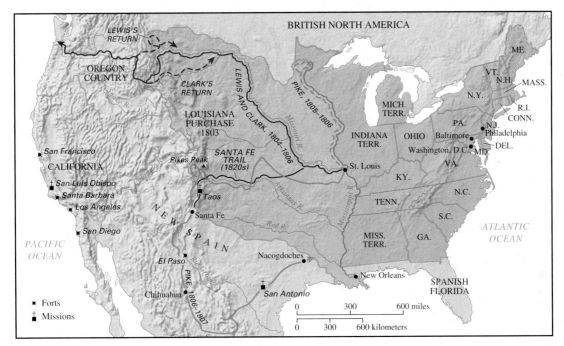

Map 9.1   Louisiana Purchase

The Louisiana Purchase (1803) doubled the area of the United States and opened the trans-Mississippi West for American settlement.

plants, and animals. He was also interested in finding "the shortest & most convenient route of communications between the U.S. & the Pacific Ocean."

In 1803 Jefferson sent an expedition headed by Meriwether Lewis and William Clark to the Pacific

LEWIS AND CLARK

coast via the Missouri and Columbia Rivers. The expedition had political as well as scientific import, for British exploration in Canada had raised fears that the British would dominate the West. Lewis and Clark officially started their journey in May 1804. They traveled up the Missouri River and wintered at Fort Mandan in present-day North Dakota. Here they selected their twenty-nine-member corps, called the Corps of Discovery, and were joined by Indian guides. In April 1805 they resumed their journey. At times they lost their way, tumbled down steep mountain trails, and slept in the snow. In November 1805 they reached the Pacific Ocean in present-day Oregon, where they wintered, and the following March they began the re-

turn trek. Lewis and Clark split up to explore alternate routes and reunited in August 1806. They arrived home in St. Louis on September 23, 1806.

Online Study Center **Improve Your Grade**
Primary Source: The President's Instructions to Meriwether Lewis

The original Corps of Discovery reflected American diversity. It included army regulars and young

CORPS OF DISCOVERY

adventurers from Kentucky. Among them were half-French, half-Omaha, and half-Shawnee men. Clark brought his slave, York. Immigrants included an Irishman and a German. Later, at the Mandan villages, Lewis and Clark took on the French Canadian trader Toussaint Charbonneau because they wanted his pregnant fifteen-year-old Shoshone wife, Sacagawea, who knew the languages of the mountain Indians. She proved invaluable as a guide and translator.

Headed by army officers, the expedition followed military rules. At times, however, it was more informal and democratic than army regulations or even civilian society allowed. When trouble arose, Lewis and Clark held courts-martial to discipline corps members for such infractions as drunkenness. Contrary to army rules, enlisted men sat on the court. And in November 1805, to determine where to locate winter quarters on the Pacific coast, all voted, including the slave York and the Indian woman Sacagawea. Yet issues of race and gender were present. At the end of the journey, the names of York and Sacagawea were not on the roster Lewis submitted to the War Department, and neither received pay for their indispensable work.

Although some Americans still believed that the West was uninhabited, Lewis and Clark knew better. They anticipated a crowded wilderness and hoped to cement U.S. relations with Indians. The explorers carried gifts for Native American leaders, both to establish goodwill and to stimulate interest in trading for American manufactured goods. They brought back stories not only of various peoples but also of fauna and flora unknown to the western scientific community. Lewis sent boxes of natural-history specimens to Jefferson, including plant and tree cuttings. The two also mapped the West and, with their reports and specimens, furthered dreams of a continental empire.

Online Study Center Improve Your Grade
Interactive Map: Louisiana Purchase and the Lewis and Clark Expedition

Other explorations followed Lewis and Clark's. In 1805 and 1806 Lieutenant Zebulon Pike sought

EXPLORATION OF THE WEST

the source of the continent-cutting river and a navigable water route to the Far West. When Pike and his men wandered into Spanish territory to the south, the Spanish held them captive for several months in Mexico. After his release, Pike wrote an account of his experiences that set commercial minds spinning. Over the next few decades, Americans avidly read accounts of western exploration. A road to the Southwest opened with the Santa Fe Trail in the 1820s, and settlement followed the trail.

New Spain's Tejas (Texas) province bordered the Louisiana Territory. Provincial officials welcomed

Americans, some of whom fought as volunteers with Indians and Mexican rebels in a twelve-year war with Spain that ended with Mexican independence in 1821. The establishment of an independent Mexico inspired these Americans to dream of an independent Texas nation—a place for white Americans. Envisioning the West as uninhabited, they did not imagine a place for Mexicans or indigenous peoples in the "empire of liberty."

A New Political Culture

Jefferson described his presidency as the beginning of a new era. Although the electorate was limited mostly to white males over age twenty-one who held property, the Democratic-Republicans had taken their appeals to the people in the elections of 1800. While Federalists thought that for candidates to debate their merits in front of voters was demeaning, a subversion of the natural political order, the Democratic-Republicans did not. Now in office, they worked hard to keep public opinion on their side.

One way to control public opinion was through the press. The new president persuaded the *National Intelligencer* to move from Philadel-

THE PARTISAN PRESS

phia to Washington, and during the ensuing Democratic-Republican administrations, it served as the official voice. In 1801 Alexander Hamilton launched the *New-York Evening Post* as the Federalist voice. While boosting Federalists, it often called Jefferson a liar and depicted him as head of a slave harem. Newspapers circulated widely and were often read aloud in taverns, coffeehouses, and hotels. Like the political parties, they helped build a national political culture. In 1800 the nation had 260 newspapers; by 1810 it had 396. Editors were outrageously partisan.

After the Federalist defeat in 1800, a younger generation of Federalists began to imitate the Democratic-Republicans. Led by such men as Josiah Quincy, a Massachusetts congressman, the Younger Federalists presented their faction as the people's party, portraying Democratic-Republicans as autocratic planters. In attacking frugal government, the Younger Federalists played on fears of a weakened army and navy. Eastern merchants depended on a strong navy to protect ocean trade; westerners looked to the army to defend them as they encroached on Indian territory.

For Democratic-Republicans, distinctive regional interests inspired a new style of campaigning, symbolized by the political barbecue.

GRASSROOTS CAMPAIGNING

In New York, campaigners roasted oxen; on the New England coast, they held clambakes. Guests washed down their meals with beer and punch and listened to the lengthy orations of candidates. The speakers attacked their opponents' character, resorting to slander and gossip and often making wild accusations. Some historians have speculated that these developing party rituals helped contain more violent expression.

The Federalists never mastered the art of campaigning. Older Federalists remained opposed to popular appeals. And though strong in Connecticut, Delaware, and a few other states, the Federalists were weak at the national level and could not manage sustained competition. The extremism of some Older Federalists discredited most of the rest. For instance, Timothy Pickering, a Massachusetts congressman and former secretary of state, opposed the Louisiana Purchase, feared Jefferson's reelection, and urged the secession of New England in 1803 and 1804. He won some support, but most Federalists balked at his plan for secession. Ever the opportunist, Vice President Aaron Burr, intrigued with Pickering's idea, fantasized about leading New York into secession, with other states following. But when Burr lost his bid to become governor of New York in 1804, dreams of a northern confederacy evaporated.

The controversies surrounding Burr illustrate the convergence of the political and the personal. In the election of 1800, he understood he

BURR AND PERSONAL ANIMOSITY

was the vice-presidential candidate, but when all seventy-three of the Democratic-Republican electors cast ballots for both Jefferson and Burr, Burr challenged Jefferson for the presidency. The Constitution required that because neither had a plurality, the contest be decided in the House of Representatives, with each state's congressmen voting as a unit. It took thirty-five ballots for the House, still with a Federalist majority, to decide that Jefferson would be a lesser evil than Burr. In response

to the tangle, the Twelfth Amendment to the Constitution (1804) changed the method of voting in the electoral college to allow for a party ticket.

For Burr it was a short step from personal animosity into violence. He and the hothead Alexander Hamilton had long despised each other. Hamilton thwarted Burr's attempt to steal the election of 1800 from Jefferson, and in the 1804 mudslinging New York gubernatorial race, he backed Burr's Democratic-Republican rival. When Hamilton accused Burr of being a liar, Burr challenged him to a duel. With his honor at stake, Hamilton accepted even though his son Philip had died in 1801 from dueling wounds. Because New York had outlawed dueling, the two men met across the Hudson River at Weehawken, New Jersey, in July 1804. Hamilton did not fire, and he paid for that decision with his life. Burr was indicted for murder.

His political career in ruins, Burr schemed to create in the Southwest a new empire carved out of the Louisiana Territory. With the collusion of General James Wilkinson, the U.S. commander in the Mississippi valley, Burr planned to raise a private army to grab land from the United States or from Spain (his exact plans remain unknown). Wilkinson switched sides and informed President Jefferson of Burr's devious intention. Jefferson personally assisted the prosecution in Burr's 1807 trial for treason, over which Chief Justice Marshall presided. The jury acquitted Burr, who fled to Europe.

Campaigning for reelection in 1804, Jefferson took credit for the restoration of republican values and

ELECTION OF 1804

the acquisition of the Louisiana Territory. The Democratic-Republicans claimed they ended the Federalist threat to liberty by repealing the Alien and Sedition and Judiciary Acts and boasted of reducing the size of government by cutting spending. American trade with Europe was flourishing, allowing Jefferson to demonstrate support for commerce too.

Jefferson's opponent in 1804 was Charles Cotesworth Pinckney, a wealthy South Carolina lawyer and former Revolutionary War aide to George Washington. As Adams's running mate in 1800, Pinckney had inherited the Federalist leadership. Jefferson and his running mate, George Clinton of New York, easily won the election.

Indian Resistance

*L*ewis and Clark's account testified to the Indian presence in the West, and most Americans viewed Native Americans, no matter where they lived, as obstacles to American settlement. Violations of treaties and coerced new ones forcing Indians to cede ever more land continually shrank Indian territory.

In the early 1800s two Shawnee brothers, Prophet (1775–1837) and Tecumseh (1768–1813), challenged

THE PROPHET

further American encroachment by fostering a pan-Indian federation that stretched from the Old Northwest to the South. Prophet's early life typified Indians' experiences in the Old Northwest. Born in 1775, Prophet, called Lalawethika ("Noisemaker"), was expelled as a young man to Ohio with

other Shawnees under the 1795 Treaty of Greenville (see Chapter 7), and he later moved to Indiana. Within Prophet and Tecumseh's own lifetimes, the Shawnees had lost most of their Ohio land. Displacement left Lalawethika forlorn, and he turned to whiskey for escape. He also turned to traditional folk knowledge and remedies and in 1804 became a tribal medicine man. His medicine, however, could not stop the white man's diseases from ravaging his village.

Lalawethika emerged from his own battle with illness in 1805 as a new man, called Tenskwatawa ("the Open Door"), or "the Prophet." Claiming to have died and been resurrected, he traveled widely in the Ohio River valley, attacking the decline of moral values among Native Americans, warning of damnation for those who drank whiskey, and condemning intertribal battles. He urged Indians to return to the

■ The Shawnee chiefs Tecumseh *(left)* and Prophet *(right)*. The two brothers led a revival of traditional Shawnee culture and preached Native American federation against white encroachment. In the War of 1812 they allied themselves with the British, but Tecumseh's death at the Battle of the Thames (1813) and British indifference thereafter caused Native Americans' resistance and unity to collapse.   (Left: MPI/Hulton Archives/Getty Images; Right: © Smithsonian American Art Museum, Washington, D.C./Art Resource, NY)

old ways and abandon white customs. Prophet's outspoken opposition to federal Indian policy drew others into his camp, and as his message spread to southern tribes, the federal government and white settlers became alarmed.

By 1808 Prophet and his older brother, Tecumseh, talked less about spiritual renewal and more about

TECUMSEH | resisting American aggression. Together they invited Indians from all nations to settle in pan-Indian towns in Indiana, first at Greenville (1806–1808) on the Wabash, called Prophetstown by whites, and then at Tippecanoe (1808–1812). The new towns challenged the treaty-making process, and the Americans viewed them as places promoting Indian resistance. In effect, Tecumseh was turning Prophet's religious movement into a political one. In repudiating land cessions to the government under the Treaty of Fort Wayne (1809), Tecumseh told Indiana's governor, William Henry Harrison, at Vincennes in 1810 that "the only way to check and stop this evil is, for all the red men to unite in claiming a common and equal right in the land, . . . for it . . . belongs to all, for the use of each. . . . No part has a right to sell, even to each other, much less to strangers."

Tecumseh, a towering six-foot warrior and charismatic orator, sought to unify northern and southern Indians by traveling widely, preaching Indian resistance. And he warned Harrison that Indians would resist white occupation of the 2.5 million acres on the Wabash River that they had ceded in the Treaty of Fort Wayne.

But the Indians could not match the armed might of the United States. In November 1811, while Tecumseh was recruiting support in the South, Harrison moved against the Prophet and his followers. In the Battle of Tippecanoe, the army burned the town and dispersed Prophet's and Tecumseh's supporters. The spiritual and political movement initiated by the brothers began to unravel.

American Shipping Imperiled

"*P*eace, commerce, and honest friendship with all nations, entangling alliance with none," President Jefferson had proclaimed in his first inaugural address. Jefferson's efforts to stand aloof from European conflict were successful until 1805. Thereafter, the United States could not escape the web of European hostilities.

The economy of the early republic relied heavily on shipping, and the commercial fleet extended

U.S. COMMERCE | American trade not only to Britain but around the world. American fishermen explored the Atlantic, while whalers hunted in the Atlantic and Pacific. Americans exported cotton, lumber, sugar, and other commodities to Europe, and brought back manufactured goods. The slave trade lured American sailing ships to Africa. Boston, Salem, and Philadelphia merchants opened trade with China, sending cloth and metal to swap for furs with Chinook Indians on the Oregon coast, then sailing to China to trade for porcelain, tea, and silk.

The root of America's problems lay in the May 1803 renewal of the Napoleonic wars between France and Britain. Initially American commerce benefited from the conflict, as the United States became the chief supplier of grain to Europe. American merchants also gained control of most of the West Indian trade. But by 1806, France and Britain, locked in a military stalemate, launched a commercial war, blockading each other's trade. As a trading partner of both countries, the United States paid a high price.

All tension focused on the high seas as Britain suffered a severe shortage of sailors, and those in

IMPRESSMENT OF AMERICAN SAILORS | service, demoralized by harsh treatment, frequently deserted. The Royal Navy resorted to stopping American vessels and impressing, or forcibly detaining, British deserters, British-born naturalized American seamen, and other unlucky sailors suspected of being British. Perhaps six to eight thousand Americans were impressed in this way between 1803 and 1812.

Anglo-American relations steadily deteriorated. Then in June 1807, the forty-gun frigate U.S.S.

CHESAPEAKE AFFAIR | *Chesapeake* left Norfolk, Virginia, and while still inside American territorial waters met the fifty-gun British frigate *Leopard*. When the *Chesapeake* refused to be searched for deserters, the *Leopard* repeatedly fired its cannon broadside into the American ship. Three Americans were killed and eighteen wounded. The British seized four deserters from the Royal Navy—three of them

American citizens. Damaged and humiliated, the *Chesapeake* returned to port.

Had the United States been better prepared militarily, the ensuing howl of public indignation might have brought about a declaration of war. But the still-fledgling country was no match for the British navy. With Congress in recess, Jefferson was able to avoid hostilities. In July the president closed American waters to British warships and soon after increased military and naval expenditures. In December 1807 Jefferson again put economic pressure on Great Britain by invoking the Non-Importation Act, followed eight days later by a new restriction, the Embargo Act.

The Embargo Act forbade all exports from the United States to any country, an action that Jefferson perceived as a short-term measure to avoid war. Exports dropped by some 80 percent in 1808. Mercantile New England, a bastion of Federalist opposition to Jefferson, was especially hard hit, and in the winter of 1808–1809 talk of secession spread from one port to another.

EMBARGO ACT

Few American policies were as well intentioned and as unpopular and unsuccessful as Jefferson's embargo. Moreover, the embargo had little impact on Britain, and France used the policy as an excuse to set privateers against American ships that had evaded the embargo. The French cynically claimed that such ships were British vessels in disguise because the embargo prevented American ships from sailing.

Although general unemployment soared, U.S. manufacturers received a boost from the embargo, since the domestic market became theirs exclusively, and merchants began to shift their capital from shipping to manufacturing. Factories were still new in America. English immigrant Samuel Slater set up the first American textile mill in Rhode Island in the 1790s. It used water-powered spinning machines that he had built from memorized British models. Although Federalists like Alexander Hamilton had pushed the United States to promote manufacturing, Jefferson envisioned an "empire of liberty" that was agricultural and commercial, not industrial. Democratic-Republican policy did not promote industry, but disruption in commerce made domestic manufactures profitable. In 1807 there were

DOMESTIC MANUFACTURING

twenty cotton and woolen mills in New England; by 1813 there were more than two hundred.

As the election of 1808 approached, the Democratic-Republicans faced factional dissent and dissatisfaction in seaboard states hobbled by the embargo. Jefferson followed Washington's lead in renouncing a third term. He supported James Madison, his secretary of state, as the Democratic-Republican standard-bearer. Madison won the endorsement of the party's congressional caucus and with his running mate, Vice President George Clinton, defeated the Federalist ticket.

ELECTION OF 1808

Under the pressure of domestic opposition, the embargo eventually collapsed. In its place, the Non-Intercourse Act of 1809 reopened trade with all nations except Britain and France, and it authorized the president to resume trade with Britain or France if either ceased to violate neutral rights. Although the new law solved the problems created by the embargo, it did not prevent further British and French interference with American commerce.

NON-INTERCOURSE ACT

When the Non-Intercourse Act expired in 1810, Congress substituted Macon's Bill Number 2, which reopened trade with both Great Britain and France but provided that when either nation stopped violating American commercial rights, the president could suspend American commerce with the other. Madison, eager to avoid war, fell victim to French duplicity. When Napoleon accepted the offer, Madison declared nonintercourse with Great Britain in 1811. The French, however, continued to seize American ships, and nonintercourse failed a second time. But because the Royal Navy dominated the seas, Britain, not France, became the main focus of American hostility.

"Mr. Madison's War"

*a*lthough unprepared for war in 1812, the United States under President Madison, having exhausted all efforts to alter British policy and fearing for the survival of American independence, seemed unable to avoid it. The Democratic-Republican "War Hawks," elected to Congress in

Industrial Piracy

Although Americans pride themselves on inventiveness and hard work, their start in industrial development depended on importing technology, sometimes by stealth. Great Britain, which in the late eighteenth century had pioneered the invention of mechanical weaving and power looms, knew the value of its head start in the industrial revolution and prohibited the export of textile technology. But the British-born brothers Samuel and John Slater, their Scottish-born power-loom-builder William Gilmore, and Bostonians Francis Cabot Lowell and Nathan Appleton evaded British restrictions and patents to establish America's first textile factories.

As an apprentice and then a supervisor in a British cotton-spinning factory, Samuel Slater had mastered the machinery and the process. Britain forbade the export of textile technology, so Slater emigrated to the United States disguised as a farmer. In 1790 in Pawtucket, Rhode Island, on the Blackstone River, he opened the first water-powered spinning mill in America, rebuilding the complex machines from memory. With his brother John and their Rhode Island partners, Moses and Obadiah Brown and William Almy, Slater later built and oversaw mills in Rhode Island and Massachusetts. In 1815 he hired a recent immigrant, William Gilmore, to build a water-powered loom like those used in Britain. Later in the 1820s, the Slaters introduced British steam-powered looms. Spinning and weaving would now be done in New England factories organized on British models.

In 1810 Francis Cabot Lowell had the same idea as the Slaters: to build modern mills with mechanical, water-powered looms. Lowell took a family vacation to Britain, and, in Edinburgh, Scotland, he met fellow Bostonian Nathan Appleton. Impressed by the textile mills they had seen in Britain, they laid plans to introduce water-powered mechanical weaving into the United States. They knew they had to acquire the "improved manufactures" from Britain that had made Manchester famous as a textile center. Lowell went to Manchester, during the day visiting and observing the factories and meeting the factory managers. At night, he returned to his hotel to sketch from memory the power looms and processes he saw. Back in the United States, he and others formed the Boston Associates, which created the Waltham-Lowell Mills based on Lowell's industrial piracy. The Lowell boarding houses, however, were intended as an alternative to the tenements and slums of Manchester. Within a few years, textiles would be a major American industry, and the Associates would dominate it.

Thus, the modern American industrial revolution began with international links, not homegrown American inventions. Ingenuity and industrial piracy put the United States on the road to industrial advancement.

This contemporary painting shows the Boston Manufacturing Company's 1814 textile factory at Waltham, Massachusetts. All manufacturing processes were brought together under one roof, and the company built its first factories in rural New England to tap roaring rivers as a power source.   (Courtesy of Gore Place Society, Waltham, Mass.)

1810, cried loudest for war. Britain's response came too late. In spring 1812, the admiralty ordered British ships not to stop, search, or seize American warships. Then in June, Britain reopened the seas to American shipping. Hard times had hit the British Isles: the Anglo-French conflict had blocked much British commerce to the European continent, and exports to the United States had fallen 80 percent. But two days after the change in British policy and before word of it had crossed the Atlantic, Congress declared war.

In his message to Congress on June 1, 1812, President Madison enumerated familiar grievances: impressment, interference with neutral trading rights, and British alliances with western Indians. More generally, the Democratic-Republicans resolved to defend American independence and honor, but some Americans saw an opportunity to conquer and annex British Canada.

DEBATE ON THE WAR

The war Congress was a partisan one. Most militant were the War Hawks, land-hungry southerners and westerners, all Democratic-Republicans, led by John C. Calhoun of South Carolina and House Speaker Henry Clay of Kentucky. Most representatives from the coastal states opposed war because armed conflict with the Royal Navy would interrupt American shipping. On the vote in Congress, not a single Federalist favored war. However, both houses of Congress voted for war, and President Madison signed the bill on June 19. Critics instantly called it "Mr. Madison's War."

During these years, politics and personal animosities were often so intense that political compromise and cooperation, essential to politics, seemed almost impossible. But social events at the Executive Mansion, dominated by the magnetic Dolley Madison, provided the site for political compromises. She had, said one observer, "the magic power of converting enemies into friends." At state dinners, she sat at the head of the table and made socializing a state craft. Under Dolley Madison, the White House took on its modern role as the focus of presidential politics. Her Wednesday evening socials brought all political factions together, the only place where political enemies talked cordially. James Madison lacked Jefferson's intellect, but with his wife in the lead, he

DOLLEY MADISON AND FEMALE POLITICAL WORK

was a far more successful politician than Jefferson had been.

Jefferson's warning that "our constitution is a peace establishment—it is not calculated for war" proved true. Although the U.S. Navy had a corps of experienced officers who had proved their mettle in the Barbary War, it was no match for the Royal Navy. The U.S. Army had neither an able staff nor an adequate force of enlisted men. Senior army officers were aged Revolutionary War veterans or political hacks. The army depended on political leaders and state militias to recruit volunteers, and not all states cooperated. The government offered enlistees a sign-up bonus of $16, monthly pay of $5, a full set of clothes, and a promise of three months' pay and rights to purchase 160 acres of western land upon discharge. Forty-two percent of the enlistees were illiterate.

RECRUITMENT

Canada was tempting, and Americans expected to take it quickly. The mighty Royal Navy could not reach the Great Lakes because there was no direct access to them from the Atlantic. Canada's population was just 0.5 million, the United States's 7.5 million. Canada had 7,000 regulars in uniform; the United States, 12,000. And Americans hoped that the French in Canada might welcome U.S. forces.

INVASION OF CANADA

Begun with high hopes, the invasion of Canada ended in disaster. The American strategy concentrated on the West, aiming to split Canadian forces and isolate the pro-British Indians. At the outset of the war, Tecumseh joined the British, who promised him in return an Indian nation in the Great Lakes region. U.S. general William Hull, territorial governor of Michigan, marched his troops into Upper Canada, with the goal of conquering Montreal. Hull had surrounded himself with newly minted colonels as politically astute and militarily ignorant as he was. He waged a timid campaign, losing Mackinac Island, Fort Dearborn in Chicago, and Fort Detroit and leaving the entire Midwest exposed to the enemy. By the winter of 1812–1813, the British controlled about half of the Old Northwest.

The United States had no greater success on the Niagara front, where New York borders Canada. At the Battle of Queenstown, Canada, north of Niagara, the U.S. Army met defeat because the New York militia refused to leave New York. This frustrating scenario was repeated near Lake Champlain when the New York militia refused to cross into Canada, and tenacious opposition from British regulars, their Indian allies, and Canadians, many of them loyalists who had fled the American Revolution, foiled American plans to attack Montreal.

The navy provided the only good news in the first year of the war. The U.S.S. *Constitution,* the U.S.S. *Wasp,* and the U.S.S. *United States* all bested British warships on the Atlantic Ocean. However, in the first year of war, the Americans lost 20 percent of their ships, while in defeat the British lost just 1 percent. With only seventeen ships in 1812, the United States could not prevent Britannia from ruling the waves. By 1814, a Royal Navy blockade covered nearly all American ports. After 1811, American trade overseas had declined nearly 90 percent, and the decline in revenues from customs duties threatened to bankrupt the federal government and prostrate New England.

NAVAL BATTLES

The contest for control of the Great Lakes, the key to the war in the Northwest, evolved as a shipbuilding race. Under Master Commandant Oliver Hazard Perry and shipbuilder Noah Brown, the United States outbuilt the British on Lake Erie and defeated them at the bloody Battle of Put-in-Bay on September 10, 1813. With this costly victory, the Americans gained control of Lake Erie.

GREAT LAKES CAMPAIGN

General William Henry Harrison then began what proved to be among the most successful U.S. land campaigns in the war. Harrison's force of forty-five hundred men took Detroit. Then they crossed to Canada, defeating the British, Shawnee, and Chippewa forces on October 5 at the Battle of the Thames. The United States regained control of the Old Northwest. Moreover, Tecumseh died in the battle, and with his death, Native American unity expired.

After defeating Napoleon in Europe in April 1814, the British launched a land counteroffensive against the United States, concentrating on the Chesapeake Bay region. Royal troops occupied Washington, D.C., in August and set it ablaze. The attack on the capital was only a diversion, however. The major battle occurred in September 1814 at Baltimore, where the Americans held firm. Francis Scott Key, detained on a British ship, watched the bombardment of Fort McHenry from Baltimore harbor and the next morning wrote the verses of "The Star-Spangled Banner" (which became the national anthem in 1931). Although the British inflicted heavy damage both materially and psychologically, they achieved little militarily. They halted their offense, and the war was stalemated.

BURNING OF WASHINGTON

The last campaigns of the war took place in the South, against the Creeks along the Gulf of Mexico and against the British around New Orleans. The Creeks had responded to Tecumseh's call to resist U.S. expansion. In December 1812 General Andrew Jackson raised his Tennessee militia to fight the Creeks. Jackson's men defeated the Creek nation at the Battle of Horseshoe Bend in Mississippi Territory in March 1814. As a result, the Creeks ceded two-thirds of their land and withdrew to the southern and western part of Mississippi Territory (what is now Alabama); the removal of Indians from the South had begun. Jackson became a major general in the regular army and continued south toward the Gulf of Mexico. After seizing Pensacola in Spanish Florida and securing Mobile, he marched to New Orleans.

CAMPAIGN AGAINST THE CREEKS

Early in December, the British fleet landed troops east of the city of New Orleans, hoping to seize the mouth of the Mississippi River and thus strangle the lifeline of the American West. They faced American regulars, Tennessee and Kentucky volunteers, and two companies of free African American volunteers from New Orleans. On January 8, 1815, after three weeks of cat-and-mouse, the two forces met head-on. Jackson's poorly trained army held its fortified position against a British contingent of six thousand. At day's end, more than two thousand British soldiers lay dead or wounded; Americans suffered only twenty-one casualties. Andrew Jackson emerged a national hero, and Americans memorialized the battle in song and paintings. The Battle of New Orleans actually took place after the end of the war. Unknown to the participants, a treaty had been signed in Ghent, Belgium, two weeks before the battle.

BATTLE OF NEW ORLEANS

Peace and Consequences

The Treaty of Ghent, ratified by the Senate on February 17, 1815, essentially restored the prewar status quo. It provided for an end to hostilities, release of prisoners, restoration of conquered territory, and arbitration of boundary disputes. It made no mention of impressment, blockades, or other maritime rights for neutrals, nor did it satisfy any British demands.

Why did the negotiators settle for so little? Events in Europe had made peace and the status quo acceptable at the end of 1814, as they had not been in 1812. Napoleon's defeat allowed the United States to abandon its demands, since impressment and interference with American commerce had become moot issues. Similarly, war-weary Britain, its treasury nearly depleted, stopped pressing for a military victory.

The War of 1812 affirmed the independence of the American republic and ensured Canada's independence from the United States.

CONSEQUENCES   Although conflict with Great Britain over trade and territory continued, it never again led to war. The experience strengthened America's resolve to steer clear of European politics because the Anglo-French conflagration had drawn the United States into war. At the same time, with Indian resistance broken, U.S. expansion would spread south and west, not north to Canada.

Conflict carried disastrous results for most Native Americans. The ninth article of the Treaty of Ghent pledged the United States to end hostilities and restore "all the possessions, rights, and privileges" that Indians had enjoyed before the war. Midwestern Indians signed more than a dozen treaties with the United States in 1815, but they had little meaning. With the death of Tecumseh, the Indians had lost their most powerful political and military leader; with the withdrawal of the British, they had lost their strongest ally. The Shawnees, Potawatomis, Chippewas, and others had lost the means to resist American expansion.

The war exposed contradictions and American fears about the growing African American population. In the Deep South, fear of arming slaves kept them out of the military except in New Orleans, where a free black militia dated back to Spanish control of Louisiana. The British army recruited slaves, offering them freedom in return for joining their side. Thus, the British assault on Washington and Baltimore included former slaves. Ironically, the United States made the same offer to slaves in Canada, and both sides gave freedom to slaves in the Old Northwest who joined the military. New York State offered freedom to slaves who enlisted and compensated their masters. In Philadelphia black leaders formed a "Black Brigade" to defend the city.

The war also exposed weaknesses in defense and transportation at home. American generals had found U.S. roads inadequate to move troops and supplies. Thus, improved transportation and a well-equipped army became national priorities in the postwar years. In 1815 Congress voted a standing army of ten thousand men—three times the size of the army during Jefferson's administration. In 1818 the National Road reached Wheeling, Virginia (now West Virginia), from its Cumberland, Maryland, beginning.

Perhaps most important of all, the war stimulated economic growth. The prewar trade restrictions and the war itself spurred the production of manufactured goods because New England capitalists began to invest in home manufactures and factories. The effects of these changes were far-reaching.

Finally, the conflict sealed the fate of the Federalists. Realizing that they could not win a presidential election in wartime, the Federalists joined renegade Democratic-Republicans in supporting New York City mayor DeWitt Clinton in the election of 1812. Federalist organization peaked at the state level as the Younger Federalists campaigned hard. The Federalists nevertheless lost to President Madison. They gained some congressional seats, but their star was waning.

With the war stalemated and their region's economy shattered, delegates from New England met in

HARTFORD   Hartford, Connecticut, in the winter of 1814–1815 to discuss revising
CONVENTION   the national compact or pulling out of the republic. Moderates prevented a resolution of secession, but the convention condemned the war and the embargo and endorsed radical changes in the Constitution, such as restricting the presidency to one term and requiring a two-thirds congressional vote to admit new states to the Union. The delegates plotted to preserve

New England Federalist political power as electoral strength shifted to the South and West.

The timing of the Hartford Convention proved lethal. The victory at New Orleans and news of the peace treaty made the convention look ridiculous, if not treasonous. Although Federalists survived in a handful of states until the 1820s, the faction dissolved.

Summary *Online Study Center* **ACE the Test**

The 1800 election marked the peaceful transition in power from the Federalists to the opposition Democratic-Republicans. New president Thomas Jefferson sought both to unify the nation and to solidify Democratic-Republican control of the government. Jeffersonians favored frugal government.

The Supreme Court under Chief Justice John Marshall remained a Federalist bastion. Marshall would ensure, until 1835, the dominance of Federalist principle: federal supremacy over the states and the protection of commerce and capital. In *Marbury v. Madison* (1803), the Supreme Court established its power of judicial review.

With the acquisition of Louisiana Territory, the United States doubled its size. Lewis and Clark's Corps of Discovery practiced "buckskin diplomacy" while exploring the land, flora, fauna, and people west of the Mississippi. Increasingly Americans looked westward.

Both the Federalists and the Democratic-Republicans competed at the grassroots level for popular support. Political conflict was bitter, and, assisted by the partisan press, political intensity began to build a national political culture.

Despite internal divisions, the greatest threats came from abroad. In both the war with the Barbary states and the War of 1812, the United States sought to guard its commerce and ships on the high seas. The Treaty of Ghent, ending the War of 1812, reaffirmed American independence. The war also broke Indian resistance in the West and South. At the same time, embargoes and war forced Americans to look toward domestic markets and jump-started American manufacturing.

LEGACY FOR A PEOPLE AND A NATION
States' Rights and Nullification

When the Constitution replaced the Articles of Confederation, the United States had a much stronger central government, but its exact relationship with the states was ambiguous because Constitutional Convention delegates could not agree on whether states or nation should prevail in the event of irreconcilable conflict. The Tenth Amendment to the Constitution offered only a slight clarification: powers not delegated to the central government, it said, were reserved to the states or to the people. Who would determine which powers had been delegated to which authority remained to be defined.

When New England Federalists met in Hartford at the end of 1814, they drew on the doctrine of nullification, first announced sixteen years earlier in Jefferson's Kentucky Resolution and Madison's Virginia Resolution. Opposing the Alien and Sedition Acts, these resolutions had asserted that if the national government assumed powers not delegated to it by the Constitution, states could nullify federal actions—that is, declare them inoperative within state borders. At Hartford, Federalist representatives of New England states discussed taking nullification a step further by seceding, or withdrawing from the Union. They backed away from this extreme step, but their formulation of the rights of states to evaluate and nullify federal authority left a legacy for dissent that would be played out in crises to the present day.

In the following decade, South Carolina nullified federal tariffs that it opposed, and in 1861 southern states threatened by Abraham Lincoln's election to the presidency claimed the right of secession. Although the Civil War supposedly settled the issue—states could neither nullify federal law nor secede—southern states opposing the Supreme Court's 1954 ruling in favor of school integration again claimed the right to nullify "unauthorized" federal policy within their borders. In the 1990s, some western states sought to nullify federal envi-ronmental laws. The Hartford Convention's legacy for a people and a nation provides Americans who dissent from national policy a model for using state governments as vehicles for their protests.

NATIONALISM, EXPANSION, AND THE MARKET ECONOMY 1816–1845

*T*he Hutchinson Family from rural New Hampshire was the most popular singing group in nineteenth-century America. Abby, Asa, Jesse, John, and Judson Hutchinson performed the patriotic, religious, and sentimental songs that had dominated popular music since the Revolution. Unlike most other musical groups, the Hutchinsons not only sang but also presented well-rehearsed and elaborately produced performances. They used folk tunes, but their lyrics explored controversial topics such as abolition and temperance.

The Hutchinson Family traveled by rail, performing across the expanding United States, but drawing their largest audiences in the growing cities of the North. The family's fee for a single night in the 1840s reached $1,000, about four hundred times a worker's daily wage. They had an entourage of managers, agents, and publishers. Hawkers sold sheet music, portraits, and songbooks at the Hutchinsons' concerts. The Hutchinson Family made a business of music and entertainment, selling nostalgia and reform.

The Hutchinsons' concert tours exemplified the market economy, in which goods and services sold in cash or credit transactions created a network of exchange that bound distant enterprises together. The family performed in western areas in the 1840s that had had no American settlements twenty years before. The canals and railroads that carried them increasingly linked the nation's regions after the War of 1812. People moved inland from the seacoast. Grain went east to coastal cities, slave-grown cotton went to Europe, and ready-made men's garments from New York and Cincinnati sold across the nation. Increasingly, farmers turned to staple-crop agriculture, and city people worked not for themselves but for others, for wages. These large-scale enterprises needed capital, and new financial institutions amassed and loaned it. Mechanization took hold; factories and precision-made machinery put home workshops and handcrafters out of business. In turn, the increased specialization

Online Study Center
This icon will direct you to interactive map and primary source activities on the website
http://college.hmco.com/pic/nortonbrief7e

C H R O N O L O G Y

1815 • Madison proposes internal improvements

1816 • Second Bank of the United States chartered
• Tariff of 1816 imposes first substantial duties
• Monroe elected president

1817 • Rush-Bagot Treaty limits British and American naval forces on Lake Champlain and Great Lakes

1819 • *McCulloch v. Maryland* establishes supremacy of federal over state law
• Adams-Onís Treaty with Spain gives Florida to U.S. and defines Louisiana territorial border

1819–23 • Hard times bring unemployment

1820 • Missouri Compromise creates formula for admitting slave and free states
• Monroe reelected

1820s • New England textile mills expand

1823 • Monroe Doctrine closes Western Hemisphere to European intervention

1824 • *Gibbons v. Ogden* affirms federal over state authority in interstate commerce
• Monroe proposes Indian removal

1825 • Erie Canal completed

1830 • Railroad era begins
• Congress passes Indian Removal Act

1830s • McCormick reaper, Deere steel plow patented

1830s–40s • Cotton production shifts to Mississippi valley

1831 • Trail of Tears begins with the forced removal of the Choctaws
• Cherokees turn to courts to defend treaty rights in *Cherokee Nation v. Georgia*

1832 • Marshall declares Cherokee nation a distinct political community in *Worcester v. Georgia*

1834 • Women workers strike at Lowell textile mills

1835–42 • Seminoles successfully resist removal in Second Seminole War

1836 • Second Bank of the United States closes

1837 • *Charles River Bridge v. Warren Bridge* encourages new enterprises
• Panic of 1837 begins economic downturn

1839–43 • Hard times strike again

1842 • *Commonwealth v. Hunt* declares strikes lawful

1844 • Government grant sponsors first telegraph line

in agriculture, manufacturing, transportation, and finance further fired the engines of the new nationwide, capitalist, market-oriented economy.

The end of the War of 1812 unleashed this growth. A new nationalist spirit encouraged the economy and promoted western expansion at home, trade abroad, and assertiveness throughout the Western Hemisphere. Economic growth and territorial expansion, however, generated sectional conflicts over slavery and economic development. Migration and changes in the ways people worked also created new tensions. Journeyman tailors, displaced by retailers and cheaper labor, found their trades disappearing. New England farm daughters who became wage workers found their

world changing no less radically. Moreover, nationwide boom-and-bust cycles wrenched livelihoods and lives. Mills, factories, roads, canals, and railroads altered or destroyed the landscape.

Everywhere Americans were on the move. Settlement moved to the interior, and farms and cities, linked first by rivers, then by roads, canals, and railroads, stretched to the Ohio and Mississippi River valleys and beyond. The Indian inhabitants attempted to hold their ground but were in the end removed to the West, pushed off their lands by the same drive for profit—a nationalist spirit reshaping national politics and the dynamic American economy. ■

Postwar Nationalism

*N*ationalism surged after the War of 1812. Self-confident, Americans asserted themselves at home and abroad as Democratic-Republicans borrowed from the Federalists' agenda and encouraged economic growth. In his December 1815 message to Congress, James Madison recommended economic development and military expansion. His agenda included a national bank (the charter of the first bank had expired in 1811) and improved transportation. To raise government revenues and foster manufacturing, Madison called for a protective tariff—a tax on imported goods designed to protect American manufactures. Yet his program acknowledged Jeffersonian republicanism: only a constitutional amendment, Madison argued, could authorize the federal government to build local roads and canals.

A new generation of congressional leaders, with a new national outlook, saw Madison's program as a way of unifying the country.

NATIONALIST PROGRAM — Democratic-Republican John C. Calhoun of South Carolina and House Speaker Henry Clay of Kentucky believed that the tariff would stimulate industry. The agricultural South and West would sell cotton to the churning mills of New England and food to its millworkers. Goods would move on roads and canals, and tariff revenues would provide money to build them. A national bank would handle the transactions.

In 1816 Congress enacted much of the nationalist program. It chartered the Second Bank of the United States, which, like its predecessor, mixed public and private ownership: the government provided one-fifth of the bank's capital and appointed one-fifth of its directors. Congress also passed a protective tariff to aid industries. The Tariff of 1816 levied taxes on imported woolens and cottons and on iron, leather, hats, paper, and sugar, in effect raising their prices in the United States. Foreshadowing a growing trend, support for the tariff divided along sectional lines: New England and the western and Middle Atlantic states stood to benefit and applauded it, but the South did not.

The South did press for better transportation. It was Calhoun who promoted roads and canals to "bind the republic together." However, Madison vetoed Calhoun's internal improvements (public works) bill as unconstitutional. The president did approve funds for extending the National Road to Ohio, deeming it a military necessity.

JAMES MONROE — James Monroe, Madison's successor and the last president to have attended the Constitutional Convention, continued Madison's domestic program, supporting tariffs and vetoing internal improvements. Monroe was a most ordinary and colorless man who rarely had an original idea. But in 1816 he easily defeated the last Federalist presidential nominee, Rufus King. A Boston newspaper dubbed this one-party period the "Era of Good Feelings."

MCCULLOCH V. MARYLAND — Led by Federalist chief justice John Marshall, the Supreme Court became the bulwark of a nationalist point of view. In *McCulloch v. Maryland* (1819), the Court struck down a Maryland law taxing banks within the state that were not chartered by the Maryland legislature—a law aimed at hindering the Baltimore branch of the federally chartered Second Bank of the United States, which had refused to pay the tax and sued. At issue was state versus federal jurisdiction. Speaking for a unanimous Court, Marshall asserted the supremacy of the federal government over the states.

In his opinion, Marshall went on to consider whether Congress could issue a bank charter. The Constitution did not spell out such power, but Marshall noted that Congress had the authority to pass "all laws which shall be necessary and proper for carrying into execution" the enumerated powers of the government. Marshall ruled that Congress could legally exercise "those great powers on which the welfare of the nation essentially depends." The bank charter was declared legal. *McCulloch v. Maryland* thus joined nationalism and economics. By asserting federal supremacy, Marshall protected the commercial and industrial interests that favored a national bank. The decision was only one in a series of rulings that cemented the federalist view.

JOHN QUINCY ADAMS — Monroe's secretary of state, John Quincy Adams, matched the self-confident Marshall Court in assertiveness and nationalism. From 1817 to 1825 he brilliantly managed the nation's foreign policy, stubbornly pushing for expansion, fishing rights for Americans in Atlantic waters, political distance from the Old World, and peace. An ardent expansionist, he nonetheless believed that expansion must come about through negotiations, not war, and that newly acquired territories must bar slavery.

Adams faced major diplomatic challenges. U.S. northern and southern borders were not clearly defined and were a potential source of conflict with Great Britain and Spain. Still, Great Britain was the largest buyer of American exports, and British textile mills depended on American cotton; both sides looked to commerce to cement better relations. The United States also sought to prevent European conflicts from spilling over into the New World.

Although an Anglophobe, Adams worked to strengthen the peace with Great Britain negotiated at Ghent (1814). In 1817 the two nations agreed in the Rush-Bagot Treaty to sharply limit their naval forces on Lake Champlain and the Great Lakes. This first disarmament treaty of modern times led to the demilitarization of the border between the United States and Canada. Adams then pushed for the Convention of 1818, which fixed the United States–Canadian border from Lake of the Woods in Minnesota westward to the Rockies along the 49th parallel (see Map 10.1). When they could not agree on the boundary west of the Rockies, Britain and the United States settled on joint occupation of Oregon for ten years (renewed indefinitely in 1827).

Adams next moved to settle long-term disputes with Spain. During the War of 1812 the United States had seized Mobile and the remainder of West Florida. After the war, Adams took advantage of Spain's preoccupation with domestic and colonial troubles to

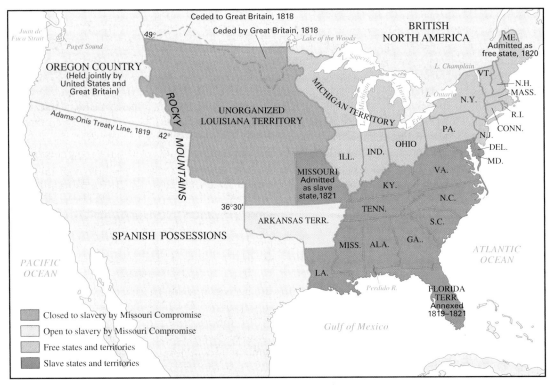

Map 10.1   Missouri Compromise and the State of the Union, 1820

The compromise worked out by House Speaker Henry Clay established a formula that avoided debate over whether new states would allow or prohibit slavery. In the process, it divided the United States into northern and southern regions.

negotiate for the purchase of East Florida. During the 1818 talks, General Andrew Jackson occupied much of present-day Florida on the pretext of suppressing Seminole raids against American settlements across the border. Adams was furious with Jackson but defended his brazen act.

The following year, Don Luís de Onís, the Spanish minister to the United States, agreed to cede Florida to the United States without payment, while the United States agreed to renounce its dubious claims to northern Mexico (Texas) and assume $5 million of claims by American citizens against Spain. The Adams-Onís, or Transcontinental, Treaty also defined the southwestern boundary of the Louisiana Purchase and set the southern border of Oregon at the 42nd parallel (see Map 10.1). Expansion was achieved at little cost and without war. In Florida, some planter-slaveholders and traders welcomed the American flag. Creeks and Seminoles, free blacks, runaway slaves, and Spanish-speaking town dwellers did not.

John Quincy Adams's desire to insulate the United States and the Western Hemisphere from European conflict brought about his greatest

INDEPENDENT STATES IN LATIN AMERICA

achievement: the Monroe Doctrine. Between 1808 and 1822, the United Provinces of the Río de la Plata (present-day northern Argentina, Paraguay, and Uruguay), Chile, Peru, Colombia, and Mexico all broke free from Spain. Monroe and Adams moved cautiously, seeking to avoid conflict with Spain and to be assured of the stability of the new regimes. But in 1822 the United States became the first nation outside Latin America to recognize the new states.

To the United States, Europe again offered potential threats to the stability of the New World. After France, to bolster the weak Spanish monarchy against domestic rebellion, occupied Spain, the United States feared that France would return the new Latin American states to colonial rule. Great Britain, similarly distrustful of France, proposed a joint United States–British declaration against European intervention in the Western Hemisphere and a joint disavowal of territorial ambitions in the region. Adams rejected the British overture, following George Washington's admonition to avoid foreign entanglements. He also interpreted Britain's proposal to disavow territorial ambitions as an attempt to thwart American expansion.

President Monroe presented the American position—the Monroe Doctrine—to Congress in December 1823. His message called

MONROE DOCTRINE

for noncolonization of the Western Hemisphere by European nations, a principle that addressed American anxiety not only about Latin America but also about Russian expansion beyond Alaska and settlements in California. He also demanded nonintervention by Europe in the affairs of independent New World nations, and he pledged noninterference by the United States in European affairs, including those of Europe's existing New World colonies.

Monroe's words, however, carried no force. Indeed, the policy depended on the support of the British, who wanted to keep other European nations out of the hemisphere to protect their dominance in the Atlantic trade. Europeans ignored the Monroe Doctrine; it was the Royal Navy they respected, not American policy.

Online Study Center Improve Your Grade
Primary Source: Monroe Doctrine

While nationalism brought Americans together, slavery divided them. Since the drafting of the Constitution, political leaders had tried

"FIRE BELL IN THE NIGHT"

to avoid the issue. The one exception was an act ending the foreign slave trade after January 1, 1808, which passed without much opposition. Slavery was dying out in the North, but not in border and southern states. In 1819 the question crept onto the political agenda when Missouri residents petitioned Congress for admission to the Union as a slave state. For two and a half years, the issue dominated Congress. "This momentous question," wrote Thomas Jefferson, "like a fire bell in the night, awakened and filled me with terror."

The debate transcended slavery in Missouri. Five new states had joined the Union since 1812: Louisiana, Indiana, Mississippi, Illinois, and Alabama. Of these, Louisiana, Mississippi, and Alabama permitted slavery. Because Missouri was on the same latitude as free Illinois, Indiana, and Ohio (a state since 1803), its admission as a slave state would thrust slavery farther northward. It would also tilt the uneasy political balance in the Senate toward the slave states. In 1819 the Union consisted of eleven slave and eleven free states.

If Missouri joined as a slave state, slave states would have a two-vote edge in the Senate.

Moral issues made slavery an explosive question. Settlers from slave states—Kentuckians and Tennesseans—made up most of the new Missourians. But many northerners had concluded that slavery was evil. When Representative James Tallmadge Jr. of New York proposed gradual emancipation in Missouri, a passionate and sometimes violent debate ensued. The House, which had a northern majority, passed the Tallmadge amendment, but the Senate rejected it. The two sides were deadlocked.

House Speaker Henry Clay promoted a compromise in 1820. Maine, carved out of Massachusetts, would become a free state balancing Missouri. In the rest of the Louisiana Territory north of latitude 36°30′ (Missouri's southern boundary), slavery would be prohibited forever (see Map 10.1). The compromise carried, but the agreement almost unraveled in November when Missouri submitted a constitution that barred free blacks from entering the state. In 1821 Clay produced a second compromise: Missouri guaranteed that none of its laws would discriminate against citizens of other states. (Once admitted to the Union, however, Missouri twice banned free blacks.)

The Market Economy and Government's Role

Before canals and railroads, farmers had geared production to their own needs and to local and foreign, not national, markets. Farm families produced much of what they needed and traded for or purchased items they could not produce, such as cooking pots and tea. The market for staple products—cotton, lumber, and sugar—was international, not domestic.

In the years after the War of 1812, Americans increasingly became involved in the market economy—growing crops and producing goods specifically for cash and buying items produced by other people. Farms and slave plantations produced crops for market sales. Farm women gave up spinning and weaving and purchased cloth made by wage-earning farm girls in Massachusetts textile mills. Nonfarm men and women sold not goods but their labor for cash, work-

ing for wages. By buying goods at market, free farmers and workers increased the demand for manufactured things. Such a system encouraged specialization. It also energized transportation.

Mechanization, the division of labor, new methods of financing, and improvements in transportation

EFFECTS OF BOOM AND BUST

all fueled the expansion of the economy. Goods and services multiplied. This growth in turn prompted new improvements and greater opportunities for wage labor. The pace of economic growth, however, was uneven. Prosperity reigned during two long periods, from 1823 to 1835 and from 1843 to 1857. But there were long stretches of economic contraction as well. Contraction and deflation (decline in the general price level) occurred during the hard times of 1819–1823 and 1839–1843. During these periods, banks collapsed, businesses went under, wages and prices declined, and jobs were hard to find or to keep.

In 1819 the postwar boom collapsed. Expansion had been built on easy credit; state banks had printed notes freely, fueling speculative buying of western land. Foreign investment in the United States had soared. When manufacturing fell in 1818, prices spiraled downward. The Second Bank of the United States cut back on loans, thus further shrinking the economy. With urban workers, farmers, and southern planters having less money to spend, the economy declined.

The contraction devastated workers and their families. As a Baltimore physician noted in 1819, working people felt hard times "a thousand fold more than the merchants." They could not build up savings during boom times to get them through the hard times; often they could not make it through the winter without drawing on charity for food, clothing, and firewood.

The 1820s and 1830s were boom times. Internal improvement projects—streets, turnpikes, canals, and railroads—made regular work plentiful, as did building construction. In the 1830s foreign investment soared; from 1832 through 1839, the United States had a net capital inflow of $189 million, or $12 for every man, woman, and child.

The Panic of 1837 led to a bust cycle from 1839 through 1843. Money became tight. Internal savings and foreign investment declined sharply. In the Panic of 1837 many banks could not repay depositors, and states, facing deficits because of the decline in the economy, defaulted on their bonds. European, especially British, investors were furious, became suspicious of all U.S. loans, and withdrew money from the United States.

Hard times had come. In New York crowds of laborers gathered at closed banks demanding their deposits. Then, Philip Hone noted in his diary, "A deadly calm pervades this lately flourishing city. No goods are selling, no businesses stirring." The hungry formed bread lines in front of soup societies, and beggars crowded the sidewalks. In Baltimore in 1839, when hundreds of small manufacturers closed their doors, tailors, milliners, and shipyard and construction workers lost their jobs. Ninety miles to the north, Philadelphia took on an eerie aura. "The streets seemed deserted," Sidney George Fisher observed in 1842, "...there is no business...no money, no

confidence." In smaller cities like Lynn, Massachusetts, shoemakers weathered the hard times by fishing and tending gardens while laborers became scavengers, digging for clams and harvesting dandelions.

What caused the boom-and-bust cycles that brought about such suffering? Generally they were a direct result of the market economy.

CAUSES OF BOOM AND BUST Prosperity stimulated demand for manufactured goods. Increased demand led not only to higher prices and production but also, because of business optimism and expectation of higher prices, to speculation in land. Investment money was plentiful as Americans saved regularly and foreign, mostly British, investors bought U.S. bonds and securities. Then production surpassed demand, causing prices and wages to fall; in response, land and stock values collapsed, and investment money flowed out of the United States.

■ E. Didier painted *Auction in Chatham Street* in 1834. Auction houses in New York and other cities boomed during hard times. (Museum of the City of New York)

Some considered this process beneficial—a self-adjusting cycle that eliminated unprofitable economic ventures. In theory, people concentrated on the activities they did best, and the economy as a whole became more efficient. Believers in the system also argued that it enhanced individual freedom, since theoretically each seller, whether of goods or of labor, determined the price. But in fact, the system tied workers to a perpetual roller coaster; they became dependent on wages—and on the availability of jobs—for their very survival.

The market economy also ushered in another type of boom-and-bust cycle: harvest and destruction. Canals and railroads spurred demand for distant resources, then accelerated the destruction of forests, natural waterways, and landscape features. Railroads made possible large-scale lumbering of pinewood forests in Michigan and Wisconsin. During the 1840s, lumber companies deforested millions of acres, leaving most of that land unfit even for agriculture. The process of harvest and destruction would eventually change the ecology of the United States.

The idea of a market economy drew on eighteenth-century republicanism. It emphasized economic liberty and individualism. Limited government, adherents argued, fostered economic expansion as individuals pursuing their private interests benefited the nation as a whole. Nonetheless, the federal government played an active role in technological and industrial growth. Federal arsenals pioneered new manufacturing techniques that helped develop the machine-tool industry. The U.S. Post Office fostered the circulation of information, a critical element in a market economy. The post office also played a brief but crucial role in the development of the telegraph, financing the first telegraph line, from Washington to Baltimore, in 1844. The government protected inventions and domestic industries. Patent laws gave inventors a seventeen-year monopoly on their inventions, and tariffs protected American industry from foreign competition.

Government policy also fostered farm life. Republicanism associated farming with virtue, independence, and productivity, essential values in the new republic, and the federal government surveyed public land and opened it to settlement. Internal improvements such as harbors, roads, and canals—some underwritten by government—linked new farms in the

GOVERNMENT'S ECONOMIC ROLE

West to markets in the East. When Indians got in the way of expansion, the federal government moved them across the Mississippi River.

The federal judiciary validated government promotion of the economy and encouraged business enterprise and risk taking. In *Gibbons v. Ogden* (1824), the Supreme Court overturned a New York State law that gave Robert Fulton and Robert Livingston a monopoly on the New York–New Jersey steamboat trade. Aaron Ogden, their successor, lost the monopoly when Chief Justice John Marshall ruled that the congressional power to license new enterprises took precedence over New York's grant of monopoly rights to Fulton and Livingston. Marshall declared that Congress's power under the commerce clause of the Constitution extended to "every species of commercial intercourse," including transportation. In defining interstate commerce broadly, the Marshall Court expanded federal powers over the economy while restricting the ability of states to control economic activity within their borders.

LEGAL FOUNDATIONS OF COMMERCE

Federal and state courts, in conjunction with state legislatures, also encouraged the proliferation of corporations—organizations entitled to hold property and transact business as if they were individuals. Corporation owners, called shareholders, were granted *limited liability,* or freedom from responsibility for the company's debts beyond their original investments. In 1800 the United States had three hundred incorporated firms; by 1830, the New England states alone had issued nineteen hundred charters.

CORPORATIONS

Legislative action allowed the creation of corporations, but the courts played a crucial role in extending their powers and protecting them. Two Massachusetts cases in 1819, for instance, upheld the limited liability of stockholders. And the U.S. Supreme Court in *Charles River Bridge v. Warren Bridge* (1837) paved the way for new enterprises and technologies, favoring competition over monopoly and the public interest over implied privileges in old contracts.

CHARLES RIVER BRIDGE CASE

The Massachusetts legislature had chartered the Charles River Bridge Company in 1785 and six years later extended its charter for seventy years. In return for building a bridge between Charlestown and Boston, the owners received the right to collect tolls. In 1828 the legislature chartered another company to build the Warren Bridge across the Charles nearby; the new bridge could collect tolls for six years, after which the bridge would be turned over to the state and be free of tolls. The Charles River Bridge Company sued in 1829, claiming that the new bridge breached the earlier charter.

Speaking for a 4-to-3 majority, Marshall's successor, Roger Taney, declared that the original charter did not confer the privilege of monopoly and that exclusivity could not therefore be implied. Taney ruled that charter grants should be interpreted narrowly and that ambiguities would be decided in favor of the public interest. New enterprises should not be restricted by old charters.

In promoting the economy, state governments far surpassed the federal government. From 1815 through the 1840s, for example, government money, mostly from the states, financed three-fourths of the nearly $200 million invested in canals. In the 1830s the states started to invest in rail construction. Although the federal government played a larger role in constructing railroads than in building canals, state and local governments provided more than half of the capital for southern rail lines. State governments also invested in corporate and bank stocks, providing much-needed capital. In fact, states' investments equaled or exceeded those of private enterprise.

STATES' SUPPORT FOR THE ECONOMY

Political controversy raged over questions of state versus federal activity, but all parties agreed on the general goal of economic expansion. Indeed, during these years, the major restraint on government action was not philosophical but financial: the public purse was small. As the private sector grew more vigorous, entrepreneurs looked less to government for financial support, and the states played less of a role in investment.

Transportation Links

*I*mproved transportation facilitated economic growth. Outside the South states invested heavily in roads, canals, and railroads, with much of the financing borrowed from Europe. With regional and national financial institutions increasingly concentrated in New York, Boston, and Philadelphia, northeastern seaboard cities became the center of American commerce. New York financial and commercial houses dominated the American export trade, not only of New England textiles but also of southern cotton. The Deep South, with most of its capital invested in slave labor and land, built fewer canals, railroads, and factories and remained mostly rural.

Water routes provided the cheapest and most available transportation. However, as settlement extended beyond the river links, the federal and state governments, followed by private corporations, invested heavily in alternative transportation modes.

In the 1820s new arteries opened up east-west travel. The National Road, which originated in Cumberland, Maryland, reached Columbus, Ohio, in 1833. More important, the Erie Canal, completed in 1825, linked the Great Lakes with New York City and the Atlantic Ocean. Railroads and later the telegraph would solidify these east-west links. Other than the coastal trade, links between the Deep South and the North were rare.

EAST-WEST LINKS

The 363-mile-long Erie Canal was a visionary enterprise. When the state of New York authorized its construction in 1817, the longest American canal was only 28 miles long. Vigorously promoted by Governor DeWitt Clinton, the Erie shortened the journey between Buffalo and New York City from twenty to six days and reduced freight charges from $100 to $5 a ton.

CANALS

The success of the Erie Canal triggered an explosion of canal building. By 1840 canals crisscrossed the Northeast and Midwest, and total canal mileage reached 3,300. None of these canals enjoyed the financial success of the Erie. As the high cost of construction combined with an economic contraction, investment in canals began to slump in the 1830s. By midcentury more miles were being abandoned than built. The canal era had ended.

Meanwhile, railroad construction boomed. The railroad era in the United States began in 1830 when Peter Cooper's locomotive, "Tom Thumb," first steamed along 13 miles of Baltimore and Ohio Rail-

RAILROADS

The United States as a Developing Nation

In the early nineteenth century, the United States was a "developing nation" as its economy slowly shifted from dependence on agriculture and raw materials to producing manufactured goods. In order to develop economically, the United States imported capital to finance international trade, internal improvements, and early factories.

American political and economic leaders in the early part of the nineteenth century talked as if they were masters of their own fate. In many ways, however, the United States remained economically dependent on its former mother country, Great Britain. The political independence that the United States won in the Revolutionary War and affirmed in the War of 1812 was not matched in the economic sphere.

Following the War of 1812, Americans depended on Britain for capital investment. Ninety percent of all U.S. foreign capital came from Britain, and around 60 percent of all British capital exports flowed to the United States. Americans used British capital to develop first the canals, then the railroads that facilitated American industrial development. For instance, from 1817 to 1825 the British invested $7 million in New York State bonds to finance the Erie Canal. Altogether, European investors

provided 80 percent of the money to build the Erie, and the United States depended on mostly British capital to finance America's internal improvements.

As a developing nation, the United States imported more goods than it exported. In other words, Americans consumed more than they produced. It was able to do so because imported capital balanced the trade deficit. As in most developing countries, exports were concentrated in agricultural commodities; 50 percent of the value of all exports was in cotton. And British credit financed cotton sales.

As a developing nation, U.S. dependency on international capital was highlighted when imported capital was interrupted, as in the Panics of 1819 and 1837. Though the financial crises began in the United States, the hard times were made worse in both cases when British investors and creditors squeezed Americans. Economic crises in England led investors to pull out capital from the United States while merchants demanded that Americans pay what they owed to British creditors. Money became tight, and the economy declined.

Thus both economic development and hard times revealed the significance of international capital links to the United States, a developing nation.

In the 1820s, canals like the Erie linked the West with eastern cities and the Atlantic Ocean, and thus world trade. U.S. exports were concentrated in agriculture, and the Erie and other canals carried grain to the world market. Charles Klackner published this view of a canal boat and its passengers, based on a contemporary painting by Edward Lamson Henry. Canal boats carried gentlemen and ladies as well as more modest citizens, many of them immigrants on their way to settling western lands.
(Chicago Historical Society Neg #ICHi-35979/Painter—Ralph Dille)

road track. By 1850 the United States had nearly 9,000 miles of track.

The earliest railroads connected nearby cities; not until the 1850s did railroads offer long-distance service at reasonable rates. The early lines had to overcome technical problems. In addition, the lack of a common standard for the width of track thwarted development of a national system. A journey from Philadelphia to Charleston, South Carolina, involved eight different track widths (called gauges), which meant that passengers and freight had to change trains seven times.

Technology and investments in transportation dramatically reduced travel time and shipping cost.

REDUCTION IN TRAVEL TIME AND COST Before 1815 river transportation was the only feasible route for long-distance journeys. In 1815 a traveler took four days to go by stagecoach from New York City to Baltimore. By 1830 the journey took a day and a half, while the Erie Canal reduced the New York–Detroit journey from four weeks to two. Before the War of 1812, wagon transportation cost 30 to 70 cents per ton per mile. By midcentury, railroads had brought the cost of land transportation down 95 percent and reduced the journey to one-fifth the time.

Commercial Farming

lthough manufacturing increased steadily, agriculture remained the backbone of the economy and American exports. But increasingly the market economy altered farming. Although the plantation system had always been market oriented, self-sufficient farm households were becoming market oriented too. Equally important, the center of commercial farming moved westward. In the 1830s and after, the plantation South shifted toward the Mississippi River valley, while commercial farming came to dominate the Old Northwest and the Ohio River valley, then moved even farther westward to the prairies.

After the 1820s, northeastern agriculture began to decline. Eastern farmers had cultivated all the land available to them. Moreover, small

NORTHEASTERN AGRICULTURE New England farms, with their uneven terrains, did not lend themselves to the new labor-saving farm implements introduced in the 1830s—mechanical sowers, reapers, and threshers.

As a result, many northern farmers either moved west or gave up farming for jobs in the merchant houses and factories.

The farmers who remained in New England, as well as those in the Middle Atlantic, adapted to the changed environment. By the 1850s, many of these farm families had abandoned the commercial production of wheat and corn. Instead, they improved their livestock, especially cattle, and specialized in vegetable and fruit production and dairy farming. They financed these initiatives through land sales and debt. Indeed, increasing land values, not farming, promised the greatest profit.

Farm women had a distinctive role in the market economy. Many sold eggs, dairy products, and garden

WOMEN'S PAID LABOR produce in local markets, and their earnings became essential to household incomes. Butter and cheese making replaced spinning and weaving; farm women now sold commodities and bought cloth. The work was physically demanding and added to regular home and farm chores. Yet women took pride in their work, often gaining from it a sense of independence that was as valuable as their profits.

Women's success at butter and cheese making led some farms to specialize in dairy production. After the Erie Canal opened, Ohio dairy farms had access to New York's export trade. Ohio entrepreneurs put cheese into factory production in the 1840s. Canals and railroads took the cheese to eastern ports, where wholesalers sold it around the world.

Individually and collectively, Americans still valued agrarian life. State governments energetically promoted commercial agriculture to spur economic growth and sustain the values of an agrarian-based republic. Massachusetts in 1817 and New York in 1819 began to subsidize agricultural prizes and county fairs. New York required contestants to submit written descriptions of how they grew their prize crops; the state then published the essays to encourage new methods and specialization. The post office circulated farm journals that helped familiarize farmers with developments in agriculture.

Gradually the Old Northwest replaced the Northeast as the center of American family agriculture.

MECHANIZATION OF AGRICULTURE Farms in the Old Northwest were large, flat, and suited to the new mechanized farming implements.

Cyrus McCormick had invented the horse-drawn mechanical reaper in 1831. He built a factory in Chicago that by 1847 sold a thousand reapers a year. Midwestern farmers bought reapers on credit and paid for them with the profits from their high yields. Similarly, John Deere's steel plow, invented in 1837, replaced the traditional iron plow; steel blades kept the soil from sticking and were tough enough to break the roots of prairie grass.

And just in time. The Midwest was becoming one of the leading agricultural regions of the world. Midwestern farms fed the cities in the East, bursting with growing immigrant populations, and still produced enough to export to Europe.

At the end of the eighteenth century, southern agriculture was diverse. Indeed, cotton was profitable

THE COTTON SOUTH only for planters in the Sea Islands of South Carolina and Georgia, where slaves grew the long, silky variety. Then Whitney's cotton gin (1793), by efficiently removing the seeds from the short-staple cotton that would grow in the interior, transformed southern agriculture, revived and expanded slavery, and boosted export of both cotton and cloth.

After 1800 the cultivation of short-staple cotton spread rapidly. By the 1820s there were cotton plantations in the fertile lands of Louisiana, Mississippi, Alabama, Arkansas, and Tennessee. Each decade after 1820, the total crop doubled. By 1825 the slave South was the world's dominant supplier of cotton, and the white fibers were America's largest export. Southerners with capital bought more land and more slaves and planted ever more cotton.

No other region was more tied to international markets than the South, yet the region seemed immune to the transforming potential of foreign trade. Most southern capital remained concentrated in land and slaves. It could not shift easily to support manufacturing and commerce. In many ways, the cotton economy resembled a colonial economy. Planters depended on distant agents to represent them and handle their finances, which often included loans. Thus, critical market decisions were made by bankers, financiers, and brokers, all outside the South. The South was engaged in the new market economy, but at a distance.

The cotton boom, dependent on slave labor, defined the South's economy and society as it moved westward. Slaveholders were oriented to the market economy, like commercial farmers, merchants, and entrepreneurs in the North. But they did not pay wages for labor; they bought laborers. Ultimately this distinctive system (see Chapter 13) would separate the South from the national economy and the nation.

The Rise of Manufacturing and Commerce

British visitors to the 1851 London Crystal Palace Exhibition, the first modern world's fair, were impressed by American design and fine tooling of working parts. American companies displayed hundreds of American machines and wares. Most impressive to the Europeans were Alfred C. Hobb's unpickable padlocks, Samuel Colt's revolvers, and Robbins and Lawrence's rifles. All were machine-tooled rather than handmade, products of what the British called the American system of manufacturing.

The American system of manufacturing used precision machinery to produce interchangeable parts

AMERICAN SYSTEM OF MANUFACTURING that did not require individual adjustment to fit. Eli Whitney had promoted the idea of interchangeable parts in 1798 when he contracted with the federal government to make ten thousand rifles in twenty-eight months. By the 1820s the U.S. Ordnance Department had contracted with private firms to introduce machine-made interchangeable parts for firearms. The American system quickly spread beyond the arsenals, creating the machine-tool industry—the manufacture of machines for purposes of mass production. One outcome was an explosion in consumer goods that were inexpensive yet of uniformly high quality.

Even larger than the machine-tool industry was the textile industry. New England mills began processing and weaving slave-grown

TEXTILE MILLS cotton in the same decade that Whitney patented his gin. Boosted by embargo and war, then protected by the tariff, the textile industry boomed with the expansion of cotton cultivation after the war.

The Boston Manufacturing Company, chartered in 1813, radically transformed textile manufacturing. The owners, Francis Cabot Lowell and other Boston merchants, erected their factories in Waltham, Massachusetts, bringing all the manufacturing processes to a single location. They employed a resident manager to run the mill, thus separating ownership from management. By the 1840s a cotton mill resembled a modern factory, and textiles were the most important industry in the nation. Cotton cloth production rose from 4 million yards in 1817 to 323 million in 1840. The industry employed around eighty thousand workers in the mid-1840s, more than half of them women.

The early mills, dependent on waterpower, sprung up in rural areas. By erecting dams and watercourses, mill owners diverted water from farmers and destroyed fishing, an important resource in rural and village America. To protect their customary rights, fishermen and farmers fought the manufacturers in New England state legislatures, but petitions from job seekers in the mill environs supported the manufacturers. The ensuing compromises promoted mill development.

Textile manufacturing changed New England and had its greatest impact on Lowell, Massachusetts. The population of Lowell, the "city of spindles" and the prototype of early American industrialization, grew from twenty-five hundred to thirty-three thousand between 1826 and midcentury. The largest of the cotton-mill towns and the front runner in technological change, Lowell boasted the biggest work force, the greatest output, and the most capital invested.

In addition to leading many women to begin purchasing inexpensive cloth rather than making their

READY-MADE CLOTHING

own, the success of the textile factories spawned the ready-made clothing industry. Before the 1820s, women sewed most clothing at home. Some people purchased used clothing, and tailors and seamstresses made wealthy men's and women's clothing to order. By the 1820s and 1830s, much clothing was mass-produced. Manufacturers used two methods. In one, the clothing was made in a factory; in the other, at home, through the putting-out system. In this arrangement, a journeyman tailor—a trained craftsman employed by a master tailor who owned the workshop—cut the fabric panels in the factory, and the masters "put out" the sewing at piece rates to women working in their own homes. The work itself was familiar, but the change was significant: women were producing goods for wages and for the market, not primarily for their families.

Most of the early mass-produced clothes, crude and loose fitting, were made for men who lived in city boarding and rooming houses. Improvements in fit and changes in men's fashion eventually made ready-to-wear apparel more acceptable to clerks and professional men. In the 1840s, men began wearing the short sack coat. This forerunner of the modern suit jacket fit loosely and needed little custom tailoring. Now even upper-class men were willing to consider ready-made apparel. Most women made their own clothes, but those who could afford to do so employed seamstresses.

Retail clothing stores began to stock ready-made clothes in the 1820s. Their owners often bought goods

RETAIL MERCHANTS

wholesale, though many manufactured shirts and trousers in their own factories. Lewis and Hanford of New York City boasted of cutting more than 100,000 garments in the winter of 1848–1849. The firm sold most of its clothing in the South and owned its own retail outlet in New Orleans. In the West, Cincinnati became the center of the new men's clothing industry, which employed fifteen hundred men and ten thousand women by midcentury.

Commerce expanded hand in hand with manufacturing. Cotton, for instance, had once been traded

SPECIALIZATION OF COMMERCE

by plantation agents, who sold the raw cotton and bought manufactured goods that they then sold to plantation owners, extending them credit when necessary. Cotton exports rose from 83 million pounds in 1815 to more than 1 billion pounds in 1849. Gradually some agents came to specialize in finance alone: they were cotton brokers, who for a commission brought together buyers and sellers. Similarly, wheat and hog brokers sprang up in the West—in Cincinnati, Louisville, and St. Louis. The distribution of finished goods also became more specialized as wholesalers bought large quantities of particular items from manufacturers, and jobbers broke down the wholesale lots for retail stores and country merchants.

Commercial specialization transformed some traders in big cities, especially New York, into virtual merchant princes. After the Erie Canal opened, New York City became a stop on every major trade route from Europe, the southern ports, and the West. New

York traders were the middlemen for southern cotton and western grain. Merchants in other cities played a similar role within their own regions. Some traders invested their profits in factories, further stimulating urban manufacturing. Some cities specialized: Rochester became a milling center, and Cincinnati—"Porkopolis"—became the first meatpacking center.

Financial institutions played a significant role in the expansion of manufacturing and commerce.

BANKING AND CREDIT SYSTEMS

Banks, insurance companies, and corporations linked savers—those who deposited money in banks—with producers and speculators who wished to borrow money. After 1816, the Second Bank of the United States injected a national perspective into finance, but many farmers, local bankers, and politicians denounced the bank as a monster serving national, not local, interests. Western landowners suffered severe losses when the Second Bank reduced loans in the western states during the Panic of 1819. In 1836 critics finally succeeded in killing the bank (discussed in Chapter 11).

The closing of the Second Bank in 1836 caused a nationwide credit shortage, which, in conjunction with the Panic of 1837, led to fundamental reforms in banking. Michigan and New York, and soon other states, introduced charter laws promoting what was called free banking. Previously every new bank had needed a special legislative charter to operate; thus, each bank incorporation involved a political process. Under the new laws, any proposed bank that met certain minimum conditions—amount of capital invested, number of notes issued, and types of loans offered—would receive a state charter automatically, allowing banks to incorporate more easily.

Free banking proved to be a significant stimulus to the economy in the late 1840s and 1850s. New banks sprang up everywhere, providing merchants and manufacturers with the credit they needed. Free-banking laws also served as a precedent for general incorporation statutes that allowed manufacturing firms to receive state charters without special legislative acts.

Workers and the Workplace

Loud the morning bell is ringing,
   Up, up sleepers, haste away;

Yonder sits the redbreast singing,
   But to list we must not stay.

. . . .

Sisters, haste, the bell is tolling,
   Soon will close the dreadful gate;
Then, alas! We must go strolling,
   Through the counting-room too late.

. . . .

Now the sun is upward climbing,
   And the breakfast hour has come;
Ding, dong, ding, the bell is chiming,
   Hasten, sisters, hasten home.

The poet, writing in 1844 in the *Factory Girl's Garland*, uses the sound of the factory bell as a refrain to emphasize its incessant control, announcing when the workers are to wake, eat, begin work, stop work, and go to sleep. Night and day, the millworkers felt the stress of factory schedules.

The first generation of young single women who left New England villages and farms to work in the mills arrived with great optimism. The mills offered steady work and good pay, plus airy boarding houses, prepared meals, and cultural activities such as evening lectures. Sisters and cousins often worked and lived in the same mill and boarding house. They helped each other adjust, and their letters home drew kin to the mills. Most arrivals were sixteen and stayed only about five years. When they left the mills to marry, other younger women took their places.

In the hard times from 1837 to 1842, most mills ran only part time. Subsequently, managers pressured

BOOM AND BUST IN THE TEXTILE MILLS

workers by means of the speed-up, the stretch-out, and the premium system. The speed-up increased the speed of the machines, the stretch-out increased the number of machines each worker had to operate, and premiums paid to the overseers whose departments produced the most cloth encouraged them to pressure workers for greater output. In the race for profits, owners lengthened hours, cut wages, tightened discipline, and packed the boarding houses. Some mill workers began to think of themselves as slaves.

New England mill workers responded to their deteriorating working conditions by organizing and

PROTESTS

striking. In 1834, in reaction to a 25 percent wage cut, they unsuccessfully "turned out" (struck) against the

Lowell mills. Two years later, when boarding house fees increased, they turned out again. In the 1840s, Massachusetts mill women joined other workers to press for state legislation mandating a ten-hour day. They also aired their complaints in worker-run newspapers.

The women's labor organizations were weakened by worker turnover. Few of the militant native-born mill workers stayed on to fight the managers and owners, and gradually fewer New England daughters entered the mills. In the 1850s, Irish immigrant women who lived at home replaced them. Technological improvements in the looms and other machinery had made the work less skilled and more routine. The mills could thus pay lower wages and draw from a reservoir of unskilled labor.

A growing gender division in the workplace, especially in the textile, clothing, and shoemaking

GENDER DIVISIONS IN WORK

industries, was one important outcome of large-scale manufacturing. Although women and men in traditional agricultural and artisan households tended to perform different tasks, they worked as a family unit. As wage work spread, however, men's and women's work cultures became increasingly separate. The women and girls who left home for jobs in textile mills worked and lived in a mostly female world. In the clothing and shoemaking industries, whose male artisans had once worked at home assisted by unpaid family labor, men began working outside the home while women continued to work at home through the putting-out system. Tasks and wages too became rigidly differentiated: women sewed, whereas men shaped materials and finished products, receiving higher wages in shops employing men only.

The market economy had an impact on unpaid household labor as well. As home and workplace became separate and labor came to be defined in terms of wages (what could be sold in the marketplace) rather than production (what could be made by hand), the unpaid labor of women was devalued. Yet the family depended on women's work within the household, ever more so as sons and even daughters sought wage work outside the home and had less time for household tasks. Thus, gender defined household labor, and in the market economy, it went unrecorded, seemed to be worth little, and was taken for granted.

The new textile mills, shoe factories, iron mills, and railroads were the antithesis of traditional work-

shop and household production. In factories, authority was hierarchically organized. Factory workers lost

CHANGES IN THE WORKPLACE

their sense of autonomy as impersonal market forces seemed to dominate their lives. Their jobs were insecure, as competition frequently led to layoffs and new machines and division of labor allowed replacement by cheaper, less-skilled workers or even children. Moreover, the formal rules of the factory contrasted sharply with the informal atmosphere of artisan shops and farm households. When master craftsmen turned their workshops into small factories and became managers, journeymen became factory operatives. In large factories, paid supervisors directed the workers, who never saw the owners. Mill workers had to tolerate the roar of the looms, and all workers on power machines risked accidents that could maim or even kill. Perhaps most demoralizing, opportunities for advancement in the new system were virtually nil.

Wage workers felt distanced from traditional culture as well. As wage work became common, the republican virtues associated with independent craft traditions eroded. The rigid rules of factory work and the swings in employment brought on by boom-and-bust cycles restricted individual freedom.

In response, some workers organized to resist the changes wrought by the market economy and factories and to regain control of their work and their lives. Women textile workers organized into unions

LABOR PARTIES

and demonstrated for better wages and conditions or lobbied legislatures for relief. Male workers also organized and protested, but because they were eligible to vote, they also organized political parties. Labor parties first formed in Pennsylvania, New York, and Massachusetts in the 1820s and then spread elsewhere; they advocated free public education and abolishing imprisonment for debt and opposed banks and monopolies.

Organized labor's greatest achievement during this period was to gain relief from the threat of conspiracy laws. When journeyman shoemakers organized during the first decade of the century, their

EMERGENCE OF A LABOR MOVEMENT

employers accused them of criminal conspiracy. Although the courts acknowledged the journeymen's right to organize, judges viewed strikes as illegal until a Massachusetts case, *Commonwealth v. Hunt* (1842), ruled that Boston journeyman bootmakers could strike "in such manner as best to subserve their own interests."

Yet permanent labor organizations were difficult to sustain. Most workers outside the crafts were unskilled or semiskilled at best. Moreover, religion, race, ethnicity, and gender divided workers, and labor organizations excluded African Americans and women. (Massachusetts mill women organized their own unions.) The first unions arose among urban journeymen in printing, woodworking, shoemaking, and tailoring. They tended to be local; the strongest resembled medieval guilds in that members sought to protect themselves against the competition of inferior workmen by regulating apprenticeship and establishing minimum wages. Umbrella organizations composed of individual craft unions, like the National Trades Union (1834), arose in several cities in the 1820s and 1830s, but they failed during hard times. Labor organizations remained weak, and after 1830 workers' share of the national wealth declined.

Americans on the Move

*A*fter the War of 1812, the United States grew in size and population. The Louisiana Purchase (1803) had doubled the land area of the United States, and acquisitions in the 1840s nearly doubled it again. Throughout the Atlantic world, population soared, and that of the United States grew by a third in each decade. Between 1820 and 1845, the U.S. population increased from 9.6 million to 20.2 million.

The United States expanded outward, mostly westward, from its original seaboard base. The
WESTWARD MOVEMENT admission of new states tells the story: Indiana, Mississippi, Illinois, Alabama, Maine, and Missouri brought the Union to twenty-four states by the 1820s. Arkansas and Michigan followed in the 1830s, as did Florida, Texas, Iowa, and Wisconsin in the following decade.

During the first two decades of the century, Americans poured into the Ohio River valley; starting in the 1820s, they moved into the Mississippi River valley and beyond. By midcentury, two-thirds of Americans lived west of the Appalachians. Mostly young and hard working, they had visions of establishing family farms and achieving economic security.

Some 5 to 10 percent of Americans moved each year. Restless, they settled only temporarily and then moved on. Although most people lived on farms, there was also a steady rural-to-urban migration.

After the 1820s, the heart of cotton cultivation and the plantation system shifted from the coastal states to Alabama and the newly settled Mississippi valley—Tennessee, Louisiana, Arkansas, and Mississippi. Southerners brought their in-
THE SOUTH stitutions; they forced slaves to move with them, and yeoman farmers followed.

The shift was dramatic. The population of Mississippi soared from 73,000 in 1820 to 607,000 in 1850, with African American slaves in the majority. Across the Mississippi River, the population of Arkansas went from 14,000 in 1820 to 210,000 in 1850. Indian removal made this expansion possible. After the United States acquired Florida and attempted to colonize and suppress the Indian peoples there, southerners poured into the new territory. And while Texas was still part of Mexico in 1835, 35,000 Americans, including 3,000 slaves, lived there. Texas independence in 1836 spurred further American immigration. By 1845 the Anglo population was 125,000. Statehood that year opened the floodgates.

Not all moves were westward. A steady stream drifted from the Upper South to the Ohio valley, from slave to free states. Though northern black people moved westward as well, thousands of free people of
MOVES NORTH color moved to northern states and Canada in the 1830s following the adoption of black codes and mob violence in the South. Fugitives from slavery too went north. In the Southwest, when the U.S. Army suppressed the Comanches, Apaches, Navajos, and Utes, Hispanic migration accelerated north into areas of Texas and present-day New Mexico and Utah.

Online Study Center **Improve Your Grade**
Interactive Map: Settled Areas of the United States, 1820 and 1840

Settlers needed land and credit. Reflecting the nationalist outlook, the federal government hoped to fill
LAND GRANTS the West with non-Indian peoples
TO STATES and thus promote republican virtue. Some public lands were granted as

rewards for military service: veterans of the War of 1812 received 160 acres. After 1819 the government reduced the price of public land to an affordable $1.25 an acre, with a minimum purchase of 80 acres.

Some eager pioneers settled land before it had been surveyed and offered for sale. Such illegal settlers, or squatters, then had to buy the land at auction and faced the risk of being unable to purchase it. In 1841, to facilitate settlement and end property disputes, Congress passed the Pre-emption Act, which legalized settlement prior to surveying.

Since most settlers needed to borrow money, private credit systems arose. Nearly all economic activity
CREDIT in the West involved credit, from land sales to produce shipments to railroad construction. In 1816 and 1836 easy credit boosted land prices. When tight credit, high interest, low prices, or destructive weather squeezed farmers' income, land values collapsed, ending the speculative bubble. Mortgage bankers and speculators then purchased land cheaply. As a consequence, many farmers became renters instead of owners of land. Tenancy became more common in the West than it had been in New England.

From the start, newly settled western areas depended on their links with towns and cities. Ohio River
FRONTIER CITIES cities—Louisville and Cincinnati— and the old French settlements— Detroit on the Great Lakes, St. Louis on the Mississippi River—predated and promoted the earliest western settlements. So too in the South, from New Orleans to Natchez to Memphis, towns spearheaded settlement and economic growth. Steamboats connected the river cities with eastern markets and ports, carrying grain east and returning with finished goods. Like cities in the Northeast, these western cities eventually developed into manufacturing centers.

Native American Resistance and Removal

I ndians were also on the move, but in forced migrations. To make way for white expansion, the indigenous cultures of the eastern and southern woodlands were uprooted. Perhaps 100,000 eastern and southern Indian people were removed between 1820 and 1850; about 30,000 died in the process. Those who remained became virtually invisible.

In theory, under the U.S. Constitution, the federal government recognized and treated Indian nations
TREATY MAKING as sovereign foreign nations. Indeed the United States received Indian delegations with pomp and ceremony. Agreements between Indian nations and the United States were signed, sealed, and ratified like other international treaties. In practice, however, treaty making and Indian sovereignty were fictions. The United States imposed conditions on Indian representatives, and as the nation expanded, new treaties replaced old ones, shrinking Indian landholdings. Eventually, under President Andrew Jackson, wholesale removal would be the order of the day.

To maintain independence and preserve traditional ways, many Indian nations tried to accommodate to
INDIANS IN THE MARKET ECONOMY the expanding market economy. In the first three decades of the century, the Choctaw, Chickasaw, and Creek peoples in the lower Mississippi became suppliers and traders. Under treaty provisions, Indian commerce took place through trading posts and stores that provided Indians with supplies and purchased or bartered Indian-produced goods. The trading posts extended credit to chiefs, who fell into debt. With pelt prices falling, the debts grew enormously and often could be paid off only by selling land to the federal government. By 1822 the Choctaw nation had sold 13 million acres but still carried a debt of $13,000. The Indians struggled to adjust, but with the loss of land came dependency. The Choctaws came to rely on white Americans not only for manufactured goods but also for food.

Dependency facilitated removal of American Indian peoples to western lands. While the population of other groups increased greatly, the Indian population fell. War, forced removal, disease (especially smallpox), and malnutrition reduced many Indian nations by 50 percent. More than half of the Pawnees, Omahas, Otoes, Missouris, and Kansas died in the 1830s alone.

The wanderings of the Shawnees illustrate the uprooting of Indian people. After giving up 17 million
SHAWNEES acres in Ohio in the 1795 Treaty of Greenville, the Shawnees scattered

to Indiana and eastern Missouri. After the War of 1812, Prophet's Indiana group withdrew to Canada under British protection. In 1822 other Shawnees sought Mexican protection and moved from Missouri to present-day eastern Texas. As the U.S. government promoted removal to Kansas, Prophet returned from Canada to lead a group to the new Shawnee lands in eastern Kansas in 1825. When Missouri achieved statehood in 1821, Shawnees living there were also forced to move to Kansas, where in the 1830s other Shawnees removed from Ohio or expelled from Texas joined them. By 1854, however, Kansas was open to white settlement, and the Shawnees had to cede seven-eighths of their land, or 1.4 million acres.

Removal had a profound impact on all Shawnees. The men lost their traditional role as providers; their methods of hunting woodland animals were useless on the prairies of Kansas. As grain became the tribe's dietary staple, Shawnee women played a greater role as providers, supplemented by government aid under treaty provisions. Remarkably, the Shawnees preserved their language and culture in the face of these drastic changes.

Ever since the early days of European colonization, whites had sought to assimilate American Indians through education and Christianity. Westward expansion reinvigorated this goal. In 1819, in response to missionary lobbying, Congress appropriated $10,000 annually for "civilization of the tribes adjoining the frontier settlements." Protestant missionaries administered the "civilizing fund" and established mission schools. Catholic missions were already established in the Southwest and California.

ASSIMILATION AND EDUCATION

Within five years, thirty-two boarding schools enrolled Indian students. They substituted English for American Indian languages and taught agriculture alongside the Christian Gospel. But at the program's peak, schools across the United States enrolled fewer than fifteen hundred students, and to settlers eyeing Indian land, assimilation through education seemed too slow a process. Thus, wherever native peoples lived, illegal settlers disrupted their lives. Although obligated to protect the integrity of treaty lands, the federal government did so only halfheartedly. With government supporting westward expansion, legitimate Indian claims had to give way to the advance of white civilization. In the 1820s, it became apparent

that Indians could not be persuaded to cede enough acreage to satisfy land-hungry whites.

In late 1824, President James Monroe proposed to Congress that Indians be moved beyond the Mississippi River. Monroe's proposition targeted the Cherokees, Creeks, Choctaws, and Chickasaws, who unanimously rejected it.

INDIAN REMOVAL AS FEDERAL POLICY

Pressure from Georgia had prompted Monroe's policy. Cherokees and Creeks lived in northwestern Georgia, and in the 1820s the state accused the federal government of not fulfilling its 1802 promise to remove the Indians in return for the state's renunciation of its claim to western lands. Neither Monroe's removal messages nor further cessions by the Creeks satisfied Georgia. In 1826, under federal pressure, the Creek nation ceded all but a small strip of its Georgia acreage. Georgians were unmoved: only the removal of the Georgia Creeks to the West could resolve the conflict between the state and the federal government.

Adapting to American ways could not forestall removal. No people met the challenge of assimilating more thoroughly than the Cherokees. Between 1819 and 1829 the tribe became economically self-sufficient and politically self-governing; the twelve to fifteen thousand adult Cherokees came to think of themselves as a nation, not a collection of villages. Sequoyah, a self-educated Cherokee, devised an eighty-six-character alphabet that made possible a Cherokee-language Bible and a bilingual tribal newspaper, *Cherokee Phoenix*. Between 1820 and 1823 the Cherokees created a formal government with a bicameral legislature, a court system, and a salaried bureaucracy. In 1827 they adopted a written constitution, modeled after that of the United States. Cherokee land laws, however, differed from U.S. law. The tribe collectively owned all Cherokee land and forbade land sales to outsiders. Economic change paralleled political adaptation. Many Cherokees became individual farmers and slaveholders in an economy of commodity trade based on barter, cash, and credit. By 1833 they held fifteen hundred black slaves.

CHEROKEES

But Cherokees' political and economic changes failed to win respect or acceptance from southerners. In the 1820s, Georgia pressed them to sell the 7,200 square miles of land they held in the state. When the

Cherokees declined to negotiate cession, Georgia annulled their constitution, extended the state's sovereignty over them, prohibited the Cherokee National Council from meeting except to cede land, and ordered their lands seized. The discovery of gold on Cherokee land in 1829 whetted Georgia's appetite for Cherokee territory.

Backed by sympathetic whites but not by the new president, Andrew Jackson, the Cherokees under

CHEROKEE NATION V. GEORGIA

Chief John Ross turned to the federal courts to defend their treaty with the United States and to prevent Georgia from seizing more land. In *Cherokee Nation v. Georgia* (1831), Chief Justice John Marshall ruled that under the federal Constitution, an Indian tribe was neither a foreign nation nor a state and therefore had no standing in federal courts. Nonethe-

less, said Marshall, the Indians had an unquestionable right to their lands; they could lose title only by voluntarily giving it up. A year later, in *Worcester v. Georgia*, Marshall defined the Cherokee position more clearly. The Indian nation was, he declared, a distinct political community in which "the laws of Georgia can have no force" and into which Georgians could not enter without permission or treaty privilege. Georgia refused to comply.

President Andrew Jackson refused to interfere because the case involved a state action. Keen to open up new lands for settlement, Jackson favored expelling the Cherokees. In the Removal Act of 1830, Congress had provided Jackson with the funds he needed to negotiate new treaties and resettle the resistant tribes west of the Mississippi (see Map 10.2).

The Choctaws went first; they made the forced journey from Mississippi and Alabama to the West

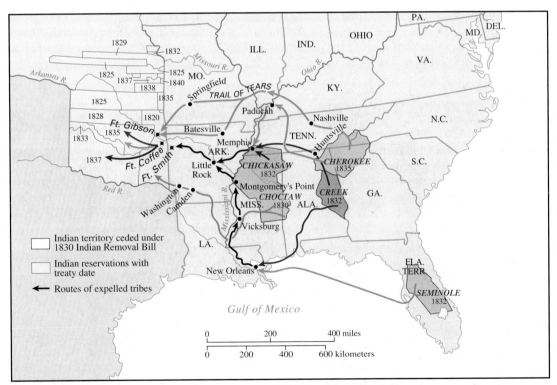

Map 10.2   Removal of Native Americans from the South, 1820–1840

Over a twenty-year period, the federal government and southern states forced Native Americans to exchange their traditional homes for western land. Some tribal groups remained in the South, but most settled in the alien western environment.

in the winter of 1831 and 1832. The Creeks in Alabama resisted removal until 1836, when the army pushed them westward. A year later, the Chickasaws followed.

Having fought removal in the courts, the Cherokees were divided. Some believed that further resistance was hopeless and accepted removal as the only chance to preserve their civilization. The leaders of this minority agreed in 1835 to exchange their southern home for western land in the Treaty of New Echota. Most, though, wanted to stand firm. John Ross, with petitions signed by fifteen thousand Cherokees, lobbied the Senate against ratification of the treaty. They lost. But when the time for evacuation came in 1838, most Cherokees refused to move. President Martin Van Buren sent federal troops to round them up. About twenty thousand Cherokees were evicted, held in detention camps, and marched to Indian Territory in present-day Oklahoma under military escort. Nearly one-quarter of them died of disease and exhaustion on what came to be known as the Trail of Tears.

When the forced march to the West ended, the Indians had traded about 100 million acres east of the Mississippi for 32 million acres west of the river plus $68 million. Only a few scattered remnants, among them the Seminoles in Florida and the Cherokees in the southern Appalachian Mountains, remained in the East and South.

Forced removal had a disastrous impact on the displaced tribes. In the West they encountered an alien environment; lacking traditional ties, few felt at peace with the land. The animals and plants they found were unfamiliar. Unable to live off the land, many became dependent on government payments for survival. Removal also brought new internal conflicts. The Cherokees in particular experienced violence between pro- and antitreaty factions. Moreover, conflict arose between Native American groups migrating from the South and East and Indians already living in the West, as they were forced to share land and scarce resources.

In Florida a small band of Seminoles continued to resist. Some Seminole leaders agreed in the Treaty

SECOND SEMINOLE WAR

of Payne's Landing to relocate to the West within three years, but others opposed the treaty. A minority under Osceola, a charismatic leader,

■ *The Trail of Tears,* by twentieth-century Pawnee artist Brummet Echohawk. About twenty thousand Cherokees were evicted in 1838–1839, and about one-quarter of them died on the forced march to present-day Oklahoma.   (Gilcrease Museum, Tulsa, OK)

refused to vacate their homes and fought the pro-treaty group. When federal troops were sent to impose removal in 1835, Osceola waged a fierce guerrilla war against them. Osceola was captured under a white flag of truce and died in an army prison in 1838, but the Seminoles continued the fight. In 1842 the United States abandoned the removal effort. Most of Osceola's followers agreed to move west to Indian Territory in 1858, but many Seminoles remained in the Florida Everglades, proud of having resisted conquest.

Summary *Online Study Center* ACE the Test

Nationalism and self-confidence accompanied the end of the War of 1812. Under the Democratic-Republicans the federal government fostered expansion and economic growth through internal improvements, tariffs, the Second Bank of the United States, land sales, and Indian removal. The Supreme Court and American diplomats, too, asserted nationalism. John Quincy Adams negotiated peace and secure borders with Great Britain and Spain, and through the Monroe Doctrine insulated the Western Hemisphere from European conflict.

But sectionalism accompanied nationalism and geographical expansion. Conflicts over tariffs, economic hard times, and slavery brought discord. The Missouri Compromise was a stopgap measure to avoid the explosive issue of slavery.

From 1816 through 1845, the United States experienced explosive growth. Population increased six-fold and moved westward. New farms grew cotton and grain for the market, and cities followed. In the process, Indians were pushed aside.

Agriculture remained the dominant industry, though by midcentury a booming manufacturing sector challenged farming. And agriculture itself was becoming market oriented and mechanized. The market economy brought sustained growth; it also ushered in cycles of boom and bust that brought hard times and unemployment. The growing economy also meant growing destruction of the environment.

Large-scale manufacturing altered traditional patterns of production and consumption. Farm families began to purchase goods formerly made at home, and geared production to faraway markets. Farm women increasingly contributed income from market sales to the household purse. In New England many young women left the family farm to become the first factory workers in the new textile industry. In the new mills and factories, workplace relations became more impersonal, working conditions grew harsher, and men's and women's work became increasingly dissimilar. Industrial jobs began to attract large numbers of immigrants, and some workers organized labor unions.

LEGACY FOR A PEOPLE AND A NATION
A Mixed Economy

How active should the U.S. government be? Should it run, regulate, or leave to the market system health care, Social Security and private pensions, corporate concentration, and stock trading and investments? In other words, to what degree should the government be responsible for the well-being of the economy and individuals?

The Articles of Confederation limited government, the Constitution empowered it, and the Bill of Rights restricted it in specific areas. While Americans have continuously debated the appropriate role of government, the United States has generally occupied a middle ground: a mixed economy.

In the early nineteenth century, government played an active role in economic and social expansion. Federal and state governments built roads and canals, developed harbors, and operated post offices and the early telegraph. More commonly the government intervened to stimulate and regulate the private sector.

In the late nineteenth century, advocates of laissez-faire, or hands-off, government, challenged the pre–Civil War tradition of active government. Laissez faire dominated briefly until the 1880s and 1890s, when large corporations and trusts accumulated so much power that governments stepped in to regulate railroads and business concentration.

After the turn of the century, the federal government extended regulation to food, drugs, the environment, working conditions, and fair business practices. In the 1930s, the crisis of the Great Depression, followed in the 1940s by World War II, would lead the federal government to establish the modern welfare state, which operates through a mixed public-private structure.

Early in the twenty-first century, Americans again debate the appropriate role of government.

Conservatives view government as the problem rather than the solution, arguing that government regulation hampers individual freedom and distorts the law of supply and demand. Advocates of an activist government argue that only the government has the power and resources to check economic concentration and to protect health, safety, and the environment. The framework of this debate is a legacy from before the Civil War.

REFORM AND POLITICS IN THE AGE OF JACKSON 1824–1845

"**I** proceed, Gentlemen, briefly to call your attention to the present state of Insane persons confined within this Commonwealth," Dorothea Dix petitioned the 1843 Massachusetts legislature, "in cages, closets, stalls, pens! Chained, naked, beaten with rods and lashed into obedience."

A year earlier, in a visit to a Newburyport almshouse, Dix had discovered one man residing in a shed whose door opened to the local "dead room," or morgue; his only companions were corpses. Shocked, she heard from an attendant about another insane inmate: "a woman in a cellar." Dix asked to see her. The superintendent warned Dix that the woman "was dangerous to be approached." Dix pressed on. They unlocked the doors and entered an underground cell. In the shadows Dix saw "a female apparently wasted to a skeleton, partially wrapped in blankets." She was withered, wrote Dix, "not by age, but by suffering." When the inmate saw the visitors, she wailed with despair: "Why am I consigned to hell? . . . I used to pray, I used to read the Bible. . . . I had friends; why have all forsaken me!—my God! my God! why hast thou forsaken me?"

Dix described in the most personal and vivid terms her visits to jails, almshouses, and private homes, and the cruel treatment of the insane. Her petition to the General Court of Massachusetts was so graphic and shocking that the legislature voted to reprint it as a government pamphlet. Part petition, part sermon, and part autobiography, it made riveting reading.

Dix epitomized much of early-nineteenth-century reform. She started with a religious belief in individual self-improvement and human perfectibility that led her to advocate collective responsibility. She made reform her career, fearlessly entering the public arena. Investigating asylums, petitioning the Massachusetts legislature, and lobbying other states and Congress, Dix moved from reform to politics, and she helped create a new public role for women, in the process broadening the base of political participation.

Online Study Center
This icon will direct you to interactive map and primary source activities on the website
http://college.hmco.com/pic/nortonbrief7e

CHRONOLOGY

1790s–1840s • Second Great Awakening spreads religious fervor

1820s • Reformers in New York and Pennsylvania establish model penitentiaries

1824 • No presidential candidate wins a majority in the electoral college

1825 • House of Representatives elects Adams president

1826 • American Society for the Promotion of Temperance founded
• Morgan affair is catalyst for Antimasonry movement

1828 • Tariff of Abominations passed
• Jackson elected president

1830 • Webster-Hayne debate explores the nature of the Union

1830s–40s • Democratic-Whig competition gels in second party system

1831 • Garrison begins abolitionist newspaper *The Liberator*
• First national Antimason convention

1832 • Jackson vetoes rechartering of the Second Bank of the United States
• Jackson reelected president

1832–33 • South Carolina nullifies tariffs of 1828 and 1832, prompting nullification crisis

1836 • Republic of Texas established after breaking from Mexico
• Specie Circular ends credit purchase of public lands
• Van Buren elected president

1837 • Financial panic ends boom of the 1830s

1838–39 • United States and Canada mobilize their militias over Maine–New Brunswick border dispute

1839–43 • Hard times spread unemployment and deflation

1840 • Whigs win presidency under Harrison

1841 • Tyler assumes the presidency after Harrison's death
• "Oregon fever" attracts settlers to the Northwest and intensifies expansionism

1843 • Dix petitions Massachusetts legislature regarding deplorable condition of insane asylums

1844 • Polk elected president

1845 • Texas admitted to the Union

1848 • Woman's Rights Convention at Seneca Falls, New York, calls for women's suffrage

The religious and reform fervor of the period arose both as part of the spiritual renewal known as the Second Great Awakening and as a response to the enormous transformation the United States experienced after the War of 1812. Immigration, the spread of a market economy, growing inequality, the westward advance of settlement, and territorial expansion all contributed to remaking the United States.

Anxieties wrought by rapid change drove the impulse to reform society. Men and women organized to end the abuses of alcohol and prostitution, improve conditions in prisons and asylums, oppose secret and antidemocratic societies, end slavery, and achieve equal rights for women. Inevitably reform movements pushed men and women into politics, though only men voted. Opponents of reform were equally concerned about social problems. They were, however, skeptical about human perfectibility, and they distrusted the exercise of power.

Two issues in particular bridged reform and politics: the short-lived Antimasonry frenzy against secret societies and the intense, uncompromising crusade for an immediate end to slavery. Though Antimasons organized the first third-party movement, abolition eventually overrode all other concerns.

The Jacksonians too saw themselves as reformers. They opposed special privileges and the Second Bank of the United States. President Andrew Jackson believed that a strong federal government restricted individual freedom by favoring one group over another. Social and religious reformers disagreed. Wanting a more active federal role, they rallied around the new Whig Party. Democrats and Whigs constituted a new party system, characterized by strong organizations, intense loyalty, and energetic religious and ethnic competition.

Both parties eagerly promoted expansionism during the prosperous 1840s. Democrats saw the agrarian West as an antidote to urbanization and industrialization; Whigs focused on the new commercial opportunities it offered. Expanding the nation to the Pacific seemed to be the manifest destiny of the United States. ■

From Revival to Reform

*R*eligion was probably the strongest motivation behind organized benevolence and reform. Beginning in the late 1790s religious revivals galvanized Protestants, especially women, into social action. At camp meetings, sometimes lasting a week with thousands in attendance, preachers exhorted sinners to repent and become genuine Christians. They offered salvation to all through personal conversion. At a time when only a minority could read and write, itinerant evangelists were democratizing American religion, making it available to all.

Resembling the Great Awakening of the eighteenth century (see Chapter 4), the movement came to be called the Second Great Awakening. It raised hopes for the Second Coming of the Christian messiah and the establishment of God's Kingdom on earth. Revivalists resolved to speed the Second Coming by combating the forces of evil and darkness. Some believed that the United States had a special mission in God's design and a special role in eliminating evil. Under revivalist influence, the role of churches and ministers in community life diminished as lay participation increased, and evangelical Christians across the country tried to right the wrongs of the world.

SECOND GREAT AWAKENING

In the South, huge numbers of people regularly attended revivals, but they especially drew women and African Americans, free and slave. The call to personal repentance and conversion invigorated Protestantism, giving southern churches an evangelical base and evangelicalism a southern accent. In essence, the Second Great Awakening turned the South into the Bible belt. It also mostly ignored slavery, thus accommodating to it.

In the North, New York lawyer Charles G. Finney led the revival movement. After his 1821 soul-shaking conversion, Finney abandoned the law to convert souls. Salvation could be achieved, Finney preached, through spontaneous conversion like his own. He mesmerized his audiences and in everyday language preached that "God has made man a moral free agent." In other words, evil was avoidable: Christians were not doomed by original sin, and anyone could achieve salvation.

Revivalism had a particularly strong base among Methodists and Baptists, and these denominations grew the most because their structure maximized democratic participation and drew their ministers from ordinary folk. As Methodists and Baptists moved west, migration patterns spread not only religion but also the impulse for moral reform. All revivalists shared a belief in individual self-improvement, and the doctrine of perfectibility demanded that Christians actively organize and convert others. Thus, the Second Great Awakening bred reform, and evangelical Protestants became missionaries for both religious and secular salvation, generating new religious groups and voluntary reform societies. New sects like the

Mormons arose out of this ferment. So did associations that addressed the pressing issues of the day: temperance, education, Sabbath observance, dueling, and later slavery.

More women than men answered the call of Christianity, sustaining the Second Great Awakening and invigorating local churches.

EVANGELICAL WOMEN

Gradually women brought their families and sometimes their husbands into church and reform. Women, more than men, tended to feel personally responsible for counteracting the secular orientation of the expanding market economy. Emotionally charged conversion could return women to what they believed was the right path. It also offered them communal ties with other women.

Female missionary societies motivated organized religious and benevolent activity on an unprecedented scale. For women and some men, reform represented their first political involvement at a time when women did not vote. In reform organizations, women represented themselves; by participating directly in service activities, they pioneered new, visible, public roles for women.

An exposé of prostitution in New York City illustrates how reform led to political action. In response to an 1830 report documenting

FEMALE REFORM SOCIETIES

widespread prostitution in the city, New York businessmen and politicians defended the city's good name against "those base slanders." Women, moved by the plight of "fallen women," organized to fight prostitution. But whereas male reformers targeted the prostitutes, the newly organized Female Moral Reform Society focused on the men who victimized young women, publicizing the names of brothel clients.

During the 1830s, the New York society expanded. Calling itself the American Female Moral Reform Society, by 1840 it had 555 affiliated chapters across the nation. The society also entered the political sphere. In New York State in the 1840s, it successfully lobbied for criminal sanctions against men who seduced women into prostitution, as well as against prostitutes themselves.

One of the most successful reform efforts was the campaign against alcohol. Americans in 1800 consumed alcohol at the formidable

TEMPERANCE

annual rate of 5 gallons per capita, and alcohol played a significant role in men's social lives. Why then did temperance become such a vital issue? Like all nineteenth-century reform, temperance had a strong religious foundation.

Evangelicals considered drinking sinful, and forsaking alcohol was frequently part of conversion. The sale of whiskey often violated the Sabbath; many workers labored for six days and spent Sunday at the public house drinking and socializing. Alcoholism also destroyed families and caused poverty and crime. In the early 1840s, thousands of ordinary women formed Martha Washington societies to protect families by reforming alcoholics, raising children as teetotalers, and spreading the temperance message. Employers complained that drinkers took "St. Monday" as a holiday to recover from Sunday. In the new world of the factory, drinking was unacceptable.

As the temperance movement gained momentum, its goal shifted from moderation to voluntary abstinence and finally to prohibition. The American Society for the Promotion of Temperance, organized in 1826 to promote pledges of abstinence, became a pressure group for state prohibition legislation. By the mid-1830s five thousand state and local temperance societies touted teetotalism, and more than 1 million people had taken the pledge. As the movement spread, per capita consumption of alcohol fell from 5 gallons to below 2 gallons in the 1840s. Moreover, a number of northern states followed Maine in outlawing the sale of alcohol except for medicinal purpose.

From the 1820s on, many reformers expressed their prejudices by regarding alcohol as an evil introduced by Catholic immigrants. Rum and immigrants, they claimed, defiled the Sabbath, brought poverty, and supported the feared papacy. In fact, many Catholics took the pledge of abstinence. But even Catholic teetotalers tended to oppose state regulation of drinking. They favored self-control, not state coercion.

As Dorothea Dix urged, moral reform also stimulated the construction of institutions to house prisoners, the mentally ill, orphans,

PENITENTIARIES AND ASYLUMS

delinquent children, and the poor. Such institutions were needed, reformers argued, to shelter victims of society's turbulence and impose on them familial discipline. Through discipline and the banning of idleness, inmates might become self-reliant and responsible.

■ As the temperance movement spread, the evils of alcohol became a major theme in popular culture. This 1830s lithograph, *Mortgaging the Farm,* hints at drinking's potential destructiveness. Drunken, idle farmers sit in the shadow of the gallows holding the tavern's signboard.   (Old Sturbridge Village)

In the 1820s New York and Pennsylvania rejected incarceration to punish criminals or remove them from society, introducing instead regimens to rehabilitate them. New York's Auburn prison placed prisoners in individual cells but brought them together in common workshops. Pennsylvania's prisons isolated prisoners completely, forcing them to eat, sleep, and work in their individual cells and allowing them contact only with guards and visitors.

Insane asylums, hospitals, and orphanages instituted similar approaches. Formerly the prescribed treatment had removed disturbed individuals from society and isolated them among strangers, many with criminals. The new asylums were clean and orderly. In response to Dorothea Dix's crusade and reform societies, twenty-eight of the thirty-three states had public institutions for the mentally ill by 1860.

Critical to reform movements was building networks. Reform and literary societies brought national speakers like Dorothea Dix, abolitionist Frederick Douglass, and hundreds of others to cities and towns to preach reform. Annual conventions increased personal contacts and motivated supporters. Reformers made use of new technology, such as the new steam presses that permitted mass publication of their newspapers and pamphlets, to spread their word.

More intense than the asylum movement was the briefer crusade against Freemasonry, a secret fraternity that had come to the United States from England in the eighteenth century. Sons of the Enlightenment such as Benjamin Franklin and George Washington were attracted to Masonry, because it emphasized individual belief in a deity (as opposed to organized religion or a single church's doctrine). In the early nineteenth century Freemasonry attracted men prominent in commerce and civic affairs.

ANTIMASONRY

Opponents of Masonry believed that its secrecy and appeal to elites were antidemocratic and antirepublican. Publications such as the *Anti Masonic Almanac* attacked Masonic initiation rites. Evangelicals labeled the order satanic. Antimasons argued that Masonry threatened the family because it excluded women and encouraged men to neglect their families for alcohol and ribald entertainments at Masonic lodges. The political arena quickly absorbed Antimasonry, and its short life illustrates the close association of politics and reform in the 1820s and after.

The catalyst for Antimasonry as an organized movement was the suspected murder of William Morgan, a disillusioned Mason who published an exposé in 1826. Even before the book appeared, a group of Masons abducted Morgan in Canandaigua, New York. It was widely believed that his kidnappers murdered him, though his body was never found.

MORGAN AFFAIR

Events seemed to confirm Masonry's antidemocratic character. Prosecutors who were Masons appeared to obstruct the investigation of Morgan's abduction. The public pressed for justice, and a series of notorious trials from 1827 through 1831 led many to suspect a cover-up. Antimasonry coalesced overnight in western New York, and it quickly became a political movement that spread to other states.

With growing popular support, the Antimasons held conventions in 1827 to select candidates to oppose Masons running for office. The next year, the conventions supported John Quincy Adams for president

CONVENTION SYSTEM

and opposed Andrew Jackson because he was a Mason. The Antimasons held the first national political convention in Baltimore in 1831, and a year later they nominated William Wirt as their presidential candidate. Thus, the Antimasons became a rallying point for anti-Jacksonians. Their electoral strength lay in New England and New York. Antimasonry found little support in the slave South.

By the mid-1830s, Antimasonry had lost momentum. A single-issue party, the Antimasons declined along with Freemasonry. Yet the movement left its mark on the politics of the era. As a moral crusade focused on public officeholders, it inspired broad participation in the political process. The Antimasons also changed party organization by pioneering the convention, rather than the caucus, for nominating candidates for office and by introducing the party platform.

Abolitionism and the Women's Movement

*a*ntimasonry foreshadowed and had much in common with abolitionism. To abolitionist William Lloyd Garrison, both slavery and Masonry undermined republican values. Eventually the issue of slavery consumed all other reforms and threatened the nation itself. Those who advocated immediate emancipation saw slavery as, above all, a moral issue—the ultimate sin.

Free blacks in the North had demanded an end to slavery since the Revolution. In 1800 Richard Allen, the first bishop of the African Methodist Episcopal (AME) Church, eulogized former president George Washington for freeing his slaves, and his sermon on immediatism— an immediate end to slavery—was widely circulated as a pamphlet. To free blacks, slavery was both a moral issue and a personal one; while slavery was legal, they were always at risk of being seized as fugitives. David Walker's *Appeal . . . to the Colored Citizens* (1829) was a clarion call for immediatism and helped politicize many abolitionists. Walker, a southern-born free black, was Boston's leading abolitionist until his death in 1830. By then fifty black abolitionist societies in the United States were assisting fugitive slaves, lobbying for emancipa-

AFRICAN AMERICAN ABOLITIONISTS

◾ Women played an activist role in reform, especially in abolitionism. A rare daguerreotype from August 1850 shows women and men, including Frederick Douglass, on the podium at an abolitionist rally in Cazenovia, New York.   (Collection of J. Paul Getty Museum, Los Angeles, California)

tion, and exposing slavery's evils. A free black press spread the word.

Few whites, however, advocated the abolition of slavery before the 1830s. In the North, where by 1820 slavery had been virtually abolished, whites took little interest in the issue. Antislavery sentiment appeared strongest in the Upper South. The American Colonization Society, founded in 1816, advocated gradual, voluntary emancipation and resettlement of former slaves in Africa, establishing the colony of Liberia for that purpose in the 1820s. Society members did not believe that free blacks had a place in the United States, and they included Jefferson and other slaveholders, some evangelicals and Quakers, and (briefly) a few blacks.

During the 1830s, however, a small number of white reformers, driven by moral urgency, joined the

GRADUAL EMANCIPATION

The International Antislavery Movement

The heart of the international antislavery movement had been in Great Britain, but in the 1830s, many of Britain's local antislavery societies thought they had accomplished their mission and disbanded. In 1833 Parliament ended slavery in the British Empire, and over the previous three decades, the international slave trade had greatly diminished. At the same time, however, abolitionism in the United States was on the rise, and now militant American black abolitionists revived the international movement to end slavery where it still existed: in Spanish possessions like Cuba, in independent and colonial South America, in Africa and Asia, and in the United States.

Seeking to raise money and put international pressure on the United States to abolish slavery, African American abolitionists in the 1840s toured Britain regularly to appeal for support. Especially effective were ex-slaves, who recounted their firsthand experiences of slavery and bared their scarred bodies. In 1845 Frederick Douglass began a nineteen-month tour, giving three hundred lectures in Britain.

In 1849 black abolitionists William Wells Brown, Alexander Crummell, and J. W. C. Pennington were among the twenty American delegates at the international Paris Peace Conference. There, Brown likened war and slavery, telling the eight hundred delegates from western Europe and the United States that "it is impossible to maintain slavery without maintaining war." His scheduled brief lecture tour in Britain turned into a five-year exile because, after passage of the 1850 Fugitive Slave Law, he feared being seized and sent back to slavery if he returned to the United States. In 1854 British abolitionists purchased his freedom from his former master.

Gandy, Douglass, Brown, and dozens of other former slaves helped revive abolitionism as an international issue. They energized the British and Foreign Anti-Slavery Society, founded in 1839, and hundreds of more militant, local societies. By the early 1850s national abolitionist movements succeeded in abolishing slavery in Colombia, Argentina, Venezuela, and Peru. As advocates of women's rights, international peace, temperance, and other reforms, the United States's black abolitionists also linked Americans to reform movements around the world.

William Wells Brown's autobiography stirred abolitionists in the United States and England. In 1849 Brown was among the American delegates to the Paris Peace Conference, then spent the next five years as an exile in Britain, fearing being sent back to slavery under the 1850 Fugitive Slave Act. He returned to the United States only after British abolitionists purchased his freedom from his former master. (Documenting the American South [http://docsouth.unc.edu], The University of North Carolina at Chapel Hill Libraries)

black crusade for immediate emancipation. Soon the immediatists, who demanded immediate, complete, and uncompensated emancipation, surpassed the gradualists as the dominant strand of abolitionism. The most prominent and uncompromising immediatist was the incendiary William Lloyd Garrison. In 1831 Garrison began publishing *The Liberator,* in whose first issue he declared, "I am in earnest—I will not equivocate—I will not excuse—I will not retreat a single inch—and *I will be heard.*"

Garrison's refusal to work with anyone who tolerated the delay of emancipation isolated him from other white opponents of slavery. Still, by his actions and rhetorical power, Garrison helped to push antislavery onto the national agenda, though he had no specific plan for abolishing slavery.

It is difficult to differentiate between those who became immediatists and those who did not. Immedi-

IMMEDIATISTS

atists were often young evangelicals active in benevolent societies in the 1820s; many became ordained ministers; and many had personal contact with free blacks. They were convinced that slaveholding was a sin. They also shared great moral intensity and were unwilling to compromise.

In the 1840s escaped slaves Frederick Douglass and Harriet Tubman joined forces with white reformers in the American Anti-Slavery Society. Those who had experienced slavery firsthand, like Douglass and Sojourner Truth, wrote personal narratives that mobilized northerners. Most benevolent workers and reformers, however, kept their distance from the immediatists. They shared the view that slavery was a sin but believed in gradual emancipation. They feared that if they moved too fast or attacked sinners too harshly, they would destroy the harmony and order they sought.

Immediatists' greatest recruitment successes resulted from defending their own constitutional rights,

OPPOSITION TO ABOLITIONISTS

not the rights of slaves. Wherever they went, immediatists found their free speech threatened by hostile crowds. Mob violence peaked in 1835 with more than fifty riots aimed at abolitionists or African Americans. In 1837 in Alton, Illinois, a mob murdered abolitionist editor Elijah P. Lovejoy. Public outrage at Lovejoy's murder increased antislavery support in the North.

In the South, mobs blocked the distribution of antislavery tracts. Steam-powered presses and tech-

nological developments in papermaking in the 1830s enabled the American Anti-Slavery Society to publish millions of pamphlets. The state of South Carolina intercepted and burned abolitionist literature. In 1835 proslavery assailants killed four abolitionists in South Carolina and Louisiana and forty supposed insurrectionists in Mississippi and Louisiana.

At a rally in Boston in 1835, former Federalist Harrison Gray Otis portrayed abolitionists as subversives. Abolitionists, he predicted, would turn to politics, causing unforeseeable calamity. "What will become of the Union?" Otis asked.

Abolitionists were already bombarding Congress with petitions to abolish slavery and the slave trade in

GAG RULE

the District of Columbia, which Congress governed. The House in 1836 adopted what abolitionists labeled the "gag rule," which automatically tabled abolitionist petitions, effectively preventing debate on them. In a dramatic defense of the right of petition, former president John Quincy Adams, now a representative from Massachusetts, took to the floor again and again to speak against the gag rule. (Its repeal in 1844 was anticlimactic.)

The Missouri Compromise, censorship of the mails, and the gag rule represented attempts to keep the issue of slavery out of the political arena. Yet the more that national leaders, especially Democrats, worked to avoid the matter, the more antislavery forces hardened their resolve.

Abolitionism was highly factionalized, and its adherents fought one another as often as they fought the defenders of slavery. They were divided between Garrison's emphasis on "moral suasion"—winning over the hearts of slaveowners rather than coercing them—and the practical politics of James G. Birney, the Liberty Party's candidate for president in 1840 and 1844. They also disagreed about the place of free blacks in American society. And the movement split over other reforms, especially the roles and rights of women.

Women had been prominent in the antislavery movement from the start, in many cases as active and

WOMEN ABOLITIONISTS

politically involved as men. Lydia Maria Child, Maria Chapman, and Lucretia Mott served on the American Anti-Slavery Society's executive committee; Child and Chapman served as editors of its official paper, the *National Anti-Slavery Standard.* Garrison's moral suasion attracted many women because it gave them a platform from which to oppose slavery. Yet some politically active societies excluded women because they could not vote and opposed women's roles in reform.

In the 1830s abolitionists Angelina and Sarah Grimké were attacked for speaking to mixed audiences. One pastoral letter declared that women should obey, not lecture, men. This reaction turned the Grimkés' attention from the condition of slaves to the condition of women. Born into a Charleston, South Carolina, slaveholding family, both sisters had experienced conversion, became outspoken abolitionists, moved north, and found a home in Garrison's immediatism. Now they confronted the concept of "subordination to man," insisting that men and women had the "same rights and same duties." Together the Grimkés initiated a new reform movement to secure legal and social equality of women.

Online Study Center
Improve Your Grade
Primary Source: Rules for Husbands and Wives

Public participation in religious revival and 25p10.5-reform had led some women to reexamine their positions in society. As the predominant group in the Second Great Awakening, women began to challenge male domination in religion. Revivals brought ordinary women into the public sphere. Female societies and reform networks, convention participation, and advocacy opened new roles to women. The market economy also created new occupations for women outside their homes.

WOMEN'S RIGHTS

Women abolitionists were among the leaders on behalf of women's rights. In July 1848 Elizabeth Cady Stanton, Lucretia Mott, and Lucy Stone organized the Woman's Rights Convention at Seneca Falls, New York. Three hundred women and men reformers gathered to demand political, social, and economic equality for women. They protested women's legal disabilities—inability to vote, limited property rights—and their social restrictions—exclusion from advanced schooling and from most occupations. Their Declaration of Sentiments indicted the injustices suffered by women and launched the women's rights movement. "All men and women are created equal," the declaration proclaimed. If women had the vote, participants argued, they could protect themselves and realize their full potential as moral and spiritual leaders.

Advocates of women's rights were slow to garner support, especially from men, who held most of the political and legal power. In the 1840s the question of women's suffrage split the antislavery movement. Some men joined the ranks, notably Garrison and Frederick Douglass, but most men actively opposed a vote for women.

Jacksonianism and Party Politics

*I*n the 1820s, reform pushed its way into politics. No less than reformers, politicians sought to control the direction of change in the expanding nation. The 1824 presidential election ignited a political fire that reformers, abolitionists, and expansionists would continuously stoke. By the 1830s, politics had become the great American pastime.

The election of 1824, in which John Quincy Adams and Andrew Jackson faced off for the first time, heralded a more open political system. From 1800 through 1820 the system in which a congressional caucus chose the Democratic-Republican nominees (Jefferson, Madison, and Monroe) had worked well. That it limited voters' involvement in choosing candidates was not an anomaly because in 1800, only five of the sixteen states selected presidential electors by popular vote. In most of the others, state legislatures selected the electors. By 1824, however, eighteen of twenty-four states chose electors by popular vote.

The Democratic-Republican caucus in 1824 chose William H. Crawford of Georgia, secretary of the treasury, as its presidential candidate. But other Democratic-Republicans, emboldened by the chance to appeal directly to voters, put themselves forward as sectional candidates. John Quincy Adams drew support from New England, while westerners backed House Speaker Henry Clay of Kentucky. Secretary of War John C. Calhoun hoped for support from the South and from Pennsylvania. The Tennessee legislature nominated Andrew Jackson, a popular military hero of unknown political views. Jackson had the most widespread support. By boycotting the caucus and attacking it as undemocratic, these men and their supporters ended the role of Congress in nominating presidential candidates.

ELECTION OF 1824

In the four-way presidential election of 1824, Andrew Jackson led in both electoral and popular votes, but no candidate received a majority in the electoral college. Adams finished second, and Crawford and Clay trailed far behind (Calhoun had dropped out of the race before the election). Under the Constitution, the House of Representatives, voting by state delegation, one vote to a state, selected the next president from among the candidates. Clay, who had received the fewest votes, was dropped. Crawford, a stroke victim, never received serious consideration. The influential Clay backed Adams, who received the votes of thirteen of the twenty-four state delegations to win. Clay then became Adams's secretary of state, the traditional steppingstone to the presidency.

Angry Jacksonians denounced the outcome as a "corrupt bargain." The Democratic-Republican Party split. The Adams wing emerged as the National Republicans; the Jacksonians became the Democrats and immediately began planning for 1828.

After taking the oath of office, Adams proposed a strong nationalist policy incorporating Henry Clay's "American System," a program of protective tariffs, a national bank, and internal improvements. Brilliant as a diplomat and secretary of state, Adams was an inept president. He underestimated the lingering effects of the Panic of 1819 and the resulting staunch opposition to a national bank and protective tariffs. Meanwhile, supporters of Andrew Jackson sabotaged Adams's administration at every opportunity.

The 1828 election campaign, pitting Adams against Jackson, was rowdy and intensely personal.

THE ELECTION OF 1828 — Jackson's supporters accused Adams, when he was envoy to Russia, of having secured prostitutes for the czar. Anti-Jacksonians published reports that Rachel Jackson had had an affair with and married Jackson before her first husband divorced her. After the election, Rachel Jackson discovered a pamphlet defending her, and she was shocked by the extent of the charges. When she died of a heart attack in December 1828, Jacksonians charged that she was "murdered."

Jackson swamped Adams, carrying 56 percent of the popular vote and winning in the electoral college by 178 to 83 votes. He and his supporters believed that the will of the people had finally been served. Through a lavishly financed coalition of state parties, political leaders, and newspaper editors, a popular movement had elected the president, and a new era had begun. The Democratic Party became the first well-organized national political party in the United States, and tight party organization became the hallmark of nineteenth-century American politics.

Nicknamed "Old Hickory" after the toughest of American hardwoods, Andrew Jackson was a rough-and-tumble, ambitious man. He rose from humble beginnings to become a wealthy planter and slaveholder and the first president from the West. He had an instinct for politics and picked both issues and supporters shrewdly.

ANDREW JACKSON AND THE DEMOCRATS

Jackson and his supporters viewed the strong federal government advocated by John Quincy Adams as the enemy of individual liberty. The Democrats represented a wide range of views but shared a fundamental commitment to the Jeffersonian concept of an agrarian society.

Jacksonians feared the concentration of economic and political power. They believed that government intervention in the economy benefited special-interest groups and created corporate monopolies that favored the rich. They sought to restore the independence of the individual—the artisan and the ordinary farmer—by ending federal support of banks and corporations and restricting the use of paper currency, which they distrusted.

Jackson and his supporters opposed reform as a movement. Reformers eager to turn their programs into legislation called for a more activist government. But Democrats tended to oppose programs like educational reform and a public education system. They believed, for instance, that public schools restricted individual liberty by interfering with parental responsibility and undermined freedom of religion by replacing church schools. Nor did Jackson share reformers' humanitarian concerns.

Jacksonians considered themselves reformers in a different way. By restraining government and emphasizing individualism, they sought to restore traditional republican virtues, such as prudence and economy. Jackson sought to encourage self-discipline and self-reliance, traits undermined by economic and social change.

JACKSONIANS AS REFORMERS

Like Jefferson, Jackson strengthened the executive branch of government even as he weakened the federal role. In combining the roles of party leader and chief of state, he centralized power in the White

House. Jackson relied on political friends, his "Kitchen Cabinet," for advice; he rarely consulted his official cabinet. By rotating officeholders, Jackson introduced a spoils system that rewarded his followers handsomely and thereby strengthened party organization and loyalty.

Jackson rejected elitism and special favors and stressed popular government. Time and again he declared that sovereignty resided with the people, not with the states or the courts. In this respect, Jackson was a reformer; he returned government to majority rule. Yet it is hard to distinguish between Jackson's belief in himself as the instrument of the people and demagogic arrogance.

Animosity between Jackson's supporters and opponents grew year by year. Massachusetts senator Daniel Webster feared the men around the president; Henry Clay most feared Jackson himself. They contended that rotation in office, with appointments based on loyalty rather than competence, corrupted government. Opponents mocked Jackson as "King Andrew I," charging him with abuse of power by ignoring the Supreme Court's ruling on Cherokee rights, using the spoils system, and consulting his Kitchen Cabinet. Critics also accused him of recklessly destroying the economy.

Amid this agitation, Jackson invigorated the philosophy of limited government. In 1830 he vetoed the Maysville Road bill, which would have funded construction of a 60-mile turnpike from Maysville to Lexington, Kentucky. A federally subsidized internal improvement confined to one state was unconstitutional, he charged; such projects were properly a state responsibility. The veto undermined Henry Clay's nationalist program and personally embarrassed Clay because the project was in his home district.

Federalism at Issue: The Nullification and Bank Controversies

Soon Jackson had to face directly the question of the proper division of sovereignty between state and central governments. The slave South feared federal power, no state more so than South Carolina. Southerners also resented protectionist tariffs, one of the foundations of Clay's American System, which in 1824 and 1828 protected northern factories by imposing import duties on manufactured cloth and iron. But the tariff raised the costs of these goods to southerners, who labeled the high tariff of 1828 the Tariff of Abominations.

South Carolina's political leaders went so far as to reject the 1828 tariff, invoking the doctrine of nul-

NULLIFICATION

lification, according to which a state had the right to overrule, or nullify, federal legislation. Nullification was based on the idea expressed in the Virginia and Kentucky resolutions of 1798 (see Chapter 8)—that the states, representing the people, have a right to judge the constitutionality of federal actions. Jackson's vice president, John C. Calhoun of South Carolina, argued in his unsigned *Exposition and Protest* that in any disagreement between the federal government and a state, a special state convention—like the conventions called to ratify the Constitution—should decide the conflict by either nullifying or affirming the federal law. Only the power of nullification, Calhoun asserted, could protect the minority against the tyranny of the majority.

In public, Calhoun let others advance nullification. He hoped to avoid embarrassing the Democratic

WEBSTER-HAYNE DEBATE

ticket and to win Jackson's support as the Democratic presidential heir apparent. Thus, in early 1830, Calhoun presided silently over the Senate and its packed galleries when Senator Daniel Webster of Massachusetts and Senator Robert Y. Hayne of South Carolina debated states' rights and the nature of the Union, with nullification a subtext. At the climax of the debate, Webster invoked two powerful images. One was the outcome of nullification: "states dissevered, discordant, belligerent; on a land rent with civil feuds, or drenched . . . in fraternal blood!" The other was a patriotic vision of a great nation flourishing under the motto "Liberty and Union, now and forever, one and inseparable."

Though sympathetic to states' rights and distrustful of the federal government, Jackson rejected the idea of state sovereignty. Believing deeply in the Union, he shared Webster's dread of nullification. Soon after the Webster-Hayne debate, the president made his position clear at a Jefferson Day dinner with the toast "Our Federal Union, it must and shall be preserved." Vice President Calhoun, when his turn came, toasted, "The Federal Union—next to our liberty the most dear." Calhoun thus revealed his adherence to states' rights.

Tension resumed when Congress passed a new tariff in 1832 reducing some duties but retaining high

NULLIFICATION CRISIS

taxes on imported iron, cottons, and woolens. Though a majority of southern representatives supported the new tariff, South Carolinians refused to go along. More than the duties, they feared that the act could set a precedent for congressional legislation on slavery. In November 1832 a South Carolina state convention nullified both tariffs, making it unlawful for federal officials to collect duties in the state.

Old Hickory responded quickly. In December he issued a proclamation opposing nullification. He moved troops to federal forts in South Carolina and prepared U.S. marshals to collect the required duties. At Jackson's request, Congress passed the Force Act, which authorized the president to call up troops but also offered a way to avoid force by collecting duties before foreign ships reached Charleston's harbor. At the same time, Jackson extended an olive branch by recommending tariff reductions.

Calhoun, disturbed by South Carolina's drift toward separatism, resigned as vice president and soon won election to represent South Carolina in the U.S. Senate. There he worked with Henry Clay to draw up the compromise Tariff of 1833. Quickly passed by Congress and signed by the president, the new tariff lengthened the list of duty-free items and reduced duties over nine years. Satisfied, South Carolina's convention repealed its nullification law. In a final salvo, it also nullified Jackson's Force Act. Jackson ignored the gesture.

Nullification offered a genuine debate on the nature and principles of the republic. Each side believed it was upholding the Constitution. Neither side won a clear victory, though both claimed to have done so. It took another crisis, over a central bank, to define the powers of the federal government more clearly.

The Second Bank of the United States, whose twenty-year charter was scheduled to expire in 1836,

SECOND BANK OF THE UNITED STATES

served as a depository for federal funds, its notes circulating as reliable currency that could be exchanged for gold; it kept state banks honest by refusing to accept the bank notes of any bank lacking sufficient gold reserves. Most state banks resented the central bank's police role: by presenting a state bank's notes for redemption all at once, the Second Bank could easily ruin a bank. Moreover, with less money in reserve, state banks found themselves unable to compete on an equal footing with the Second Bank.

Many state governments also regarded the national bank as unresponsive to local needs. Westerners and urban workers remembered with bitterness the bank's conservative credit policies during the Panic of 1819. As a private, profit-making institution, its policies reflected the interest of its owners. Its president, Nicholas Biddle, was an eastern patrician who symbolized all that westerners found wrong with the bank.

The bank's charter was valid until 1836, but with the 1832 presidential campaign in view, Henry Clay, the National Republican presidential candidate, persuaded Biddle to ask Congress to approve an early rechartering. Clay intended to pressure Jackson to sign the rechartering bill or to face an override of his veto. The plan backfired, however, when the Senate failed to override the president's veto. Jackson's veto message was an emotional attack on the undemocratic nature of the bank. With the bank the prime issue in the 1832 campaign, and with Jackson denouncing special privilege and economic power, he won reelection easily.

In 1833 Jackson moved to dismantle the Second Bank of the United States. He deposited federal funds

JACKSON'S SECOND TERM

in state-chartered banks (critics called them his "pet banks"). Without federal money, the Second Bank shriveled. When its federal charter expired in 1836, it became just another Pennsylvania-chartered private bank. Five years later, it closed its doors.

As the bank died, Congress passed the Deposit Act of 1836. The act authorized the secretary of the treasury to designate one bank in each state and territory to provide the services formerly performed by the Bank of the United States. The act provided that the federal surplus in excess of $5 million be distributed to the states as interest-free loans beginning in 1837.

The surplus had derived from wholesale speculation in public lands: speculators borrowed money to

SPECIE CIRCULAR

purchase public land, used the land as collateral for credit to buy additional acreage, and repeated the cy-

■ This 1830 Ralph E. W. Earl oil painting of President Andrew Jackson, entitled *Tennessee Gentleman,* captures the complexity of Jackson's image. The first president from the West and the first born in a log cabin, Jackson nonetheless poses as an aristocrat with his plantation house, The Hermitage, in the background.   (Courtesy, The Hermitage—The Home of Andrew Jackson)

1836, only specie—gold or silver—or Virginia scrip (paper money) would be accepted as payment for land. By ending credit sales, it significantly reduced purchases of public land and the federal budget surplus. As a result, the government suspended payments to the states soon after they began.

The policy was a disaster. The increased demand for specie squeezed banks. Credit contracted as banks issued fewer notes and loans. In the waning days of Jackson's administration, Congress voted to repeal the circular, but the president pocket-vetoed the bill by holding it unsigned until Congress adjourned. Finally in May 1838, a joint resolution of Congress overturned the circular.

The first six presidents had vetoed nine bills; Jackson alone vetoed twelve. Previous presidents had

USE OF THE VETO

believed that vetoes were justified only on constitutional grounds, but Jackson considered policy disagreement legitimate grounds as well. Using the veto to control Congress, in effect, Jackson made the executive for the first time a rival branch of government, equal in power to Congress.

The Whig Challenge and the Second Party System

*M*ost historians view the 1830s and 1840s as an age of reform and popularly based political parties. As the passions of reformers and abolitionists spilled over into politics, party differences became paramount, and party loyalties solidified. For the first time in American history, grassroots political groups, organized from the bottom up, set the tone of political life.

Opponents of the Democrats found shelter under a common umbrella, the Whig Party, in the 1830s.

WHIG PARTY

From 1834 through the 1840s, the Whigs and the Democrats competed on a nearly equal footing at local and national levels and achieved a stability previously unknown in American politics. The political competition of this period—known as the second party system—was more intense and well organized than the first party system of Democratic-Republicans versus Federalists. As political interest

cle. The state banks providing the loans issued bank notes. Jackson, who opposed paper money, feared that the speculative craze threatened the stability of state banks and undermined the interests of settlers, who could not compete with speculators in bidding for the best land.

Reflecting his hard-money instincts, the president ordered Treasury Secretary Levi Woodbury to issue the Specie Circular. It provided that after August broadened, states expanded white male voting. By 1840 only seven of twenty-six states had property restrictions for male suffrage.

Increasingly the parties diverged. Whigs favored economic expansion through an activist government, Democrats through limited central government. Whigs supported corporate charters, a national bank, and paper currency; Democrats were opposed to all three. Whigs also favored more humanitarian reforms than did Democrats, including public schools, abolition of capital punishment, prison and asylum reform, and temperance. Whigs were generally more optimistic than Democrats and more enterprising. The chartering of corporations, they argued, expanded economic opportunity for everyone, laborers and farmers alike. Democrats, distrustful of concentrated economic power and moral and economic coercion, held fast to the Jeffersonian principle of limited government.

WHIGS AND REFORMERS

Religion and ethnicity, not economics and class, most influenced party affiliation. The Whig Party won the favor of evangelical Protestants and the small number of free black voters and was the vehicle of revivalist Protestantism. Indeed, Whigs practiced a kind of political revivalism. Their rallies resembled camp meetings; in their speeches, they employed pulpit rhetoric, and their programs embodied the perfectionist beliefs of reformers.

In their appeal to evangelicals, Whigs alienated members of other faiths. The evangelicals' ideal Christian state had no room for Catholics, Mormons, Unitarians, Universalists, or religious freethinkers. Those groups opposed Sabbath laws and temperance legislation in particular and state interference in moral and religious questions in general. As a result, more than 95 percent of Irish Catholics, 90 percent of Reformed Dutch, and 80 percent of German Catholics voted Democratic.

Jackson handpicked Vice President Martin Van Buren to head the Democratic ticket in the 1836 presidential election. The Whigs, not yet organized into a national party, entered three sectional candidates: Daniel Webster of New England, Hugh White of the South, and William Henry Harrison of the West. By splintering the vote, they hoped to throw the election into the

ELECTION OF 1836

House of Representatives. Van Buren, however, comfortably captured the electoral college despite an edge of only 25,000 votes out of 1.5 million cast.

Van Buren took office just weeks before the American credit system collapsed. In response to the impact of the Specie Circular, New York banks stopped redeeming paper currency with gold in mid-1837. Soon all banks suspended payments in hard coin. Thus began a downward economic spiral that curtailed bank loans and strangled business confidence. Hard times persisted from 1839 until 1843.

VAN BUREN AND HARD TIMES

Ill-advisedly, Van Buren followed Jackson's hard-money policies. He cut federal spending, which caused prices to drop further, and he opposed a national bank, which would have expanded credit. Even worse, the president proposed a new regional treasury system for government deposits. The treasury branches would accept and pay out only gold and silver coin; they would not accept paper currency or checks drawn on state banks. Van Buren's independent treasury bill became law in 1840. By increasing the demand for hard coin, it deprived banks of gold and further accelerated price deflation.

With the nation in the grip of hard times, the Whig strategy for the election of 1840 was simple: hold on to loyal supporters and win over independents by blaming hard times on the Democrats. The Whigs rallied behind a military hero, General William Henry Harrison, conqueror of the Shawnees at Tippecanoe Creek in 1811. The Democrats renominated President Van Buren.

WILLIAM HENRY HARRISON AND THE ELECTION OF 1840

Harrison, or "Old Tippecanoe," and his running mate, John Tyler of Virginia, ran a "log cabin and hard cider" campaign—a people's crusade—against the aristocratic president in "the Palace." In a huge turnout, 80 percent of eligible voters cast ballots. Harrison won the popular vote by a narrow margin but swept the electoral college by 234 to 60.

Within a month of his inauguration, Harrison died of pneumonia. His successor, John Tyler, had left the Democratic Party to protest Jackson's nullification proclamation. Tyler turned out to be more Democrat than Whig. He repeatedly vetoed

PRESIDENT TYLER

Henry Clay's protective tariffs, internal improvements, and bills to revive the Bank of the United States. Two days after Tyler's second veto of a bank bill, the entire cabinet resigned except Secretary of State Daniel Webster, who was busy with treaty negotiations; he left shortly after. Tyler became a president without a party, and the Whigs lost the presidency without losing an election.

Hard times in the late 1830s and early 1840s deflected attention from a renewal of Anglo-American

ANGLO-AMERICAN TENSIONS

tensions that had multiple sources: northern commercial rivalry with Britain, the default of state governments and corporations on British-held debts during the Panic of 1837, rebellion in Canada, boundary disputes, southern alarm over West Indian emancipation, and American expansionism.

One problem disrupting Anglo-American relations was an old border dispute between Maine and New Brunswick. When Canadian lumbermen cut trees in the disputed region in the winter of 1838–1839, the citizens of Maine attempted to expel them. The lumbermen captured a Maine land agent and posse, both sides mobilized their militias, and Congress authorized a call-up of fifty thousand men. Ultimately, a truce was arranged, and no blood was spilled. The two sides compromised on their conflicting land claims in the Webster-Ashburton Treaty (1842).

The border dispute with Great Britain prefigured conflicts that were to erupt in the 1840s over the expansion of the United States. With Tyler's succession to power in 1841 and James K. Polk's Democratic victory in the presidential election of 1844, federal activism in the domestic sphere ended for the rest of the decade, as attention turned to territorial expansion.

Manifest Destiny and Expansionism

*T*he belief that American expansion westward and southward was inevitable, just, and divinely ordained was first labeled "manifest destiny" in 1845 by John L. O'Sullivan, editor of the *United States Magazine and Domestic Review*. The annexation of Texas, O'Sullivan wrote, was "the fulfillment of our manifest destiny to overspread the continent allotted by Providence for the free development of our yearly multiplying millions."

As the proportion of Americans living west of the Appalachians grew, both national parties joined the popular clamor for expansion. Agrarian Democrats sought western land to balance urbanization. Enterprising Whigs looked to the new commercial opportunities the West offered. Southerners envisioned the extension of slavery and more slave states.

Fierce national pride spurred the quest for land. Americans were convinced that theirs was the greatest country on earth, with a special role to play in the world. To Americans, expansion promised to extend the benefits of a republican system of government to the unfortunate and the inferior.

In part, racism contributed to manifest destiny. The impulse to colonize and develop the West was based on the belief that Euro-Americans could use the land more productively than American Indians or Hispanics. Euro-Americans viewed these peoples as inferior, best controlled or conquered. Thus, the same racial attitudes that justified slavery and discrimination against black people supported expansion in the West.

Among the long-standing objectives of expansionists was Texas, which in addition to present-day

REPUBLIC OF TEXAS

Texas included parts of Oklahoma, Kansas, Colorado, Wyoming, and New Mexico (see Map 11.1). After winning independence from Spain in 1821, Mexico encouraged the development of its remote northern province, offering large tracts of land virtually free to U.S. settlers called *empresarios*. The settlers in turn agreed to become Mexican citizens, adopt Catholicism, and bring hundreds of American families into the area.

By 1835 thirty-five thousand Americans, including many slaveholders, lived in Texas. As the new settlers' numbers and power grew, they tended to ignore their commitments to the Mexican government. In response, dictator General Antonio López de Santa Anna tightened control over the region. In turn, the Anglo immigrants and *Tejanos*—Mexicans living in Texas—rebelled. At the Alamo mission in San Antonio in 1836, fewer than two hundred Texans made a heroic but unsuccessful stand against three thousand Mexicans under General Santa Anna. With

Map 11.1 Westward Expansion, 1800–1860

Through exploration, purchase, war, and treaty, the United States became a continental nation, stretching from the Atlantic to the Pacific.

Legend:
- U.S. territory, 1783
- Louisiana Purchase, 1803
- Florida annexed, 1819–1821
- Texas, 1845
- Oregon Country, 1846
- Mexican Cession, 1848
- Gadsden Purchase, 1853
- OHIO 1803 States admitted, 1800–1860
- Western trails

"Remember the Alamo" as their rallying cry, the Texans won independence by the end of the year.

Texas established the independent Lone Star Republic but soon sought annexation to the United States. The issue quickly became politically explosive. Southerners favored annexing proslavery Texas; abolitionists, many northerners, and most Whigs opposed annexation. In recognition of the political dangers, President Jackson reneged on his promise to recognize Texas, and President Van Buren ignored annexation. Texans then talked about closer ties with the British and extending their republic to the Pacific coast. President Tyler, concerned that a Texas alliance with Britain might threaten American independence and also hoping to gain southern support for an 1844 election bid, pressed for annexation.

As southerners sought expansion to the Southwest, northerners looked to the Northwest. In 1841 "Oregon fever" struck thousands who, lured by the glowing reports of missionaries, took to the Oregon Trail. The 2,000-mile journey took six months or more, but within a few years, five thousand settlers had arrived in the fertile Willamette valley.

OREGON FEVER

Britain and the United States had jointly occupied the disputed Oregon Territory since the Convention of 1818. Beginning with the administration of President John Quincy Adams, the United States had tried to fix the boundary at the 49th parallel, but Britain had refused. In 1843 a Cincinnati convention of expansionists demanded the entire Oregon Country for the United States, up to its northernmost border at latitude 54°40'. Soon "Fifty-four Forty or Fight" became the rallying cry of American expansionists.

With antislavery forces favoring both expansion into Oregon and rejection of annexing Texas, anxious southern leaders persuaded the 1844 Democratic convention to adopt a rule requiring the presidential nominee to receive two-thirds of the convention votes. In effect, the southern states acquired a veto, which they wielded to block Van Buren's nomination because of his opposition to slavery and Texas an-

POLK AND THE ELECTION OF 1844

nexation. Instead, the party chose House Speaker James K. Polk, a hard-money Jacksonian, avid expansionist, and slaveholding cotton planter from Tennessee. The Whigs and their nominee, Henry Clay, argued that the Democrats' belligerent nationalism would lead the nation into war with Great Britain or Mexico, or both. Clay favored expansion through negotiation.

With a well-organized campaign, Polk won the election by 170 electoral votes to 105. He won the popular vote by just 38,000 out of 2.7 million votes cast and New York's 36 electoral votes by only 6,000 popular votes. Abolitionist James G. Birney, the Liberty Party candidate, had drawn almost 16,000 votes away from Clay, handing New York and the election to Polk.

Interpreting Polk's victory as a mandate for annexation, President Tyler proposed that Texas be admitted by joint resolution of Congress. The resolution passed, and three days before leaving office, Tyler signed it. Mexico, which did not recognize Texas independence, immediately broke relations with the United States. In October the citizens of Texas ratified annexation, and Texas joined the Union in December 1845.

ANNEXATION OF TEXAS

Summary   **Online Study Center** ACE the Test

Religion, reform, and expansionism shaped politics from 1824 through the 1840s. As the Second Great Awakening spread through villages and towns, the converts, especially women, organized to reform a rapidly changing society. Religion imbued men and women with zeal to right the wrongs of American society and the world. Reformers pursued perfectionism and republican virtue by battling with the evils of slavery, prostitution, and alcohol. In the process, women entered the public sphere as advocates of reform. Two issues in particular—the comet of Antimasonry and the smoldering fire of abolitionism—aroused passions that transformed moral crusades into political movements. With women's rights and nationalism contributing, the mix of issues made politics far more critical and engaging than just voting at elections.

The organized parties of the 1820s and the struggles between the National Republicans and the Democrats, then between the Democrats and the Whigs, stimulated even greater interest in campaigns and political issues. The Democrats, who rallied around Andrew Jackson, and Jackson's opponents, who came together under the Whig tent, competed almost equally for the loyalty of voters. Both parties favored economic expansion. Their worldviews, however, differed fundamentally. Whigs were more optimistic and favored greater centralized government initiative. Democrats harbored a deep-seated belief in limited government. The controversies over the Second Bank of the United States and nullification allowed Americans to debate the principles of the republic.

Many Americans caught the fever of expansionism. Euro-American farmers sought land, slaveholders wished to extend slavery, and millions itched to move westward. The admission of Texas into the Union in 1845 served one destiny—expansion—but also sharpened the nation's increasing divisions over slavery.

LEGACY FOR A PEOPLE AND A NATION
The Bible Belt

Had an eighteenth-century visitor to North America asked for the Bible belt, she would have been directed to New England. By the 1830s, however, the South was the most churched region. The Second Great Awakening spread like wildfire through the South. By the 1830s, more than half of white and one-quarter of black southerners had undergone a conversion experience, and religion and the South formed a common identity.

Religion helped define southern distinctiveness. Southern Protestant liturgy and cadences were as much African as European; thus, southern and northern denominations grew apart. They formally separated in the 1840s when Southern Baptists and Methodists withdrew from the national organizations that had barred slaveowners from church offices. Presbyterians withdrew later. After the Civil War, evangelical denominations remained divided into northern and southern organizations.

Southern religion maintained tradition and resisted modern ways. Mostly evangelical, it emphasized conversion and a personal battle against sin. By the twentieth century, fundamentalism, which stressed a literal reading of the Bible, reinforced resistance to modernism. Yet southern Protestantism lost ground as a political force in opposing evolution and in alliances with nativist, anti-immigrant groups.

But evangelicalism rose again in the 1960s, especially after a Catholic—John F. Kennedy—won the Democratic nomination for president. Many evangelicals began to vote their religion, moving to the Republican Party, and in 1964 Republican Barry Goldwater won the Bible belt states, breaking up the solid Democratic block. His conservative rhetoric resonated with southerners concerned about desegregation and erosion of religious values.

In the 1980s and 1990s, the Bible belt became the base of mobilized evangelical political action led by the Moral Majority. Religious and cultural issues rallied southern evangelicals: defending the traditional family, advocating prayer in schools, and opposing abortion, the Equal Rights Amendment, and gay rights legislation. In their own eyes, fundamentalist evangelical Protestants were defending biblical principles.

Thus, the revivals that began in the early 1800s have rippled in ever wider circles across the South for two centuries, shaping the distinctive southern blend of culture and politics.

PEOPLE AND COMMUNITIES IN THE NORTH AND WEST 1830–1860

*a*t eight o'clock on a snowy St. Patrick's Day morning in Lowell, Massachusetts, in 1841, more than one hundred members of the Irish Benevolent Society prepared to march through the mill town with a brass band. Each year, across the United States and around the world, Irish settlers and their descendants expressed their Irish pride by celebrating St. Patrick's Day. In colonial America, mostly Scots-Irish Protestants toasted Ireland and Britain at banquets. After the War of 1812, the banqueters and marchers, mostly middle-class Irish, represented charities and raised money to assist immigrants. New arrivals were mostly Catholic, and the parades and banquets brought together Catholics and Protestants.

But events in Ireland made the American Irish community increasingly Catholic. After a failed revolution against Britain in 1798, the 1800 Act of Union merged Ireland into the United Kingdom, eliminated the Irish Parliament, and disfranchised Catholics, making them powerless. Declining farm sizes and a population explosion impoverished them. Visiting Ireland in 1835, a stunned Alexis de Tocqueville wrote to his father, "You cannot imagine what a complexity of miseries five centuries of oppression and disorders and religious hostility have piled up on this poor people."

While many struggled in Ireland, others left their country. In England, industrial Manchester and London offered jobs, but more distant America offered political and religious freedom as well as economic opportunities. Thus, in the 1820s and 1830s, St. Patrick's Day increasingly became identified with Irish Catholics. Recent immigrants were poorer, and they could not pay for banquets. But parades were an opportunity to express their solidarity as well as their appreciation for America. They marched against the British and for equal rights in Ireland, often wearing red, white, and blue as well as green, to demonstrate their identity. Both Americans and the Irish had suffered, they

Online Study Center
This icon will direct you to interactive map and primary source activities on the website
http://college.hmco.com/pic/nortonbrief7e

CHRONOLOGY

1830 • Smith founds Mormon Church
  • First National Negro Convention

1830s–50s • Urban riots commonplace

1832 • Rice debuts in New York minstrel show

1835 • Arkansas passes first women's property law

1837 • Boston employs paid policemen

1837–48 • Mann heads the Massachusetts Board of Education

1838 • Mormons driven out of Missouri

1841–47 • Brook Farm combines spirituality, work, and play in a utopian rural community

1842 • Knickerbocker baseball club formed

1844 • Nativist riots peak in Philadelphia
  • Smith brothers murdered in Illinois

1845 • Irish potato blight begins
  • *Narrative of the Life of Frederick Douglass* appears

1846–47 • Mormon trek to the Great Salt Lake

1847–57 • Immigration at peak pre–Civil War levels

1848 • Abortive revolution in German states
  • U.S. acquires Alta California in Treaty of Guadalupe Hidalgo
  • Gold discovered in California

1849 • California gold rush transforms the West Coast

1852 • Stowe's *Uncle Tom's Cabin* published

1854 • Large-scale Chinese immigration begins
  • Germans replace Irish as largest group of new arrivals

1855 • New York establishes Castle Garden as immigrant center

pointed out, from British tyranny. St. Patrick's Day speakers reminded audiences that "republicanism" was both an American and Irish principle. Editor Thomas O'Connor, who described himself as an "Irishman by birth" and an "American by adoption," toasted "America as she is, Ireland as she ought to be." St. Patrick's Day linked American and Irish causes.

But increasingly American Irish Protestants stayed away from such events. They identified with Britain, not the Irish opposition. In the 1820s, they began to skip St. Patrick's Day parades and march instead on July 12, commemorating the English victory of William of Orange in the Battle of the Boyne in 1690. They purposefully distanced themselves from the new immigrants, becoming Whigs while the new immigrants gravitated to Andrew Jackson. Then, in

the 1840s and 1850s, as potato blight and famine stalked Ireland, nearly 2 million Irish immigrants—almost all Catholics—arrived in the United States. Now St. Patrick's Day marches attracted not hundreds but thousands, and nativists jeered the marchers, occasionally assaulting them.

The huge Irish immigration was only part of a worldwide population movement. From the 1830s through the 1850s, millions of Europeans arrived on America's shores, transforming the American nation. Within large cities and in the countryside, whole districts became ethnic and religious enclaves.

The cultural traditions of European immigrants differed from those in the American colonial past, and some white Americans came to see the differences as racial rather than cultural. Black Americans

became racial outsiders, as did Hispanics in the Southwest. In a society growing ever more diverse and complex, conflict became common.

The market economy both energized and accentuated the differences among Americans. In the nation's cities, both wealth and poverty reached extremes unknown in the countryside. Ethnicity, race, religion, and class divided Americans as well. Farm families attempted to maintain cohesive, rural villages, while utopians and groups like the Mormons sought to create self-governing communal havens.

The market economy altered family life too. As commerce and industry grew, the home lost its function as a workplace. Goods formerly made at home were now mass-manufactured in factories and bought in stores. Public schools took over much of the family's traditional role as prime educator. Leisure became a commodity to be purchased by those who could afford it. Families shrank in size, and more people lived outside family units. ■

Country Life

*R*ural life changed significantly in the first half of the nineteenth century. Farm population in the coastal states declined as towns grew and manufacturing expanded. Farm families sought more fertile and cheaper land in the West. Market-oriented communities arose there, linked to eastern markets by the new transportation networks.

The railroad depot and post office in the farm village linked farmers with the rest of the world. But in

FARM COMMUNITIES

these villages, with their churches, general stores, and taverns, communal values still ruled. Families gathered on one another's farms to accomplish as a community what they could not manage individually. Barn-raisings regularly brought people together. The neighbors came by buggy to help a farm family raise the walls and build a roof. Afterward everyone celebrated with a hearty communal feast and singing, dancing, and

games. Similar gatherings took place at harvest time and on special occasions.

Farm men and women had active social lives. Men met frequently at general stores, weekly markets, and taverns, and they hunted and fished together. Some women also attended market. More typically they met at after-church dinners, prayer groups, sewing and corn-husking bees, and quilting parties. These were cherished opportunities to exchange experiences, thoughts, and spiritual support and to swap letters, books, and news.

Traditional country bees had their town counterparts. Fredrika Bremer, a Swedish visitor, described

BEES

a sewing bee in Cambridge, Massachusetts, in 1849, at which neighborhood women made clothes for "a family who had lost all their clothing by fire." Yet town bees were not the all-day family affairs of the countryside, and those who moved from farm to town missed the country gatherings. In town, people were wage earners and consumers, and the market economy shaped and controlled their daily lives.

Most Americans came to accept these changes, but some tried to resist. One opposition path was to restore traditional work and social cohesion by living in rural utopian communities. Some groups, like the Shakers, had originated in eighteenth-century Europe, while others, like the Mormons, arose out of the religious ferment of the Second Great Awakening. What they shared in common was a commitment to rural communal living as members experimented with innovative (sometimes shocking) family arrangements and more egalitarian gender roles in a cooperative rather than competitive environment.

Online Study Center
Improve Your Grade

Primary Source: Oneida Sisters Comment on Love and Labor

The Shakers, the largest of the communal utopian experiments, reached their peak between 1820 and

SHAKERS

1860 when six thousand members lived in twenty settlements in eight states. Founder Ann Lee, who advocated celibacy, had brought the sect to America in 1774. Shakers got their name from the singing and dancing in their worship service.

In religious practice and social relations, Shakers offered an alternative to changing urban and rural life.

■ *The Lackawanna Valley* (1855) by George Inness. Hired by the Lackawanna Railroad to paint a picture showing the company's new roundhouse at Scranton, in northeastern Pennsylvania, Inness combined landscape and locomotive technology into an organic whole. Industrialism, Inness seems to say, belonged to the American landscape; it would neither overpower nor obliterate the land.   (Gift of Mrs. Huttleston Rogers, © 1996 Board of Trustees, National Gallery of Art, Washington, D.C.)

They lived communally, abolishing individual families. Leaders tended to be women. However, the settlements depended on constant recruitment. In addition to their celibacy, most members stayed only a short time, being temporary refugees from hardship or abuse, or families who found themselves unsuited to communal living. In the middle of the nineteenth century, Shaker communities began a slow but steady decline.

The Church of Jesus Christ of Latter-Day Saints, known as the Mormons, was the most successful communitarian experiment and, like the Shakers, restructured family life. During the religious ferment of the 1820s in western New York, Joseph Smith,

MORMON COMMUNITY OF SAINTS

a young farmer, reported that an angel called Moroni had given him engraved divine gold plates. Smith published his revelations as the *Book of Mormon* and organized a church in 1830. The next year the community moved west to Ohio to await the second coming of Jesus. Angry mobs drove them from Ohio to Missouri, where in 1838 the governor gathered evidence to indict Smith and other Mormon leaders for treason.

Smith and his followers resettled in Nauvoo, Illinois. The state legislature gave them a city charter that made them self-governing and authorized a local militia. But hostility arose again, especially after Smith introduced the practice of polygamy in 1841. In 1842 Smith became mayor, and Nauvoo petitioned the fed-

eral government to be a self-governing territory, further antagonizing opponents. After Smith and his brother were charged with treason, jailed, and then murdered in 1844, the Mormons left Illinois to seek security in the wilderness. In 1847 they arrived in the Great Salt Lake valley, in the unorganized territory of Utah, and established a patriarchal, cooperative "community of saints." Now led by Brigham Young, they achieved religious freedom and political autonomy.

In Utah the Mormons distributed agricultural land according to family size. An extensive irrigation system, constructed cooperatively, transformed the arid valley into a rich oasis. As the colony developed, the church elders gained control of water, trade, industry, and eventually the territorial government of Utah.

Though short-lived (1841–1847), the Brook Farm cooperative near Boston played a significant role

AMERICAN RENAISSANCE

in the flowering of a national literature. Its members were inspired by transcendentalism—the belief that the physical world is secondary to the spiritual realm, which can be reached only by intuition. During these years Nathaniel Hawthorne, Ralph Waldo Emerson, and Margaret Fuller (editor of the leading transcendentalist journal, *Dial*) joined Henry David Thoreau, Herman Melville, and others in a literary outpouring known today as the American Renaissance. In philosophical intensity and moral idealism, their work was both distinctively American and an outgrowth of the European romantic movement. Their themes were universal, their settings and characters American.

The essayist Ralph Waldo Emerson was the prime mover of the American Renaissance and a pillar of the transcendental movement. "We live in succession, in division, in parts, in particles," Emerson wrote. "We see the world piece by piece, as the sun, the moon, the animal, the tree; but the whole, of which these are the shining parts, is the soul." Intuitive experience of God is attainable, insisted Emerson, because "the Highest dwells" within every individual in the form of the "Over-Soul."

The West

n the 1840s a trickling stream of migrants followed the Oregon Trail to the West Coast. Then, in 1848, gold was discovered in California. The next year a pioneer observed that the Oregon Trail "bore no evidence of having been much traveled." Traffic flowed south instead, and California drew population to the Pacific slope.

When the United States acquired Alta California from Mexico in the 1848 Treaty of Guadalupe Hi-

GOLD RUSH

dalgo (covered in Chapter 14), the province was inhabited mostly by Indians, with some Mexicans living on large estates. A chain of small settlements surrounded military forts (*presidios*) and missions. That changed almost overnight after James Marshall, a carpenter, spotted gold particles in the millrace at Sutter's Mill (northwest of Sacramento) in January 1848. Word of the discovery spread, and Californians rushed to scrabble for instant fortunes.

By 1849 the news had sped around the world, and hundreds of thousands of fortune seekers, mostly young men, streamed into California. Gold mining seemed to offer instant riches, and indeed, some did make fortunes. Most "forty-niners," however, never found enough gold to pay their expenses. "The stories you hear frequently in the States," one gold seeker wrote home, "are the most extravagant lies imaginable—the mines are a humbug." Many found work in California's cities and agricultural districts more profitable. Meanwhile, enterprising merchants rushed to supply, feed, and clothe the new settlers. One such merchant was Levi Strauss, a German Jewish immigrant, whose tough mining pants found a ready market among the prospectors.

The forty-niners had to be fed. Thus began the great California agricultural boom. Farmers preferred

FARMING

wheat for its minimal investment and quick return at the end of a relatively short growing season. California farmers eagerly imported horse-drawn machines, since labor was scarce (and expensive). By the mid-1850s, California exported wheat and had become firmly linked, through commerce, to the rest of the United States. Farmers on the West Coast cleared the land and, because success often depended on their access to water, sought to divert streams and rivers to irrigate their land.

Most men in California came alone, drawn by a sense of adventure and personal opportunity. Women who accompanied their husbands—only one-seventh of the travelers on the overland trails were women—experienced migration differently. Their lives drastically

Gold in California

When James Marshall discovered gold in Sutter's Mill, California, in January 1848, word spread quickly—and quite literally around the world. Within a year, tens of thousands of adventurers from other countries had rushed to California, the new "land of opportunity." Soon it was as cosmopolitan as any other American place.

In an era before the telegraph crossed the oceans, it is surprising how fast the news traveled. Mexicans heard of the gold strike first. Overland travelers brought the news south to Baja California and Sonora in Mexico. By spring 1849 some six thousand Mexicans were panning for gold in California.

Sailing ships brought news of California gold to Hawai'i. "Honolulu has never before witnessed such an excitement as the gold fever has created," the newspaper *Honolulu Polynesian* reported in the summer of 1848. Gold seekers and merchants sailed from Hawai'i to California, and their letters home recruited others to come.

A ship brought news of California gold discoveries to Valparaiso, Chile, in August 1848. More dramatically, a few weeks later, another sailing vessel landed with $2,500 in gold dust aboard. Before the end of the year, two thousand Chileans had left for California, and many Chilean merchants opened branch stores in San Francisco.

Word of gold reached Australia in December 1848, and by 1850 every ship in Sydney harbor was destined for California. News had already reached China in mid-1848. A San Francisco merchant headed for the gold fields, Chum Ming, had written a cousin about his hopes for wealth. Four months later, the cousin arrived in San Francisco, with fellow villagers he had recruited. After the upheavals of the Taiping Revolution in 1850, Chinese migration soared. By the mid-1850s, one in five gold miners was Chinese.

Californians, new and old, foreign and native-born, expressed amazement at the ethnic variety. One described it as "the most curious Babel of a place imaginable." In 1850 the new state of California had nearly 40 percent foreign-born inhabitants, the majority non-European. Through word of mouth, rumor, letters home, and newspaper reports, the discovery of gold in 1848 linked California to millions of ordinary people around the globe.

This 1855 Frank Marryat drawing of a San Francisco saloon dramatizes the international nature of the California gold rush. Like theater performers, the patrons of the saloon dress their parts as Yankees, Mexicans, Asians, and South Americans. (© Collection of the New York Historical Society)

changed as they left behind networks of friends and kin to journey, often with children, along an unknown and hazardous path to a strange environment. Yet in the West, their domestic skills were in great demand. They received high fees for cooking, laundering, and sewing, and they ran boarding houses and hotels.

City Life

Irish and other European immigrants and rural migrants made cities, especially northern ones, expand geometrically. Europeans spread westward, and small rural settlements quickly became towns. In 1830 the nation had only 23 cities with 10,000 or more people and only 7 with more than 25,000. By 1860, 93 towns exceeded 10,000, 35 towns had more than 25,000, and 9 exceeded 100,000 (see Map 12.1).

Some cities became great metropolitan centers. By 1830 New York City had been the nation's most populous city and major commercial center for twenty years. At midcentury, Baltimore and New Orleans dominated the South, and San Francisco was the leading West Coast city. In the Midwest, the new lake cities (Chicago, Detroit, and Cleveland) began to pass the frontier river cities (Cincinnati, Louisville, and Pittsburgh) founded a generation earlier.

As the nation's premier city, New York grew from 202,000 people in 1830 to over 814,000 in 1860. The immigrant port city was mostly Irish and German by the 1850s. Across the East

NEW YORK CITY

River, Brooklyn tripled in size between 1850 and 1860, becoming the nation's third-largest city, with a population of 279,000. Many people were short-term residents of the two cities; the majority did not stay ten years. Thus, New York was ever changing, full of energy, reeking of sweat, horse dung, and garbage—and above all, teeming with people.

By modern standards, nineteenth-century cities were disorderly, unsafe, and unhealthy. Expansion occurred so rapidly that few cities could handle the

URBAN PROBLEMS

problems it brought. For example, migrants from rural areas were accustomed to relieving themselves outside and throwing refuse in vacant areas. In the city, such waste smelled, spread disease, and polluted water. New York City partially solved the problem in the 1840s by abandoning wells in favor of reservoir water piped into buildings and outdoor fountains. In some districts, scavengers and refuse collectors carted away garbage and human waste, but in much of the city, it just rotted on the ground. Only one-quarter of New York City's streets had sewers by 1857.

Cities lacked adequate taxing power to provide services for all. The best the city could do was to tax property adjoining new sewers, paved streets, and water mains. Thus, basic services depended on residents' ability to pay. As a result, those most in need of services got them last. Private companies could be chartered to sell basic services. This plan worked well for gas lighting. Baltimore first chartered a private gas company in 1816; by midcentury, every major city was lit by a private gas supplier. The private sector, however, lacked the capital to build adequate citywide water systems. City governments therefore had to assume that responsibility.

Cities led in offering public education. In 1800 only New England had public schools; by 1860 every state offered some public education to whites. Under

HORACE MANN AND PUBLIC SCHOOLS

Horace Mann, secretary of the state board of education from 1837 to 1848, Massachusetts established a minimum school year of six months and formalized the training of teachers.

Mann advocated free, state-sponsored education. "If we do not prepare children to become good citizens," Mann argued, "if we do not develop their capacities, . . . then our republic must go down to destruction." Universal education, Mann proposed, would end misery and crime. Mann and others responded to the changes wrought by the market economy, urbanization, and immigration. The typical city dweller was a newcomer, from abroad or from the country. Public schools would take the children of strangers and give them shared values. Few states, however, included free black children in public schools.

Free public schools altered the scope of education. Schooling previously had focused on literacy, religious training, and discipline. Under Mann's leadership, the curriculum became more secular and appropriate for America's future clerks, farmers, and workers. Students studied geography, American

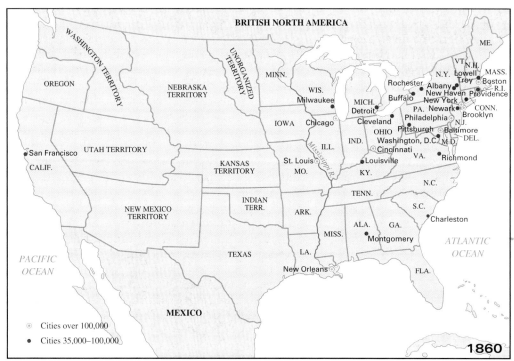

Map 12.1 Major American Cities in 1830 and 1860

The number of Americans who lived in cities increased rapidly between 1830 and 1860, and the number of large cities grew as well. In 1830 only New York City had a population exceeding 100,000; thirty years later, eight more cities had surpassed that level.

history, arithmetic, and science. Schools retained moral education, but they dropped direct religious indoctrination.

Catholics, immigrants, blacks, and workers sought to control their own schools, but the state legislatures established secular statewide standards under Protestant educators. Catholics in New York responded by building their own educational system over the next half-century. When Los Angeles became a city in 1850, it attempted to establish bilingual Spanish-English instruction, but the idea was dropped because trained bilingual teachers could not be found.

Towns and cities created new patterns of leisure as well as work. In rural society, social activities and work often took place at home. But in cities, dedi-

LEISURE

cated spaces—streets, theaters, sports fields—constituted a public sphere where people could socialize. Through the sale of admission tickets or membership in associations, leisure became a commodity to be purchased and reflected ethnic, racial, and class divisions. Even in cities, however, some traditional rural pursuits continued. Fishing remained popular, men played games of strength and skill in taverns, and churches served as social centers.

Americans read more too. Thanks to the expansion of public education, the vast majority of native-born white Americans were literate by the 1850s. For

READING

the reading public, fiction and autobiographies competed with religious tracts as popular literature. Newspapers and magazines printed fiction, and bookstores in large cities sold novels and autobiographies. Frederick Douglass's powerful attack on slavery in his 1845 autobiography sold widely. Many popular novels, some written by women, often for women, were set in the home and upheld Christian values. Yet they also can be read as a challenge to prevailing values. Although Susan Warner's *The Wide, Wide, Wide World* (1850), Nathaniel Hawthorne's *The House of the Seven Gables* (1851), and Fanny Fern's *Ruth Hall* (1855) did not challenge women's traditional domestic roles, they accorded women a special moral bearing. In giving a positive cast to notions of community and republican virtue, they implicitly criticized the growing market economy. By the 1850s popular fiction circulated widely. Harriet Beecher Stowe's antislavery novel, *Uncle Tom's Cabin,*

or Life Among the Lowly (1852), sold 300,000 copies in book form in its first year.

A theater was often the second public building constructed in a town—after a church. Large cities boasted

THEATER

two or more theaters catering to different classes. Some plays cut across class lines. Shakespeare was performed so often and appreciated so widely that even illiterate theatergoers knew his plays well. In the 1840s, musical and dramatic presentations took on a more professional tone; newly popular minstrel shows and traveling circuses offered carefully rehearsed routines including dancing and music.

By the 1840s, hundreds of traveling minstrel troupes presented a European version of African American culture. Minstrel acts had

MINSTREL SHOWS

first appeared twenty or thirty years earlier, when white men, in burned cork makeup, imitated African Americans in song, dance, and patter. In the early 1830s, Thomas D. Rice of New York became famous for his role as Jim Crow, an old southern slave. In ill-fitting patched clothing and torn shoes, the blackface Rice shuffled, danced, and sang on stage.

Minstrelsy stereotyped black people by exaggerating physical features. It also portrayed African Americans as being sensual and lazy. The fictional representation of blacks on stage defined not only "blackness" but also "whiteness." Whiteness as a racial category took on meaning as laughing white audiences distinguished themselves from the black characters. The net effect was to stoke the fires of racism and thereby further the growing racial tensions in the United States.

Increasingly, urban recreation and sports became formal commodities to be purchased. One had to buy

SPORTS

a ticket to go to the theater, the circus, the racetrack, or the ballpark. Spectator sports surged. In addition to horseracing, boxing and baseball attracted large, urban male crowds. News of an 1849 Maryland boxing match was so much in demand that a round-by-round account of the fight was telegraphed throughout the East. In baseball, organized leagues replaced spontaneity, and in 1845 the Knickerbocker Club, which had been formed in 1842, drew up rules for the game.

■ Thomas D. Rice playing Jim Crow in blackface at the Bowery Theater in New
York City, 1833. The rowdy audience climbed on the stage, leaving Rice little
room to perform. In representing African Americans on stage, Rice and other
minstrels contributed to establishing black and white as racial categories.
(© Collection of the New York Historical Society)

Ironically, public leisure soon developed a private dimension. Exclusive private associations provided space and occasions for leisure apart from crowds and rowdiness.

CITY CULTURE

While old-stock middle- and upper-class Americans were isolating themselves, members of various ethnic, racial, and religious groups formed their own associations. The Irish formed the Hibernian Society, the Germans brought Turnvereine physical-cultural clubs across the Atlantic, Jews founded B'nai B'rith, and African Americans started chapters of the Prince Hall Masons in their communities. Women too organized their own associations, ranging from literary clubs to benevolent societies. Associations brought together like people, but they also formalized divisions.

A youth culture emerged on New York's Bowery, an entertainment strip, in the 1840s. Older New Yorkers feared the "Bowery boys and gals," whose ostentatious dress and behavior seemed threatening to them. A Bowery boy had long hair, often greased into a roll. He wore a broad-brimmed black hat and as much jewelry as he could afford. His swaggering gait frightened many in the middle class. Equally disturbing to old New Yorkers were the young working women who strolled the Bowery. Unlike more genteel ladies, who wore modest veils or bonnets, Bowery "gals" flaunted outlandish costumes and ornate hats.

Most working people spent much of their lives outdoors; they worked in the streets as laborers, shopped in open markets, paraded, and socialized on sidewalks; they courted, argued, and defended their turf in public places. Increasingly, urban streets served as a political arena as crowds formed to listen to speakers, respond and demonstrate, and sometimes take mob action.

In the 1830s riots became commonplace as professionals, merchants, craftsmen, and laborers vented their rage against political and economic rivals. "Gentlemen of property and standing," unnerved by antislavery proponents, sacked abolitionist and antislavery organizations, even murdering newspaper editor Elijah Lovejoy in Alton, Illinois, in 1837. In the 1840s "respectable" citizens drove the Mormons out of Missouri and Illinois. In Philadelphia ongoing racial and ethnic conflict came to a head in 1844 when Protestant skilled workers attacked Irish Catholics. Smaller cities too became battlegrounds as nativist riots peaked in the 1850s. By 1860 more than 1,000 people had died in urban riots.

URBAN RIOTS

As public disorder spread, Boston hired uniformed policemen in 1837 to supplement its part-time watchmen and constables, and New York in 1845 established a uniformed force. Nonetheless, middle-class city dwellers did not venture out alone at night. In the midst of so much noise, crime, and conflict, the lavish uptown residences of the very rich rose like an affront to those struggling to survive.

Extremes of Wealth

After visiting America in 1831 and 1832, Alexis de Tocqueville characterized the United States as primarily a place of equality and opportunity for white males. Tocqueville attributed American equality—the relative fluidity of the social order—to Americans' mobility and restlessness. Geographic mobility, he felt, offered people a chance to start anew regardless of where they came from or who they were.

Others disagreed with this egalitarian view of American life. *New York Sun* publisher Moses Yale Beach believed a new aristocracy based on wealth and power was forming. Beach listed 750 New Yorkers with assets of $100,000 or more in 1845. John Jacob Astor, with a fortune of $25 million, led the list of 19 millionaires. Ten years later, Beach reported more than 1,000 New Yorkers worth $100,000, among them 28 millionaires. Tocqueville himself, sensitive to conflicting trends in American life, had described the new industrial wealth. The rich and well educated

GREAT FORTUNES

"come forward to exploit industries," Tocqueville wrote, and become "more and more like the administrators of a huge empire. . . . What is this if not an aristocracy?"

Wealth throughout the United States was becoming concentrated in the hands of a relatively small number of people. In New York City between 1828 and 1845, the richest 4 percent of the city's population increased their holdings from an estimated 63 percent to 80 percent of all individual wealth. By 1860 the top 5 percent of American families owned more than half of the nation's wealth.

From 1826 until his death in 1851, Philip Hone, one-time mayor of New York, kept a diary, meticulously recording the life of an American aristocrat. On February 28, 1840, for instance, Hone attended a masked ball at the Fifth Avenue mansion of Henry Breevoort Jr. and Laura Carson Breevoort. The five hundred invited ladies and gentlemen wore costumes adorned with ermine and gold. Like their counterparts in Boston, Philadelphia, Baltimore, and Charleston, the New York elite lived in mansions attended by servants and could escape the city for country estates or grand tours of Europe.

URBAN ELITE

Much of this wealth was inherited. For every John Jacob Astor who made millions in the western fur trade, ten others had inherited or married money. Many of the wealthiest New Yorkers bore the names of the colonial commercial elite: Breevoort, Roosevelt, Van Rensselaer, and Whitney. These rich New Yorkers were not idle; they worked at increasing their fortunes and power by investing in commerce and manufacturing. Wealth begat wealth, and marriage cemented family ties.

But just a short walk from this wealth, native-born working poor, newly arrived immigrants, and free blacks jostled in crowded streets with thieves, beggars, and prostitutes. Poor working men and women fretted continually that hard times were imminent. They dreaded poverty, chronic illness, disability, and old age. With good reason, women feared raising children without a spouse, as few women's jobs paid enough to support a family.

New York City's Five Points section, a few blocks from City Hall, lacked running water and sewers and was notorious for its physical and moral squalor. Dominated by the

URBAN SLUMS

Old Brewery, converted to housing, the neighborhood was predominantly Irish but also home to a few free black people. Contemporaries estimated that more than a thousand people lived in the Old Brewery's rooms and cellars. Throughout the city, workers' housing was at a premium. Houses built for two families often held four; tenements built for six families held twelve. Families took in lodgers to help pay the rent.

Meanwhile, a small but distinct middle class appeared on the urban scene—city businessmen, traders, and professionals serving the growth and specialization of trade. Middle-class families enjoyed new consumer items: wool carpeting, fine wallpaper, rooms full of furniture, and indoor toilets. They filled the family pews in church on Sundays; their male children went to college. They were as distant from Philip Hone's world as from that of the working class and the poor. Increasingly they looked to the family and home as the core of middle-class life.

THE MIDDLE CLASS

Family Life

*a*s urban families in the nineteenth-century market economy began to lose their role as producers, the result was sweeping change in the household economy as men increasingly worked for wages outside the home, and so did their offspring.

English common law gave husbands absolute control over the family. Men owned their wives' personal property, they were legal guardians of the children, and they owned whatever family members produced or earned. A father still had the legal authority to oppose his daughter's choice of husband. Nonetheless, most American women, with their parents' blessing, chose their own marriage partners.

LEGAL RIGHTS

Married women made modest gains in property and spousal rights from the 1830s on. Arkansas in 1835 passed the first married women's property law, and by 1860 sixteen more states had followed suit. In those states, when a wife inherited, earned, or acquired property, it was hers, not her husband's, and she could write a will. In the 1830s states began to liberalize divorce, adding cruelty and desertion as grounds for divorce. Nonetheless, divorce was rare.

In working-class families, women left their parental homes as early as age twelve, earning wages most of their lives, with only short respites for bearing and rearing children. Primarily unmarried girls and women worked as domestic servants in other women's homes; married and widowed women worked as laundresses, seamstresses, and cooks. Some hawked food and wares on city streets; others did piecework sewing at home in the putting-out system; and some became prostitutes. Few of these occupations enabled women to support themselves, let alone a family, at a respectable level.

WORKING WOMEN

Middle-class Americans, however, sought to keep women close to home. They idealized the family as a moral institution characterized by selflessness and cooperation. The world of work—the market economy—was seen as an arena of conflict identified with men and dominated by base self-interest. If young girls left home to work—in New England's textile mills, in new urban stores as clerks—it was only for a brief interval before marriage.

The domestic ideal restricted the paying jobs available to middle-class women, but one occupation was considered consistent with genteel femininity: teaching. In 1823 the Beecher sisters, Catharine and Mary, established the Hartford Female Seminary and offered history and science to the traditional women's curriculum of domestic arts and religion. A decade later Catharine Beecher successfully campaigned for teacher-training schools for women. By 1850 many women worked for a time as teachers, usually for two to five years. Unmarried women earned about half the salary of male teachers.

TEACHERS

The market economy brought economic insecurity and altered family life. As the American population moved west, kin became separated, and multigenerational families in the same household became less common. And all families, regardless of class or region, were shrinking in size. In 1830 American women bore an average of five or six children; by 1860 the figure had dropped to five. This decline occurred despite the arrival of many immigrants with large-family traditions; thus, the birth rate among native-born women declined even more steeply.

FAMILY SIZE

A number of factors account for reduced family size. Small families were viewed as increasingly desirable in an economy in which the family was a unit of consumption rather than production. In smaller families, parents could give children more attention, better education, and more financial help. Evidence suggests many wives and husbands deliberately limited the size of families.

The demographic data suggest that changes in childbearing reduced family size. Average age at marriage rose, thus shortening the period of potential childbearing. The age at which women bore their last child dropped from around forty in the mid-eighteenth century to around thirty-five in the mid-nineteenth.

But couples also limited family size through birth control. Traditional practices continued—coitus interruptus (withdrawal of the male before completion of the sexual act), breast-feeding to prolong infertile periods, and rhythm methods. Traditional remedies from American Indian to African folk medicine spread as well. Cheap rubber condoms became available in the 1850s. Douching after intercourse was also practiced. None of the methods was particularly reliable.

As formerly private concerns began to be discussed publicly, women shared and purchased information on limiting reproduction. If

ABORTION

all else failed, women resorted to abortions, especially after 1830. Ineffective folk methods of self-induced abortion had been around for centuries, but in the 1830s abortionists, mostly women, advertised surgical services in large cities. To protect women from unqualified abortionists, and in response to reformers opposed to abortion, states began to regulate the procedure. By 1860 twenty states had either restricted late-term abortions or prohibited abortion altogether.

Smaller size and fewer births changed the family. At one time, birth and infant care had occupied nearly the entire span of women's adult lives. In smaller families, individual children received greater attention, and childhood gradually came to be perceived as a distinct period in the life span.

Many single men lived and worked outside traditional families. In urban areas, rooming and boarding

SINGLE MEN AND WOMEN

houses provided them with places to sleep and eat. The expansion of cities and the market economy led more women to live outside families as well. Women like Louisa May Al-

cott (1832–1888), author of *Little Women* (1868), who lived most of her life in Massachusetts, followed an independent path. Her father never adequately provided for his family. Louisa May Alcott supported the family by working as a seamstress, governess, teacher, and housemaid before her writing brought her success. "I think I shall come out right, and prove that . . . I can support myself," she wrote her father in 1856. "I like the independent feeling; and though not an easy life, it is a free one, and I enjoy it."

To foreswear marriage and a family was not easy in a society that considered family the appropriate foundation of a moral life for women. But Alcott and other unmarried women managed to pursue careers and lives defined by female relationships. Given the difficulty women had finding ways to support themselves, they undertook independence at great risk. Nonetheless, the proportion of single women in the population increased significantly in the nineteenth century. Independent white women, in sum, were taking advantage of new opportunities offered by the market economy and urban expansion. At the same time communitarian ventures in rural America, like the Shakers and Mormons, offered experimentation in new family relationships.

Immigrant Lives in America

The 5 million immigrants who came to the United States between 1830 and 1860 outnumbered the entire population of the country recorded in the first census in 1790. The vast majority were European (see Figure 12.1). During the peak period of pre–Civil War immigration, from 1847 through 1857, 3.3 million immigrants entered the United States; 1.3 million were from Ireland and 1.1 million from the German states. By 1860, 15 percent of the white population was foreign-born.

This massive migration had been set in motion decades earlier. At the turn of the nineteenth century, the Napoleonic wars gave rise to one of the greatest population shifts in history; ultimately it lasted more than a century. War, revolution, famine, religious persecution, and the lure of industrialization led many Europeans to leave home. From the other side of the world, 41,000 Chinese, nearly all men, entered the United States from 1854 through 1860. The United States attracted immigrants as its economy offered jobs and its

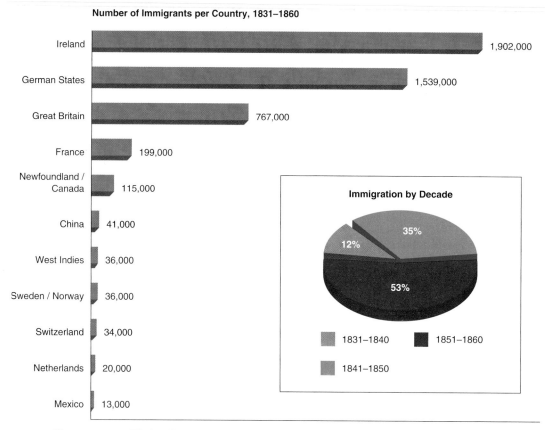

Number of Immigrants per Country, 1831–1860

Country	Immigrants
Ireland	1,902,000
German States	1,539,000
Great Britain	767,000
France	199,000
Newfoundland / Canada	115,000
China	41,000
West Indies	36,000
Sweden / Norway	36,000
Switzerland	34,000
Netherlands	20,000
Mexico	13,000

Immigration by Decade

35% — 1831–1840
12% — 1841–1850
53% — 1851–1860

Figure 12.1   Major Sources of Immigration to the United States, 1831–1860

Most immigrants came from two areas: Great Britain, of which Ireland was a part, and the German states. These two areas sent more immigrants between 1830 and 1860 than the inhabitants of the United States enumerated at the first census in 1790. By 1860, 15 percent of the white population was of foreign birth.   (Source: Data from Stephan Thernstrom, ed., *Harvard Encyclopedia of American Ethnic Groups* [Cambridge, Mass., and London: Harvard University Press, 1980], 1047.)

Constitution protected religious freedom. Not all planned to stay permanently, and many, like the Irish, saw themselves as exiles from their homeland.

Online Study Center **Improve Your Grade**
Interactive Map:
Origin and Settlement of Immigrants, 1820–1850

The market economy needed workers. Large construction projects and mining operations sought strong young men, and textile mills sought young women. Both private firms and governments recruited

PROMOTION OF
IMMIGRATION

European immigrants. Midwestern and western states lured potential settlers to promote economic growth. In the 1850s Wisconsin, for instance, appointed a commissioner of emigration, who advertised the state's advantages in European newspapers. Europeans' awareness of the United States grew as employers, states, and shipping companies promoted opportunities across the Atlantic. Often the message was stark: work and prosper in America, or starve in Europe. The price of passage across the ocean after 1848 was within easy reach of millions of Europeans.

Immigrants endured the hardships of travel and of living in a strange land. The average transatlantic crossing took six weeks; in bad weather, it could take three months. Disease spread unchecked among people packed together like cattle in steerage. More than seventeen thousand immigrants, mostly Irish, died from "ship fever" in 1847. On arrival, con artists and swindlers preyed on newcomers. In response, New York State established Castle Garden as an immigrant center in 1855. There, at the tip of Manhattan Island, the major port for European entry, immigrants were somewhat sheltered from fraud. Authorized transportation companies maintained offices in the large rotunda and assisted new arrivals with their travel plans.

Most immigrants gravitated toward cities, and many stayed in New York City itself. By 1855, 52

SETTLING IN

percent of its 623,000 inhabitants were immigrants—28 percent from Ireland and 16 percent from the German states. Boston also took on a European tone; throughout the 1850s the city was about 35 percent foreign born, of whom more than two-thirds were Irish. In the West, St. Louis and San Francisco had foreign-born majorities. Southern cities like Charleston and Savannah had significant Irish settlements.

Some immigrants settled in rural areas, though they tended to avoid the rural South, with its predominance of slave labor. German, Dutch, and Scandinavian farmers, in particular, headed toward the Midwest. Greater percentages of Scandinavians and Netherlanders took up farming than did other nationalities; both groups came mostly as religious dissenters and migrated in family units.

Not all arrivals found success in the United States; hundreds of thousands returned to their homelands

IMMIGRANT DISENCHANTMENT

disappointed. Before the famines of the late 1840s hit Ireland, American recruiters had lured many Irish to work on American canals and railroads and in construction. The promise that "he should soon become a wealthy man" lured Michael Gaugin, who had worked for thirteen years as an assistant engineer in the construction of a Dublin canal. The Irish agent for a New York firm convinced him to quit his job to come to America. But Gaugin landed in New York City during the financial panic of 1837. He could not find work, and within two months he was broke, struggling to find the means to return to Ireland.

Before the great famine, caused by a blight that ruined the potato crop, Ireland's food staple, there

IRISH IMMIGRANTS

had been a substantial outmigration from Ireland, mostly to English cities, but also a steady stream to the United States. From 1845 to 1849, death from starvation, malnutrition, and typhus spread in Ireland. In all, 1 million died and about 1.5 million scattered around the world, two-thirds of them to the United States. In every year but one between 1830 and 1854, the Irish constituted the largest group of immigrants.

Although most Irish made an economic decision to leave their homeland, they often viewed themselves as political exiles, forced to flee because of British tyranny. While nature caused the potato blight, they blamed British misrule for the events that led to famine. Thus, settlers of the Irish diaspora—in the United States, Canada, Australia, South Africa, Argentina, and even England—tended to be politically active. In the United States especially, as in St. Patrick's Day parades, they displayed their two national identities.

Most of the new immigrants from Ireland were young, female, poor, from rural counties, and Roman Catholic. In America, these women found work in textile mills and households. Young Irishmen worked in transportation and construction. The Irish supported their families back home and in Irish enclaves in cities, built Catholic churches and schools, and established networks of charitable and social organizations.

This wave of Irish immigrants, descended from the ancient Celts who spoke Gaelic, differed greatly

RACIAL IDEAS

from the Protestant Scots-Irish who had migrated earlier to the American colonies. Many considered the Celts inferior. The British had thought them barbaric, and colonists carried those views to America. Dr. Robert Knox of the Edinburgh College of Surgeons believed "the source of all evil lies in the race, the Celtic race of Ireland." Many Americans agreed. They talked about Celtic racial characteristics: a small, upturned nose, high forehead, and black tint of skin. As scientists like Knox began to classify peoples into biological types, scientific theory buttressed the developing notion of race.

With the immigration of new groups to the United States—Celts, Jews, and Catholics, for instance—with the black population expanding, and with territorial expansion bringing in Hispanics and more Indians, native-born white Americans were increasingly confronted with people who did not look like them. Many considered these non-British, non-European, non-Protestant people separate races. Ralph Waldo Emerson asserted the importance of race in *English Traits* (1856). To Emerson, a race passes on to its members its physical, intellectual, and moral characteristics. "Race avails . . . that all Celts are Catholics," Emerson wrote. "Race is a controlling influence in the Jew. . . . Race in the negro (sic) is of appalling importance."

Closely related to racial stereotyping in its causes and nasty effects was anti-Catholicism, which became

ANTI-CATHOLICISM

strident in the 1830s and was most overt and cruel in Boston with its many Irish. Anti-Catholic riots were almost commonplace. In Lawrence, Massachusetts, for instance, a mob leveled the Irish neighborhood in 1854.

The native-born whites who rejected the Irish and hated Catholics were motivated in part by economic competition and anxiety. Competition was stiffest among the lowest paid and least desirable jobs. To apprehensive workers, racializing the Irish as Celts was a way to keep them out of the running. Irish Catholics were also blamed for nearly every social problem, from immorality and alcoholism to poverty and economic upheaval. Impoverished native-born workers complained to the Massachusetts legislature in 1845 that the Irish displaced "the honest and respectable laborers of the State." American workers, they claimed, "not only labor for the body but for the mind, the soul, and the State."

In emphasizing "the soul, and the State," native-born workers added a political dimension to their racial expression. Republicanism depended on broad participation and the consent of the governed, and it seemed to American nativists that the Irish, a non-white, non-British "race," were not fit to participate.

By and large Americans viewed most Germans, unlike the Irish, as white, especially the majority

GERMAN IMMIGRANTS

Protestant group. They shared a racial stock with the English. Americans stereotyped Germans as hard working, self-reliant, and intelligent, attributes also applied to white

people. Many believed that Germans fit more easily than the Irish into American culture.

In 1854 Germans replaced the Irish as the largest group of new arrivals. Potato blight also prompted emigration from the German states in the 1840s, as did other hardships. Many came from regions where small landholdings made it hard to eke out a living. Craftsmen displaced by the industrial revolution sought jobs in America's expanding market economy. Political refugees—liberals, freethinkers, socialists, communists, and anarchists—fled to the United States after the abortive revolutions of 1848.

In the South, Germans were peddlers and merchants; in the North and West, they worked as farmers, urban laborers, and businessmen. Their tendency to migrate as families and groups helped them maintain German customs and institutions. Many settled in small towns and rural areas, where they could preserve their language and regional German cultures. In larger cities, their tendency to cluster together transformed the tone of communities like Cincinnati and Milwaukee.

Non-Protestant Germans did not fare so well. A significant number of German immigrants were Jewish, and Jews were considered a separate race. Anti-Catholics attacked German immigrants who were Catholic. The Sunday tradition of urban German families gathering at beer gardens to eat and drink, dance and sing, and sometimes play cards outraged Protestants, who viewed this behavior as violating the sanctity of the Lord's day.

From Florida to Texas and the Southwest to California, Hispanic inhabitants of the borderlands became "immigrants" without actually moving; treaties

HISPANICS

placed them in the United States. Some Mexicans were unhappy to find themselves in a new country, while others welcomed the political self-government the United States seemed to promise.

But reality denied promise. In Nueces County, Texas, at the time of the Texas Revolution (1836), Mexicans held all the land; twenty years later, they had lost it. The new Anglo owners produced crops for the market economy; *rancheros* and *vaqueros*—cowboys—became obsolete. Although many Mexicans, called *Tejanos*, had fought for Texas's independence, new Anglo settlers tended to treat them as inferiors and foreigners. They became second-class citizens on land where they had lived for generations. Still, they retained their culture. They held fast to their language, Roman Catholic religion, and cultural traditions.

In California—unlike in Texas, New Mexico, and Arizona—Hispanic society and political power quickly gave way to American and European culture. *Californios*, the Mexican population, numbered 10,000 in 1848, or two-thirds of the non-Indian population. By the end of the century, the Hispanic population was 15,000 out of 1.5 million, and Hispanic culture was only a remnant.

White Americans considered Hispanics, a group descended from Indians and Spaniards, as a separate, nonwhite race. Anglo-Americans also inherited the British view of Spaniards as inferior, lazy, and decadent, stereotypes they applied to Hispanics. Racializing Hispanics helped to justify the attitudes and actions of aggressive whites.

Free People of Color

Blacks, slave and free, were the most visible nonwhite group in the early nineteenth century. As their numbers grew, from 2.3 million in 1830 to 4.4 million in 1860, whites increasingly viewed them as a racial group, a people apart. In law and society, most black people found themselves outsiders in the land of their birth.

GROWTH OF THE BLACK POPULATION

The free African American population grew from 320,000 in 1820 to almost 500,000 in 1860. Nearly half lived in the urban North and almost an equal number in the Upper South, where, outside of Baltimore—the nation's largest black community—most were rural. A scattering of free people of color lived in the Deep South. Despite differences in occupation, wealth, education, religion, and social status, the necessity of self-defense promoted solidarity among free blacks.

Ex-slaves constantly increased the ranks of free people of color in the North. Some, like Frederick Douglass and Harriet Tubman, were fugitives. Tubman, a slave in Maryland, escaped to Philadelphia in 1849. Over the next two years, she returned twice to free her two children, her sister, her mother, and her brother and his family. Some slaves received freedom in owners' wills. And some owners freed their children born of liaisons or forced relations with slaves or released elderly slaves rather than support them in old age.

AFRICAN AMERICAN COMMUNITIES

Black people, free and slave, forged their own communities and culture. Swept up by the Second Great Awakening, blacks turned increasingly to religion, most often to Christianity. But as they founded their own churches and denominations, like the African Methodist Episcopal (AME) Church (1816), they reshaped ritual and practice. Services reflected black musical traditions, and they gave theological prominence to themes of equality, exodus, and freedom. Black churches and preachers, both male and female, played central roles in their communities. Ministers were political leaders and abolitionists, united in their opposition to the enslavement of other black people, sometimes their own kin.

A network of voluntary associations became the hallmark of black communities. Besides the churches, men and women organized reform societies, fraternal and benevolent associations, literary societies, and schools. In Philadelphia in the 1840s, more than half of the black population belonged to mutual beneficiary societies. Many black leaders believed these mutual aid societies would encourage thrift, industry, and morality, thus assisting their members in improving themselves. But no amount of effort could completely counteract the burden of white racism, which impinged on every aspect of their lives.

POLITICAL ACTIVISM

In the majority of states where free blacks were excluded from the ballot, they formed organizations to fight for equal rights. Among the early efforts was the Negro Convention movement. From 1830 to 1835, and irregularly thereafter, free blacks held national conventions with delegates drawn from city and state organizations. Under middle-class leadership, the convention movement served as a forum to attack slavery and agitate for equal rights. Militant new black newspapers joined the struggle.

DISCRIMINATION AND EXCLUSION

Activists fought their second-class status and the continuation of slavery. Although the Bill of Rights and the Constitution promised protection of civil rights, eighteenth-century political theory had defined the republic as being for whites only (see Chapter 7), and early federal legislation excluded blacks from common rights. The first naturalization law in 1790 limited citizenship to "free white persons." And after 1821, every new state admitted until the Civil War, free and slave, banned blacks from voting. Finally, when Congress organized the Oregon and New Mexico Territories, it reserved public land grants for whites. Clearly free people of color were defined as an alien race.

Even in the North, states attempted to exclude African Americans. Many states barred free blacks or required them to post bonds ranging from $500 to $1,000 to guarantee their good conduct. Only in Massachusetts, New Hampshire, Vermont, and Maine could blacks vote on an equal basis with whites throughout the early nineteenth century. In 1842 African Americans gained the right to vote in Rhode Island, but they had lost it earlier in Pennsylvania and Connecticut. Only Massachusetts permitted blacks to serve on juries. Four midwestern states and California did not allow African Americans to testify against whites. In Oregon blacks could not own real estate, make contracts, or sue in court.

Black people also faced economic restrictions. They were excluded from the new factory and clerical jobs of the expanding market economy. In the North and Upper South, black women, who were more likely to work for wages than white women, whether married or single, worked as house servants, cooks, washerwomen, and child nurses. Most black men were construction workers, porters, longshoremen, and day laborers. All suffered frequent unemployment.

Some black men and women turned service occupations into businesses. In the growing cities, blacks opened restaurants, taverns, hotels, barber shops, and employment agencies for domestic servants. A few became very successful economically, like sail maker James Forten (Philadelphia), barber Samuel Mordechai (St. Louis), and ship captain Paul Cuffee. With professionals—ministers, teachers, physicians and dentists, lawyers, and newspaper editors—they formed a growing black middle class.

While free people of color sought economic and political security, they forged their own cultural identity. They began to call themselves

African American Culture

"Colored Americans" rather than "Africans." Like the Irish on St. Patrick's Day, they acknowledged a dual identity as African descendants and as Americans. There is much evidence that they mixed African and American cultures in distinct ways. They dressed up for church, wearing their "Sunday go-to-meetin' clothes." They modified African hairstyles in cutting, wrapping, and braiding their hair. Africans brought the banjo and drum to the New World, introducing new rhythms to Europeans. Black brass bands created what Walt Whitman called "grand American opera."

Most expressive was African American dance. From Congo Square in New Orleans on Sundays to the integrated "dives" in Five Points, New York, visitors observed African-based dance movements unknown to Europeans. Frederick Bremer in South Carolina in 1850 described such movements in a black church. They sang "with all their souls and with all their bodies in unison, for their bodies wagged, their heads nodded, their feet stamped, their knees shook, their elbows and their hands beat time to the tune." Here were the African traditions of polyrhythms, improvisation, and intensive physicality.

In the late 1840s and 1850s the mood of many free blacks turned pessimistic. They felt frustrated by the failure of the abolitionist movement and angered by the passage of the stringent Fugitive Slave Act of 1850 (discussed in Chapter 14). Some fled to Canada. Many more were swept up in a wave of black nationalism that stressed racial solidarity, self-help, and a growing interest in Africa. Before this time, efforts to send African Americans "back to Africa" had originated with whites seeking to rid the United States of blacks, and nearly all African American leaders had been opposed. But in the 1850s, some participated in emigrationist conventions led by abolitionists Henry Bibb and Martin Delany. With the coming of the Civil War, the status of blacks would move onto the national political agenda.

Summary   *Online Study Center*   ACE the Test

The American people and communities in the North and West were far more diverse and turbulent in the 1850s than they had been in the 1820s. The market economy and westward movement altered rural and urban life and class structure; heavy immigration, growing racial ideas, and the anguished position of free people of color added to the tensions. Inequality increased, as did the gap between the haves and the have-nots. As the nation grew more populous and the market economy upset work and social relations, many felt a loss of tradition and community. Some longed to return to old values. Utopians like the Shakers, Mormons, and Brook Farmers sought to counter isolation and individualism.

Increasingly cities became the center of American life, with New York the predominant metropolis. Growing populations brought new problems, however, and cities struggled to provide adequate public health, safety, and education for their residents. Large cities offered rich leisure activities, but people divided along class, ethnic, and racial lines.

In the midst of these changes, families adapted to the urban, market economy. They became consumers rather than producers, and they shrank in size as women had fewer children. Middle-class families sought to insulate their homes from the competition of the market economy. Increasingly cities offered opportunities for people to live outside of families.

Famine and oppression in Europe propelled millions of people across the Atlantic. American expansion added Hispanics to the nation. Diversity, competition, and religious and scientific thought fueled racial ideas. Many European descendants began to view the Irish, Hispanics, and African Americans as inferior races.

LEGACY FOR A PEOPLE AND A NATION
White Fascination with and Appropriation of Black Culture

White Americans' fascination with and appropriation of black culture blossomed in the early nineteenth century. Whites performed songs and dances from blackface minstrel reviews, while urban young people imitated black language, dress, and hairstyles. In the 1850s white songwriter Stephen Foster's "Old Folks at Home," "Susanna," and "Camptown Races" were enormously popular.

American popular culture combined African, European, and African American traditions. Its emphasis on performance, improvisation, strong rhythms, vernacular language, multiple meanings,

and integration into everyday life is evidence of strong African ties. These elements appealed to whites because of their expressive power. Whites also believed that black cultural forms were "exotic" and offered "natural" forms of expression.

Black traditions continue to influence popular culture today. Minstrelsy turned into vaudeville and Broadway theater. Popular dance and music, performed mostly by whites, drew heavily on black gospel, slave spirituals, the blues, and jazz. Black traditions influenced the swing bands of the 1930s, and after World War II, they shaped rhythm and blues, rock 'n' roll, and, later, rap, hip-hop, and ska.

Until recently, most whites experienced black culture as appropriated by whites. But in the late twentieth century, a synthesis of black and white traditions became notable. In the early 1950s Bill Haley and the Comets, a white group, combined black rhythm and blues with white country and western music. Their 1954 sensation, "Shake, Rattle & Roll," for instance, was a sanitized version of Big Joe Turner's rhythm and blues hit. White audiences responded enthusiastically, and when Haley and the Comets played "Rock Around the Clock" in the 1955 movie *Blackboard Jungle*, rock 'n' roll took off. Elvis Presley too synthesized rhythm and blues and gospel with country music and middle-of-the-road popular music. Rap and hip-hop built on the talking blues, call and response, and urban black and Chicano/a dance styles of the 1970s. White suburban youth made them dominant popular forms.

Popular music and dance, with its African American roots, is uniquely American. Young people fostered this popular culture and used its expressive elements to define themselves. Thus, African American culture has given the people and the nation a unique cultural legacy.

₽EOPLE AND COMMUNITIES IN A SLAVE SOCIETY: THE SOUTH 1830–1860

₽ierce Butler was broke. It was late winter 1859, fear of disunion dominated national life, and Butler's slave auction had all of coastal Georgia and South Carolina talking. Butler had divided his time between the family's ostentatious home in Philadelphia and 1,500 acres of cotton plantations in Georgia, worked by eight hundred slaves. By 1859 Butler had squandered a fortune of $700,000 through speculation and gambling.

Most of Butler's properties and possessions in Philadelphia were sold to satisfy his creditors. Then came the largest slave auction in American history. In the last week of February, 436 Butler slaves were taken to Savannah by railroad and steamboat. People of all ages—infants, husbands, wives, children, grandparents—huddled in fearful expectation. The auction lasted an agonizing two days in a driving rainstorm.

If possible, families were sold intact for group prices; thus, the old and infirm could still be liquidated, while the closest kin stayed together. A seventeen-year-old "Prime woman" and her three-month-old son went for $2,200. A nineteen-year-old "prime young man" netted $1,295. Some families of four brought only $1,600 together. At the end of the second day of what blacks in the region called the "weeping time," Butler had amassed $303,850 by selling 436 human beings.

As long as slavery was perceived as a peculiarly southern institution, it did not seem to bother many northerners at first glance. But as slavery spread westward, its worst elements, such as the Butler auction, threatened and disturbed growing numbers of restless Americans. And on the ground in the South, slaves struggled to survive and resist.

By the 1830s, the North was an emerging market economy embarking on an industrial revolution. The South, with a different kind of growth and pros-

Online Study Center
This icon will direct you to interactive map and primary source activities on the website http://college.hmco.com/ pic/nortonbrief7e

CHRONOLOGY

1810–20 • 137,000 slaves are forced to move from North Carolina and the Chesapeake to Alabama, Mississippi, and other western regions

1822 • Vesey's insurrection plot is discovered in South Carolina

1830s • Vast majority of African American slaves are native-born in America

1830s–40s • Cotton trade grows into largest source of commercial wealth and America's leading export

1831 • Turner leads a violent slave rebellion in Virginia

1832 • Virginia holds the last serious debate in the South about the future of slavery; gradual abolition is voted down
• Publication of Dew's proslavery tract, *Abolition of Negro Slavery*

1836 • Arkansas gains admission to the Union as a slave state

1845 • Florida and Texas gain admission to the Union as slave states
• Publication of Douglass's *Narrative of the Life of Frederick Douglass, An American Slave*

1850 • Planters' share of agricultural wealth in the South is 90 to 95 percent

1850–60 • Of some 300,000 slaves who migrate from Upper to Lower South, 60 to 70 percent go by outright sale

1857 • Publication of Helper's *The Impending Crisis*, denouncing the slave system

1860 • 405,751 mulattos in the United States, 12.5 percent of the African American population
• Three-quarters of all southern white families own no slaves

1861 • South produces largest cotton crop ever

---

perity, also participated in the market revolution. New lands were settled and new states peopled, and steadily the South emerged as the world's most extensive and vigorous slave economy, linked to an international cotton trade and textile industry. Slavery had a far-reaching influence on all of southern society. The Old South's wealth came from export crops, land, and slaves, and its population was almost wholly rural. ■

The Distinctive South?

Certain American values such as materialism, individualism, and faith in progress have been associated with the North in the nineteenth century, and values such as tradition, intolerance, and family loyalty with the South. The South, so the stereotype has it, was static, and the North dynamic. There are many measures of just how different the South was from the North in the antebellum era, and at the same time there were many Souths: low-country rice and cotton regions with dense slave populations; mountainous regions of small farmers, plantation culture, and subsistence agriculture; Texas grasslands; cities with bustling ports and merchants.

The South was distinctive because of its commitment to slavery, but it was also much like the rest of the nation. The South and the North were roughly the same size geographically. By the 1830s, white southerners shared a heritage from the era of the American Revolution with their fellow free citizens in the North. Southerners spoke the same language, worshiped the same Protestant God, and lived under the same cherished

SOUTH-NORTH SIMILARITY

Constitution as northerners, and they shared common attitudes toward government. Down to the 1840s, northerners and southerners both invoked the doctrine of states' rights against federal authority. A faith in the future fueled by a sense of American mission and the dreams inspired by westward movement were as much a part of southern as of northern experience. But as slavery and the plantation economy expanded, the South did not become a land of individual opportunity in quite the same manner as the North.

Research has shown that slavery was a profitable labor system for planters. As it grew, the slave-based economy of money-crop agriculture reflected planters' rational choices. More land and more slaves generally converted into more wealth. By the eve of the Civil War in 1860, the distribution of wealth and property in the two sections was almost identical: 50 percent of free adult males owned only 1 percent of real and personal property, while the richest 1 percent owned 27 percent of the wealth. Both North and South had ruling classes, and entrepreneurs in both sections, whether planters in the Mississippi Delta or factory owners in New England, sought their fortunes in a shared and expanding market economy.

But there were also important differences between the North and the South. The South's climate and longer growing season gave it an unmistakable rural and agricultural destiny. Its people, white and black, developed an intense attachment to place, to the ways people were related to the land and to one another. It developed as a biracial society of brutal inequality, where the liberty of one race directly depended on the enslavement of another.

SOUTH-NORTH DISSIMILARITY

Cotton growers spread out over as large an area as possible to maximize production and income. Population density was low; by 1860, there were only 2.3 people per square mile in vast and largely unsettled Texas and 18.0 in Georgia. Population density in the nonslaveholding states east of the Mississippi River was almost three times higher. The Northeast had an average of 65.4 people per square mile, Massachusetts 153.1, and New York City 86,400.

Where people were scarce, it was difficult to finance and operate schools, churches, libraries, or even inns and restaurants. Southerners were strongly committed to their churches, and some believed in the importance of universities, but all such institutions were far less developed than those in the North. Factories were rare because planters invested most of their capital in slaves. And despite concerted efforts, the South had only 35 percent of the nation's railroad mileage in 1860.

The South did have urban centers, especially ports like New Orleans and Charleston, which became bustling crossroads of commerce and small-scale manufacturing. But slavery slowed urban growth. And because of the lack of jobs, the South did not attract immigrants as readily as the North did.

Like most northerners, antebellum southerners practiced evangelical Christianity. But southern evangelicalism was distinct from northern practice. In the South, Baptists and Methodists concentrated on personal rather than social improvement. By the 1830s in the North, evangelicalism was a major wellspring of reform movements; but in the states where blacks were so numerous and unfree, religion, as one scholar has written, preached "a hands-off policy concerning slavery." The only reform movements that did take hold in the South, such as temperance, focused on personal behavior, not social reform.

Perhaps in no other way was the South more distinctive than in its embrace of a particular worldview, a system of thought and meaning held especially by the planter class but influencing all groups of whites. At the heart of the proslavery argument was a deep and abiding racism. The persistence of modern racism in all sections of the United States is all the more reason to comprehend antebellum southerners' justifications for human slavery.

A SOUTHERN WORLDVIEW AND THE PROSLAVERY ARGUMENT

By 1830, white southerners defended slavery as a "positive good," not merely a "necessary evil." They used the Bible and its many references to slaveholding, as well as the ancient roots of slavery, to foster a historical argument for bondage. Slavery, they deemed, was the natural status of blacks. Whites were the more intellectual race, in this view, and blacks the more inherently physical, and therefore destined for labor.

Some southerners defended slavery in practical terms; they saw their bondsmen as an economic necessity in their quest for prosperity. Others argued that slaveholding was essentially a matter of property rights. James Henry Hammond of South Carolina spoke for many southerners in his unwillingness to "deal in abstractions" about the "right and wrong" of slavery: property was sacred, and slaves were legal property—end of argument.

2 The deepest root of the proslavery argument was a hierarchical view of the social order as slavery's defenders believed God or nature had prescribed it. Southerners cherished stability, duty, and honor, believing social change should come in slow increments, if at all. When the Virginia legislature debated the gradual abolition of slavery in 1831–1832, Thomas R. Dew, a slaveholder and professor of law and history, contended, "There is a time for all things, and nothing in this world should be done before its time." Dew's widely read work, *Abolition of Negro Slavery* (1832), ushered in an outpouring of proslavery writing that would intensify over the next thirty years. Dew declared black slavery part of the "order of nature," indispensable to the "deep and solid foundations of society," and the basis of the "well-ordered, well-established liberty" of white Americans. Dew's well-ordered society also included his conception of the proper division of men and women into separate spheres and functions.

Proslavery advocates held very different views from those of northern reformers on the concepts of freedom, progress, and equality. They turned natural-law doctrine to their favor, arguing that the natural state of mankind was inequality of ability and condition, not equality. Proslavery writers believed that people were born to certain stations in life; they stressed dependence over autonomy, and duty over rights, as the human condition.

Hence, many slaveholders believed that their ownership of people bound them to a set of paternal obligations in a familial relationship between masters and slaves. Although contradicted by countless examples of slave resistance and escape, planters needed to believe in, and exerted great energy in constructing, the idea of the contented slave. Slaveholders needed to justify endlessly how much the freedom and profits of whites depended on the bondage of blacks.

What the South had become by the 1830s, and grew even more fully into by 1860, was not merely a society with slaves, but a *slave soci-*

A SLAVE SOCIETY

ety (see Chapter 3). Slavery and race affected everything in the Old South. Whites, slaveholding or not, and blacks, slave or free, all grew up, were socialized, married, reared children, and honed their most basic habits of behavior under the influence of slavery. Slavery shaped the social structure of the South, fueled almost anything meaningful in its economy, and came to dominate its politics.

The South was interdependent with the North and the West and even with Europe in a growing capitalist market system. Southerners relied on northern banks, northern steamship companies, and northern merchants to keep the cotton trade flowing. But there were elements of that system that southerners increasingly rejected during the antebellum era, especially urbanism, the wage labor system, a broadening right to vote, and any threats to the racial and class order on which they so depended.

Just how distinctive the South was will always be debated. Culturally, the South developed a proclivity to tell its own story. Its ruralness and its sense of tradition may have given southerners a special habit of telling tales. "Southerners . . . love a good tale," said Mississippi writer Eudora Welty. The South's tragic and distinct story begins in the Old South. The story was distinctive and national all at once.

Free Southerners: Farmers, Free Blacks, and Planters

a large majority of white southern families (three-quarters in 1860) owned no slaves. Some lived in towns, but most were yeoman farmers who owned their own land and grew their own food. The social distance between different groups of whites was great. Still greater was the distance between whites and blacks.

Yeoman farmers were individualistic and hard working, but their status as a numerical majority did

YEOMAN FARMERS

not mean that they set the political or economic direction of the slave society. Self-reliant and often isolated, always absorbed in the work of their farms, they operated both apart from and within the slave-based staple-crop economy.

Yeomen pioneered the southern wilderness, moving into undeveloped regions—or Indian land after removal—and building log cabins. After the War of 1812, they moved in successive waves down the southern Appalachians into the Gulf lands. In large sections of the South, small, self-sufficient farms were

■ Eastman Johnson's *Fiddling His Way* (1866) depicts rural life by representing the visit of an itinerant black musician to a farm family. Expressions and gestures suggest remarkable ease between the races at the yeoman level of southern society.   (Eastman Johnson [American, 1824–1906] *Fiddling His Way,* 1866, oil on canvas, 24¼ x 36½ inches. Bequest of Walter P. Chrysler, Jr., Chrysler Museum of Art, Norfolk, VA 89.60)

the norm. Lured by stories of good land, many men uprooted their wives and children repeatedly.

On the southern frontier, men worked hard to fields and establish farms, while their wives labored in the household economy and patiently re-created the social ties—to relatives, neighbors, fellow churchgoers—that enriched everyone's experience. Women seldom shared the men's excitement about moving. They dreaded the isolation and loneliness of the frontier.

Some yeomen acquired large tracts of level land, purchased slaves, and became planters. They forged part of the new wealth of the boom states of Missis-sippi and Louisiana, the region to which the southern political power base shifted by the 1840s and 1850s. Others clung to familiar mountainous areas or kept moving as independent farmers.

The yeomen enjoyed a folk culture based on fam-ily, church, and local region. They flocked to religious revivals called camp meetings, and in between got together for house-raisings, logrollings, quilting bees, corn-shuckings, and hunting for both food and sport. Such occasions combined work with fun and fellowship.

YEOMAN FOLK CULTURE

A demanding round of work and family respon-sibilities shaped women's lives in the home. In addi-tion to preparing and preserving food, they worked in the fields to an extent that astonished travelers such as Frances Trollope, who believed yeomen had rendered their wives "slaves of the soil." Household tasks continued during frequent pregnancies and childcare. Primary nursing and medical care also fell to mothers, who often relied on folk wisdom.

Among the men were many who aspired to wealth, eager to join the race for slaves and cotton profits. Others were content with their independence, family, religion, and recreation. All worked hard.

YEOMAN LIVELIHOODS

North Carolinian Ferdinand L. Steel, who took up farming in Mississippi, was a typical yeoman. Steel rose every day at five and worked until sundown. With the help of his family, he raised corn, wheat, pork, and vegetables. Cotton was his cash crop: he sold five or six bales (about 2,000 pounds) a year to obtain money for sugar, coffee, salt, calico, gunpowder, and a few other store-bought goods.

Thus, Steel entered the market economy as a small farmer, but with mixed results. He complained that cotton cultivation was brutal work and not profitable. He felt like a serf in cotton's kingdom. When cotton prices fell, a small grower like Steel could be driven into debt and lose his farm.

Steel's life in Mississippi in the 1840s retained much of the flavor of the frontier. He made all the family's shoes; his wife and sister sewed dresses, shirts, and "pantaloons." The Steel women also rendered their own soap and spun and wove cotton into cloth; the men hunted game. As the nation fell deeper into crisis over the future of slave labor, this independent southern farmer never came close to owning a slave.

The focus of Steel's life was family and religion. Family members prayed together daily, and Steel studied Scripture for an hour after lunch. He borrowed histories and religious books from his church. Eventually he became a traveling Methodist minister. "My life is one of toil," he reflected, "but blessed be God that it is as well with me as it is."

Toil with even less security was the lot of two other groups of free southerners: landless whites and free blacks. A sizable minority of white southern workers—from 25 to 40 percent—were unskilled laborers who owned no land and worked for others in the countryside and towns. Their property consisted of a few household items and some animals—usually pigs—that could feed themselves on the open range. The landless included some immigrants, especially Irish, who did heavy and dangerous work such as building railroads and digging ditches.

LANDLESS WHITES

In the countryside, white farm laborers struggled to purchase land in the face of low wages or, if they rented, unpredictable market prices for their crops. By scrimping and saving and finding odd jobs, some managed to climb into the ranks of yeomen. When James and Nancy Bennitt of North Carolina succeeded in their ten-year struggle to buy land, they decided to avoid the unstable market in cotton and raised extra corn and wheat as sources of cash.

By 1860, as the South anticipated war to preserve its society, between 300,000 and 400,000 white people in the four states of Virginia, North and South Carolina, and Georgia lived in genuine poverty, approximately one-fifth of the total white population. Their lives were harsh to say the least.

For the nearly quarter-million free blacks in the South in 1860, conditions were often little better than the slaves'. They usually did not own land and had to labor in someone else's fields, often beside slaves. By law, free blacks could not own a gun, buy liquor, violate curfew, assemble except in church, testify in court, or (throughout the South after 1835) vote. Despite these obstacles, a minority bought land, and others found jobs as skilled craftsmen.

FREE BLACKS

A few free blacks prospered and bought slaves, most of them purchasing their own wives and children (whom they could not free, since laws required newly emancipated blacks to leave their states). In 1830 there were 3,775 free black slaveholders in the South; 80 percent lived in the four states of Louisiana, South Carolina, Virginia, and Maryland, and approximately half of the total lived in the two cities of New Orleans and Charleston.

Online Study Center
Improve Your Grade
Primary Source: Black Recollections of Freedom's Impact

In the cotton and Gulf regions, a large proportion of free blacks were mulattos, the privileged offspring of wealthy white planters. Not all planters freed their mixed-race offspring, but those who did often recognized a moral obligation and gave their children a good education and financial backing. In a few cities like New Orleans, Charleston, and Mobile, extensive interracial sex, as well as migrations from the Caribbean, had produced a mulatto population that was recognized as a distinct class.

FREE BLACK COMMUNITIES

In many southern cities by the 1840s, free black communities formed, especially around an expanding number of churches. By the late 1850s, Baltimore had fifteen churches, Louisville nine, and Nashville and St. Louis four each, and most of them were African Methodist Episcopal. Class and race distinctions were important to southern free blacks, but outside a few cities, which developed fraternal orders of skilled craftsmen and fellowships of light-skinned people, most mulattos experienced hardship. In the United States, "one drop" of black "blood" made them black, and potentially enslaveable.

At the top of the southern social pyramid were slaveholding planters. As a group they lived well,

PLANTERS

but most lived in comfortable farmhouses, not on the opulent scale that legend suggests. A few statistics tell the story: in 1850, 50 percent of southern slaveholders had fewer than five slaves; 72 percent had fewer than ten; 88 percent had fewer than twenty. Thus, the average slaveholder was not a wealthy aristocrat but an aspiring farmer, and usually of humble origins.

The richest planters used their wealth to model genteel sophistication. Extended visits, parties, and balls to which women wore the latest fashions provided opportunities for friendship, courtship, and display. These entertainments were especially important as diversions for plantation women, and at the same time they sustained a rigidly gendered society. Young women relished social events to break the monotony of their domestic lives.

Most of the planters in the cotton-boom states of Alabama and Mississippi were newly rich by the 1840s. As one historian put it, "a number of men mounted from log cabin to plantation mansion on a stairway of cotton bales, accumulating slaves as they climbed." And many did not live like rich men. They put their new wealth into cotton acreage and slaves even as they sought refinement and high social status.

Slaveholding men dominated society and, especially among the wealthiest and oldest families, justified

SOUTHERN PATERNALISM

their dominance over white women and black slaves through a paternalistic ideology. Instead of stressing the profitable aspects of commercial agriculture, they focused on their obligations, viewing themselves as custodians of the welfare of society in general and of the black families they owned in particular. The paternalistic planter saw himself not as an oppressor but as the benevolent guardian of an inferior race.

Paul Carrington Cameron, North Carolina's largest slaveholder, exemplifies this mentality. After a period of sickness among his one thousand North Carolina slaves (he had hundreds more in Alabama and Mississippi), Cameron wrote, "I fear the Negroes have suffered much from the want of proper attention and kindness under this late distemper . . . no love of lucre shall ever induce me to be cruel."

It was comforting to rich planters to see themselves in this way, and slaves—accommodating to the realities of power—encouraged their masters to think their benevolence was appreciated. Paternalism also served as a defense against abolitionist criticism. Still, paternalism often covered harsher assumptions. As talk of paternalistic duties increased, theories about the complete and permanent inferiority of blacks multiplied. In reality, paternalism grew as a give-and-take relationship between masters and slaves, each extracting from the other what they desired: owners took labor from the bondsmen, while slaves expected from masters a measure of autonomy and living space. But it also evolved as a theory of black slavery and white dominance.

Even Paul Cameron's benevolence vanished with changed circumstances. After the Civil War, he bristled at African Americans' efforts to be free. Writing on Christmas Day 1865, Cameron showed little Christian charity (but a healthy profit motive) when he declared, "I am convinced that the people who gets rid of the free negro first will be the first to advance in improved agriculture. Have made no effort to retain any of mine [and] will not attempt a crop beyond the capacity of 30 hands." With that he turned off his land nearly a thousand black people, rented his fields to several white farmers, and invested in industry.

Relations between men and women in the planter class were similarly paternalistic. The upper-class southern woman was raised and educated to be a wife, mother, and subordinate companion to men. South Carolina's Mary Boykin Chesnut wrote of her husband, "He is master of the house. To hear is to obey. . . . All the comfort of my life depends upon his being in a good humor." In a social system based on the coercion of an entire race, women were not allowed to challenge society's rules on sexual or racial relations.

"King Cotton" in the World Economy

The economy of the Old South was deeply intertwined with international trade. Cash crops such as cotton were exported, and the fate of this slave society depended on world trade, especially with Europe.

The American South so dominated the world's supply of cotton that the size of the U.S. crop normally determined the price in an international market where demand continued to skyrocket. This circumstance gave southern planters enormous confidence that the cotton boom was permanent and that the industrializing nations of England and France in particular would always bow to "King Cotton."

American cotton doubled in yield each decade after 1800 and provided three-fourths of the world's supply by the 1840s. Southern staple crops were fully three-fifths of all American exports by 1850, and one of every seven workers in England depended on American cotton for a job. Indeed, cotton production made slaves the single most valuable financial asset in the United States—greater in dollar value than all of America's banks, railroads, and manufacturing combined.

The Old South never developed its own banking and shipping capacity to any degree. If it had, its effort to be an international cartel might have succeeded longer. Most southern bank deposits were in the North, and southern cotton planters became ever more dependent on New York for shipping.

Until 1840 the cotton trade furnished much of the export capital to finance northern economic growth. After that date, however, the northern economy expanded without dependence on cotton profits. Nevertheless, southern planters and politicians continued to boast of King Cotton's supremacy. "No power on earth dares . . . to make war on cotton," James Hammond lectured the U.S. Senate in 1858. "Cotton is king." Although the South produced 4.5 million bales in 1861, its greatest cotton crop ever, this link to the world was about to collapse in a civil war. Thereafter, cotton was more a shackle to the South than a king.

Cotton traded to England would be returned to the United States in fabric collections called sample books, such as this Norwich Textile Sample Book. Orders were placed and then shipped to Americans. (Courtesy, The Henry Francis du Pont Winterthur Library: Joseph Downs Collection of Manuscripts & Printed Ephemera)

Planters' daughters usually attended one of the South's rapidly multiplying boarding schools. There they formed friendships with other girls and received an education. Typically the young woman could entertain suitors whom her parents approved. But very soon she had to choose a husband and commit herself for life to a man whom she generally had known only briefly. Young women were often alienated and emotionally unfulfilled. They had to follow the wishes of their families, especially fathers. "It was for me best that I yielded to the wishes of papa," wrote a young North Carolinian in 1823. "I wonder when my best will cease to be painful and when I shall begin to enjoy life instead of enduring it."

MARRIAGE AND FAMILY AMONG THE PLANTER CLASS
Upon marriage, a planter class woman ceded to her husband most of her legal rights, becoming part of his family. Most of the year she was isolated on a large plantation, where she had to oversee the cooking and preserving of food, manage the house, supervise care of the children, and attend sick slaves. It is not surprising that a perceptive young white woman sometimes approached marriage with anxiety.

Childbearing often involved grief, poor health, and death. In 1840 the birth rate for white southern women in their childbearing years was almost 30 percent higher than the national average. By 1860 the average southern white woman could expect to bear six children, with one or more miscarriages likely. For women who wanted to plan their families, methods of contraception and medical care were uncertain. Complications of childbirth were a major cause of death, occurring twice as often in the hot, humid South as in the Northeast.

Sexual relations between planters and slaves were another source of problems that white women had to endure but were not supposed to notice. "Violations of the moral law . . . made mulattoes as common as blackberries," protested a woman in Georgia, but wives had to play "the ostrich game." "A magnate who runs a hideous black harem," wrote Mrs. Chesnut, ". . . poses as the model of all human virtues to these poor women whom God and the laws have given him."

Southern men tolerated little discussion by women of the slavery issue. In the 1840s and 1850s, as abolitionist attacks on slavery increased, southern men published a barrage of articles stressing that women should restrict their concerns to the home. The *Southern Quarterly Review* declared, "The proper place for a woman is at home. One of her highest privileges, to be politically merged in the existence of her husband."

But some southern women were beginning to seek a larger role. A study of women in Petersburg, Virginia, revealed behavior that valued financial autonomy. Over several decades before 1860, the proportion of women who never married, or did not remarry after the death of a spouse, grew to exceed 33 percent. Likewise, the number of women who worked for wages, controlled their own property, and ran millinery or dressmaking businesses increased. In managing property, these and other women benefited from legal changes; to protect families from the husband's indebtedness during business panics and recessions, reforms gave married women some property rights.

Slave Life and Labor

For African Americans, slavery was a burden that destroyed some people and forced others to develop modes of survival. Slaves knew a life of poverty, coercion, toil, and resentment. They provided the physical strength, and much of the know-how, to build an agricultural empire. But their daily lives embodied the nation's most basic contradiction in the world's model republic: they were on the wrong side of a brutally unequal power relationship.

SLAVES' EVERYDAY CONDITIONS
Southern slaves enjoyed few material comforts beyond the bare necessities. Although they generally had enough to eat, their diet was plain and monotonous and lacking in nutrition. Clothing was plain, coarse, and inexpensive. Few slaves received more than one or two changes of clothing for hot and cold seasons and one blanket each winter. Children of both sexes ran naked in hot weather and wore long cotton shirts in winter. Many slaves had to go without shoes until December. Their bare feet were often symbolic of their status—one reason why, after freedom, many black parents were so anxious to provide their children with shoes.

Some of the richer plantations provided substantial houses, but the average slave lived in crude ac-

■ Thomas S. Noble's painting *The Last Sale of Slaves* depicts the public drama and family horror of slave auctions. Noble's work stimulated a heated newspaper debate in St. Louis over its abolitionist message. The sight of people treated as property and bills of sale signed on the table leave slavery's most haunting images.   (Missouri Historical Society, St. Louis)

commodations, usually one-room cabins. The gravest drawback of slave cabins was their unhealthfulness. Each dwelling housed one or two families. Crowding and lack of sanitation fostered the spread of infection and contagious diseases such as typhoid fever, malaria, and dysentery.

Hard work was the central fact of slaves' existence. The long hours and large work gangs that

SLAVES' WORK ROUTINES

characterized Gulf Coast cotton districts operated almost like factories in the field. Overseers rang the morning bell before dawn. And as one woman recalled when interviewed in the 1930s, "it was way after sundown fore they could stop that field work. Then they had to hustle to finish their night work [such as watering livestock or cleaning cotton] in time for supper, or go to bed without it."

Working "from sun to sun" became a norm in much of the South. As one planter put it, slaves were the best labor because "you could command them and make them do what was right." Profit took precedence over paternalism. Slave women did heavy fieldwork, often as much as the men and even during pregnancy. Old people were kept busy caring for young children, doing light chores, or carding, ginning, and spinning cotton.

Slave children were the future of the system and were widely valued. In 1858 an unidentified slave-owner calculated that a slave girl he purchased in 1827 for $400 had three sons now worth $3,000 as his working field hands. Slave children gathered kindling, carried water to the fields, lifted cut sugar-cane stalks into carts, chased birds away from sprouting rice plants, and labored at many levels of cotton and tobacco production.

Incentives too were part of the labor regime and the master-slave relationship. Planters in the South Carolina and Georgia low country used a task system whereby slaves were assigned measured amounts of work to be performed in a given amount of time. So much cotton on a daily basis was to be picked or so many rows hoed or plowed in a particular slave's specified section. When their task and "clock time" was up, slaves' time was their own, for working in garden plots, tending to hogs, or even hiring out their own extra labor. The system's incentives afforded many slave families life-sustaining material benefits and personal space. From this experience, slaves often developed their own sense of property ownership.

Incentives notwithstanding, the slaveowner enjoyed a monopoly on force and violence. Whites

VIOLENCE AGAINST SLAVES

throughout the South believed that slaves "can't be governed except with the whip." Evidence suggests that whippings were less frequent on small farms than on large plantations. But beatings symbolized authority to the master and tyranny to the slaves, who made them a benchmark for evaluating a master. In the words of former slaves, a good owner was one who did not "whip too much"; a bad owner "whipped till he's bloodied you and blistered you."

The master wielded virtually absolute authority on his plantation, and terrible abuses could and did occur. Courts did not recognize the word of chattel. Pregnant women were whipped, and there were burnings, mutilations, tortures, and murders. Yet physical cruelty may have been less prevalent in the United States than in other slaveholding parts of the New World. Especially in some of the sugar islands of the Caribbean, treatment was so poor and death rates so high that the heavily male slave population shrank. In the United States, by contrast, the slave population experienced a steady natural increase as births exceeded deaths.

The worst evil of American slavery was not its physical cruelty but the nature of slavery itself: coercion, belonging to another person, virtually no hope for mobility or change. A woman named Delia Garlic made the essential point: "It's bad to belong to folks that own you soul an' body. I could tell you 'bout it all day, but even then you couldn't guess the awfulness of it."

The great majority of American slaves retained their mental independence and self-respect despite their bondage. Contrary to popular belief at the time, they were not loyal partners in their own oppression. They had to be subservient and speak honeyed words to their masters, but they talked and behaved quite differently among themselves. The evidence of their resistant attitudes comes from their actions and their own life stories. In his autobiography (1845), Frederick Douglass wrote that most slaves, when asked about "their condition and the character of their masters, almost universally say they are contented, and that their masters are kind." Slaves did this, said Douglass, because they were governed by the maxim that "a still tongue makes a wise head," especially in the presence of unfamiliar people.

Some former slaves remembered warm feelings between masters and slaves, but the prevailing attitudes were distrust and antagonism.

SLAVE-MASTER RELATIONSHIPS Slaves saw through acts of kindness. One woman said her mistress was "a mighty good somebody to belong to" but only "'cause she was raisin' us to work for her." Another observed that his master "fed us reg'lar on good, 'stantial food, just like you'd tend to your horse, if you had a real good one."

Slaves were alert to the thousand daily signs of their degraded status. One man recalled the general rule that slaves ate cornbread and owners ate biscuits. A former slave recalled, "Us catch lots of 'possums," but "the white folks at 'em." If the owner took his slaves' garden produce to town and sold it for them, the slaves often suspected him of pocketing part of the profits.

Suspicion often grew into hatred. When a yellow fever epidemic struck in 1852, many slaves saw it as God's retribution. An elderly ex-slave named Minnie Fulkes cherished the conviction that God was going to punish white people for their cruelty to blacks. She described the whippings that her mother had to endure, and then she exclaimed, "Lord, Lord, I hate white people and the flood waters goin' to drown some more."

Slave Culture

a people is always "more than the sum of its brutalization," wrote the African American novelist Ralph Ellison in 1967. The resource that enabled slaves to maintain hope and defiance was their culture: a body of beliefs, values, and practices born of their past and maintained in the present. As best they could, they built a community knitted together by stories, music, a religious worldview, leadership, the smells of their cooking, the sounds of their voices, and the tapping of their feet. Thus slaves endured and found loyalty and strength among themselves.

Slave culture changed significantly after 1800, as fewer and fewer slaves were African-born. By

AFRICAN CULTURAL SURVIVAL the 1830s, the vast majority of slaves in the South were native-born Americans.

Despite lack of firsthand memory, African influences remained strong, especially in appearance and forms of expression. Some slave men plaited their hair into rows and fancy designs; slave women often wore their hair "in string"—tied in small bunches with a string or piece of cloth. A few men and many women wrapped their heads in kerchiefs of West African styles and colors.

Music, religion, and folktales were parts of daily life for most slaves. Borrowing partly from their African background, as well as forging new American folkways, they developed what scholars have called a "sacred world-view" that affected all aspects of work, leisure, and self-understanding. Slaves made musical instruments with carved motifs that resembled African stringed instruments. Their drumming and dancing followed African patterns that made whites marvel. One visitor to Georgia in the 1860s described a ritual dance of African origin: "A ring of singers is formed. . . . They then utter a kind of melodious chant, which gradually increases in strength, and in noise, until it fairly shakes the house."

Many slaves continued to believe in spirit possession. Their belief resembled the African concept of the living dead—the idea that deceased relatives visit the earth for many years until the process of dying is complete. Slaves also practiced conjuration and quasi-magical root medicine. By the 1850s, the most notable conjurers and root doctors were reputed to live in South Carolina, Georgia, Louisiana, and other isolated coastal areas with high slave populations.

These cultural survivals provided slaves with a sense of their separate past and special ways. Such practices and beliefs were not static "Africanisms" or mere "retentions." They were cultural adaptations, living traditions re-formed in the Americas in response to new experience. African American slaves in the Old South were a people forged by two centuries of cultural mixture in the Atlantic world, and the South itself melded many African and European cultural forces.

As they became African Americans, slaves also developed a sense of racial identity. In the colonial period, Africans had arrived in America from many different states and kingdoms, represented by distinctive languages, body markings, and traditions. Planters had used ethnic differences to create occupational hierarchies. By the early antebellum period, however, old ethnic identities were giving way as American slaves increasingly saw themselves as a single group unified by race. Africans had arrived in the

New World with virtually no concept of "race"; by the antebellum era, their descendants had learned that race was now the defining feature of their lives.

With the maturing of African American culture, more and more slaves adopted Christianity. But they fashioned Christianity into an instrument of support and resistance. Theirs was a religion of justice and deliverance, quite unlike the religious propaganda their masters directed at them. "You ought to have heard that preachin'," said one man. "'Obey your master and mistress, don't steal chickens and eggs and meat,' but nary a word about havin' a soul to save." Slaves believed that Jesus cared about their souls and their plight. For them, Christianity was a religion of personal and group salvation. Many slaves nurtured an unshakable belief that God would enter history and end their bondage. This faith—and the joy and emotional release that accompanied worship—sustained them.

SLAVES' RELIGION AND MUSIC

Slaves also adapted Christianity to African practices. In West African belief, devotees are possessed by a god so thoroughly that the god's own personality replaces the human personality. In the late antebellum era, Christian slaves experienced possession by the Protestant "Holy Spirit." The combination of shouting, singing, and dancing that seemed to overtake black worshipers formed the heart of their religious faith. "The old meeting house caught fire," recalled an ex-slave preacher. "The spirit was there. . . . God saw our need and came to us." And out in brush arbors or in meetinghouses, slaves took in the presence of God and sang away their woes.

Rhythm and physical movement were crucial to slaves' religious experience. In their own preachers' chanted sermons, which reached out to gather the sinner into a narrative of meanings and cadences along the way to conversion, an American tradition was born. The chanted sermon was both a message from Scripture and a patterned form that required audience response punctuated by "yes sirs!" and "amens!" But it was in song that the slaves left their most sublime gift to American culture.

Tension and sudden change between sorrow and joy animates many of the slave songs: "Sometimes I feel like a motherless chile . . . / Sometimes I feel like an eagle in the air, / Spread my wings and fly, fly, fly!" Many songs also express a sense of intimacy and closeness with God. Some songs display an unmistak-

able rebelliousness, such as the enduring, "He said, and if I had my way / If I had my way, if I had my way, / I'd tear this building down!" And some spirituals reached for a collective sense of hope in the black community as a whole:

> O, gracious Lord! When shall it be,
> That we poor souls shall all be free;
> Lord, break them slavery powers—
> Will you go along with me?
> Lord break them slavery powers,
> Go sound the jubilee!

In many ways, American slaves converted the Christian God to themselves. They sought an alternative world in which they could live. In a thousand variations on the Br'er Rabbit folktales in which the weak survive by wit and power is reversed, and in the countless refrains of their songs, they fashioned survival and resistance out of their cultural imagination.

American slaves clung tenaciously to the personal relationships that gave meaning to life. Although American law did not recognize slave families, masters permitted them; in fact, slaveowners expected slaves to form families and have children. As a result, even along the rapidly expanding edge of the cotton kingdom, there was a normal ratio of men to women, young to old.

THE BLACK FAMILY IN SLAVERY

Following African kinship traditions, African Americans avoided marriage between cousins. By naming their children after relatives of past generations, African Americans emphasized their family histories. If they chose to bear the surname of a slaveowner, it was often the name of the owner under whom their family had begun their bondage in America.

For slave women, sexual abuse and rape by white masters were ever-present threats. By 1860 there were 405,751 mulattos in the United States, 12.5 percent of the African American population, and the majority were the offspring of involuntary relationships. Buying slaves for sex was all too common at the New Orleans slave market. In what was called the "fancy trade" (a "fancy" was a young attractive slave girl or woman), females were often sold for prices as much as 300 percent higher than the average. At such auctions for young women, slaveholders exhibited some of the ugliest values at the heart of the slave system.

Slave women had to negotiate this confused world of desire, threat, and shame. Harriet Jacobs spent much of her youth and early adult years dodging her owner's relentless sexual pursuit. In recollecting her desperate effort to protect her children, Jacobs asked a haunting question that many slave women carried with them to their graves: "Why does the slave ever love? Why allow the tendrils of the heart to twine around objects which may at any moment be wrenched away by the hand of violence?"

Separation from those they loved by violence, sexual appropriation, and sale was what slave fami-

THE DOMESTIC SLAVE TRADE

lies feared and hated most. Many struggled for years to keep their children together and, after emancipation, to reestablish contact with loved ones lost by forced migration and sale. Between 1820 and 1860, an estimated 2 million slaves were moved into the region extending from western Georgia to eastern Texas. When the Union Army registered thousands of black marriages in Mississippi and Louisiana in 1864 and 1865, fully 25 percent of the men over age forty reported that they had been forcibly separated from a previous wife.

Many antebellum white southerners made their living from the slave trade. In South Carolina alone, by the 1850s there were over one hundred slave-trading firms selling an annual average of approximately 6,500 slaves to southwestern states. Although southerners often denied it, vast numbers of slaves moved west by outright sale, not by migrating with their owners.

Slave traders were practical, roving businessmen. They were sometimes considered degraded by white planters, but many slaveowners did business with them. Traders did their utmost to make their slaves appear young, healthy, and happy, cutting gray whiskers off men and forcing people to dance and sing as buyers arrived for an auction. When transported to the southwestern markets, slaves were often chained together in "coffles," which made journeys of 500 miles or more on foot.

The complacent mixture of racism and business among traders is evident in their own language. "I refused a girl 20 year[s] old at 700 yesterday," one trader wrote to another in 1853. "If you think best to take her at 700 I can still get her. She is very badly whipped but good teeth." Some sales were transacted at owners' requests. "Bought a cook yesterday that was to go out of state," wrote a trader; "she just made the people mad that was all."

Slave Resistance and Rebellion

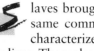laves brought to their efforts at resistance the same common sense and determination that characterized their struggle to secure their family lives. The scales were weighted heavily against overt revolution, and the slaves knew it. But they seized opportunities to alter their work and life conditions.

Sometimes slaves slacked off work when they were not being watched. Sometimes they manifested

STRATEGIES OF RESISTANCE

their discontent by sabotaging equipment, stealing food, or being wantonly careless about work. Many male, and some female, slaves acted out their defiance by violently attacking overseers or even their owners. Southern court records and newspapers are full of accounts of these resistant slaves who gave the lie to the image of docile bondsmen. The price they paid was high. Such lonely rebels were customarily secured and flogged, sold away, or hanged.

Many individual slaves attempted to run away to the North, and some received assistance from the loose network known as the Underground Railroad (discussed in the next chapter). But it was more common for slaves to run off temporarily and hide in the woods. Approximately 80 percent of runaways were male; women could not flee as readily because of their responsibility for children. Fear, disgruntlement over treatment, or family separation might motivate slaves to risk all in flight. Only a minority of those who tried such escapes ever made it to freedom in the North or Canada.

American slavery produced some fearless revolutionaries. Gabriel's Rebellion involved as many as a thousand slaves when it was discovered in 1800 (see Chapter 8). According to controversial court testimony, a similar conspiracy existed in Charleston in 1822, led by a free black named Denmark Vesey. According to one long-argued interpretation, Vesey was a heroic revolutionary determined to free his people or die trying. But in a recent challenge, historian Michael Johnson points out that the court testimony is the only reliable source on the alleged insurrection. The court, says Johnson, built its case on rumors and intimidated witnesses, and "conjured into being" an insurrection not about to occur in reality. Whatever the facts, when the arrests and trials were over, thirty-seven "conspirators" were executed, and more than three dozen others were banished from the state.

Online Study Center **Improve Your Grade**
Interactive Map: Escaping from Slavery

The most famous rebel of all, Nat Turner, struck for freedom in Southampton County, Virginia, in

NAT TURNER'S
INSURRECTION

1831. The son of an African woman who passionately hated her enslavement, Nat Turner was a precocious child who learned to read when he was very young. Encouraged by his first owner to study the Bible, he enjoyed certain privileges but also endured hard work and changes of masters. His father successfully escaped to freedom.

Eventually young Nat became a preacher with a reputation for eloquence and mysticism. After nurturing his plan for several years, Turner led a band of rebels from farm to farm in the predawn darkness of August 22, 1831. The group severed limbs and crushed skulls with axes or killed their victims with guns. Before they were stopped, Turner and his followers had slaughtered sixty whites of both sexes and all ages in forty-eight hours. The rebellion was put down, Turner hanged, and an estimated two hundred African Americans, including innocent victims, killed by vengeful whites. In the wake of the insurrection, many states stiffened legal codes against black education and religious practices.

Harmony and Tension in a Slave Society

From 1830 to 1860, slavery impinged on laws and customs, individual values, and, increasingly, every aspect of southern politics. In all things, from their workaday movements to Sunday worship, slaves fell under the supervision of whites. State courts held that a slave "has no civil right" and could not hold property "except at the will and pleasure of his master." Revolts like Nat Turner's tightened the legal straitjacket even more. As political conflicts between North and South deepened, fears of slave re-

volt grew, and restrictions on slaves increased accordingly.

State and federal laws aided the capture of fugitive slaves and required nonslaveholders to support the slave system. All white male citizens had a legal duty to participate in slave patrols. Ship captains, harbor masters, and other whites were required to scrutinize the papers of African Americans who might be attempting to escape bondage.

Slavery deeply affected southern values precisely because it was the main determinant of wealth. Own-

SLAVERY,
WEALTH, AND
SOCIAL
STANDING

ership of slaves guaranteed the labor to produce cotton and other crops on a large scale. Slaves were a commodity and an investment, much like gold; people bought them on speculation, hoping for a steady rise in their market values. Wealth in slaves also translated into political power: a solid majority of political officeholders were slaveholders, and the most powerful were usually large-scale planters.

Slavery's influence spread throughout the social system until even the values and mores of nonslaveholders bore its imprint. The availability of slave labor tended to devalue free labor: where strenuous work under supervision was reserved for an enslaved race, few free people relished it. When Alexis de Tocqueville crossed from Ohio into Kentucky in his travels in 1831, he observed that on "the right bank of the Ohio [River] everything is activity, industry; labor is honoured; there are no slaves. Pass to the left bank and . . . the enterprising spirit is gone. There, work is not only painful; it is shameful." Tocqueville's own class impulses, however, were at home in the South, where he found a "veritable aristocracy."

The values of the aristocrat—lineage, privilege, pride, and refinement of person and manner—com-

ARISTOCRATIC
VALUES AND
FRONTIER
INDIVIDUALISM

manded respect throughout the South. Many of those qualities were in short supply, however, in the recently settled portions of the cotton kingdom, where the frontier values of courage and self-reliance ruled. Independence and defense of one's honor became highly valued traits for planter and frontier farmer alike. Thus, instead of gradually disappearing, as it did in the North, dueling, which required men to defend their honor through violence, lasted much longer in the South.

Other aristocratic values of the planter class were less acceptable to less wealthy whites. In their pride, planters expected not only to wield power but to receive deference from poorer whites. But the sternly independent yeoman class resented infringements of their rights. Also conscious of national democratic ideals, yeomen sometimes challenged or rejected the political pretensions of planters, whose claims to a republican ideal of white men leading other white men was built on a foundation of black slave labor.

Class tensions emerged in the western, nonslaveholding parts of the seaboard states by the 1830s.

YEOMAN DEMANDS AND WHITE CLASS RELATIONS

There, yeoman farmers resented their underrepresentation in state legislatures and the corruption in local government. After vigorous debate, the reformers won many battles. Voters in more recently settled states of the Old Southwest adopted white manhood suffrage and other electoral reforms, including popular election of governors, legislative apportionment based on white population only, and locally chosen county government.

Slaveowners knew that a more open government structure could permit troubling issues to arise. In Virginia, it was nonslaveholding westerners who petitioned and initiated the 1831–1832 debate over the gradual abolition of slavery in the wake of Nat Turner's Rebellion.

Given such tensions, why were class confrontations among whites so infrequent? One of the most important factors was race. The South's racial ideology stressed the superiority of all whites to blacks. Thus, slavery became the basis of equality among whites, and racism inflated the status of poor whites and gave them a common interest with the rich. Family ties also linked some nonslaveholders to wealthy planters, especially on the expanding frontier. And the Old South was a fluid society in which constant mobility and the westward-expanding cotton kingdom gave yeomen the hope of rising in status by acquiring land and slaves.

Most important, in their daily lives, yeomen and slaveholders were seldom in conflict. Before the Civil War, most yeomen were able to pursue their independent lifestyle unhindered. They worked their farms, avoided debt, and marked progress for their families that in their rural habitats was unrelated to slaveholding. Likewise, slaveholders pursued their goals quite independent of yeomen.

Suppression of dissent also played an increasing role. After 1830, white southerners who criticized the slave system out of moral conviction or class resentment were intimidated, attacked, or legally prosecuted. By the 1850s, the defense of slavery's interests exerted an ever more powerful influence on southern politics and society.

Still, there were signs that the relative lack of conflict between slaveholders and nonslaveholders

HARDENING OF CLASS LINES

was coming to an end in the late antebellum period. As cotton lands filled up, nonslaveholders saw their opportunities beginning to narrow; meanwhile, wealthy planters enjoyed expanding profits. The risks of entering cotton production were becoming too great and the cost of slaves too high for many yeomen to rise in society. From 1830 to 1860, the percentage of white southern families holding slaves declined steadily from 36 to 25 percent. Yet with slaveowners a smaller portion of the population, planters continued to own 90 to 95 percent of the South's agricultural wealth.

Urban artisans and mechanics felt the pinch acutely. Their numbers were few, and in bad times, they were often the first to lose work as markets collapsed. Moreover, they faced stiff competition from urban slaves, whose masters wanted to hire them out to practice trades. White workers protested, demanding that economic competition from slaves be forbidden, but they were ignored. However, their angry protests resulted in harsh restrictions on free African American laborers and craftsmen. Pre–Civil War politics reflected these tensions as well. Anticipating possible secession and the prospect of a war to defend slavery, slaveowners expressed growing fear about the loyalty of nonslaveholders. Schemes to widen the ownership of slaves were discussed, including reopening the African slave trade. In North Carolina, a bitter controversy erupted over the combination of high taxes on land and low taxes on slaves. When nonslaveholder Hinton R. Helper denounced the slave system in *The Impending Crisis*, published in 1857, discerning planters feared the eruption of such controversies in every southern state.

But for the moment slaveowners stood secure. In the 1850s, they occupied from 50 to 85 percent of the seats in state legislatures and a similarly high percentage of the South's congressional seats. Planters' interests controlled all the other major social institutions. Professors who criticized slavery had been dismissed; schoolbooks that contained "unsound" ideas had been replaced. And almost all the Methodist and Baptist clergy had become slavery's most vocal defenders.

Summary *Online Study Center* **ACE the Test**

During the thirty years before the Civil War, the South grew as part of America's westward expansion. Ideologically and economically, the southern states developed in many distinctive ways; at the same time, they were also deeply enmeshed in the nation's heritage and political economy. Far more than the North, the antebellum South was a biracial society; whites grew up directly influenced by black folkways and culture, and blacks, the vast majority of whom were slaves, became predominantly native-born Americans and the cobuilders with whites of a rural, agricultural society. From the Old South on to modern times, white and black southerners have always shared a tragic, mutual history.

With the sustained cotton boom, the South grew fatefully into a much larger slave society than it had been early in the century. The coercive influence of slavery affected virtually every element of southern life and politics. Despite the white supremacy that united them, the democratic values of yeomen often clashed with the profit motives of aristocratic planters. The benevolent self-image and paternalistic ideology of slaveholders ultimately had to stand the test of the slaves' own judgments. African American slaves responded by fashioning over time a rich, expressive folk culture and a religion of personal and group deliverance.

By 1850, through their own wits and on the backs of African labor, white southerners had aggressively built one of the last profitable, expanding slave societies on earth. North of them, deeply intertwined with them in the same nation, market economy, constitutional system, and history, a different kind of society had grown even faster—one driven by industrialism and free labor. The clash of these two deeply connected yet divided societies was about to explode in political storms over how the nation would define its future.

LEGACY FOR A PEOPLE AND A NATION
Reparations for Slavery

How should the United States come to terms with 250 years of racial slavery? Does the nation owe a long-overdue debt to black people for their oppression?

In the wake of emancipation in 1865 and rooted in vague federal promises, many former slaves believed they were entitled to "forty acres and a mule," but these never materialized. As the leader of a planters' association put it in 1865, "The emancipated slaves own nothing, because nothing but freedom has been given to them."

Recently a widespread debate over "reparations" for slavery has emerged. Since the 1960s, Americans have learned a great deal about how slave labor created American wealth: how insurance companies insured slaves, how complicitous the U.S. government was in slavery's defense and expansion, and how slaves built the U.S. Capitol while their owners received $5 a month for their labor.

The debate is fueled by a wealth of analogies: the reparations paid to Japanese Americans interned in World War II, the reparations paid to several Native American tribes for their stolen land, and a suit settled in 1999 that will pay an estimated $2 billion to some twenty thousand black farmers for discrimination practiced by the Agriculture Department in the early twentieth century.

On the other side, some argue that because there are no living former slaves or slaveholders, reparations for slavery can never take the form of money. But in 2002, a lawsuit was filed against three major corporations that allegedly profited from slavery, and the National Reparations Coordinating Committee promises a suit against the

U.S. government itself. Critics argue that resources would be better spent "making sure black kids have a credible education" and in rebuilding inner cities. The movement for reparations has strong support in grassroots black communities, and the issue has become the subject of a broad public debate. The legacy of slavery for a people and a nation promises to become America's most traumatic test of how to reconcile its history with justice.

SLAVERY AND AMERICA'S FUTURE: THE ROAD TO WAR 1845–1861

*T*he delegates who filed into the Musical Fund Hall in Philadelphia on June 17, 1856, knew they had created something special in American politics. The first national nominating convention of the Republican Party met to approve a platform and select their presidential ticket. Formed just two years earlier, in 1854, the party drew together a broad coalition of northern politicians who opposed the expansion of slavery and the growing power of the South in the federal government. Republicans had come to Philadelphia to offer the American electorate a genuinely antislavery future.

Their coalition combined former Democrats; former founding members of the American Party, a group that wanted to prohibit foreigners, especially Catholics, from settling in the United States; and many former Whigs, whose party had been shattered by the crisis over slavery and its expansion. They consisted of conservatives, moderates, and radicals; some believed slavery a moral evil, while others saw it as a political problem.

At this convention, a radical temper prevailed. The convention was only minutes old when the temporary chairman used the Declaration of Independence to label slavery a great political danger to the nation's future. Speaker after speaker declared that their party would render "freedom national" and "slavery sectional" by using the power of Congress to outlaw human bondage in all western territories.

The convention's platform committee was chaired by David Wilmot, a former Democrat who was no friend of black civil and political rights. But Wilmot, like the others, was firmly opposed to slavery's expansion and endorsed the protection of free white men's labor and landownership across the continent. At the heart of the platform was the short, direct credo calling on Congress to "prohibit in the territories those twin relics of barbarism—polygamy and slavery." The Republicans nominated John C. Frémont, the

Online Study Center
This icon will direct you to interactive map and primary source activities on the website http://college.hmco.com/pic/nortonbrief7e

CHRONOLOGY

1846 • War with Mexico begins
   • Oregon Treaty negotiated
   • Wilmot Proviso inflames sectional divisions

1847 • Cass proposes idea of popular sovereignty

1848 • Treaty of Guadalupe Hidalgo gives United States new territory in the Southwest
   • Free-Soil Party formed
   • Taylor elected president

1849 • Gold discovered in California, which applies for admission to Union as free state

1850 • Compromise of 1850 passed in separate bills

1852 • Stowe publishes *Uncle Tom's Cabin*
   • Pierce elected president

1854 • Kansas-Nebraska Act wins approval and ignites controversy
   • Republican Party formed
   • Return of fugitive Burns from Boston to slavery in Virginia

1856 • Bleeding Kansas troubles nation
   • Brooks attacks Sumner in Senate chamber

   • Buchanan elected president, but Republican Frémont wins most northern states

1857 • *Dred Scott v. Sandford* endorses southern views on black citizenship and slavery in territories
   • Economic panic and widespread unemployment begins

1858 • Kansas voters reject Lecompton Constitution

1859 • Brown raids Harpers Ferry

1860 • Democratic Party splits in two; southern Democrats demand "Slave Code for the Territories"
   • Lincoln elected president
   • Crittenden Compromise fails
   • South Carolina secedes from Union

1861 • Six more Deep South states secede
   • Confederacy established at Montgomery, Alabama
   • Attack on Fort Sumter begins Civil War
   • Four states in the Upper South join the Confederacy

famous western explorer and former California senator, for president. In the election that followed, Americans began to vote by section and not by party as never before. The Republican coalition began to unify the North around keeping the West free and alarmed the South, which now saw the future of its slave society endangered by a political movement determined to limit, if not destroy, slavery. Frémont lost the 1856 election, but the Republicans made the best showing a newly born party ever had in its first presidential bid.

Meanwhile, in Kansas territory, open warfare had exploded between proslavery and antislavery settlers. On the floor of the U.S. Senate, a southern representative beat a northern senator senseless. A new fugitive slave law sent thousands of blacks, fearing for their liberty and their lives, fleeing to Canada. The tradition of compromise on political problems related to slavery teetered on the brink of complete collapse. Within a year the Supreme Court had issued a dramatic decision about slavery, its constitutionality in westward expansion, and the status of African American citizenship—to the delight of most southerners and the dread of most northerners. And abolitionist John Brown was planning a raid into Virginia to start a slave rebellion.

The political culture of the American republic was disintegrating. As the 1850s advanced, slavery pulled Americans, North and South, into a maelstrom that its best statesmen ultimately could not subdue. A prosperous nation, riven by stark contradictions, was on the road to a terrible war.

Slavery had aroused passions that could be neither contained nor resolved. What began as a dark cloud over the territories became a storm engulfing the nation. Between 1845 and 1853, the United States added Texas, California, Oregon Country, and the Southwest to its domain and launched the settlement of the Great Plains. Each time the nation expanded, it confronted a thorny issue: should new territories and states be slave or free?

The ensuing political storms gave rise to a feeling in both North and South that America's future was at stake. The new Republican Party believed that America's future depended on the unbound labor of free men. They charged southerners with using the power of the federal government to make slavery legal throughout the Union. Southern leaders defended slavery and charged the North with unconstitutional efforts to destroy it. For blacks, the growing dispute brought hope and despair. They could take heart that the country's political strife over slavery might somehow lead to their liberation. But in a nation now trying to define its future, blacks had to wonder whether they had a future at all in America. ■

The War with Mexico and Its Consequences

In the 1840s, territorial expansion surged forward under the leadership of President James K. Polk. The annexation of Texas just before his inauguration did not necessarily make war with Mexico inevitable, but by design and through a series of calculated decisions, Polk brought the conflict on. Polk was determined to fulfill the nation's "manifest destiny" to rule the continent. He wanted Mexico's territory all the way to the Pacific, and all of Oregon Country as well.

During the 1844 campaign, Polk's supporters had threatened war with Great Britain to gain all of Oregon. As president, however, Polk turned first to diplomacy. Not

OREGON

wanting to fight Mexico and Great Britain at the same time, he tried to avoid bloodshed in the Northwest, where America and Britain had jointly occupied disputed territory since 1818. Dropping the demand for a boundary at latitude 54°40', he pressured the British to accept the 49th parallel. In 1846 Great Britain agreed. The Oregon Treaty gave the United States all of present-day Oregon, Washington, and Idaho and parts of Wyoming and Montana.

Toward Mexico, Polk was more aggressive. In early 1846, he ordered American troops to march south and defend the contested border of the Rio Grande. Polk had earlier encouraged Texas to claim the Rio Grande as its southern and western border. He especially desired California as the prize in his expansionist strategy, and he attempted to buy from Mexico a huge tract of land extending to the Pacific. When that effort failed, Polk waited for war. Negotiations between troops on the Rio Grande proved fruitless. The situation became increasingly tense, and on April 24, 1846, Mexican cavalry ambushed a U.S. cavalry unit on the north side of the river; eleven Americans were killed and sixty-three taken captive.

"MR. POLK'S WAR"

Polk now drafted a message to Congress: Mexico had "passed the boundary of the United States, had invaded our territory and shed American blood on American soil." Polk deceptively declared that "war exists by the act of Mexico itself" and summoned the nation to arms. Two days later, on May 13, the House recognized a state of war with Mexico by a vote of 174 to 14, and the Senate by 40 to 2, with numerous abstentions. Some antislavery Whigs in Congress had tried to oppose the war but were barely allowed to speak. Since Polk withheld key facts, what had happened on the distant Rio Grande was not fully known. But the theory and practice of manifest destiny had launched the United States into its first major war on foreign territory.

The idea of war unleashed great public celebrations. Huge crowds gathered in southern cities to voice support for the war effort. Twenty thousand Philadelphians and even more New Yorkers rallied in the same spirit. After news came of General Zachary Taylor's first two battlefield victories at Palo Alto

FOREIGN WAR AND THE POPULAR IMAGINATION

and Resaca de la Palma, volunteers swarmed recruiting stations. The advent of daily newspapers, printed on new rotary presses, boosted sales by giving the war a romantic appeal.

Here was an adventurous war of conquest in a far-off, exotic land. Here was the fulfillment of Anglo-Saxon–Christian destiny to possess the North American continent and to take "civilization" to the "semi-Indian" Mexicans. For many, racism fueled the expansionist spirit. In 1846 an Illinois newspaper justified the war on the basis that Mexicans were "reptiles in the path of progressive democracy."

The war spawned an outpouring of poetry, song, drama, and lithographs that captured the popular imagination and glorified the conflict. Most of the war-inspired flowering in the popular arts was patriotic. But not everyone cheered. The abolitionist James Russell Lowell considered the war a "national crime committed in behoof of slavery, our common sin." Even proslavery spokesman John C. Calhoun saw the

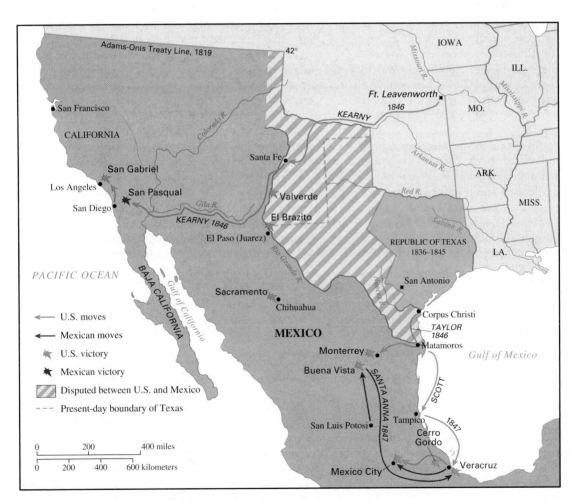

Map 14.1 The War with Mexico

This map shows the territory disputed between the United States and Mexico. After U.S. gains in northeastern Mexico and in New Mexico and California, General Winfield Scott captured Mexico City in the decisive campaign of the war.

perils of expansionism. Mexico, he said, was "the forbidden fruit; the penalty of eating it would be to subject our institutions to political death."

U.S. forces made significant gains early in the war. In May 1846 Colonel Stephen Kearny and a

CONQUEST

small detachment invaded the remote and thinly populated provinces of New Mexico and California.

Taking Santa Fe without opposition, Kearny pushed into California, where he joined forces with rebellious American settlers led by Captain John C. Frémont and with a couple of U.S. naval units. General Zachary Taylor's forces attacked and occupied Monterrey, which surrendered in September, securing northeastern Mexico (see Map 14.1). American soldiers established dominion over distant California before the end of 1846. General Winfield Scott now carried the war to the enemy's heartland. Landing at Veracruz, he led fourteen thousand men toward Mexico City. After a series of hard-fought battles, U.S. troops captured the Mexican capital.

Representatives of both countries signed the Treaty of Guadalupe Hidalgo in February 1848. The

TREATY OF GUADALUPE HIDALGO

United States gained California and New Mexico (including present-day Nevada, Utah, and Arizona and parts of Colorado and Wyoming) and recognition of the Rio Grande as the southern boundary of Texas.

In return, the American government agreed to settle the claims of its citizens against Mexico ($3.2 million) and pay Mexico a mere $15 million. On the day Polk received the treaty from the Senate, a mob in Paris forced Louis Philippe to abdicate the throne of France. As the 1848 nationalistic revolutions against monarchy spread to Italy, Austria, Hungary, and Germany, republican America seized an empire.

The costs of the war included the deaths of thirteen thousand Americans and fifty thousand Mexicans and U.S.-Mexican enmity that endured into the twentieth century. The war also sharply divided public opinion in the United States. Southwesterners were enthusiastic, as were most southern planters; New Englanders strenuously opposed the war. Whigs in Congress charged that Polk, a Democrat, had "provoked" an unnecessary war and "usurped the power of Congress." An Illinois Whig named Abraham Lincoln called Polk's justifications the "half insane mumbling of a fever-dream."

These charges fed northern fear of the so-called Slave Power. Abolitionists had long warned of a slave-

"SLAVE POWER CONSPIRACY"

holding oligarchy that controlled the South and intended to dominate the nation through its hold on federal power. These dangerous aristocrats had forced the gag rule on

Congress in 1836 and threatened northern liberties. To many white northerners, even those who saw nothing wrong with slavery, it was the battle over free speech that first made the idea of a Slave Power credible. The War with Mexico deepened such fears. Had this questionable war, asked antislavery northerners, not been launched for vast, new slave territory?

Northern opinion on the expansion of slavery began to shift, but the impact of the war on southern opinion was even more dramatic. At first some southern leaders criticized the War with Mexico, and few southern congressmen saw slavery as the paramount issue. Many whites in both North and South feared that large land seizures would bring thousands of nonwhite Mexicans into the United States and upset the racial order. An Indiana politician did not want "any mixed races in our Union, nor men of any color except white, unless they be slaves." Despite their racism, however, many statesmen soon saw other prospects in the outcomes of the war.

In August 1846, David Wilmot, a Pennsylvania Democrat, proposed an amendment, or proviso, to

WILMOT PROVISO

a military appropriations bill: that "neither slavery nor involuntary servitude shall ever exist" in any territory gained from Mexico. Al-

though the proviso never passed both houses of Congress, it transformed the debate. Southerners suddenly circled their wagons to protect the future of a slave society. John C. Calhoun asserted a radical new southern position. The territories, Calhoun insisted, belonged to all the states, and the federal government could do nothing to limit the spread of slavery there. Southern slaveholders had a constitutional right rooted in the Fifth Amendment, Calhoun claimed, to take their slaves (as property) anywhere in the territories.

This position, often called "state sovereignty," was a radical reversal of history. In 1787 the Confederation Congress had excluded slavery from the Northwest Territory; Article IV of the federal Constitution had authorized Congress to make "all needful rules and regulations" for the territories, and the Missouri Compromise had barred slavery from most of the Louisiana Purchase. Now, however, southern leaders demanded protection and future guarantees for slavery.

In the North, the Wilmot Proviso became a rallying cry for abolitionists. Eventually the legislatures of fourteen northern states endorsed it—and not because all its supporters were abolitionists. David Wilmot, significantly, was neither an abolitionist nor an antislavery Whig. His goal was to defend "the rights of white freemen" and to obtain California "for free white labor."

Fear of the Slave Power, however, was building a potent antislavery movement that united abolitionists and antiblack voters. At stake was an abiding version of the American Dream: the free individual's access to social mobility through opportunities in the West and the sacred ideal of free labor. Slave labor, thousands of northerners had come to believe, would degrade the honest toil of free men and render them unemployed and propertyless. The West must therefore be kept free of slaves and open to free white men.

The slavery question could not be kept out of national politics. After Polk renounced a second term as president, the Democrats nominated Senator Lewis Cass of Michigan for president. Cass, a party loyalist, had devised in 1847 the idea of "popular sovereignty" for the territories—letting residents in the territories decide the question of slavery for themselves. His party's platform declared that Congress lacked the power to interfere with slavery. The Whigs nominated General Zachary Taylor, a southern slaveholder and war hero. The Whig convention similarly refused to assert that Congress had power over slavery in the territories.

The Election of 1848 and Popular Sovereignty

New York Democrats committed to the Wilmot Proviso rebelled against Cass and nominated former president Martin Van Buren. Antislavery Whigs and former supporters of the Liberty Party then joined them to organize the Free-Soil Party, with Van Buren as its candidate. This party, whose slogan was "Free Soil, Free Speech, Free Labor, and Free Men," won almost 300,000 northern votes. Taylor polled 1.4 million votes to Cass's 1.2 million and won the White House, but the results were more ominous than decisive. The war with Mexico turned the political issue of slavery expansion into a moral issue. Politics had split along sectional lines as never before. Religious denominations too were splitting into northern and southern wings. As the 1850s dawned, the legacies of the Mexican War and the conflicts of 1848 dominated national life and threatened the nature of the Union itself.

1850: Compromise or Armistice?

The first sectional battle of the new decade involved California. More than eighty thousand Americans flooded into California during the gold rush of 1849. With Congress unable to agree on a formula to govern the territories, President Taylor urged these settlers to apply directly for admission to the Union. They promptly did so, proposing a state constitution that banned slavery. Southern politicians objected because California's admission as a free state would upset the equal balance of fifteen free and fifteen slave states in the Senate. At a minimum, southerners wanted the Missouri Compromise line extended to the Pacific.

Henry Clay, the venerable Whig leader, sensed that the Union was in peril. Twice before—in 1820 and 1833—Clay had taken the lead in shaping sectional compromise; now he struggled one last time to preserve the nation. Clay presented a series of compromise measures in the winter of 1850. Over the weeks that followed, he and Senator Stephen A. Douglas of Illinois steered their omnibus bill, or compromise package, through debate and amendment.

Debate over Slavery in the Territories

The package addressed difficult problems. Would California, or part of it, become a free state? How should the territory acquired from Mexico be organized? Texas, a slave state, claimed large portions of it as far west as Santa Fe. Southerners complained that fugitive slaves were not being returned as the Constitution required, and northerners objected to the sale of human beings in the nation's capital. Most troublesome of all was the status of slavery in the territories.

In Lewis Cass's idea of popular sovereignty Clay and Douglas discovered what one historian called a "charm of ambiguity" that appealed to practical politicians. Ultimately Congress would have to approve statehood for a territory, but "in the meantime," said Cass, it should allow the people living there "to regulate their own concerns in their own way."

Those simple words proved all but unenforceable. When could settlers prohibit slavery? To avoid dissension within their party, northern and southern Democrats explained Cass's statement to their constituents in two incompatible ways. Southerners claimed that neither Congress nor a territorial legislature could bar slavery. Only late in the territorial process, when settlers were ready to draft a state constitution, could they take that step. Northerners, however, insisted that Americans living in a territory were entitled to local self-government and thus could outlaw slavery at any time.

The cause of compromise gained a powerful supporter when Senator Daniel Webster committed his prestige and eloquence to Clay's bill. "I wish to speak today," Webster declaimed on March 7, "not as a Massachusetts man, nor as a Northern man, but as an American. I speak today for the preservation of the Union." When, after months of labor, Clay and Douglas finally brought their legislative package to a vote, they lost. With Clay sick and absent from Washington, Douglas reintroduced the compromise measures one at a time. Although there was no majority for compromise, Douglas shrewdly realized that different majorities might be created for the separate measures. The strategy worked, and the Compromise of 1850 became law.

The compromise had five essential measures: California became a free state; the Texas boundary

COMPROMISE OF 1850   was set at its present limits (see Map 14.2) and the United States paid Texas $10 million for the loss of New Mexico territory; the territories of New Mexico and Utah were organized on a basis of popular sovereignty; the fugitive slave law was strengthened; and the slave trade was abolished in the District of Columbia. Jubilation greeted passage of the compromise; crowds in Washington and other cities celebrated the happy news.

In reality, there was less cause for celebration than people hoped. As one historian has argued, the Compromise of 1850 was more an "armistice," delaying greater conflict, than a compromise. It had two basic flaws. The first concerned the ambiguity of territorial legislation: how exactly was popular sovereignty to be enforced? Southerners insisted there would be no prohibition of slavery during the territorial stage, and northerners declared that settlers could bar slavery whenever they wished. The compromise even allowed the appeal of a territorial legislature's action to the Supreme Court.

The second flaw lay in the Fugitive Slave Act, which gave new—and controversial—protection to slavery. The law empowered slave-

FUGITIVE SLAVE ACT   owners to go into court in their own states to present evidence that a slave who owed them service had escaped. The resulting transcript and a description of the fugitive would then serve as legal proof of a person's slave status, even in free states and territories. Penalties made it a felony to harbor fugitives. And the fees paid to U.S. marshals favored slaveholders: $10 if the alleged fugitive was returned to the slaveowner, $5 if not returned.

Abolitionist newspapers quickly attacked the Fugitive Slave Act as a violation of fundamental American rights. Why were alleged fugitives denied a trial by jury? Why were they given no chance to present evidence or cross-examine witnesses? Why did the law give authorities a financial incentive to send suspected fugitives into bondage? These arguments led to protest meetings all over the North.

Between 1850 and 1854, violent resistance to slave catchers occurred in dozens of northern towns. Sometimes a captured fugitive was broken out of jail or taken from slave agents by abolitionists, as in the case of Shadrach Minkins in 1851 in Boston, who was spirited by a series of wagons and trains across Massachusetts, up through Vermont, to Montreal, Canada. Also in 1851, the small black community in Lancaster County, Pennsylvania, rose up in arms to defend four escaped slaves from a federal posse charged with reenslaving them. At this "Christiana riot," the fugitives shot and killed Edward Gorsuch, the Maryland slaveowner who sought the return of his "property."

At this point, a novel portrayed the humanity and suffering of slaves in a way that touched millions of northerners. Harriet Beecher

UNCLE TOM'S CABIN   Stowe, whose New England family had produced many prominent ministers, wrote *Uncle Tom's Cabin* out of deep moral conviction. Her story, serialized in 1851 and published as a book in 1852, conveyed the agonies that slave families faced. Stowe also portrayed slavery's evil effects on slave-holders, indicting the institution itself more harshly than she indicted the southerners caught in its web. By mid-1853, *Uncle Tom's Cabin* had sold over 1 million copies. Through her book, Stowe brought home the evil of slavery to many who had never before given it much thought.

The popularity of *Uncle Tom's Cabin* alarmed anxious southern whites. In politics and now in popular literature, they saw threats to their way of life. Behind the South's aggressive claims about territorial rights lay the fear that if nearby areas outlawed slavery, they would be used as bases from which to spread abolitionism into the slave states.

Slaveholders were especially disturbed by the 1850s over what was widely called the Underground

THE UNDERGROUND RAILROAD

Railroad. This loose, illegal network of civil disobedience, spiriting runaways to freedom in safe houses, had never been very organized. Thousands of slaves did escape by these routes, but largely through their own wits and courage and through the assistance of black vigilance committees in some northern cities.

Online Study Center

Improve Your Grade
Primary Source: Levi Coffin Remembers the Underground Railroad

Moreover, Harriet Tubman, herself an escapee in 1848, returned to her native Maryland and to Virginia nearly twenty times, and through clandestine measures helped as many as three hundred slaves to freedom. Maryland planters were so outraged at her heroic success that they offered a $40,000 reward for her capture.

In Ohio numerous white abolitionists joined with blacks as agents of slave liberation at various points along the river border between slavery and freedom. The Underground Railroad also had numerous maritime routes out of Virginia and the Carolinas and from New Orleans. Some slaves who escaped by sea went to the Caribbean or to England. Many had escaped over the decades to Florida and across the Mexican border. In Mexico they entered a country that had abolished slavery; in Florida many were fully assimilated into the Seminole communities. This constant, dangerous flow of humanity was a testament to

■ In *Still Life of Harriet Tubman with Bible and Candle*, we see the youthful, calm, determined leader of the Underground Railroad. Appearing gentle, Tubman was in her own way a revolutionary who liberated nearly three hundred of her people.   (© psihoyos.com)

human courage and the will for freedom. It never reached the scale that some angry slaveholders believed or that of the countless safe houses and hideaways claimed by hundreds of northern towns and local historical societies today. But in reality and in legend, the Underground Railroad emphasized the slavery crisis and provided slaves with a focus for hope.

The 1852 election gave southern leaders hope for the security of slavery. Franklin Pierce, a Democrat

ELECTION OF 1852 AND THE COLLAPSE OF COMPROMISE

from New Hampshire, handily defeated the Whig nominee, General Winfield Scott. Pierce defended each section's rights as essential to the nation's unity, and southerners hoped that his firm support for the

Compromise of 1850 might end the season of crisis. His easy victory suggested widespread support for the compromise.

Pierce's victory, however, derived less from his strengths than from the Whig Party's weakness. The Whigs were a congressional and state-based party that never had achieved much success in presidential politics. By 1852 sectional discord had rendered the Whig Party all but dead.

President Pierce's embrace of the compromise appalled many northerners. His actions in a fugitive slave case provoked outrage and fear of the Slave Power. The slave Anthony Burns had fled Virginia by stowing away on a ship in 1852. In heavily abolitionist Boston, Burns began a new life. But in 1854 federal marshals found and placed him under guard in Boston's courthouse. An interracial crowd of abolitionists attacked the courthouse, killing a jailer, in an unsuccessful attempt to free Burns.

Pierce moved decisively to enforce the Fugitive Slave Act. He telegraphed local officials to "incur any expense to insure the execution of the law" and sent federal forces to Boston. U.S. troops marched Burns to Boston harbor through streets draped in black. At a cost of $100,000, a single black man was returned to slavery through the power of federal law.

This demonstration of federal support for slavery radicalized opinion. Textile manufacturer Amos A. Lawrence observed that "we went to bed one night old fashioned, conservative, Compromise Union Whigs & waked up stark mad Abolitionists." In New England, states began to pass personal-liberty laws absolving local judges from enforcing the Fugitive Slave Act, in effect nullifying federal authority. What northerners now saw as evidence of a dominating Slave Power, outraged slaveholders saw as the legal defense of their rights.

Pierce seemed unable to avoid sectional conflict in other arenas as well. His proposal for a transcontinental railroad derailed when congressmen fought over its location, North or South. His attempts to acquire foreign territory stirred more trouble. An annexation treaty with Hawai'i failed because southern senators would not vote for another free state, and efforts to acquire slaveholding Cuba angered northerners. In the Pacific, Commodore Matthew Perry's mission to establish trade relations with the Japanese also caused division at home over just how far American expansion should extend. In 1854 Perry negotiated two ports as coaling stations for American ships, but trading arrangements were slow in coming. Then another territorial bill embroiled Congress and the nation, and the Compromise of 1850 fell into complete collapse.

Slavery Expansion and Collapse of the Party System

The new controversy began in a surprising way. Stephen A. Douglas, one of the architects of the Compromise of 1850, introduced a bill to establish the Kansas and Nebraska Territories. Talented and ambitious for the presidency, Douglas was known for compromise, but he was willing to risk some controversy to benefit Illinois, his home state. A transcontinental railroad would encourage settlement of the Great Plains and stimulate the economy of Illinois, but no company would build it before Congress organized the territories it would cross. To promote the construction of such a railroad, Douglas introduced a bill that inflamed sectional passions.

The Kansas-Nebraska bill exposed the conflicting interpretations of popular sovereignty. Douglas's bill left "all questions pertaining to slavery in the Territo-

THE KANSAS-NEBRASKA BILL

ries . . . to the people residing therein." Northerners and southerners, however, still disagreed violently over what territorial settlers could constitutionally do. Moreover, the Kansas and Nebraska Territories lay north of latitude 36°30', where the Missouri Compromise prohibited slavery (see Map 14.2). If popular sovereignty were to mean anything in Kansas and Nebraska, it had to mean that the Missouri Compromise was no longer in effect and that settlers could establish slavery there.

Southern congressmen, anxious to establish slaveholders' right to take slaves into any territory, demanded an explicit repeal of the 36°30' limitation as the price of their support. During a carriage ride with Senator Archibald Dixon of Kentucky, Douglas debated the point at length. Finally he made an impulsive decision: "By God, Sir, you are right. I will incorporate it in my bill, though I know it will raise a hell of a storm."

His bill thus threw open to slavery land from which it had been prohibited for thirty-four years. Opposition from Free-Soilers and antislavery forces

Annexation of Cuba

One of the most contentious issues in antebellum American foreign relations was the annexation of Cuba. As a strategic bulwark against Britain and France in the Western Hemisphere, for its massive sugar wealth, and as a slave society that might reinforce the security of southern slavery, the Spanish-controlled island fired the imagination of manifest destiny.

In the early republic, Presidents Jefferson and Madison had explored acquisition. But until the 1840s, the United States officially supported Spanish rule for stability and the preservation of slavery. The prospect of slave insurrection and the spread of abolitionism drove many southerners and three Democratic administrations to shift course and pursue acquisition of Cuba. Slaveholding politicians viewed Cuba as critical to expansion; human bondage, they believed, had to expand southward and westward, or it might die.

In 1848 President Polk authorized $100 million to purchase Cuba. The Spanish foreign minister, however, bluntly refused. During the crisis over the Kansas-Nebraska Act in 1854, some southerners planned to seize Cuba by force. Although the expedition never embarked, its prospect outraged antislavery Republicans eager to halt slavery's expansion.

So did the Ostend Manifesto of October 1854. Written after a meeting among the American foreign ministers to Britain, France, and Spain, the document advocated conquest of Cuba if it could not be purchased. The ministers predicted that Cuba "would be Africanized and become a second St. Domingo, with all its attendant horrors to the white race." But antislavery northerners saw schemes of the "Slave Power." The Ostend controversy forced temporary abandonment of annexation efforts, but in 1858, President Buchanan reignited Cuba fever. A fierce Senate debate over yet another purchase offer in early 1859 ended in bitter division over the extension of slavery's domain.

"I want Cuba, and I know that sooner or later we must have it . . . for the planting or spreading of slavery," said Mississippian Albert G. Brown in 1858. Too many northerners, however, understood Brown's intentions. In America's links to the world, in this case only 90 miles from the Florida coast, just as in domestic affairs, the expansion of slavery poisoned the body politic.

This cartoon portrays Sam Houston, the famed Texan and proponent of American expansion, rowing the boat for a harpoonist in quest of the whale, Cuba. The dream of appropriating Cuba to the United States died very hard in the antebellum era. *Vanity Fair,* New York, June 1860. (© Bettmann/Corbis)

was immediate and enduring. The titanic struggle in Congress lasted three and a half months. Douglas eventually prevailed: the bill became law in May 1854 by a vote that demonstrated the dangerous sectionalization of American politics.

But the storm was just beginning. Abolitionists charged sinister aggression by the Slave Power, and northern fears of slavery's influence deepened. Opposition to the Fugitive Slave Act grew dramatically; between 1855 and 1859, Connecticut, Rhode Island, Massachusetts, Michigan, Maine, Ohio, and Wisconsin passed personal-liberty laws. These laws enraged southern leaders by providing counsel for alleged fugitives and requiring trial by jury. More important was the devastating impact of the Kansas-Nebraska Act on political parties. The weakened Whig Party broke apart into northern and southern wings that could no longer cooperate nationally. The Democrats survived, but their support in the North fell drastically in the 1854 elections.

Online Study Center **Improve Your Grade**
Interactive Map: The Kansas-Nebraska Act and Slavery Expansion, 1854

BIRTH OF THE
REPUBLICAN
PARTY

The beneficiary of northern voters' wrath was a new political party. During the summer and fall of 1854, antislavery Whigs and Democrats, Free-Soilers, and other reformers throughout the Old Northwest met to form the new Republican Party, dedicated to keeping slavery out of the territories. The influence of the Republicans rapidly spread to the East, and they won a stunning victory in the 1854 elections: in their first appearance on the ballot, Republicans captured a majority of northern House

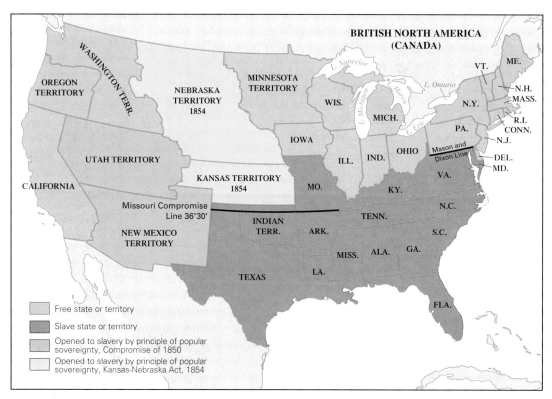

Map 14.2   The Kansas-Nebraska Act and Slavery Expansion, 1854

The vote on the Kansas-Nebraska Act in the House of Representatives demonstrates the sectionalization of American politics due to the slavery question.

seats. Antislavery sentiment had created a new party and caused roughly a quarter of northern Democrats to desert their party. For the first time, too, a sectional party had gained significant power in the political system. Now the Whigs were gone, and only the Democrats struggled to maintain national membership. The Republicans absorbed the Free-Soil Party and grew rapidly in the North. Indeed, the emergence of the Republican coalition of antislavery interests is the most rapid transformation in party allegiance and voter behavior in American history. This fact alone attests to the centrality of slavery expansion in the causation of the Civil War.

Republicans also drew into their coalition a fast-growing nativist movement that called itself the

KNOW-NOTHINGS

American Party, or Know-Nothings (because its first members kept their purposes secret, answering, "I know nothing," to all questions). This group exploited nativist fear of foreigners and Catholics. Between 1848 and 1860, nearly 3.5 million immigrants entered the United States—proportionally the heaviest inflow of foreigners ever in American history.

In 1854 anti-immigrant fears gave the Know-Nothings spectacular success in some northern states. They triumphed especially in Massachusetts, electing 11 congressmen, a governor, all state officers, all state senators, and all but 2 of 378 state representatives. The temperance movement also gained new strength early in the 1850s with its promises to stamp out the evils associated with liquor and immigrants (a particularly anti-Irish campaign). In this context, the Know-Nothings strove to reinforce Protestant morality and restrict voting and officeholding to the native-born. But like the Whigs, the Know-Nothings could not keep their northern and southern wings together, and they dissolved after 1856.

With nearly half of the old electorate up for grabs, the demise of the Whig Party ensured a major

PARTY REALIGNMENT AND THE REPUBLICANS' APPEAL

realignment of the political system. The remaining parties made appeals to various segments of the electorate. Immigration, temperance, homestead bills, the tariff, and internal improvements all played important roles in attracting voters during the 1850s. The Republicans appealed strongly to those interested in the economic develop-

ment of the West. Commercial agriculture was booming in the Ohio–Mississippi–Great Lakes area, and residents of that region desired more canals, roads, and river and harbor improvements. They also favored a homestead program through which western land would be made available free to individual farmers. The Republicans seized on these political desires, promising internal improvements and land grants as well as backing higher tariffs for industrialists.

Partisan ideological appeals became the currency of the realigned political system. As Republicans preached "Free Soil, Free Labor, Free Men," they captured a self-image of many northerners. These phrases resonated with traditional ideals of equality, liberty, and opportunity.

"Free Soil, Free Labor, Free Men" seemed an appropriate motto for a northern economy that was en-

REPUBLICAN IDEOLOGY

ergetic, expanding, and prosperous. The key to progress appeared to many people to be free labor—the dignity of work and the incentive of opportunity. Any hard-working and virtuous man, it was thought, could improve his condition and achieve economic independence by seizing opportunities that the country had to offer. Republicans argued that the South, with little industry and slave labor, was backward and retrograde by comparison. Their arguments captured much of the spirit of the age in the North. Traditional republicanism hailed the virtuous common man as the backbone of the country. Republicans portrayed their party as the guardian of economic opportunity, giving individuals a chance to work, acquire land, and attain success.

At stake in the enveloping crises of the 1850s were thus two competing definitions of "liberty": southern planters' claims to protection of their liberty in the possession and transport of their slaves anywhere in the land, and northern workers' and farmers' claims to protection of their liberty to seek a new start on free land, unimpeded by a system that defined labor as slave and black. Thus, a growing number of northerners expressed the fear that the rising political storm was an "irrepressible conflict."

Opposition to the extension of slavery had brought the Republicans into being, but party members carefully broadened their appeal by adopting the causes of other groups. As the editor Horace Greeley wrote in 1860, "an Anti-Slavery man per se cannot be elected." But, he added, "a Tariff, River-and-Harbor,

Pacific Railroad, Free Homestead man, may succeed although he is Anti-Slavery." As these elements joined the Republican Party, they also grew to fear slavery even more.

In the South, the disintegration of the Whig Party had left many southerners at loose ends politi-

SOUTHERN DEMOCRATS

cally. Some gravitated to the American Party, but not for long. In the increasingly tense atmosphere of sectional crisis, these people were highly susceptible to strong states' rights positions and defense of slavery. In the 1850s, most formerly Whig slaveholders converted to the Democrats.

Since Andrew Jackson's day, however, nonslaveholding small farmers had been the heart of the Democratic Party. Democratic politicians, though often slaveowners themselves, lauded the common man and argued that their policies advanced his interests. According to the southern version of republicanism, white citizens in a slave society enjoyed liberty and social equality because black people were enslaved. As Jefferson Davis put it in 1851, slavery elevated every white person's status and allowed the nonslaveholder to "stand upon the broad level of equality with the rich man." Southern Democrats warned that the issue was, "Shall negroes govern white men, or white men govern negroes?" They also portrayed the well-ordered South as the true defender of constitutional principles.

Racial fears and traditional political loyalties helped keep the political alliance between yeoman farmers and planters largely intact through the 1850s. Across class lines, white southerners joined together against what they perceived as the Republican Party's capacity to cause slave unrest in their midst. In the South, no viable party emerged to replace the Whigs. The result was a one-party system that emphasized sectional issues and loyalty. In the South as in the North, political realignment sharpened sectional identities.

Political leaders of both sections used race in their arguments about opportunity. The *Montgomery* (Alabama) *Mail* warned southern whites in 1860 that the Republicans intended "to free the negroes and force amalgamation between them and the children of the poor men of the South." Republicans warned northern workers that if slavery entered the territo-

ries, the great reservoir of opportunity for ordinary citizens would be poisoned.

In the territory of Kansas, the Kansas-Nebraska Act spawned hatred and violence. Abolitionists and religious groups sent in armed Free-Soil settlers; southerners sent in their reinforcements to establish slavery and prevent "northern hordes" from stealing Kansas away. Conflicts led to bloodshed, and soon the whole nation was talking about "Bleeding Kansas."

Politics in the territory resembled war more than democracy. During elections for a territorial legisla-

BLEEDING KANSAS

ture in 1855, thousands of proslavery Missourians invaded the polls and ran up a large fraudulent majority for slavery candidates. The resulting legislature legalized slavery, and in response Free-Soilers held an unauthorized convention at which they created their own government and constitution. In the spring of 1856, a proslavery posse sent to arrest the Free-Soil leaders sacked the Kansas town of Lawrence, killing several people. In revenge, John Brown, a radical abolitionist, and some followers murdered five proslavery settlers living along Pottawatomie Creek. Soon, armed bands of guerrillas roamed the territory.

These passions brought violence to the U.S. Senate in May 1856, when Charles Sumner of Massachusetts denounced "the Crime against Kansas." Radical in his antislavery views, Sumner bitterly assailed the president, the South, and Senator Andrew P. Butler of South Carolina. Soon after, Butler's cousin, Representative Preston Brooks, approached Sumner at the latter's Senate desk, raised his cane, and beat Sumner on the head until he collapsed, bleeding, to the floor.

Shocked northerners recoiled from what they saw as another southern assault on free speech and proof of southerners' readiness to use violence. Popular opinion in Massachusetts supported Sumner; voters in South Carolina reelected Brooks and sent him dozens of commemorative canes. The country was becoming polarized.

The election of 1856 showed how extreme that polarization had become. The Democrats chose James Buchanan of Pennsylvania, whose chief virtue was that for the past four years, he had been ambassador to Britain and uninvolved in territorial controversies. Superior party organization helped Buchanan win the election, but he owed his victory to southern support. The Republican candidate, John C. Frémont, won eleven of sixteen free states; Republicans had become the dominant party in the North. The Know-Nothing candidate, Millard Fillmore, won almost 1 million votes in that party's last hurrah. The coming battle, with voter turnouts as high as 75 to 80 percent in many states, would pit a sectional Republican Party against an increasingly divided Democratic Party.

Slavery and the Nation's Future

For years the issue of slavery in the territories had convulsed Congress, which had tried to settle the issue with vague formulas. In 1857 a different branch of government, the Supreme Court, stepped into the fray and attempted to silence controversy with a definitive verdict.

A Missouri slave named Dred Scott had sued his owner for his freedom. Scott based his claim on the

DRED SCOTT CASE

fact that his former owner, an army surgeon, had taken him for several years into Illinois, a free state, and into the Wisconsin Territory, from which slavery had been barred by the Missouri Compromise. Scott first won but then lost his case as it moved on appeal through the state courts, into the federal system, and finally to the Supreme Court.

This case involved substantive issues related to slavery and its extension in the territories, which Chief Justice Roger B. Taney of Maryland addressed when, in March 1857, he delivered the majority opinion of a divided Court. Taney declared that as a black slave, Scott was not a citizen of either the United States or Missouri and so was ineligible to sue in federal court; that residence in free territory did not make Scott free; and that Congress had no power to bar slavery from any territory. The decision not only overturned a sectional compromise (the Missouri Compromise of 1820) that had been honored for thirty-seven years; it also invalidated the basic ideas of the Wilmot Proviso and popular sovereignty.

The Slave Power seemed to have won a major constitutional victory. African Americans were especially dismayed, for Taney's decision asserted that the nation's founders had never intended for black people to be citizens, regarding them, the chief justice

wrote, "as beings of an inferior order" with "no rights which the white man was bound to respect." Taney was mistaken; African Americans had been citizens in several of the original states and had voted.

Nevertheless, the ruling seemed to shut the door permanently on black hopes for justice and equal rights. In northern black communities, rage and despair prevailed. Many who were still fugitive slaves sought refuge in emigration to Canada, the Caribbean, or even Africa. One black abolitionist said the *Dred Scott* decision had made slavery "the supreme law of the land and all descendants of the African race denationalized." Uncertain and fearful, blacks contemplated whether they had any future in America.

A storm of angry reaction broke in the North. The decision seemed to confirm every charge against the aggressive Slave Power. "There is such a thing as the slave power," warned the *Cincinnati Daily Commercial*. "It has marched over and annihilated the boundaries of the states." The economic and racial anxieties of poor northern whites reached a peak. The *Cincinnati Freeman* asked, "What security have the Germans and the Irish that their children will not, within a hundred years, be reduced to slavery in this land of their adoption?"

To Abraham Lincoln, the territorial question affected every citizen. "The whole nation," he had declared as early as 1854, "is interested

ABRAHAM LINCOLN AND THE SLAVE POWER

that the best use shall be made of these Territories. We want them for homes of free white people. This they cannot be, to any considerable extent, if slavery shall be planted within them." The territories must be reserved, he insisted, "as an outlet for free white people everywhere."

More important, Lincoln warned of slavery's increasing control over the nation. The founders had created a government dedicated to freedom, Lincoln insisted. Admittedly they had recognized slavery's existence, but the public mind, he argued in 1858, had always rested in the belief that slavery would die either naturally or by legislation. The next step in the unfolding Slave Power conspiracy, Lincoln alleged, would be a Supreme Court decision "declaring that the Constitution does not permit a State to exclude slavery from its limits." This charge was not pure hyperbole, for lawsuits soon challenged state laws that freed slaves brought within their borders.

Lincoln's most eloquent statement against the Slave Power was his famous "House Divided" speech, in which he declared:

> "A house divided against itself cannot stand." I believe this government cannot endure, permanently half slave and half free. I do not expect the Union to be dissolved—I do not expect the House to fall—but I do expect it to cease to be divided. It will become all one thing or all the other. Either the opponents of slavery will arrest the further spread of it, and place it where the public mind shall rest in the belief that it is in the course of ultimate extinction; or its advocates will push it forward, till it shall become alike lawful in all the States, old as well as new, North as well as South.

Politically, these forceful Republican arguments offset the difficulties that the *Dred Scott* decision posed. By endorsing the South's doctrine of state sovereignty, the Court had in effect declared that the Republican Party's central position—no extension of slavery—was unconstitutional. Republicans could only repudiate the decision, appealing to a "higher law," or hope to change the personnel of the Court. They did both and gained politically.

For northern Democrats like Stephen Douglas, the Court's decision posed an awful dilemma. North-

THE LECOMPTON CONSTITUTION AND SECTIONAL DISHARMONY AMONG DEMOCRATS

ern voters were alarmed by the prospect that the territories would be opened to slavery. To retain their support, Douglas had to find some way to reassure them. Yet, given his ambitions to lead the national Democratic Party and become president, Douglas could not afford to alienate southern Democrats.

Douglas chose to stand by his principle of popular sovereignty, even if the result angered southerners. In 1857 Kansans voted on a proslavery constitution that had been drafted at Lecompton. It was defeated by more than ten thousand votes in a referendum boycotted by most proslavery voters. The evidence was overwhelming that Kansans did not want slavery, yet President Buchanan tried to force the Lecompton Constitution through Congress. Breaking with the administration, Douglas threw his

weight against the Lecompton Constitution. He gauged opinion in Kansas correctly, for in 1858 voters there rejected the constitution again. But his action infuriated southern Democrats. Increasingly, many southerners believed their sectional rights and slavery would be safe only in a separate nation.

Meanwhile, as the territorial process floundered in Kansas, it also collapsed in Utah. For their practice

THE "MORMON WAR" IN UTAH

of polygamy and their theocratic government, the Mormons who settled Utah were among the most persecuted peoples in America. Under the church-centered leadership of seer and prophet Brigham Young, the Mormons claimed the doctrine of popular sovereignty as their basis of independent rule while seeking recognition from Congress of territorial status and polygamy. But a series of corrupt territorial court justices appointed by Presidents Pierce and Buchanan failed to rein in the frontier society.

In 1857 Buchanan dispatched 2,500 troops, one-sixth of the U.S. Army, to suppress Young, who as one historian describes him, ruled "like a traitor in rebellion against the United States." Blocked by winter in the Rockies, the army never reached Utah. The massacre of a wagon train of 120 settlers by the Mormons and Indian allies notwithstanding, the "Mormon War" ended in Young's withdrawing his forces and Buchanan sending peace commissioners and offering amnesty in 1858. The struggle over federal authority, as well as the Mormons' own "peculiar institution" in Utah, would continue for years.

Disunion

t is worth remembering that in the late 1850s, most Americans were not caught up daily in the slavery crisis. They were preoccupied with personal affairs, especially coping with the effects of the economic panic that began in the spring of 1857. They were worried about widespread unemployment, the plummeting price of wheat, declining wages at a textile mill, or sons who needed land.

The panic had been caused by shortcomings of the unregulated American banking system, frenzied speculation in western lands and railroads, and a weak and overburdened credit system. By 1858 Philadelphia had 40,000 unemployed workers, and New York

City nearly 100,000. Fear of bread riots and class warfare gripped many cities in the North. True to form, blame for such economic woe became sectionalized, as southerners saw their system justified by the temporary collapse of industrial prosperity, and northerners feared even more the incursions of the Slave Power on an insecure future.

Soon, however, the entire nation's focus would be thrown on a new dimension of the slavery question: armed rebellion. John Brown had been raised by staunchly religious and antislavery parents. He relied on an Old Testament conception of justice—"an eye for an eye"—and he had a puritanical obsession with the wickedness of others, especially southern slaveowners. Brown believed that violence in a righteous cause was a holy act. To Brown, the destruction of slavery in America required revolutionary ideology and revolutionary acts.

JOHN BROWN'S RAID ON HARPERS FERRY

On October 16, 1859, Brown led a small band of eighteen whites and blacks in an attack on the federal arsenal at Harpers Ferry, Virginia. Hoping to trigger a slave rebellion, Brown failed miserably and was quickly captured, tried, and executed. Yet his attempted insurrection struck fear into the South. Then it became known that Brown had received financial backing from several prominent abolitionists. When northern intellectuals such as Ralph Waldo Emerson and Henry David Thoreau praised Brown as a holy warrior who "would make the gallows as glorious as the cross," white southerners' outrage multiplied. Most troubling to southerners, perhaps, was that while Republican politicians condemned Brown's crimes, they did so in a way that deflected attention onto the still greater crime of slavery.

Many Americans believed that the election of 1860 would decide the fate of the Union. The Democratic Party was the only party truly national in scope. But at its 1860 convention in Charleston, South Carolina, the Democratic Party split. Stephen A. Douglas wanted his party's presidential nomination, but he could not afford to alienate northern voters by accepting the southern position on the territories. Southern Democrats, however, insisted on recognition of their rights and moved to block Douglas's nomination. When Douglas obtained a majority for his version of

ELECTION OF 1860

the platform, delegates from the Deep South walked out of the convention. After efforts at compromise failed, the Democrats presented two nominees: Douglas for the northern wing, and Vice President John C. Breckinridge of Kentucky for the southern. The Republicans nominated Abraham Lincoln, and a Constitutional Union Party, formed to preserve the nation but strong only in the Upper South, nominated John Bell of Tennessee.

Bell's only issue in the ensuing campaign was the urgency of preserving the Union. Douglas desperately sought to unite his northern and southern supporters, while Breckinridge quickly backed away from the appearance of extremism, and his supporters in several states stressed his unionism. Although Lincoln and the Republicans denied any intent to interfere with slavery in the states where it existed, they stood firm against the extension of slavery into the territories.

The election of 1860 was sectional in character. Lincoln won, but Douglas, Breckinridge, and Bell together received a majority of the votes. Douglas had broad-based support but won few states. Breckinridge carried nine states, all in the Deep South. Bell won pluralities in Virginia, Kentucky, and Tennessee. Lincoln prevailed in the North, but in the four border states that ultimately remained loyal to the Union (Missouri, Kentucky, Maryland, and Delaware), he gained only a plurality, not a majority. Lincoln's victory was won in the electoral college.

Opposition to slavery's extension was the core issue of the Republican Party, and Lincoln's alarm over slavery's growing political power was genuine. Moreover, abolitionists and supporters of free soil in the North worked to keep the Republicans from compromising on their territorial stand. Meanwhile, proslavery advocates and secessionists in the South whipped up public opinion and demanded that state conventions assemble to consider secession.

Lincoln made the crucial decision not to soften his party's position on the territories. He wrote of the need to maintain the bond of faith between voter and candidate and of declining to set "the minority over the majority." Although many conservative Republicans—eastern businessmen and former Whigs who did not feel strongly about slavery—hoped for a compromise, the original and most committed Republicans—old Free-Soilers and antislavery Whigs—were adamant about stopping the expansion of the peculiar institution.

Senator John J. Crittenden of Kentucky tried to craft a late-hour compromise. The Crittenden Compromise proposed that the two sections divide the territories between them at latitude 36°30'. But the southerners would agree to this only if the Republicans did too. When Lincoln ruled out concessions on the territorial issue, Crittenden's peacemaking effort collapsed.

Meanwhile, the Union was being destroyed. On December 20, 1860, South Carolina passed an ordinance of secession. This step marked the inauguration of the secessionist strategy of separate-state secession. Secessionists concentrated their efforts on the most extreme proslavery state, hoping South Carolina's bold act would induce other states to follow, with each decision building momentum for disunion.

SECESSION AND THE CONFEDERATE STATES OF AMERICA

Southern extremists soon got their way in the Deep South. They called separate state conventions and passed secession ordinances in Mississippi, Florida, Alabama, Georgia, Louisiana, and Texas. By February 1861 these states had joined South Carolina to form a new government in Montgomery, Alabama: the Confederate States of America. The delegates at Montgomery chose Jefferson Davis as their president, and the Confederacy began to function independently of the United States.

This apparent unanimity was deceiving. Confused and dissatisfied with the alternatives, many southerners who in 1860 had voted in the U.S. presidential election stayed home a few months later rather than vote for delegates who would decide on

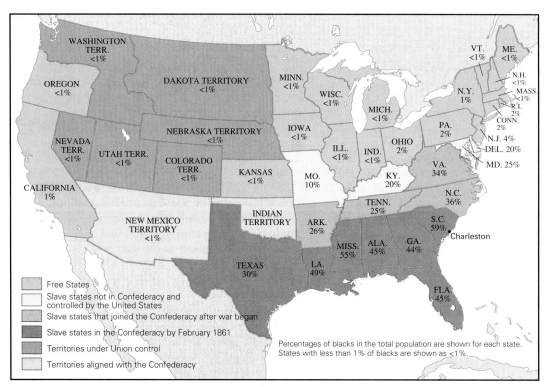

Map 14.3.   The Divided Nation—Slave and Free Areas, 1861

After fighting began, the Upper South joined the Deep South in the Confederacy. How does the nation's pattern of division correspond to the distribution of slavery and the percentage of blacks in the population?

secession. Even so, in some state conventions, the vote to secede was close, with secession decided by overrepresentation of plantation districts. Furthermore, the conventions were noticeably unwilling to let voters ratify their acts. Four states in the Upper South—Virginia, North Carolina, Tennessee, and Arkansas—flatly rejected secession and did not join the Confederacy until 1861, after fighting had begun. In the border states, popular sentiment was deeply divided; minorities in Kentucky and Missouri tried to secede, but these slave states ultimately came under Union control, along with Maryland and Delaware (see Map 14.3).

Such misgivings were not surprising. Secession raised the possibility of war and the question of where it would be fought and who would die. Analysis of election returns from 1860 and 1861 indicates

that slaveholders and nonslaveholders were beginning to part company politically. Heavily slaveholding counties strongly supported secession, but most counties with few slaves took an antisecession stance (see Figure 14.1). With war on the horizon, yeomen were beginning to consider their class interests and ask themselves how far they would go to support slavery and slaveowners.

As for why the Deep South bolted, we can look to the entreaties of the secession commissioners sent out by the seven seceded states to try to convince the other slave states to join them. Repeatedly they stressed independence as the only way to preserve white racial security and the slave system. Only secession, contended the Alabama commissioner, Stephen Hale, could sustain the "heaven-ordained superiority of the white over the black race."

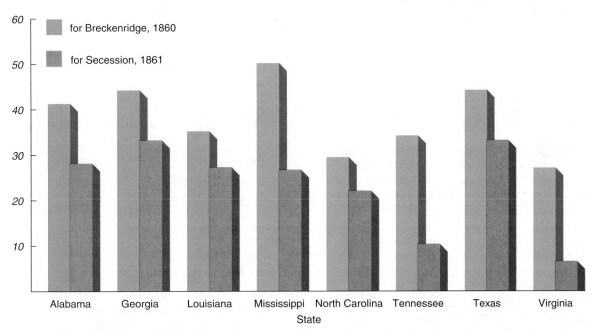

Figure 14.1   Voting Returns of Counties with Few Slaveholders, Eight Southern States, 1860 and 1861

This graph depicts voting in counties whose percentage of slaveholders ranked them among the lower half of the counties in their state. How does voters' support for secession in 1861 compare with support for John Breckinridge, the southern Democratic candidate in 1860? Why was their support for secession so weak? At this time counties with many slaveholders were giving increased support to secession.

The dilemma facing President Lincoln on inauguration day in March 1861 was how to maintain the

FORT SUMTER AND OUTBREAK OF WAR

federal government's authority without provoking war. Proceeding cautiously, he sought only to hold on to forts in the states that had left the Union, reasoning that he could thus assert federal sovereignty while waiting for a restoration. But Jefferson Davis, who could not claim to lead a sovereign nation if the Confederate ports were under foreign (that is, U.S.) control, was unwilling to be so patient. A collision was inevitable.

It arrived in the early morning hours of April 12, 1861, at Fort Sumter in Charleston harbor. A federal garrison there ran low on food, and Lincoln notified the South Carolinians that he was sending a ship to resupply the fort. The Montgomery government, facing the choice of attacking the fort or acquiescing to Lincoln's authority, ordered local commanders to obtain a surrender or attack. After two days of heavy bombardment, the federal garrison finally surrendered. Confederates permitted the U.S. troops to sail away on unarmed vessels while Charlestonians celebrated wildly. The Civil War had begun.

Summary   Online Study Center   ACE the Test

*T*hroughout the 1840s and 1850s, most people, North and South, had hoped to keep the nation together. As late as 1858, even Jefferson Davis had declared, "This great country will continue united," saying that "to the innermost fibers of my heart I love it all, and every part."

Why had all efforts to prevent war failed? The conflict that slavery generated was fundamental. The emotions bound up in attacking and defending slavery's future were too powerful, and the interests it affected too vital, for compromise. North and South had fundamentally different attitudes toward the institution. The logic of Republican ideology tended in the direction of abolishing slavery, even though Republicans denied any such intention. The logic of southern arguments led toward establishing slavery everywhere, though southern leaders too denied such a motive. Lincoln put these facts succinctly. In a postelection letter to his old friend Alexander Stephens of Georgia, Lincoln wrote, "You think slavery is right

and ought to be expanded; while we think it is wrong and ought to be restricted. That I suppose is the rub."

Territorial expansion generated disputes so frequently that the nation never enjoyed an extended breathing space during the 1850s. Every southern victory increased fear of the Slave Power, and each new expression of Free-Soil sentiment made alarmed slaveholders more insistent in their demands. Eventually even those opposed to war could see no way to avoid it. In the profoundest sense, slavery was the root of the war. But as the fighting began, this, the war's central issue, was shrouded in confusion. How would the Civil War affect slavery, its place in the law, and African Americans' place in society?

LEGACY FOR A PEOPLE AND A NATION
Terrorist or Freedom Fighter?

The greatest significance of John Brown's raid on Harpers Ferry in 1859 rests in its aftermath in American memory. Brown is as important as a symbol as he is for his deeds. He has been one of the most beloved and most loathed figures in American history. In the song that bears his name, "John Brown's Body," a popular marching tune during the Civil War, his "soul goes marching on."

In the wake of his execution, in painting, song, and poetry, people constructed a John Brown mythology. Was he a Christ-like figure who died for the nation's sins? Or was he a terrorist thief who murdered in the name of his own peculiar vision of God's will? Brown can be disturbing and inspiring, majestic and foolish, a monster or a warrior saint. He represented the highest ideals and the most ruthless deeds. He killed for justice.

Over the years, many organizations have adopted John Brown as their justifying symbol, from left-wing students opposing American foreign policy to anti-abortion groups that target clinics and doctors. Today, terrorism and revolutionary violence are often in the news: a federal building explodes in Oklahoma City; suicide bombers attack buses and restaurants in Israel; the Irish Republican Army plants explosives in London subways; and on September 11, 2001, four hijacked passenger airplanes bring terrorism to American soil as never before. The story of John Brown's raid in 1859 forces us to ask when and how revolutionary violence—violence in the name of a political or spiritual end—is justified. That is his legacy for a people and a nation.

TRANSFORMING FIRE: THE CIVIL WAR 1861–1865

*H*e was an ordinary twenty-seven-year-old store clerk from a New England town, who went off to war. In spring 1861, Charles Brewster left his mother and two sisters behind and joined Company C of the Tenth Massachusetts Volunteers. Brewster had no idea of his capacity for leadership or his ability to uphold such values as courage and manliness.

In more than two hundred sometimes lyrical letters to his mother and sisters, Brewster, who rose to lieutenant and adjutant of his regiment, left a trove of commentary on the meaning of war, why slavery had to be destroyed, and, especially, the values of common, mid-nineteenth-century American men. Brewster was as racist as many southerners in his perceptions of blacks. He was no "desperate hero" about battlefield courage, and he nearly died of dysentery twice. He was personally eager for rank and recognition, and eventually held only contempt for civilians who stayed at home. He was often miserably lonely and homesick, and he described battlefield carnage with an honest realism.

Most telling, Brewster's attitudes toward race transformed. In 1862 he defied orders and took in a seventeen-year-old ex-slave as his personal servant. In 1864, after some of the worst battles of the war in Virginia destroyed his regiment, Brewster, frightened of civilian life, reenlisted to be a recruiter of black troops. In this new role, Brewster worked from an office in Norfolk, Virginia, where his principal job was writing "love letters" for illiterate black women to their soldier husbands at the front. In imagining Brewster sitting at a table with a lonely freedwoman, swallowing his prejudices toward blacks and women, and repeatedly writing or reciting the phrases "give my love to . . ." and "your Husband untall Death," we can glimpse the enormous potential for human transformation at work in this war.

The Civil War's astonishing, unexpected changes in North and South obliterated normal patterns of life. Millions of men were swept away into training camps and battle units. Armies of hundreds of thousands marched

Online Study Center
This icon will direct you to interactive map and primary source activities on the website
http://college.hmco.com/pic/nortonbrief7e

CHRONOLOGY

1861 • Battle of Bull Run
- McClellan organizes Union Army
- Union blockade begins
- U.S. Congress passes first confiscation act
- *Trent* affair

1862 • Union captures Fort Henry and Fort Donelson
- U.S. Navy captures New Orleans
- Battle of Shiloh shows the war's destructiveness
- Confederacy enacts conscription
- McClellan's Peninsula Campaign fails to take Richmond
- U.S. Congress passes second confiscation act, initiating emancipation
- Confederacy mounts offensive in Maryland and Kentucky
- Battle of Antietam ends Lee's drive into Maryland in September
- British intervention in the war on Confederate side is averted

1863 • Emancipation Proclamation takes effect
- U.S. Congress passes National Banking Act
- Union enacts conscription
- African American soldiers join Union Army
- Food riots occur in southern cities
- Battle of Chancellorsville ends in Confederate victory but Jackson's death
- Union wins key victories at Gettysburg and Vicksburg

- Draft riots take place in New York City
- Battle of Chattanooga leaves South vulnerable to Sherman's march into Georgia

1864 • Battles of the Wilderness and Spotsylvania produce heavy casualties on both sides in the effort to capture and defend Richmond
- Battle of Cold Harbor continues carnage in Virginia
- Lincoln requests Republican Party plank abolishing slavery
- Sherman captures Atlanta
- Confederacy begins to collapse on the home front
- Lincoln wins reelection, eliminating any Confederate hopes for a negotiated end to war
- Jefferson Davis proposes emancipation within the Confederacy
- Sherman marches through Georgia to the sea

1865 • Sherman marches through Carolinas
- U.S. Congress approves Thirteenth Amendment
- Lee abandons Richmond and Petersburg
- Lee surrenders at Appomattox Court House
- Lincoln assassinated
- Death toll in war reaches 620,000

over the South, devastating countrysides. Families struggled to survive without their men; businesses tried to cope with the loss of workers. Women in both North and South took on extra responsibilities at home and moved into the work force, some joining the ranks of nurses and hospital workers.

But southern soldiers, and their families, also experienced what few other groups of Americans have— utter defeat. For most of them, hope turned to despair as countless southern farms were ruined. Late in the war, many southerners yearned only for an end to inflation, shortages, and the death that visited nearly every family.

Northern soldiers, though ultimately victorious, often resented the sacrifices demanded of them. For northern businessmen, however, the conflict ensured vast government expenditures, a heavy demand for goods, and lucrative federal contracts. *Harper's Monthly* reported that an eminent financier expected a long and profitable war, ripe with speculative opportunities. "The battle of Bull Run," predicted the financier, "makes the fortune of every man in Wall Street who is not a natural idiot."

Change was most drastic in the South, where secessionists had launched a conservative revolution for their section's national independence. Born of states' rights doctrine, the Confederacy now had to transform into a centralized nation to fight a vast war. Southern whites had feared that a peacetime government of Republicans would interfere with slavery and upset the routine of plantation life. Instead, their own actions led to a war that turned southern life upside down and imperiled the very existence of slavery.

War altered the North as well, but less sharply. Because most of the fighting took place on southern soil, northern farms and factories remained largely unscathed and busy. Workers lost ground to inflation, but the economy hummed. A new pro-business atmosphere dominated Congress. To the alarm of many, the powers of the federal government and of the president increased during the war.

Ultimately the Civil War forced on the nation a social and political revolution regarding race. Its greatest effect was to compel leaders and citizens to deal directly with the issue they had struggled over but had been unable to resolve: slavery. ■

America Goes to War, 1861–1862

Few Americans understood what they were getting into when the war began. The onset of hostilities sparked patriotic sentiments and joyous ceremonies in both North and South. Northern communities raised companies of volunteers eager to save the Union. In the South, confident recruits boasted of whipping the Yankees and returning home before Christmas.

Through the spring of 1861, both sides scrambled to organize and train their undisciplined armies.

FIRST BATTLE OF BULL RUN

On July 21, 1861, the first battle took place outside Manassas Junction, Virginia, near a stream called Bull Run. General Irvin McDowell and 30,000 Union troops attacked General P. G. T. Beauregard's 22,000 southerners. As raw recruits struggled amid the confusion of their first battle, federal forces began to gain ground. Then they ran into a line of Virginia troops under General Thomas Jackson. "There is Jackson standing like a stone wall," shouted one Confederate. "Stonewall" Jackson's line held, and the arrival of 9,000 Confederate reinforcements won the day for the South. Union troops fled back to Washington.

The unexpected rout at Bull Run gave northerners their first hint that although the United States enjoyed an enormous advantage in resources, victory would not be easy. Pro-Union feeling was growing in western Virginia, and loyalties were divided in the four border slave states: Missouri, Kentucky, Maryland, and Delaware. But the rest of the Upper South—North Carolina, Virginia, Tennessee, and Arkansas—had joined the Confederacy. Moved by an outpouring of regional loyalty, half a million southerners volunteered to fight.

Lincoln gave command of the northern army to General George B. McClellan, an officer who proved to be better at organization and training than at fighting. McClellan devoted the fall and winter of 1861 to readying the Union Army, a formidable force of a quarter-million men whose mission would be to take Richmond, established as the Confederate capital by July 1861.

While McClellan prepared, the Union began to implement other parts of its overall strategy, which

GRAND STRATEGY

called for a blockade of southern ports and eventual capture of the Mississippi River. Like a constricting snake, this "Anaconda plan" would strangle the Confederacy. At first the Union Navy had too few ships to patrol 3,550 miles of coastline effectively. Gradually, however, the navy increased the blockade's effectiveness, though it never stopped southern commerce completely.

Confederate strategy was essentially defensive. A defensive posture not only was consistent with the South's claim of independence, but acknowledged the

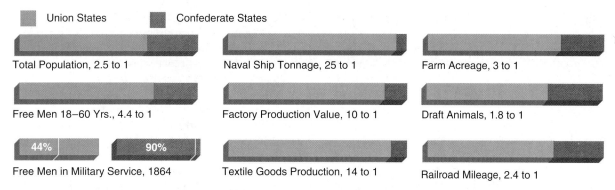

Figure 15.1   Comparative Resources, Union and Confederate States, 1861

The North had vastly superior resources. Although the North's advantages in manpower and industrial capacity proved very important, the South still had to be conquered, its society and its will crushed.   (Source: *The Times Atlas of World History.* Time Books, London, 1978. Used with permission.)

North's advantage in resources (see Figure 15.1). But Jefferson Davis called the southern strategy "offensive defensive," taking advantage of opportunities to attack and using its interior lines of transportation to concentrate troops at crucial points.

Strategic thinking on both sides slighted the importance of "the West," that vast expanse of territory between Virginia and the Mississippi River and beyond. Guerrilla warfare broke out in 1861 in the politically divided state of Missouri, and key locations along the Mississippi and other major western rivers would prove to be crucial prizes in the North's eventual victory. Beyond the Mississippi River, the Confederacy hoped to gain an advantage by negotiating treaties with the Cherokees and other Indian tribes. Meanwhile, the Republican U.S. Congress carved the West into territories in anticipation of state making. What began during the Civil War was the start of nearly three decades of offensive warfare against Indians, an enveloping strategy of conquest, relocation, and slaughter.

The last half of 1861 brought no major land battles, but the North made gains by sea. Union naval forces secured vital coastal points in the Carolinas, as well as Fort Pulaski, which defended Savannah. The coastal victories off South Carolina frightened planters, who abandoned their lands and fled. But thousands of slaves greeted

UNION NAVAL CAMPAIGN

what they hoped to be freedom with rejoicing and broke the hated cotton gins. A growing stream of runaways poured into the Union lines. The Union government, unwilling at first to wage a war against slavery, did not acknowledge the slaves' freedom. It began, however, to use their labor in the Union cause.

The coastal incursions worried southerners, but the spring of 1862 confirmed the naval threat. In April Union ships commanded by Admiral David Farragut smashed through log booms blocking the Mississippi River and fought their way upstream to capture New Orleans.

Farther west, three full Confederate regiments were organized, mostly of Cherokees from Indian Territory, but a Union victory at Elkhorn Tavern, Arkansas, shattered southern control of the region. Thereafter, dissension within Native American groups and Union advances reduced Confederate operations in Indian Territory to guerrilla raids.

WAR IN THE FAR WEST

In the westernmost campaign of the war, from February to May 1862, some 3,000 Confederate forces marched north from Texas to fight for control of New Mexico Territory. The military significance of the New Mexico campaign was limited. About 4,000 Colorado and New Mexico Unionists fought for their region, and by May 1 Confederate forces straggled down the Rio Grande River back into Texas, ending their effort.

Meanwhile, in February 1862, land and river forces in northern Tennessee won significant victories for the Union. A Union commander named Ulysses S. Grant captured Fort Henry and Fort Donelson, guarding the Tennessee and Cumberland Rivers. A path into Tennessee, Alabama, and Mississippi now lay open before the Union Army. Grant moved on into southern Tennessee and the first of the war's shockingly bloody encounters, the Battle of Shiloh. Early on April 6, Confederate general Albert Sidney Johnston attacked federal troops caught with their backs to the Tennessee River. Although Johnston was killed, southern forces almost achieved a breakthrough, but Union reinforcements arrived that night. The next day, after ten hours of terrible combat, the Confederates withdrew. Neither side won a victory at Shiloh, yet the losses were staggering. Northern troops lost 13,000 men (killed, wounded, or captured) out of 63,000; southerners sacrificed 11,000 out of 40,000. The true nature of the war was emerging.

GRANT'S TENNESSEE CAMPAIGN AND THE BATTLE OF SHILOH

On the Virginia front, President Lincoln had a different problem. General McClellan was slow to move. Habitually overestimating the size of enemy forces, McClellan called repeatedly for reinforcements and ignored Lincoln's directions to advance. Finally he chose to move by water, sailing his troops down the Chesapeake, landing them on the peninsula between the York and James Rivers, and advancing on Richmond from the east.

MCCLELLAN AND THE PENINSULA CAMPAIGN

After a bloody but indecisive battle at Fair Oaks from May 31 to June 1, the federal armies moved to within 7 miles of the Confederate capital. The Confederate commanding general, Joseph E. Johnston, was badly wounded at Fair Oaks, and President Jefferson Davis placed his chief military adviser, Robert E. Lee, in command. Lee soon foiled McClellan's legions.

First, he sent Stonewall Jackson's corps of 17,000 into the Shenandoah valley behind Union forces, where they threatened Washington, D.C., drawing some federal troops away from Richmond to protect their own capital. Then, in a series of engagements known as the Seven Days Battles, June 26–July 1, Lee forced McClellan to retreat toward the James River. By August 3 McClellan withdrew his army to the Potomac; Richmond remained safe for another two years.

Buoyed by these results, Jefferson Davis conceived an ambitious plan to turn the tide of the war and gain recognition of the Confederacy by European nations. He ordered a general offensive, sending Lee north into Maryland and Generals Kirby Smith and Braxton Bragg into Kentucky. Calling on residents of Maryland and Kentucky (still slave states) to make a separate peace with his government, Davis also invited northwestern states like Indiana, which sent much of their trade down the Mississippi to New Orleans, to leave the Union.

CONFEDERATE OFFENSIVE IN MARYLAND AND KENTUCKY

The plan was promising, but every part of the offensive failed. In the bloodiest day of the entire war, September 17, 1862, McClellan turned Lee back in the Battle of Antietam near Sharpsburg, Maryland. He also, however, indecisively allowed Lee's stricken army to retreat to safety, and Lincoln removed him from command. In Kentucky, Generals Smith and Bragg secured Lexington and Frankfurt, but were then stopped at the Battle of Perryville on October 8. Bragg's army retreated back into Tennessee. Confederate leaders had marshaled all their strength for a breakthrough but had failed. Tenacious defense and stoic endurance now seemed the South's only long-range hope.

But 1862 also brought painful lessons to the North. Confederate general J. E. B. Stuart executed a daring cavalry raid into Pennsylvania in October. Then on December 13, Union general Ambrose Burnside, now in command of the Army of the Potomac, unwisely ordered his soldiers to attack Lee's army, which held fortified positions on high ground at Fredericksburg, Virginia. Lee's men performed so efficiently in killing northerners that Lee was moved to say, "It is well that war is so terrible. We should grow too fond of it."

War Transforms the South

*T*he war caused tremendous disruptions in civilian life and altered southern society beyond all expectations. One of the first traditions to fall was the southern preference for local and limited government. States' rights had been a formative ideology for the Confederacy, but to withstand the massive power of the North, the South needed to centralize, as Jefferson Davis quickly recognized.

Promptly Davis moved to bring all arms, supplies, and troops under his control. But when the states failed

THE CONFEDERACY AND CENTRALIZATION to provide sufficient numbers of troops, Davis secured passage in April 1862 of the first national conscription (draft) law in American history. Davis also adopted firm leadership toward the Confederate Congress, which raised taxes and later passed a tax-in-kind—paid in farm products. When opposition arose, the government suspended the writ of habeas corpus (which prevented individuals from being held without trial) and imposed martial law. Despite Davis's unyielding stance, this tax system proved inadequate to the South's war effort.

Soon the Confederate administration in Richmond gained virtually complete control over the southern economy. Because it controlled the supply of labor through conscription, the administration could compel industry to work on government contracts and supply the military's needs. The Confederate Congress also gave the central government almost complete control of the railroads. A large bureaucracy sprang up to administer these operations. By the war's end, the southern bureaucracy was larger in proportion to population than its northern counterpart.

Historians have long argued over whether the Confederacy was a "rebellion," a "revolution," or

CONFEDERATE NATIONALISM the genuine creation of a "nation." Whatever label we apply, Confederates created a culture and an ideology of nationalism. In flags, songs, language, seals, school readers, and

■ In October 1862 in New York City, photographer Mathew Brady opened an exhibition of photographs from the Battle of Antietam. Although few knew it, Brady's vision was poor, and this photograph of Confederate dead was actually taken by his assistants, Alexander Gardner and James F. Gibson.   (Library of Congress)

other forms of "national characteristics," Confederates created their own story.

In its conservative crusade to preserve the social order and racial slavery and as a bulwark against centralized power, southerners believed the Confederacy was the true legacy of the American Revolution. Also central to Confederate nationalism was a refurbished defense of slavery as a benign, protective institution. And the idea of the "faithful slave" was key to southerners' nationalist cause.

In the face of defeat and devastation, forms of Confederate nationalism collapsed in the final year of the war. But much of the spirit and substance of Confederate nationalism would revive in the postwar period in a new ideology of the Lost Cause.

SOUTHERN CITIES AND INDUSTRY

Clerks and subordinate officials crowded the towns and cities where Confederate departments set up their offices. Clerks had always been males, but now "government girls" staffed the Confederate bureaucracy. The sudden population booms that resulted overwhelmed the housing supply and stimulated new construction. The pressure was especially great in Richmond, whose population increased 250 percent.

As the Union blockade disrupted imports of manufactured products, the traditionally agricultural South forged industries. Many planters shared Davis's hope that industrialization would bring "deliverance, full and unrestricted, from all commercial dependence" on the North or the rest of the world. Indeed, beginning almost from scratch, the Confederacy achieved tremendous feats of industrial development. The government also constructed new railroad lines, in many cases using as laborers slaves who had been relocated from farms and plantations.

CHANGING ROLES OF WOMEN

White women, restricted to narrow roles in antebellum society, gained substantial new responsibilities in wartime. The wives and mothers of soldiers now headed households and performed men's work. Women in nonslaveowning families cultivated fields themselves, while wealthier women suddenly had to perform as overseers and manage field work. In the cities, white women—who had been virtually excluded from the labor force—found a limited number of respectable paying jobs, and female schoolteachers appeared in the South for the first time. Some women gained confidence from their new responsibilities, but others resented their burdens. Many grew angry over shortages and resented cooking and unfamiliar contact with lower-class women.

HUMAN SUFFERING, HOARDING, AND INFLATION

For millions of ordinary southerners, change brought privation and suffering. Mass poverty descended for the first time on many yeoman families that had lost their breadwinners to the army. As a South Carolina newspaper put it, "The duties of war have called away from home the sole supports of many, many families. . . . Help must be given, or the poor will suffer." Women on their own sought help from relatives, neighbors, friends, anyone. Sometimes they pleaded their cases to the Confederate government.

The South was so sparsely populated in many places that the conscription of one skilled craftsman could work a hardship on the people of an entire county. Often they begged in unison for the exemption or discharge of the local miller, a wheelwright, or especially a blacksmith. As a petition from Alabama explained, "Our Section of County [is] left entirely Destitute of any man that is able to keep in order any kind of Farming Tules."

Inflation raged out of control, fueled by the Confederate government's heavy borrowing and inadequate taxes, until prices had increased almost 7,000 percent. Inflation particularly imperiled urban dwellers without their own sources of food. As early as 1861 and 1862, newspapers reported that "want and starvation are staring thousands in the face." Some families came to the aid of their neighbors, and "free markets," which disbursed goods as charity, sprang up in various cities. But hoarding worsened matters, and a rudimentary relief program organized by the Confederacy failed to meet the need.

INEQUITIES OF THE CONFEDERATE DRAFT

As their fortunes declined, people of once-modest means looked around and found abundant evidence that all classes were not sacrificing equally and that Confederate government policies favored the upper class. Until the last year of the war, for example, prosperous southerners could avoid military service by hiring substitutes. Well over 50,000 upper-class southerners did so. In October 1862, when the Confederate Congress exempted from military duty anyone who was supervising at least twenty slaves, protests poured in from every corner of the Confederacy, and North Carolina's legislators formally condemned the law. Its defenders argued, however, that the exemption preserved order and aided food production, and the statute remained on the books.

Dissension spread, and alert politicians and newspaper editors warned of class warfare. The bitterness of letters to Confederate officials suggests the depth of the people's anger. One woman swore to the secretary of war that unless help was provided to poverty-stricken wives and mothers, "an allwise god . . . will send down his fury . . . [on] those that are in power." War magnified existing social tensions in the Confederacy, and created a few new ones.

Wartime Northern Economy and Society

*W*ith the onset of war, change rolled over the North as well. The energies of an industrializing, capitalist society were harnessed to serve the cause of the Union, and the federal government and its executive branch gained new powers. Idealism and greed flourished together, and the northern economy proved its awesome productivity.

At first, the war was a shock to business. Northern firms lost their southern markets, and many

NORTHERN BUSINESS, INDUSTRY, AND AGRICULTURE

companies had to change their products and find new customers to remain open. Southern debts became uncollectible, jeopardizing not only northern merchants but also many western banks. In farming regions, families struggled with a shortage of labor caused by enlistments.

But certain entrepreneurs, such as wool producers, benefited from shortages of competing products, and soaring demand for war-related goods swept some businesses to new success. Secretary of War Edwin M. Stanton's list of the supplies needed by the Ordnance Department indicates the scope of government demand: "7,892 cannon, 11,787 artillery carriages, 4,022,130 small-arms, . . . 1,022,176,474 cartridges for small-arms, 1,220,555,435 percussion caps, . . . 26,440,054 pounds of gunpowder, . . . 90,416,295 pounds of lead." Stanton's list covered

only weapons; the government also purchased huge quantities of uniforms, boots, food, camp equipment, saddles, ships, and other necessities.

War aided some heavy industries in the North, especially iron and steel production. Although new railroad construction slowed, repairs caused increased manufacture of rails. Of considerable significance was the railroad industry's adoption of a standard gauge (width) for track, which eliminated the unloading and reloading of boxcars and created a unified transportation system.

The northern economy also grew because of a complementary relationship between agriculture and industry. Mechanization of agriculture had begun before the war. Wartime recruitment and conscription, however, gave western farmers an added incentive to purchase labor-saving machinery. The shift from human labor to machines created new markets for industry and expanded the food supply for the urban industrial work force. Mechanization in agriculture also meant that northern farm families whose breadwinners went to war did not suffer as much as did their counterparts in the South.

Northern industrial and urban workers did not fare as well. After the initial slump, jobs became plentiful, but inflation ate up much of a

NORTHERN WORKERS' MILITANCY

worker's paycheck. Between 1860 and 1864 consumer prices rose at least 76 percent, while daily wages rose only 42 percent. Workers' families consequently suffered a substantial decline in their standard of living.

As their real wages shrank, industrial workers lost job security. To increase production, some employers replaced workers with labor-saving machines. Other employers urged the government to promote immigration to secure cheap labor. Workers responded by forming unions and sometimes by striking. Skilled craftsmen organized to combat the loss of their jobs and status to machines; women and unskilled workers, who were excluded by the craftsmen, formed their own unions. Indeed, thirteen occupational groups—including tailors, coal miners, and railway engineers—formed national unions during the Civil War.

Hostile employers viewed labor activism as a threat to their freedom of action and accordingly formed statewide or craft-based associations to cooperate and pool information. They shared blacklists of union members and required new workers to sign "yellow dog" contracts (promises not to join a union). To put down strikes, they hired strikebreakers from among blacks, immigrants, and women, and sometimes they used federal troops to break unions.

Labor militance did not prevent employers from making profits or profiteering on government contracts. Unscrupulous businessmen took advantage of the suddenly immense demand for army supplies by selling clothing and blankets made of "shoddy"—wool fibers reclaimed from rags or worn cloth. Shoddy goods often came apart in the rain; most of the shoes purchased in the early months of the war were worthless. Contractors sold inferior guns for double the usual price and passed off tainted meat as good.

Legitimate enterprises also made healthy profits. The output of woolen mills increased so dramatically

ECONOMIC NATIONALISM AND GOVERNMENT-BUSINESS PARTNERSHIP

that dividends in the industry nearly tripled. Some cotton mills made record profits on what they sold, even though they reduced their output. Railroads carried immense quantities of freight and passengers, and railroad stocks skyrocketed in value.

Railroads also were a leading beneficiary of government largesse. With southerners absent from Congress, the northern route of the transcontinental railroad quickly prevailed. In 1862 and 1864 Congress chartered two corporations, the Union Pacific Railroad and the Central Pacific Railroad, and assisted them financially in connecting Omaha, Nebraska, with Sacramento, California. Overall, the two corporations gained approximately 20 million acres of land and nearly $60 million in loans.

Other businessmen benefited handsomely from the Morrill Land Grant Act (1862). To promote public education in agriculture, engineering, and military science, Congress granted each state 30,000 acres of federal land for each of its congressional districts. The law eventually fostered sixty-nine colleges and universities, but one of its immediate effects was to enrich a few prominent speculators.

Before the war, there was no adequate national banking, taxation, or currency. Banks operating under state charters issued no fewer than seven thousand different kinds of notes, which were difficult to distinguish from forgeries. During the war, Congress and the Treasury Department established a national

banking system empowered to issue national bank notes, and by 1865 most state banks were forced to join the national system. This process created a sounder currency, but also inflexibility in the money supply and an eastern-oriented financial structure.

In response to the war, the Republicans created an activist federal government. Indeed, with agricultural legislation, the land grant colleges, higher tariffs, and railroad subsidies, the federal government entered the economy forever.

Abraham Lincoln, like Jefferson Davis, found that war required active presidential leadership. At

EXPANSION OF PRESIDENTIAL POWER

the beginning of the conflict, Lincoln launched a major shipbuilding program without waiting for Congress to assemble. The lawmakers later approved his decision, and Lincoln continued to act in advance of Congress when he deemed such action necessary. In one striking exercise of executive power, Lincoln suspended the writ of habeas corpus for everyone living between Washington, D.C., and Philadelphia. Later in the war, with congressional approval, Lincoln repeatedly suspended habeas corpus and invoked martial law.

On occasion Lincoln used his wartime authority to bolster his own political fortunes. He and his generals proved adept at furloughing soldiers who usually voted Republican so they could vote in close elections.

In thousands of self-governing towns and communities, northern citizens felt a personal connection

THE UNION CAUSE

to representative government. Secession threatened to destroy their system, and northerners rallied to its defense. Secular and church leaders supported the cause, and in the first two years of the war, northern morale remained remarkably high.

But in the excitement of moneymaking, an eagerness to display one's wealth flourished in the largest cities. *Harper's Monthly* reported that "the suddenly enriched contractors, speculators, and stock-jobbers . . . are spending money with a profusion never before witnessed in our country." The *New York Herald* noted, "This war has entirely changed the American character. . . . The individual who makes the most money—no matter how—and spends the most—no matter for what—is considered the greatest man."

Yet idealism coexisted with ostentation. Abolitionists campaigned to turn the war into a crusade against slavery. Free black communities and churches, both black and white, responded to the needs of slaves who flocked to the Union lines, sending clothing, ministers, and teachers to aid the freed people.

Northern women, like their southern counterparts, took on new roles. Those who stayed home or-

NORTHERN
WOMEN ON
HOME FRONT
AND
BATTLEFRONT

ganized over ten thousand soldiers' aid societies, rolled bandages, and raised $3 million to aid injured troops. Women were instrumental in pressing for the first trained ambulance corps in the Union armies, and they formed the backbone of the U.S. Sanitary Commission, which provided crucial nutritional and medical aid to soldiers.

Approximately 3,200 women also served as nurses in frontline hospitals, where they pressed for better care of the wounded. Yet women had to fight for a chance to serve at all. The professionalization of medicine since the Revolution had created a medical system dominated by men, and many male physicians did not want women's aid. Even Clara Barton, famous for her persistence in working in the worst hospitals at the front, was ousted from her post in 1863.

The Advent of Emancipation

Despite the sense of loyalty to cause that animated soldiers and civilians on both sides, the governments of the United States and the Confederacy lacked clarity about the purpose of the war. Throughout the first several months of the struggle, both Davis and Lincoln studiously avoided references to slavery. Davis, realizing that emphasis on the issue could increase class conflict, told southerners that they were fighting for constitutional liberty.

Lincoln had his own reasons for not mentioning slavery. It was crucial at first not to antagonize the Union's border slave states, whose loyalty was tenuous. Also for many months, Lincoln hoped that a pro-Union majority would assert itself in the South. It might be possible, he thought, to coax the South back into the Union and stop the fighting. And not all Republicans burned with moral outrage over slavery. A forthright stand by Lincoln on the subject of slavery could split the party. No northern consensus on what to do about slavery existed early in the war.

Lincoln first broached the subject of slavery in a substantive way in March 1862, when he proposed

LINCOLN AND
EMANCIPATION

that the states consider emancipation on their own. He asked Congress to promise aid to any state that decided to emancipate, appealing especially to border state representatives. What Lincoln proposed was gradual emancipation, with compensation for slaveholders and colonization of the freed slaves outside the United States. To a delegation of free blacks, he explained that "it is better for us both . . . to be separated."

Until well into 1864, Lincoln's administration promoted an impractical scheme to colonize blacks in Central America or the Caribbean. Lincoln saw colonization as one option among others in dealing with the impending freedom of America's 4.2 million slaves.

Other politicians had different ideas. A group of Republicans in Congress, known as the Radicals,

CONFISCATION
ACTS

dedicated themselves to a war for emancipation. In August 1861, at the Radicals' instigation, Congress passed its first confiscation act. Designed to punish the Confederates, the law confiscated all property used for "insurrectionary purposes." Thus, if the South used slaves in a hostile action, those slaves were declared seized and liberated. A second confiscation act (July 1862) went much further: it confiscated the property of anyone who supported the rebellion, even those who merely resided in the South and paid Confederate taxes. Their slaves were declared "forever free of their servitude." These acts stemmed from the logic that to crush the southern rebellion, the government had to use extraordinary powers.

Lincoln refused to adopt that view in the summer of 1862. He stood by his proposal of voluntary gradual emancipation by the states and made no effort to enforce the second confiscation act. His stance provoked a public protest from Horace Greeley, editor of the powerful *New York Tribune*. In an open letter to the president entitled "The Prayer of Twenty Millions," Greeley pleaded with Lincoln to "execute the laws" and declared, "On the face of this wide earth, Mr. President, there is not one . . . intelligent champion of the Union cause who does not feel that all attempts to put down the Rebellion and at the same time uphold its inciting cause are preposterous and futile." Lincoln's reply was an explicit statement of his calculated approach to the question. "I would save the Union," announced Lincoln. "If I could save the Union without freeing any slave I would do it, and if I could save it by freeing all the slaves I would do it; and if I could save it by freeing some and leaving others alone I would also do that."

When he wrote those words, Lincoln had already decided to boldly issue a presidential Emancipation Proclamation. He was waiting, however, for a Union victory so that it would not appear to be an act of desperation.

On September 22, 1862, shortly after Union success at the Battle of Antietam, Lincoln issued the first

EMANCIPATION PROCLAMATION

part of his two-part proclamation. Invoking his powers as commander-in-chief of the armed forces, he announced that on January 1, 1863, he would emancipate the slaves in the states "in rebellion." Thus, his September proclamation was less a declaration of the right of slaves to be free than a threat to southerners: unless they put down their arms, they would lose their slaves. Lincoln had little expectation that southerners would give up their effort, but he was careful to offer them the option, thus trying to put the onus of emancipation on them.

In the fateful January 1 proclamation, Lincoln excepted (as areas in rebellion) every Confederate county or city that had fallen under Union control. Nor did Lincoln liberate slaves in the border slave states that remained in the Union. "The President has purposely made the proclamation inoperative in all places where . . . the slaves [are] accessible," charged the anti-administration *New York World*. "He has proclaimed emancipation only where he has notoriously no power to execute it."

But if as a legal document the Emancipation Proclamation was wanting, as a moral and political document, it had great meaning. Because the proclamation defined the war as a war against slavery, Radicals could applaud it, even if the president had not gone as far as Congress. Yet at the same time it protected Lincoln's position with conservatives, leaving him room to retreat if he chose and forcing no immediate changes on the border slave states.

Most important, though, thousands of slaves had already reached Union lines in various sections of the South. They had "voted with their feet" for emancipation, as many said, well before the proclamation. And now every advance of federal forces into slave society was a liberating step. This Lincoln knew in taking his own initially tentative, and then forthright, steps toward emancipation.

The need for men soon convinced the administration to recruit northern and southern blacks for the Union Army. By the spring of 1863, African American troops were answering the call of a dozen or more black recruiters barnstorming the cities and towns of the North. Lincoln came to see black soldiers as "the great available and yet unavailed of force for restoring the Union." African American leaders hoped military service would secure equal rights for their people. Once the black soldier had fought for the Union, wrote Frederick Douglass, "there is no power on earth which can deny that he has earned the right of citizenship in the United States."

In June 1864, on the eve of the Republican national convention, Lincoln called the party's chairman to the White House and instructed him to have the party "put into the platform as the keystone, the amendment of the Constitution abolishing and prohibiting slavery forever." The party promptly called for the Thirteenth Amendment. Lincoln demonstrated his commitment by lobbying Congress for quick approval of the measure. The proposed amendment passed in early 1865 and was sent to the states for ratification. The war to save the Union had also become the war to free the slaves.

It has long been debated whether Abraham Lincoln deserves the label "Great Emancipator." Was Lincoln

WHO FREED THE SLAVES?

ultimately a reluctant emancipator, following rather than leading Congress and public opinion? Or did he give essential presidential leadership to the most transformative and sensitive aspect of the war by going slow on emancipation, but once moving, never backpedaling on black freedom? Once Lincoln decided to prosecute the war to the unconditional surrender of the Confederates, he made the destruction of slavery central to the conflict's purpose.

Others have argued, however, that the slaves themselves are the central story in the achievement of their own freedom. When they were near enough to the war zones, they fled for their freedom by the thousands. Some worked as camp laborers for the Union armies, and eventually more than 180,000 black men served in the Union Army and Navy.

However freedom came to individuals, emancipation was a historical confluence of two essential forces: one, a policy directed by and dependent on the military authority of the president in his effort to win the war and two, the will and courage necessary for acts of self-emancipation.

Before the war was over, the Confederacy too addressed the issue of emancipation. Jefferson Davis

A CONFEDERATE PLAN OF EMANCIPATION

himself offered a proposal for black freedom of a kind. Late in the war, he was willing to sacrifice slavery to achieve independence. He proposed that the Confederate government purchase forty thousand slaves to work for the army as laborers, with a promise of freedom at the end of their service. Soon Davis upgraded the idea, calling for the recruitment and arming of slaves as soldiers to be freed at war's end. The wives and children of these soldiers, he made plain, must also receive freedom from the states.

Bitter debate over Davis's plan resounded through the Confederacy. When the Confederate Congress approved slave enlistments without the promise of freedom in March 1865, Davis insisted on more. He issued an executive order to guarantee that owners would emancipate slave soldiers and eventually their families.

The war ended before much could come of these desperate Confederate policy initiatives. By contrast, Lincoln's Emancipation Proclamation stimulated a vital infusion of forces into the Union armies. Before the war was over, 134,000 slaves (and 52,000 free blacks) had fought for freedom and the Union. Their participation was pivotal in victory.

The Soldiers' War

The intricacies of policymaking and social revolution were far from the minds of most ordinary soldiers. Military service completely altered their lives. Army life meant tedium, physical hardship, and separation from loved ones. Yet the military experience had powerful attractions as well. It molded men on both sides so thoroughly that they came to resemble one another far more than they resembled civilians back home. Many soldiers forged amid war a bond with their fellows and a connection to a noble purpose that they cherished for years afterward.

Soldiers benefited from certain new products, such as canned condensed milk, but blankets, clothing,

HOSPITALS AND CAMP LIFE

and arms were often of poor quality. Hospitals were badly managed at first. Rules of hygiene in large camps were scarcely enforced; latrines were poorly made or carelessly used. Water supplies were unsafe and typhoid epidemics common. About 57,000 men died from dysentery and diarrhea; in fact, 224,000 Union troops died from disease or accidents compared with 140,000 who died as a result of battle.

On both sides, troops quickly learned that soldiering was far from glorious. Before the war, few had seen violent death. Now the war exposed them to the blasted bodies of their friends and comrades. "Any one who goes over a battlefield after a battle," wrote one Confederate, "never cares to go over another. . . . It is a sad sight to see the dead and if possible more sad to see the wounded—shot in every possible way you can imagine." Much of the carnage resulted from tactics that made little sense. Still, Civil War soldiers developed deep commitments to each other and to their task. When at last the war was over, "it seemed like breaking up a family to separate," one man observed.

Online Study Center Improve Your Grade
Primary Source: Heat of Battle from the
Southern Soldier's Perspective

Advances in technology made the Civil War particularly deadly. By far the most important were the rifle

THE RIFLED MUSKET

and the "minie ball." Bullets fired from a smoothbore musket tumbled and wobbled as they flew through the air and thus were not accurate at distances over 80 yards. Cutting spiraled grooves inside the barrel gave the projectile a spin and much greater accuracy after Frenchman Claude Minie and the American James Burton developed a new kind of bullet. Civil War bullets were sizable lead slugs with a cavity at the bottom that expanded on firing so that the bullet "took" the rifling and flew accurately. With these bullets, rifles were accurate at 400 yards and useful up to 1,000 yards.

This meant that soldiers assaulting a position defended by riflemen were in greater peril than ever before. Although Civil War rifles were cumbersome to load, advancing soldiers were repeatedly exposed to accurate rifle fire. Because medical knowledge was rudimentary, even minor wounds often led to amputation and to death through infection. Never before in Europe or America had such massive forces pummeled each other with weapons of such destructive power.

At the outset of the war, racism in the Union Army was strong. Most white soldiers wanted noth-

THE BLACK SOLDIER'S FIGHT FOR MANHOOD

ing to do with black people and regarded them as inferior. "I never came out here for to free the black devils," wrote one soldier. For many, acceptance of black troops grew only because they could do heavy labor and "stop Bullets as well as white people."

But among some, a change occurred. White officers who volunteered to lead black units only to gain promotion found that the experience altered their opinions. After just one month with black troops, a white captain informed his wife, "I have a more elevated opinion of their abilities than I ever had before. I know that many of them are vastly the superiors of those . . . who would condemn them all to a life of brutal degradation." One general reported that his "colored regiments" possessed "remarkable aptitude for military training." Another observer said, "They fight like fiends."

Black troops created this change through their own dedication. They had a mission to destroy slavery and demonstrate their equality. Corporal James Henry Gooding of Massachusetts's black Fifty-fourth Regiment explained that his unit intended "to live down all prejudice against its color, by a determination to do well in any position it is put." After an engagement, he was proud that "a regiment of white men gave us three cheers as we were passing them," because "it shows that we did our duty as men should."

African American soldiers displayed courage despite persistent discrimination. Off-duty black soldiers were sometimes attacked by northern mobs; on duty, they did most of the heavy labor. The Union government, moreover, paid white privates $13 per month plus a clothing allowance of $3.50, whereas black privates earned only $10 per month less $3 for clothing. Congress eventually remedied the inequity. In this instance, at least, the majority of legislators agreed with a white private that black troops had

"proved their title to manhood on many a bloody field fighting freedom's battles."

1863: The Tide of Battle Turns

The fighting in the spring and summer of 1863 did not settle the war, but it began to suggest the outcome. The campaigns began in a deceptively positive way for Confederates, as their Army of Northern Virginia performed brilliantly in battles in central Virginia.

On May 2 and 3, west of Fredericksburg, Virginia, some 130,000 members of the Union Army of the Po-

BATTLE OF CHANCELLORSVILLE

tomac bore down on fewer than 60,000 Confederates. Boldly, Lee and Stonewall Jackson divided their forces, ordering 30,000 men under Jackson on a day-long march westward for a flank attack. Jackson's seasoned "foot cavalry" found unprepared Union troops laughing, smoking, and playing cards. The Confederate attack drove the entire right side of the Union Army back in confusion. However, as Jackson and a few officers returned at twilight from reconnoitering, southern troops mistook them for federals and fired, fatally wounding their commander. The next day, Union forces left in defeat. Chancellorsville was a remarkable southern victory but costly for the loss of Stonewall Jackson.

July brought crushing defeats for the Confederacy in two critical battles—Vicksburg and Gettysburg—

SIEGE OF VICKSBURG

that severely damaged Confederate hopes for independence. Vicksburg was a vital western citadel, the last major fortification on the Mississippi River in southern hands. After months of searching through swamps and bayous, General Ulysses S. Grant found an advantageous approach to the city. He laid siege to Vicksburg in May, bottling up the defending forces. If Vicksburg fell, Union forces would control the river, cutting the Confederacy in two and gaining an open path into its interior. Meanwhile, General Lee launched a Confederate invasion of the North.

As Lee's emboldened army advanced through western Maryland and into Pennsylvania, Confederate prospects along the Mississippi darkened. Davis repeatedly wired General Joseph E. Johnston, urging him to concentrate his forces and attack Grant's army.

Johnston, however, did little. Grant's men, meanwhile, were supplying themselves from the abundant crops of the Mississippi River valley and could continue their siege indefinitely.

In such circumstances, the fall of Vicksburg was inevitable, and on July 4, 1863, its commander surrendered. The same day, a battle that had been raging for three days concluded at Gettysburg, Pennsylvania (Map 15.1). On July 1, Confederate forces hunting for a supply of shoes had collided with part of the Union Army. After heavy fighting on the second day, federal forces occupied high ground along Cemetery Ridge, enjoying the protection of a stone wall and a clear view of their foe across almost a mile of open field.

BATTLE OF GETTYSBURG

Undaunted, Lee believed his reinforced troops could break the Union line, and on July 3 he ordered a direct assault. General James Longstreet warned Lee that "no 15,000 men ever arrayed for battle can take that position." But Lee stuck to his plan. Virginians under General George E. Pickett and North Carolinians under General James Pettigrew methodically marched up the slope in a doomed assault known as Pickett's Charge. For a moment, a few hundred Confederates breached the enemy's line, but most fell in heavy slaughter. On July 4, Lee had to withdraw, his army having suffered almost 28,000 casualties.

Southern troops displayed unforgettable courage and dedication at Gettysburg, as did the Union Army, which suffered 23,000 casualties (nearly one-quarter of the force), under General George G. Meade. But the results there and at Vicksburg were disastrous for the South. The Confederacy was split in two, and its heartland lay exposed to invasion. Lee's defeat spelled the end of major southern offensive actions. Too weak to prevail in attack, the Confederacy henceforth would have to conserve its limited resources and rely on a prolonged defense.

Map 15.1   Battle of Gettysburg

In the war's greatest battle, fought around a small market town in southern Pennsylvania, Lee's invasion of the North was repulsed. Union forces had the advantage of high ground, shorter lines, and superior numbers. The casualties for the two armies—dead, wounded, and missing—exceeded 50,000 men.

Disunity, South, North, and West

Both northern and southern governments waged the final two years of the war in the face of increasing opposition at home. The gigantic costs of a civil war that neither side seemed able to win fed the unrest. But protest also arose from fundamental stresses in the social structures of North and South.

The Confederacy's problems were both more serious and more deeply rooted than the North's. One ominous development was the planters' increasing opposition to their own government. Not only did the Richmond government impose new taxes, but Confederate military authorities also impressed

DISINTEGRATION OF CONFEDERATE UNITY

slaves to build fortifications. And when Union forces advanced on plantation areas, Confederate commanders burned stores of cotton that lay in the enemy's path. Such interference with plantation routines and financial interests was not what planters had expected of their government, and they complained bitterly.

Nor were the centralizing policies of the Davis administration popular. The increasing size and power of the Richmond government startled and alarmed planters. The Confederate constitution had in fact granted substantial powers to the central government, especially in time of war. But many planters had assumed with R. B. Rhett, editor of the *Charleston Mercury,* that the Confederate constitution "leaves the States untouched in their Sovereignty, and commits to the Confederate Government only a few simple objects, and a few simple powers to enforce them."

Years of opposition to the federal government within the Union had frozen southerners in a defensive posture. Now they erected the barrier of states' rights as a defense against change. Planters sought, above all, a guarantee that their plantations and their lives would remain untouched. As secession revolutionized their world, many were not fully committed to the cause.

For ordinary southerners, hunger and suffering were becoming a reality. Food riots occurred in the

Food Riots in Southern Cities

spring of 1863 in Atlanta, Macon, Columbus, and Augusta, Georgia, and in Salisbury and High Point, North Carolina. On April 2 a crowd assembled in Richmond to demand relief. A passerby, noticing the excitement, asked a young girl, "Is there some celebration?" "We celebrate our right to live," replied the girl. "We are starving. As soon as enough of us get together we are going to the bakeries and each of us will take a loaf of bread." Soon they did just that, sparking a riot that Jefferson Davis himself had to quell at gunpoint.

Throughout the rural South, ordinary people resisted more quietly—by refusing to cooperate with conscription, tax collection, and impressments of food. "In all the States impressments are evaded by every means which ingenuity can suggest, and in some openly resisted," wrote a high-ranking commissary officer. Conscription officers increasingly found

no one to draft. "The disposition to avoid military service is general," observed a Georgia senator in 1864.

Such discontent was certain to affect the Confederate armies. Worried about their loved ones and resentful of what they saw as a rich

Desertions from the Confederate Army

man's war, large numbers of men deserted. The problem became especially acute after 1862. In mid-1863 it was estimated that 40,000 to 50,000 troops were absent without leave and that 100,000 were evading duty in some way. By November 1863 Secretary of War James Seddon admitted that one-third of the army could not be accounted for.

The defeats at Gettysburg and Vicksburg dealt a heavy blow to Confederate morale. In desperation, President Davis and several state governors resorted to threats and racial scare tactics to drive southern whites to further sacrifice. Despite such tactics, the internal disintegration of the Confederacy quickened. A few newspapers even began to call openly for peace.

In North Carolina a peace movement grew under the leadership of William W. Holden, a popular Dem-

Antiwar Sentiment, South and North

ocratic politician and editor. Over one hundred public meetings took place in the summer of 1863 in support of peace negotiations. In Georgia early in 1864, Governor Joseph E. Brown and Alexander H. Stephens, vice president of the Confederacy, led a similar effort. Ultimately these movements came to naught. Politically, the lack of a two-party system allowed any criticism of the government to be colored with the taint of dishonor and disloyalty.

But by 1864, much of the opposition to the war had moved entirely outside the political sphere. Southerners were simply giving up the struggle and withdrawing their cooperation from the government. Deserters dominated whole towns and counties. Secret societies favoring reunion sprang up. Active dissent was particularly common in upland and mountain regions. The government was losing the support of its citizens.

In the North, opposition to the war was similar but less severe. Alarm intensified over the growing centralization of government, and by 1863, war-weariness was widespread. Resentment of the draft sparked protest, especially among poor citizens, and the Union Army struggled with a desertion rate as high as the Confederates'. But the Union was so much richer than the South in human resources that fresh recruits were always available.

Also, Lincoln possessed a talent that Davis lacked: he knew how to stay in touch with the ordinary citizen. Through letters to newspapers and to soldiers' families, he reached the common people and demonstrated that he had not forgotten them. The daily carnage, the tortuous political problems, and the ceaseless criticism weighed heavily on him. But this self-educated man of humble origins was able to communicate his suffering with words that helped contain northern discontent.

Much of the wartime protest in the North was political in origin. The Democratic Party fought to regain power by blaming Lincoln for the war's death toll, the expansion of federal powers, inflation and the high tariff, and the emancipation of blacks. Appealing to tradition, its leaders called for an end to the war and reunion on the basis of "the Constitution as it is and the Union as it was." The Democrats denounced conscription and martial law and defended states' rights. In the 1862 congressional elections, the Democrats made a strong comeback, and peace Democrats, who would go much further than others in the party to end the war, had influence in New York State and majorities in the legislatures of Illinois and Indiana.

PEACE DEMOCRATS

Led by outspoken men like Representative Clement L. Vallandigham of Ohio, the peace Democrats made themselves highly visible. Vallandigham criticized Lincoln as a dictator who had suspended the writ of habeas corpus without congressional authority and had arrested thousands of innocent citizens. He condemned both conscription and emancipation. Vallandigham stayed carefully within legal bounds, but his attacks seemed so damaging to the war effort that military authorities arrested him for treason. Lincoln wisely decided against punishment—and martyr's status—for the Ohioan and exiled him to the Confederacy.

Lincoln believed that antiwar Democrats were linked to secret traitorous organizations that encouraged draft resistance, discouraged enlistment, sabotaged communications, and plotted to aid the Confederacy. Likening such groups to a poisonous snake, Republicans sometimes branded them—and by extension the peace Democrats—as "Copperheads." Although some Confederate agents were active in the North and Canada, they never genuinely threatened the Union war effort.

More violent opposition to the government arose from ordinary citizens facing the draft, which became law in 1863. Under the law, a draftee could stay at home by providing a substitute or paying a $300 commutation fee. Many wealthy men, and some of modest means, chose these options, and in response to popular demand, clubs, cities, and states provided the money for others to escape conscription. The urban poor and immigrants in strongly Democratic areas were especially hostile to conscription. The poor viewed the commutation fee as discriminatory, and many immigrants suspected (wrongly, on the whole) that they were called in disproportionate numbers.

NEW YORK CITY DRAFT RIOTS

As a result, there were scores of disturbances and melees. Enrolling officers received rough treatment, and riots occurred in many states from New Jersey to Wisconsin. By far the most serious outbreak of violence was in July 1863 in New York City, a Democratic stronghold where racial, ethnic, and class tensions ran high. Working-class New Yorkers feared an inflow of black labor from the South and regarded blacks as the cause of the war. Poor Irish workers resented having to serve in the place of others who could afford to avoid the draft. When these tensions erupted, seventy-four people died during three days of rioting. Blacks became the special target of rioters, who rampaged through African American neighborhoods, beating residents and destroying an orphan asylum.

A civil war of another kind raged on the Great Plains and in the Southwest. By 1864 U.S. troops under Colonel John Chivington waged full-scale war against the Sioux, Arapahos, and Cheyennes to eradicate Indian title to all of eastern Colorado. Indian chiefs sought peace, but American commanders had orders to "burn villages and kill Cheyennes whenever and wherever found." A Cheyenne chief, Black Kettle, was told by the U.S. command his

WAR AGAINST INDIANS IN THE FAR WEST

people would find a safe haven by moving to Sand Creek, Colorado. But on November 29, 1864, 700 cavalrymen, many drunk, attacked the Cheyenne village. With most of the men absent hunting, 105 Cheyenne women and children and 28 men were slaughtered.

In New Mexico and Arizona Territories, the Apaches and the Navajos had for generations raided the Pueblo Indians and Hispanic peoples of the region. During the Civil War years, Anglo-American farms also became Indian targets. In 1863 the New Mexico Volunteers, commanded by former mountain man Kit Carson, defeated the Mescalero Apaches and forced them onto the Bosque Redondo Reservation.

The area's Navajos resisted from the canyons and high deserts where they lived. After Carson carried out a "scorched earth" campaign against them, three-quarters of the twelve thousand Navajos were rounded up in 1864 and forced to march 400 miles (the "Long Walk") to Bosque Redondo, suffering malnutrition and death along the way. Permitted to return to a fraction of their homelands later that year, the Navajos carried with them searing memories of the federal government's ruthless policies toward Indian peoples.

Back east, war-weariness reached a peak in the summer of 1864, when the Democratic Party nomi-

ELECTION OF 1864

nated the popular General George B. McClellan for president, inserted a peace plank into its platform, and made racist appeals to white insecurity. Lincoln concluded that it was "exceedingly probable that this Administration will not be reelected." Although relatively unified, the Republican Party faced the horrible casualty lists and battlefield stalemate of summer 1864.

The fortunes of war soon changed the electoral situation. With the fall of Atlanta and Union victories in the Shenandoah valley by early September, Lincoln's prospects rose. Decisive in the election was that Lincoln won an extraordinary 78 percent of the soldier vote. With the president taking 55 percent of the total popular vote, Lincoln's reelection—a referendum on the war and emancipation—had a devastating impact on southern morale. Without this political outcome in 1864, a Union military victory may never have been possible.

1864–1865: The Final Test of Wills

uring the final year of the war, the Confederates could still have won their version of victory if military stalemate and northern antiwar sentiment had forced a negotiated settlement to end the war. But events and northern determination prevailed.

From the outset, the North had pursued one paramount diplomatic goal: to prevent recognition of

NORTHERN DIPLOMATIC STRATEGY

the Confederacy by European nations. Foreign recognition would belie Lincoln's claim to be fighting an illegal rebellion and would open the way to financial and military aid. Both England and France stood to benefit from a divided and weakened America. Thus, to achieve their goal, Lincoln and Secretary of State William H. Seward needed to avoid both serious military defeats and controversies with the European powers.

Aware that the textile industry employed one-fifth of the British population directly or indirectly, southerners banked on British recognition of the Confederacy. But at the beginning of the war, British mills had a 50 percent surplus of cotton on hand, and later they found new sources of supply in India, Egypt, and Brazil. Refusing to be stampeded into recognition of the Confederacy, the British government kept its eye on the battlefield. France, though sympathetic to the South, was unwilling to act independent of Britain.

More than once, the Union strategy nearly broke down. An acute crisis occurred in 1861 when the overzealous commander of an American frigate stopped the British steamer *Trent* and removed two Confederate ambassadors. The British interpreted this action as a violation of freedom of the seas and demanded the prisoners' release. Lincoln and Seward waited until northern public opinion cooled and then released the two southerners.

Then the sale to the Confederacy of warships constructed in England sparked vigorous U.S. protest. A few English-built ships, notably the *Alabama,* reached open water to serve the South. Over twenty-two months, the *Alabama* destroyed or captured more than sixty Union ships.

The Civil War in Britain

Because of the direct reliance of the British textile industry on cut-off southern cotton, as well as the many ideological and familial ties between the two nations, the American Civil War was decisive in Britain's economy and domestic politics. The British aristocracy and most cotton mill owners were solidly pro-Confederate and proslavery, while a combination of clergymen, shopkeepers, artisans, and radical politicians worked for the causes of Union and emancipation. Most British workers saw their futures at stake in a war for slave emancipation. "Freedom" to the huge British working class (who could not vote) meant basic political and civil rights, and the "cotton famine" threw millhands out of work.

English aristocrats saw Americans as untutored, wayward cousins and took satisfaction in America's troubles. Conservatives believed in the superiority of the British system of government and looked askance at America's leveling tendencies. And some aristocratic British Liberals also saw Americans through their class bias and sympathized with the Confederacy's demand for "order" and independence. English racism also intensified in these years, exemplified by the popularity of minstrelsy and the employment of science in racial theory.

The intensity of the British debate over the American conflict is evident in the huge public meetings organized by both sides with cheering and jeering, competing banners, carts and floats, orators and resolutions. In a press war, the British argued over whether rebellion or secession was justified or legal, whether slavery was at the heart of the conflict, and especially over the democratic image of America. This bitter debate over America's trial became a test over reform in Britain: those eager for a broadened franchise and increased democracy were pro-Union, and those who preferred to preserve Britain's class-ridden political system favored the Confederacy.

In the end, the British government did not recognize the Confederacy, and by 1864, the English cotton lords had found new sources in Egypt and India. But in this link between America and its English roots, the Civil War was a transformation of international significance.

Some southern leaders pronounced that cotton was "king" and would bring Britain to their cause. This British cartoon shows King Cotton brought down in chains by the American eagle, anticipating the cotton famine to follow and the intense debate in Great Britain over the nature and meaning of the American Civil War. (The Granger Collection)

On the battlefield, the northern victory was far from won in 1864. General Nathaniel Banks's Red

BATTLEFIELD STALEMATE AND A UNION STRATEGY FOR VICTORY

River campaign, designed to capture more of Louisiana and Texas, quickly fell apart, and the capture of Mobile Bay in August did not cause the fall of Mobile. Union general William Tecumseh Sherman commented that the North had to "keep the war South until they are not only ruined, exhausted, but humbled in pride and spirit."

Military authorities throughout history have agreed that deep invasion is highly risky: the farther an army penetrates enemy territory, the more vulnerable are its own communications and supply lines. General Grant, by now in command of all the federal armies, decided to test this assertion—and southern will—with a strategic innovation of his own: raids on a massive scale. Grant proposed to use whole armies to destroy Confederate railroads, thus ruining the enemy's transportation and damaging the South's economy. Abandoning their lines of support, Union troops would live off the land while laying waste all resources useful to the military and to the civilian population. After General George H. Thomas's troops won the Battle of Chattanooga in November 1863 by ignoring orders and charging up Missionary Ridge, the heartland of Georgia lay open. Grant entrusted General Sherman with 100,000 men for an invasion deep into the South, toward the rail center of Atlanta.

Jefferson Davis countered by positioning the army of General Joseph E. Johnston in Sherman's

FALL OF ATLANTA

path. Davis hoped that southern resolve would lead to Lincoln's defeat and the election of a president who would sue for peace. When General Johnston slowly but steadily fell back toward Atlanta, Davis grew anxious and sought assurances that Atlanta would be held. From a purely military point of view, Johnston maneuvered skillfully, but when he continued to retreat, Davis replaced him with the one-legged General John Hood, who knew his job was to fight. Hood attacked but was beaten, and Sherman's army occupied Atlanta on September 2, 1864. The victory buoyed northern spirits, ensured Lincoln's reelection, and cleared the way for Sherman's march from Atlanta to the sea (see Map 15.2).

Sherman's army was an unusually formidable force, composed almost entirely of battle-tested vet-

SHERMAN'S MARCH TO THE SEA

erans, tanned, bearded, tough, and unkempt, who were determined, as one put it, "to Conquer this Rebelien or Die." As Sherman's men moved across Georgia, they cut a path 50 to 60 miles wide and more than 200 miles long. The destruction they caused was awesome. A Georgia woman described the "Burnt Country" this way: "The fields were trampled down and the road was lined with carcasses of horses, hogs, and cattle that the invaders, unable either to consume or to carry with them, had wantonly shot down to starve our people. . . . The stench in some places was unbearable." Such devastation sapped the South's will to resist. Indeed, the lack of popular resistance in Georgia and South Carolina indicated that southern whites had lost the will to continue the struggle.

Online Study Center Improve Your Grade
Interactive Map: Grant's Campaign Against Lee

In Virginia, too, the path to victory proved protracted and ghastly. Throughout the spring and sum-

VIRGINIA'S BLOODY SOIL

mer of 1864, intent on capturing Richmond, Grant hurled his troops at Lee's army in Virginia and suffered appalling losses: almost 18,000 casualties in the Battle of the Wilderness, more than 8,000 at Spotsylvania, and 12,000 in the space of a few hours at Cold Harbor.

Before the assault at Cold Harbor (which Grant later admitted was a grave mistake), Union troops pinned scraps of paper bearing their names and addresses to their backs, certain they would be mowed down as they rushed Lee's trenches. In four weeks in May and June, Grant lost as many men as were enrolled in Lee's entire army. Though costly, and testing northern morale to its limits, these battles prepared the way for eventual victory: Lee's army shrank until offensive action was no longer possible, while Grant's army kept replenishing its forces with new recruits.

The end finally came in the spring of 1865. From its trenches besieging Petersburg, Grant's army kept

SURRENDER AT APPOMATTOX

battering Lee, who tried but failed to break through the Union line. With the numerical superiority of Grant's army now greater than two to one, Confederate defeat was

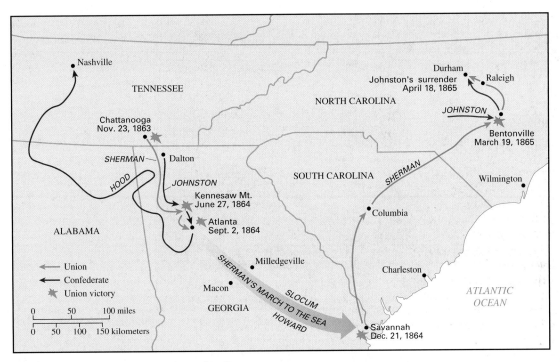

Map 15.2   Sherman's March to the Sea

The West proved a decisive theater at the end of the war. From Chattanooga, Union forces drove into Georgia, capturing Atlanta. Following the fall of Atlanta, General Sherman embarked on his march of destruction through Georgia to the coast and then northward through the Carolinas.

inevitable. On April 2 Lee abandoned Richmond and Petersburg. On April 9, hemmed in by Union troops, short of rations, and with fewer than thirty thousand men left, Lee surrendered at Appomattox Court House. Grant treated his rival with respect and paroled the defeated troops. The war was over at last. Within weeks, Confederate forces under Johnston surrendered, and Davis was captured in Georgia.

With Lee's surrender, Lincoln knew that the Union had been preserved, yet he lived to see but a few days of the war's aftermath. On the evening of Good Friday, April 14, he accompanied his wife to Ford's Theatre in Washington to enjoy a popular comedy. There, John Wilkes Booth, an embittered southern sympathizer, shot the president in the head at point-blank range. The Union had lost its wartime leader, and millions publicly mourned the martyred chief executive. Relief at the war's end mingled

hauntingly with a renewed sense of loss and anxiety about the future.

Property damage and financial costs were enormous, though difficult to tally. U.S. loans and taxes during the conflict totaled almost $3 billion, and interest on the war debt was $2.8 billion. The Confederacy borrowed over $2 billion but lost far more in the destruction of homes, crops, livestock, and other property. In southern war zones, the landscape was desolated. Over wide regions, fences and crops were destroyed; houses, barns, and bridges burned; and fields abandoned and left to erode. Factories had been looted, and two-thirds of the South's railroad system was out of service.

FINANCIAL TALLY

Estimates of the total cost of the war exceed $20 billion—five times the total expenditures of the federal government from its creation to 1861. By 1865

■ The death of President Lincoln caused a vast outpouring of grief in the North. As this Currier and Ives print shows, Lincoln's funeral train stopped at several cities on its way to Illinois to allow local services to be held.   (Anne S. K. Brown Military Collection, Brown University Library)

the federal government's spending had soared to twenty times the prewar level and accounted for over 26 percent of the gross national product. Many of these changes were more or less permanent, as wartime measures left the government deeply involved in manufacturing, banking, and transportation. If southerners had hoped to remove government from the economy, the war had now irrepressibly bound them together.

The human costs of the Civil War were staggering. The total number of military casualties on both sides exceeded 1 million—a frightful toll

DEATH TOLL

for a nation of 31 million people. Approximately 360,000 Union soldiers died. Another 275,175 were wounded. On the Confederate side, an estimated 260,000 lost their lives, and almost as many suffered wounds. More men died in the Civil War than in all other American wars combined until Vietnam.

Summary   *Online Study Center* ACE the Test

The Civil War altered American society forever. During the war, women in both North and South took on new roles. Industrialization and large economic enterprises grew in power. The character and extent of government power changed markedly. Under Republican leadership, the federal government had expanded its power not only to preserve the Union but also to extend freedom. A social revolution and government authority emancipated the slaves. A republic desperately divided against itself had survived, but in new constitutional forms yet to take shape during Reconstruction.

In the West, two civil wars raged, the second resulting in conquest of southwestern Indians by U.S. troops and land-hungry settlers. On the diplomatic front, the Union government had delicately managed to keep Great Britain and other foreign powers out of the war. Dissent flourished in both North and South, playing a crucial role in the ultimate collapse of the Confederacy, while the Union cause was only marginally affected.

It was unclear how or whether the nation would use its power to protect the rights of the former slaves. Secession was dead, but whether Americans would continue to embrace a centralized nationalism remained to be seen. How would white southerners, embittered and impoverished, respond to efforts to reconstruct the nation? How would the country care for the maimed, the orphans, the farming women without men to work their land, and all the dead who had to be found and properly buried? What would be the place of black men and women in American life? In the Civil War, Americans had undergone a transformation like nothing before in their history. The war and all its drama, sacrifice, and social and political changes left a compelling memory in American hearts and minds for generations.

LEGACY FOR A PEOPLE AND A NATION
The Confederate Battle Flag

The most widespread and controversial symbol to emerge from the Civil War era is the Confederate flag. Rather than the official flag of the Confederacy, it was a flag that soldiers carried to mark the center of a unit's position in the confusion of combat. Over time, this flag has taken on powerful emotional meanings.

At Confederate veterans' reunions and parades from the 1870s to well into the twentieth century, the flag was an emblem of the South's Lost Cause. Increasingly, Confederate remembrance merged with white supremacy at the turn of the twentieth century, and African Americans resented the flag.

In the late 1940s the flag became a fixture of popular culture with heightened racial meanings. In 1948 it was a symbol of the States' Rights ("Dixiecrat") Party. By the 1950s, waving the Confederate flag expressed defiance among southern whites against the civil rights revolution.

This flag is a loaded symbol that can be interpreted in opposite ways. Some southern whites argue that it is merely a marker of regional pride and identity. But to most blacks and many whites, it expresses racism. Some claim it represents the "nobility" of southern military tradition; others conclude that it stands for the hatred embodied in the Ku Klux Klan.

In recent times, the Confederate flag has been the center of legal and political disputes emanating from city councils, high schools, and universities over public and private uses of the flag. Most visible of all have been the debates in Georgia, South Carolina, Alabama, and Mississippi over whether to cease flying the Confederate flag at official sites or as part of state flags. At issue are important questions: free speech, equal protection under law, perception versus reality, official government endorsement of collective symbols, the significance of race and racism in our national memory, and the meaning of the Civil War itself.

ℛ ECONSTRUCTION: AN UNFINISHED REVOLUTION 1865–1877

𝒶 fter a prolonged Union bombardment, the lower half of Charleston, South Carolina, the seedbed of secession, lay burning and in ruin when most of the white population evacuated on February 18, 1865. Among the first Union troops to enter Charleston was the Twenty-first U.S. Colored Regiment, which received the surrender of the city from its mayor. In symbolic celebrations, black Charlestonians, most of whom were former slaves, proclaimed their freedom and announced their rebirth.

Still, in Charleston, as elsewhere, death demanded attention. During the final year of the war, the Confederates had converted the planters' Race Course, a horseracing track, into a prison, where Union soldiers were kept in terrible conditions without shelter. The 257 who died of exposure and disease were buried in a mass grave behind the judges' stand. After the fall of the city, Charleston's blacks organized to create a proper burial ground for the Union dead. During April, more than twenty black workmen reinterred the dead in marked graves.

Then, on the morning of May 1, 1865, a procession of ten thousand people marched around the planters' Race Course, led by three thousand children carrying armloads of roses and singing "John Brown's Body." They were followed by black women and men, members of black and white Union regiments, and white missionaries and teachers. All who could fit assembled at the gravesite; five black ministers read from Scripture, and a black children's choir sang. When the ceremony ended, the large crowd retired to the Race Course for speeches, picnics, and military festivities.

The war was over in Charleston, and "Decoration Day"—now Memorial Day, the day to remember the war dead and decorate their graves—had been founded by African Americans. Black people had created an American tradition. In their vision, they were creating the Independence Day of a Second American Revolution.

Online Study Center
This icon will direct you to interactive map and primary source activities on the website
http://college.hmco.com/ pic/nortonbrief7e

C H R O N O L O G Y

1865 • Johnson begins rapid and lenient Reconstruction
- Confederate leaders regain power
- White southern governments pass restrictive black codes
- Congress refuses to seat southern representatives
- Thirteenth Amendment ratified, abolishing slavery

1866 • Congress passes Civil Rights Act and renewal of Freedmen's Bureau over Johnson's veto
- Congress approves Fourteenth Amendment
- Most southern states reject Fourteenth Amendment
- In *Ex parte Milligan* the Supreme Court reasserts its influence

1867 • Congress passes Reconstruction Acts and Tenure of Office Act
- Seward arranges purchase of Alaska
- Constitutional conventions called in southern states

1868 • House impeaches Johnson; Senate acquits him
- Most southern states readmitted to the Union under Radical plan
- Fourteenth Amendment ratified
- Grant elected president

1869 • Congress approves Fifteenth Amendment (ratified in 1870)

1871 • Congress passes second Enforcement Act and Ku Klux Klan Act

1872 • Amnesty Act frees almost all remaining Confederates from restrictions on holding office
- Grant reelected

1873 • *Slaughter-House* cases limit power of Fourteenth Amendment
- Panic of 1873 leads to widespread unemployment and labor strife

1874 • Democrats win majority in House of Representatives

1875 • Several Grant appointees indicted for corruption
- Congress passes weak Civil Rights Act
- Democratic Party increases control of southern states with white supremacy campaigns

1876 • *U.S. v. Cruikshank* further weakens Fourteenth Amendment
- Presidential election disputed

1877 • Congress elects Hayes president
- "Home rule" returns to three remaining southern states not yet controlled by Democrats; Reconstruction considered over

Reconstruction would bring revolutionary circumstances, but revolutions can go backward. The Civil War and its aftermath wrought unprecedented changes in American society, law, and politics, but the underlying realities of economic power, racism, and judicial conservatism limited Reconstruction's revolutionary potential.

Nowhere was the turmoil of Reconstruction more evident than in national politics. Lincoln's successor, Andrew Johnson, fought bitterly with Congress over the shaping of Reconstruction policies. Though a southerner, Johnson had always been a foe of the South's wealthy planters, and his first acts as president suggested that he would be tough on "traitors." Before the end of 1865, however, Johnson's policies changed direction. Jefferson Davis stayed in prison for two years, but Johnson quickly pardoned other rebel leaders and allowed them to occupy high offices. He also ordered the return of plantations to their original owners.

Johnson imagined a lenient and rapid "restoration" of the South to the Union rather than the fundamental "reconstruction" that Republican congressmen favored. Between 1866 and 1868, the president and the Republican leadership in Congress engaged in a bitter power struggle over how to put the United States back together again. Before it ended, Congress had impeached the president, enfranchised the freedmen, and given them a role in reconstructing the South. The nation also adopted the Fourteenth and Fifteenth Amendments. But little was done to open the doors of economic opportunity to black southerners. Moreover, by 1869, the Ku Klux Klan employed extensive terror to thwart Reconstruction and undermine black freedom.

As the 1870s advanced, industrial growth accelerated, creating new opportunities and priorities. The West, with its seemingly limitless potential and its wars against Indians, drew American resources and consciousness like never before. Political corruption became a nationwide scandal, bribery a way of doing business.

Thus, Reconstruction became a revolution eclipsed. White southerners' desire to take back control of their states and of race relations overwhelmed the national interest in stopping them. But Reconstruction left enduring legacies the nation has struggled with ever since. ■

Wartime Reconstruction

*R*econstruction of the Union was an issue as early as 1863. The very idea of Reconstruction raised many questions: How would the nation be restored and southern states and leaders treated? What was the constitutional basis for readmission of states to the Union? More specifically, four vexing problems compelled early thinking and would haunt the Reconstruction era. One, who would rule in the South once it was defeated? Two, who would rule in the federal government: Congress or the president? Three, what were the dimensions of black freedom, and what rights under law would the freedmen

enjoy? And four, would Reconstruction be a preservation of the old republic or a second revolution, a reinvention of a new republic?

Online Study Center Improve Your Grade
Interactive Map: The Reconstruction

Abraham Lincoln had never been antisouthern. In his Second Inaugural Address, he had promised

LINCOLN'S 10 PERCENT PLAN

"malice toward none; with charity for all" as Americans strove to "bind up the nation's wounds." Lincoln planned early for a swift and moderate Reconstruction process. In his "Proclamation of Amnesty and Reconstruction," issued in December 1863, he proposed to replace majority rule with "loyal rule" as a means of reconstructing southern state governments. He proposed pardoning all ex-Confederates except the highest-ranking military and civilian officers. As soon as 10 percent of the voting population in the 1860 election in a given state had taken an oath and established a government, the new state would be recognized. Lincoln did not consult Congress in these plans, and "loyal" assemblies (known as "Lincoln governments") were created in Louisiana, Tennessee, and Arkansas in 1864, states largely occupied by Union troops.

Congress responded with great hostility to Lincoln's moves to readmit southern states in what

CONGRESS AND THE WADE-DAVIS BILL

seemed such a premature manner. Many Radical Republicans considered the 10 percent plan a "mere mockery" of democracy. Thaddeus Stevens of Pennsylvania advocated a "conquered provinces" theory, and Charles Sumner of Massachusetts employed an argument of "state suicide." Both contended that by seceding, southern states had destroyed their status as states. They therefore must be treated as "conquered foreign lands" and revert to the status of "unorganized territories" before Congress could entertain any process of readmission.

In July 1864, the Wade-Davis bill, named for its sponsors, Senator Benjamin Wade of Ohio and Congressman Henry W. Davis of Maryland, emerged from Congress with three specific conditions for southern readmission: one, it demanded a "majority" of white male citizens participating in the creation of a new government; two, to vote or be a delegate to constitutional conventions, men had to take an "ironclad" oath (declaring they had never aided the Confederate war effort); and three, all officers above the rank of lieutenant and all civil officials in the Confederacy would be disfranchised and deemed "not a citizen of the United States." Lincoln pocket-vetoed the bill and announced that he would not be inflexibly committed to any "one plan" of Reconstruction.

This exchange came during Grant's bloody campaign in Virginia against Lee, when the outcome of the war and Lincoln's reelection were still in doubt. Radical members of his own party, indeed, were organizing a dump-Lincoln campaign for the 1864 election. What emerged in 1864–1865 was a clear-cut debate and a potential constitutional crisis. Lincoln saw Reconstruction as a means of weakening the Confederacy and winning the war; the Radicals saw it as a longer-term transformation of the political and racial order of the country.

In early 1865, Congress and Lincoln joined in two important measures that recognized slavery's centrality to the war. On January 31, with strong administration backing, Congress passed the Thirteenth Amendment, which had two provisions: it abolished involuntary servitude everywhere in the United States, and it declared that Congress shall have power to enforce this outcome by "appropriate legislation."

THIRTEENTH AMENDMENT

The Thirteenth Amendment had emerged from a long congressional debate and considerable petitioning and public advocacy. One of the first and most remarkable petitions for a constitutional amendment abolishing slavery was submitted early in 1864 by Elizabeth Cady Stanton, Susan B. Anthony, and the Women's Loyal National League. Women throughout the Union accumulated thousands of signatures, even venturing into staunchly pro-Confederate regions of Kentucky and Missouri to secure supporters. It was a long road from the Emancipation Proclamation to the Thirteenth Amendment, but the logic of winning the war by crushing slavery, and of securing a new beginning for the nation that so many had now died to save, won the day.

Potentially as significant, on March 3, 1865, Congress created the Bureau of Refugees, Freedmen, and Abandoned Lands—the Freedmen's Bureau, an unprecedented agency of social uplift, necessitated by the ravages of the war. In the mere four years of its existence, the Freedmen's Bureau supplied food and medical services, built over

FREEDMEN'S BUREAU

four thousand schools and some colleges, negotiated several hundred thousand employment contracts between freedmen and their former masters, and tried to manage confiscated land.

The Bureau would be a controversial aspect of Reconstruction, both within the South, where whites generally hated it, and within the federal government, where politicians divided over its constitutionality. The war had forced into the open an eternal question of republics: What are the social welfare obligations of the state toward its people, and what do people owe their governments in return?

The Meanings of Freedom

Entering life after slavery with hope and circumspection, freed men and women tried to gain as much as they could from their new circumstances. Often the changes they valued the most were personal: alterations in location, employer, or living arrangements.

Online Study Center **Improve Your Grade**
Primary Source: Black Testimony on the Aftermath of Enslavement

For America's former slaves, Reconstruction had one paramount meaning: a chance to explore freedom. Former slaves remembered singing far into the night after federal troops, who confirmed rumors of their emancipation, reached their plantations. The slaves on a Texas plantation shouted for joy, their leader proclaiming, "We is free—no more whippings and beatings." One man recalled that he and others "started on the move," either to search for family members or just to exercise the human right of mobility.

THE FEEL OF FREEDOM

Many freed men and women reacted more cautiously and shrewdly, taking care to test the boundaries of their new condition. "After the war was over," explained one man, "we was afraid to move. Just like terrapins or turtles after emancipation. Just stick our heads out to see how the land lay." As slaves they had learned to expect hostility from white people, and they did not presume it would instantly disappear. Life in freedom might still be a matter of what was allowed, not what was right. One sign of

The Armed Slave, William Sprang, oil on canvas, c. 1865. This remarkable painting depicts an African American veteran soldier, musket with fixed bayonet leaning against the wall, cigar in hand indicating a new life of safety and leisure, reading a book to demonstrate his embrace of education and freedom. The man's visage leaves the impression of satisfaction and dignity.   (Courtesy of The Civil War Library and Underground Railroad Museum of Philadelphia)

wife, child, or parent. Some succeeded in their quest, sometimes almost miraculously. Others never found their loved ones.

Husbands and wives who had belonged to different masters established homes together for the first time, and, as they had under slavery, parents asserted the right to raise their own children. A mother bristled when her old master claimed a right to whip her children. She informed him that "he warn't goin' to brush none of her chilluns no more." The freed men and women were too much at risk to act recklessly, but as one man put it, they were tired of punishment and "sure didn't take no more foolishness off of white folks."

To avoid contact with overbearing whites who were used to supervising them, blacks abandoned

BLACKS' SEARCH FOR INDEPENDENCE the slave quarters and fanned out to distant corners of the land they worked. Some described moving "across the creek" or building a "saplin house . . . back in the woods." Others established small all-black settlements that still exist today along the back roads of the South.

In addition to a fair employer, what freed men and women most wanted was the ownership of land.

FREEDPEOPLE'S DESIRE FOR LAND Land represented self-sufficiency and a chance to gain compensation for generations of bondage. In February 1865 General Sherman ordered 400,000 acres in the Sea Islands region set aside for the exclusive settlement of the freedpeople. But President Johnson ordered them removed in October and returned the land to its original owners under army enforcement.

Most members of both political parties opposed genuine land redistribution to the freedmen. Even northern reformers showed little sympathy for black aspirations. The former Sea Island slaves wanted to establish small, self-sufficient farms. Northern soldiers, officials, and missionaries insisted that they grow cotton, emphasizing profit, cash crops, and the values of competitive capitalism.

"The Yankees preach nothing but cotton, cotton" complained one Sea Island black. "We wants land," wrote another, but tax officials "make the lots too big, and cut we out." Indeed, the U.S. government sold thousands of acres in the Sea Islands, 90 percent of which went to wealthy investors from the North.

their caution was the way freedpeople evaluated potential employers, wandering in search of better circumstances. A majority of blacks eventually settled as agricultural workers back on their former farms or plantations. But they relocated their houses and did their utmost to control the conditions of their labor.

Throughout the South, former slaves devoted themselves to reuniting their families, separated

REUNION OF AFRICAN AMERICAN FAMILIES during slavery or by dislocation during the war. With only shreds of information to guide them, thousands of freedpeople embarked on odysseys in search of a husband,

Ex-slaves reached out for valuable things in life that had been denied them, including education. Blacks

THE BLACK EMBRACE OF EDUCATION

of all ages hungered for the knowledge in books that had been permitted only to whites. With freedom, they started schools and filled classrooms. On log seats and dirt floors, freed men and women studied their letters in old almanacs and discarded dictionaries. Young children brought infants to school with them, and adults attended at night or after "the crops were laid by."

The federal government and northern reformers of both races assisted this pursuit of education through Freedmen's Bureau schools and others founded by private northern philanthropy. More than 600,000 African Americans were enrolled in elementary school by 1877.

Blacks and their white allies also saw the need for colleges and universities to train teachers, ministers, and professionals for leadership. The American Missionary Association founded seven colleges, including Fisk and Atlanta Universities, between 1866 and 1869. The Freedmen's Bureau helped to establish Howard University in Washington, D.C., and northern religious groups supported dozens of seminaries and teachers' colleges.

During Reconstruction, African American leaders often were highly educated individuals; many were from the prewar elite of free people of color and often blood relatives of wealthy whites; some planters had given their mulatto children an outstanding education. Francis Cardozo, who held various offices in South Carolina, had attended universities in Scotland and England. The two black senators from Mississippi, Blanche K. Bruce and Hiram Revels, possessed privileged educations. These men and many self-educated former slaves brought to political office not only fervor but useful experience.

Freed from the restrictions and regulations of slavery, blacks could build their own institutions as

GROWTH OF BLACK CHURCHES

they saw fit. The secret churches of slavery came into the open; throughout the South, ex-slaves "started a brush arbor," which was "a sort of . . . shelter with leaves for a roof," but the freed men and women worshiped in it enthusiastically. Within a few years, however, independent branches of the Methodist and Baptist denominations had attracted the great majority of black Christians in the South.

The desire to gain as much independence as possible also shaped the former slaves' economic arrangements.

RISE OF THE SHARECROPPING SYSTEM

Since most of them lacked the money to buy land, they preferred the next best thing: renting the land they worked. But the South had a cash-poor economy with few sources of credit. Therefore, black farmers and white landowners turned to sharecropping, a system in which farmers kept part of their crop and gave the rest to the landowner while living on his property. The landlord or a merchant "furnished" food and supplies needed before the harvest. Although landowners tried to set the laborers' share at a low level, black farmers had some bargaining power, at least at first. Sharecroppers would hold out, or move and try to switch employers from one year to another. As the system matured during the 1870s and 1880s, most sharecroppers worked "on halves"—half for the owner and half for themselves.

The sharecropping system originated as a desirable compromise. It eased landowners' problems with cash and credit and provided them a permanent, dependent labor force; blacks accepted it because it gave them more freedom from daily supervision. Instead of working in the hated gangs under a white overseer, as in slavery, they farmed their own plot of land in family groups. But sharecropping later proved to be a disaster. Owners and merchants developed a monopoly of control over the agricultural economy, and sharecroppers found themselves riveted into ever-increasing debt. Moreover, southern farmers concentrated on cotton, and cotton prices began a long decline.

Johnson's Reconstruction Plan

When Reconstruction began under President Andrew Johnson, many former slaveowners, as well as northern Radicals, had reason to believe that he would deal sternly with the South. Throughout his career in Tennessee, he had criticized the wealthy planters and championed the small farmers. When one Radical suggested the exile or execution of ten or twelve leading rebels to set an example, Johnson replied, "How are you going to pick out so small a number?"

Like his martyred predecessor, Johnson followed a path in antebellum politics from obscurity to power.

ANDREW JOHNSON OF TENNESSEE

With no formal education, he became a tailor's apprentice. But from 1829, while in his early twenties, he held nearly every office in Tennessee politics, including two terms as governor, and he was a U.S. senator by 1857. Although elected as a southern Democrat, Johnson was the only senator from a seceded state who refused to follow his state out of the Union. Lincoln appointed him war governor of Tennessee in 1862, hence, his symbolic place on the ticket in the president's bid for reelection in 1864.

Although a staunch Unionist, Johnson was also an ardent states' rightist. And while he vehemently opposed secession, he advocated limited government. His philosophy toward Reconstruction may be summed up in the slogan he adopted: "The Constitution as it is, and the Union as it was."

Through 1865, Johnson alone controlled Reconstruction policy, for Congress recessed shortly before he became president and did not reconvene until December. In the following eight months, Johnson put into operation his own plan, forming new state governments in the South by using his power to grant pardons.

Although never a planter, Johnson had owned house slaves. He accepted emancipation as a result of

JOHNSON'S RACIAL VIEWS

the war, but he did not favor black civil and political rights and was a thoroughgoing white supremacist. Johnson believed that black suffrage could never be imposed on a southern state by the federal government, and that set him on a collision course with the Radicals. In perhaps the most blatantly racist official statement ever delivered by an American president, Johnson declared in his annual message of 1867 that blacks possessed less "capacity for government than any other race of people."

Such racial views had an enduring effect on Johnson's policies. Where whites were concerned, however, Johnson seemed to be pursuing changes in class relations. He proposed rules that would keep the wealthy planter class at least temporarily out of power.

White southerners were required to swear an oath of loyalty as a condition of gaining amnesty or

JOHNSON'S PARDON POLICY

pardon, but Johnson barred several categories of people from taking the oath: former federal officials, high-ranking Confederate officers, and political leaders or graduates of West Point or Annapolis who had joined or aided the Confederacy. To this list Johnson added another important group: all ex-Confederates whose taxable property was worth more than $20,000. These individuals had to apply personally to the president for pardon and restoration of their political rights. It thus appeared that the leadership class of the Old South would be removed from power.

Johnson appointed provisional governors who began the Reconstruction process by calling constitutional conventions. The delegates chosen for these conventions had to draft new constitutions that eliminated slavery and invalidated secession. After ratification of these constitutions, new governments could be elected, and the states would be restored to the Union with full congressional representation. But only those southerners who had taken the oath of amnesty and been eligible to vote on the day the state seceded could participate in this process. Thus, unpardoned whites and former slaves were not eligible.

If Johnson intended to strip the old elite of its power, he did not hold to his plan. Surprisingly, he

PRESIDENTIAL RECONSTRUCTION

started pardoning aristocrats and leading rebels. These pardons, plus the rapid return of planters' abandoned lands, restored the old elite to power.

Why did Johnson allow the planters to regain power? In part, he was determined to implement a rapid Reconstruction to deny the Radicals the opportunity for the more thorough racial and political changes they desired in the South. Johnson also needed southern support in the 1866 elections. Hence, he declared Reconstruction complete only eight months after Appomattox, and in December 1865 many Confederate leaders, including the vice president of the Confederacy, traveled to Washington to claim seats in the U.S. Congress.

The election of such prominent rebels troubled many northerners. So did other results of Johnson's

BLACK CODES

program. Some of the state conventions were slow to repudiate secession; others admitted only grudgingly that slavery was dead. Furthermore, to define the status of freed men and women and control their labor, some legislatures merely revised large sections of the slave codes by substituting the word *freedmen* for *slaves*. The new black codes compelled the former slaves to carry passes, observe a curfew, live in housing provided by a landowner, and give up hope of entering many desirable occupations. Stiff vagrancy laws and restrictive labor contracts bound freedpeople to plantations.

It seemed to northerners that the South was intent on returning African Americans to servility. Thus, the Republican majority in Congress decided to call a halt to the results of Johnson's plan. On reconvening, the House and Senate considered the credentials of the newly elected southern representatives and decided not to admit them. Instead, they bluntly challenged the president's authority and established a joint committee to investigate a new direction for Reconstruction.

The Congressional Reconstruction Plan

*N*orthern congressmen were hardly unified, but they did not doubt their right to shape Reconstruction policy. The Constitution mentioned neither secession nor reunion, but it gave Congress the primary role in the admission of states. Moreover, the Constitution declared that the United States shall guarantee to each state a republican form of government. This provision, legislators believed, gave them the authority to devise policies for Reconstruction.

They soon found that other constitutional questions affected their policies. What, for example, had rebellion done to the relationship between southern states and the Union? Lincoln had always insisted that states could not secede—they had engaged in an "insurrection"—and that the Union remained intact. Not even Andrew Johnson, however, accepted the southern position that state governments of the Confederacy could simply reenter the nation. Congressmen who favored vigorous Reconstruction measures argued that the war had broken the Union and that the South was subject to the victor's will. Moderate congressmen held that the states had forfeited their rights through rebellion and thus had come under congressional supervision.

These theories mirrored the diversity of Congress itself. Northern Democrats denounced any idea of racial equality and supported John-

THE RADICALS   son's policies. Conservative Republicans favored a limited federal role in

Reconstruction. The Radical Republicans wanted to transform the South. Although a minority in their party, they had the advantage of clearly defined goals. They believed it was essential to democratize the South, establish public education, and ensure the rights of freedpeople. They favored black suffrage, supported some land confiscation and redistribution, and were willing to exclude the South from the Union for several years if necessary to achieve their goals. A large group of moderate Republicans did not want to go as far as the Radicals but opposed Johnson's leniency.

Ironically, Johnson and the Democrats sabotaged the possibility of a conservative coalition. They refused to cooperate with conservative or moderate Republicans and insisted that Reconstruction was over, that the new state governments were legitimate, and that southern representatives should be admitted to Congress. Among the Republicans, the Radicals' influence grew in proportion to Johnson's intransigence.

Trying to work with Johnson, Republicans believed a compromise had been reached in the spring of

CONGRESS VS. JOHNSON   1866. Under its terms, Johnson would agree to two modifications of his program: extension of the life of the Freedmen's Bureau for another year and passage of a civil rights bill to counteract the black codes. This bill would force southern courts to practice equality before the law by allowing federal judges to remove from state courts cases in which blacks were treated unfairly. Its provisions applied to public, not private, acts of discrimination. The civil rights bill of 1866 was the first statutory definition of the rights of American citizens.

Johnson destroyed the compromise by vetoing both bills (they later became law when Congress overrode the president's veto). All hope of presidential-congressional cooperation was now dead. In 1866 newspapers reported daily violations of blacks' rights in the South and carried alarming accounts of antiblack violence. In Memphis, for instance, forty blacks were killed and twelve schools burned by white mobs. Such violence convinced Republicans, and the northern public, that more needed to be done. A new Republican plan took the form of the Fourteenth Amendment to the Constitution, forged out of a compromise between radical and conservative elements of the party.

Of the four parts of the Fourteenth Amendment, the first would have the greatest legal significance in

FOURTEENTH AMENDMENT

later years. It conferred citizenship on the freedmen and prohibited states from abridging their constitutional "privileges and immunities." It also barred any state from taking a person's life, liberty, or property "without due process of law" and from denying "equal protection of the laws." These resounding phrases became powerful guarantees of African Americans' and all other citizens' civil rights in the twentieth century.

Nearly universal agreement emerged among Republicans on the amendment's second and third provisions. The second declared the Confederate debt null and void and guaranteed the war debt of the United States. The third provision barred Confederate leaders from holding state and federal office. Only Congress, by a two-thirds vote of each house, could remove the penalty.

The fourth part of the amendment dealt with representation and embodied the compromises that produced the document. Emancipation made every former slave a full person rather than three-fifths of a person, which would increase southern representation. Thus, the postwar South stood to gain power in Congress, and if white southerners did not allow blacks to vote, former secessionists would derive the political benefit from emancipation. So Republicans determined that if a southern state did not grant black men the vote, its representation would be reduced proportionally. This compromise avoided a direct enactment of black suffrage but would deliver future black voters to the Republican Party.

The Fourteenth Amendment specified for the first time that voters were "male," but it ignored female citizens, black and white. For this reason, it provoked a strong reaction from the women's rights movement. Prominent leaders such as Elizabeth Cady Stanton and Susan B. Anthony ended their alliance with abolitionists and fought more determinedly for themselves. Thus, the amendment infused new life into the women's rights movement and caused considerable strife among old allies.

In 1866 the major question in Reconstruction politics was how the public would respond to the congressional initiative. Johnson did his best to block the Fourteenth Amendment in both North and South. Condemning Congress for

THE SOUTH'S AND JOHNSON'S DEFIANCE, 1866

its refusal to seat southern representatives, the president urged state legislatures in the South to vote against ratification. Every southern legislature except Tennessee's rejected the amendment by a wide margin.

To present his case to northerners, Johnson boarded a special train for a "swing around the circle" that carried his message into the Northeast, the Midwest, and then back to Washington. In city after city, he criticized the Republicans in a ranting, undignified style. Increasingly audiences rejected his views and hooted and jeered at him.

The elections of 1866 were a resounding victory for Republicans in Congress. Radicals and moderates whom Johnson had denounced won reelection by large margins, and the Republican majority grew to two-thirds of both houses of Congress. The North had spoken clearly: Johnson's policies were prematurely giving the advantage to rebels and traitors. Thus, Republican congressional leaders won a mandate to pursue their Reconstruction plan.

After some embittered debate, Congress passed the First Reconstruction Act in March 1867. This plan, under which the southern states were readmitted to the Union, incorporated only a part of the Radical program. Union generals, commanding small garrisons of troops and charged with supervising all elections, assumed control in five military districts in the South (see Map 16.1). Confederate leaders designated in the Fourteenth Amendment were barred from voting until new state constitutions were ratified. The act guaranteed freedmen the right to vote in elections for state constitutional conventions and in subsequent elections. In addition, each southern state was required to ratify the Fourteenth Amendment, ratify its new constitution by majority vote, and submit it to Congress for approval. The Second, Third, and Fourth Reconstruction Acts, passed between March 1867 and March 1868, provided the details of operation for voter registration boards, the adoption of constitutions, and the administration of "good faith" oaths on the part of white southerners.

RECONSTRUCTION ACTS OF 1867–1868

In the words of one historian, the Radicals succeeded in "clipping Johnson's wings." But they had hoped Congress could do much more. Thaddeus Stevens, for example, argued that economic opportunity

FAILURE OF LAND REDISTRIBUTION

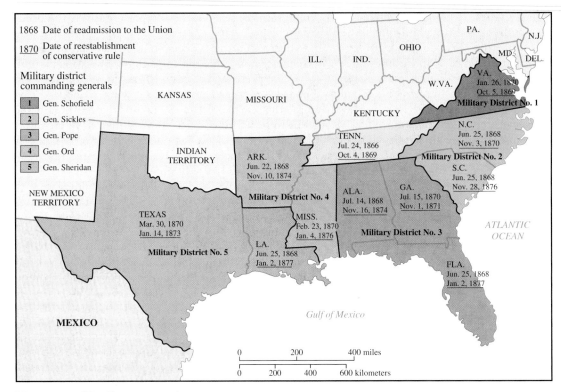

Map 16.1   The Reconstruction

This map shows the five military districts established when Congress passed the Reconstruction Act of 1867. As the dates within each state indicate, conservative Democratic forces quickly regained control of government in four southern states. So-called Radical Reconstruction was curtailed in most of the others as factions within the weakened Republican Party began to cooperate with conservative Democrats.

was essential to the freedmen. Stevens therefore drew up a plan for extensive confiscation and redistribution of land. Only one-tenth of the land affected by his plan was earmarked for freedmen, in forty-acre plots. The rest was to be sold to generate money for Union veterans' pensions, compensation to loyal southerners for damaged property, and payment of the federal debt.

But plans for property redistribution were unpopular measures, and virtually all failed. Northerners were accustomed to a limited role for government, and the business community staunchly opposed any interference with private property rights, even for former Confederates.

Congress's quarrels with Johnson grew more bitter. To restrict Johnson's influence and safeguard its

CONSTITUTIONAL CRISIS

plan, Congress passed a number of controversial laws. First, it limited Johnson's power over the army by requiring the president to issue military orders through the General of the Army, Ulysses S. Grant, who could not be dismissed without the Senate's consent. Then Congress passed the Tenure of Office Act, which gave the Senate power to approve changes in the president's cabinet. Designed to protect Secretary of War Edwin M. Stanton, who sympathized with the Radicals, this law violated the tradition that a president controlled appointments to his own cabinet. These measures, as well as each of the Reconstruction Acts, were passed by a two-thirds override of presidential vetoes.

Johnson took several belligerent steps of his own. He issued orders to military commanders in the South limiting their powers and increasing the powers of the civil governments he had created in 1865. Then he removed military officers who were conscientiously enforcing Congress's new law, preferring commanders who allowed disqualified Confederates to vote. Finally, he tried to remove Secretary of War Stanton. With that attempt the confrontation reached its climax.

Twice in 1867, the House Judiciary Committee had considered impeachment of Johnson, rejecting

IMPEACHMENT OF PRESIDENT JOHNSON

the idea once and then having its recommendation by a 5-to-4 vote decisively defeated by the House. After Johnson tried to remove Stanton, a third attempt to impeach the president carried easily in early 1868. The indictment concentrated on his violation of the Tenure of Office Act, though many modern scholars regard his efforts to impede enforcement of the Reconstruction Act of 1867 as a far more serious offense.

Johnson's trial in the Senate began promptly and lasted more than three months. The prosecution attempted to prove that Johnson was guilty of "high crimes and misdemeanors." But they also argued that the trial was a means to judge Johnson's performance, not a judicial determination of guilt or innocence. The Senate ultimately rejected such reasoning, which could have made removal from office a political weapon against any chief executive who disagreed with Congress. Although a majority of senators voted to convict Johnson, the prosecution fell one vote short of the necessary two-thirds majority. Johnson remained in office, politically weakened and with only a few months left in his term.

In the 1868 presidential election Ulysses S. Grant, running as a Republican, defeated Horatio Seymour,

ELECTION OF 1868

a New York Democrat. Grant was not a Radical, but his platform supported congressional Reconstruction and endorsed black suffrage in the South. (Significantly, Republicans stopped short of endorsing it in the North.) The Democrats vigorously denounced Reconstruction.

Participating in their first presidential election ever on a wide scale, blacks voted en masse for General Grant.

In office Grant acted as an administrator of Reconstruction but not as its enthusiastic advocate. He vacillated in his dealings with the southern states, sometimes defending Republican regimes and sometimes currying favor with Democrats. On occasion Grant called out federal troops to stop violence or enforce acts of Congress. But he never imposed a true military occupation on the South. The later legend of "military rule," so important to southern claims of victimization during Reconstruction, was steeped in myth.

In 1869, in an effort to write democratic principles into the Constitution, the Radicals passed the

FIFTEENTH AMENDMENT

Fifteenth Amendment. This measure forbade states to deny the right to vote "on account of race, color, or previous condition of servitude." Such wording did not guarantee the right to vote. It deliberately left states free to restrict suffrage on other grounds so that northern states could continue to deny suffrage to women and certain groups of men—Chinese immigrants, illiterates, and those too poor to pay poll taxes. Although several states outside the South refused to ratify, three-fourths of the states approved the measure, and the Fifteenth Amendment became law in 1870.

With passage of the Fifteenth Amendment, many Americans, especially supportive northerners, considered Reconstruction essentially completed. "Let us have done with Reconstruction," pleaded the *New York Tribune* in April 1870. "The country is tired and sick of it. . . . Let us have Peace!"

Reconstruction Politics in the South

*F*rom the start, Reconstruction encountered the resistance of white southerners. In the black codes and in private attitudes, many whites stubbornly opposed emancipation, and the former planter class proved especially unbending. In 1866 a Georgia newspaper frankly observed that "most of the white citizens believe that the institution of slavery was right, and . . . they will believe that the condition, which comes nearest to slavery, that can now be established will be the best."

Fearing loss of control over their slaves, some planters attempted to postpone freedom by denying or misrepresenting events. Former slaves reported that their owners "didn't tell them it was freedom" or "wouldn't let [them] go." To hold onto their workers, some landowners claimed control over black children and used guardianship and apprentice laws to bind black families to the plantation. Whites also blocked blacks from acquiring land. After President Johnson encouraged the South to resist congressional Reconstruction, some white conservatives worked hard to capture the new state governments, while others boycotted the polls in an attempt to defeat Congress's plans.

WHITE RESISTANCE

Very few black men stayed away from the polls. Enthusiastically and hopefully, they voted Republican. Most agreed with one man who felt he should "stick to the end with the party that freed me." Illiteracy did not prohibit blacks (or uneducated whites) from making intelligent choices. A Mississippi black testified that he and his friends had no difficulty selecting the Republican ballot. "We stood around and watched," he explained. "We saw D. Sledge vote; he owned half the county. We knowed he voted Democratic so we voted the other ticket so it would be Republican."

BLACK VOTERS AND THE SOUTHERN REPUBLICAN PARTY

Thanks to a large black turnout and the restrictions on prominent Confederates, a new southern Republican Party came to power in the constitutional conventions of 1868–1870. Republican delegates consisted of a sizable contingent of blacks (265 out of the total of just over 1,000 delegates throughout the South), some northerners who had moved to the South, and native southern whites who favored change. The new constitutions were more democratic. They eliminated property qualifications for voting and holding office, and they turned many appointed offices into elective posts. They provided for public schools and institutions to care for the mentally ill, the blind, the deaf, the destitute, and the orphaned.

The conventions broadened women's rights in property holding and divorce. Usually the goal was not to make women equal to men but to provide relief to thousands of suffering debtors. In families left

■ Thomas Nast, in this 1868 cartoon, pictured the combination of forces that threatened the success of Reconstruction: southern opposition and the greed, partisanship, and racism of northern interests.
(Library of Congress)

poverty stricken by the war and weighed down by debt, it was usually the husband who had contracted the debts. Thus giving women legal control over their own property provided some protection to their families. The goal of some delegates, however, was to elevate women with the right to vote.

Under these new constitutions, the southern states elected Republican-controlled governments. For the first time, the ranks of state legislators in 1868 included some black southerners. But in most states, whites were in the majority, and former slaveowners controlled the

TRIUMPH OF REPUBLICAN GOVERNMENTS

best land and other sources of economic power. James Lynch, a leading black politician from Mississippi, explained why African Americans shunned the "folly" of disfranchisement of ex-Confederates. Unlike northerners who "can leave when it becomes too uncomfortable," landless former slaves "must be in friendly relations with the great body of the whites in the state."

Far from being vindictive toward the race that had enslaved them, most southern blacks treated leading rebels with generosity and appealed to white southerners to adopt a spirit of fairness and cooperation. In this way, the South's Republican Party condemned itself to defeat if white voters would not cooperate. Within a few years, Republicans were reduced to the embarrassment of making futile appeals to whites while ignoring the claims of their strongest supporters, blacks. But for a time, some propertied whites accepted congressional Reconstruction as a reality and declared themselves willing to compete under the new rules. All sides found an area of agreement in economic policies.

Reflecting northern ideals and southern necessity, the Reconstruction governments enthusiastically pro-

INDUSTRIALIZATION

moted industry. Reconstruction legislatures encouraged investment with loans, subsidies, and exemptions from taxation for periods up to ten years. The southern railroad system was rebuilt and expanded, and coal and iron mining made possible steel plants in Birmingham, Alabama. Between 1860 and 1880, the number of manufacturing establishments in the South nearly doubled. This emphasis on big business, however, produced higher state debts and taxes, drew money away from schools and other programs, and multiplied possibilities for corruption.

Policies appealing to African American voters never went beyond equality before the law. In fact, the

REPUBLICANS AND RACIAL EQUALITY

whites who controlled the southern Republican Party were reluctant to allow blacks a share of offices proportionate to their electoral strength. Aware of their weakness, black leaders did not push very far for revolutionary economic or social change. In every southern state, they led efforts to establish public schools, although they did not press for integrated facilities.

Economic progress was uppermost in the minds of most freedpeople. Black southerners needed land, and much land did fall into state hands for nonpay-

ment of taxes and was offered for sale in small lots. But most freedmen had too little cash to bid against investors or speculators. Any widespread redistribution of land had to arise from Congress, which never supported such action. The lack of genuine land redistribution remained the significant lost opportunity of Reconstruction.

Within a few years, as centrists in both parties met with failure, white hostility to congressional Reconstruction began to dominate.

MYTH OF "NEGRO RULE"

Taking the offensive, conservatives charged that the South had been turned over to ignorant blacks and deplored "black domination," which became a rallying cry for a return to white supremacy.

Such inflammatory propaganda was part of the growing myth of "Negro rule." African Americans participated in politics but hardly dominated or controlled events. They were a majority in only two out of ten state constitution–writing conventions (transplanted northerners were a majority in one). In the state legislatures, only in the lower house in South Carolina did blacks ever constitute a majority; among officeholders, their numbers generally were far fewer than their proportion in the population. Sixteen blacks won seats in Congress before Reconstruction was over, but none was ever elected governor. Only eighteen served in a high state office such as lieutenant governor, treasurer, superintendent of education, or secretary of state. However, elected officials, such as Robert Smalls in South Carolina, labored tirelessly for cheaper land prices, better health care, access to schools, and the enforcement of civil rights for their people.

Conservatives also assailed the allies of black Republicans. Their propaganda denounced whites from

CARPETBAGGERS AND SCALAWAGS

the North as "carpetbaggers," greedy crooks planning to pour stolen tax revenues into their sturdy luggage made of carpet material. In fact, most northerners who settled in the South had come seeking business opportunities, as schoolteachers, or to find a warmer climate and never entered politics. Those who did enter politics generally wanted to democratize the South and introduce northern ways, such as industry, public education, and the spirit of enterprise.

Conservatives also coined the term *scalawag* to discredit any native white southerner who cooperated with the Republicans. A substantial number did so. Most scalawags were yeoman farmers, men from mountain areas and nonslaveholding districts who saw that they could benefit from the education and opportunities promoted by Republicans. Banding together with freedmen, they pursued common class interests and hoped to make headway against the power of long-dominant planters. A majority of scalawags, however, did not support racial equality. The black-white coalition was thus vulnerable on the race issue.

Taxation was a major problem for the Reconstruction governments. Republicans wanted to maintain prewar services, repair the

TAX POLICY AND CORRUPTION AS POLITICAL WEDGES

war's destruction, stimulate industry, and support important new ventures such as public schools. But the Civil War had destroyed much of the South's tax base. Thus, an increase in taxes was necessary even to maintain traditional services, and new ventures required still higher taxes. Republican tax policies aroused strong opposition, especially among yeomen.

Corruption was another serious charge levied against the Republicans. Unfortunately, it often was true. Many carpetbaggers and black politicians engaged in fraudulent schemes, sold their votes, or padded expenses, taking part in what scholars recognize was a nationwide surge of corruption. Corruption carried no party label, but the Democrats successfully pinned the blame on unqualified blacks and greedy carpetbaggers among southern Republicans.

All these problems hurt the Republicans, but in many southern states the deathblow came through violence. The Ku Klux Klan began in

KU KLUX KLAN

Tennessee in 1866; it spread through the South and rapidly evolved into a terrorist organization. Violence against African Americans occurred from the first days of Reconstruction but became far more organized and purposeful after 1867. Klansmen sought to frustrate Reconstruction and keep the freedmen in subjection. Nighttime harassment, whippings, beatings, rapes, and murder became common, and terrorism dominated some counties and regions.

The Klan's main purpose was political. Lawless nightriders targeted active Republicans. Leading white and black Republicans were killed in several states. After freedmen who worked for a South Carolina scalawag started voting, terrorists visited the plantation and, in the words of one victim, "whipped every nigger man they could lay their hands on." Klansmen also attacked Union League clubs—Republican organizations that mobilized the black vote—and schoolteachers who aided the freedmen.

Klan violence was not a spontaneous outburst of racism; very specific social forces shaped and directed it. In North Carolina, for example, the sites of the worst Klan violence were Alamance and Caswell Counties. There, slim Republican majorities rested on cooperation between black voters and white yeomen, who together had ousted officials long entrenched in power. The wealthy and powerful men who had lost their accustomed political control then organized a deliberate campaign of terror. The campaign of intimidation and murder weakened the Republican coalition and restored a Democratic majority.

Klan violence injured Republicans across the South. One in ten of the black leaders who had been delegates to the 1867–1868 state constitutional conventions was attacked, seven fatally. A single attack on Alabama Republicans in the town of Eutaw left four blacks dead and fifty-four wounded. According to historian Eric Foner, the Klan "made it virtually impossible for Republicans to campaign or vote in large parts of Georgia."

Thus, a combination of difficult fiscal problems, Republican mistakes, racial hostility, and terror

FAILURE OF RECONSTRUCTION

brought down the Republican regimes. In most southern states, "Radical Reconstruction" lasted only a few years (see Map 16.1). The most enduring failure of Reconstruction, however, was not political; it was that Reconstruction failed to alter the South's social structure or its distribution of wealth and power. Without land of their own, freedpeople were at the mercy of white landowners. Armed only with the ballot, they had little chance to effect significant changes.

Reconstruction Reversed

*N*ortherners had always been more interested in suppressing rebellion than in aiding southern blacks, and by the early 1870s the North's commitment to bringing about change in the South weakened. In one southern state after another, Democrats regained control. And for one of only a few times in American history, violence and terror emerged as a tactic in normal politics.

In 1870 and 1871, the violent campaigns of the Ku Klux Klan forced Congress to pass two Enforce-

POLITICAL
IMPLICATIONS
OF KLAN
TERRORISM

ment Acts and an anti-Klan law. These laws made actions by individuals against the civil and political rights of others a federal criminal offense for the first time. They also provided for election supervisors and permitted martial law and suspension of the writ of habeas corpus to combat murders, beatings, and threats by the Klan. Federal prosecutors used the laws rather selectively. In 1872 and 1873, Mississippi and the Carolinas saw many prosecutions, but in other states where violence flourished, the laws were virtually ignored. Southern juries sometimes refused to convict Klansmen.

Some conservative but influential Republicans opposed the anti-Klan laws. Rejecting other Republicans' arguments that the Thirteenth, Fourteenth, and Fifteenth Amendments had made the federal government the protector of citizens' rights, these dissenters echoed an old Democratic charge that Congress was infringing on states' rights. This opposition foreshadowed a more general revolt within Republican ranks in 1872.

Disenchanted with Reconstruction, a group calling itself the Liberal Republicans bolted the party in

LIBERAL
REPUBLICAN
REVOLT

1872 and nominated Horace Greeley, the well-known editor of the *New York Tribune,* for president. The Liberal Republicans were a varied group, including civil service reformers, foes of corruption, and advocates of a lower tariff. Normally such disparate elements would not cooperate, but two popular and widespread attitudes united them: distaste for federal intervention in the South and an elitist desire to let market forces and the "best men" determine events, in both the South and Washington. The Democrats also gave their nomination to Greeley in 1872. The combination was not enough to defeat Grant, who won reelection, but it reinforced Grant's desire to avoid confrontation with white southerners.

Dissatisfaction with Grant's administration grew during his second term. Strong-willed but politically naive, Grant made a series of poor appointments. His secretary of war, his private secretary, and officials in the Treasury and Navy Departments were involved in bribery or tax-cheating scandals. Instead of exposing the corruption, Grant defended the culprits. In 1874, as Grant's popularity and his party's prestige declined, the Democrats recaptured the House of Representatives.

The effect of Democratic gains in Congress was to weaken legislative resolve on southern issues. Already,

A GENERAL
AMNESTY

in 1872, Congress had adopted a sweeping Amnesty Act, which pardoned most of the remaining rebels, lifting the political disabilities of the Fourteenth Amendment, and left only five hundred barred from political office. In 1875 Congress passed a Civil Rights Act purporting to guarantee black people equal accommodations in public places, such as inns and theaters, but the bill was watered down and contained no effective provisions for enforcement. And by 1876, the Democrats had regained control in all but three southern states. Meanwhile, new concerns were capturing the public's attention.

Both industrialization and immigration were surging, hastening the pace of change in national life.

RECONCILIATION
AND INDUSTRIAL
EXPANSION

Within only eight years, postwar industrial production increased by an impressive 75 percent. For the first time, nonagricultural workers outnumbered farmers, and only Britain's industrial output was greater than that of the United States. Lured by employment prospects in the expanding economy, 3 million immigrants entered the country between 1865 and 1873.

Then the Panic of 1873 ushered in over five years of economic contraction. Three million people lost their jobs, and the clash between labor and capital became the major issue of the day. Class attitudes diverged, especially in large cities. Debtors and the unemployed sought easy-money policies to spur economic expansion. Businessmen, disturbed by the widespread strikes and industrial violence that accompanied the panic, fiercely defended property rights and demanded "sound money" policies. The chasm between farmers and workers and wealthy industrialists grew ever wider.

Nowhere did the new complexity and violence of American race relations play out so vividly as in the

THE WEST,
RACE, AND
RECONSTRUCTION

West. Across the West, the federal government pursued a policy of containment against Native Americans. In California, where white

The Grants' Tour of the World

On May 17, 1877, two weeks after his presidency ended, Ulysses S. Grant and his wife, Julia, embarked from Philadelphia on a grand tour of the world that would last twenty-six months. Portrayed as a private vacation, the trip was a very public affair. The small entourage included John Russell Young, a reporter for the *New York Herald* who recorded the journeys in the two-volume illustrated *Around the World with General Grant.*

The Grants spent many months in England attending a bewildering array of banquets, one with Queen Victoria. In Newcastle, thousands of workingmen conducted a massive parade in Grant's honor. Grant was viewed as a warrior statesman, the savior of the American nation, the liberator of slaves, and a celebrity—a measure of the American presence on the world stage. On the European continent, the pattern continued as every royal or republican head of state hosted the Grants.

The Grants next went to Egypt, where they rode donkeys into remote villages along the Nile. They traveled by train to the Indian Ocean and embarked for India. They encountered British imperialism in full flower in Bombay and that of the French in Saigon. Northward in Asia, the grand excursion went to China and Japan. In Canton, Grant passed before an assemblage of young men who, according to a reporter, "looked upon the barbarian with . . . contempt in their expression, very much as our young men in New York would regard Sitting Bull or Red Cloud."

"I am both homesick and dread going home," Grant wrote in April 1879. Sailing across the Pacific, the Grants landed in San Francisco in late June. The former president would spend his final years a war hero and a national symbol. No American president would again establish such personal links to the world until Woodrow Wilson at the end of World War I.

On their tour of the world, Ulysses and Julia Grant sat here with companions and guides in front of the Great Hypostyle Hall at the Temple of Amon-Ra in Karnak in Luxor, Egypt, 1878. The Grants' extraordinary tour included many such photo opportunities, often depicting the plebeian American president, and now world celebrity, in exotic places with unusual people. (Library of Congress)

farmers and ranchers often forced Indians into captive labor, some civilians practiced a more violent form of "Indian hunting." By 1880, thirty years of such violence left an estimated 4,500 California Indians dead at the hands of white settlers.

In Texas and the Southwest, the rhetoric of national expansion still deemed Mexicans and other mixed-race Hispanics to be debased, "lazy," and incapable of self-government. And in California and other states of the Far West, thousands of Chinese immigrants became the victims of brutal violence. Few whites had objected to the Chinese who did the dangerous work of building railroads through the Rocky Mountains. But when the Chinese began to compete for urban, industrial jobs, great conflict emerged. Anticoolie clubs appeared in California in the 1870s, seeking laws against Chinese labor and organizing vigilante attacks on Chinese workers and the factories that employed them. Western politicians sought white votes by pandering to prejudice, and in 1879 the new California constitution denied the vote to Chinese.

During Reconstruction, America was undergoing what one historian has called a "reconstruction" of the very idea of "race" itself. And as it did so, tumbling into some of the darkest years of American race relations, the turbulence of the expanding West reinforced a resurgent white supremacy, a new nationalism, and the reconciliation of North and South.

Following the Civil War, pressure for expansion reemerged, and in 1867 Secretary of State William H.

FOREIGN EXPANSION

Seward arranged the purchase of Alaska from the Russian government. Opponents ridiculed Seward's $7.2 million venture, but he convinced important congressmen of Alaska's economic potential, and other lawmakers favored the dawning of friendship with Russia.

Also in 1867 the United States took control of the Midway Islands, a thousand miles northwest of Hawai'i. And in 1870 President Grant tried unsuccessfully to annex the Dominican Republic.

Meanwhile, the Supreme Court played its part in the northern retreat from Reconstruction. During the

JUDICIAL RETREAT FROM RECONSTRUCTION

Civil War, the Court had been cautious and inactive. Reaction to the *Dred Scott* decision (1857) had been so violent, and the Union's wartime emergency so great, that the Court avoided interference with government actions. In 1866, however, *Ex parte Milligan* reached the Court.

Lambdin P. Milligan of Indiana had plotted to free Confederate prisoners of war and overthrow state governments. For these acts, a military court sentenced Milligan, a civilian, to death. Milligan claimed that he had a right to a civil trial. The Supreme Court declared that military trials were illegal when civil courts were open and functioning, and its language indicated that the Court intended to reassert its authority.

In the 1870s the Court successfully renewed its challenge to Congress's actions when it narrowed the meaning and effectiveness of the Fourteenth Amendment. The *Slaughter-House* cases (1873) began in 1869, when the Louisiana legislature granted one company a monopoly on the slaughtering of livestock in New Orleans. Rival butchers in the city promptly sued. Their attorney argued that the Fourteenth Amendment had revolutionized the constitutional system by bringing individual rights under federal protection. This argument articulated an original goal of the Republican Party: to nationalize civil rights and guard them from state interference.

The Court rejected the argument and thus dealt a stunning blow to the scope and vitality of the Fourteenth Amendment. State citizenship and national citizenship were separate, the Court declared. National citizenship involved only matters such as the right to travel freely from state to state and to use the nation's navigable waters, and only these narrow rights were protected by the Fourteenth Amendment.

The Supreme Court also concluded that the butchers who sued had not been deprived of their rights or property in violation of the amendment's due-process clause. The Court's majority declared that the framers of the recent amendments had not intended to "destroy" the federal system, in which the states exercised "powers for domestic and local government, including the regulation of civil rights." Thus, the justices severely limited the amendment's potential for securing and protecting the rights of black citizens—its original intent.

The next day the Court decided *Bradwell v. Illinois,* a case in which Myra Bradwell, a female attorney, had been denied the right to practice law in Illinois on account of her gender. Pointing to the Fourteenth Amendment, Bradwell's attorneys contended that the state had unconstitutionally abridged her "privileges and immunities" as a citizen. The Supreme Court rejected her claim, alluding to women's traditional role in the home.

In 1876 the Court weakened the Reconstruction era amendments even further by emasculating the enforcement clause of the Fourteenth Amendment and revealing deficiencies inherent in the Fifteenth Amendment. In *U.S. v. Cruikshank* the Court overruled the conviction under the 1870 Enforcement Act of Louisiana whites who had attacked a meeting of blacks and conspired to deprive them of their rights. The justices ruled that the Fourteenth Amendment did not give the federal government power to act against these whites. The duty of protecting citizens' equal rights, the Court said, "rests alone with the States." Such judicial conservatism had a profound impact down through the next century, blunting the revolutionary potential in the Civil War amendments.

The 1876 presidential election confirmed that the nation was increasingly focused on economic issues and that the North was no longer willing to pursue the goals of Reconstruction. Samuel J. Tilden, the Democratic governor of New York, ran strongly in the South and needed only one more electoral vote to triumph over Rutherford B. Hayes, the Republican nominee. Nineteen electoral votes from Louisiana, South Carolina, and Florida (the only southern states yet "unredeemed" by Democratic rule) were disputed; both Democrats and Republicans claimed to have won in those states despite fraud committed by their opponents. One vote from Oregon was undecided because of a technicality (see Map 16.2).

DISPUTED ELECTION OF 1876 AND THE COMPROMISE OF 1877

To resolve this unprecedented situation Congress established a fifteen-member electoral commission, with membership to be balanced between Democrats and Republicans. Since the Republicans held the majority in Congress, they prevailed 8 to 7 on every attempt to count the returns, along strict party lines. Hayes would become president if Congress accepted the commission's findings.

Congressional acceptance was not certain, and many citizens worried that the nation had entered a major constitutional crisis and would slip once again into civil war. The crisis was resolved when Democrats acquiesced in the election of Hayes based on a

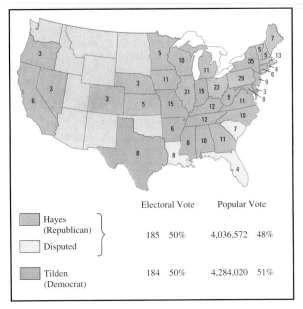

	Electoral Vote		Popular Vote	
Hayes (Republican)	185	50%	4,036,572	48%
Disputed				
Tilden (Democrat)	184	50%	4,284,020	51%

Map 16.2   Presidential Election of 1876 and the Compromise of 1877

In 1876 a combination of solid southern support and Democratic gains in the North gave Samuel Tilden the majority of popular votes, but Rutherford B. Hayes won the disputed election in the electoral college, after a deal satisfied Democratic wishes for an end to Reconstruction.

"deal" cut in a Washington hotel between Hayes's supporters and southerners who wanted federal aid to railroads, internal improvements, federal patronage, and removal of troops from southern states. Northern and southern Democrats simply decided they could not win and did not contest the election of a Republican who was not going to continue Reconstruction. Thus, Hayes became president.

Southern Democrats rejoiced, but African Americans grieved over the betrayal of their hopes for equality. To many of these people, the only hope lay outside the South. Thus, from South Carolina, Louisiana, Mississippi, and other southern states, thousands gathered up their possessions and migrated to Kansas. They were called Exodusters, disappointed people still searching for their share in the American dream. Even in Kansas they met disillusionment as the wel-

BETRAYAL OF BLACK RIGHTS

come extended by the state's governor soon gave way to hostility among many whites.

Blacks now had to weigh their options, which were not much wider than they had ever been. Frederick Douglass looked back on fifteen years of unparalleled change for his people and worried about the hold of white supremacy on America's historical memory: "If war among the whites brought peace and liberty to the blacks, what will peace among the whites bring?" Douglass's question would echo down through American political culture for decades.

Summary *Online Study Center* ACE the Test

*R*econstruction left a contradictory record. It was an era of tragic aspirations and failures, but also of unprecedented legal, political, and social change. The Union victory brought about an increase in federal power, stronger nationalism, sweeping federal intervention in the southern states, and landmark amendments to the Constitution. But northern commitment to make these changes endure had eroded, and the revolution remained unfinished.

The North embraced emancipation, black suffrage, and constitutional alterations strengthening the central government. But it did so to defeat the rebellion and secure the peace. As the pressure of these crises declined, strong underlying continuities emerged and placed their mark on Reconstruction. The American people and the courts maintained a preference for state authority and a distrust of federal power. The ideology of free labor dictated that property should be respected and that individuals should be self-reliant. Racism endured and transformed into the even more virulent forms of Klan terror. Concern for the human rights of African Americans was strongest when their plight threatened to undermine the interests of whites, and reform frequently had less appeal than moneymaking in an individualistic, enterprising society.

In the wake of the Civil War, Americans faced two profound tasks: the achievement of healing and the dispensing of justice. Both had to occur, but they never developed in historical balance. Making sectional reunion compatible with black freedom and equality overwhelmed the imagination in American political culture, and the nation still faced much of this dilemma more than a century later.

LEGACY FOR A PEOPLE AND A NATION
The Fourteenth Amendment

Before the Civil War, no definition of civil rights existed in America. Reconstruction legislation, especially the Fourteenth Amendment, changed that forever. Approved by Congress in 1866, the Fourteenth Amendment enshrined in the Constitution the ideas of birthright citizenship and equal rights. The Fourteenth Amendment was designed to secure and protect the rights of the freedpeople. But over time, the "equal protection of the law" clause has been used at times to support the rights of states, cities, corporations, immigrants, women, religious organizations, gays and lesbians, students, and labor unions. It has advanced both tolerance and intolerance, affirmative action and anti-affirmative-action programs. It provides the legal wellspring for the generations-old civil rights movement in the United States.

The amendment as originally written required individuals to pursue grievances through private litigation, alleging state denial of a claimed federal right. At first, the Supreme Court interpreted it conservatively, especially on racial matters, and by 1900, the idea of color-blind liberty in America was devastated by Jim Crow laws, disfranchisement, and unpunished mob violence.

But Progressive reformers used the equal-protection clause to advocate government support of health, union organizing, municipal housing, and the protection of woman and child laborers. In the 1920s and 1930s, a judicial defense of civil liberties and free speech took hold. The Supreme Court expanded the amendment's guarantee of equality by a series of decisions upholding the rights of immigrant groups to resist "forced Americanization," especially Catholics in their creation of parochial schools. And from its inception in

1910, the National Association for the Advancement of Colored People waged a long campaign to reveal the inequality of racial segregation in schooling and every other kind of public facility. Led by Charles Houston and Thurgood Marshall, this epic legal battle culminated in the *Brown v. Board of Education* desegregation decision of 1954. In the Civil Rights Act of 1964, the equal-protection tradition was reenshrined into American law. Since 1964, Americans have lived in a society where the Fourteenth Amendment's legacy is the engine of expanded liberty for women and all minorities, as well as a political battleground for defining the nature and limits of human equality, and for redistributing justice long denied.

APPENDIX

Documents

DECLARATION OF INDEPENDENCE IN CONGRESS, JULY 4, 1776

When, in the course of human events, it becomes necessary for one people to dissolve the political bonds which have connected them with another, and to assume, among the powers of the earth, the separate and equal station to which the laws of nature and of nature's God entitle them, a decent respect to the opinions of mankind requires that they should declare the causes which impel them to the separation.

We hold these truths to be self-evident: That all men are created equal; that they are endowed by their Creator with certain unalienable rights; that among these are life, liberty, and the pursuit of happiness; that, to secure these rights, governments are instituted among men, deriving their just powers from the consent of the governed; that whenever any form of government becomes destructive of these ends, it is the right of the people to alter or to abolish it, and to institute new government, laying its foundation on such principles, and organizing its powers in such form, as to them shall seem most likely to effect their safety and happiness. Prudence, indeed, will dictate that governments long established should not be changed for light and transient causes; and accordingly all experience hath shown that mankind are more disposed to suffer, while evils are sufferable, than to right themselves by abolishing the forms to which they are accustomed. But when a long train of abuses and usurpations, pursuing invariably the same object, evinces a design to reduce them under absolute despotism, it is their right, it is their duty, to throw off such government, and to provide new guards for their future security. Such has been the patient sufferance of these colonies; and such is now the necessity which constrains them to alter their former systems of government. The history of the present King of Great Britain is a history of repeated injuries and usurpations, all having in direct object the establishment of an absolute tyranny over these states. To prove this, let facts be submitted to a candid world.

He has refused his assent to laws, the most wholesome and necessary for the public good.

He has forbidden his governors to pass laws of immediate and pressing importance, unless suspended in their operation till his assent should be obtained; and, when so suspended, he has utterly neglected to attend to them.

He has refused to pass other laws for the accommodation of large districts of people, unless those people would relinquish the right of representation in the legislature, a right inestimable to them, and formidable to tyrants only.

He has called together legislative bodies at places unusual, uncomfortable, and distant from the depository of their public records, for the sole purpose of fatiguing them into compliance with his measures.

He has dissolved representative houses repeatedly, for opposing, with manly firmness, his invasions on the rights of the people.

He has refused for a long time, after such dissolutions, to cause others to be elected; whereby the legislative powers, incapable of annihilation, have returned to the people at large for their exercise; the state remaining, in the mean time, exposed to all the dangers of invasions from without and convulsions within.

He has endeavored to prevent the population of these states; for that purpose obstructing the laws for naturalization of foreigners; refusing to pass others to encourage their migration hither, and raising the conditions of new appropriations of lands.

He has obstructed the administration of justice, by refusing his assent to laws for establishing judiciary powers.

He has made judges dependent on his will alone, for the tenure of their offices, and the amount and payment of their salaries.

He has erected a multitude of new offices, and sent hither swarms of officers to harass our people and eat out their substance.

He has kept among us, in times of peace, standing armies, without the consent of our legislatures.

He has affected to render the military independent of, and superior to, the civil power.

He has combined with others to subject us to a jurisdiction foreign to our constitution, and unacknowledged by our laws, giving his assent to their acts of pretended legislation:

For quartering large bodies of armed troops among us;

For protecting them, by a mock trial, from punishment for any murders which they should commit on the inhabitants of these states;

For cutting off our trade with all parts of the world;

For imposing taxes on us without our consent;

For depriving us, in many cases, of the benefits of trial by jury;

For transporting us beyond seas, to be tried for pretended offenses;

For abolishing the free system of English laws in a neighboring province, establishing therein an arbitrary government, and enlarging its boundaries, so as to render it at once an example and fit instrument for introducing the same absolute rule into these colonies;

For taking away our charters, abolishing our most valuable laws, and altering fundamentally the forms of our governments;

For suspending our own legislatures, and declaring themselves invested with power to legislate for us in all cases whatsoever.

He has abdicated government here, by declaring us out of his protection and waging war against us.

He has plundered our seas, ravaged our coasts, burned our towns, and destroyed the lives of our people.

He is at this time transporting large armies of foreign mercenaries to complete the works of death, desolation, and tyranny already begun with circumstances of cruelty and perfidy scarcely paralleled in the most barbarous ages, and totally unworthy the head of a civilized nation.

He has constrained our fellow-citizens, taken captive on the high seas, to bear arms against their country, to become the executioners of their friends and brethren, or to fall themselves by their hands.

He has excited domestic insurrection among us, and has endeavored to bring on the inhabitants of our frontiers the merciless Indian savages, whose known rule of warfare is an undistinguished destruction of all ages, sexes, and conditions.

In every stage of these oppressions we have petitioned for redress in the most humble terms; our repeated petitions have been answered only by repeated injury. A prince, whose character is thus marked by every act which may define a tyrant, is unfit to be the ruler of a free people.

Nor have we been wanting in our attentions to our British brethren. We have warned them, from time to time, of attempts by their legislature to extend an unwarrantable jurisdiction over us. We have reminded them of the circumstances of our emigration and settlement here. We have appealed to their native justice and magnanimity; and we have conjured them, by the ties of our common kindred, to disavow these usurpations, which would inevitably interrupt our connections and correspondence. They, too, have been deaf to the voice of justice and of consanguinity. We must, therefore, acquiesce in the necessity which denounces our separation, and hold them, as we hold the rest of mankind, enemies in war, in peace friends.

We, therefore, the representatives of the United States of America, in General Congress assembled, appealing to the Supreme Judge of the world for the rectitude of our intentions, do, in the name and by the authority of the good people of these colonies, solemnly publish and declare, that these United Colonies are, and of right ought to be, FREE AND INDEPENDENT STATES; that they are absolved from all allegiance to the British crown, and that all political connection between them and the state of Great Britain is, and ought to be, totally dissolved; and that, as free and independent states, they have full power to levy war, conclude peace, contract alliances, establish commerce, and do all other acts and things which independent states may of right do. And for the support of this declaration, with a firm reliance on the protection of Divine Providence, we mutually pledge to each other our lives, our fortunes, and our sacred honor.

———

ARTICLES OF CONFEDERATION

(The text of the Articles of Confederation can be found at college.hmco.com.)

———

CONSTITUTION OF THE UNITED STATES OF AMERICA AND AMENDMENTS*

Preamble

We the people of the United States, in order to form a more perfect union, establish justice, insure domestic tranquillity, provide for the common defense, promote the general welfare, and secure the blessings of liberty to ourselves and our posterity, do ordain and establish this Constitution for the United States of America.

Article I

Section 1 All legislative powers herein granted shall be vested in a Congress of the United States, which shall consist of a Senate and a House of Representatives.

Section 2 The House of Representatives shall be composed of members chosen every second year by the people of the several States, and the electors in each State shall have the qualifications requisite for electors of the most numerous branch of the State Legislature.

---

*Passages no longer in effect are printed in italic type.

No person shall be a Representative who shall not have attained to the age of twenty-five years, and been seven years a citizen of the United States, and who shall not, when elected, be an inhabitant of that State in which he shall be chosen.

Representatives and direct taxes shall be apportioned among the several States which may be included within this Union, according to their respective numbers, *which shall be determined by adding to the whole number of free persons, including those bound to service for a term of years and excluding Indians not taxed, three-fifths of all other persons.* The actual enumeration shall be made within three years after the first meeting of the Congress of the United States, and within every subsequent term of ten years, in such manner as they shall by law direct. The number of Representatives shall not exceed one for every thirty thousand, but each State shall have at least one Representative; *and until such enumeration shall be made, the State of New Hampshire shall be entitled to choose three, Massachusetts eight, Rhode Island and Providence Plantations one, Connecticut five, New York six, New Jersey four, Pennsylvania eight, Delaware one, Maryland six, Virginia ten, North Carolina five, South Carolina five, and Georgia three.*

When vacancies happen in the representation from any State, the Executive authority thereof shall issue writs of election to fill such vacancies.

The House of Representatives shall choose their Speaker and other officers; and shall have the sole power of impeachment.

Section 3 The Senate of the United States shall be composed of two Senators from each State, *chosen by the legislature thereof,* for six years; and each Senator shall have one vote.

Immediately after they shall be assembled in consequence of the first election, they shall be divided as equally as may be into three classes. The seats of the Senators of the first class shall be vacated at the expiration of the second year, of the second class at the expiration of the fourth year, and of the third class at the expiration of the sixth year, so that one-third may be chosen every second year; and if vacancies happen by resignation or otherwise, during the recess of the legislature of any State, the Executive thereof may make temporary appointments until the next meeting of the legislature, which shall then fill such vacancies.

No person shall be a Senator who shall not have attained to the age of thirty years, and been nine years a citizen of the United States, and who shall not, when elected, be an inhabitant of that State for which he shall be chosen.

The Vice-President of the United States shall be President of the Senate, but shall have no vote, unless they be equally divided.

The Senate shall choose their other officers, and also a President *pro tempore*, in the absence of the Vice-President, or when he shall exercise the office of President of the United States.

The Senate shall have the sole power to try all impeachments. When sitting for that purpose, they shall be on oath or affirmation. When the President of the United States is tried, the Chief Justice shall preside: and no person shall be convicted without the concurrence of two-thirds of the members present.

Judgment in cases of impeachment shall not extend further than to removal from the office, and disqualification to hold and enjoy any office of honor, trust or profit under the United States: but the party convicted shall nevertheless be liable and subject to indictment, trial, judgment and punishment, according to law.

Section 4 The times, places and manner of holding elections for Senators and Representatives shall be prescribed in each State by the legislature thereof; but the Congress may at any time by law make or alter such regulations, except as to the places of choosing Senators.

The Congress shall assemble at least once in every year, and such meeting *shall be on the first Monday in December, unless they shall by law appoint a different day.*

Section 5 Each house shall be the judge of the elections, returns and qualifications of its own members, and a majority of each shall constitute a quorum to do business; but a smaller number may adjourn from day to day, and may be authorized to compel the attendance of absent members, in such manner, and under such penalties, as each house may provide.

Each house may determine the rules of its proceedings, punish its members for disorderly behavior, and with the concurrence of two-thirds, expel a member.

Each house shall keep a journal of its proceedings, and from time to time publish the same, excepting such parts as may in their judgment require secrecy; and the yeas and nays of the members of either house on any question shall, at the desire of one-fifth of those present, be entered on the journal.

Neither house, during the session of Congress, shall, without the consent of the other, adjourn for more than three days, nor to any other place than that in which the two houses shall be sitting.

Section 6 The Senators and Representatives shall receive a compensation for their services, to be ascertained by law and paid out of the treasury of the United States. They shall in all cases except treason, felony and breach of the peace, be privileged from arrest during their attendance at the session of their respective houses, and in going to and returning from the same; and for any speech or debate in either house, they shall not be questioned in any other place.

No Senator or Representative shall, during the time for which he was elected, be appointed to any civil office under the authority of the United States, which shall have been created, or the emoluments whereof shall have been increased, during such time; and no person holding any office under the United States shall be a member of either house during his continuance in office.

Section 7   All bills for raising revenue shall originate in the House of Representatives; but the Senate may propose or concur with amendments as on other bills.

Every bill which shall have passed the House of Representatives and the Senate, shall, before it become a law, be presented to the President of the United States; if he approve he shall sign it, but if not he shall return it with objections to that house in which it originated, who shall enter the objections at large on their journal, and proceed to reconsider it. If after such reconsideration two-thirds of that house shall agree to pass the bill, it shall be sent, together with the objections, to the other house, by which it shall likewise be reconsidered, and, if approved by two-thirds of that house, it shall become a law. But in all such cases the votes of both houses shall be determined by yeas and nays, and the names of the persons voting for and against the bill shall be entered on the journal of each house respectively. If any bill shall not be returned by the President within ten days (Sundays excepted) after it shall have been presented to him, the same shall be a law, in like manner as if he had signed it, unless the Congress by their adjournment prevent its return, in which case it shall not be a law.

Every order, resolution, or vote to which the concurrence of the Senate and House of Representatives may be necessary (except on a question of adjournment) shall be presented to the President of the United States; and before the same shall take effect, shall be approved by him, or being disapproved by him, shall be repassed by two-thirds of the Senate and House of Representatives, according to the rules and limitations prescribed in the case of a bill.

Section 8   The Congress shall have power

To lay and collect taxes, duties, imposts, and excises, to pay the debts and provide for the common defense and general welfare of the United States; but all duties, imposts and excises shall be uniform throughout the United States;

To borrow money on the credit of the United States;

To regulate commerce with foreign nations, and among the several States, and with the Indian tribes;

To establish an uniform rule of naturalization, and uniform laws on the subject of bankruptcies throughout the United States;

To coin money, regulate the value thereof, and of foreign coin, and fix the standard of weights and measures;

To provide for the punishment of counterfeiting the securities and current coin of the United States;

To establish post offices and post roads;

To promote the progress of science and useful arts by securing for limited times to authors and inventors the exclusive right to their respective writings and discoveries;

To constitute tribunals inferior to the Supreme Court;

To define and punish piracies and felonies committed on the high seas and offenses against the law of nations;

To declare war, grant letters of marque and reprisal, and make rules concerning captures on land and water;

To raise and support armies, but no appropriation of money to that use shall be for a longer term than two years;

To provide and maintain a navy;

To make rules for the government and regulation of the land and naval forces;

To provide for calling forth the militia to execute the laws of the Union, suppress insurrections, and repel invasions;

To provide for organizing, arming, and disciplining the militia, and for governing such part of them as may be employed in the service of the United States, reserving to the States respectively the appointment of the officers, and the authority of training the militia according to the discipline prescribed by Congress;

To exercise exclusive legislation in all cases whatsoever, over such district (not exceeding ten miles square) as may, by cession of particular States, and the acceptance of Congress, become the seat of government of the United States, and to exercise like authority over all places purchased by the consent of the legislature of the State, in which the same shall be, for erection of forts, magazines, arsenals, dockyards, and other needful buildings; —and

To make all laws which shall be necessary and proper for carrying into execution the foregoing powers, and all other powers vested by this Constitution in the government of the United States, or in any department or officer thereof.

Section 9   *The migration or importation of such persons as any of the States now existing shall think proper to admit shall not be prohibited by the Congress prior to the year 1808; but a tax or duty may be imposed on such importation, not exceeding $10 for each person.*

The privilege of the writ of habeas corpus shall not be suspended, unless when in cases of rebellion or invasion the public safety may require it.

No bill of attainder or ex post facto law shall be passed.

No capitation, or other direct, tax shall be laid, unless in proportion to the census or enumeration herein before directed to be taken.

No tax or duty shall be laid on articles exported from any State.

No preference shall be given by any regulation of commerce or revenue to the ports of one State over those of another; nor shall vessels bound to, or from, one State, be obliged to enter, clear, or pay duties in another.

No money shall be drawn from the treasury, but in consequence of appropriations made by law; and a regular statement and account of the receipts and expenditures of all public money shall be published from time to time.

No title of nobility shall be granted by the United States: and no person holding any office of profit or trust under them, shall, without the consent of the Congress, accept of any present, emolument, office, or title, of any kind whatever, from any king, prince, or foreign state.

Section 10   No State shall enter into any treaty, alliance, or confederation; grant letters of marque and reprisal; coin money; emit bills of credit; make anything but gold and silver coin a tender in payment of debts; pass any bill of attainder, ex post facto law, or law impairing the obligation of contracts, or grant any title of nobility.

No State shall, without the consent of Congress, lay any imposts or duties on imports or exports, except what may be absolutely necessary for executing its inspection laws: and the net produce of all duties and imposts, laid by any State on imports or exports, shall be for the use of the treasury of the United States; and all such laws shall be subject to the revision and control of the Congress.

No State shall, without the consent of Congress, lay any duty of tonnage, keep troops or ships of war in time of peace, enter into any agreement or compact with another State, or with a foreign power, or engage in war, unless actually invaded, or in such imminent danger as will not admit of delay.

Article II

Section 1   The executive power shall be vested in a President of the United States of America. He shall hold his office during the term of four years, and, together with the Vice-President, chosen for the same term, be elected as follows:

Each State shall appoint, in such manner as the legislature thereof may direct, a number of electors, equal to the whole number of Senators and Representatives to which the State may be entitled in the Congress; but no Senator or Representative, or person holding an office of trust or profit under the United States, shall be appointed an elector.

The electors shall meet in their respective States, and vote by ballot for two persons, of whom one at least shall not be an inhabitant of the same State with themselves. And they shall make a list of all the persons voted for, and of the number of votes for each; which list they shall sign and certify, and transmit sealed to the seat of government of the United States, directed to the President of the Senate. The President of the Senate shall, in the presence of the Senate and House of Representatives, open all the certificates, and the votes shall then be counted. The person having the greatest number of votes shall be the President, if such number be a majority of the whole number of electors appointed; and if there be more than one who have such majority, and have an equal number of votes, then the House of Representatives shall immediately choose by ballot one of them for President; and if no person have a majority, then from the five highest on the list said house shall in like manner choose the President. But in choosing the President the votes shall be taken by States, the representation from each State having one vote; a quorum for this purpose shall consist of a member or members from two-thirds of the States, and a majority of all the States shall be necessary to a choice. In every case, after the choice of the President, the person having the greatest number of votes of the electors shall be the Vice-President. But if there should remain two or more who have equal votes, the Senate shall choose from them by ballot the Vice-President.

The Congress may determine the time of choosing the electors and the day on which they shall give their votes; which day shall be the same throughout the United States.

No person except a natural-born citizen, *or a citizen of the United States at the time of the adoption of this Constitution,* shall be eligible to the office of President; neither shall any person be eligible to that office who shall not have attained to the age of thirty-five years, and been fourteen years a resident within the United States.

In cases of the removal of the President from office or of his death, resignation, or inability to discharge the powers and duties of the said office, the same shall devolve on the Vice-President, and the Congress may by law provide for the case of removal, death, resignation, or inability, both of the President and Vice-President, declaring what officer shall then act as President, and such officer shall act accordingly, until the disability be removed, or a President shall be elected.

The President shall, at stated times, receive for his services a compensation, which shall neither be increased nor diminished during the period for which he shall have been elected, and he shall not receive within that period any other emolument from the United States, or any of them.

Before he enter on the execution of his office, he shall take the following oath or affirmation:—"I do solemnly swear (or affirm) that I will faithfully execute the office of President of the United States, and will to the best of my ability preserve, protect and defend the Constitution of the United States."

Section 2   The President shall be commander in chief of the army and navy of the United States, and of the militia of the several States, when called into the actual service of the United States; he may require the opinion, in writing, of the principal officer in each of the executive departments, upon any subject relating to the duties of their respective offices, and he shall have power to grant reprieves and pardons for offenses against the United States, except in cases of impeachment.

He shall have power, by and with the advice and consent of the Senate, to make treaties, provided two-thirds of the Senators present concur; and he shall nominate, and by and with the advice and consent of the Senate, shall appoint ambassadors, other public ministers and consuls, judges of the Supreme Court, and all other officers of the United States, whose appointments are not herein otherwise provided for, and which shall be established by law: but Congress may by law vest the appointment of such inferior officers, as they think proper, in the President alone, in the courts of law, or in the heads of departments.

The President shall have power to fill up all vacancies that may happen during the recess of the Senate, by granting commissions which shall expire at the end of their next session.

Section 3   He shall from time to time give to the Congress information of the state of the Union, and recommend to their consideration such measures as he shall judge necessary and expedient; he may, on extraordinary occasions, convene both houses, or either of them, and in case of disagreement between them, with respect to the time of adjournment, he may adjourn them to such time as he shall think proper; he shall receive ambassadors and other public ministers; he shall take care that the laws be faithfully executed, and shall commission all the officers of the United States.

Section 4   The President, Vice-President and all civil officers of the United States shall be removed from office on impeachment for, and on conviction of, treason, bribery, or other high crimes and misdemeanors.

Article III

Section 1   The judicial power of the United States shall be vested in one Supreme Court, and in such inferior courts as the Congress may from time to time ordain and establish. The judges, both of the Supreme and inferior courts, shall hold their offices during good behavior, and shall, at stated times, receive for their services a compensation which shall not be diminished during their continuance in office.

Section 2   The judicial power shall extend to all cases, in law and equity, arising under this Constitution, the laws of the United States, and treaties made, or which shall be made, under their authority;—to all cases affecting ambassadors, other public ministers and consuls;—to all cases of admiralty and maritime jurisdiction;—to controversies to which the United States shall be a party;—to controversies between two or more States;—*between a State and citizens of another State;*—between citizens of different States;—between citizens of the same State claiming lands under grants of different States, and between a State, or the citizens thereof, and foreign states, citizens or subjects.

In all cases affecting ambassadors, other public ministers and consuls, and those in which a State shall be party, the Supreme Court shall have original jurisdiction. In all the other cases before mentioned, the Supreme Court shall have appellate jurisdiction, both as to law and fact, with such exceptions, and under such regulations, as the Congress shall make.

The trial of all crimes, except in cases of impeachment, shall be by jury; and such trial shall be held in the State where said crimes shall have been committed; but when not committed within any State, the trial shall be at such place or places as the Congress may by law have directed.

Section 3   Treason against the United States shall consist only in levying war against them, or in adhering to their enemies, giving them aid and comfort. No person shall be convicted of treason unless on the testimony of two witnesses to the same overt act, or on confession in open court.

The Congress shall have power to declare the punishment of treason, but no attainder of treason shall work corruption of blood, or forfeiture except during the life of the person attainted.

Article IV

Section 1   Full faith and credit shall be given in each State to the public acts, records, and judicial proceedings of every other State. And the Congress may by general laws prescribe the manner in which such acts, records, and proceedings shall be proved, and the effect thereof.

Section 2   The citizens of each State shall be entitled to all privileges and immunities of citizens in the several States.

A person charged in any State with treason, felony, or other crime, who shall flee from justice, and be found in another State, shall on demand of the executive authority of the State from which he fled, be delivered up, to be removed to the State having jurisdiction of the crime.

No person held to service or labor in one State, under the laws thereof, escaping into another, shall, in consequence of any law or regulation therein, be discharged from such service or labor, but shall be delivered up on claim of the party to whom such service or labor may be due.

Section 3   New States may be admitted by the Congress into this Union; but no new State shall be formed or erected within the jurisdiction of any other State; nor any State be formed by the junction of two or more States, or parts of States, without the consent of the legislatures of the States concerned as well as of the Congress.

The Congress shall have power to dispose of and make all needful rules and regulations respecting the territory or other property belonging to the United States; and nothing in this Constitution shall be so construed as to prejudice any claims of the United States, or of any particular State.

Section 4 The United States shall guarantee to every State in this Union a republican form of government, and shall protect each of them against invasion; and on application of the legislature, or of the executive (when the legislature cannot be convened), against domestic violence.

Article V

The Congress, whenever two-thirds of both houses shall deem it necessary, shall propose amendments to this Constitution, or, on the application of the legislatures of two-thirds of the several States, shall call a convention for proposing amendments, which, in either case, shall be valid to all intents and purposes, as part of this Constitution, when ratified by the legislatures of three-fourths of the several States, or by conventions in three-fourths thereof, as the one or the other mode of ratification may be proposed by the Congress; provided *that no amendments which may be made prior to the year one thousand eight hundred and eight shall in any manner affect the first and fourth clauses in the ninth section of the first article;* and that no State, without its consent, shall be deprived of its equal suffrage in the Senate.

Article VI

All debts contracted and engagements entered into, before the adoption of this Constitution, shall be as valid against the United States under this Constitution, as under the Confederation.

This Constitution, and the laws of the United States which shall be made in pursuance thereof; and all treaties made, or which shall be made, under the authority of the United States, shall be the supreme law of the land; and the judges in every State shall be bound thereby, anything in the Constitution or laws of any State to the contrary notwithstanding.

The Senators and Representatives before mentioned, and the members of the several State legislatures, and all executive and judicial officers, both of the United States and of the several States, shall be bound by oath or affirmation to support this Constitution; but no religious test shall ever be required as a qualification to any office or public trust under the United States.

Article VII

The ratification of the conventions of nine States shall be sufficient for the establishment of this Constitution between the States so ratifying the same.

Done in Convention by the unanimous consent of the States present, the seventeenth day of September in the year of our Lord one thousand seven hundred and eighty-seven and of the Independence of the United States of America the twelfth. In witness whereof we have hereunto subscribed our names.

AMENDMENTS TO THE CONSTITUTION*

Amendment I

Congress shall make no law respecting an establishment of religion, or prohibiting the free exercise thereof; or abridging the freedom of speech, or of the press; or the right of the people peaceably to assemble, and to petition the government for a redress of grievances.

Amendment II

A well-regulated militia being necessary to the security of a free State, the right of the people to keep and bear arms shall not be infringed.

Amendment III

No soldier shall, in time of peace, be quartered in any house without the consent of the owner, nor in time of war, but in a manner to be prescribed by law.

Amendment IV

The right of the people to be secure in their persons, houses, papers, and effects, against unreasonable searches and seizures, shall not be violated, and no warrants shall issue but upon probable cause, supported by oath or affirmation, and particularly describing the place to be searched, and the persons or things to be seized.

Amendment V

No person shall be held to answer for a capital, or otherwise infamous crime, unless on a presentment or indictment of a grand jury, except in cases arising in the land or naval forces, or in the militia, when in actual service in time of war or public danger; nor shall any person be subject for the same of-

---

*The first ten Amendments (the Bill of Rights) were adopted in 1791.

fense to be twice put in jeopardy of life or limb; nor shall be compelled in any criminal case to be a witness against himself, nor be deprived of life, liberty, or property, without due process of law; nor shall private property be taken for public use without just compensation.

Amendment VI

In all criminal prosecutions, the accused shall enjoy the right to a speedy and public trial, by an impartial jury of the State and district wherein the crime shall have been committed, which district shall have been previously ascertained by law, and to be informed of the nature and cause of the accusation; to be confronted with the witnesses against him; to have compulsory process for obtaining witnesses in his favor, and to have the assistance of counsel for his defense.

Amendment VII

In suits at common law, where the value in controversy shall exceed twenty dollars, the right of trial by jury shall be preserved, and no fact tried by a jury shall be otherwise reexamined in any court of the United States, than according to the rules of the common law.

Amendment VIII

Excessive bail shall not be required, nor excessive fines imposed, nor cruel and unusual punishments inflicted.

Amendment IX

The enumeration in the Constitution, of certain rights, shall not be construed to deny or disparage others retained by the people.

Amendment X

The powers not delegated to the United States by the Constitution, nor prohibited by it to the States, are reserved to the States respectively, or to the people.

Amendment XI

[Adopted 1798]

The judicial power of the United States shall not be construed to extend to any suit in law or equity, commenced or prosecuted against one of the United States by citizens of another State, or by citizens or subjects of any foreign state.

Amendment XII

[Adopted 1804]

The electors shall meet in their respective States, and vote by ballot for President and Vice-President, one of whom, at least, shall not be an inhabitant of the same State with themselves; they shall name in their ballots the person voted for as President, and in distinct ballots the person voted for as Vice-President, and they shall make distinct lists of all persons voted for as President, and of all persons voted for as Vice-President, and of the number of votes for each, which lists they shall sign and certify, and transmit sealed to the seat of government of the United States, directed to the President of the Senate;—the President of the Senate shall, in the presence of the Senate and House of Representatives, open all the certificates and the votes shall then be counted;—the person having the greatest number of votes for President shall be the President, if such number be a majority of the whole number of electors appointed; and if no person have such majority, then from the persons having the highest numbers not exceeding three on the list of those voted for as President, the House of Representatives shall choose immediately, by ballot, the President. But in choosing the President, the votes shall be taken by States, the representation from each State having one vote; a quorum for this purpose shall consist of a member or members from two-thirds of the States, and a majority of all the States shall be necessary to a choice. And if the House of Representatives shall not choose a President whenever the right of choice shall devolve upon them, before *the fourth day of March* next following, then the Vice-President shall act as President, as in the case of the death or other constitutional disability of the President.

The person having the greatest number of votes as Vice-President shall be the Vice-President, if such number be a majority of the whole number of electors appointed; and if no person have a majority, then from the two highest numbers on the list the Senate shall choose the Vice-President; a quorum for the purpose shall consist of two-thirds of the whole number of Senators, and a majority of the whole number shall be necessary to a choice. But no person constitutionally ineligible to the office of President shall be eligible to that of Vice-President of the United States.

Amendment XIII

[Adopted 1865]

Section 1 Neither slavery nor involuntary servitude, except as a punishment for crime whereof the party shall have been duly convicted, shall exist within the United States, or any place subject to their jurisdiction.

Section 2 Congress shall have power to enforce this article by appropriate legislation.

Amendment XIV

[Adopted 1868]

Section 1 All persons born or naturalized in the United States, and subject to the jurisdiction thereof, are citizens of the United States and of the State wherein they reside. No State shall make or enforce any law which shall abridge the privileges or immunities of citizens of the United States; nor shall any State deprive any person of life, liberty, or property, without due process of law; nor deny to any person within its jurisdiction the equal protection of the laws.

Section 2 Representatives shall be apportioned among the several States according to their respective numbers, counting the whole number of persons in each State, excluding Indians not taxed. But when the right to vote at any election for the choice of Electors for President and Vice-President of the United States, Representatives in Congress, the executive and judicial officers of a State, or the members of the legislature thereof, is denied to any of the male inhabitants of such State, being twenty-one years of age and citizens of the United States, or in any way abridged, except for participation in rebellion, or other crime, the basis of representation therein shall be reduced in the proportion which the number of such male citizens shall bear to the whole number of male citizens twenty-one years of age in such State.

Section 3 No person shall be a Senator or Representative in Congress, or Elector of President and Vice-President, or hold any office, civil or military, under the United States, or under any State, who, having previously taken an oath, as a member of Congress, or as an officer of the United States, or as a member of any State legislature, or as an executive or judicial officer of any State, to support the Constitution of the United States, shall have engaged in insurrection or rebellion against the same, or given aid or comfort to the enemies thereof. Congress may, by a vote of two-thirds of each house, remove such disability.

Section 4 The validity of the public debt of the United States, authorized by law, including debts incurred for payment of pensions and bounties for services in suppressing insurrection or rebellion, shall not be questioned. But neither the United States nor any State shall assume or pay any debt or obligation incurred in aid of insurrection or rebellion against the United States, or any claim for the loss of emancipation of any slave; but all such debts, obligations, and claims shall be held illegal and void.

Section 5 The Congress shall have power to enforce, by appropriate legislation, the provisions of this article.

Amendment XV

[Adopted 1870]

Section 1 The right of citizens of the United States to vote shall not be denied or abridged by the United States or by any State on account of race, color, or previous condition of servitude.

Section 2 The Congress shall have power to enforce this article by appropriate legislation.

Amendment XVI

[Adopted 1913]

The Congress shall have power to lay and collect taxes on incomes, from whatever source derived, without apportionment among the several States, and without regard to any census or enumeration.

Amendment XVII

[Adopted 1913]

Section 1 The Senate of the United States shall be composed of two Senators from each State, elected by the people thereof, for six years; and each Senator shall have one vote. The electors in each State shall have the qualifications requisite for electors of [voters for] the most numerous branch of the State legislatures.

Section 2 When vacancies happen in the representation of any State in the Senate, the executive authority of such State shall issue writs of election to fill such vacancies: Provided, that the Legislature of any State may empower the executive thereof to make temporary appointments until the people fill the vacancies by election as the Legislature may direct.

Section 3 This amendment shall not be so construed as to affect the election or term of any Senator chosen before it becomes valid as part of the Constitution.

Amendment XVIII

[Adopted 1919; Repealed 1933]

Section 1 After one year from the ratification of this article the manufacture, sale, or transportation of intoxicating liquors within, the importation thereof into, or the exportation thereof from the United States and all territory subject to the jurisdiction thereof, for beverage purposes, is hereby prohibited.

Section 2 The Congress and the several States shall have concurrent power to enforce this article by appropriate legislation.

Section 3 This article shall be inoperative unless it shall have been ratified as an amendment to the Constitution by the legislatures of the several States, as provided by the Constitution, within seven years from the date of the submission thereof to the States by the Congress.

Amendment XIX

[Adopted 1920]

Section 1 The right of citizens of the United States to vote shall not be denied or abridged by the United States or by any State on account of sex.

Section 2 The Congress shall have power to enforce this article by appropriate legislation.

Amendment XX

[Adopted 1933]

Section 1 The terms of the President and Vice-President shall end at noon on the 20th day of January, and the terms of Senators and Representatives at noon on the 3rd day of January, of the years in which such terms would have ended if this article had not been ratified; and the terms of their successors shall then begin.

Section 2 The Congress shall assemble at least once in every year, and such meeting shall begin at noon on the 3d day of January, unless they shall by law appoint a different day.

Section 3 If, at the time fixed for the beginning of the term of the President, the President-elect shall have died, the Vice-President–elect shall become President. If a President shall not have been chosen before the time fixed for the beginning of his term, or if the President-elect shall have failed to qualify, then the Vice-President–elect shall act as President until a President shall have qualified; and the Congress may by law provide for the case wherein neither a President-elect nor a Vice-President–elect shall have qualified, declaring who shall then act as President, or the manner in which one who is to act shall be selected, and such persons shall act accordingly until a President or Vice-President shall have qualified.

Section 4 The Congress may by law provide for the case of the death of any of the persons from whom the House of Representatives may choose a President whenever the right of choice shall have devolved upon them, and for the case of the death of any of the persons from whom the Senate may choose a Vice-President whenever the right of choice shall have devolved upon them.

Section 5 Sections 1 and 2 shall take effect on the 15th day of October following the ratification of this article.

Section 6 This article shall be inoperative unless it shall have been ratified as an amendment to the Constitution by the Legislatures of three-fourths of the several States within seven years from the date of its submission.

Amendment XXI

[Adopted 1933]

Section 1 The eighteenth article of amendment to the Constitution of the United States is hereby repealed.

Section 2 The transportation or importation into any State, Territory, or Possession of the United States for delivery or use therein of intoxicating liquors, in violation of the laws thereof, is hereby prohibited.

Section 3 This article shall be inoperative unless it shall have been ratified as an amendment to the Constitution by conventions in the several States, as provided in the Constitution, within seven years from the date of submission thereof to the States by the Congress.

Amendment XXII

[Adopted 1951]

Section 1 No person shall be elected to the office of President more than twice, and no person who has held the office of President, or acted as President, for more than two years of a term to which some other person was elected President shall be elected to the office of President more than once. But this article shall not apply to any person holding the office of President when this article was proposed by the Congress, and shall not prevent any person who may be holding the office of President, or acting as President, during the term within which this article becomes operative from holding the office of President or acting as President during the remainder of such term.

Section 2 This article shall be inoperative unless it shall have been ratified as an amendment to the Constitution by the legislatures of three-fourths of the several States within seven years from the date of its submission to the States by the Congress.

Amendment XXIII

[Adopted 1961]

Section 1 The District constituting the seat of Government of the United States shall appoint in such manner as the Congress may direct:

A number of electors of President and Vice-President equal to the whole number of Senators and Representatives in Congress to which the District would be entitled if it were a State, but in no event more than the least populous State; they shall be in addition to those appointed by the States, but they shall be considered for the purposes of the election of President and Vice-President, to be electors appointed by a State; and they shall meet in the District and perform such duties as provided by the twelfth article of amendment.

Section 2 The Congress shall have the power to enforce this article by appropriate legislation.

Amendment XXIV

[Adopted 1964]

Section 1 The right of citizens of the United States to vote in any primary or other election for President or Vice-President, for electors for President or Vice-President, or for Senator or Representative in Congress, shall not be denied or abridged by the United States or any State by reason of failure to pay any poll tax or other tax.

Section 2 The Congress shall have the power to enforce this article by appropriate legislation.

Amendment XXV

[Adopted 1967]

Section 1 In case of the removal of the President from office or of his death or resignation, the Vice-President shall become President.

Section 2 Whenever there is a vacancy in the office of the Vice-President, the President shall nominate a Vice-President who shall take office upon confirmation by a majority vote of both Houses of Congress.

Section 3 Whenever the President transmits to the President pro tempore of the Senate and the Speaker of the House of Representatives his written declaration that he is unable to discharge the powers and duties of his office, and until he transmits to them a written declaration to the contrary, such powers and duties shall be discharged by the Vice-President as Acting President.

Section 4 Whenever the Vice-President and a majority of either the principal officers of the executive departments or of such other body as Congress may by law provide, transmit to the President pro tempore of the Senate and the Speaker of the House of Representatives their written declaration that the President is unable to discharge the powers and duties of his office, the Vice-President shall immediately assume the powers and duties of the office as Acting President.

Thereafter, when the President transmits to the President pro tempore of the Senate and the Speaker of the House of Representatives his written declaration that no inability exists, he shall resume the powers and duties of his office unless the Vice-President and a majority of either the principal officers of the executive department[s] or of such other body as Congress may by law provide, transmit within four days to the President pro tempore of the Senate and the Speaker of the House of Representatives their written declaration that the President is unable to discharge the powers and duties of his office. Thereupon Congress shall decide the issue, assembling within forty-eight hours for that purpose if not in session. If the Congress, within twenty-one days after receipt of the latter written declaration, or, if Congress is not in session, within twenty-one days after Congress is required to assemble, determines by two-thirds vote of both Houses that the President is unable to discharge the powers and duties of his office, the Vice-President shall continue to discharge the same as Acting President; otherwise, the President shall resume the powers and duties of his office.

Amendment XXVI

[Adopted 1971]

Section 1 The right of citizens of the United States, who are eighteen years of age or older, to vote shall not be denied or abridged by the United States or by any State on account of age.

Section 2 The Congress shall have power to enforce this article by appropriate legislation.

Amendment XXVII

[Adopted 1992]

No law, varying the compensation for the services of the Senators and Representatives, shall take effect, until an election of Representatives shall have intervened.

Presidential Elections

Year	Number of States	Candidates	Parties	Popular Vote	% of Popular Vote	Electoral Vote	% Voter Participation[a]
1789	10	**George Washington**	No party			69	
		John Adams	designations			34	
		Other candidates				35	
1792	15	**George Washington**	No party			132	
		John Adams	designations			77	
		George Clinton				50	
		Other candidates				5	
1796	16	**John Adams**	Federalist			71	
		Thomas Jefferson	Democratic-Republican			68	
		Thomas Pinckney	Federalist			59	
		Aaron Burr	Democratic-Republican			30	
		Other candidates				48	
1800	16	**Thomas Jefferson**	Democratic-Republican			73	
		Aaron Burr	Democratic-Republican			73	
		John Adams	Federalist			65	
		Charles C. Pinckney	Federalist			64	
		John Jay	Federalist			1	
1804	17	**Thomas Jefferson**	Democratic-Republican			162	
		Charles C. Pinckney	Federalist			14	
1808	17	**James Madison**	Democratic-Republican			122	
		Charles C. Pinckney	Federalist			47	
		George Clinton	Democratic-Republican			6	
1812	18	**James Madison**	Democratic-Republican			128	
		DeWitt Clinton	Federalist			89	
1816	19	**James Monroe**	Democratic-Republican			183	
		Rufus King	Federalist			34	
1820	24	**James Monroe**	Democratic-Republican			231	

Presidential Elections (continued)

Year	Number of States	Candidates	Parties	Popular Vote	% of Popular Vote	Electoral Vote	% Voter Participation[a]
		John Quincy Adams	Independent Republican			1	
1824	24	**John Quincy Adams**	Democratic-Republican	108,740	30.5	84	26.9
		Andrew Jackson	Democratic-Republican	153,544	43.1	99	
		Henry Clay	Democratic-Republican	47,136	13.2	37	
		William H. Crawford	Democratic-Republican	46,618	13.1	41	
1828	24	**Andrew Jackson**	Democratic	647,286	56.0	178	57.6
		John Quincy Adams	National Republican	508,064	44.0	83	
1832	24	**Andrew Jackson**	Democratic	701,780	54.2	219	55.4
		Henry Clay	National Republican	484,205	37.4	49	
		Other candidates		107,988	8.0	18	
1836	26	**Martin Van Buren**	Democratic	764,176	50.8	170	57.8
		William H. Harrison	Whig	550,816	36.6	73	
		Hugh L. White	Whig	146,107	9.7	26	
1840	26	**William H. Harrison**	Whig	1,274,624	53.1	234	80.2
		Martin Van Buren	Democratic	1,127,781	46.9	60	
1844	26	**James K. Polk**	Democratic	1,338,464	49.6	170	78.9
		Henry Clay	Whig	1,300,097	48.1	105	
		James G. Birney	Liberty	62,300	2.3		
1848	30	**Zachary Taylor**	Whig	1,360,967	47.4	163	72.7
		Lewis Cass	Democratic	1,222,342	42.5	127	
		Martin Van Buren	Free Soil	291,263	10.1		
1852	31	**Franklin Pierce**	Democratic	1,601,117	50.9	254	69.6
		Winfield Scott	Whig	1,385,453	44.1	42	
		John P. Hale	Free Soil	155,825	5.0		
1856	31	**James Buchanan**	Democratic	1,832,955	45.3	174	78.9
		John C. Frémont	Republican	1,339,932	33.1	114	
		Millard Fillmore	American	871,731	21.6	8	
1860	33	**Abraham Lincoln**	Republican	1,865,593	39.8	180	81.2
		Stephen A. Douglas	Democratic	1,382,713	29.5	12	
		John C. Breckinridge	Democratic	848,356	18.1	72	
		John Bell	Constitutional Union	592,906	12.6	39	
1864	36	**Abraham Lincoln**	Republican	2,206,938	55.0	212	73.8
		George B. McClellan	Democratic	1,803,787	45.0	21	

Presidential Elections (continued)

Year	Number of States	Candidates	Parties	Popular Vote	% of Popular Vote	Electoral Vote	% Voter Participation[a]
1868	37	**Ulysses S. Grant**	Republican	3,013,421	52.7	214	78.1
		Horatio Seymour	Democratic	2,706,829	47.3	80	
1872	37	**Ulysses S. Grant**	Republican	3,596,745	55.6	286	71.3
		Horace Greeley	Democratic	2,843,446	43.9	b	
1876	38	**Rutherford B. Hayes**	Republican	4,036,572	48.0	185	81.8
		Samuel J. Tilden	Democratic	4,284,020	51.0	184	
1880	38	**James A. Garfield**	Republican	4,453,295	48.5	214	79.4
		Winfield S. Hancock	Democratic	4,414,082	48.1	155	
		James B. Weaver	Greenback-Labor	308,578	3.4		
1884	38	**Grover Cleveland**	Democratic	4,879,507	48.5	219	77.5
		James G. Blaine	Republican	4,850,293	48.2	182	
		Benjamin F. Butler	Greenback-Labor	175,370	1.8		
		John P. St. John	Prohibition	150,369	1.5		
1888	38	**Benjamin Harrison**	Republican	5,447,129	47.9	233	79.3
		Grover Cleveland	Democratic	5,537,857	48.6	168	
		Clinton B. Fisk	Prohibition	249,506	2.2		
		Anson J. Streeter	Union Labor	146,935	1.3		
1892	44	**Grover Cleveland**	Democratic	5,555,426	46.1	277	74.7
		Benjamin Harrison	Republican	5,182,690	43.0	145	
		James B. Weaver	People's	1,029,846	8.5	22	
		John Bidwell	Prohibition	264,133	2.2		
1896	45	**William McKinley**	Republican	7,102,246	51.1	271	79.3
		William J. Bryan	Democratic	6,492,559	47.7	176	
1900	45	**William McKinley**	Republican	7,218,491	51.7	292	73.2
		William J. Bryan	Democratic; Populist	6,356,734	45.5	155	
		John C. Wooley	Prohibition	208,914	1.5		
1904	45	**Theodore Roosevelt**	Republican	7,628,461	57.4	336	65.2
		Alton B. Parker	Democratic	5,084,223	37.6	140	
		Eugene V. Debs	Socialist	402,283	3.0		
		Silas C. Swallow	Prohibition	258,536	1.9		
1908	46	**William H. Taft**	Republican	7,675,320	51.6	321	65.4
		William J. Bryan	Democratic	6,412,294	43.1	162	
		Eugene V. Debs	Socialist	420,793	2.8		
		Eugene W. Chafin	Prohibition	253,840	1.7		
1912	48	**Woodrow Wilson**	Democratic	6,296,547	41.9	435	58.8
		Theodore Roosevelt	Progressive	4,118,571	27.4	88	
		William H. Taft	Republican	3,486,720	23.2	8	
		Eugene V. Debs	Socialist	900,672	6.0		

Presidential Elections (continued)

Year	Number of States	Candidates	Parties	Popular Vote	% of Popular Vote	Electoral Vote	% Voter Participation[a]
		Eugene W. Chafin	Prohibition	206,275	1.4		
1916	48	**Woodrow Wilson**	Democratic	9,127,695	49.4	277	61.6
		Charles E. Hughes	Republican	8,533,507	46.2	254	
		A. L. Benson	Socialist	585,113	3.2		
		J. Frank Hanly	Prohibition	220,506	1.2		
1920	48	**Warren G. Harding**	Republican	16,143,407	60.4	404	49.2
		James M. Cox	Democratic	9,130,328	34.2	127	
		Eugene V. Debs	Socialist	919,799	3.4		
		P. P. Christensen	Farmer-Labor	265,411	1.0		
1924	48	**Calvin Coolidge**	Republican	15,718,211	54.0	382	48.9
		John W. Davis	Democratic	8,385,283	28.8	136	
		Robert M. La Follette	Progressive	4,831,289	16.6	13	
1928	48	**Herbert C. Hoover**	Republican	21,391,993	58.2	444	56.9
		Alfred E. Smith	Democratic	15,016,169	40.9	87	
1932	48	**Franklin D. Roosevelt**	Democratic	22,809,638	57.4	472	56.9
		Herbert C. Hoover	Republican	15,758,901	39.7	59	
		Norman Thomas	Socialist	881,951	2.2		
1936	48	**Franklin D. Roosevelt**	Democratic	27,752,869	60.8	523	61.0
		Alfred M. Landon	Republican	16,674,665	36.5	8	
		William Lemke	Union	882,479	1.9		
1940	48	**Franklin D. Roosevelt**	Democratic	27,307,819	54.8	449	62.5
		Wendell L. Willkie	Republican	22,321,018	44.8	82	
1944	48	**Franklin D. Roosevelt**	Democratic	25,606,585	53.5	432	55.9
		Thomas E. Dewey	Republican	22,014,745	46.0	99	
1948	48	**Harry S Truman**	Democratic	24,179,345	49.6	303	53.0
		Thomas E. Dewey	Republican	21,991,291	45.1	189	
		J. Strom Thurmond	States' Rights	1,176,125	2.4	39	
		Henry A. Wallace	Progressive	1,157,326	2.4		
1952	48	**Dwight D. Eisenhower**	Republican	33,936,234	55.1	442	63.3
		Adlai E. Stevenson	Democratic	27,314,992	44.4	89	
1956	48	**Dwight D. Eisenhower**	Republican	35,590,472	57.6	457	60.6
		Adlai E. Stevenson	Democratic	26,022,752	42.1	73	
1960	50	**John F. Kennedy**	Democratic	34,226,731	49.7	303	62.8
		Richard M. Nixon	Republican	34,108,157	49.5	219	
1964	50	**Lyndon B. Johnson**	Democratic	43,129,566	61.1	486	61.7
		Barry M. Goldwater	Republican	27,178,188	38.5	52	
1968	50	**Richard M. Nixon**	Republican	31,785,480	43.4	301	60.6
		Hubert H. Humphrey	Democratic	31,275,166	42.7	191	

Presidential Elections (continued)

Year	Number of States	Candidates	Parties	Popular Vote	% of Popular Vote	Electoral Vote	% Voter Participation[a]
		George C. Wallace	American Independent	9,906,473	13.5	46	
1972	50	**Richard M. Nixon**	Republican	47,169,911	60.7	520	55.2
		George S. McGovern	Democratic	29,170,383	37.5	17	
		John G. Schmitz	American	1,099,482	1.4		
1976	50	**James E. Carter**	Democratic	40,830,763	50.1	297	53.5
		Gerald R. Ford	Republican	39,147,793	48.0	240	
1980	50	**Ronald W. Reagan**	Republican	43,904,153	50.7	489	52.6
		James E. Carter	Democratic	35,483,883	41.0	49	
		John B. Anderson	Independent	5,720,060	6.6		
		Ed Clark	Libertarian	921,299	1.1		
1984	50	**Ronald W. Reagan**	Republican	54,455,075	58.8	525	53.3
		Walter F. Mondale	Democratic	37,577,185	40.6	13	
1988	50	**George H. W. Bush**	Republican	48,886,097	53.4	426	50.1
		Michael S. Dukakis	Democratic	41,809,074	45.6	111[c]	
1992	50	**William J. Clinton**	Democratic	44,909,326	43.0	370	55.2
		George H. W. Bush	Republican	39,103,882	37.4	168	
		H. Ross Perot	Independent	19,741,048	18.9		
1996	50	**William J. Clinton**	Democratic	47,402,357	49.2	379	49.1
		Robert J. Dole	Republican	39,196,755	40.7	159	
		H. Ross Perot	Reform	8,085,402	8.4		
		Ralph Nader	Green	684,902	0.7		
2000	50	**George W. Bush**	Republican	50,455,156	47.9	271	51.2
		Albert Gore	Democratic	50,992,335	48.4	266	
		Ralph Nader	Green	2,882,955	2.7		
2004	50	**George W. Bush**	Republican	62,039,073	50.7	286	55.3
		John F. Kerry	Democratic	59,027,478	48.2	251	
		Ralph Nader	Independent	240,896	0.2		

Candidates receiving less than 1 percent of the popular vote have been omitted. Thus the percentage of popular vote given for any election year may not total 100 percent.

Before the passage of the Twelfth Amendment in 1804, the electoral college voted for two presidential candidates; the runner-up became vice president.

Before 1824, most presidential electors were chosen by state legislatures, not by popular vote.

[a]Percent of voting-age population casting ballots.

[b]Greeley died shortly after the election; the electors supporting him then divided their votes among minor candidates.

[c]One elector from West Virginia cast her electoral college presidential ballot for Lloyd Bentsen, the Democratic Party's vice-presidential candidate.

Presidents and Vice Presidents

1. President	**George Washington**	1789–1797	
Vice President	John Adams	1789–1797	
2. President	**John Adams**	1797–1801	
Vice President	Thomas Jefferson	1797–1801	
3. President	**Thomas Jefferson**	1801–1809	
Vice President	Aaron Burr	1801–1805	
Vice President	George Clinton	1805–1809	
4. President	**James Madison**	1809–1817	
Vice President	George Clinton	1809–1813	
Vice President	Elbridge Gerry	1813–1817	
5. President	**James Monroe**	1817–1825	
Vice President	Daniel Tompkins	1817–1825	
6. President	**John Quincy Adams**	1825–1829	
Vice President	John C. Calhoun	1825–1829	
7. President	**Andrew Jackson**	1829–1837	
Vice President	John C. Calhoun	1829–1833	
Vice President	Martin Van Buren	1833–1837	
8. President	**Martin Van Buren**	1837–1841	
Vice President	Richard M. Johnson	1837–1841	
9. President	**William H. Harrison**	1841	
Vice President	John Tyler	1841	
10. President	**John Tyler**	1841–1845	
Vice President	None		
11. President	**James K. Polk**	1845–1849	
Vice President	George M. Dallas	1845–1849	
12. President	**Zachary Taylor**	1849–1850	
Vice President	Millard Fillmore	1849–1850	
13. President	**Millard Fillmore**	1850–1853	
Vice President	None		
14. President	**Franklin Pierce**	1853–1857	
Vice President	William R. King	1853–1857	
15. President	**James Buchanan**	1857–1861	
Vice President	John C. Breckinridge	1857–1861	
16. President	**Abraham Lincoln**	1861–1865	
Vice President	Hannibal Hamlin	1861–1865	
Vice President	Andrew Johnson	1865	
17. President	**Andrew Johnson**	1865–1869	
Vice President	None		
18. President	**Ulysses S. Grant**	1869–1877	
Vice President	Schuyler Colfax	1869–1873	
Vice President	Henry Wilson	1873–1877	
19. President	**Rutherford B. Hayes**	1877–1881	
Vice President	William A. Wheeler	1877–1881	
20. President	**James A. Garfield**	1881	
Vice President	Chester A. Arthur	1881	
21. President	**Chester A. Arthur**	1881–1885	
Vice President	None		
22. President	**Grover Cleveland**	1885–1889	
Vice President	Thomas A. Hendricks	1885–1889	
23. President	**Benjamin Harrison**	1889–1893	
Vice President	Levi P. Morton	1889–1893	
24. President	**Grover Cleveland**	1893–1897	
Vice President	Adlai E. Stevenson	1893–1897	
25. President	**William McKinley**	1897–1901	
Vice President	Garret A. Hobart	1897–1901	
Vice President	Theodore Roosevelt	1901	
26. President	**Theodore Roosevelt**	1901–1909	
Vice President	Charles Fairbanks	1905–1909	
27. President	**William H. Taft**	1909–1913	
Vice President	James S. Sherman	1909–1913	
28. President	**Woodrow Wilson**	1913–1921	
Vice President	Thomas R. Marshall	1913–1921	
29. President	**Warren G. Harding**	1921–1923	
Vice President	Calvin Coolidge	1921–1923	
30. President	**Calvin Coolidge**	1923–1929	
Vice President	Charles G. Dawes	1925–1929	
31. President	**Herbert C. Hoover**	1929–1933	
Vice President	Charles Curtis	1929–1933	
32. President	**Franklin D. Roosevelt**	1933–1945	
Vice President	John N. Garner	1933–1941	
Vice President	Henry A. Wallace	1941–1945	
Vice President	Harry S Truman	1945	
33. President	**Harry S Truman**	1945–1953	
Vice President	Alben W. Barkley	1949–1953	
34. President	**Dwight D. Eisenhower**	1953–1961	
Vice President	Richard M. Nixon	1953–1961	

Presidents and Vice Presidents (continued)

35. President	**John F. Kennedy**	1961–1963	40. President	**Ronald W. Reagan**	1981–1989
Vice President	Lyndon B. Johnson	1961–1963	Vice President	George H. W. Bush	1981–1989
36. President	**Lyndon B. Johnson**	1963–1969	41. President	**George H. W. Bush**	1989–1993
Vice President	Hubert H. Humphrey	1965–1969	Vice President	J. Danforth Quayle	1989–1993
37. President	**Richard M. Nixon**	1969–1974	42. President	**William J. Clinton**	1993–2001
Vice President	Spiro T. Agnew	1969–1973	Vice President	Albert Gore	1993–2001
Vice President	Gerald R. Ford	1973–1974	43. President	**George W. Bush**	2001–2009
38. President	**Gerald R. Ford**	1974–1977	Vice President	Richard Cheney	2001–2009
Vice President	Nelson A. Rockefeller	1974–1977			
39. President	**James E. Carter**	1977–1981			
Vice President	Walter F. Mondale	1977–1981			

For a complete list of Presidents, Vice Presidents, and Cabinet Members, go to college.hmco.com.

Justices of the

Supreme Court

	Term of Service	Years of Service	Life Span		Term of Service	Years of Service	Life Span
John Jay	1789–1795	5	1745–1829	Joseph P. Bradley	1870–1892	22	1813–1892
John Rutledge	1789–1791	1	1739–1800	Ward Hunt	1873–1882	9	1810–1886
William Cushing	1789–1810	20	1732–1810	*Morrison R. Waite*	1874–1888	14	1816–1888
James Wilson	1789–1798	8	1742–1798	John M. Harlan	1877–1911	34	1833–1911
John Blair	1789–1796	6	1732–1800	William B. Woods	1880–1887	7	1824–1887
Robert H. Harrison	1789–1790	—	1745–1790	Stanley Mathews	1881–1889	7	1824–1889
James Iredell	1790–1799	9	1751–1799	Horace Gray	1882–1902	20	1828–1902
Thomas Johnson	1791–1793	1	1732–1819	Samuel Blatchford	1882–1893	11	1820–1893
William Paterson	1793–1806	13	1745–1806	Lucius Q. C. Lamar	1888–1893	5	1825–1893
*John Rutledge**	1795	—	1739–1800	*Melville W. Fuller*	1888–1910	21	1833–1910
Samuel Chase	1796–1811	15	1741–1811	David J. Brewer	1890–1910	20	1837–1910
Oliver Ellsworth	1796–1800	4	1745–1807	Henry B. Brown	1890–1906	16	1836–1913
Bushrod Washington	1798–1829	31	1762–1829	George Shiras Jr.	1892–1903	10	1832–1924
Alfred Moore	1799–1804	4	1755–1810	Howell E. Jackson	1893–1895	2	1832–1895
John Marshall	1801–1835	34	1755–1835	Edward D. White	1894–1910	16	1845–1921
William Johnson	1804–1834	30	1771–1834	Rufus W. Peckham	1895–1909	14	1838–1909
H. Brockholst Livingston	1806–1823	16	1757–1823	Joseph McKenna	1898–1925	26	1843–1926
Thomas Todd	1807–1826	18	1765–1826	Oliver W. Holmes	1902–1932	30	1841–1935
Joseph Story	1811–1845	33	1779–1845	William D. Day	1903–1922	19	1849–1923
Gabriel Duval	1811–1835	24	1752–1844	William H. Moody	1906–1910	3	1853–1917
Smith Thompson	1823–1843	20	1768–1843	Horace H. Lurton	1910–1914	4	1844–1914
Robert Trimble	1826–1828	2	1777–1828	Charles E. Hughes	1910–1916	5	1862–1948
John McLean	1829–1861	32	1785–1861	Willis Van Devanter	1911–1937	26	1859–1941
Henry Baldwin	1830–1844	14	1780–1844	Joseph R. Lamar	1911–1916	5	1857–1916
James M. Wayne	1835–1867	32	1790–1867	*Edward D. White*	1910–1921	11	1845–1921
Roger B. Taney	1836–1864	28	1777–1864	Mahlon Pitney	1912–1922	10	1858–1924
Philip P. Barbour	1836–1841	4	1783–1841	James C. McReynolds	1914–1941	26	1862–1946
John Catron	1837–1865	28	1786–1865	Louis D. Brandeis	1916–1939	22	1856–1941
John McKinley	1837–1852	15	1780–1852	John H. Clarke	1916–1922	6	1857–1945
Peter V. Daniel	1841–1860	19	1784–1860	*William H. Taft*	1921–1930	8	1857–1930
Samuel Nelson	1845–1872	27	1792–1873	George Sutherland	1922–1938	15	1862–1942
Levi Woodbury	1845–1851	5	1789–1851	Pierce Butler	1922–1939	16	1866–1939
Robert C. Grier	1846–1870	23	1794–1870	Edward T. Sanford	1923–1930	7	1865–1930
Benjamin R. Curtis	1851–1857	6	1809–1874	Harlan F. Stone	1925–1941	16	1872–1946
John A. Campbell	1853–1861	8	1811–1889	*Charles E. Hughes*	1930–1941	11	1862–1948
Nathan Clifford	1858–1881	23	1803–1881	Owen J. Roberts	1930–1945	15	1875–1955
Noah H. Swayne	1862–1881	18	1804–1884	Benjamin N. Cardozo	1932–1938	6	1870–1938
Samuel F. Miller	1862–1890	28	1816–1890	Hugo L. Black	1937–1971	34	1886–1971
David Davis	1862–1877	14	1815–1886	Stanley F. Reed	1938–1957	19	1884–1980
Stephen J. Field	1863–1897	34	1816–1899	Felix Frankfurter	1939–1962	23	1882–1965
Salmon P. Chase	1864–1873	8	1808–1873	William O. Douglas	1939–1975	36	1898–1980
William Strong	1870–1880	10	1808–1895	Frank Murphy	1940–1949	9	1890–1949

Justices of the Supreme Court (continued)

	Term of Service	Years of Service	Life Span		Term of Service	Years of Service	Life Span
Harlan F. Stone	1941–1946	5	1872–1946	Abe Fortas	1965–1969	4	1910–1982
James F. Byrnes	1941–1942	1	1879–1972	Thurgood Marshall	1967–1991	24	1908–1993
Robert H. Jackson	1941–1954	13	1892–1954	*Warren C. Burger*	1969–1986	17	1907–1995
Wiley B. Rutledge	1943–1949	6	1894–1949	Harry A. Blackmun	1970–1994	24	1908–1998
Harold H. Burton	1945–1958	13	1888–1964	Lewis F. Powell Jr.	1972–1987	15	1907–1998
Fred M. Vinson	1946–1953	7	1890–1953	*William H. Rehnquist*	1972–2005	33	1924–2005
Tom C. Clark	1949–1967	18	1899–1977	John P. Stevens III	1975–	—	1920–
Sherman Minton	1949–1956	7	1890–1965	Sandra Day O'Connor	1981–	—	1930–
Earl Warren	1953–1969	16	1891–1974	Antonin Scalia	1986–	—	1936–
John Marshall Harlan	1955–1971	16	1899–1971	Anthony M. Kennedy	1988–	—	1936–
William J. Brennan Jr.	1956–1990	34	1906–1997	David H. Souter	1990–	—	1939–
Charles E. Whittaker	1957–1962	5	1901–1973	Clarence Thomas	1991–	—	1948–
Potter Stewart	1958–1981	23	1915–1985	Ruth Bader Ginsburg	1993–	—	1933–
Byron R. White	1962–1993	31	1917–	Stephen Breyer	1994–	—	1938–
Arthur J. Goldberg	1962–1965	3	1908–1990	John G. Roberts	2005–	—	1955–

Note: Chief justices are in italics.

*Appointed and served one term, but not confirmed by the Senate.

INDEX